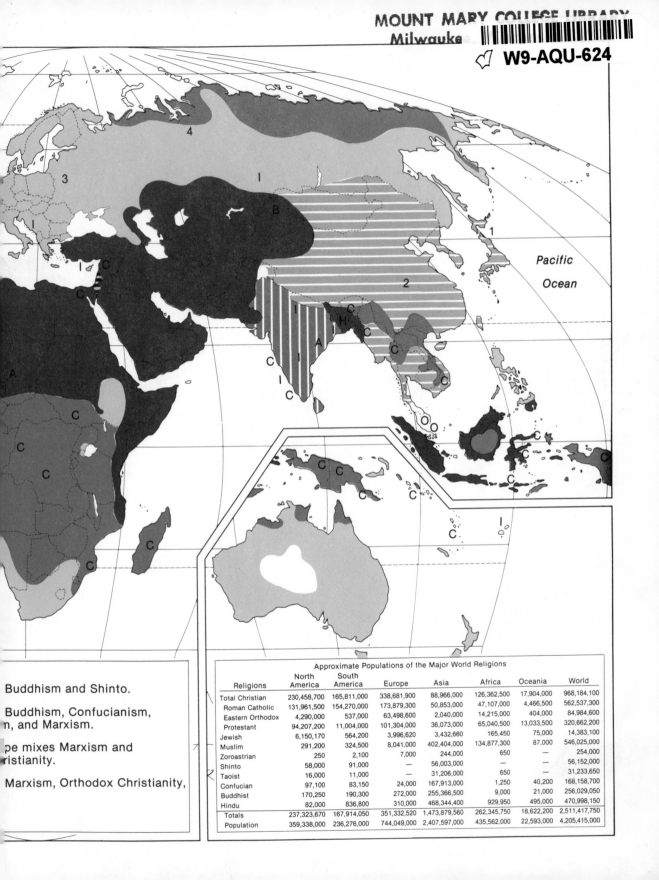

Pacific

Ocean

Buddhism and Shinto.

Buddhism, Confucianism,
n, and Marxism.

pe mixes Marxism and
ristianity.

Marxism, Orthodox Christianity,

Approximate Populations of the Major World Religions							
Religions	North America	South America	Europe	Asia	Africa	Oceania	World
Total Christian	230,458,700	165,811,000	338,681,900	88,966,000	126,362,500	17,904,000	968,184,100
Roman Catholic	131,961,500	154,270,000	173,879,300	50,853,000	47,107,000	404,000	562,537,300
Eastern Orthodox	4,290,000	537,000	63,498,600	2,040,000	14,215,000	—	84,984,600
Protestant	94,207,200	11,004,000	101,304,000	36,073,000	65,040,500	13,033,500	320,662,200
Jewish	6,150,170	564,200	3,996,620	3,432,660	165,450	75,000	14,383,100
Muslim	291,200	324,500	8,041,000	402,404,000	134,877,300	87,000	546,025,000
Zoroastrian	250	2,100	7,000	244,000	650	—	254,000
Shinto	58,000	91,000	—	56,003,000	—	—	56,152,000
Taoist	16,000	11,000	—	31,206,000	650	—	31,233,650
Confucian	97,100	83,150	24,000	167,913,000	1,250	40,200	168,158,700
Buddhist	170,250	190,300	272,000	255,366,500	9,000	21,000	256,029,050
Hindu	82,000	836,800	310,000	468,344,400	929,950	495,000	470,998,150
Totals	237,323,670	167,914,050	351,332,520	1,473,879,560	262,345,750	18,622,200	2,511,417,750
Population	359,338,000	236,276,000	744,049,000	2,407,597,000	435,562,000	22,593,000	4,205,415,000

WAYS TO THE CENTER

AN INTRODUCTION TO WORLD RELIGIONS

Of related interest . . .

BETWEEN TIME AND ETERNITY: THE ESSENTIALS OF JUDAISM, *Jacob Neusner*
JUDAISM: DEVELOPMENT AND LIFE, second edition, *Leo Trepp*

The Religious Life of Man Series   Frederick Streng, editor

UNDERSTANDING RELIGIOUS LIFE, second edition, *Frederick Streng*
THE HOUSE OF ISLAM, second edition, *Kenneth Cragg*
THE WAY OF TORAH, third edition, *Jacob Neusner*
THE HINDU RELIGIOUS TRADITION, *Thomas J. Hopkins*
THE CHRISTIAN RELIGIOUS TRADITION, *Stephen Reynolds*
CHINESE RELIGION, third edition, *Laurence G. Thompson*
JAPANESE RELIGION, second edition, *H. Byron Earhart*
THE BUDDHIST RELIGION, second edition, *Richard H. Robinson and Willard L. Johnson*
ISLAM FROM WITHIN, *Kenneth Cragg and R. Marston Speight*
LIFE OF TORAH, *Jacob Neusner*
CHINESE WAY IN RELIGION, *Laurence G. Thompson*
RELIGION IN THE JAPANESE EXPERIENCE, *H. Byron Earhart*
THE BUDDHIST EXPERIENCE, *Stephan Beyer*

WAYS TO THE CENTER
AN INTRODUCTION TO WORLD RELIGIONS

Denise Lardner Carmody
Wichita State University

John Tully Carmody
Wichita State University

Wadsworth Publishing Company
Belmont, California
A Division of Wadsworth, Inc.

Religion Editor: Sheryl Fullerton
Production Editor: Helen Sweetland
Designer: Janet Wood
Copy Editor: Paul Monsour
Cover Art: Janet Wood
Cartographer: Larry Jansen

Endpaper map adapted with permission of Macmillan Publishing Company, Inc. *from Historical Atlas of the Religions of the World* by Ismael R. Al Faruqi and David E. Sopher. Copyright © 1974 by Macmillan Publishing Company, Inc.

Printed in the United States of America
2 3 4 5 6 7 8 9 10—85 84 83 82 81

Library of Congress Cataloging in Publication Data
Carmody, Denise Lardner, 1935–
    Ways to the center.
    Bibliography: p.
    Includes index.
    1. Religions. I. Carmody, John, 1939–   joint author. II. Title.
BL80.2.C34   291   80-20257
ISBN 0-534-00890-9

In Memory of

Catherine R. Carmody
Stephen J. Carmody
Denis Lardner
Martha Comen Lardner

Contents

PART TWO: ASIAN RELIGIONS 95

Contents

Preface

This book derives from the numerous courses we have taught, singly and together, in the world religions. The following observations will indicate our intentions in writing it.

First, our main audience is college students. We do not assume prior courses in religion, and we have tried to use direct, clear prose.

Second, we have emphasized history and structural (philosophical and comparative) analysis, which seem to us the richest beginning approaches to the religions. The introduction explains our rationale, which we hope will give our work a distinctive character.

Third, a textbook has a secondary audience—the teachers who use it. For them (and the more adventurous students) we offer a sizable number of references, usually to recent sources. Because the journals *History of Religions* and *Journal of the American Academy of Religion* are easily available, we have frequently referred to articles in these journals, which we abbreviate in citations as *HR* and *JAAR*. The annotated bibliography at the back of the book, intended for students, emphasizes interesting works that are nontechnical.

Fourth, we explicitly discuss women's experiences with the world religions, because most treatments give short shrift to the female population. Religion has been a major influence on women's cultural roles everywhere, so such neglect can impede liberation.

Fifth, the book is designed for a fifteen-week semester. Shorter courses might emphasize Chapters 1, 4–6, and 8–10.

Last, our deepest hope is that the book invites the reader to the mysterious center of human experience, where authentic religion offers all of us our best names.

We take pleasure in gratefully acknowledging help from the following persons and institutions: Robert L. Cohn, Thomas V. Peterson, John Pickering, the Institute for the Arts and Humanistic Studies of the Pennsylvania State University, the Institute for Ecumenical and Cultural Research (Collegeville, Minn.), the Mabelle McLeod Lewis Memorial Fund, the Office of Research and Sponsored Programs of Wichita State University, and the Research Office of the College of Liberal Arts of the Pennsylvania State University.

We are also indebted to the scholars who reviewed our manuscript at various stages and provided valuable suggestions:

Willard Johnson, San Diego State University; M. Gerald Bradford, University of California at Santa Barbara; Gene R. Thursby, University of Florida; Robert F. Streetman, Montclair State College; Thomas V. Peterson, Alfred University; Nancy K. Frankenberry, Dartmouth College; Gary Davis, Northwest Missouri State University; W. Richard Comstock, University of California at Santa Barbara; Richard Paulson, Fresno City College; William B. Huntley, University of Redlands; R. Lanier Britsch, Brigham Young University; Robert S. Michaelsen, University of California at Santa Barbara; and Glenn Yocum, Whittier College.

Symbols Used on Chapter-Opening Pages

INTRODUCTION & CONCLUSION   *A contemporary sign for friendship between man and woman*

CHAPTER 1   *Egyptian symbol for divine wisdom*

CHAPTER 2   *Australian aboriginal hunting symbol*

CHAPTER 3   *Zoroastrian fire symbol representing purity*

CHAPTER 4   *Hindu Om: Mantra expressing the unity of reality*

CHAPTER 5   *Lotus: Buddhist symbol for pure nirvana in the midst of besmirched samsara*

CHAPTER 6   *Chinese character for Tao ("Way")*

CHAPTER 7   *Torii: Gateway to Shinto Shrines*

CHAPTER 8   *Star of David*

CHAPTER 9   *Cross of Christ*

CHAPTER 10   *Crescent and star: Ancient Byzantine symbols taken over by victorious Islam*

Introduction

RELIGIOUS WISDOM: TWENTY-FIVE KEY DATES

CA. 1500 B.C.E.	VEDAS
CA. 1360	HYMNS OF AKHENATON
1000–500	REDACTIONS OF PENTATEUCH
800–400	UPANISHADS
750–550	HEBREW PROPHETS
550	OLDEST PARTS OF ZOROASTRIAN *AVESTA*
500	OLDEST PARTS OF *ANALECTS*
400–250	JOB; ECCLESIASTES; *BHAGAVAD GITA*
CA. 350	PLATO'S *LAWS; TAO TE CHING*
CA. 330	ARISTOTLE'S *METAPHYSICS*
CA. 160	BUDDHIST *PRAJNA-PARAMITA*
CA. 80	*LOTUS SUTRA,* KEY BUDDHIST TEXT

On the Study
of World Religions

The religious life of humanity is a vast spectacle that is hard to keep in perspective. Therefore, we should make our goals and methods clear from the outset. Our primary goal is to make clear how the world's religious traditions have oriented billions of human lives. Our primary method is to place the study of religion in the context of the humanities and approach the traditions with a consistent format. Let us explain these notions in more detail.

THE NATURE OF RELIGION

Picture yourself in New Delhi. You are outside *Rajgat*, the memorial to Mahatma Gandhi, the politician and holy man who led India to freedom from British colonial rule. Before you, squatting on the broken sidewalk, are three small boys with wooden flutes. They are piping tunes directed toward round wicker baskets, and when they lift the baskets' covers, three silver cobras slowly weave their way out. You watch for several minutes, fearful but entranced. Then the boys shove the cobras back under their arms and approach you for their fee. A few rupees seem fair enough—you don't want to upset those cobras.

Does this picture shine a light on the exotic East? Is it a minor revelation of Indian culture? Yes, but only if you know a little background. In India, as in many other countries with ancient cultures, serpents have been potent symbols (think of the story in Genesis, chapter 3). Perhaps because they appear menacing or phallic (penislike), they have stood for something very basic, something very close to the life force. For centuries, groups of Indians have specialized in snake handling, and the skills have been passed along from father to son. Their profession has combined show business and a bit of crude religion. It has been both entertainment and an occasion to shiver about the implications of death and life.

Now picture yourself in medieval England. In 627 c.e. ("common era" = a.d.)

the monk Paulinus came to King Edwin in northern England and urged him to convert his people to Christianity. After some debate, one of Edwin's counselors stood up and said: "Your majesty, on a winter night like this, it sometimes happens that a little bird flies in that far window, to enjoy the warmth and light of our fire. After a short while it passes out again, returning to the dark and the cold. As I see it, our human life is much the same. We have but a brief time between two great darknesses. If this monk can show us warmth and light, we should follow him."[1]

For medieval Europe, the warmth and light that made life seem good radiated from Jesus Christ. At the core of Europe's complex and in many ways crude culture at that time, there was a faith that a personal father God so loved the world that he had given his son to heal and enlighten it. When they shared that faith, European monks, kings, and kings' counselors largely agreed on their conception of life. Monks, for instance, were willing to give up family life in order to bear witness to God's love. Kings tried to show that their rule derived from what God had done through Jesus, and counselors tried to show commoners how the kings' rule mediated God's will. Often, of course, monks and kings and counselors did things that we find hard to square with Jesus, pursuing wealth and power by means of guile. But their culture forced them all to confront Christian warmth and light, as Indian culture forced Indians to confront sex, death, and life.

Our two pictures are not quite compatible. The modern Indian scene stressed rather primitive sexual or vital energies, while the medieval English scene stressed lofty love and vision. Westerners have tended to view Indian and European life in that way, as the writings of early Christian missionaries to India suggest. However, the past century of scholarship in religious studies has shown the deficiencies of such an attitude, so we must add a few comments on the two scenes.

First, drawing a picture of medieval Europe that is raw and primitive would not

Figure 1   Head of Christ, attributed to Rembrandt (1606–1669). The Metropolitan Museum of Art, Mr. and Mrs. Isaac D. Fletcher Collection, bequest of Isaac D. Fletcher, 1917.

be hard. In Ingmar Bergman's movies of the medieval period, such as *The Seventh Seal* and *The Virgin Spring*, death and sex and life are jammed together like serpents in a basket. Because of the Black Death, the plague that killed about three-quarters of the late medieval European population, monks and commoners marched in processions while they beat themselves, scourging their flesh with whips to do penance for their sins and to keep death away. The harshness of medieval life also led to brutal wars and brutal rapes. The knight and the squire of *The Seventh Seal*, who watch the procession of penitents, have kept company with death since they went to war as Crusaders. The young girl who is raped and killed in *The Virgin*

Spring sums up medieval primitiveness. Sex and death pour out in her blood, and only after her father has slain the rapists do we see hope for new life trickle forth in a fresh spring. Medieval Europe, Bergman suggests, was as raw as India has ever been.

Second, were we to go inside the memorial to Gandhi and look at the scene at his commemorative stone, the sublimity of Indian culture and its visions of warmth and light would rise up and parallel those of Christian Europe. *Rajgat* blends green grass, elegant black marble, and fresh flower petals of orange and pink. They symbolize the beautiful spirit of the Mahatma, the little man of great soul. Gandhi was a politician who moved people by *satyagraha*—the force of truth. Without military arms, much money, or even much respect from British leaders, he forced the whole world to take notice. When he vowed to take no food until India's just claims were met, the world held its breath. When he led groups of nonviolent *satyagrahis* into the midst of club-swinging soldiers, he upset the conscience of the world. By the simple rightness, the sheer justice, of his cause, Gandhi showed how his Hindu conception of God could be very powerful. His God was "Truth," and it finally shamed the British into withdrawal.

Snakes and scourges, love and truth—they have shot through India, Europe, and most other parts of the world. In contemporary America, they or their offspring live with us yet. For instance, our nuclear missiles are for many citizens and analysts eerie phallic symbols. Like cobras we are trying to get back in their baskets, the missiles give us shivers. Many people see the missiles' thrust, their destructive power, and the claims that they give us security or economic life as brutalizing and raping our culture. From Hiroshima to Three Mile Island, nuclear power muddles our wellsprings and hope.

So too with the ways that we whip ourselves for guilt, the ways that we still crave love, the ways that we search after light. Our guilt keeps psychiatrists in business. Our searches for light fill churches and schools. Clearly we are sisters and brothers to religious Indians and Europeans. Clearly their snakes and saviors relate to our own.

Religion is the issue of ultimate meaning that this discussion of cobras and monks spotlights. It is the part of culture—Eastern, Western, or contemporary American—that we study when we ask about a people's deepest convictions. For instance, Hinduism is the animating spirit, the soul, the way of looking at the world, that has tied snake handling and *satyagraha* together for most Indians. Christianity is the way of looking at the world that has joined scourging to Jesus for most Europeans. Religion, then, is what you get when you investigate striking human phenomena to find the ultimate vision or set of convictions that gives them their sense. It is the cast of mind and the gravity of heart by which a people endures or enjoys its time between the two great darknesses.

STUDYING RELIGION

Certain attitudes should be cultivated in all study, but the study of religion demands more self-awareness and personal engagement with its materials than most other disciplines do. For instance, although reducing physical science to "objective" observing and testing is simplistic, since all knowledge is ultimately personal,[2] physical science does not make great demands on a student's inner experiences of suffering or love. The humanities (those disciplines that study our efforts at self-expression and self-understanding) involve more of such inner experiences, because suffering and love shape so much of history and literature, yet even the humanities seldom deal with direct claims about ultimate meaning. Only in philosophy and religion does one directly encounter systems about God, evil, and humanity's origin and end. Philosophy deals with such concepts principally in their rational forms, while religious studies meet them

more concretely in the myths, rituals, mysticisms, behavior patterns, and institutions through which most human beings have been both drawn to ultimate meaning and terrified of it.

More than in any other discipline, the student in a religious studies course is confronted with imperative claims. The religions are not normally warehouses where you pay your money and take your choice. Rather, they are impassioned heralds of ways of life. More than most people initially like, the religions speak of death, ignorance, and human viciousness. However, they also speak of peace and joy, forgiveness and harmony. Whatever they discuss, though, they are *mystagogic*, which etymologically means "mystery working." The religions work mystery. Their preoccupations, when they are healthy, are nature's wonder, life's strange play of physical death and spiritual resurrection, and the possibility of order in the midst of chaos. The religions say that the kingdom of God is in your midst, because you are a being who can pray, "Abba, Father." They say that the *Tao* ("the Way") that can be named is not the real *Tao*. Above all, they say that the person who lives divorced from the mysteries of rosy-fingered dawn and wintery death is less than fully human. So Sioux Indians revered the East, because dawn symbolizes the light of conscience. So Jewish scripture speaks of love as strong as death. So, finally, Islam speaks for all religions when it says that Allah—Muslim divinity—is as near as the pulse at our throats. Clearly, then, we cannot study the religions well if we are afraid of mystery or in flight from death and life.

We also cannot study the religions well if we insist on forcing them into the categories of our own faith. We must first take them on their own terms, giving their experiences and problems a sympathetic hearing. After we have listened to the wisdom of a scripture such as the Hindu *Bhagavad Gita*, we may and should compare it with the wisdom of our Western faiths. Unless we then say with the Christians' Saint Peter, "I see now how true it is that God has no favorites, but that in every nation the person who is God-fearing and does what is right is acceptable" (Acts 10:34), we risk acting with prejudice and condescension.

A second reason for remembering life's mystery, then, is that it helps us clear away prejudice. Talk of the New Testament superseding the Old or of revealed religion besting paganism—without strong qualifications— is self-serving and naive. Used as a word of God, Jewish scriptures open onto a divinity ever new, ever fresh, and ever free. Taken in its experiential vividness, a Zen Buddhist's enlightenment *(satori)* tears the veil of ignorance and comes as revelation and grace.[3] As Thomas Aquinas insisted, we do not know what God is. As John Calvin knew, the mind without mystery is a factory of idols. The most authoritative Western theologians have counseled against prejudice.

It is worth pointing out that the religious studies course offered here is not theology, at least not the theology of a church. Church theology tends to be a search for an understanding of one's own faith that is directed by the particular creed or commitment of an individual or group. Spontaneously the search spreads to a probing of all life's dimensions in terms of such a commitment. So, there develops a theology of art, a theology of history, and even a theology of the world religions.[4] In these theologies, however, a goal is to square data with one's own faith or religious group. Moreover, a church theology's ultimate goal is to promote its own faith. It studies art, history, or the world religions in order to beautify, advance, or defend its own vision of things, whether the church be Muslim, Buddhist, Jewish, or Christian. The understanding that theology seeks in such study is not necessarily distorted, but it is in the service of preaching, ministering, and counseling. When it is not in such service, church theology becomes divorced from the life of its community.[5]

In a university, however, neither students nor teachers are expected to confess their faith (or nonfaith). We, the authors, have argued elsewhere[6] that it is proper and healthy to make clear one's position on the *implications*, for thought and action alike, to which a course's studies lead. In other words, there is nothing wrong and much right with teachers and students becoming personal—dealing with concrete, practical implications. There is much wrong, however, in university courses that place their own values on other people's art, history, or religion and thereby distort them. One must listen with an open mind before judging and deciding.

So we urge you to get inside the religions' experiences and values and to compare them with your own. In fact, we very much hope that your study will enrich your appreciation of nature, increase your wonder about life's meaning, and increase your resources for resisting evil. But we do not set these hopes in the framework of any one faith. We are not, in other words, doing church theology. You may be Christian, Jewish, Buddhist, agnostic, atheistic, or anything else. To us such labels do not matter. What matters is that you be human: a man or woman trying to hear the Delphic oracle's "know thyself," a person humble with the Confucian virtue of sympathy or "fellow feeling" *(jen).*

What benefits will this effort to study humanistically bring you? At least two spring to mind. First, you will be able to grapple with some of the most influential and wisest personalities of the past. Second, you will better understand the world of the present, in which all peoples on the globe are much closer than they have ever been before.

To illustrate the first benefit, let us call on the Chinese sage Confucius. In his time (551–479 B.C.E.) people were advancing the dictum that it is better to pay court to the stove (to practicalities) than to heaven (to ideals) (see *Analects* 3:3). Confucius batted their dictum back. If you do not pay court to heaven, he said, you will have no recourse when practicalities fail to bring you good life. In other words, the mystery of life is more than food and drink, more than shelter and pleasure. Important as those things are, they do not make truly good life. Only moving in the Way *(Tao)* of heaven makes us humans what we ought to be and what we most deeply want to be. If we settle for the stove, we halve our potential riches.

To illustrate the second benefit of the humanistic study of religion, we must comment briefly on current history. Today it is a commonplace observation that the world is becoming one. That does not mean that all peoples are agreeing on a common government, economy, or philosophy. It does mean that communications, transportation, economics, and other forces are tying all nations together. Thus, commentators speak of a "global village" or a "planetary culture." They remind us of the novelty of the twentieth century, the only time when it could have happened that when Gandhi fasted, the world held its breath; that when Mao died, his funeral reached every capital. Further, in our nuclear age all curtains can be raised. In our age of escalating population and hunger, all the silos of Kansas cast shadows on East Africa.

All the implications of the current state of affairs are too numerous to detail. We may be on the verge of a new phase of evolution; the human sciences may just be approaching their maturity. Or the outer complexity of human affairs may just be developing a self-consciousness among humans so that they can cope with these affairs. In either case, religion acquires an added significance, because we cannot learn much about the evolution or self-consciousness of the global village unless we listen to its members' deepest perceptions and convictions. Religion shows a people's deepest perceptions and convictions. Hinduism, Buddhism, Christianity, and Islam form the souls of a majority of the world's population today. To live together in the future, humans will have to understand the world religions very well.

ORGANIZATION OF THE BOOK

This book is divided into three parts. Part One deals with ancient religions. In it our goal is to introduce the basic religious elements—what we find from the dawn of history. Specifically, we begin by discussing the ancient religious mind—the concerns and modes of thought that dominate both prehistoric religion and oral (nonwriting) societies of the present. Next, we look at a few oral religious peoples—American Indians, Eskimos, Africans, and Australians. They should strengthen the conviction underlying humanistic religious studies that other peoples are as human as we. Our last topic is religion in the lands of the early civilizations, such as Egypt, Persia, and Greece. By considering the world views of the people of these lands, we can clarify what happened to religion during the development of agriculture, writing, early science, and fine art.

Part Two deals with Asian religions: Hinduism, Buddhism, Chinese religion, and Japanese religion. Hinduism and Buddhism arose in India, the motherland of religious and philosophic speculation. However, most Indians have not been philosophers, so we shall pay attention to the Hindu myths, Buddhist rituals, and Indian folk religion that have shaped the lives of the majority. Our chapters will only scratch the surface, but they will make clear that Indian ways of being human have differed markedly from those of most of our American ancestors.

Buddhism emigrated from India to East Asia, where it mingled with the native traditions of China, Japan, and other countries. In East Asia, as in India, the richness of religious thought, ceremonies, devotional practice, political influence, and so on, can seem overwhelming. Thus, we only lay out the major religious features of the cultures through history and structural analysis. For example, we underscore the importance of nature and aesthetics. In China the physical world has been esteemed quite differently than in either India or Europe. Because neither individual salvation nor a personal cre-

Figure 2   Head of Avalokitesvara, Khmer artifact from Temple of Prah Khan, twelfth century. Nelson Gallery–Atkins Museum, Kansas City, Missouri (Nelson Fund).

ator God has been a pressing concern, China's prevailing search has been for harmony—for the sense, as one scholar phrases it, that human beings are part of a natural gestalt, a patterned cosmological flow.[7]

Part Three deals with world religions from the Near East: Judaism, Christianity, and Islam. In Israelite (early Jewish) religion, we first focus on prophecy—people feeling called to speak God's "word." Using prophecy to characterize Judaism, Christianity, and Islam, we can say that Indian and East Asian religions, by contrast, are sapiential—concerned more with *wisdom*. Such a contrast is only partially true, but it is a useful way to first distinguish religions in Asia and the Near East.

Christians developed certain Israelite notions about prophecy, history, and messianism (the expectancy of an anointed leader), producing a rich culture of thought and institutions. Islam, perhaps the fullest prophetic religion, proceeded from Judaism and Christianity, and in its own eyes superseded them. Islam has experienced great waves of military triumph and culture, but also considerable stagnation. Today it is on the march, winning much of Africa and pressing on the West through its petrodollars.

These three Near Eastern religions, with their offshoots and cousins (for example, Sikhism and Baha'i), account for almost half the world's people. In the West, Judaism and Christianity, with Greek and Roman culture, remain our heritage.

The book concludes with reflections somewhat similar to those with which we began this introduction. Having surveyed the major religious traditions, we shall at the end pause again to take stock. First, we will look back at the religions' unity and diversity. Second, we will have some thoughts on the uses of religion—on the services religion has tendered through the centuries. Third, we will reflect on being an American citizen of the religious world—a contemporary at least somewhat tutored by the mysterious humanity of the past. In that way, perhaps, our book will complete its circle and make a *mandala*—a symbol of wholeness.

Our material content is as comprehensive as our space allows. To organize all this information, though, we have employed a format that has three aspects. First, wherever possible, we will describe how the religion under consideration appears. In other words, we will try to describe what it looks like and its atmosphere. From travel and study, we will offer vignettes of Hindu temples, Buddhist monasteries, Confucian government, and Muslim art. Ideally, these vignettes will launch you into each religion briskly, engaging your interest and whetting your taste.

The second aspect of the format is history. Having dealt with the religion's appearance, we will tell its story—trace how it evolved. Historical explanation is now a staple in Western studies. You use its cause-effect reasoning every day. There are problems in analyzing ancient and Eastern religious traditions historically, because they frequently have not recorded their pasts nor conceived of their identities as Westerners do. Nevertheless, we can describe Eastern traditions fairly well. For prehistoric and oral peoples, stressing description and analysis is more profitable.

The last aspect of our format is structural analysis: asking how a religion puts together its world view.[8] For example, how does it tend to think and feel about the physical world? As you will see, Hinduism tends to think about the physical world differently than Japanese Buddhism or medieval Christianity does. Similarly, if we investigate a religion's sense of society, self, or divinity, we will find illuminating likenesses and unlikenesses. Structural analysis and comparison, then, enable us to sharpen differences and discern similarities.

Finally, a few pedagogical comments. Our three-aspect format stems from what we have discovered about the mind's patterns of inquiry. In inquiry, the mind regularly moves from experience, through understanding and judgment, to decision.[9] That is, human knowing begins in wonder, from information that teases and beguiles. Then it works to grasp and affirm reality—to achieve an understanding of how the information makes sense, to achieve an insight or "click." Finally, this understanding leads to a decision: What am I going to do about this insight; what action does it command? Thus, our format moves from soliciting your interest in a religion, to explaining how it arose, to analyzing it structurally so that you can decide what it might mean for your own life.

Our job, finally, is to structure the material so that you may understand it and decide well. Your job is to be attentive, intelligent, reflective, and decisive. If you do so, you will make progress toward your center. If we do our job well, you will see how the religions themselves are but ways to the Center. The coincidence of your center and the Center is that peak experience which T. S. Eliot described as being "at the still point of the turning world." We human beings are so made that all our significant times, good and bad, take us into mystery. Mystery is more intimate to us than we are to ourselves. Mystery is closer than the pulse at our throats. Centering in mystery and recognizing that only ultimate reality can give us our lives, religious persons the world over have been paramount humanists. To follow their ways, even just in one's mind, is therefore a great chance for liberal—freeing—education. We will be happy if we increase your likelihood of seizing such a chance.

Study Questions

1. What would it mean for you to say, "Religious studies are integral to liberal education"?

2. Are the world religions more significant today than they were a generation ago?

3. How would you relate the history of religious traditions to their comparative analysis?

4. Can you describe your mind's movement from experience to understanding to judgment to decision?

Part One:

ANCIENT RELIGIONS

Before we begin our study of the most ancient levels of religion, a few preliminary notes may be helpful. The first concerns terminology. "The wise person does not care about terms," Aquinas said, but we all know at least a few people who are not so wise as we.

When we are wise, precisely what we *call* the oldest levels of religion makes little difference. When we are wise, our effort is just to describe the intense, vivid, highly imaginative world of ancient humans who are "younger," less sophisticated, and perhaps healthier than we. They saw the world with fresh vision. They had not rigidly distinguished the experience of dreams from the experience of work, the experience of songs from the experience of schooling. For them, all experience flowed together, and any part of it could be greatly significant.

Not too many years ago, scholars referring to prehistoric humanity or oral peoples of the present used such terms as *savage* and *primitive*. Such scholars found early humans more than a little repulsive or embarrassing, as though in them Darwin's ape had leapt onto the porch. To be sure,

primitive can have positive connotations, as when we call the paintings of Grandma Moses primitive. Further, the more we learn about the damage that tradition and "civilization" can do to talent and to the earth, the more we can make the word *primitive* a sign of vitality and power. Nonetheless, subjects of "primitive religion," such as American Indians, have rightly felt that the term was not used in praise.

The problem, though, is what term to employ instead. At one stage in this book, we opted for *archaic*. Our intent was to stress the antiquity and the deep psychic influence that the oldest levels reveal. However, *archaic* seems almost as bad as *primitive* to some people, so we have used the weaker but, we hope, less offensive term *ancient*. Even here, though, the situation is not wholly happy, because in Part One we place together "ancient" peoples and religious outlooks, styles, and notions that are more disparate than those we place together in Parts Two and Three. To explain why this is so may further help you to begin your study of ancient religion.

The oral peoples, whom we consider

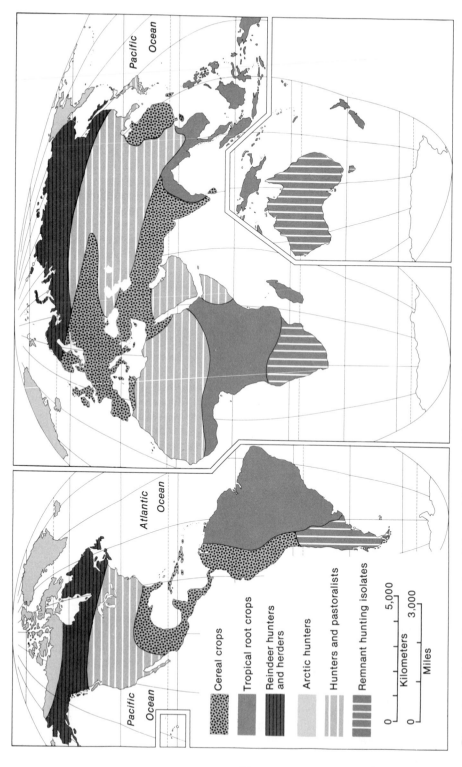

Figure 3   Original economies of the world. Adapted from The Times Atlas of World History, edited by Geoffrey Barraclough, 1979. © Hammond, Inc., Maplewood, New Jersey 07040. Reprinted by permission of The London Times, New York, N.Y. 10017.

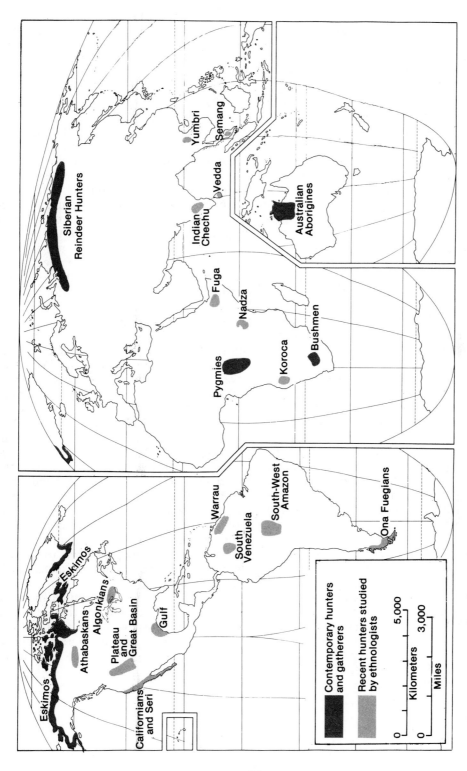

Figure 3a   Modern hunters. Adapted from The Times Atlas of World History, edited by Geoffrey Barraclough, 1979.
© Hammond, Inc., Maplewood, New Jersey 07040. Reprinted by permission of The London Times, New York, N.Y. 10017.

in Chapter 2, are much more than ancient. Although we can defend grouping prehistoric humanity, which is the subject of Chapter 1, with the early civilizational religions, which we take up in Chapter 3, we have to sing and dance a little to sell the propriety of having oral peoples between them. There is an anomaly in moving from Paleolithic people to Eskimos or Africans of the present and then back to early Greeks or Egyptians.

Prehistoric humanity was largely comprised of hunters and gatherers. Its religion derived from and begot the close connection with the animal world that hunting demands. Between prehistoric hunters and the great early civilizations of Egypt and Greece lay the dawn of agriculture and writing, which was the threshold to history. Therefore, one can picture the relations involved among the three groups of subjects rather simply. First, there was the ancient religious mind, the ultimate meanings that go back so far into our race's origins that they slip out of sight. Second, after the glaciers melted, there was the progressive discovery of agriculture, writing, and a spate of new tools such as the wheel. Together, they revolutionized humanity's world. Third, there were the cultures that rose from the greater population and the sedentary life, which agriculture made possible (see Figures 3 and 3a on pages 12–13). Those cultures involved a proliferation of specialists—farmers, soldiers, craftspersons, and priests—and the beginnings of a progressive collection of lore.

Where, though, do the peoples of oral societies, who often still focus on hunting and gathering, fit in? They may have a keen memory, but because they lack writing, they are not ''historical'' as we normally use that word. Further, despite all the changes they experienced in the thousands of years before they encountered Europeans and in the time after European contact infiltrated their traditions, oral peoples have often kept some

quite ancient traditions. Indeed, they have greatly illumined what we know of prehistoric humanity from its European remains. Therefore, too incautiously but with some good reason, anthropologists and religious historians have tried to link oral peoples even of recent times with the world view that they believe was held by humans who lived before agriculture and writing. That is a major reason for our linking them.

However, we have also chosen to insert oral peoples after our first chapter on the ancient religious mind because the similarities seem pedagogically useful. That is, despite the problems involved, we find that beginning students in world religions are helped when the closeness between prehistoric themes and the themes of contemporary oral peoples is underscored, for instance, by focusing on a religious functionary like the shaman or medicine man.

Finally, were we to treat other traditions exhaustively, the anomaly mentioned above might seem less severe. We would have to question the basis for linking Hinduism and Japanese religion and for linking Christianity and Islam. In other words, we would have to point out that *Asian* and *Near Eastern* are also rather imprecise terms and that they carry as much baggage as *ancient*. Indeed, we could even emphasize how thin the doctrinal and affectional bonds have become among some groups of Buddhists or Christians and so call those terms up for a more critical review. On balance, then, the structural similarities between oral and prehistoric religious peoples seem to us sufficient to offset their temporal distances for our purposes here.

So, do not worry overmuch about this term *ancient*. Sufficient for this day is the task of seeing how prehistoric people, Australians, and Persians contribute to a portion of the religious story that more than merits your close study.

Chapter One

THE ANCIENT RELIGIOUS MIND: TWENTY-FIVE KEY DATES

4.6 BILLION YEARS AGO	FORMATION OF THE EARTH
3.6 BILLION YEARS AGO	RISE OF LIFE
4 MILLION YEARS AGO	*AUSTRALOPITHECUS,* ADVANCED HOMINID IN AFRICA
2 MILLION YEARS AGO	*HOMO HABILIS;* STONE TOOLS
1.5 MILLION YEARS AGO	*HOMO ERECTUS;* MORE SOPHISTICATED TOOLS
500,000 YEARS AGO	USE OF FIRE
100,000 YEARS AGO	*HOMO SAPIENS;* RITUAL BURIAL
75,000 YEARS AGO	MOUSTERIAN CAVE DWELLERS; CLOTHING TO SURVIVE NORTHERN WINTERS
40,000 YEARS AGO	*HOMO SAPIENS SAPIENS,* "MODERN MAN," FULL HUNTING CULTURE
35,000 YEARS AGO	CLOTHING ADEQUATE FOR LIFE IN SIBERIA
30,000 YEARS AGO	PREHISTORIC PAINTING AND SCULPTURE
30,000–25,000 YEARS AGO	MIGRATIONS ACROSS BERING STRAIT TO NEW WORLD

The Ancient Religious Mind

20,000 YEARS AGO	COLONIZATION OF EUROPE, JAPAN
15,000 YEARS AGO	EXTENSIVE CEREAL COLLECTING
10,500 YEARS AGO	HUMANS THROUGHOUT SOUTH AMERICA
9,500–6,500 YEARS AGO	CEREAL CULTIVATION, DOMESTICATION OF ANIMALS
8,000 B.C.E.	FULL WITHDRAWAL OF GLACIERS
8350–7350 B.C.E.	JERICHO, FIRST WALLED TOWN (10 ACRES)
6250–5400	CATAL HUYUK (TURKEY), LARGE CITY (32 ACRES)
CA. 6000	RICE CULTIVATION IN THAILAND; POTTERY AND WOOLEN TEXTILES IN CATAL HUYUK
CA. 5000	IRRIGATION OF MESOPOTAMIAN ALLUVIAL PLAINS
CA. 4000	BRONZE CASTING IN MIDDLE EAST
CA. 3500	MEGALITHS IN BRITTANY, IBERIAN PENINSULA, BRITISH ISLES; INVENTION OF WHEEL
CA. 3100	PICTOGRAPHIC WRITING IN SUMER
CA. 3000	SPREAD OF COPPER WORKING

We begin our study of the world religions by trying to understand the mentality of prehistoric human beings and oral (nonliterate) peoples living today. *Prehistoric* implies having no literature or writing, insofar as we moderns require writing for a critical, trustworthy account of what happened—a history. The ancient religious mind is the mentality that we hypothesize has characterized humanity when it is without written records. It is the oldest human mentality, because the first human beings did not write. It is also the newest human mentality in that it is the "beginner's mind" with which humans first met the world.[1]

To feel sympathy for the earliest religionists, we must be convinced that they were as human as we are. In a way, the description that follows will argue this case, but it will also assume it. Right now, then, we need a quick and brilliant proof—a case that will slash all doubt. Consider the cripple of Shanidar.

From excavations at a Paleolithic cave ("Shanidar cave") in northern Iraq, archeologists have reported on the skeleton of a man whose arm had been severed in his youth. He must have been useless for hunting or self-defense. He could not drag fuel, extend a territory, or stalk or stun a foe. Life at that time was hand-to-mouth, and there was little extra food to go around. Surely, then, he was a liability. Like animals, his fellow cave-dwellers should have let him lie where the accident occurred.

They did not. The cripple must have had something about him, something more than the ability to hunt and gather. Maybe he sang, bringing cheer to the dark night. Maybe he loved children—was patient, kind, quick to tell stories. Maybe he was a great wit, or a great lover, or a great reader of signs. Or maybe he was just a good man in pain—a man whose smile broke your heart. Whatever, his family kept him on, made sure he got food and clothing. He did not die by famine or by beast. He died in a cave-in, at home in his family circle.

That acceptance of nonutility, that valuing of humanity just for itself, indicates that prehistoric people were more than our peers. Sometimes they were our superiors.[2]

PREHISTORIC RELIGION

What we are calling ancient religion spans from the oldest remains of human culture to the present. Since humanoid beings have been walking the earth for perhaps 3,500,000 years, and since true humans *(Homo sapiens)* surely existed 100,000 years ago,[3] this is an enormous time span. On the basis of archeological evidence, scholars are persuaded that religion is virtually as old as humanity itself.[4] The earliest forms of religion are quite vague, but since the time of what we might call "developed" human beings (capable of abstraction and calculation), which began at least with the Aurignacian era 32,000 years ago,[5] there likely has been a reflective religion that we ourselves could recognize.

Indeed, as we shall show, we moderns continue to manifest many facets and interests of ancient religion, and psychoanalytic theory suggests that strata of early evolutionary experiences live on in our unconscious.[6] Because we have become aware of this, and because anthropological studies have shown contemporary oral tribes to be as natively intelligent as ourselves, contemporary attitudes toward ancient religion are very different from attitudes during the formative years of academic religious studies, when the so-called classical approaches emerged.[7] Then a scholar such as K. T. Preuss, who flourished at the turn of the century, could locate ancient religion in what he called "primitive stupidity" *(Urdummheit)*. Bedeviled by the evolutionary perspective that had burst on the scene with Darwin's

---

Authors' Note   Because of limited sources, we obviously cannot compose anything like a close history of the ancient religious mind. Detail is available in Chapter 3. Here the emphasis is structural.

On the Origin of Species (1859), many of the classicists considered ancient humans to be savages, more bestial than rational.

But rational they were, and such remains as cave paintings and rock incisions lead us to conclude that they were thoroughly absorbed in making religious sense of their condition. It is perilous to generalize about a regular or typical ancient religious mentality (in North America alone, prior to the coming of whites, there were up to 2,000 separate cultures, many of them based on mutually unintelligible languages),[8] but Native Americans, Africans, Australians, and others do seem to have shared some basic beliefs. From these we can tender a few hypotheses about early human culture. We can also realize that our ancestors—whether tribal or organized in great early cultures such as the Aztec, Incan, or Mayan—were far from primitive.[9]

What do scholars of prehistoric religion say about the earliest human mentality? That its most absorbing issues were birth, subsistence, and death.[10] The first human concern was survival, which meant food and children. The first religious interest, consequently, was how to get the mysterious surrounding powers to provide food and children. Developing this thesis, the British scholar John Bowker has proposed that early religion clarifies the general biological or evolutionary situation, in which a species must sufficiently crack its "compound of limitations" to gain another generation's worth of life.[11] By "compound of limitations" Bowker means the set of factors that threaten a species' existence. It includes needing food, being liable to disease, being vulnerable to natural disaster, and the like. For human beings it also includes spiritual vulnerabilities: madness, loss of hope, and noncooperation.

At first Bowker's theory, which owes much to computer science, seems very sophisticated, but it soon works out to be rather basic: The first human beings strove mightily to survive. They hunted and gathered for food; they did what they could to avert sickness and cure disease; they begot

Figure 4   Mayan incense burner, Palenque region, ca. 500 C.E. The Cleveland Museum of Art, purchase from the J. H. Wade Fund.

children and tried to protect them. Part of their recourse in these efforts, though, went beyond what we might call practical means. There is evidence, for instance, that more than 500,000 years ago, in the Dragon Bone Hill caves of China near Peking, humans were buried in hope of an afterlife.

Some of the earliest peoples, then, tried to break death's stranglehold by imagining that something in them survived death. That something might be the part that traveled in dreams, that could fantasize and construct realities other than the physical. It might be like the smoke that wood releases when it is destroyed by fire, or like the part of plants that makes them flower again after winter. Whatever, these prehistoric peoples used their imagination and at least rudimentary reflection to project meanings that could overcome their biological weakness and mortality.

At this stage of human existence, the hard distinctions between nature and human beings that we have been taught did not exist. Rather, the art of prehistoric caves suggests that animals and plants were fellow creatures, close links to humans in the chain of life. What happened to plants in the spring might well illumine what would happen to human dead in the next turn of their cycle. So as prehistoric people mourned their dead, treasured their frail offspring, or marveled at sexuality, they probably drew on a sense of the life chain, the continuum of plants, animals, and themselves. We know that they anointed their dead with substances like red ochre, which resembles life-giving blood. As well, they probably saw hunting and gathering as sacred affairs, dealings with nature's awesome powers of life and death. Nature, then, was the great interest and educator of ancient peoples. Much more than we moderns, they felt part of the seasonal cycles, dominated by sun and cold.

This concern with nature seems to have made potent symbols of certain objects related to fecundity, hunting magic, and the cult of the dead. Whether ancient peoples thought in terms of a single, overarching power (a "God") that would organize these symbols is still debated. More likely, their most general conception was a universal bounty—a source of life that kept being replenished. Two apparent repositories of this providential power were the sky and the earth. The sky vaulted over everything, was in a position to observe and perhaps control, and contained the sun and the rain; thus, it regularly attracted the ancient mind's search for an ultimate principle. From the experience of human birthing, the earth seems to

have assumed a maternal modality very early—to have become a Great Mother.

Much of the cult of early humanity, much of its worship, probably focused on generative powers and the Great Mother. Relics from a swath of land extending from Siberia to the Near East attest to the prehistoric use of figurines of pregnant women and to the likely conception of God as a woman.[12] In the same way, numerous relics attest to a concern with hunting magic and animal fertility. In the cave called Trois Frères, near St. Girons in Ariège, France, explorers found the head of a lion engraved on a stalactite. The presence of numerous arrows suggests that the lion head functioned as a target in a ritual of hunting magic. The famous "sorcerer" painting discovered elsewhere in the same cave depicts a figure who may have presided over such hunting magic. His legs are human, his eyes are those of an owl, and he has reindeer antlers, the paws of a bear, the tail of a horse, and prominent genitals. Some scholars suggest that he is a "master of the animals,"[13] who led a dance or ritual in which his people expressed their needs and hopes for the hunt.

So prehistoric peoples probably understood their world largely in terms of quite concrete, emotion-laden interactions with the life powers. From oral peoples living today, we can infer that prehistoric peoples probably developed stories about the origin of the world and of themselves on the basis of their observations of human and animal birth. Moreover, because they could create by making things and so sensed their special powers of consciousness, prehistoric peoples may frequently have claimed to have a special soul—a source of more than biological life. Such a soul may have been thought to linger after death, giving ancestors a semiphysical presence, something more than just their children's memories. Because of this conception of a soul, they may have thought of death as a passageway, a threshold to a new level of existence. As one passed thresholds at birth and puberty, so one might pass a last threshold at death. In death one might even curve to a new phase in a circle, which led the soul to return to life someday—one's life force would animate another breathing creature, even another human body.

In this way, the fascination and dread experienced by early humans in their encounters with death could have risen to a new plane. As a result, these people may have tried to explain both the interconnectedness of living things, which often take life from one another, and the apparent end signified by an individual's death. Because they felt so dependent on the sky and the earth, early humans may well have petitioned their aid, asking the sky and earth to carry the dying across to a new life. Thus, the cyclical conflict of life and death probably formed the center of prehistoric religion.

THE SACRED

Life and death dominated prehistoric religion as they dominate much religion today, but the broadest notion in the ancient mind remains what we call the sacred or the holy. The Oxford English Dictionary defines *sacred* as "set apart for or dedicated to some religious purpose." For ancient peoples it meant the realm of the truly real, the realm of the gods or venerable powers.

This idea of the sacred was vital among the first humans. We believe this because oral peoples today sense that one can live in passionate connection with what is most real and valuable or in disassociation from it. They sense that they ought to be in harmony with the power that courses through sky and earth and sea and that they often are not. Further, they, and no doubt the first humans, have seen the destruction that disharmony can bring—natural disasters, disease, slaughter, and death. So the realm of ultimacy, the realm of power and the truly real, has been both concrete and mysterious. It has been the massive given with which ancient peoples have had to contend. They may not have abstracted its powers into a "realm" or personified it as an expression of

a primordial will, but they have completely turned their spirits towards its puzzles and sway.[14]

The experience of the sacred, in Rudolf Otto's celebrated description, involves the sense of a mystery that is both fearsome and fascinating.[15] It has been most vivid in nature's manifestations of power, but it might also occur in initiation rites, ceremonial ecstasy, or other intense experiences. With modifications, we can glimpse the experience of the sacred in the accounts of enlightenment and peak experiences from religious and psychological literature. The visions of Isaiah (6 : 1–13), Ezekiel (1 : 1–29), and Revelation (1 : 1–29) show some of the sacred's biblical expressions. In all these cases, we can see what is finally an ancient imagination dazzled by the pure power that makes everything that is. Perhaps this power, Van der Leeuw has argued, is religion's central object.[16]

As many scholars have shown, the sacred can touch any aspect of creation or life. Van der Leeuw himself deals with stones, trees, water, fire, sky, mother, father, demon, angel, king, life, death, preacher, priest, community, family, church, nation, soul, and more. The sacred may even focus on human hair and fingernails.[17] Clearly, ancient humanity felt the power of creation, the awesome force of life and being, everywhere. During a storm, the power could be manifested as thunder and lightning. More tranquilly, it could play on the waters.[18] Regularly it would rush in at birth and death. Hunting, planting, weaving, metalworking—all occupations felt power's touch. Thus, ancient peoples lived with a fact that the early Greek scientist Thales only glimpsed in a vision: "The world is full of gods." For them nothing that one saw or did was without its heavenly archetype.

This omnipresence of sacred power is perhaps our best thread through the labyrinth of the ancient religions. To dramatize the omnipresence, let us draw on some examples of sacredness that Mircea Eliade has assembled in his thematic sourcebook *From Primitives to Zen*.[19] The Dayak of Borneo, for instance, thought of themselves as a sacred people. Their land was sacred, too, because it had been given to them by the divinity, which made it from the remains of the sun and the moon. For the Delaware Indians of North America, the four directions of the compass were sacred and merited prayers of thanksgiving. They thanked the east for the morning, when the light is bright and everyone feels good. They thanked the west for the end of day, when the sun goes down and everyone can again feel good. To the north they owed thanks for the wind, whose cold coming reminds us that we have lived to see the leaves fall again. To the south they owed thanks for the warm winds that make the grass turn green.

Thus, the land and its directions were regularly thought of as manifestations of creation's holy power. So, too, were the phases of life. The Ngaju Dayak of South Borneo saw marriage as a sacred stage in life's unfolding. Therefore, the two marital partners were made to die symbolically so that they could be reborn by sticking the stem of the Tree of Life, represented by a spear, in a human head taken in a raid or from a slave. Thus, the couple was made vividly aware that their new state dealt with awesome powers. (Recently the head has been replaced by a coconut.)

For the Naskapi Indians of Labrador, hunting was especially sacred, since it was their most important occupation. The Naskapi believed that the animals they hunted had emotions and purposes like their own, and that in the beginning animals could talk like humans. So the Naskapi would sing and drum to them as to friends. Similarly, they would take great care not to mutilate certain bones of the elk or beaver believed to enclose an inner soul, a spirit like the hunter's own. Indeed, at death the animals gathered in their animal realm, just as human spirits gathered in the human realm. Both realms were conceived as stages in a cycle of reincarnation (rebirth in a new form), and so both sets of spirits were bound together. If the hunters did not know the behavioral

principles governing their sacred connections with the animals, all sorts of misfortune could ensue. The hunt would be fruitless, the people would be without food, or sickness and even death might descend.

As hunting peoples considered their pursuit of game sacred, so agricultural peoples considered farming sacred. Zoroastrians, for instance, taught that for the land to bear fruit, it had to be sown in the way that a husband lovingly fertilizes his wife. The Native Americans who raised corn (maize) reverenced it as the gift of the Corn Maiden and harvested it ceremonially.[20] Other Native Americans insisted on treating the earth especially gently in the spring, for then it was like a woman pregnant with new life. To plow it, even to walk or run on it without care, would have been to mistreat a full womb.

The Jains of India inculcated a reverence for all living things, however tiny. They considered injuring the earth or water to be like maiming a blind man. In fact, even the dust and the dung heap merited respect, for they housed living creatures. Many Jains carefully swept the path in front of themselves in order to clear away living things on which they might step. In this way, they preserved themselves from the bad *karma* (spiritual effect) that comes from doing violence to the chain of life, which is most precious and sacred.

In a word, just about every aspect of human experience has at some time been held sacred. Thought and sex, trees and waters, stones and ancestors—all have been considered manifestations of power or holiness. We can say, therefore, that the sacred is the ultimate or deepest significance that any thing, place, or person can manifest if seen at the right angle. For instance, the beggar can seem to wear a coat of holiness. Usually a marginal if not contemptible figure, he or she can, with a shift of vision, become a source of blessing. Then God is held to cherish the poor, and one hears stories of almsgivers meeting with angels or Christs in disguise. On the other end of the social scale, chieftains and kings have regularly been reverenced as sacred. In fact, the king has been not only a ruler by divine right but also a frequent sacrificial figure, killed for the sake of his people.[21]

More understandably, perhaps, the shamans, yogis, and medicine men who are prominent in ancient societies' dealings with the sacred take on auras of holiness. Because they are mediums for encountering the venerable powers, they themselves are venerated and feared. Normally ancient peoples feel that the sacred itself is a good or at least an indifferent force. If one is not in harmony with it, however, it can be destructive. Therefore, one has to approach sacred functionaries with some caution.

A story by the contemporary Native American storyteller Durango Mendoza captures this feeling of caution.[22] Two children make fun of an old man. He has a reputation for witchcraft—the ability to turn special powers against his enemies. When one of the children later becomes sick, the story suggests an almost palpable presence of evil. As studies of Navaho witchcraft have shown, this evil (power turned malevolent) is often a strong component of the American Indian world view.[23] In dealing with the holy, human beings risk being consumed in burning flames. If humans are not protected, the holy can destroy them.

As discussed later in this chapter, it is part of the shaman's training to gain knowledge of the sacred's ways and so come to power over evil. Only because the shaman has supposedly died to ordinary life and been reborn to sacredness can he or she guide the dead to their resting place, cure the sick of what evil spirits have done to them, or represent the tribe before the goddess who is withholding the fish. So, too, the Native American medicine man must purify himself of ordinary thoughts before he begins to cure. In a sweat lodge or by fasting and withdrawing into solitude, he must cleanse his spirit of what could interfere with its being a pure carrier of the sacred.

Many ancient aversions and taboos (irrational or magical forbiddings of contact with items thought to be dangerous) can be explained by this belief that the sacred demands purity. Contact with the dead, for instance, is often a source of pollution. This is a major theme in Shinto. Because many peoples have considered contact with a menstruating woman to be polluting, ancient woman was a powerful figure.[24] In neither case is the pollution something moral—it is not a matter of bad will, bad choice, or sin. Rather, it is a matter of being out of phase with the sacred and so endangered.

It is difficult for us in modern technological societies to appreciate this ancient sense of the sacred. However, our own interests in the occult, astrology, demonology, and parapsychology indicate that we still sense part of its world. Indeed, the ancient world portrayed so effectively by Carlos Castaneda forces us to realize how much our own reality is the product of social consensus and the inner dialogue that we constantly carry on.[25] If we lived in the midst of people who were awestruck by the sun, we, too, would likely reverence its rays.

Today simple vegetative forces remain quite tremendous, quite capable of humbling us. For instance, Annie Dillard reports that a single plant of winter rye grass can send forth 378 miles of roots with 14 billion root hairs. One cubic inch of its soil can contain 6,000 miles of root hairs.[26] The power coursing through the natural world is staggering, and when we are staggered, we are open to the sacred.

MYTH AND RITUAL

Ancient peoples have usually described the sacred through myth and ritual. A *myth* is a story, an explanation of what has happened. History began in the tendency of peoples to tell myths explaining how they came to be where and what they were. Of course, contemporary critical history distances itself from myth by rigorously controlling sources and arguments. Nonetheless, critical history could not have developed without the capacity of human beings to remember what had happened to them and what that meant.

Ritual refers to the conduct of ceremonies. In the ancient context, it consists of the dances and dramatic presentations by which tribes displayed their mythic histories and realities. Together, myth and ritual constitute the characteristic means by which ancient peoples have explained the world, interacted with the sacred, solidified their community, and baffled many scientific observers. If one takes ancient cultures seriously, without presuming that they are inferior or subhuman, one has to search for the meaning of their myths and rituals.[27] Let us see what that might entail.

Until the French anthropologist Marcel Griaule was tutored by a blind tribal elder, he could only deal superficially with the culture of the Dogon, an ancient tribe living near the Upper Volta region of northwestern Africa.[28] But when Ogotemmeli, the elder, led him through thirty-three days of indoctrination, Griaule came to realize that this "primitive" people had an amazingly complex traditional lore through which they explained all the important facets of their life. Essentially, their explanations were stories of how each thing or practice came to be.

Weaving and smithery, for instance, were considered activities of heavenly origin. The weaver's ginning iron and the smith's hammer both reflected the celestial granary, which symbolized the whole world system. Because the granary contained seeds, and the heavenly smith brought these seeds to humans on his hammer, and because the ginning iron both resembled the smith's hammer and dealt with seeds (cotton), the smiths (men) and the weavers (women) could be confident that their work had come from heaven and was supremely significant. In the same way, the weaver's carding stick was like the rod on which the archetypal smith sprinkled water on his fire, while the skin on which a woman spun was like the sun, because the first leather belonged to the bellows of the smithy, and the smithy contained the solar fire.

Clearly, the mythic mentality of the Dogon gives them a reality that is very different from what modern imagination gives us. The logic governing the Dogon world, like most mythic worlds, is a logic of correspondences. Blacksmithing and weaving correspond because their tools are similarly shaped and their materials are used in similar ways. Further, they both fit into more comprehensive patterns used by the heavenly forces who formed the world by design. As a result, things are more "alive" than they are in a scientific culture. A scientific culture tends to fix relationships to universal patterns. Unless items correlate according to these patterns, they are not considered real but merely imaginary or fabulous. Like the centaur, the phoenix, or the unicorn, they can be represented but are not truly real.

Ogotemmeli does not follow such patterns. His ancestors explained the world to him in terms of what the Nummo, the heavenly forces, did in creating and ordering it, and this explanation has served him well. It has given smithery, weaving, harvesting, and his people's other occupations dignity and coherence. What could be more dignified than a work designed by the gods? What could be more coherent than a culture in which all occupations relate, in which all occupations are strands in a single tapestry? Ogotemmeli's world is not simply a cartoon that is colorfully imagined. His mythic mentality knows as well as the scientific that human relations and farming are objective and demand common sense. But often such a mentality brings a different, indeed a more creative, sensitivity to such common sense.

For example, the Dogon view speech as a means of organization, and as such it is essentially good. Nonetheless, from the start of the world speech has loosed disorder. This is because the jackal, God's deluded and deceitful son, desiring speech, laid hands on the skirt (where speech was hidden) of his mother the earth and so began an incestuous relation that set the world careening. As a result, there are many bad words whose utterance has quite physical effects. To Ogotemmeli they actually smell, and their smell travels from the nose to the throat and liver, and then to the sexual organs, where it affects potency and procreation. Is this not a vivid way of symbolizing our human psychosomatic constitution? Does it not make us rethink the effect that bad words of lust or hate have on children, both in the womb and out?

Creation Myths

The myths of other ancient peoples prompt similar thoughts. For example, though American Indian creation myths are no scientific competition to current astronomy, they offer considerable insight into our condition as creatures. The Winnebago, for instance, picture creation as a process of pure divine thought. When the Father, the Earthmaker, came to consciousness, he cried because he did not know what to do. Noticing that his tears, which had fallen from heaven, had become the waters, he realized that by wishing he could make other things become. So he wished light and earth, which became. Then he made a likeness of himself from earth, and when it did not answer him he made for it a mind and soul and breathed into it so that it could reply. Thus, in one myth, the Winnebago teach that the world was made by design and that humans were made in God's image to converse with him.

Creation is the subject of the most basic myth, which ritual frequently uses to integrate a people with the sacred. Scholars have lavished much attention on this type of myth and have found explanations of creation involving thought, sacrifice, masturbation, a cosmic egg, and diving into the primeval waters. The Boshongo, a Bantu tribe of central Africa, say that the creator Bumba produced the world because he had a stomachache. In pain, he vomited up the sun, the moon, living creatures, and finally humans. The Babylonians, on the other hand, thought that the heavens and the earth had once been part of a whole. They were separated when Marduk, champion of the new generation of gods, defeated Tiamat, the Great Mother and sea. He then split her body into above and below, heaven and earth. From the blood of Kingu, Tiamat's leading soldier, he fashioned the people of Mesopotamia.

The Scandinavian creation epic speaks of a time when gods lived but no sea, sand, earth, heaven, or grass existed—only a void. The gods worked like a busy construction crew, fashioning what we now see. This is all destined for destruction, though, for in the cosmic struggle between good and evil, the world tree and the gods will be overcome by fire and flood. Then they will be reborn, for creation is a great wheel that keeps turning.

A whole group of peoples—Indians, Iranians, Germans, Romans, Greeks, Old Russians, and even Chinese—explained the world's origin in terms of an Indo-European myth.[29] The likely origin of this myth was the pastoral society of Indo-Irania, which was comprised of primordial man and primordial animal. The physical world resulted from the sacrifice of this primal couple—from the ritualistic killing of both human and animal life. Archeological evidence suggests that this myth, whose most famous version can be found in the Hindu Rig Veda (10.90 : 6–16), was the basis for human and animal sacrifices in the fourth and fifth millennia. (In later periods, Indo-Europeans offered vegetables or liquids instead.) In the Indo-European case, then, the link between myth and ritual is especially clear. The mythic version of how things came to be furnished ritual with its basic material. Ritual, in turn, ceremonialized the Indo-European convictions, as seasons and needs pushed one and then another to the fore.

A primary cluster of ancient rituals, not just in Europe but also elsewhere, involves sacrifice. Theories of the meaning of sacrifice—the killing of something as a way of giving it to the venerable powers—have abounded. There is probably no simple explanation, since sacrifice seems to be a complex process. It may include "gift exchange, tribute, propitiation, penitence, atonement, submission, purification, communion, symbolic parricide or filicide, impetration . . . the offering of a gift or the immolation of a victim."[30] Psychologically, it could symbolize the destruction of the socially bound self in order to liberate the freer, more antistructural self and so renew society's basic energies. That is, by sacrificing something valuable, one renounces treasured flaws (such as antagonism or pride), in order to release new energies that can revivify the tribe. That is Victor Turner's theory.

Turner's theory rests on fieldwork among the Ndembu, an African tribe of Zambia. That he can correlate what he found in contemporary Africa with what scholars have discovered about ancient Roman sacrifice shows something of the ancient mind's universality. In very many places, ritual's intent has been to integrate people with heavenly patterns. As we saw with the Dogon, this has meant symbolizing many of the activities of daily life: smithery, weaving, ginning, and so forth. The myth that is most important to both festivals and daily life, however, is the cosmogony, the story of

Figure 5   Sacred Ashanti stool, Ghana. According to tradition, the power and well-being of the Ashanti state were vested in a stool thrown down from the heavens. Nelson Gallery–Atkins Museum, Kansas City, Missouri (Nelson Fund).

creation. The cosmogony, then, is the primal archetype that ancient ritual tries to apply to the present.[31]

For instance, for many peoples the cosmogony is applied in the construction of new dwellings. It is retold as the building proceeds in order to harmonize the construction with the construction that built the world itself. Relatedly, the cosmogony is the substance of the new year festivals that most peoples celebrate. In such festivals there is a return to precreational chaos through orgies and sexual rites and then a renewal of order, discipline, and cosmos (a world of structure). Occasionally, the cosmogony is even used in healing rituals. An Akkadian myth tells of the origin of toothache: A worm was given our gums as its food. Part of the cure for a toothache was to recite this part of the creation story. The dentist would tell the story, do his work (seize the worm?), and repeat the gods' rejection of the worm's right to infect the gums.[32] And so it was with other ancient rituals—installing a king, erecting a temple, and even starting a military campaign.

Rites of Passage

Lastly, we should mention rituals that scholars call "rites of passage." These are ceremonies of the life cycle, religious dramas for birth, puberty, marriage, and death. For ancient peoples, each of these times is the threshold to a new stage of development, a new stage of intimacy with the sacred. As the gods did at the beginning, ancient peoples give birth, pass over to adulthood, marry, and bury their dead. Most impressive are the rites for puberty. Rites for young men regularly stress enduring suffering. Those for young women stress preparing for feminine tasks, as the particular society conceives of them. For both sexes, puberty is a time to learn about sexuality, the tribal gods, and the discipline that adulthood demands.

In Black Elk's account of the seven rites of the Oglala Sioux,[33] the pattern for the female puberty rite was set by a vision of a buffalo calf being cleansed by its mother.

Out of this grew the traditional ways that young women were cleansed (as the Sioux thought necessary for their fertility power) so that they could bear children and raise them in a sacred manner, and so that their fertility power would not conflict with the killing power of Sioux males (who were hunters and warriors).

For the BaMbuti, the forest pygmies of the northeastern Congo, female puberty rites are less solemn. These rites, called the *elima*, consist of dancing and singing in praise of life.[34] Since the BaMbuti have a quite positive view of the life that their forest gives them, the *elima* is but one of a number of occasions on which they sing with their *molimo* (a long tubal instrument that produces hauntingly beautiful sounds and is thought to represent the forest animals' collective voice). What emerges in the *elima* is the equality of men and women among the BaMbuti. This is reflected in the economic cooperation among the pygmies, but during the *elima* it emerges as something more basic—an instance of androgyny, of the ancient conviction that both sexes are needed for a complete, fully human life that will mirror divinity.[35]

THE SHAMAN

The central figure of ancient religion, the shaman, is the most striking example of meeting the sacred with a mythoritualistic consciousness. According to Mircea Eliade,[36] the shaman is a specialist in archaic techniques of ecstasy. Specifically, tribes of Siberia and central Asia (which scholars consider the most purely shamanistic) often select their shamans for psychological features and capacities that render them apt for ecstasy—for going outside themselves. The typical prospect is sensitive, introverted, inclined to solitude, and perhaps sickly (perhaps epileptic or given to fainting). By adolescence he (males predominate in Siberian shamanism) is thought different—peculiar, brooding, religious. If he has an emotional crisis or if something strange happens to him (such as getting very sick or being struck by lightning), elders will consider him appropriate for initiation into shamanism. That will entail learning tribal lore and ecstatic techniques and then passing an initiatory ordeal.

In Siberia the initiatory ordeal amounts to a ritualized experience of suffering, death, and resurrection. The candidate's body is dismembered; he dies and is transported to the realm of the gods. There his organs are replaced or renewed, sometimes with special stones or other tokens of his visit added. Depending on the beliefs of his tribe, he may fly to heaven as a bird, climb a sacred pole or tree (the *axis mundi* connecting earth to heaven), or travel up the rainbow. Which organ is replaced seems to depend on what his tribe thinks is the organ that ultimately quickens us. Bone and blood are popular choices. The constant feature of the ordeal is bodily sundering and death. As noted, the death usually takes place in the realm of the gods, after a flight or ascent, and a benefactor god or ally typically reconstitutes the candidate's body (replaces the removed organ) and returns him to life.

This experience takes place while the candidate is in ecstasy, standing outside his normal consciousness. If the initiation is public, the community gets a running narration of how it is going, with descriptions of the ascent, the celestial realm, the dismembering, and sample voices of the gods. A modern Westerner would probably call the proceedings imaginary, but ancient peoples tend to equate the real with the vividly experienced, so they consider it quite real.[37] Further, studies show shamans to be the healthiest members of their tribes psychologically, not the most schizoid, hysterical, or neurotic. Performing his duties makes the shaman feel good and heals him of his ills, so whenever he is out of sorts, the shaman will sing or drum and go out of himself to the gods.

When the candidate has passed his initiatory ordeal, he is usually accepted by his community and can start functioning as a shaman. His principal functions are healing, guiding the dead to the afterworld, and acting as a medium between the living and the dead. These functions show much of what a shaman's tribe believes, which is essentially that the universe and the human being are both dualistic. The universe is dual because it includes the human realm, where the shaman's body remains, and the spiritual realm, to which his spirit travels. The human being is dual because he or she has both a bodily and a spiritual part. The spirit's "travel" is the shaman's colorful experience of ecstasy.

Ordinarily, a shaman goes into ecstasy in order to gain knowledge or power. He must find out from the gods what is ailing a patient or what the right medicine is. (For ancient peoples, illness is as much a spiritual matter as a physical one.) Similarly, to find where the game has gone, the shaman must be able to go to the gods who keep the game. For example, to the coastal Eskimos, this meant swimming to the depths of the sea, where the goddess Sedna, who ruled the seals and the fish, had fenced them in. To guide the souls of the departed, the shaman must also be able to travel to the land of rest. If a tribal member suffers soul loss (which causes sickness), the shaman must be able to trace the soul and retrieve it.

Wherever he goes, the shaman reports on his progress. His functioning therefore recreates the community in two senses: (1) He helps his people reassert their view of the world, and (2) he gives them an entertaining account of his plunge to the bottom of the sea, his fight to get past Sedna's vicious watchdog, and so forth. When he returns from a mission, he often requires the community to renew itself. Sedna may be withholding the fish because someone has broken a taboo—a hunter may have mistreated a seal, two brothers may have had a violent fight, or spouses may have aborted a fetus. Such a violation of the tribe's ethic must be atoned, for it has ruptured their harmony with nature. Thus, the skillful shaman creates a forum in which his people can confess their guilts and express their regrets and fears. He tries to reconcile enemies and convince the whole tribe to reaffirm its ethical ideals.

How do shamans gain their tribe's confidence to do this? Some develop paranormal powers, including clairvoyance and clairaudience (seeing and hearing beyond the normal range). Others possess an impressive knowledge of herbs, drugs, tribal traditions, or special vocabulary. Probably the shamans' greatest success, though, comes from their mastery of techniques of suggestion, which are especially effective with peoples of vivid imagination.

Eliade's description of shamanism stresses ecstasy and the shaman's ability to go into a trance and travel to the realm of the sacred powers. Other scholars interpret shamanism more loosely, stressing its social dynamics.

Some functionaries in ancient societies give guidance by taking in a spirit. In other words, rather than going out to the gods, the gods come into them. That is the case for much of the shamanism in China and Japan. Typically shamans there sing songs and go into a trance as a way of being taken over, being temporarily inhabited or possessed. Significantly, such shamanism has been practiced more by women than by men. In China, the female shaman's song to her guiding spirit has a romantic tone, as though a beloved were pining for her lover.[38] In Japan, the *kami*, or spirits, who come are erotically intimate. In both places, the possessed shaman performs divination, discerning what the spirits want or what the future will require. Additionally, the Japanese shamans used to band together and walk a regular beat through the local villages, offering personal advice and medical healing. In performing this work, they developed teaching techniques that contributed to Japanese theater and dance.[39]

I. M. Lewis's anthropological study of spirit possession and shamanism[40] reveals important sociological aspects. Lewis finds that many of the spirit-possessed live on the margins of society. This contrasts with Eliade's theory, in which the shaman is a key social figure. Part of the contrast may lie in the fact that Lewis deals more with modern societies, whose power structures are more differentiated and complex. Another part may lie in Lewis's concentration on the "enthusiasm" of "little people" (marginals) in highly developed religious traditions (including Islam and Christianity).

Etymologically, *enthusiasm* means "being filled with the god." In Lewis's study it tends to mean emotional exaltation, as we can observe in rural American religion, where the devout may swoon, sing ecstatically, or dance. Interestingly, societies that grant women little status tend to have a substantial number of female enthusiasts. Most likely, such women use their religious experience to gain a little respect and influence. So, too, with the powerless people prominent among other groups of ecstatics. Their religion may be genuine, but the attention they receive can be very welcome.

If shamanism is to be considered in general terms, the phenomena of visions and tutelary spirits must be considered. Among Native Americans the vision quest is a regular feature of an adolescent's passage to maturity. This quest is especially clear for men (it is less clear for women), and some of its most famous examples are in *Black Elk Speaks*.[41] There we read that even before adolescence and without a quest, Black Elk was taken into the air on a cloud, saw groups of prancing horses, was told by "grandfathers" about his people's sad future, and finally was taught the sacredness of his nation's hoop—the circle representing all the Sioux.

This vision stayed with Black Elk throughout his life, dominating his interpretation of all that he observed and experienced. After he had grown old and witnessed many sadnesses, he climbed Harney Peak (for the Oglala Sioux the center of the world), prayed to the grandfatherly spirits, and confronted for the last time the broken hoop, the withering of the tribal tree. As if in answer to the tearful conclusion of his life, a raincloud appeared in the clear sky—a dramatic expression of the Great Spirit. Perhaps a majority of Native Americans were shamans in this way (though not necessarily in such dramatic fashion), for many of them lived by a personal vision and spirit.

Not all shamanist figures are exalted personalities or seers. Some are charlatans who perform for applause or money, and some are "black" shamans, who solicit the powers of evil to inflict harm. In fact, shamans run the full gamut: from holy persons, expert in venerable lore, stooped from bearing the tribe's burdens, to quacks and half-mad mutterers. (Films show Nepalese shamans performing the crudest of cures, with filthy fetishes [objects believed to have protective power] and the blood of cocks. No doubt they offer some psychological comfort to their people, but they must be hygienic disasters. Similarly, films of Yanomamo shamans, who practice among the fierce people living at the border of Venezuela and northern Brazil, indicate that their visions come from ingesting hallucinogenic snuff. The snuff induces visions of *hekura*, tiny humanoid figures who may be used for healing friends or making enemies sick. The Yanomamo shaman's vocation demands some dedication—periods of celibacy, for instance—but most Yanomamo shamans practice in order to ingest snuff and fight.)[42]

Shamanism is so widespread that it cannot be explained by cultural diffusion from a single original center. Eliade's study treats central and northern Asia, North and South America, Southeast Asia and Oceania, central Europe, Tibet, China, and East Asia. Edmans's volume *Studies in Shamanism* studies Eskimos, North Americans, Nepalese, people of Kalash-Kaffir, Israelites (on the basis of biblical evidence), Hungarians, and Swedes.[43] Other studies have dealt with Greek and Malay cases. If the definition of shamanism is extended to include divination by trance, we could cite many African instances, including some influenced by devotional Islam (Sufism).

What does this worldwide phenomenon suggest? That shamanist ecstasy accomplishes something that most peoples have desired. To go out of oneself in order to deal with supernatural powers is a way of extending one's world. Many peoples find it a way to encounter the sacred, a way to experiences both tremendous and fascinating. Surely that is why so many different tribes have employed shamanism.

THE PERSISTENCE OF ANCIENT THEMES

The persistence of ancient themes into our time is almost too evident. Astrology, witchcraft, and the occult are ready examples, but they do not necessarily recommend the ancient mind. Meditation, physical exercise (as a spiritual activity), and ecology may be more appealing. With creative science and art, they exemplify the contemporary search for harmony, ecstasy, guidance, and the holy.

Robert Ornstein has argued that it is time for ancient and esoteric (secret) disciplines to cooperate with modern science.[44] Robert Pirsig has argued that we shall only be sane when we marry our technology to spiritual discipline.[45] To be a developed human being, to come of age, requires more than a slide rule or a pill box. It requires wonder, humility, honesty, and even suffering love—quite ancient virtues.

Why? Because the world continues to give us signs, wonders, and ordeals. We have quoted Annie Dillard on the facts of winter rye to demonstrate the overwhelming wonders of nature. We could quote Lewis Thomas on the mites that live in us, which show how our very blood is not our own.[46] Even in a postancient age, nature and our own bodies remain a mystery. So do our selves. Despite the centuries, the Delphic oracle's command "Know thyself" remains terribly difficult to follow. As the Danish philosopher Søren Kierkegaard saw, the self is a relation to the absolute. It cannot be understood unless the world, society, and its projection toward eternal fulfillment make sense.

No sense can be made of the evil that humans produce. It is the mystery of iniquity; in Paul's words, "The good that I would do I do not, and the evil that I would not I do" (Rom. 7 : 15). Because of this evil, we are unhappy and waiting for rescue. In Jean-Paul Sartre's famous play *No Exit,* there is no rescue. His characters, who represent contemporary men and women, go round and round, hurting each other. For Albert Camus, another celebrated French existentialist, we are like Sisyphus, the Greek mythological figure condemned to keep rolling a stone up a hill, only to have it roll back down. In a dark mood, Camus suggested that posterity will describe us by saying, "They fornicated and read the newspapers." Thus, whatever our advances over ancient culture, these Nobel Prize–winning authors do not find our life more meaningful. For them, we remain savages, pathetic primitives.

Central to our contemporary plight is the fact that we have not solved the ancient problem of God.[47] The question of ultimate reality haunts us still. For ancient society, divinity, if not a single god, was unquestioned. Not to try to live in tune with sacredness was madness. The theologian Paul Tillich has demonstrated how religious impulses linger in modern secularists, whose ultimate concerns can entail as much faith as did the ancients'. Indeed, whatever deeply absorbs an individual or group involves the same energies that ancient peoples directed to sacred nature and that medieval peoples directed to God.

Tillich's interpretation of faith is creative and illuminating, but many adherents of traditional religions mistrust it. For them God is quite alive without such interpretation. Some of these adherents are street corner chanters or campus crusaders, but others are simply quiet folk who put on a prayer shawl or slip into a back pew to pray to the Master of the Universe in secret. About "God" these latter people can be quite modest. Poetically, God is a furnace of silence or a difficult friend.[48] Prosaically, God is a father, a mother, human beings' refuge and hope. With time, the prayer of quiet folk is simplified, tending to wordless communion. Hardly realizing it, they join the mainstream of ancient humanity, for whom meditating on the sacred was the soul's deepest hunger.

Thus, the sacred persists in many contemporary lives. The mystery of goodness and evil, the mystery that anything exists at all—these continue to absorb many souls. Martin Heidegger speaks of the *Seinsfrage:* the question of being.[49] It lies in Florida sunsets, in otters sporting off Point Lobos, in a lover's eyes—in all poetic human experiences. There is no place we can fly, the psalmist says, where divine mystery does not hover. The very structure of our mind raises the question of God.[50]

As a consequence, we retain a sense of the profane, the nonsacred. It comes from losing oneself in cooking, clerking, welding, or tennis—from gaining bread or freeing sweat. Our surfeit of busy-ness and pragmatism is a major form of profanity. Perhaps because of it, we have few awesome shrines, our woods are not full of helper spirits. We still intuitively distinguish the sacred from the profane, however, for we still sense that some things are truly real and others are but passing.

We also still make myths and ritualize the life cycle,[51] though few commentators find our myths effective or our rituals profound. For decades, Americans lived a civil myth now called "manifest destiny." It began with the Pilgrims' errand in the wilderness, moved west to establish a New Israel, and finally led us to think we were guardians of the free world, able to destroy villages in order to save them. The shattering of this myth was close to a national trauma, suggesting how powerful ancient peoples' self-definition through stories must have been. Whether we shall fashion a new myth or a ritual cycle to make our children brave remains to be seen. We could do better than the current New Year's Day, Memorial Day, Fourth of July, and Thanksgiving or the current American way of wedding and dying. We could learn from feminist religionists' revolt from tradition and return to the goddess.[52] We could tell stories from E. F. Schumacher's *Small Is Beautiful.*[53]

Last, what about shamanism today? Are there still ecstatic people able to communicate with the sacred? The poet T. S. Eliot was rather doubtful. In *The Cocktail Party*, he made the psychiatrist our priest. One could do worse, though, than a Robert Coles or Erik Erikson. They know a great deal about the spirit's quests. Similarly, Michael Polanyi and Eric Voegelin suggest the religious import of creative scholarship; Doris Lessing, Lawrence Durrell, Walker Percy, Patrick White, Isaac Singer, Saul Bellow, and many others show the art and mystery of modern love. Shamanism is not dead. Its essence lives in such tribal comforters.

To be sure, these people offer no panacea, no unguent for every bruise. With Aeschylus, they know that wisdom comes through suffering. But they keep heaven open, so they are deeply encouraging. Beating their drums, spinning their tales, they climb the cosmic pillar. Had we eyes to see, we might follow them to an ancient beauty, a wonder viable yet.

Study Questions

1. Does it explain much about prehistoric religion to say that the most absorbing problems of the earliest humans were birth, subsistence, and death?

2. Could you describe an experience of the sacred that people might have in the last two decades of the twentieth century?

3. Write a brief myth about your own rise to prominence as a scholar or warrior.

4. Write a brief ritual for a contemporary young person's passage to adulthood.

5. Why would you like or not like to be a shaman?

6. Is it possible for an ancient religious emphasis to complement or stabilize the modern scientific mind?

Chapter Two

RELIGIONS OF ORAL PEOPLES: TWENTY-FIVE KEY DATES

100,000 YEARS AGO	*HOMO SAPIENS* IN AFRICA
70,000–50,000 YEARS AGO	*HOMO SAPIENS* IN AUSTRALIA
30,000–25,000 YEARS AGO	MONGOLOID PEOPLES CROSS BERING STRAIT
8500 B.C.E.	MONGOLOID PEOPLES THROUGHOUT SOUTH AMERICA
5000	AGRICULTURE AND DOMESTICATED CATTLE IN NILE DELTA
4000	INTENSE HUNTING, GATHERING, FISHING IN BOREAL REGIONS
3000	FARMING IN CENTRAL AFRICA
2000	METALWORKING IN PERU
1500	MAIZE FARMING IN CENTRAL AMERICA
1100	LAPITA CIVILIZATION IN POLYNESIA
1000	COLONIZATION OF ARCTIC
900	FOUNDATION OF NUBIAN KINGDOM OF KUSH

Religions of Oral Peoples

We have seen something of the ancient religious mind. In this chapter, we examine four oral peoples from different parts of the world: American Indians, Eskimos, Africans, and Australians. Each area has many cultural subgroups, so what we can say about each group as a whole is limited. Nonetheless, this chapter should give us a better understanding of religions that formed specific ancient peoples.

AMERICAN INDIANS

Today few American Indians live as their great-grandparents did due to their contact with white culture, which has altered their reality markedly. However, on the western reservations enough of the old traditions and native mentality remains to distinguish Indian children from those of other ethnic groups. At least, that is what child psychiatrist Robert Coles concluded after extensive contacts with Pueblo and Hopi children of New Mexico.[1] They showed an instinctive reverence for the land, a living relationship with their departed ancestors, and a revelatory dream life that he had not found in black, white, or Chicano children. All these characteristics indicate ancient beliefs, but the most significant is the orientation to the land. As Coles himself puts it:

Figure 6 Indian Boy *by George Catlin (1796–1872). Nelson Gallery–Atkins Museum, Kansas City, Missouri (Nelson Fund).*

There is a seemingly impersonal quality to the words and gestures a Pueblo or Hopi parent uses when pointing at some element in the surrounding landscape. There is a pantheistic side to Indian life—an emphasis by parents upon the sacral quality of both the living and the inanimate world. And, too, there is a subdued but persistent eroticism that is expressed in the contemplative wonder and awe that Indian children learn to feel when they stare at the sky, the horizon, the land both near and far. A thunderstorm, a windstorm, or simply a bright, clear day—and the Pueblo or Hopi child is happy, is ready (if it were possible) to reach out and touch with great satisfaction the sun, the dark clouds, the air rushing by so noisily.[2]

Consider what the life of a Pueblo Indian even fifty years ago might have been like. For years, he or she would have been living "on the roof of the world," absorbed by the sun, the sky, and the mountains. In youth, there would have been leisurely, wonderful ceremonies that drew the young person into the meanings and mysteries of the sun, the sky, and the mountains. In adulthood, much of life was arranged so one could contemplate these elements—think on them from the heart. Increasingly the elements came to dominate one's life. The sun, was it not a great god? Were not all humans children of its light and warmth? The mountains—did they not give us water and make us the streams necessary for life?

All that such an Indian cared for came together in the ceremonies and contemplation. Dancing and gazing, the Indian did his or her part of the holy work. Ultimately the Pueblos believed that the world itself would cease to function if they did not observe their religion: The sun would not travel the sky; the mountains would not stand tall. In the utterly clear air, this belief was absolutely certain. Without thanks and exchange, the forces of the world would not abide human beings, would not function. Indians and sun, then, kept a holy compact. All that gave Indians life came from the sun, the sky, and the mountains. Yet, Indians had great dignity, for Indians kept nature going, kept furnishing it a reason to be.[3]

For our purposes, these attitudes link contemporary American Indians with their most ancient forebears, who probably came from Siberia across a land bridge at the Bering Strait as much as 30,000 years ago. Upon contact with Europeans in the fifteenth century, native North Americans comprised several distinct geographical groups.[4] In the East were woodland tribes, who both hunted and planted. Southeastern tribes cultivated the land extensively, midwestern Plains tribes were primarily buffalo hunters, and southwestern tribes lived in pueblos or were nomads. Along the Pacific Northwest coast, fishers predominated. In each case, the tribal economy determined the life-style. Depending on the buffalo meant a life quite different from that which depended on salmon or corn. Nonetheless, scholars think that some basic attitudes were held by all North Americans.[5]

At the core of these attitudes lay belief in a primary holy force. For the Sioux it was *wakan;* for the Algonquin, *orenda.* Other tribes gave it other names. But shamans throughout the continent agreed that a holy force held all things together. North American Indian life largely revolved around this force. It made nature alluring and intimidating, a source of parental influences that on occasion turned severe. Perhaps the key goal of these tribes was to keep harmony with such holy natural power, to move with its cosmic pulse. Harmony was the way to fertility of both tribe and field, to success in both hunting and war, to a full life. By contrast, disharmony led to disaster: ruined crops, sickly children, defeat in war. As a dramatic exercise in disharmony, witchcraft caused a perceptible shudder. It ventured against the natural rhythm, deliberately tempting power to run amok. Death was too good for a witch.

As noted, these ideas originated many millennia in the past. In fact, many of the myths, rituals, and beliefs of the native North Americans resemble those of Siberian tribes, and the two groups share numerous physical characteristics. The North Americans' original myths, rituals, and beliefs likely developed in a culture centered on hunting, warfare, and shamanistic activities, which North Americans pursued until recent times.[6] Even today Navaho ritual

---

Authors' Note Because of the lack of written sources, the historical discussion in this chapter is fragmentary.

attempts cures by singing, and Zuni ritual shows traces of hunting ceremonies (though the Zuni have been settled agriculturalists for some time).

Divinity

For the most part, ancient North Americans did not worship a supreme "God." For them, the categories "nature" and "divinity" were largely indistinguishable. Some of the agricultural tribes thought of a supreme power associated with the sky or the sun, but most peoples worshipped several powers. For instance, scholars studying Indian myths find a variety of creator spirits. Earth Diver (an animal or bird who brings the earth up out of the water) is a common one, but the Zuni tell of numerous workers who disappeared once the world was organized. According to the creation myth of the Maidu of California, a turtle collaborated with a heavenly spirit called "Earth Initiate" to pull the land up out of the waters. The turtle wanted a place to rest from his ceaseless swimming, so he volunteered to dive down for some earth. Earth Initiate held a rope tied to the turtle's left arm. The turtle went down, stayed six years, and returned covered with green slime. Under his fingernails was some sand, which Earth Initiate rolled into a ball that swelled up and became the earth.[7] In the slightly different version of the Yauelmani Yokuts of California, a duck and an eagle replace the turtle and Earth Initiate.

Less revered than deities are the myths' culture heroes, whose function is to socialize the tribe. Often they are twins to whom the people trace their arts and crafts. Another superhuman figure in many tribal mythologies is the spirit who owns the animals. Unless the people reverence this spirit, they will not have good hunting or fishing. A third character in North American mythology is the antihero called Trickster. He is both a cunning person and a dupe, a principle of both order and disorder, the founder of convention and yet its chief defier. Typically, he has enlarged intestines, an insatiable appetite, and an extended, uncontrolled penis that goes off on adventures of its own. Trickster will not control his bowels or bladder, and he makes practical jokes and humbles the haughty. In short, he is human impulsiveness, the psychoanalytic id, set free as an entertainer.[8]

By contrasting divinity with lesser figures such as Trickster or culture heroes, we can focus on the more comprehensive North American notions of divinity. These include the Dakota Wakan Tanka, the Lenape Mani, and the Pawnee Tirawa. Wakan Tanka is the oneness of all holy *(wakan)* beings. Mani, on the other hand, is the chief among many gods who function as his agents. Most Lenape prayers address these agents, but the greatest ceremonies address Mani himself. Tirawa seems more like Wakan Tanka than like Mani. Though "Father Above" is one of its titles, Tirawa is usually impersonal. Perhaps we can best conceive of it as the power in all creation that sustains all things.

These native divinities, of course, were not principally ideas. If we imply that they are philosophical conclusions or abstract inferences, we misrepresent them. Rather, they have been the stuff of story telling, song, and dance. North Americans lived with them, spoke to them from the heart, and sought access to their sacredness through traditional ceremonies. Perhaps such ceremonies are the best introduction to the American Indians' religious sense of both society and self.

Ceremonies

Some ceremonies, which we might call negative, emphasized the dangers of falling out of harmony with sacred power. For instance, warriors and homicides had to be purified, lest they infect the tribe; relatives of dead persons had to be protected against ghosts. Even scalping ceremonies were negative, insofar as they were efforts to tame and tap the male spirit power, which resided in the head. Death, then, was a time of crisis demanding ritual protection to restore the harmony it had upset.

Much other Native American ritual, however, was positive, aiming at intimacy with a benevolent supernatural power. A good example of this is the vision quest. Many North American Indians strenuously sought a vision of a guiding spirit. (South Americans accepted visions that came but tended not to pursue them.) The vision quest became a rite of passage, a threshold to maturity. Without a vision as a guiding experience, one could not walk with direction or live with full purpose. If a young man's vision quest failed, he might become a tribal marginal, forced to dress in women's clothing and barred from male roles.

Along the Great Lakes and Mississippi Valley, the vision quest was largely used to train boys. In the Plains, men used it throughout life, whenever they felt the need. On the Pacific coast, it often took the form of spirit possession.[9] When the vision quest was used as training, children as young as seven years learned to fast. Boys heard that they would amount to nothing if they did not see a spirit and obtain its guidance. Girls could quest until puberty, when a different kind of power came, the power of motherhood.

As Charles Eastman, a Santee Sioux, tells it, a young man would begin the vision quest with a steam bath, putting off all worldly thoughts. Then he would ascend the most commanding summit, strip to his moccasins and breechcloth, and stand erect and motionless for several days.[10] To prove his sincerity, he might cut off his little finger or offer strips of flesh from his arm. When his vision came, it usually included a promise for his tribe, a glimpse of a tutelary animal (often a wolf or eagle), and a token (perhaps a feather or hair), which became his most prized possession. Finally, the youth would also receive his song—the particular chant that he alone could sing on important occasions. If he had other visions in the future, he could accumulate a "medicine bundle" of

tokens. Often shamans who were great healers relied on them to work cures.

An important variation on this vision theme was the Hopi representation of spirits through ceremonial masks. In that tribe, children up to eight or nine believed the *kachinas*, or masked dancers, to be real spirits in their midst. The crisis of the Hopi passage to adulthood occurred when the dancers dropped their masks, for then the young person had to accept that the reality of the *kachinas* was not physical but completely spiritual. In a painting by Louis Aiken,[11] the *kachina* has horns, a marionette face, a block nose, speakerlike ears, and a collar of fur. Emory Sekaquaptewa has described how Hopi adults assumed the characters of the masks they wore by projecting themselves into the spirit world and becoming what they were representing.[12]

Other tribes achieved this projection through the use of narcotics. Peyote is the best known, but at the time of Columbus, American Indians used perhaps a hundred substances.[13] Far fewer were available in the Old World, which may explain why the vision quest was much less common there.

Largely through their visions, Native American shamans functioned as healers, prophets, and diviners. As healers, they tended to suck from victims' bodies objects thought to be the tools of witches or ghosts. Shamans from Navaho and other tribes of the Southwest stressed healing by ritual singing, while holy people of planting tribes specialized in spells for crop fertility. The Pueblos of New Mexico were agriculturalists who shifted from shamanist, rather individualistic, ceremonies to more formalized, priestly rituals. However, even their lengthy chants for healing and fertility retained ecstatic elements from a preagricultural, nomadic past.

Constantly, then, American Indian peoples interacted with spirits, divinities, and animals, since their principal goal was to be in balance with them. Tribal rituals served this end, for they kept human beings on the right path. No North Americans seem to have thought in terms of original sin or a fall, but all tribes recognized a need for discipline and renewal. A religious ceremony such as the sun dance combined such social and personal functions, renewing the tribe's good standing with sacred nature and giving warriors stoic courage.

The Self and Destiny

Among hunting tribes, the concept of the self or soul was not well defined. Humans were thought to have several souls, one or more of which might live on after death. In fact, the Sioux were exceptional in not fearing the dead. Other tribes would have a child "adopt" a deceased relative to tame the relative's loosed soul. Reincarnation was a common belief, and the Hopi buried dead infants in the hope that their souls would return in future children. The Pueblos had a singularly clear and happy conception of the afterlife. For them the dead would either join the *kachinas* or become rain clouds. More typical was the Hopis' muted hope—they buried women in their wedding dresses, anticipating the women's passage to the next world.

Despite the importance of these notions, Native Americans were less concerned with salvation in a future heaven than with a good life in the present. Happiness or success was to enjoy the beautiful land, to have many children, and to know the spirits intimately. Our modern notions of getting ahead would have meant little to a traditional Native American. Far more important than possessions was the power to see.

Recent Movements

In the nineteenth century, a pantribal movement called the Ghost Dance responded to Indians' depression and temporarily lifted their spirits. It was a cult based on trance and a spiritual message promising that if the Indians renewed the old ways and danced the new dance, they would defeat the whites and witness the return of the buffalo. In 1886 a Paiute named Wowoka rallied hundreds of Paiutes, Kiowas, and Cheyenne in Nevada. By 1890 the Sioux, who had lost 9 million acres of their best land, turned to the Ghost Dance as a last resort. Across the country, Indians sang of the message brought by a spotted eagle: The dead are returning; the nation is coming; the Father will return the elk, the deer, and the buffalo. But the whites killed Sitting Bull, and the movement ended in the tragedy of Wounded Knee.[14]

Today one of the most interesting Native American religious movements is the Peyote religion. It was introduced in the late nineteenth century by Apaches, who traded for peyote across the Mexican border. Slowly a body of rituals developed, many of them from the Plains Indians, until there was a complete ceremonial of confession, singing, drumming, and praying. The movement incorporated some Christian elements, reached many tribes of the Plains and the Southeast, and filled some of the void left by the Ghost Dance. Today, incorporated as the Native American Church, the Peyote religion offers Indians the legal right to take peyote as their ritual sacrament.

In these and other ways, some of the tribes are preserving their traditions. Pueblos, Navahos, and Hopis have retained some of their rituals, while in the Plains the Sun Dance ceremony of dedication and endurance is being revived. On the reservations, though, the main heritage seems to be the intimacy with nature that Coles witnessed and the concern for living at the center of nature that has so impressed Christian observers.[15] With the Native American understanding of suffering,[16] this heritage makes for a powerful, underappreciated religious resource. American scholars still have a hard time appreciating the holistic, more-than-rational character of American Indian religion.[17] Perhaps for that reason, foreign scholars have worked more vigorously to show the importance of American Indian religion.[18] But a desire for greater intimacy with earth powers has brought feminist writers such as Margaret Atwood to an American Indian psychology,[19] and ecological concerns may bring more of us to it in the future.[20]

ESKIMOS

Far north of the American Indians, but having some contact and a common Siberian past, have lived the Eskimos, our next ancient religious group. The Eskimo groups differ significantly, especially the coastal and inland groups. However, most of the 50,000 or so who call themselves "Inuit" understand one another. From Greenland, across Canada and Alaska, and to the Bering Strait, their life has traditionally revolved around fishing and hunting. Naturally, their culture is most shaped by their environment. Because sheer survival is a formidable feat, Eskimo children learn to disregard egocentric or self-indulgent impulses. From their earliest years, they are part of a group dominated, regulated, and challenged by the wind, the river, the tundra, and, above all, the snow and ice.

What sort of a personality does a child brought up in such a world have? Were you to ask Eskimo children about the world, you might be discomfited by the answer. They might quietly summarize the ruin that whites have brought Eskimo culture (especially Alaskan Eskimo culture), and they might describe a confrontation with death that the elements seldom force on us in warmer climates.

If the children draw you pictures, the pictures will probably strike you as abstract: no people, a few uncontrolled lines, and a few bleak colors. Such a picture may well represent a storm that no one survived, the last moments of a village, or the child's own final day. Frequently, it will show only a little blue fighting an immensity of white. The white is winning—the snow, the ice, the cold.

In a strange way, this clear acknowledgment of icy death may liberate Eskimo children. They see the harshness of life so clearly that the behavior demanded by their

Figure 7   Alaskan house post, Haida, Sukkwan Island, ca. 1850. Nelson Gallery–Atkins Museum, Kansas City, Missouri (Nelson Fund).

41

parents makes sense. Further, the opportunities to express kindness and friendliness are all the more precious. Wary yet full of grace, children may grow up and carve wonderful seals or spirits in ivory or stone. Or, they may grow up and try to drown their pain in alcohol.[21]

The Supernatural

The full history of the Eskimos' habitation in the far north is beyond recovery. Their location, physical characteristics, and culture argue for a North Asian origin. Like that of traditional, shamanist Siberian tribes, traditional Eskimo life was dominated by the supernatural. Spirits and powers were as real as ice and snow. Eskimo notions of creation, however, were rather vague. North Alaskans held that when Great Raven was sitting in darkness, he came to consciousness and was moved to create trees and humans.[22]

Eskimos of northern Canada had a myth of Sedna, goddess of the sea and source of the sea animals. Originally, Sedna was a handsome girl who proudly spurned prospective suitors. One spring a fulmar flew in from across the ice and wooed her; his song described the soft bearskins she would rest on and the good food she would never lack were she to become his wife. However, the new bride found herself in the most wretched conditions, bitterly lamenting her rejection of previous human suitors. To avenge her, Sedna's father killed the lying fulmar; but he and Sedna then became objects of the other fulmars' wrath. While Sedna and her father were fleeing from an attack, a heavy storm arose, and her father decided to surrender Sedna to the birds by throwing her overboard. She clung to the side of the boat, but he cut off her fingers. The first joints became whales, the second joints became seals, and the stumps became ground animals. The storm subsided and Sedna returned to the boat with a fierce hatred for her father. While he was sleeping, she had her dogs gnaw off his feet and hands. He cursed her, the dogs, and himself, whereupon the earth opened and swallowed them all. Ever since, they have lived in the nether world, where Sedna is mistress of sea life.[23]

In a Greenland version of this myth, Arnaquagsaq, the old woman living in the ocean depths, sits in her dwelling in front of a lamp and sends out the animals that Eskimos hunt. Sometimes, however, parasites settle on her head, and in her anger she keeps back the game. Then the *angakoq* (shaman) must brave the way to her and remove the parasites. To do this, he must cross a turning wheel of ice, negotiate a kettle of boiling water, skirt terrible guardian animals, and finally navigate a bridge as narrow as a knife's edge.[24] He narrates this journey to the community, who follow the tale breathlessly in their mind's eye.

On traditional Eskimo earth live the goblin people—dwarfs, giants, trolls, shadows, and the like—who can help travelers or carry them off to torture. Below the earth is an underworld—a warm, comfortable place where the dead can enjoy what they liked in life. The sky is usually considered a good place, too, although western Greenlanders pictured it as being cold and deserted. When the northern lights appeared in the sky, the dead were believed to be playing football with a walrus head.[25]

Eskimos traditionally regarded rocks, animals, food, and even sleep as alive. Their whole world was alive, though only humans and animals had true souls. The basic image for those souls was either a shadow or a breath. The souls were miniatures of what they animated; thus, they were pictured as tiny humans, tiny caribou, and so on. A child was named for a dead person in the belief that he or she inherited that person's soul and qualities. For that reason, the Caribou Eskimo called a child who had inherited an ancestor's name "grandmother" or "grandfather." Many Eskimos also believed in animal reincarnation. For instance, the fish soul was thought to dwell in the intestines, so they threw fish intestines back into the water to replenish the schools.

The most general Eskimo religious conception, however, was "Sila." Najagneq, a shaman whom the explorer Knud Rasmussen met in Nome, described Sila as "a great spirit, supporting the world and the weather and all life on earth, a spirit so mighty that his utterance to mankind is not through common words, but by storm and snow and rain and the fury of the sea; all the forces of nature that men fear."[26] On the other hand, Sila could also express himself gently, by sunlight or calm of the sea. Frequently, he spoke to small children. Since many of his messages warned of danger, children were directed to alert the shaman. When all was well, Sila dwelt in endless nothingness, apart from everything. He was a mystery, whether he was close or far away. Thus, Najagneq concluded, "No one has ever seen Sila; his place of being is a mystery."[27]

The Shaman

Normally, the shaman mediates between Sedna or Sila and the tribe. Another of Rasmussen's informants, Igjugarjuk, said this about shamanist power: "All true wisdom is only to be learned far from the dwellings of men, out in the great solitudes; and is only to be attained through suffering. Privation and suffering are the only things that can open the mind of man to those things which are hidden from others."[28] The hidden powers themselves choose the persons who are to deal with them, often through revelations in dreams.

Igjugarjuk, for instance, became a shaman because of strange visions he had at night, which marked him as a potential *angakoq*. He was therefore given an instructor. In the dead of winter, his instructor placed him in a tiny snow hut and left him without food or drink. His only provision was an exhortation to think of the Great Spirit. Five days later the instructor returned and gave him some lukewarm water. Again he exhorted him to think of the Great Spirit and left. Fifteen days later, the instructor gave Igjugarjuk another drink of water and a small piece of meat. After ten more days—a total of thirty days of nearly complete solitude and fasting—Igjugarjuk saw a helping spirit in the form of a woman. For five months after this he was kept on a strict diet and forbidden sexual intercourse to consoli-

date his new power. Throughout his later career, he fasted whenever he wanted to see his spirit and gain her help.

Other Eskimo shamans have reported initiations involving being shot through the heart or drowned. One who was drowned described being tied to a pole and carried out onto a frozen lake. His instructor cut a hole in the ice and thrust him into it, so that he stood on the bottom with his head under water. He claimed to have been left in this position for five days, and when he was hauled up, his clothes were not wet. He had overcome death and become a great wizard.[29]

In these accounts, we can see something of the pattern that Eliade found in Siberian shamanism. The Eskimo shaman's way to power is through an initiatory ordeal that often has a death-resurrection motif. Eliade's own materials on Eskimo shamans detail other initiatory techniques.[30] For instance, a neophyte may have to rub stones over and over until helping spirits come, or an older shaman may extract the neophyte's soul from his eyes, brain, or intestines, so that the spirits may determine what is best in him. Through this process, the neophyte learns how to draw out the soul himself, so as to travel on mystical journeys. Still another initiatory motif focuses on sudden illumination. In the shaman's brain flashes a sort of searchlight or luminous fire that enables him to see in the dark, perceive coming events, or read others' secret thoughts. Finally, Iglulik Eskimos speak of the shaman's ability to see himself as a skeleton, all of whose parts he can name in a special language. The skeleton represents elemental human stuff, that which can best resist sun, wind, weather, and even death. By going in spirit to his skeleton, the shaman strips himself of perishable flesh and blood and readies himself to deal with the holy.

World View

In traditional Eskimo religion, then, divinity, nature, and self were all related. If Sila represented a force moving through the universe, it could be personified as a woman who was especially concerned that humans treat the animals kindly. The mythic Eskimo mentality sensed Sila or divinity in a wide variety of places, and it did not specify the status of spirits, ghosts, or Sedna. More important was the typical ancient conviction that nature is alive, willful, holy, and dangerous. Because the shaman came into contact with this dimension of life most directly, the shaman best exemplifies the Eskimo self. "Animistic," "impressionable," and even "hallucinatory" are tags that commentators have used, but these terms are probably more confusing than explanatory. Quite simply, these very practical people, who often expressed themselves in exceptionally skillful hunting, sewing, and art, were, like American Indians, extraordinarily aware of the elements' impact on their psyches.

Traditional Eskimo society focused on survival: gaining shelter against the cold and obtaining the seal, fish, or deer that furnished food and clothing. The basic social unit was the married couple, and the male hunted and the female sewed. Both the hunting and the sewing took place in the midst of complex taboos. As interpreted by the shaman, these taboos formed a system for dealing with the spirits. Shamanist ecstasy, then, served social as well as individual ends. The shaman fasted, danced, or ingested tobacco to gain for the tribe access to the control center of the natural world.

This culture may go back beyond the Bronze Age.[31] Since that time, Eskimos have been hunters, and the elaborate taboo system that they developed seems designed to conciliate the game who had to suffer so that the Eskimos could live. As one Iglulik shaman put it, "Life's greatest danger lies in the fact that man's food consists entirely of souls."[32] Therefore, great precautions were taken to placate the spirits of the game and avoid their anger. For instance, Eskimos poured water on the snout of the ringed seal when they killed it, because it lived in salt water and was thirsty. The harpoon had to stand by the blubber lamp the first night after the kill so that the soul still in the har-

poon head might stay warm. If one killed a bearded seal or bear, no one could work for three days; also, such a prize deserved presents—for example, sole skin for the bear, because bears walk so much. The Bering Sea Eskimos spent a month preparing for their festival of the bearded seal, during which they returned to the sea the bladders of all seals caught in the preceding year.[33] In honor of the whale, they held masked dances and gave gifts.

The Eskimos of central Canada had taboos to separate land animals from sea animals. For instance, eating walrus and caribou meat on the same day was forbidden. Before seal hunting on ice could begin, the hunters had to smoke their weapons over fires of seaweed to remove the smell of the land. Similarly, all sewing of caribou skins had to cease on a particular day.

Such a taboo system depends on a network of relations among the different forms of life. Because of those relations, many Eskimos carried amulets or fetishes—bits of bone, feathers, or the like. An amulet represented a power bond between the wearer and the animal of origin. One might give a baby some owl claws so that the baby would have strong fists. A man would wear a piece of caribou ear to gain sharp hearing. Even soot was given to impart strength, since it is strong enough to extinguish fire.

Many analyses of Eskimo culture linger somewhat pruriently over marriage.[34] According to Freuchen, Eskimo marriage began by the man's "capturing" the woman (carrying her off more or less against her will). It was not sexually exclusive, for a man might offer his wife to a visiting friend, regularly arrange to share her with other men, take another man's wife hunting with him if his own were pregnant, and so on. Some groups practiced polygamy, and the general attitude was that sexual desire is just another appetite like hunger.

In part, these marital arrangements usually reflected a shortage of women. Fathers prized male children, and many female infants were killed by strangling or exposure because raising them and providing a dowry loomed as too great a burden. In daily life, however, women were indispensible. They cooked the food and made all the clothing, often chewing for hours on an animal skin to soften it for sewing. Women went on dogsled trips, and some could handle the dogs better than men. Eskimo men feared menstrual blood, so women were forbidden to hunt. For the same reason, men isolated women who were in labor. In fact, both birth and death were awesome events involving dangerous forces. A new mother was restricted in what she could eat, whom she could see, what clothing she could wear, and more. Only certain persons could touch the dead, and, if possible, a person died outdoors. If death occurred indoors, everything in the house had to be destroyed.[35]

The "spirit songs" recorded by Rasmussen offer our final glimpse into the Eskimo mind.[36] They breathe both loneliness and sensitivity. Fighting their vast, barren land, Eskimos remind us about how many trials ancient peoples endured. Their lives were short, their labors heavy. Eskimo children often died in birth, and Eskimo hunters were frequently lost at sea or frozen in storms. Nonetheless, the Eskimo human spirit devised implements for building igloos at breakneck speed and for hunting, fishing, and traveling by sled. It also produced a somber yet poetic thought world. Although that world was poorer mythologically than those of the American Indian or African, it was equally impressive in imagining life's elemental forces. Sitting on their ice floes and working animal skins, Eskimo men and women did what had to be done to survive. Their wisdom about Sila was no cheap grace; Sila was in both storm and quiet. It moved the bear as well as the child. Knowing Sila, one could call life good. Knowing Sila, one could be glad to be an Eskimo.

AFRICANS

As American Indians and Eskimos have been shaped by their environments, so traditional Africans have been shaped by their land. They have been forest people, such as the BaMbuti, or mountain people, such as the Ik. In fact, the habitat of Africans has even determined their sense perception, how they see and hear the world. Anthropologists have found Africans who could not see things in perspective at far distances. For instance, one anthropologist took a BaMbuti friend from the forests of Zaire on a trip to the Ruwenzori Mountains of Uganda. At home in his forest, the Pygmy was a skillful hunter, able to pick his way through the dense growth with ease. He knew dozens of plants at a glance, and very little escaped his gaze. The trip was a great adventure for the Pygmy, who was shrewd, alert, and interested in every detail.

In the mountains, no trees blocked the Pygmy's view for the first time. The anthropologist only realized how significant this was when they stood looking down over miles of grassland. Several miles away, yet clearly in view, was a herd of grazing buffalo. "What are those insects?" the Pygmy asked. The anthropologist thought he was joking until he realized that the Pygmy had never had to make much allowance for distance when he judged something's size. The same thing happened later when they were viewing a distant lake; the Pygmy refused to believe that a large boat was in the middle, insisting that it was just a floating piece of wood.[37]

The Africa most germane to our study in this chapter is south of the Sahara.[38] In the north, Islam is now the major influence, while in the south, ancient religion mingles with Christianity. A 1971 census estimated that 75 million Africans were Christians, 140 million were Muslims, and 120 million adhered to traditional ancient ways.[39] However, those figures are deceptive. Ancient notions persist so strongly that African Islam and Christianity differ markedly from their counterparts elsewhere.[40]

Because they were oral peoples, no materials are available for a history of the cultural development of traditional Africans. Still, some analysts of African mythology find indications of very ancient thought patterns, as well as of extensive cross-cultural influences. For instance, one analyst sees in Ogotemmeli's Dogon thought world evidence of a time of hunting and gathering, a time of early land cultivation, a time of grain cultivation, and a time of contact with Hellenistic culture.[41] Another analyst, in a famous study of Near Eastern kingship, draws extensive parallels between Egyptian notions more than 4,000 years old and twentieth-century African views.[42] A third, like scholars of ancient peoples generally, underscores the conservatism and tenacity of oral traditions. Some African tribes have kept a ritual language that is different from contemporary speech and that goes back countless generations, just as liturgical Latin or Old Slavonic does.[43]

World View

In analyzing traditional African religion, one first notes that most tribes have had a Supreme Being. In East Africa, its most common name has been Mulungu, which connotes an impersonal spirit that is far away.[44] Mulungu is creative, omnipotent, and omnipresent. It may be heard in thunder and seen in lightning. Originally Mulungu was intimate with the world, but in later days it withdrew. When personified, Mulungu is envisioned as having a wife and family. He molds human bodies and gives all life its breath.

Under Mulungu are subordinate powers.[45] Africans reverence both these powers and their own departed ancestors. The most important of the subordinate natural powers are the spirits of the storm, but earth spirits, water spirits, and spirits associated with crafts (such as blacksmithing and weaving) exert considerable influence, as do gods associated with divination.

West Africans have families of gods and build temples. They tend to pray every day, using simple, personal words, and frequently they pray at one of the many shrines that dot the countryside. Usually their prayers are quite practical—petitions for health, security, good farming, or safe travel. They commonly sacrifice something to a god, usually offering a liquid or cereal. The first-fruits offering at harvest time is especially important. Special occasions may prompt an animal sacrifice, and in ancient days humans apparently were sacrificed, largely to provide companions for deceased kings.[46] (Kings were crucial mediators of cosmic harmony, and so somewhat divine.)

The ox sacrifice of the Nuer shows African religious ceremony in high style. It only takes place on such important occasions as weddings or feud settlements. Once the ox has been brought in, the ceremony unfolds in four phases: presentation, consecration, invocation, and immolation (killing). The animal is tethered to a stake; officiants rub ashes on it to consecrate it; a priest raises his spear and invokes the spirit; he then spears the animal, and all members of the community eat from it.[47] (Africans in general show great regard for cattle, and the main idea in cattle sacrifice seems to be to revere and tap the powers of procreation that bulls and cows represent.)

Traditionally Africans also emphasize rites of passage, investing birth, adolescence, marriage, and death with religious significance and giving the self a sense of development. Usually these rites are performed at home under the guidance of a family elder. At a birth, the family will make offerings to the ancestors. They will also divine to which deity the child should be dedicated. Adolescent ceremonies stress endurance. They are ordeals designed to toughen children into adults and to impart adult sacred lore. Frequently they take the form of circumcision or clitoridectomy.

Many tribes are polygynous, and so African women often are cowives. As the operation of a women's society such as the Sande of Sierra Leone shows, one of the purposes of clitoridectomy is to develop deep sisterly ties, lest husbands play women off against one another. Thus, the painful excision of the initiate's clitoris is performed amid strong group support; other women console the initiate with food, songs, and dances, promising her that her present suffering will ensure her future fertility and be a sign to her husband of her moral and religious maturity. It is also likely that clitoridectomy is thought to remove any maleness (since the clitoris is perceived as a penislike organ), allowing the woman to fit into her female social status more easily.[48] Anthropologists furnish similarly interesting accounts of African circumcision.[49]

Almost all Africans consider marriage a sacred duty, and children are a great blessing. For that reason, the menarche (first menstruation) can be a time of tribal rejoicing and such celebrations as the Pygmies' *elima* feast for young women. Indeed, female fertility is linked directly to tribal prosperity. With no social security system, African parents see many children as their hedge against old age. Thus, polygyny and large families are frequent. Westerners trying to lower the birth rate find themselves upsetting an old economic system.[50]

Funeral rites are intended to separate the dead from the living without offense. One must perform them most carefully, for they can influence the dead person's peace in the spirit world. Funerals keep the living in view, too, stirring up consoling memories and reminding the bereaved that all life is fleeting.

Representative Myths

African religions are especially rich mythologically, so studying the tribes' tales has become a preferred way of understanding the African social outlook. In a Yoruba creation myth, the supreme God sends to a marsh an artisan who is carrying a bag that lay between the great God's thighs. From this bag he shakes out soil and then a cock and pigeon, which scratch the soil until the marsh is covered. Thus, their land is holy, given from above. The Dogon say that God created the sun and moon like pots with copper rings. To make the stars he flung pellets of clay into space, and he also made the earth of clay. The Fon think that a great snake gathered the earth together after God made it

and that the earth still rests on this snake's coils. For the Gikuyu of Kenya, God is the divider of the universe. He made Mount Kenya, the "Mountain of Brightness," as evidence of his wonders and as a divine resting place. The Luyia say that God first made the moon brighter and bigger than the sun. The sun became jealous, and the two fought. The moon was thrown into the dirt, resulting in its muddy face.[51]

Through many images, then, traditional Africans made their world sacred. It was a living whole, not our science's objective collection of matter. Perhaps relatedly, African art tends to avoid representing the supreme God. Indeed, there are numerous myths of his withdrawal to the distant heaven. The Mende of Sierra Leone say that God moved away because humans were always bothering him. Ghanans and Nigerians say that humans became too familiar with God. Originally God's heaven was just above their heads, but children came to wipe their hands on it, women hit it when pounding grain, and finally a woman with a long pole hit heaven in the eye. God then moved away. The Burundi of central Africa say that God went off because a crippled baby was born, and some humans wanted to kill God, whom they held responsible. In African mythology, God often leaves by climbing a spider's thread. If there were a great emergency, humans might be able to find the thread and obtain God's help again.

Though these stories stress God's distance and so reflect an African sense of a fall from heavenly grace, African prayers show that divinity is still thought to be present and operative, in ordinary times through intermediary gods and in times of crisis through the high God. Thus, a prayer to Imana, creator God of the Ruanda-Urundi, begs, "Give me offspring, give me as you give to others! Imana, what shall I do, where shall I go? I am in distress, where is there room for me? O Merciful, O Imana of mercy, help this once."[52]

A hymn to Mwari, God of the Mashona of Southern Rhodesia, recites his attributes and accomplishments (he piled the rocks into mountains and sewed the heavens like cloth), then asks a hearing and mercy. A South African bushman asks his God Gauwa for help in hunting, complains that Gauwa is cheating him, but concludes on a note of hope: "Gauwa will bring something for us to kill next day, after he himself hunts and has eaten meat, when he is full and feeling well."[53]

The African God, then, is both far and near, both inscrutable and able to be petitioned. In general, he is considered kind and good, a father or friend. He creates and sustains all things, but no one has ever seen him. In a number of myths, he creates humans out of the ground. The Zulu of South Africa and the Thonga of Mozambique both have a tradition that the first man and woman came out of an exploded reed bed. A Pygmy story says that the chameleon heard a strange, whispering noise in a tree. When it cut the tree open, out came a flood of water, which spread over the earth, and the first humans, who were light-skinned. The Ashanti of Ghana revere Mondays and Tuesdays, because the leopard, who is sacred to some clans, emerged on those days. Also, the first human leader consoled his followers, who were frightened on coming out from under the earth. Because that leader was killed on Wednesday, Wednesday is a feared day.[54]

Overall, Africans seem to experience nature as being bountiful and good, unlike the Eskimos. Perhaps as a result, Africans show little tendency towards asceticism. God's heavenly world is but a larger and happier version of their present good life. Many tribes hope that after death there will be a rebirth from the world of ghosts into another part of the sunlit earth.

Because nature is bountiful, natural processes, including sex, are accepted without great question. The Ashanti of Ghana say sexual knowledge came when the python sent man and woman to lie together. Consequently, many Ashanti thank the python for their children. If they find a dead python, they sprinkle it with white clay and give it a ritual burial. Africans tend to fear abnormal births, however, and disfigured persons become outcasts. Twins are regarded differently by different tribes. Some tribes expose them to die, but others welcome and honor them. Like Eskimos, Africans think that souls are numerous, that the world is alive, and that a new child may inherit a soul from an ancestor.

Several of the most poignant African myths deal with life's troubles. A Zambian story tells of an old woman who wanted to follow her dead relatives because she had been left all alone. First she cut down tall trees and piled them on top of one another, trying to reach the sky. When this failed, she went looking for the road to heaven, which appears to touch the earth at the horizon. She could not find it, but in her travels she met many tribes. They assured her that suffering is normal. A myth of the Chaga of Kenya tells of a man determined to shoot God because his sons had died. When he found God, however, there were his sons, more glorious than they had been on earth.

From these and other sources, it follows that many Africans have attributed death to a mistake. The Kono of Sierra Leone, for instance, explain death as the failure of a messenger dog. God gave the dog new skins for humans, but the dog put them down in order to join a feast and a snake stole them. Since then the snake has been immortal, changing skins, while humans have died—and tried to destroy snakes.

Divination

The African religious functionary who merits most attention is probably the diviner. One scholar has suggested that there are several levels of African divination, and that the diviner at the deeper levels is equivalent to a profound shaman.[55] The two polar categories this scholar uses are "possession" and "wisdom." In possession, the diviner is filled by a spirit that reads omens, interprets movements of sacred animals, and so on. In wisdom, the spirits, gods, and the diviner's own personality are subordinate to the cosmic order. Thus, wisdom is a protoscience or cosmology—an effort to set the facts of nature and experience into some overarching scheme. Often through wisdom the diviner arrives at the notion of a Supreme Being who intelligently controls all cosmic flux. In other words, the diviner of wisdom is an intellectual, not an ecstatic or spirit-possessed functionary. His or her religious talent is to conceive a comprehensive view of how all events fit into a sacred scheme.

However, possession and wisdom are not clearly differentiated. Intermediate forms lie between them. The Mwari cultists of the Matopo Hills of Rhodesia, for instance, believe that God speaks through mediums whom he possesses deep in certain caves, and that these messages give a comprehensive view of his operations in the world.

Also, there are numerous African intuitive diviners, famed for their ability to find lost articles, identify thieves, recognize witches, and so on. Whether they are inspired by a spirit or instinctively sense particular events is unclear. Perhaps neither explanation is adequate. These diviners show high intelligence, can pick up oblique clues from their clients' stories, and give evidence of extrasensory perception.

Evan Zuesse suggests that Ogotemmeli is a wisdom diviner, insofar as the mythoscientific scheme that he reveals functions, with its archetypes and creation accounts, as the Dogon's most profound way of situating themselves in the world. The myths of the scheme's first level, which are made known to noninitiates, have themes such as the loss of paradise and the withdrawal of God, which are common to hunters and gatherers. A second level deals with the marriage of heaven and earth, which is a theme typical of early cultivators. The third-level myths of the cosmic egg have been found among grain cultivators, while the highest esoteric knowledge, concerning the "Word," suggests the *logos* (Word) of Hellenistic culture. Therefore, through the centuries Dogon sages likely assimilated the deepest insights of each new culture with which they came into contact, weaving them into their own philosophy.[56]

Another evidence that African world views reflect centuries of cultural exchange is the common divinatory systems that stretch from Zaire to South Africa. In one system, for example, a basket containing 205 pieces of bone or wood represents all reality. To answer a question, the diviner shakes the basket and analyzes the pattern into which the pieces fall. The possible combinations are enormous, so students travel long distances to study with famous teachers. In effect, the basket and its pieces are a microcosm of the African world's social institutions and forces. The diviner can feed into this system the problem at hand and then read out an answer. As with the shaman's report from the gods, the diviner's answer often becomes a means to healing or reconciliation.

With the witch doctor, who is a sort of physician, the diviner supports the forces of good, just as witches (to be distinguished from witch doctors) and sorcerers are agents of evil. Most tribes think that witches work at night, are usually women, and inherit or buy from demons a power to inflict harm.[57] The sorcerer taps the power that witch doctors use, but turns it to harm. He or she may make potions, cast spells, or put pins in an image of the victim. Needless to say, sorcerers and witches are greatly feared and hated.[58]

AUSTRALIANS

Australians lived far from the influence of the madding European crowd until the end of the eighteenth century. Of the settlement that followed Cook's exploratory voyage of 1770 it has recently been said: "The spread of settlement proved a disaster to the delicate ecology of aboriginal civilisation, which perished from all but the centre and far north almost before it was noticed, let alone understood."[59] Consequently, the reconstruction of how native Australian religious culture must have first appeared takes considerable imagination.[60]

The prime impression that the natives made on observers was of living in a different sort of time. Australian natives were not just sensitive to the seasons—they seemed to have a different set of aspirations. Their apparent listlessness seemed to grow more intense with age. A young man or woman who was manifestly alert and able to solve practical problems steadily became more dreamlike.

The first European observers did not know that this psychological makeup had a firm rationale. Were the native informants really to have spoken, they might have said something like the following: "In our religious ceremonies, we are initiated ever more deeply into the dream time of the eternal ancestors. That is the world's own time, by which creation moves. Around us, at the places in the landscape that we memorialize, the ancestors exert the pull of this dream time. Slowly, they return us all to our origins, to where we were before this life. How strange that you whites rush and bustle. You must not know the dream time, must not want to return. Too bad. Life is for returning. We are as the ancestors have dreamed us."

Historically, the Australian aborigines probably migrated from Southeast Asia (southern India and Sri Lanka) about 50,000 years ago. They spread throughout the continent and were isolated from outside influences until the arrival of Europeans in the eighteenth century. From the time of Cook's voyage interest grew, and in 1778 the British settled a penal colony in the area that is now Sydney. At the time of European contact, the aborigines probably numbered about 350,000. Some aspects of their culture suggest that they had had contact with peoples of Melanesia and New Guinea. Presently they number about 120,000, and about 45,000 are of pure stock. In the semidesert northern region, they maintain much of their original culture, which is based on hunting and gathering and which was fairly uniform across the numerous tribes.

World View

The secrecy and foreignness of much Australian lore have made it hard for Western investigators to penetrate its history or philosophic structure. Nevertheless, E. A. Worms has suggested a list of the original religion's essential features, which include the belief in a personal sky being, belief in helping spirit beings, belief in holy, powerful objects left by the sky being, ritual drama to renew divine creativity, initiation rites for both sexes, sacrifice and prayer, and a medicine man leader.[61]

T. G. H. Strehlow has complemented this list by sketching the beliefs that were held over the entire continent.[62] According to Strehlow, most tribes believed in eternal supernatural beings, whom they linked with totemic animals, plants, or natural phenomena. In fact, the concept of totem came into religious studies largely as a result of research in Australia.[63] As Webster defines it, a totem is "an animal, plant, or other object serving as the emblem of a family or clan." The eternal supernatural beings were therefore ancestors and clan founders.

In the beginning, many tribes say, these supernatural beings slept under the earth's crust. Time began when they were "born out of their eternity" and burst to the surface. According to the Unambal of northwestern Australia, in the beginning Ungud lived in the earth as a snake, while in the sky was Wallanganda, the Milky Way. During the night they created everything through a creative dream. Ungud transformed himself into the beings that he dreamed; Wallanganda threw out a spiritual force, shaped it into images, and projected them onto the rocks of the present landscape.[64] Next, spirits arose, shaped as either animals or humans and based on Wallanganda's images. In turn, they shaped the rest of the earth—mountains, sand hills, plains, and so on. The ancestors were also responsible for the aborigines' sacred songs and rituals, which were preserved with great care.

The ancestors were restrained only by a vague superior force that could punish any crimes, although they were also subject to age, sickness, and decay. Eventually they sank back into their first state of sleep, having produced the sun, moon, stars, death, labor, and pain. In the Northern Territory, scholars have found cults and art honoring the ancestors' fertility. In other regions, natives venerate rocks, trees, and *tjurunga* (distinctive slabs of wood) as sites where ancestors left supernatural powers.

Thus, Australians parceled divinity among several supernatural figures. Central Australians believed that human beings came into existence as semiembryonic masses that were joined together by the hundreds. The totemic ancestors then sliced these masses into individual infants. The traces of these masses left in the landscape became a principle of human life, for pregnant women would receive them and pass them on to the unborn. In other words, a soul could enter the fetus from a certain point in the landscape. It would be an immortal gift from one of the ancestors, the ancestor's own reincarnation. The newborn was thus a being of high dignity. Also, the newborn had strong links to a particular rock or tree, since from it had come the ancestor's spirit.

If humans were linked with eternal ancestors, why did they die? According to the Wotjubaluk of southeastern Australia, originally the moon raised the dead. Then an old man said, "Let them remain dead." So now only the moon itself returns to life. An Aranda myth says that the dead used to emerge from the grave for a second round of life, but a magpie who witnessed this became angry, grasped a heavy spear, thrust it into the neck of a dead man, and shoved the man back into the grave, saying, "Remain rooted down for all time."[65]

Now mortal, humans pass through a temporal circuit. Life begins when one's parent perceives the coming of the ancestor's spirit to the womb. This most often occurs in a dream but may be prompted by morning sickness or even birth pangs. During initiation into maturity, one partially reenters the dreamtime—the time when he or she originated out of eternity. Adult life means returning deeper and deeper into this time through religious ceremonies. At death one crosses the final threshold and again becomes a sacred spirit in the sky.[66]

Ritual

Puberty rites were a crucial occasion. Scholars first thought that they existed only for men, but more recent scholarship suggests that menstruation and childbirth were ritualized as religious experiences.[67] Puberty rites took place in considerable secrecy on sacred ground. Often this sacred ground represented the world as it was in the beginning, for in the puberty ceremonies the participants relived the time of creation. In the puberty rites of the Kamilaroi, for instance, the time when their god Baiame was on earth and founded their ceremonies was reenacted; in this way the tribe reactualized his presence and regenerated the world.

Accordingly, the Kamilaroi prepared the sacred ceremonial ground in terms of a cosmic symbolism. The dominant features were two circular enclosures. The larger enclosure, about 23 meters in diameter, had a pole about 3 meters high with emu feathers on top. In the smaller circle were two young trees with their roots in the air. The Kamilaroi drew figures on the ground or modeled them in clay. The largest was a five-meter representation of Baiame. Then they pantomimed the sacred history of Baiame's creative acts. For the adolescent initiates, this was the first exposure to the tribal lore of how things were in the beginning. For the adults who directed the ceremony, it was a renewal of faith.

One tribe, the Kurnai, separated adolescent boys from their mothers matter of factly, but most tribes even today begin the ceremonies with much weeping and lamentation. Initiates may vary in age from six to fourteen, and they undergo various bodily operations. Most ceremonies follow a regular pattern of segregation of the initiates, instruction, bodily operations, revelation of some sacred objects and ceremonies, washing, and returning to ordinary life.[68] The dominant symbolism of the entire ceremony is death and resurrection. The novice dies to the child's world of irresponsible ignorance and is reborn as a mature, spiritual being. Supposedly the mothers take the death motif literally. Thinking hostile supernatural beings have killed their sons, they mourn as at a funeral. When the boys return, the women treat them as new beings, quite different from what they were.

During the ceremony, the boys are covered with branches or rugs. They may not use words, only sounds and signs. In the ritual operations deadly supernatural beings act upon them. When the bullroarer (a slat of wood tied to the end of a thong that roars when whirled) is sounded, the supernatural beings may knock out a tooth, pull out hair, or scar the body. Circumcision is the key act, however, because it is a direct slash at a life source.

Six months to three years after circumcision, many tribes perform a second operation called subincision. Students of Australian religion debate its significance. Subincision involves slitting the underside of the penis and permanently opening the urethra. Some tribes give it overtones of bisexuality, likening the wound to a vulva. In that case, it may represent males' efforts to arrogate powers of mothering. Supporting this is the sociological fact that the boys pass from female to male control at this time. Other evidence indicates that subincision is a way to gather blood, which is needed for other ceremonials. From this perspective the act approximates menstruation. Eliade explains this ritual as follows: "Just as the women get rid of 'bad blood' through menstruation, the initiate can expel his mother's blood by laceration of the subincision wound."[69] The deeper goal of all these initiation ceremonies, however, is to instruct the young men in the sacred lore necessary for an adult male life.

Girls' initiations are tailored more for the individual, since they are triggered by the onset of menstruation. Older women teach the girl songs and myths relating to female dignity and duties in seclusion. After this instruction, they lead the young woman to a fresh lagoon for a ritual bath and then display her to the community as an adult. In some tribes, a girl's initiation includes defloration with some sort of dildo, followed by ritual intercourse with a group of men. No doubt this act has more than a sadistic or carnal motive, but its exact religious significance is unclear. Certainly ancient peoples treat sexuality as a dimension of tribal life, so perhaps this aspect of the ceremony is a way of tying the potential mother to the gods' and tribe's forces.

The female puberty rite is only the first rite in an Australian woman's life. Marriage, childbearing, menopause, and old age occasion further instruction in the nature of the sacred. As the revelations become more profound, the ceremonies become more secret. Westerners have found a pattern in the women's rituals similar to that in the men's—the reenactment of mythical events from the time of creation.

In early times, women apparently played important parts in the men's rituals. Myths speak of female ancestors who were more powerful than male ancestors and of men stealing songs, powers, and artifacts that had belonged to the women. The bullroarer is one of the artifacts that the men supposedly stole. Women may have originally functioned in the male circumcision rites, for among some tribes today the initiate gives his foreskin to his sister, "who then dries it, anoints it with ochre, and suspends it from her neck."[70] No myth speaks of women stealing important religious items or doctrines from men. Most likely, then, in earlier times religious collaboration between the sexes was greater than it has been recently. In modern times, women have not been privy to male lore. For that reason, men say that women do not progressively reenter the sacred dream time—that female ceremonies are not a steady return to spiritual existence in the sky.

The Medicine Man

The principal figure in Australian ritual life is the medicine man, who derives his healing powers from visionary contacts with supernatural beings. Usually he possesses magical items that symbolize these powers: quartz crystals, pearl shells, stones, bones, or the like. Mircea Eliade has described the ecstatic, highly imaginary making of a medicine man among the Wiradjuri of southeastern Australia.[71] First his father places two large quartz crystals against the boy's breast. They disappear into his body, making him clever and "able to bring things up." These crystals feel warm, but other ones that the boy drinks look like ice and taste sweet. From this time on, the boy can see ghosts.

During the boy's puberty rites, after a tooth has been knocked out, he learns to go down into the ground and bring up quartz crystals. The initiators take him to a grave, where a dead man rubs him to make him clever. The dead man also gives him a personal totem, a tiger snake. By following the snake, the boy and his father find the living places of various gods. At the initiation's climax, they climb a thread to Baiame's place in the sky. Baiame looks like an old man with a long beard, and from his shoulders extend two great quartz crystals.

Evidently, the medicine man is a sort of shaman whose healing powers derive from his ability to "travel to heaven." They are represented by his quartz crystals, which are part of divinity itself, and his animal spirit, the tiger snake, helps him in his tasks. An Unmatjera medicine man from central Australia reported that an old doctor threw crystals at him during his initiation and then cut out his insides. He was dead until the old man put more crystals in his body, covered it with leaves, and sang over him. The singing caused him to swell up. Then the old man gave him new internal organs and brought him back to life. From that time the medicine man was able to produce quartz crystals within himself at will, and they gave him the power to heal.

Thus, Australian ancient religion bound people to the land and to one another through imaginative myths and rituals that brought them into contact with ancestral totemic spirits or divinities. Its basic goal was to keep harmony with these powers. By integrating with them through ritual, a person supported nature as well as personal and tribal life. Death broke one's ties with the supernatural beings, so funeral rites had two functions—consoling the bereaved and helping the deceased to find his or her new station. The Aranda believed that finding one's new station entailed the immortal soul's going back to the place where it first passed into the fetus. The dead person's second, mortal soul turned into a ghost and was capable of malicious acts. Consequently, the mourning ceremonies tried to mute any anger that the deceased might have borne against relatives and friends. After a stated time, the ghost was incapable of mischief, because it departed for other haunts or faded away.

SUMMARY

Let us reflect on some of the similarities and differences among these four oral religions by examining the role of the shaman and the rites of passage of each.

The Shaman

If oral religion—and thus prehistoric religion—has a single dominant figure, it is the shaman. However, as we have seen, this figure is not clearly defined. We have used Mircea Eliade's definition, which emphasizes ancient techniques of ecstasy—of "going out" of oneself. Still, not all ancient religious functionaries fit this pattern, and it is clear that social as well as personal forces are involved in the shaman's work.

Nevertheless, the shaman remains a useful constant in the varied cultures of the American Indians, Eskimos, Africans, and Australians. The shaman is most clearly realized among the Eskimos, probably because of the close ties between Eskimos and the people of Siberia. Eskimos seem to have realized most fully the range of techniques, images, and beliefs that ancient ecstasy could entail.

The Eskimo use of cold and sensory deprivation, tobacco, dancing, and singing underscores how shamanism changes ordinary perception. Because they saw the world differently, heard new inner words, or felt uniquely alive, shamans called particular times or practices sacred. Thus, Eskimos fought their brutal environment with an altered perception, accepting the challenge of the elements, even increasing the force of the darkness and cold in order to turn that force to better use. The result was an appreciation of wisdom by suffering, and a strong belief that the shaman had access to Sedna or Sila—to the force that controlled their fate.

The information we have on Australians is too scanty, while that on the American Indians and Africans really bears on dozens of quite different tribes. However, other oral groups, like the Eskimos, had a vividly imagined spiritual world that was quite real, and they used their central religious figures, who were somewhat shamanist, as intermediaries with that world. For some Australians an ecstatic death-resurrection ritual was the key to becoming a mediator, and tokens of contact with the gods, such as the medicine man's crystals, became a sort of license to operate.

Native American and African religious functionaries were more varied than Eskimo and Australian, perhaps because of their greater numbers. At any rate, the several different cultural groups in pre-Columbian America did not all have shamans of the Siberian or Eskimo type. However, they did all prize spiritual experiences—communion with animals, oneness with the living earth, contemplation of the Great Spirit, and ecstatic dance. Their lives were mysterious, for they saw symbols of deep meaning everywhere. They communicated with spiritual powers or with the dead through dreams, and they believed that ecstasy, at least in the sense of spiritual exaltation, would provide their lives with direction.

The African world seems to have housed a number of fearsome spirits, which perhaps explains the heavy African interest in witchcraft, although other peoples, such as the American Navahos, share this interest. Clearly the African thought world was rich in myth and symbol, and divining the

future was a central interest. To create their myths and to divine, Africans needed mental, imaginative, or spiritual experiences at least analogous to those of shamanist ecstasy. The environment of most Africans was lush and bountiful, so their reaction was understandably different than that of the Eskimos. Nonetheless, through diviners, sacred kings, priests, and witch doctors (agents of good magic), Africans, too, took direction from people of changed, extraordinary perception. The shaman, then, is the ancient religious world's equivalent to Eastern religion's sage or Western religion's prophet. Like those figures, the shaman is familiar with ultimate meaning and divinity.

Rites of Passage

In ancient societies, all people strove for ultimate meaning. Ancient ritual was more a participatory than a spectator sport. Though certain persons directed the proceedings, everyone took part. Tribal life revolved around religious ceremonies, some of which were geared to the seasons, such as those that focused on hunting or wild crops. Equally significant ones, though, focused on the human life cycle. Indeed, the basic characteristic of oral (and prehistoric) societies is that their members all sought intimacy with ultimate meaning or divinity through rites of passage. That is, both men and women sought to realize the patterns that the sacred powers wanted them to follow. All people, then, were to be shamans, in the sense of being familiar with the holy.

The oral peoples stressed birth, puberty, marriage, and death. In addition, they tended to develop rites, with accompanying mythic lore, for tribal subgroups: young men, old women, fishers, and nurses. In some cases, as with the Dogon Ogotemmeli, there was layer upon layer of secret learning, each entailing its own initiation. The same seems to be true of Australians, whose whole lives could become a deeper and deeper entry into the dream time. Carlos Castaneda's initiation at the hands of Don Juan, which became as public as a supermarket bookstand, showed this pattern among American Indians. The Eskimo parallel might be the great Eskimo shaman's moving ever more deeply into Sila's mystery.

Rites of passage, though, were a common tribal possession. Such rites said that the clock whose tick most counted was biological. There is no way to defeat aging. For all that ancient myths struggle with death, they make life the central human issue. At birth, the question is where life comes from. At death, the question is where life goes. When people connected birth and death, existence became a great circle. Then it was but a step to the Eastern doctrine of transmigration, in which the life force merely passes from one entity to another. Whatever its relation to death, though, birth begs us for meaning. What end will this new life serve? Ancient peoples ritualized birth much more than we. By comparison, our baptisms and circumcisions often seem perfunctory.

The oral peoples we have studied all treasure their rites of passage, though Eskimo ceremonial may be somewhat scanty. American Indians, Africans, and Australians all spotlight puberty. Thus, they all quite explicitly wonder about sex. Sex gives them not only the mystery of a primal human difference—femaleness and maleness—but

also power that is ambiguous, linking life and death. Most ancient peoples disciplined their adolescents strictly, forcing them to develop stamina and learn the traditions.

Marriage completed this task of maturation. Procreation was stressed more than individual fulfillment. Spouses did have some rights, but essentially marriage was a way of coordinating men and women to produce and care for children. It was the gateway to another generation of survival, another round of songs and tears.

The aged Eskimo departing to an ice floe to wait for death is perhaps the most dramatic last rite of passage; aged Indians set out for the swamp or the prairie, and Australians and Africans were similarly forthright in facing death. For them all, death was the final mystery and was rather private. To be sure, all groups had mourning ceremonies, but often these involved placation of the departed, lest the dead person stay around to haunt the survivors. Thus, precisely because it was ultimate, death moved ancient people so far from their ordinary perception that the living found it disturbing, perhaps even polluting. We carry this attitude yet. The rite of passage to death is a foreign travel. If only because of death, we and ancient peoples remain fellow travelers.

Study Questions

1. What does Robert Coles mean by the "persistent eroticism" that Pueblo and Hopi children show toward physical nature?

2. What was the function of the vision quest for American Indians?

3. What does the character of Sedna tell you about Eskimo religion?

4. Would it be beneficial for Americans today to imitate Eskimo shamans and contemplate themselves as skeletons?

5. Does the shaping of a Pygmy's sense of vision by life in the forest mean that physical habitat is destiny?

6. What seems to be the purpose of clitoridectomy and circumcision?

7. Analyze the initiation or making of an Australian medicine man, paying special attention to the quartz crystals.

Chapter Three

RELIGIONS OF ANCIENT CIVILIZATIONS: TWENTY-FIVE KEY DATES

CA. 6500 B.C.E.	FIRST FARMING IN GREECE AND AEGEAN COUNTRIES
CA. 5000	AGRICULTURAL SETTLEMENTS IN EGYPT
CA. 3100	UNIFICATION OF EGYPT; MEMPHITE THEOLOGY
2700–2200	OLD KINGDOM IN EGYPT
2590	GREAT PYRAMIDS AT GIZA
2050–1800	MIDDLE KINGDOM IN EGYPT
2000	BEGINNING OF MINOAN CIVILIZATION IN CRETE
1570–1165	NEW KINGDOM IN EGYPT
CA. 1500	IRANIAN-SPEAKING PEOPLES RISE
1370	AKHENATON'S "MONOTHEISTIC" REFORM
1200	COLLAPSE OF MYCENAEAN CIVILIZATION IN GREECE
776	FIRST OLYMPIC GAMES

Religions of
Ancient Civilizations

The passage from oral, hunting societies to literate, urban civilizations was momentous. For oral Paleolithic peoples, the world was alive with animistic powers. For the civilized peoples who followed in the wake of the Sumerians' invention of writing (about 3100 B.C.E.), the world was still mysterious, but in a different way, in part because many plants and animals had been domesticated. Between Paleolithic and civilized peoples lay millennia of cultural evolution and significant technological and religious developments. Before dealing with three impressive religious civilizations—Egypt, Iran, and Greece—let us briefly consider those developments.

DEVELOPMENTS BEFORE CIVILIZATION

By now, you should realize that early humanity forged an impressive spiritual world. The pivotal discovery by prehistoric humanity was agriculture. Before we analyze the antecedents and consequents of that discovery, let us try to imagine how agricultural religion appeared.

Consider a prehistoric farmer. Most likely, the farmer is a woman. Centuries before, her forebears advanced from gathering seeds to planting them. Slowly they came to control a small number of crops and learned to make them thrive. So the farmer does her work confidently because she knows her craft. She still talks to the plants, as people did before agriculture, but many of her fellow farmers consider that outmoded. They know that the individual plants do not determine the harvest as much as the Great Mother, from whom all life issues. If she does not give, all fields will be barren. Our farmer knows this, too, but she still likes to talk to the plants.

It is a good time to be a woman. With a clearer understanding of the Mother has come a better appreciation of women's worth. Many tribes now have a matriarchal structure, and inheritance often passes along the female line. Further, the women's groups and temples form strong bonds among the women. Serving the Mother, many women are deeply content. In rites of praise or holy sex, they affirm their own woman power and need a man only briefly. The important work proceeds secretly, as it does under the earth.

Patiently the farmer cares for her field. Soon the child she is carrying may be helping. She hopes it will be another maker of life, another daughter for the Mother. The warm sun soothes the farmer's neck, and her strained muscles unknot. She wipes her brow and speaks again toward the Mother. "Care for my child, holy Mother. See that my field grows well. I am your daughter, consecrated to you. Give my days full measure. The first fruits I gather have always been yours. They will always be. When you help me, all my work is easy. Help me, then, all days."

Before Agriculture

For the more prosaic, and more certain, aspects of the history of religion before civilization, a useful guide is the first volume of Mircea Eliade's history of religious ideas.[1] In it, Eliade, a very influential historian of religion, summarizes the major religious advances from prehistory to the time of the city-state. At the beginning, more than 2 million years ago, our ancestors pondered life's mysteriousness—largely in terms of the implications of hunting. Living off animal flesh, they both established a mystical bond with the animal world and made a significant change in their own evolution: "Hunting determined the division of labor in accordance with sex, thus reinforcing 'hominization'; for among the carnivora, and in the entire animal world, no such difference exists."[2] Thus, well before 600,000 B.C.E. (the date of the first documented use of fire), humans had moved into a world of self-generated meanings by developing tools for hunting and home use.

The earliest remains believed to be used for religious purposes are bones, and those from the Mousterian period (70,000–50,000 B.C.E.) indicate the practice of burial, probably with hopes for an afterlife. The problem in interpreting ancient artifacts (many of them much older than the Mousterian), though, is that they are "opaque": Their meanings are uncertain. Without written texts or at least semididactic ("teaching") art, we can only imagine how Paleolithic people used such artifacts—what the people thought, why they sang and danced, and so on. The situation is somewhat better in the Paleolithic period (30,000–9000 B.C.E.), since many cave paintings reflect the theme of animal life. They make it clear that Paleolithic peoples were bonded to animals out of need, reverence, and fear.

Some of the motifs in the cave paintings correspond to what we know from shamanist hunting peoples of modern times. For instance, many paintings combine animal and human forms (the shaman often identifies with a bird or wolf), and the "X-ray" paintings manifest an interest in skeletal structures (many shamans meditate on skulls and bones, which they consider the crucial animal elements).

We mentioned these ancient views of life in our first two chapters, but Eliade's survey gives their chronological order more clearly. For example, certain motifs arise in remains from the Mesolithic period, after the last glacial period (about 9000 B.C.E.). The first motif is a marked concern with women and human fertility, as evidenced by many statues of females who either are pregnant or have exaggerated sexual features. Along with excavations of a Paleolithic village in Siberia, in which men and women lived in different quarters, this motif suggests an increased interest in human procreation and sexual complementariness. Such complementariness no doubt had more than human significance. Likely it meshed with these hunting peoples' views of animal life, calculations of astronomical cycles, dances, mythic-ritualistic accounts of creation, and so on.

If the apparent similarities between certain Paleolithic remains and the arts of ancient peoples living today are valid, we can infer that Mesolithic tribes had a complex world of signs and symbols—a cosmos (ordered whole) with many sacred layers. We know that shamanist ecstasy is a prehistoric phenomenon. We can guess that a more enduring wonder about the human language lent great imaginative power to such ecstasy, as it did to ritual and myth. From at least Mesolithic times, then, human beings have tried to coordinate sex, sacrifice, death, animals, the moon, and the stars—all the striking, impressive phenomena of their lives.

Moreover, the end of the Ice Age seems to have marked a division between prehistoric peoples and their ancestors. From Mesolithic times there is mention of a golden era, a paradise when human relations with heaven and the animals were more harmonious. Probably this idea represents the culmination of hunting peoples' myths and reflection—an early form of mythic speculation on the ways things ought to be. In any case, when the glaciers melted, the flood brought the world's periodicity into sharper focus. Also, questions arose of moral responsibility and guilt: What caused the flood? How did we lose paradise? Ancestors, believed to linger on as ghosts or spiritual presences, also stimulated such questions: What is our relationship to our predecessors who knew better times? To increase their chances of living in a good age, ancient hunters likely developed a code of behavior and a cluster of taboos that they attributed to their ancestors: "Live this way and you will prosper."

After Agriculture

The great practical advances of the Mesolithic period were settled communities and the domestication of plants and animals. In the Near East, especially in Palestine, these advances created a period of strong cultural activity, as people strove to understand and express the far-reaching changes in their life-styles. The remains of the Natufian culture at Wadi en-Natuf, for instance, show a people who built a village of circular huts, harvested wild cereals with stone sickles, and ground seeds with mortar and pestle. (There is evidence that cereals were a dietary staple in the valley of the upper Nile as early as 13,000 B.C.E.) By 6500 B.C.E. different Near Eastern communities had domesticated sheep, goats, and pigs. The Mesolithic period also produced numerous important inventions, among them the bow, cords, nets, hooks, and boats.

In Eliade's view, such inventions have more than just practical or economic effects. When people work with different materials imaginatively and creatively, they develop a sophisticated sense of the many possibilities in matter—the many analogies between tools and artifacts, human work and natural processes. Thus, they easily create rich symbolisms or mystiques. We have seen how Ogotemmeli viewed the blacksmith, the granary, and the spindle. Other ancient peoples gave mining, harvesting, or sewing the same sort of densely symbolic value. A fairly direct line runs from their prehistoric world to that of the medieval alchemist and even that of the modern engineer.

Before the Mesolithic turn to agriculture and a more settled life, nomadic cultures depended on hunting, blood sacrifices, and a close identification with animals. In later times, these Paleolithic themes continued to play in the background. Through military groups, myths of the days of nomadic life, hunting for sport, and occasional orgies (with frenzied tearing of animals and eating of raw flesh), agricultural peoples kept contact with their past. Nonetheless, after village life came "vegeculture" (the cultivation of roots, tubers, and rhizomes), and then agriculture (the cultivation of cereals and grasses). The religious impact of these cultures was revolutionary.

For instance, as producers of food, human beings had to calculate the seasons much more accurately. This led to astronomical calculations, astrology, and the worship of planets and stars. Further, agriculture meant a more intimate knowledge of the regular cycle of death and rebirth. In the typical myth of Hainuwele, from New Guinea, we can see the ancient struggle to comprehend this new set of mysteries.[3] By her murder and dismemberment, the semidivine Hainuwele allowed tuberous plants to spring forth. In other words, vegeculture depended on a primordial murder. More deliberately than hunters, who find available animals, cultivators bury life in order to secure their food. Summarizing the psychic impact of this new situation, Eliade says, "All responsible activities (puberty ceremonies, animal or human sacrifices, cannibalism, funerary ceremonies, etc.) properly speaking constitute a recalling, a 'remembrance,' of the primordial murder. It is significant that the cultivator associates with a murder the essentially peaceful labor that insures his existence, whereas in societies of hunters the responsibility for slaughter is attributed to *another*, to a 'stranger.' "[4]

Succeeding the mystical solidarity between hunters and animals, then, is a mystical solidarity between cultivators and plants. Whereas in earliest times blood and bone were the essential, most sacred elements of life, in agricultural times the generative elements—masculine sperm and feminine blood—became most sacred. Above all, women dominated agricultural life, and "mother earth" was the prime focus. Through the millennia, before the biology of reproduction became clear, the earth was believed to give birth independently, without need of any male. Because women developed agriculture and controlled it, and because women issued all human life, Mesolithic culture valued women as it did mother earth and gave women great religious and political power. Thus, from this period the best-known great goddesses came; during this period matriarchy thrived. Sexuality became a sacred drive and process, because all nature—the whole cosmos—moved through a religious cycle of conception, gestation, birth, nurturance, growth, decline, and then death (which may be a new conception).

Houses, villages, shrines, and burial vaults all reflected the womb architecturally. The earth itself is uterine: from it we come, to it we return. Accordingly, myths of human creation speak of first ancestors crawling forth from mines or caves, and funerary rituals consign the dead offspring back to the Great Mother. During this initial period of agriculture, there was an increased stress on polarities—earth and sky, dirt and rain, yin and yang (the Chinese dual elements).

This stress on the earth of the Mesolithic continued into Neolithic times, when village life developed into city life, agriculture became more extensive and secure, and arts and crafts such as pottery, weaving, and tool manufacturing were established. Also, in the Neolithic period, cults of fertility and death assumed even greater prominence. From sanctuaries excavated in Anatolia (modern Turkey), we know that around 7000 B.C.E. worship involved skulls and various gifts, such as jewels, weapons, and textiles. The principal divinity was a goddess, who was manifested in three forms: a young woman, a mother, and a crone (old woman). Figurines represent her giving birth, breasts adorn her cave sites, and drawings portray her among animals, especially bulls and leopards. In many caves the double ax, symbol of the storm god, underscores the fertility theme (stormy rain fecundates mother earth).

Representations of bees and butterflies relate this fertility theme to the burial skulls and gifts, since both bees and butterflies pass through distinct stages in their life cycles. Worshippers likely tried to fit death into such a scheme—to see it as another transformation of the life force, another stage. Subordinate to the goddess was a male god, a boy or youth, who seems to be her child and lover and who has some correlations with the bull.

With the discovery of bronze about 3500 B.C.E. in the Middle East, new weapons and tools came into use. Also, more specialized work developed, such as mining, smelting, and casting metal. In turn, this work created more efficient farming implements, which led to the production of surplus food.

Surplus food allowed a new class of religious specialists (who were agriculturally unproductive) to arise, while the metals "industry" stimulated the exploration and colonization of new territories for raw materials.

From 1900 to 1400 B.C.E., following the Hittite invention of tempering, iron came into widespread use, and the production of bronze and iron further stimulated the human imagination and increased the symbolic content of mother earth. Whereas the earliest iron was a gift from the sky (coming in the form of meteorites), mined iron came from the womb of the earth. Indeed, miners developed regimes of fasting, meditation, and purification, since they had to go into sacred depths and extract a new form of life. Their mythology spoke of elves, fairies, genies, and spirits who inhabited the underground, assisting or witnessing the slow gestation of mother earth's strangest children, the ores. Metallurgists, like blacksmiths and potters, had to be "masters of fire," which associated them with the shamans, who were masters of inner, magical heat. Also, metallurgists took on some of the paradoxical nature of metal itself. Coming from mother earth and a boon to humanity, metal was sacred. However, being invulnerable and easily an instrument of death, metal was too close to evil for humans to handle comfortably. Thus, the smith entered the mythology of the gods, fashioning weapons for their heavenly battles and tools for their heavenly enterprises. In India, Tvastr made Indra's weapons for the fight against Vrtra; in Greece Hephaestus forged the thunderbolt that enabled Zeus to triumph over Typhon.

Megaliths

The Bronze and Iron Ages begot the first great civilizations, and their religions will be our major interest. Before discussing them, however, we should survey one last prehistoric phenomenon, the megaliths. *Megalith* means "great stone," and it brings to mind the prehistoric European cultures that left remains such as the famous crom-lech (circle of huge stones) at Stonehenge in England. Actually, prehistorians speak of a megalithic cultural complex, centered at Los Millares in southeastern Spain and covering Portugal, half of France, western England, and parts of Ireland, Denmark, and Sweden. In some cases, prehistoric peoples in these areas arranged either cromlechs or *dolmens* ("immense capstone[s] supported by several upright stones arranged to form a sort of enclosure or chamber")[5] from slabs weighing as much as 300 tons.

What was the point to all this labor? Apparently the megalith was the major symbol for a cult of the dead. For Neolithic peasants of the fifth and fourth millennia B.C.E., stone was the symbol of permanence—of resistance to change, decay, or death. Unlike peoples in central Europe and the Near East, who strictly separated themselves from the dead, megalithic tribes sought close communion with the deceased, probably because they regarded death as a state of security and strength. To these people, ancestors could be powerful helpers and great allies. With the discovery of agriculture, human life probably seemed even more frail than it had before. Like that of the plant, it was ephemeral, bound to a cycle of birth, life, and death. By associating with "ancestral" stones—the bones of mother earth—humans might overcome their frailty and impermanence.

The megaliths represent burial vaults or ritual areas where this faith was practiced. At Stonehenge, for instance, the cromlech was in the middle of a field of funeral mounds. (Stonehenge was also a sophisticated instrument that could be used for making astronomical calculations.) At Carnac in Brittany, there was an avenue large enough for thousands to parade. Both sites were likely ceremonial centers or unenclosed temples—both were likely areas of sacred space for communing with ancestral stones.

Practically the whole island of Neolithic Malta was a megalithic sanctuary system. There a great goddess presided as the guardian divinity of a cult of the dead. One necropolis, now called the Hypogeum, has yielded bones of more than 7,000 people. Previously, scholars thought that this cultural complex, like the European ones, derived from a cultural basin around the Aegean Sea. However, radiocarbon datings show that the megaliths are older than the remains from the prehistoric Aegean, so western Europeans apparently developed their megalithic death cult independently.

Moreover, megaliths later cropped up in a vast geographic area extending from Algeria to Korea and North America. Thus, huge stones probably prompted certain ideas about death, ancestors, permanence, and escape from time and decay to all peoples. If most prehistoric peoples were moved to ponder their mortality more deeply because of agriculture, perhaps they tended to use stone to assist in this contemplation. Indeed, studies of megalithic societies that continued into the twentieth century confirm this hypothesis. In Indonesia and Melanesia, stone monuments defended the soul during its journey to the beyond, ensured an eternal existence after death, linked the living and the dead, and fertilized the crops and animals through their sacred durability. Certain customs of European peasants in megalithic areas further confirm this hypothesis. As late as the early twentieth century, peasant women in parts of France slid along stones or rubbed themselves against stones to stimulate conception. For them as for women who lived in their locales 5,000 years earlier, stone was powerful and fertilizing.

The New Religious Mentality

Clearly, then, the ancient religious mind of prehistoric oral peoples produced a variety of cultures well worth our study and appreciation. The majority of them depended on hunting and gathering or relatively simple agriculture and thus tended to be nomadic and loosely organized. In anthropological terminology, they tended to be societies of small scale. The rest of this chapter addresses settled societies of larger scale—

cultures that evolutionists classify as "higher" or "more developed." Extensive agriculture, estimable art and technology, city life, and complex government are some of the characteristics of societies so classified.

Equally important, though, is the development of writing, which led to history, literature, and other forms of communication that radically altered how human beings thought about themselves and the world. Written records enabled people to control trade, administer a large realm, and chart the movements of the stars. Therefore, our main interest in most of this chapter is the new religious mentality that arose when humanity became literate and superseded the ancient religious mentality.

In examining that new religious mentality, we shall study the rich, complex cultures of three ancient civilizations: Egypt, Iran, and Greece. These civilizations merit special attention because of the elaborateness of their religious systems and their influence on the modern world. They exhibit quite different orientations, so by the end of this chapter the term *ancient civilization* should be a complex, broadly defined term. Also by the end of this chapter we hope to have clarified Eric Voegelin's pregnant concept, "the cosmological myth," which explains much about ancient religious consciousness, particularly the pervading ancient notion that the world is a single living whole.[6] No ancient civilization ever broke the cosmological myth completely, but the differing attempts by the Egyptian Akhenaton, the Iranian Zoroaster, and the Greek Plato are key moments in their respective peoples' cultural histories and in humanity's religious march.

Many other cultures might have been studied in this chapter had space allowed. Ancient Mesopotamia, for instance, was probably the birthplace of writing, and its anxiety-ridden, very human religious culture contrasts instructively with Egypt's stability and optimism.[7] Both the Mesopotamian creation account *(Enuma Elish)* and the heroic *Epic of Gilgamesh* deserve their

renown as masterpieces of ancient thought, and an ideal, leisurely introduction would surely review them carefully. Similarly, Roman religion would be a valuable subject. As perhaps the paramount empire of Western antiquity, Rome is a striking instance of civil religion. All ancient civilizations combined religion and politics, but Rome developed a legal and military efficiency that makes its blend especially striking.[8] Since civil religion has become a rallying point in recent analyses of bicentennial American religion,[9] studying the imperial Roman product could be quite timely.

Ideally we would also take up the religions of ancient Europe and the New World. Though these peoples did not develop full writing systems, they did produce estimable technologies and arts fully informed by their religious notions. In pre-Christian Europe, Germanic, Celtic, and Slavic peoples lived close to a wild, hearty nature and were shamanist, priestly, kingly, and folkloric. They had matriarchal societies, practiced some human sacrifice, and were vigorously concerned with magic and fertility. Because the ideas of these people have entered our own cultural blood, often less obviously than those from Israel, Greece, Rome, and Christianity, they could have the special fascination of mysteries ingredient in our own psyches.[10]

In the New World, the great cultures of ancient Mexico and Peru beg for comparison with North American ancient cultures. Why, for instance, did the Aztecs develop such a rich system of myths and sacraments concerning gods who traded with human beings? Why did that trade balance slip toward the end of the pre-European period and human sacrifice arise? The ancient Incan civilization of Peru, which predated European contact by more than 2,000 years, integrated the human life cycle with nature's fertility rhythms almost classically. The Peruvian *huaca*, like the Sioux *wakan*, was a divine force present in all holy things. Yet, archeological excavations have shown traces of both an early creator god and later

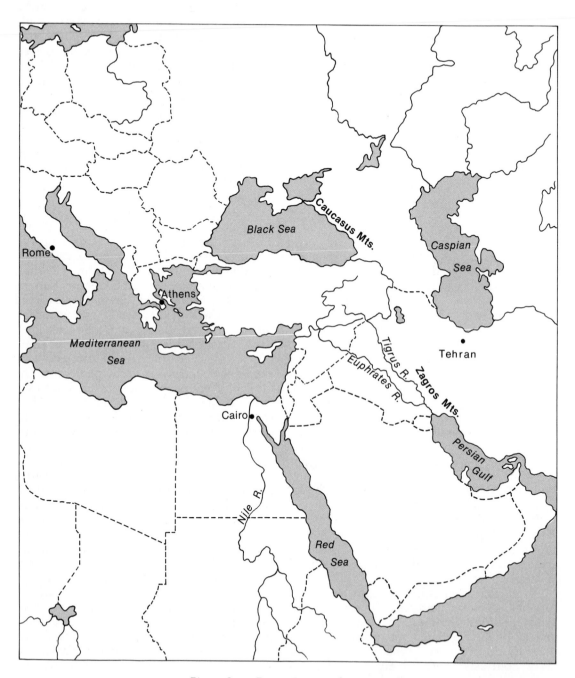

Figure 8   Egypt, Iran, and Greece.

animal divinities, such as snakes, condors, and cats. Thus, a full account of human religiosity would discuss old America.[11]

EGYPT

Today Egypt is a powerful center of Arab and Muslim culture. Taxi drivers careen through Cairo with a Qur'an on the dashboard to protect them; common people lay rugs in the train station and kneel at the call to prayer. Yet the treasures of Tutankhamen, the Giza pyramids, and above all the Nile tie modern Cairo to the pre-Islamic Egypt of more than 5,000 years ago. Merely follow the Nile by train to Alexandria and you will see in its delta *fellah* (peasants)

drawing water with buffalo much as they did in the Old Kingdom.

The Nile itself is a principal player in Egyptian history. Its moods, both varying and constant,[12] reflect the Egyptian soul. Historically, the Egyptian soul appears ageless. For the best part of 2,500 years Egyptian life remained the same. At the Great Pyramids near the Sphinx, the desert seems to have mimicked the Nile's behavior. The endless sand, like the river water, changes with the wind. Actually, though, little changes. Sky, sun, sand, and water—they all endure. Like stable props, they are set on every stage.

On the Egyptian stage, pharaohs and *fellah* enacted a mortality play. As the pyramids show, death kept adamant hold on this

Figure 9   *Great Sphinx near Giza pyramids, outside Cairo, Egypt.*
Photo by J. T. Carmody.

people's soul. Beyond life under the sun, life in the flesh, lay deathlessness. The tomb then was an archway through which everybody passed. Sanity was preparing to pass well.

Standing before the Sphinx, an Egyptian might offer this prayer: "O god of the puzzle, well do you symbolize our situation. Strong as a lion, winged like thought, you beguile us like a woman. In this flesh, we mainly know contradiction. Body and thought, we go diverse ways. Clearly, though, all ways end in the underworld. Help us stand judgment there before Osiris. Help us enter Re's course through the sky. May our time in the sun go smoothly. May our afterlife be content. Help us solve our riddle."

Religious History

Scholars debate the history of Egyptian religion, but the major events are clear. Unification of Upper (southern) and Lower (northern) Egypt occurred about 3100 B.C.E., and with it began the central Egyptian religious dogma—divine kingship.[13] In the prehistoric years before unification, Neolithic culture gradually developed small-town life, characterized by domestic animals, significant crafts (especially pottery), and probably the burial of the dead with hopes of an afterlife. From the beginnings of Egyptian history, local gods had great influence, and throughout the long dynasties they comprised a pantheon (assembly of divinities). It is well established that ancient Egypt was amazingly stable culturally. Divine kingship, concern with an afterlife, and a rather unorganized complex of gods exemplify that stability, for they characterized the entire 2,000 years of the native dynasties.

Egyptian splendor began vigorously in the period 3100–2200 B.C.E., which historians divide into the Early Dynasties (3100–2700 B.C.E.) and the Old Kingdom (2700–2200 B.C.E.). A famous product of Old Kingdom religion is the Memphite theology, developed to justify the new, unified kingdom centered at Memphis. Central to the justification is that the god of Memphis, Ptah, is the foremost creator god. Ptah originated Atum, the supreme god of the older cosmogony, and the other gods by an idea in his heart and a command on his tongue. Scholars are fascinated by this notion, because it suggests that 2,000 years before the Hebrews or Greeks came up with the notion of a first spiritual cause, an Egyptian had more than suspected it.[14]

From about 2200 to 2050 B.C.E., there was an intermediate period of disorder. The social order rooted in the permanence of nature and the gods gave way to chaos. We catch overtones of that upheaval in the famous "Dispute over Suicide," a remarkable text from the end of the third millennium. A man says to his soul, "To whom can I speak today? My fellows are evil, my friends do not love, . . . the land is left to those who do wrong." So, he considers suicide: "Death faces me today like the recovery of a sick man, like going out into the open after a confinement, . . . like the longing of a man to see his home again, after many years in captivity."[15] Clearly the prehistoric Egyptian hope of a happy afterlife with the gods functioned for this desolate writer as a way to justice—a way to symbolize the friendship and social order that life must have if it is not to seem absurd.

The Middle Kingdom (2050–1800 B.C.E.) was centered at Thebes. It nurtured several trends that brought important changes, although they worked below the surface constancy of Egyptian life. The most important of these trends was a democratization of certain religious rights, as the distance between the pharaoh and the common people narrowed. Also, there was an effort to elevate the more important gods and an increasing inclination to worship gods who were in the form of animals,[16] two phenomena that we shall observe below when we analyze the complex Egyptian sense of divinity. The most important religious rights that democratization brought the middle classes were privileges in the afterlife and a chance to participate in ceremonies that had been confined to the king and a few priests.

A second intermediate period (1800–1570 B.C.E.) dissolved the Middle Kingdom and included a century or so of rule by the Hyksos (shepherd kings), who were probably Syrians. The New Kingdom (1570–1165 B.C.E.) began with the famous XVIII dynasty, which made Egypt a true empire that stretched to the Euphrates. For our limited review of the high points in later Egyptian religious history, the New Kingdom's speculation on monotheism and a purer divinity is important. In the XIX dynasty under Akhenaton (1369–1353 B.C.E.), there was a move to make Aton, previously just the sun disk, the sole deity. Apparently Akhenaton himself bullied through this change (Egypt quickly reverted to polytheism after his death) because of his own spiritual perceptions.

Eric Voegelin calls Akhenaton " a new voice in history, the voice of a man intimately sympathetic with nature, sensitive to the splendor of light and its life-spending force, praising the god and his creature."[17] In a joyful climax, one of Akhenaton's hymns cries out: "The Aton is the creator-god: O sole god, like whom there is no other! Thou didst create the world according to thy desire, while thou wert alone."[18] Moreover, Aton was not the god of Egypt alone. Akhenaton saw that a true creator god must have established all peoples, whatever their country, speech, culture, or skin. This was truly a remarkable leap toward universalism, especially coming from the leader of a resolutely ethnocentric people, and it was the centerpiece in the so-called Armarna Revolution that gave the New Kingdom a great charge of cultural energy.

Another high point of New Kingdom theology was the Amon hymns, which probably date from the reign of Ramses II (1290–1224 B.C.E.). They illustrate a return to Amon and the demise of Aton, as well as a deep sense that the first creator god must be mysterious. Amon is "far from heaven, he is absent from the underworld, so that no gods know his true form. His image is not displayed in writings. No one bears witness to him. . . . He is too mysterious that his majesty might be disclosed, he is too great that men should ask about him, too powerful that he might be known."[19] Along with the hymns of Akhenaton, these praises of Amon represent the greatest advance in Egyptian theology.

For the most part, the Egyptians were not a speculative, intellectually probing people. They easily tolerated many gods and relied almost unquestioningly on ethical maxims and proverbs. In the Amon hymns, however, we see traces of a negative theology—a rising of the mind to the true nature of divinity by denying that creatures can represent it adequately. Because negative theology is a paramount way of breaking the cosmological myth, the Amon hymns show how close Egypt came to the revolutions that Israel and Greece accomplished.

In the centuries after the New Kingdom, the capital moved to Tanis, Bubastis, and Saïs—a good indication of the political turmoil of that era. Persians ruled Egypt from 525 to 405 B.C.E., and the last native dynasties (405–332 B.C.E.) ended with the conquest of Alexander. In the period from Alexander to about 30 B.C.E., the Hellenistic Ptolemies ruled, and the city of Alexandria was the luminary of the eastern Mediterranean. Christian influence rose in the Roman and Byzantine periods (30 B.C.E.–641 C.E.), bequeathing Egypt the Coptic church. Since 641, Egyptian culture has been largely Muslim, but its native orientations have never completely died.

World View

In analyzing the Egyptian religious mentality, we quickly realize that studying any single portion of such a long-lived culture is bound to be inadequate. Therefore, the remarks below about the basic attitudes of Egyptians are just generalizations.

With regards to divinity, the proliferation of gods and symbols is overwhelming.

The basic hieroglyph for God was a pole with a flag—the emblem flying in front of major temples, which designated purity and the creative life force. Since the Egyptians sensed purity and creativity in many places, they split divinity into many gods. The gods most important in the old cosmogony were four male-female pairs. The males bore the head of a frog, and the females the head of a snake—symbols, apparently, of self-renewal (the frog begins as a tadpole, while the snake sheds its skin). The belief (before the Memphite theology established Ptah as the creator) was that an invisible wind moved over primal waters and used these four pairs of gods to make life.

Throughout Egyptian history, the most important gods were associated with the sun and death-resurrection. Their names and images varied from cultural center to cultural center, but the most common name for the sun-god was Re, symbolized by either the sun's disk or the falcon. Another name was Khepri, represented by a scarab pushing the sun disk; a third name was Atum, whom people at Heliopolis worshipped and represented by the setting sun. In the mythology of Heliopolis, Atum generated himself on the primordial hill of creation (the great pyramids of the Old Kingdom represented this hill). He conquered chaos, took charge of the world, and established *maat*, the eternal cosmic order. The *Book of the Dead* (17 : 3–5), from the New Kingdom, says that Re became king of the gods in the earliest times by defeating all his opponents. Maat is his daughter but also his mother, because in his course through the sky, the sun-god follows her cosmic order.

That course determined Egyptian reality. The west was the land of the dead, and the east was where the daily miracle of the sun's return from the dead occurred.[20] On the walls of royal tombs near Luxor, twelve sections divide the night realm, or underworld, through which the sun-god's boat travels. Although the sun-god is dead during this time, he still possesses the power of resurrection. Middle night is the realm of Sokaris, who appears in human form with the head of a falcon. His area is a desert through which Re's boat has to be dragged before the sun can reemerge into the light.

It was Osiris, however, around whom the funerary cult developed that made the underworld almost an Egyptian obsession. Nowhere is the myth of his descent to the underworld detailed, but it probably had the following plot. Osiris and Seth were brothers, and Isis was Osiris' sister and wife. Osiris ruled the world as a good regent, but Seth hated him and killed him by guile. He got Osiris into a coffin and sent it down the Nile. Isis recovered Osiris' corpse and uttered a soulful dirge (which inspired litanies used in Osiris' worship). This dirge had a magic power that revived Osiris. Once again Seth moved against Osiris, this time hacking Osiris' body into fourteen pieces and then scattering them. Isis recovered them all and buried each piece properly wherever she found it (this explained the many Osirian sanctuaries). Further, Isis conceived a son Horus by the dead Osiris and brought Horus up in the marshes to hide him from Seth.

When Horus reached manhood, Isis arranged for a trial at which Seth was condemned for murdering Osiris and Horus was recognized as Osiris' heir. Osiris himself remained in the underworld, accepting the roles of lord of the nether realm and judge of the dead. Osiris seems to represent the growing power of vegetation, which roots in the earth, and he relates to all buildings that are set on the earth, to the moon, and to the dead. Isis represents the throne, the sacred seat of the king. As such, she "makes" the king and is his mother. For instance, on a relief in a temple at Abydos, the pharaoh sits in Isis' lap. Thus, Horus and the pharaoh are correlated. As Horus owed his throne to his mother Isis, so did the pharaoh.

Horus had many appearances, but most frequently he wore the head of a falcon. He was the model son but shows traces of an older sky god. In the Osiris myth, Horus fought Seth and lost an eye, while depriving Seth of his testicles. They reconciled, however, to suggest that life and death, too, can agree. Thoth, originally a moon god, was the agent of their reconciliation. Usually Thoth was represented as a baboon or ibis. He was also a god of the dead and is thought to have found Horus' lost eye and have returned it to him. This eye became a token of life returned from the dead.

The prime attribute of Egyptian divinity, then, was life. It shone in the sun, who daily accomplished the miracle of being resurrected from darkness, bestowing life-giving light and warmth. Life flowed in the Nile, whose annual flooding was necessary for crops to grow. Even the underworld became a realm of life. Osiris ruled there, judgment took place there, and vegetation rooted there.

Nature and Society

From this association of divinity with life, it follows that nature itself had a potent sacredness. Henri Frankfort, in fact, has analyzed Egyptian divinity in terms of the sun's power of creation, the power of procreation in cattle, and the power of resurrection in the earth.[21] We have seen a little of the sun and the Osirian earth. Apis, the bull god, was a focus of procreative power, as was Min, a mummy with a huge projecting phallus.

By the "cosmological myth," we mean the tendency to run these various sacred forces together so that nature and divinity are coextensive. Apart from the brief ventures behind the hymns to Aton and Amon, Egypt little doubted the cosmological myth. It could support so many gods because, like oral ancient peoples, Egyptians sensed sacredness everywhere. Unlike Jews, Christians, and Muslims, however, they did not fashion a popular, effective negative theology that said, "True divinity is actually in no one place—it is beyond all place, all time, all this worldly containment." As a result, nature's cycles and changes all represented aspects of the basic Egyptian divinity, which was the world itself. This cosmos of rocks and trees, water and land, living things and dying things—this was the ultimate reality.

The Egyptian people participated in the sacred cosmos through their king, who to them was quite literally divine. The king represented Horus, Re, or Osiris. In the analytic terms of Western scholars, he mediated between nature's divine order and his people. Society and politics were part of one natural circuit; the *maat* (goddess of order) that gave the world its law or reason ran from heaven through the pharaoh to the people. Thus, the pharaoh was under *maat* and yet, for the common people, the source of *maat*. Psychologically, this order was a major reason for the stability of the Egyptian culture. With divinity in their midst, what need the people fear?

Through many agricultural ceremonies and many regal rituals, these beliefs took dramatic form.[22] At first the common people had limited access to most kingly ceremonies, but in the later centuries their participation increased. The greatest threat to social stability, understandably, was the king's death. Consequently, the most influential mythic cycle was that of Osiris and Isis, which explained where the king (identified with Osiris) had gone at death. Relatedly, the most important ceremonies were the old king's burial and the new king's accession. For a hint of how effective this mythic-ritualistic faith was, consider the pyramids. The common people supplied the immense, brutal labor needed to build the pyramids, which assured the kings' happy afterlife and the state's continuance.

Ancient Egypt had a powerful caste of priests, and at times, despite the dogma of the king's divinity, it clashed with the crown. The conflict between Akhenaton and the priests of the old god Amon was a vivid instance of such friction, but conflict was almost always on the verge of breaking out. When Akhenaton moved the capital from Thebes to Amarna, he bruised theological, class, and local sensitivities all at once. The local priesthood, fighting for its own gods and people, consistently defended those sensitivities. As a result, the priesthood was a powerful sociological force.

Women were quite subordinate in Egyptian society, but not without influence and religious importance. The goddesses Hathor, Nut, Neith, Maat, and Isis represented the feminine aspects of divinity, while the queen had vital roles in the political theology.[23] Hathor, Nut, and Neith were forms of the mother goddess—both sacred representations of fertility and figures of comfort. Maat ruled cosmic justice, while Isis was sister and wife of the god as king. On rare occasions a queen could rule (Hatshepsut, 1486–1468 B.C.E., is the most famous instance), and as the source of the divine king, the queen mother was much more than just another harem wife.

Egyptian proverbs encouraged husbands to treat their wives well so that their property would prosper, but they also pictured women as "frivolous, flirtatious, and unreliable, incapable of keeping a secret, untruthful and spiteful as well as naturally unfaithful. To the storytellers and moralists [women were] the epitome of all sin and an endless source of mischief."[24] Women of the New Kingdom served in the temples and as popular entertainers, but in both cases they risked reputations as prostitutes. In both formal and popular religion, Isis was a focal point for women's own religion, especially in Hellenistic times. Related to Osiris, she was the ideal wife (and a potent exemplar of grief); related to Horus, she was the ideal mother. Through Isis, then, women in ordinary roles participated in divinity.

Perhaps due to this divinity, legal documents from about 500 B.C.E. suggest that Egyptian women had the right to own property, buy or sell goods, and testify in court. They were taxpayers and could sue; they could inherit from parents or husbands.[25] On the other hand, husbands could dismiss wives at their pleasure (but not vice versa), and concubinage, adultery, and prostitution were widespread. Because many Egyptian women worked the fields or had other important economic roles, their lot was better than that of women in other ancient civilizations (Mesopotamia, for instance). Still, women were not equal to men, in part because of a prevailing male suspicion of

woman: "She is a deep water whose twisting men know not."[26]

The Self

The religious conception of the self relates intimately to the Egyptian concern with death, burial, and the afterlife. That concern, John Wilson insists,[27] was a result not of gloom but of optimism. The ancient Egyptians loved life, despite its dependence on such uncertain phenomena as the Nile's proper rising, and they looked forward to another, better chapter after death. The remains of many burial sites, well preserved because of the desert sand and dry climate, show that the departed took with them favorite utensils and even favorite servants. The *ba* was that aspect of a person that continued after death, which contrasts with the *ka*, or vital force, the impersonal power animating the living. A third concept, the *akh*, was the shining, glorious aspect of the dead in heaven. With these three notions, the Egyptians had a sense of what moves the living and what continues on after death.

As indicated in our outline of the myth, Osiris judged the dead in the underworld. The pyramid texts of the Old Kingdom, coffin texts of the Middle Kingdom, and *Book of the Dead* from the New Kingdom show a constant concern with judgment and hence a certain awareness of personal responsibility. The *Book of the Dead* contains a famous "negative confession" that illustrates both the posthumous trial Egyptians imagined and some of their principal ethical concerns. The deceased claims before Osiris: "I have not committed evil against men. . . . I have not mistreated cattle. . . . I have not blasphemed a god. . . . I have not done violence to a poor man. . . . I have not made anyone weep. . . . I have not killed. . . . I have not defamed a slave to his superior. . . . I have not had sexual relations with a boy." In all, thirty-six declarations of innocence are made.[28] Then, to complete his show of religious virtuosity, he gives each of the forty-two divine jurors, by name, a specific assurance. For example, "O Embracer-of-Fire, who comes forth from Babylon, I have not stolen. O Eater-of-Entrails, who comes forth from the thirty [judges in the world of the living], I have not practised usury. O Eater-of-Blood, who comes forth from the execution block, I have not slain the cattle of the god."[29]

In ancient Egypt, then, the gods were everywhere. Economics, politics, the arts, nature—all aspects of life were religious. In symbolically mythic ways, nobles and peasants alike looked to the king, tried to discern *maat*, and hoped for mercy before Osiris. The sun, the river, and the land all witnessed the interplay of death and resurrection with comfort. Each dawn, each annual flood, each spring sprouting was a pledge of hope. Therefore, one could live optimistically and even with good humor; on most days, life was good.

IRAN

Contemporary Iran is a nation in the throes of choosing its identity and direction. On first view, the principal factors are Western secularism (almost unavoidable because of Iran's massive petroleum industry) and a volatile form of traditional Islam. These factors alone are more than enough to bewilder analysts, but the snowcapped mountains rimming Tehran suggest there is much more—the long history of culture that crossed the Iranian plain. When one sees Iranian women draped in black, showing only a panel of dark eyes, something flickers more ancient than Islam.

That something is the spirit of Zoroaster, priest and prophet. In the mind's eye, it burns toward Truth. Picture Zoroaster as being fiery, choleric, fierce of face. He is angry that some Iranians do not accept his Wise Lord. In their dimness, they stick to the old vital forces. Zoroaster, though, knows better—he knows the battle between Evil and Good.

The battle between Evil and Good absorbs Zoroaster completely, and in every conflict he sees its mark. His vision brings forth symbols of judgment. The wicked, who reject the Wise Lord, will never cross Paradise Bridge. Paradise Bridge is sharp as a razor and cuts all deceit to the quick. But the Evil Spirit is a powerful enemy, and his handiwork, the Lie, is everywhere. Thus, Zoroaster redoubles his insistence on Truth. Rugged as the Elburz Mountains in the distance, he is highly disciplined. This is a man who has discovered the utter clarity of conscience's call to the light. Expect from him no compromise, no accommodation. Thus spake Zarathustra (the Greek form of the name), who formed ancient Iran.

Ask about Zoroaster on the streets of Tehran today, however, and you will likely be rebuked: "We are Muslims!" the typical residents will say. True enough, less than 10,000 Zoroastrians remain in Iran (perhaps 100,000 remain in India). Nonetheless, Zoroaster was the greatest religious influence in the epochal Persian Empire, the strongest molder of the Iranian spirit. As well, he was the first son of Asia adopted by the West.[30]

Zoroaster first intrigued the Greeks, whose explorers encountered his culture 400 years before Christ. Much later he impressed Western historians, philosophers, and artists as a cultural hero—a founder of civilization and conscience.

The Founding of Zoroastrianism

The historical influence of Zoroaster stretches from the tenth century C.E., when the Arab military conquest of the seventh century began to affect Iranian culture, back beyond 1500 B.C.E., when speakers of Indo-Iranian filtered through the Caucasus Mountains to the Iranian plateau. Before that date, "cave man," as Ghirshman calls him, lived around that plateau in holes dug into wooded mountainsides.[31] Indeed, archeological remains suggest that humans have inhabited Iran since the beginning of a dry period, twelve to seventeen thousand years ago.

According to Ghirshman, in primitive agricultural societies that developed on alluvial deposits, such as on the Iranian plateau, women had an economic, political, and religious superiority. Indo-European conquerers probably adopted their matriarchal social structure from these first inhabitants of present-day Iran.

Those first inhabitants were great potters, and archeologists have found among their relics designs and figurines of a naked goddess, whose mate was likely a god who was her son. This belief would be the most direct explanation for the early Iranian customs of marriage between blood relations, descent through the female line, and, in certain tribes (for example, the Guti of Kurdistan), female army commanders. Later archeological remains, dating back to 2000 B.C.E., suggest a people both artistic and hopeful, for impressive pendants, earrings, bracelets, and the like found in gravesites imply a strong belief in an afterlife.

In the second millennium B.C.E., Indo-Europeans, pressured by population shifts in the areas around them, left their homelands in the plains of southern Russia and migrated southeast across Iran. Some of them eventually ended up as far south as India.[32] In the west they established the Hittite Empire, sacked Babylon, and confronted the Egyptians. From the east, tribes called the Mittani conquered northern Mesopotamia and allied themselves with Egypt in about 1450 B.C.E. Linguistic, religious, and social parallels suggest that pre-Zoroastrian Iranian culture, as well as the culture of the peoples who conquered the Indus Valley in India and produced the Vedic culture, derived from the Mittani, Hittite, and other Indo-European "Aryans" (from an Indo-European word meaning "noble"). In particular, the Iranian and Indian Aryans had similar gods and similar social structures. (French scholar Georges Dumezil has argued that the Aryan gods correlated with a three-part social structure—priests, warriors, and agriculturalists—in which each social class had both a legal and a magical aspect.)[33]

The native Iranian religion that Zoro-aster challenged was probably controlled by Median priests (the Medes were a later Aryan tribe) from western Iran called *magi*. Apparently that religion was an animistic polytheism (devotion to many divine spirits) similar to that of early Aryan India. After Zoroaster's death, the magi fused their old ideas onto his new notions, making Zoroastrianism a hodgepodge of conflicting gods and practices.

Zoroaster is estimated to have lived from 628 to 551 B.C.E., but the only direct source for his message is a fragment of the sacred Zoroastrian liturgical text, the *Avesta*. That portion, called the *Gathas*, along with later Greek and Persian traditions, suggests that Zoroaster's enemies (magi and men's societies of the old religion) forced him to flee from his native western Iran eastward into ancient Chorasmia (the area today of Khurasan, western Afghanistan, and the Turkmen Republic of the Soviet Union). There, when about forty years old, he found a patron in King Vishtapa and his message began to have social effect.

R. C. Zaehner has suggested the following summary of Zoroaster's main doctrines:[34] (1) There is a supreme God, the Wise Lord (Ahura Mazdah), who has thought all things into existence by his Holy Spirit. The Wise Lord is holy, righteous, and generous, and he expresses himself through the Holy Spirit, Good Mind, and Truth—three entities inseparable from his essence. Wholeness, Immortality, and Right-Mindedness are his attributes. (2) The world is divided between Truth and the Lie. Ahura Mazdah made Truth, but Zoroaster does not say who made the Lie. (3) Creatures of the Wise Lord (spiritual beings and humans) are free to choose between Truth and the Lie. Angra Mainyu (the Destructive Spirit), twin brother of the Holy Spirit, chooses to do evil. "This he does of his own free will as do the *daevas*, the ancient gods whom, on account of the violence associated with their worship, Zarathustra considered to be evil powers." (4) Because human beings are free, they are responsible for their ultimate fates. By good deeds they win the eternal reward of possessing Wholeness and Immortality; by evil deeds they merit eternal pain in hell. (5) The great outward symbol of Truth is fire, and the center of the Zoroastrian cult is the fire altar.

When we set these doctrines in the context of Zoroaster's times, they are striking for their interiority. Before this prophet, little in Indo-European, Mesopotamian, or Egyptian religion focused on the mental concepts of truth and lie, the spiritually intuitive concepts of immortality and right-mindedness. In a way that prefigures the Greek philosophers' more radical discovery of reason, Zoroaster generates his images of divinity and human destiny from the operations of his own spirit. He turns away almost completely from nature toward the inner light of human conscience. In so doing he steps at least halfway out of the cosmological myth.

Two verses from perhaps the most autobiographical of Zoroaster's hymns suggest the religious experience at the core of his preaching:

As the holy one I recognized thee, O Wise Lord,
When I saw thee at the beginning, at the birth of existence,
Appoint a recompense for deed and word:
Evil reward to the evil, good to the good,
Through thy wisdom, at the last turning-point of creation [43 : 5].[35]

As the holy one I recognized thee, O Wise Lord,
When he came to me as Good Mind.
To his question: "To whom wilt thou address thy worship?"
I made reply: "To thy fire! While I offer up my veneration to it,
I will think of the Right to the utmost of my power" [43 : 9].[36]

In Iran in the early sixth century B.C.E., only an exceptional personality could have cut through the welter of Aryan gods, spells, and semimagical practices and discerned a clear religious call to identify divinity with justice. Similarly, only an exceptional personality could have lingered over abstractions such as Good Mind and the Right and made these terms God's best names.

It is true, as most scholars remind us, that Zoroaster's revelations had a social background and significance;[37] for instance, he championed the farmer over the nomad. Nonetheless, the deeper explanation of Zoroaster's religious power is the interior, spiritual experiences indicated by the *Gathas*. Like Buddha and Muhammad, Zoroaster met a holy, compelling divinity or ultimate reality. His mission was simply to spread the truth of this divinity far and wide. The origins of Zoroastrian history, then, are the visions and the religious insights of a founding genius. Through all its later changes, Zoroastrianism and the world religions that it influenced kept some aspect of Zoroaster's Wise Lord.

Zoroastrianism after Zoroaster

The great leaders of the Achaemenid empire who followed Zoroaster were the Persians Cyrus II (559–530 B.C.E.), Cambyses II (530–522 B.C.E.), and Darius I (522–486 B.C.E.). They conquered eastern Iran, the prophet's initial sphere of influence, and we can read in inscriptions that they left something of Zoroastrianism's function as the religious rationale for a new, energetic empire. Eric Voegelin cites these inscriptions as products of what he calls the "ecumenic age," when the new, transnational kingdoms precipitated the problem of how many peoples could be equally human.[38]

Spiritually, the new kings were neither fish nor fowl. On the one hand, they could not quite see themselves in the role of an Egyptian pharaoh or a Babylonian king. Both the ethnic complexity of the new Persian Empire, which contained several peoples, and Zoroaster's insights into God's universality went against Egyptian and Babylonian beliefs that Egypt and Babylon were the center of all creation. On the other hand, the Achaemenids still tended to think of the *ecumene,* the inhabited world, in terms of the countries that they had conquered. That is, they still failed to see that the true *ecumene,* the more profound "inhabited world,"

is not a matter of territories but of reason and spirit. Thus, they did not develop Zoroaster's spadework on the human soul's openness to a universal God by adopting a political philosophy in which no people are closer to divinity than any other, and no functionary (king, clerk, or peasant) is closer to God than any other.

However, as the inscriptions of Darius at Behistun and Naqsh-i-Rustam indicate, the Achaemenids did make Ahura Mazdah the source of their success, sensing the universal outreach of Ahura Mazdah's kingdom of truth. (Unfortunately, they also identified their opponents with the realm of the Lie.) For example, a Naqsh-i-Rustam inscription says of Darius' work:

A great god is Ahuramazda [Ahura Mazdah]
who has created this all-surpassing work,
that has become visible,
who has created the peace for men,
who has endowed with wisdom and good-being Darius the King.[39]

In Voegelin's view, this inscription represents a definite, if incomplete, step away from the political theology of the cosmological myth: "The substance of order that fills the far-flung empire through the conquering and administrative action of the king is no longer cosmic but the spiritual and moral substance of Ahura Mazda."[40] Xerxes, Darius' successor, building on this order, opposed his rule to that of certain rebels in terms of a clash between his Zoroastrian divine commission and their demonic worship of pre-Zoroastrian *daevas,* or lower gods. Unlike Egyptian political theology, the Persian political theology of the Achaemenids made the king the mediator of a divine truth that came from beyond the natural world. The pharaoh was the conduit of *maat*—cosmic order. The Persian king was the champion of Ahura Mazdah's Truth, which was precosmic and transcosmic, the enemy of the Destructive Spirit's realm of the Lie.

If the advance or decline in clarifying

reality marks the importance of a given epoch, the Achaemenid empire represented a very significant time. In it humanity advanced toward definitions of nature, divinity, and society that stem from wise judgment. We today have yet to secure those definitions, but we would be even less advanced had there been no Zoroaster or Persian culture.

Following Alexander's victory over Darius III in 331 B.C.E., the Achaemenids gave way to the Greek Seleucids. Under the Seleucids, for almost a century, Hellenistic cultural ideals blended with Persian. Zoroastrian influence probably declined, being overshadowed by a Greek-Iranian syncretism (combination of two forms of belief). While the practice of pure Zoroastrianism seems to have remained in Fars (the southern province called Persis), the old Iranian goddess Anahita, fused with the Mesopotamian goddess Nanai, complicated the religious picture in other provinces.

Also complicating the picture was the

Greek hero Heracles, who joined with local gods. Heracles was the patron of the gymnasium, the place of physical exercise, an important feature of Hellenistic culture. Also, he was one of several "savior" gods (gods who made life whole) whose influence grew apace with the disintegration of the previously secure city-state religions. The *Avesta* was probably still evolving at this time, incorporating hymns to the god Mithra, who had existed before Zoroaster and later became an important savior god for the Romans. In the *Avesta*, Mithra's main functions are to preserve cattle, sanctify contracts, and render judgment on human actions.[41]

The Era of Many Religions

The Greek Seleucids yielded to the Parthians, who entered Iran from the area southwest of the Caspian Sea. The Parthians dominated Iran, bit by bit, from the first conquest by Arsaces in about 238 B.C.E. until about 226 C.E. While sources are scanty, Zoroastrianism apparently made some gains against syncretism under the Parthians, achieving a privileged status. Richard Frye relates this to the influence of the magi: "We may suspect that Magi, in various parts of Iran, upheld the worship of Ahura Mazda and/or other old Aryan gods in varying forms and degrees of piety."[42] Nonetheless, in Parthian times the cultures of the different geographic areas varied considerably. Coins, art, and other remains indicate different local preferences for a variety of gods. Ahura Mazdah and Mithra certainly were influential, but the cult of the goddess Anahita was probably the most important.[43] The northern magis' custom of exposing the bodies of the dead on mountains (burial would pollute the earth) spread as far south as Susa, capital of the old Elamite kingdom. We also know that the Parthians were tolerant of religious minorities, so much so that Jews regarded them as great protectors.

The history of Zoroastrianism under the Parthians remains rather vague. Under the Sassanians (ca. 226–637 C.E.), it is more definite, as is the story of Persian culture

generally. The early Sassanian king Papak probably was the director of the shrine to Anahita at Istakhr in Persis (south central Iran), and his successor Shapur had quite liberal religious policies. That soon changed, however, largely due to the influence of Kartir, a zealous Zoroastrian priest. By the last third of the third century, he had made Zoroastrianism the established Persian "church." Kartir favored proselytizing, establishing fire temples for worship and instruction, purging Zoroastrian heretics, and attacking all non-Zoroastrian religions. Consequently, he persecuted Jews, Buddhists, Hindus, Christians, and Manichaeans, destroying their centers and proscribing their faiths. From his time marriage between blood relations became a common Zoroastrian practice, and the Zoroastrian clergy were a political power.

The Manichaeans—followers of the native Iranian prophet Mani—were the chief heretics. Under Shapur I, Mani had been free to travel and preach, but soon after Shapur's death the Zoroastrians martyred him. Nonetheless, his ideas gained considerable acceptance, both in Iran and throughout the Roman Empire. They stressed a dualism of good and evil, equating good with the spirit and evil with matter. Consequently, Manichaeans denigrated the body, sex, marriage, women, and food—anything perceived as carnal. As we shall see, Manichaeanism had an exciting effect on Christians, influencing Augustine and spawning several medieval heresies. At the end of the fifth century C.E., Persian Manichaeans led a socioeconomic movement called Mazdakism (after its leader Mazdak), which preached a sort of communism that included the division of wealth and the sharing of wives and concubines. Many poor people embraced this movement, but Prince Chosroes Anosharvan massacred the Mazdakite leaders about 528 C.E.[44]

By the last decades of Sassanian rule, the Zoroastrian church sanctioned a rigid caste system based, somewhat like that of India, on an ideal division of society into priests, warriors, scribes, and commoners. Ritual tended toward a sterile formalism, and a number of speculative or gnostic (relating to secret knowledge) tendencies emerged. At the beginning of the Sassanian period, Zurvanism had become the dominant Zoroastrian theology, in good part because of an increasing interest in the problem of evil. Zurvan is Infinite Time. Slowly, he displaced Ahura Mazdah (now called Ohrmazd) as the first principle. Ohrmazd then became identical with Holy Spirit, and Zurvan became his father, as well as the father of Holy Spirit's twin, Destructive Spirit. Thus, Zurvanism begot a dualism: Holy Spirit and Destructive Spirit. However, unlike Mani's dualism, Zurvanism did not make matter evil. For Zurvanite Zoroastrians, nature remained God's good creation.

After Muslims conquered Persia in the seventh century, Zoroastrianism lingered on for some time. The province of Fars, for instance, remained Zoroastrian into the tenth century. Gradually, however, the Zoroastrians retreated into ghettoes, and by 945, when Shiite Muslims took Baghdad, the end was near. Zoroastrian elements remained culturally important through the tenth-century renaissance of Persian letters, but thenceforth Islam was Iran's religion. Today perhaps 10,000 Zoroastrians remain in Iran around Gizd and Kerman. In the eighth century significant numbers emigrated to India to avoid Muslim rule. Their descendants have survived, retaining the original scriptures and much of the traditional doctrine. Known as Parsis, they now number about 150,000, with the largest concentration in Bombay. They keep the fire sacrifice, expose the dead in "towers of silence" where vultures may strip their flesh, and are one of India's best educated and most prosperous groups.

Zoroastrian World View

Before Zoroaster, Iran acknowledged a number of *ahuras*—good celestial spirits. The most prominent were lucidity (the brightness that glances off the waters or that leaps from fire); the sacred liquor *haoma*, used in the old Aryan cult; and plain water, symbol of purity and motherliness. Zoroaster pushed one wise Ahura to the fore, whose special qualities, such as Wholeness and Good Mind, were expressions of divine being. In later Zoroastrianism, these qualities became angelic beings who served Ohrmazd and influenced humans.

Opposing the good angels were powerful, antidivine forces led by the evil one, Ahriman. According to speculation after Zoroaster, Ohrmazd realized that to destroy Ahriman, he would have to lure him out of eternal time (Zurvan) into finite time. Zoroastrian theology thus became highly eschatological (interested in the last events of humanity) and developed imaginative doctrines of judgment, heaven, and hell. Ultimately Ohrmazd and goodness would triumph, and hell would cease after the wicked had been purged of their sins.[45]

If Ohrmazd and Zurvan represent the most refined aspects of Zoroastrian divinity, Mithra and Anahita express aspects no less influential. Both relate divinity to nature— Mithra to the sky and sun, Anahita to water. On the folk level, Anahita was very powerful, in effect giving Iran a great goddess. For instance, in one *Avestan* text (*Yasht* 5:17), Ahura Mazdah asks Anahita to make Zoroaster think, speak, and act according to good religion. Clearly, then, there was considerable confusion in developed Zoroastrian theology. Pressed by pre-Zoroastrian traditions and by outside cultural influences, Zoroastrianism tried to accommodate a variety of divinities within its monotheistic stress on Wise Lord. As a result, the goddess of plenty, the god of wind, the star Sirius, the Fravashis (the preexistent souls of good men and women), and more were objects of veneration. Thus, we might call Zoroastrianism an impure monotheism.

Though Zoroaster's theology turned away from nature and toward mental processes, the physical elements continued to shape Iranian religion. Mental processes and physical elements conspired in practical living, since the basic ethical imperative was to maintain goodness and life by fighting against evil and death.[46] As a result, Zoroastrianism frowned on fasting, asceticism, and celibacy. Rather, humans were to foster the powers of generation in nature and humanity alike. One basis for this view was Zoroaster's own stress on the holiness of agriculture, which to him was a cooperation with Ahura Mazdah. The farmer who sows corn, he said, "feeds the religion" of the Wise Lord.

Ancient Iran established a pronounced caste system, but most of its cultic practices cut across class distinctions. Some common people were quite interested in magic, but the orthodox leaders feared the occult, treating sorcerers and witches as criminals. Superstitions and totemic practices (for example, rubbing oneself with the wing of a falcon to ward off an evil spell) flourished, in part because of contact with Mesopotamia. Both divination and astrology were common, and other nations considered Persian magis to be specialists in dream interpretation. Finally, to add a little excitement now and then, there was trial by fire or molten lead (if the person survived, he or she was deemed innocent).

Zoroaster himself seems to have disapproved of blood sacrifices, going out of his way to try to protect cattle. Blood sacrifices survived in later Zoroastrianism, though, the most important being the bull sacrifice. Also important to later Zoroastrians was the preparation and offering of *haoma*, the sacred liquor, which until recently served as a sort of sacrament for the dying. The most important sacrifice and cultic focus, however, was the fire sacrifice. The flame had to be "pure," (obtained by burning "pure" materials such as sandalwood), and it had to pass to another flame before its fuel became embers. The fire sacrifice has overtones of an ancient wonder at the source of light and heat, but its major emphasis has always been to symbolize the divine.

Through their several sacrifices, Zoroastrians kept a sense of righteousness before Ahura Mazdah. For individuals, rites of passage at maturity, marriage, and death were important, as were various purifications. At maturity, both men and women apparently received a sacred thread and shirt. The thread was a compound symbol: cosmically, it stood for the Milky Way, the thread of the stars through the heavens; mythologically, it recalled Ahura Mazdah's gift of *haoma*; personally, it symbolized taking up adult responsibilities. The shirt was white, to symbolize purity and the garment that the soul dons after death.

Death and bloodshed were prime occasions for purification, because they were prime pollutants. As noted, Zoroastrians exposed the dead so as not to defile other persons, the earth, fire, or water. In some periods of Zoroastrianism, blood from a cut, extracted tooth, or even menstrual flow could render one ritually unclean. Emily Culpepper, who has surveyed Zoroastrian menstrual taboos, suggests a strong ancient element in this concern with purity.[47] (Complicated rites in which bodily impurities were passed through bull's urine, sand, and water also evidence this concern.)[48] In general, women played only a small part in the Zoroastrian world. Their part in redemption was to furnish males to fight against Ahriman. Most of the tradition held that in the beginning women defected to the Destructive Spirit. Theologically, then, Zoroastrianism viewed the female nature as unholy.

Conclusion

Zoroastrianism is important beyond its own confines. Because its eschatology attracted Jews, Christians, and Muslims, it has influenced perhaps half the world's believers. That is its historical prestige. In terms of philosophical prestige, where the issue is wisdom—the clarification of reality—Zoroaster is a prime religious figure because he made a strong contribution to the discovery of order. Order is the proper perspective on reality that only comes when we determine the relations among nature, society, self, and divinity.[49]

In cosmological civilizations, such as Egypt, the spirituality or reason of the human self remained unclear. As a result, Akhenaton's view of Aton and the Amon hymns to the unknown God were historical dead ends. Zoroaster, however, impressed upon Iranian culture a permanent sense of human and divine spirituality—a glimpse of a reality independent of matter, sense, or imagination. His insight was only partial, and it never dominated Iranian life. Nonetheless, it makes Zoroastrianism a significant, history-changing step. For if order is our goal, Zoroaster is a hero, and Iran is a country of wonders.

GREECE

Egypt amazes the world historian by the stability of its civilization. Iran-Persia impresses the historian of religion by Zoroastrianism's contribution to the clarification of order and its influence on Judaism, Christianity, and Islam. Greece, the third land of ancient religious civilization that we study, dazzles both world historians and historians of religion with its cultural diversity and splendor. Like classical Egyptian and classical Iranian religious culture, classical Greek religious culture has passed from the scene. Its influence in modern Greece lies under the surface of Eastern Orthodox Christianity, much as classical Egyptian religion lies under present-day Egyptian Islam and classical Zoroastrianism lies under present-day Iranian Islam. It is dead, but not without its influence.

Moreover, the influence of classical Greek religion is active in a different sense than that of its Egyptian or Iranian counterparts. Through the philosophy, science, literature, politics, and art that it nurtured, classical Greece became tutor to the West. For example, it furnished Christianity and Islam with many of their intellectual categories. Insofar as those categories have been developed in modern science and technology, classical Greece has been absolutely instrumental in shaping the present global society.

In addition, the Greek love of wisdom clarified the nature of human reason, prompting a momentous step toward right order—far greater than Zoroaster's. Classical Greece was the climax of ancient efforts to discern how human spirit is consubstantial ("of the same stuff") with God. Since the Greek dramatists, the wisdom to manage human spirit has been closely associated with suffering. Since Socrates, Plato, and Aristotle, human thought has reached into the mind of God.

The cultural splendor of Greece blazed forth in a land of great beauty. If the Athens of today suffers disturbing pollution, the Athens of yesterday still glimmers on the Acropolis and bustles in the streets of its port, Piraeus. Indeed, leave Piraeus by boat, or Athens by bus, and in less than two hours pre-Christian Greece is upon you. What do you feel? That it is, above all, a place of vision—of incredibly clear light and unbounded blue sea. On Cape Sounion or one of the islands, this beautiful clarity remains today. John Fowles describes the scene:

It was a Sunday in late May, blue as a bird's wing. I climbed up the goat-paths to the island's ridge-back, from where the green froth of the pine-tops rolled two miles down to the coast. The sea stretched like a silk carpet across the shadowy wall of mountains on the mainland to the west, a wall that reverberated away south, fifty or sixty miles to the horizon, under the vast bell of the empyrean. It was an azure world, stupendously pure, and as always when I stood on the central ridge of the island and saw it before me, I forgot most of my troubles.[50]

The natural beauty of classical Greece, above all in Athens, stimulated poets, artists, philosophers, and politicians to make a human counterpart—a beautiful society. Perhaps the clearest way to sketch the history of Greek religion is to show its ascent to the pinnacle of fourth century B.C.E. Athens and its descent to the Hellenistic syncretism of the early centuries C.E.

Religion of Minoan Crete

In his world history, Arnold Toynbee locates the beginnings of Greek culture about the middle of the third millennium B.C.E., when Sumerian and Egyptian influences apparently stimulated civilization in Crete.[51] Sir Arthur Evans, the foremost archeologist of ancient Crete, called the Bronze Age culture that had developed by 2000 B.C.E. "Minoan" after Minos, the legendary king of Crete. By about 1700 B.C.E. the Minoans had a linear script, and in the period 1580–1450 B.C.E. a splendid civilization flourished. The first true Greeks, called Minyans, were Aryan-speaking Indo-Europeans. They established relations with Minoan Crete, and between 1450 and 1400 B.C.E., at which time they were known as Mycenaeans, the Greeks had settled at the capital city of Knossos. The Mycenaean period (1400–1150 B.C.E.) constituted Crete's last glory; the Dorians invaded from northern Greece and cast a "dark age" over the Aegean from 1100 to 650 B.C.E.

During that period, literacy largely passed from the Greek scene. Consequently, much of our knowledge of Minoan religious culture comes from archeological excavations. These reveal that caves were great cultural centers from Neolithic times, serving as dwellings, cemeteries, and churches all in one. (Insofar as they gave rise to the mythic labyrinth, Cretan caves influenced the Greek religious psyche permanently.)[52] As the archeological excavations show quite clearly, the foremost deity of Cretan cave religion was a goddess, whose primary features were fertility and mastery of animals. This corresponds with remains found on Cretan mountains, where Minoans also celebrated fertility.

However, the goddess cult probably did more than simply venerate natural life. The many burial remains, symbols of butterflies and bees (change-of-state beings), and other artifacts suggest a complex veneration of life, death, and rebirth. Probably participants underwent initiation into these mysteries, much as ancient Africans or Australians have long done. The remains or artistic representations of bull horns, double axes, trees, animals, cosmic pillars, and blood sacrifices testify to a particularly rich Neolithic agricultural goddess religion like that described on pages 60–61.

In light of later Greek initiations—for example, those of the Eleusinian and Orphic mysteries—it is likely that the Minoan goddess cult aimed at insuring a happy afterlife.[53] If so, it probably had conceptions of immortality that continued through the dark age and served as a counterpoint to Zeus and the Olympian gods. In the Olympian scheme, the afterlife was only a shadowy, dismal existence. The mystery religions that offered a more hopeful view may well have derived from the Cretan earth goddess.

At any rate, as the script that archeologists have discovered and called Linear B shows, people spoke Greek on Crete from 1400 B.C.E. By that time, Minoan and Mycenaean cultural forces were interacting. One important effect was that later Greek religious culture appropriated Minoan Crete as its golden age. For instance, according to Olympian legend, Zeus was born on Crete, and Apollo, Heracles, and Demeter (and even the non-Olympian Dionysus) performed prodigies or had high adventures in Crete. Crete thus became the *omphalos*, the navel or birth center, of the classical Hellenic world. At the end of his life and literary career, when he composed his masterpiece the *Laws*, Plato placed his characters on Crete, walking from Knossos into the hills to the temple cave of Zeus.

Olympian Religion

The Cretan or Minoan strand of Greek religious history wove itself deep into the Hellenic fiber. The Mycenaean strand, however, was throughout more predominant.

Linear B shows that the people who invaded Crete were Indo-Europeans—the people that shaped both Iran and India. One of the outstanding characteristics of Indo-European religion was its interest in sky phenomena—storms, wind, lightning, the sun, and stars. Zeus, the prime Greek Olympian god, is a close relative of both Vedic and Iranian sky gods. (In proto-Indo-European religion, Mother Earth was polar to Father Sky but less powerful.) Further, the Indo-Europeans were much concerned with the human word—in sacrifices, chanting, spells, and sagas. Their traditions were largely oral, and they opposed writing when they first encountered it among Near Eastern peoples. It is worth underscoring that they had a powerful, double sense of the sacred—the sacred was both charged with divine presence and forbidden to human touch. Throughout its later development, Greek religion never lost this sense of awe-filled untouchability. Lastly, as we noted in connection with Iran, Indo-Europeans divided their society and gods into three groups. As a result, Vedic India, Aryan Iran, and preclassical Greece all thought in terms of priests, warriors, and commoners (though in Greece the priestly class was underdeveloped), as did Celts and Romans.

If both Crete and mainland Greece maintained earlier traditions during the dark age,[54] we can assume that the emergence of Homeric, Olympian religion was quite slow. By the time of Homer, however, the Indo-European religion had a distinctively Greek flavor. For instance, Zeus had acquired a mythological lineage. According to Hesiod's *Theogony*, he was born in the third generation of gods, after the original period of Earth and Heaven and the second period of the Titans. When Zeus overthrew his father Kronos, the present world resulted. (Eliade sees in the rather violent mythology of the *Theogony* a Greek account of creation. Heaven and earth separate; nature's forces assume their present order.)[55]

Zeus came to preeminence slowly. Most likely, his many liaisons with local goddesses represent a religious and political takeover, as a unified Greek culture emerged out of local traditions. These local traditions did not disappear, but instead entered the larger complex of Greek religious notions, enriching both Greek mythology and religious practices. For instance, the local Cretan dances of armed youths during their initiation ceremonies became part of the colorful story of the infant Zeus' birth in Crete. The noise of the youths' clashing shields drowned out the infant's cries, and so saved him from Kronos, who wanted to devour him. Further, the Cretan Zeus merged with the child and lover of the Cretan goddess, linking him to the island's Neolithic past.

In classical Greece, Zeus was first among the gods dwelling on Mount Olympus, as Homer portrayed him. He was the father of humans, the ruler of their destinies, and, despite his own moral waywardness, the ultimate upholder of justice. In addition to Zeus, the roster of the foremost Olympian gods includes Hera, Zeus' wife; Poseidon, god of the sea; Hephaestus, the divine blacksmith; Apollo, god of law and order; Hermes, the divine messenger; Artemis, mistress of wild beasts; Athena, patroness of feminine and practical arts; and Aphrodite, goddess of love.

Apollo and Dionysus

Of these gods and goddesses, Apollo deserves special mention, because he came to symbolize many virtues that seem typically Greek, such as serenity, harmony, balance, and order.[56] Through his oracle at Delphi, Apollo gave counsel on matters of liturgical propriety and ritual purification. For example, Apollo had charge of purifying homicides, who had to cleanse themselves of their "pollution." One would take serious matters needing counsel to Apollo's pythia (priestess) at Delphi. In trance, she would exclaim the wisdom with which Apollo filled her. The origins of the pythia's exclamation may lie in shamanism, but by classical times Apollonian wisdom had distanced itself from the emotional and irrational, becoming primarily intellectual *theoria*—relatively serene religious contemplation. As epitomized in the Delphic oracle's command "Know thyself," Apollonian religion deified thought and spirit. For that reason, it encouraged science, art, philosophy, and music.

Somewhat the antithesis of Apollo was Dionysus, an eccentric among the gods of the Olympian period. A son of Zeus by a mortal woman, Dionysus apparently always remained an outsider. His cult was not native to central Greece, while psychologically its concern with the irrational and emotional made many fear it. In his well-known study *The Greeks and the Irrational*, E. R. Dodds associates Dionysus with "the blessings of madness."[57] Unlike the ecstasy of the Apollonian pythia, that of the followers of Dionysus (for example, of the women called maenads)[58] was wild, frenzied, and orgiastic. Such ecstasy represented the enthusiasm (being filled with divine force) that could come from dancing and wine drinking.

For Eliade, Dionysus conjures up "the totality of life, as is shown by his relations with water and germination, blood or sperm, and by the excess of vitality manifested in his animal epiphanies (bull, lion, goat)."[59] Finally, Dionysus was a god of vegetation who would disappear to the underworld and then spring back to life. The most influential literary source on the Dionysian cult, Euripides' play the *Bacchae*, portrays the god's followers as wildly joyous. If the play is accurate, their mountain revels culminated in tearing apart live animals and then eating their flesh raw (so as to commune with the god of animal life).

Strangely enough, the Greeks recognized something essential in Dionysus. Call it the need for madness, reverence for the life force, or the value of temporarily escaping one's mortal bonds—they blessed it and called it good. As a result, Apollo vacated Delphi during the three winter months and allowed Dionysus to reign.

Heroes

The Olympian religion had another category of influential figures called heroes, who include Heracles, Achilles, Theseus, Odysseus, and Orestes. These heroes were the subjects of much mythology and folklore. In the hands of Homer and the playwrights, their stories became the most profound reflections of classical literature. Aeschylus' *Oresteia*, for instance, has become a literary classic.

Eliade notes that the heroes tended to be active in the time of human beginnings, when things were unsettled. They had superhuman capacities and illustrated the heights and depths of achievement that history usually levels. Further, heroes typically suffered dramatic deaths, were great warriors or athletes, were expert at visions or the healing arts, or founded cities and clans. They created many of humanity's greatest achievements, such as city laws, writing, metallurgy, songs, and military tactics.

Indeed, as popular religion developed initiation rites and various mysteries, heroes became the mythological founders or patrons. For example, Theseus, prime hero of the Athenians, was the paradigm of the ritually initiated warrior because of his exploits in the labyrinth with the Minotaur. So, using history and their striking imagination, the Greeks made a world of fascinating characters who were larger than life. As exemplars of human potential, the heroes excited a will to excel, to push bone and spirit to the limits, that made *arete* (excellence) a Greek watchword.

Mortality

Excellence, like justice, raises the issue of anthropology—the conception of human nature. Olympian religion generally regarded humans rather bleakly. The prime attribute of an Olympian god is immortality, so according to Olympian religion human nature is from the outset defective. Gods are different from humans because they do not know death, the most striking aspect of the human condition. As Homer says, humans are but leaves scattered by the wind. They suffer many pains, abuses, and injustices. Because of this heavy burden, it would be a mercy not to be born or not to live in such an uncertain, mysterious, unjust world. Human life lies in the hands of the gods or of a less personalized fate.[60] Therefore, one can only hope that the gods are just. As the Homeric tales show only too clearly, however, divine justice is far from certain. Consequently, a theological purification set in. By the time of Euripides, Socrates, and Plato, justice was virtually identified with divinity. As a fragment from Euripides puts it, "If the gods do anything base, they are not the gods."

Whether divine justice is perfect or imperfect, though, humans have to submit to it. A major belief of official Greek religion supported the maxim "Nothing to excess"— no wild leaps of Dionysian enthusiasm, no hubris (overweening pride) that forgets human fallibility, no striving for immortality. Rather, we should accept our mortality and try to live nobly the brief span that fate has spun for us. Paradoxically, perhaps, this attitude led to affirming, even sanctifying, mortal life. In fact, it led to a *joie de vivre*: a delight in the human body, in festivals, sports, song, and dance.

Socrates, the restless prober of traditions, came to his calm before death by pressing Greek joy to the hilt. His sole tutor in wisdom, he claimed, was the great god Eros. However, Eros takes much of his flame from our certitude of dying. He urges us toward the perishing beauty of this work, that lovely person. Right now they have fine, precious life. Right now we can celebrate their wondrous luster. If the afterlife is but a place of shades, the here and now—the glorious sea, the dazzling sun—is all the more precious, all the more holy.

Earthly Religion

However, the sky-oriented Olympian religion never was the whole story. From the Minoans and the psyche came an earthly religion to balance the sky. Certainly the Dionysian cult was a major manifestation. So, too, were the many mother goddesses. Hera, Artemis, and Aphrodite, for example, all relate to fertility and mother earth. In Hesiod's *Theogony*, Gaea (earth) actually precedes and produces heaven. In popular religion, Demeter and Persephone were very influential. In fact, Demeter's search for Persephone in the underworld was a major theme of the Eleusinian mysteries, which are described below.

The result of this earth-oriented counterweight to the somewhat overbearing Olympians was a view that humans should aim to become, in Plato's phrase, "as much like God as possible." Through contact with the forces of life and fertility (in the Eleusinians' case) and with the forces of intellectual light (in the philosophers' case), the limits of mortality were challenged. "No," many Greeks said, "we are made for more than a few days in the sun. If we truly know ourselves, we can find undying life."

The Eleusinian mysteries were practiced in Athens from about 600 B.C.E. on, though they clearly originated much earlier. They evolved from the myth of Demeter's search for Persephone in the underworld,[61] which included a subplot about Demeter's unsuccessful (because of human folly) attempt to make Demophoon, the infant prince of Eleusis, an immortal. Thus, the mysteries consisted of rites and revelations that gave initiates precious knowledge in this life and bliss in the world to come.

We do not know the particulars of the mysteries, which were strictly secret, but the mysteries probably grafted Neolithic agricultural ideas onto the Olympian theme that the gods are immortal. If so, the mysteries moved beyond the myths of the Hainuwele type, in which agriculture entailed ritual murder and gods that die. The result was a new, powerful synthesis of sexuality and death (as reflected in Persephone being carried to the underworld by Pluto) and of agriculture and a happy existence beyond the grave (as in Demeter representing mother earth). This religious synthesis made Eleusis an important cultic center for almost 2,000 years. Adherents to the Eleusinian mysteries lived in all parts of the Greek world and came from all social classes. Anyone who spoke Greek and had "clean hands" (including women, children, and slaves) could take part. Poets of the stature of Pindar and Sophocles praised the mysteries, and they were a powerful force in Greek life.

The background of the Orphic rites was a mythology somewhat like that of Demeter and Persephone.[62] Orpheus was a prominent Thracian hero, the son of Calliope by Apollo. His great gift was for music—when he played the lyre wild beasts grew calm, trees danced, and rivers stood still. Orpheus married the nymph Eurydice, who died from snakebite while fleeing Aristaeus, another son of Apollo. Orpheus could have regained Eurydice from the underworld if he had been able to resist looking at her. But he had to wander inconsolably until followers of Dionysus tore him apart (because of his devotion to Apollo). From this background Guthrie concludes: "The story throws light upon the Orphic religion because that is exactly what, in its main features, it stood for, a blend of the Thracian belief in immortality with Apolline ideas of *katharsis* [purification]. From the one it took *ekstasis*, enthusiasm, and a deep spiritual hope; from the other a formalizing influence, an almost legal atmosphere of rules and regulations."[63]

The direct basis for the doctrines elaborated in the Orphic rites, however, was another myth, that of Dionysus Zagreus, the son of Zeus and Persephone. Zeus proposed to make Dionysus ruler of the universe, but the Titans were so enraged that they dismembered and devoured him. Athena saved Dionysus' heart and gave it to Zeus, who swallowed it and then destroyed the Titans with lightning. Dionysus Zagreus was born anew from that heart, while from the ashes of the Titans came the human race, which was thus part divine (from Dionysus) and part evil (from the Titans). Consequently, the Orphics believed in the divine origin of the human soul but also in the need to leave

behind the soul's Titanic inheritance through ritual initiation and reincarnation.

For eternal blessedness, Orphics preached, one had to follow a strict moral code, abstain from the flesh of living creatures, and cultivate the Dionysian part of human nature. When fully pure, the soul would be reincarnated no more. No more would it drink of the spring of Lethe (forgetfulness), but, light as air, it would live in union with the divine mind. The Orphics appealed to persons of refinement, and Orphism certainly influenced Plato, the natural philosopher Empedocles, and the Roman epic poet Vergil.

Both the Eleusinian mysteries and the Orphic rites sought immortality, the one by a profound ritualization of the life force, the other by purifying the divine soul. Together, they were a strong counterforce to the pessimism fostered by heaven-oriented Olympianism. Another counterforce to the sky was the *chthonioi*, the spirits who lived in the dark recesses of the earth.[64] Though they were hardly mentioned in Homer, in popular religion they tended to spell out the twofold function of mother earth: fertility and rule of the dead. For the most part, the *chthonioi* were local spirits, concerned with a particular town's crops or deceased. Sometimes their cult blended with the cult of a local hero. Other times sacrifices to the *chthonioi* had overtones of devotion to Gaea, Demeter, Pluto, or Trophonious—divinities of fertility or Hades. Whether the *chthonioi* were gods or shady figures imagined to populate the afterlife is not clear. Regardless, they elicited considerable fear, and the common people tried not to offend them.

Popular Religion

Our last topic before we consider philosophy is the emotional religion of the ordinary ancient Greek.[65] If we confine our study to the literary sources of the classical period we get a false picture of Greek religion. By that time, the intellectuals were quite refined. Homer, Hesiod, and the early poets and philosophers had moved from gods who were simple nature forces, to gods who were anthropomorphic (personified), to a divinity that had to be pure—more just, more intelligent, and less limited than what the traditional myths described. The great playwrights (Aeschylus, Sophocles, and Euripides) and the great philosophers (Socrates, Plato, and Aristotle) completed this movement.

However, from prehistoric times well into the Christian era, over a span of perhaps 4,000 years, the nonintellectuals—the poor, ordinarily illiterate Greek peasantry—lived with a lively, emotional, hopelessly complicated blend of hopes and fears. Of the Olympians, they favored Hermes, whose Trickster quality, concern for travelers, closeness to shepherds, sexuality, and fondness for human beings made him unthreatening. Indeed, he was even the companion and patron of thieves. The other Olympians seem to have become less and less impressive, finally giving way to the *chthonioi*. Certainly local patron gods continued to be important; all Athenians, high and low, reached out to Athena. But the fertility forces, heroes (such as Asclepius the healer), and Apollo and Dionysus in their most popular aspects dominated the religion of most ordinary Greeks.

Most ordinary Greeks also believed in other, often malevolent, forces:[66] *keres*, whose function was to harm; *erinyes*, whose function was to punish; and *daimones*, spirits of the dead or inner voices who populated the world of intuition, suspicion, and dread. Committing any of several offenses might make one polluted, which would require ritual cleansing. Magic, personal prayer, and sacrifice were employed for various reasons.

These beliefs and practices were maintained throughout pre-Christian Greek history. Indeed, when Christianity became popular, this prevailing Greek religion largely looked upon it as just a new set of instruments: saints, blessings, and ceremonies. To the present day, peasants relate Christ to their old fertility religion. At Easter vigil, they have been heard to say, "If Christ does not rise tomorrow, we shall have no harvest this year."[67] Among the Greek people, then, divinity has remained close to the earth.

Philosophy

The common people did not build Athenian culture or make the breakthrough called philosophy. Rather, an aristocratic elite, working for several centuries, slowly distinguished the realms of myth and reason and in so doing wrote a pivotal chapter in the history of human consciousness. Before philosophy, the concept of reason was vague. We have seen the prehistoric suspicion that something can travel in dreams, rise in shamanist flight, and survive the grave. In Egypt, the Amon hymns exhibited a strong sense of transcendence—of the human mind pressing beyond materiality to divine mystery itself. In Iran, Zoroaster's interior dualism (the battle between Truth and the Lie) revealed a striking grasp of the abstract spirit.

Although many cultures thus showed some awareness of reason and spirit, the culture of the Greek city-state identified reason and controlled it. Only the line of pre-Socratic thinkers—most prominently, Pythagoras, Xenophanes, Parmenides, and Heraclitus—so disciplined their dissatisfaction with Olympian culture that they saw human mind *(nous)* itself as being divine and real. As we shall see, India approached this belief but never came away with Greece's balancing belief in the material world.

The story of the pre-Socratics, which weaves into that of the dramatists and Sophists (teachers of shallow philosophy), is a fascinating chapter in religion.[68] Partly from interior experimentation and partly from an empirical study of nature, the early philosophers moved beyond what most previous peoples had meant by the word *god*. As we have seen, peoples believing in the cosmological myth considered the world to be a living whole. With the rise of civilized religion, Mesopotamians, Egyptians, Iranians, and others focused on the political aspect of the cosmos. In other words, divinity to them

*Figure 10   The Parthenon, remains of a prime symbol of
Athens' golden age. Photo by J. T. Carmody.*

was in good part a symbolic representation of their own society. Even Ahura Mazdah had a strong political function. For Darius I, Ahura Mazdah sanctioned the building of an empire of Truth.

Out of its dark age, Greek creativity produced a pantheon—a roster of gods—that was neither natural nor political. The Olympians were anthropomorphic, evidencing human aspects. To be sure, Zeus was a sky god and Athena fought for Athens. But although nature and politics played important roles, they did not make the Olympians distinctive. What made the Olympians distinctive was the rich, anthropomorphic mythology surrounding them. In these divine characters or personalities, human passions were blown up to divine stature. Contemplating such divinity, ruminating on the Olympian mythology, the Greek geniuses clarified

where and how *mythos* shatters on *logos*—where story must yield to analytic reason.

Of course, this realization was prompted by historical events. It did not spawn at a seaside resort. Looking around them, the Greek geniuses of the fifth and fourth centuries B.C.E. saw a succession of empires. The decline of Babylon, Egypt, and Persia evoked the question, "What is the meaning of history's process?" As a result, historians such as Herodotus and Thucydides wanted a break with myth, an explanation of the flux in political affairs.[69] As a result, Socrates, Plato, and Aristotle labored heroically to produce such a break.

When the Athenians sentenced Socrates to death for impiety, they shocked Plato to the depths of his soul. If Athens could reject the one wise person who might save it, what chance did truth have?[70] Eventually

Plato correlated the Athenian city-state experience with the flux of empires and came to wonder about the possibility for human order. The *Republic* and *Laws*, which constitute about 40 percent of Plato's writings, testify to how long and deeply problems of political order absorbed him. His great problem, in fact, was the disorder of most humanity—citizens, empire builders, the great and small alike. Grappling with this problem, Plato saw that all order—personal, sociopolitical, and historical—depends on a truth only luminous from god. Since Plato's great problem remains our own, we do well to attend to his insight.

From instinct, observation, and reflection, Plato decided that history means more than wars and power struggles. Restricted to that level, history is literally absurd—a cause for despair—and yields no ordering truth (except negatively as an analysis of cultural destruction).

Rather, we must become aware of a reality that is not distorted by our lusts; divine mystery must shine forth an ordering light. Where warmongers and powerbrokers close themselves, philosophers must be receptive and willing to change. Where politicians restrict reality to money and influence, philosophers must go to the center of things—to the soul's passion for justice and love. Like a new Prometheus firing humanity's soul, the Platonic lover of wisdom made justice and love humanity's great passion. The presence or absence of that passion makes health or disease. Plato minces no words: one either admits divine mystery or faces disaster.

The fire and order of the Platonic soul clarified human reality. From Plato's time, some persons have realized that the meaning of their existence was to move through experience toward the intellectual light of God. Thus, the process of human questioning—human searching for flashes of insight and then sustained visions—has been a primary task for those seriously religious since Plato. The Western development of science, philosophy, and the humanities was made pos-sible by the Greek consecration of this task.

Plato himself used myth and symbols to suggest the psychology, politics, and natural philosophy of the newly clarified human consciousness. These uses were deliberate, calculated attempts to keep touch with the whole field of human awareness, to keep from getting lost in abstraction. Aristotle, more prosaic, commonsensical, and scientific than Plato, analyzed the new clarification of consciousness in drier, more technical terms.[71] As he saw it, a person first experiences ignorance about the meaning of human existence. This ignorance, however, is peculiar: It is knowing that one does not know—being aware that one is in the dark. Instinctively we seek release from the tension that this realization produces. Aware of our confusion, upset that we do not know how our lives make sense, we are moved to clarify things. If distractions, whether personal or social, do not interfere, we will pursue enlightenment, and our search will become inner directed. We will grope forward by an intuition or foreknowledge of what we seek, just as we work a math problem by a knowing ignorance that enables us to recognize when our answer is correct.

Likewise, in the profound problem of human understanding that Aristotle was working on, there is a sense of the answer or goal from the beginning. Looking for the reality that will order both ourselves and our world, questioning and following the thoughts of our mind, we slowly advance toward the divine light, the divine mind, the divine being. Indeed, divinity itself, Aristotle finally realized, had been attracting him from the beginning. From the first, his glimmerings of light, of intellectual understanding, had been sharings in God. Developing this Platonic and Aristotelian insight, the Christian theologians Augustine and Aquinas wrote a new treatise on the image of God, stating that our intellectual light is a share in the activities of the Father, the Son, and the Holy Spirit.[72]

This is not the place to review all the

other changes resulting from the classical philosophers' achievement. We must underscore, though, that classical Greek philosophy made a quantum leap in the search for divinity. With the philosophers' new tools of self-awareness and analysis, immortality and becoming godlike became more than symbols from the mystery religions. Rather, they became substantial themes of the contemplative life *(bios theoretikos).*[73] Aristotle placed the contemplative life at the pinnacle of human achievement, for in such a life he saw human beings most directly cooperating with God. Seeking the explanation for all things, humans would sometimes be drawn into an overwhelming fullness of life. For Aristotle, God was the explanation for all things, and God's life was "thought thinking itself." After Aristotle, human beings could rejoice or groan at the calling to participate in divine self-thinking. After Aristotle, the contemplative life was a potent symbol of human perfection.

The Hellenistic Religions

Following the cultural flowering of Greek religion in drama and philosophy, the Hellenistic religions dominated. This period resulted from Alexander the Great's conquests (*Hellenism* is the term for his vision of an ecumenical, transnational culture). The Hellenistic era extended from Alexander (who died in 323 B.C.E.) well into the Roman and Christian periods. According to historians who love classical Greek culture, it was not a time of glory. Gilbert Murray, for instance, speaks of a "failure of nerve," while E. R. Dodds speaks of a "fear of freedom."[74] From our standpoint, perhaps the most significant feature of Hellenistic religion was its syncretism. In an imperial area populated by numerous ethnic groups, many different gods, beliefs, and rituals all became alike. We can conclude our historical survey of Greek religion by describing the most important aspects of this syncretism.

Alexander himself was something of a visionary, for what lured him to empire building was the idea of an ideal realm in which conquered peoples "were to be treated not as uncivilized and barbarous members of subject races but as equals with whom one must live in concord."[75] Prior to Alexander, the Greeks had some knowledge of foreign religions through travel and trade, but, in general, oriental deities had made little impact on their own piety. (One exception might be Cybele, a mother goddess imported from Phrygia [central Turkey], who was identified with Rhea, the mother of Zeus.) However, from the time of the Diadochi, Alexander's successor rulers, oriental cults began to spread. By the beginning of the second century B.C.E., they were predominant. The most popular gods were Cybele, Isis, and Serapis. In the later Roman period, Mithra also flourished.

As noted, Cybele was a mother goddess (and mistress of the animals). Usually she was accompanied by her young lover, Attis. (We may hypothesize that to the Greeks Cybele and Attis echoed the Minoan cave goddess and her consort.) She was severe and vengeful, and accompanied by lions. When Attis was unfaithful, she drove him insane. Eventually Cybele became a maternal deity such as Demeter, Hera, and Aphrodite—a patroness of life, protectress of particular cities, and defender of women.

In her ceremonies devotees reenacted Attis' insanity and consequent self-castration. They would take the pine tree (Attis' symbol), bury it, mourn for the dead god, and then observe his resurrection. Resurrected, Attis would rejoin Cybele, which was cause for great feasting. The cult seems to have promoted fertility, and its rituals have overtones of the vegetative cycle and sexuality. Celebrants went to emotional extremes, dancing, scourging themselves, and even on occasion imitating Attis' castration. We could say that the worship of Cybele attracted Dionysian energies.

In ancient Egypt, Isis was the wife of Osiris and the mother of Horus. In the Hellenistic period she achieved a wider influence, often in the company of Serapis.

Serapis was an artificial creation, the result of the Greeks' aversion to the Egyptian tendency of worshipping gods in animal form. Fusing Osiris with his symbol (Apis, the bull), the Greeks made a new god: Serapis. He was bearded and seated on a throne, like Zeus, Hades, and Asclepius, some of whose functions he shared (such as rule of the sky, rule of the underworld, and healing). Joined with Isis, Serapis was primarily a fertility god, bedecked with branches and fruit.

Isis rather overshadowed Serapis, for she became a full-fledged, several-sided deity. As the consort of Osiris-Serapis, she was the heavenly queen of the elements, the ruler of stars and planets. Because of such power, she could enter the underworld to help her devotees or to stimulate the crops. Indeed, as a vegetative goddess she blended with Demeter and also the moon goddess Selene. Perhaps her most important role, though, was to represent feminine virtues. In distress, she had sought the slain Osiris and brought him back to life. Sensitive and compassionate, she would do the same for her followers. As the mother of Horus (she was often represented as suckling him), she would help women in childbirth and child raising. Unlike Cybele, the Hellenistic Isis was soft and tender. Yet, as recent scholarship has shown,[76] her devotees assumed a code of high ethics and her cult was strikingly upright.

Like those for Cybele and Attis, the ceremonies for Isis and Osiris-Serapis amounted to a cycle of mourning and rejoicing. Mourning, followers reenacted Isis' search for Osiris and her discovery of his dismembered parts. Rejoicing, they celebrated Osiris' resurrection and the return of Isis' joy. Apuleius' famous account gives some of the details of the rituals, which included bathings, ten days of abstinence from sex, "approaching the gates of death," and entering the presence of the gods.[77] Clearly, the ceremonies were elaborate and effective, much as the Eleusinian mysteries must have been. Through the cycle of Osiris' death and resurrection, followers would gain confidence that their own lives were in good

hands. Through the dramatic symbolization of the afterlife, they could anticipate security and bliss.

Mithra, whom we know from Iran, never took strong hold among the Hellenistic Greeks, but he did become important among the Romans influenced by Hellenism, especially the Roman soldiers. Indeed, his transformation illustrates almost perfectly the religious hodgepodge that cross-cultural contact produced at this time. In Mithra's Romanization, Jupiter (Zeus) took on attributes of Ahura Mazdah and became a great champion of Truth. Mithra, in turn, became Jupiter-Ahura Mazdah's faithful helper in the battle against the Lie. In this later mythology, Mithra was born of a rock (symbol of the celestial vault), and from birth carried a bow, arrows, and dagger (much like a Persian noble). He shot the arrows into the heavens from time to time to produce a heavenly spring of pure rain water. Very important was his sacrifice of the bull, from whose blood sprouted the corn (symbol of vegetation).

Thus, Mithra was both a celestial deity (later associated particularly with the sun) and a fertility god. His followers would trace his circuit through the sky, reenact the mythology of his birth, and celebrate a bull sacrifice in his name. After the sacrifice they would feast together, believing that the bull's meat and blood contained the substance of eternity. As the Mithraic doctrine developed, it generated a complicated astrology, by which the progress of initiates' souls through the heavens was shown. At its peak, Mithraism ran underground "churches" and schools. Today excavations under Christian churches, including St. Clement's in Rome, reveal statuary, classrooms, and altars used by Mithraists.

In summary, the Hellenistic period was a time of profuse religious activity. Onto Greek and then Roman religious culture, a cosmopolitan era grafted elements from the Egyptians, Persians, Phrygians, and others. (We have not even mentioned the Syrian cults of the mother goddess Adonis and of various baals [Canaanite and Phoenician local deities], which constituted another strand of Hellenistic fertility religion.)[78] Beyond doubt, a certain cultural confusion underlay all this excitement. Thrown into close contact with foreigners, all persons in the new empires had to face new divinities and beliefs. Partly as a result, many persons felt great need for signs of salvation or assurances of a happy afterlife. The upshot was a frenzy of mysteries through which devotees could feel stirring emotions or see marvelous sights. With a rush of sorrow, sexual excitement, or hope for rebirth, an initiate would feel passionately alive. In a time of disarray and ceaseless warfare, when the city-state or clan no longer offered security or guidance, such a sense of vitality was more than welcome.

Structural Analysis

Nature and divinity run together in Greek religion. Throughout its history, the Greek religious mind associated all major natural phenomena with particular gods. As noted, the sky, sea, and earth were powerful deities. The major stress was on fertility (which was the focus of most local festivals), perhaps due to the poor quality of the rocky Greek soil. The Homeric hymns, for instance, sing praise to mother earth, who feeds all creatures and blesses humans with good crops. Relatedly, they make the man with good crops a symbol of prosperity. The earth, mother of the gods and wife of the starry heavens, has blessed him—his children can play merrily.[79] As a result of its prehistoric roots, then, Greece saw much divinity in natural growth.

In social terms, Greek religious culture reflects the ethical ideas that bound first the early clanspeople and then the citizens of the city-state. The ethics of the early historical period evolved from the extended family. There was no money, and banditry was rife, so a man's great virtue was to provide food, shelter, and defense—whether by just means or otherwise. Consequently, most men (it was a patriarchal culture) petitioned the gods for material prosperity and success

in arms. They called one of their number good *(agathos)* and praised him for excellence *(arete)* if he was a survivor. The more elevated notions of justice later developed by philosophers clashed with this less moral tradition. Since early Greek religion did not associate godliness with justice, the philosophers called for its overthrow.

Another primitive concept that died hard was "pollution." This was the dangerous state of being unclean, or at odds with the natural powers because of some dread deed. Homicide was especially polluting, but incest, contact with a dead person, or even a bad dream or childbirth could also be polluting, each in varying degrees. Washing in a spring would cleanse away a bad dream; purification by fire and the offering of pig's blood cleansed a homicide. The concept of pollution seems to have been a way for the Greeks to deal with dreadful, amoral happenings that might bring destructive contact with the sacred, even though they were unintentional. Since polluted persons could contaminate others, they were often banished.

Greek cults used magical formulas, prayers, sacrifices, dances, and dramatic scenes—a wealth of creative expressions. Magical formulas probably were most prominent in agricultural festivals, where peasants mixed models of snakes and phalluses with decomposing, organic materials, such as pine branches and remains of pigs, to excite powers of fertility. Greek prayers would recall a god's favors and the sacrifices that the praying person had offered previously. This implied a sort of barter: We will honor you and offer a sacrifice if you give us success in crops (or war, or family life, or whatever). Occasionally texts indicate pure admiration for divine power or beauty, but the ordinary attitude was quite practical. Since the gods were not necessarily rational or holy, they had to be cajoled. Indeed, a Greek tended to pray and sacrifice rather parochially, addressing the family Apollo or Athena, who might remember fat sacrifices offered in the past. Each family or city-state had its own traditions, customs, myths, and gods, which served both to bind the members together and to maintain the splintering among the different tribes.

Sacrifice was a primary way to keep local religion in good health. By giving the local god good things, one could expect prosperity in return. (Significantly, this implied that the gods blessed those who were wealthy and had good things to sacrifice and that those who sacrificed and met bad luck had secret sins or wicked ancestors. Either way, human success and goodness were rather arbitrary.) In a sacrifice, usually parts of an animal were offered and the rest was consumed. According to a Homeric account, for instance, a pig was cut up, pieces of each limb were wrapped in fat and thrown on the fire, and barley grains were sprinkled on the fire. The meal that followed was a mode of communion with the deities.

Greek cults produced many priests, but their status and functions were limited. In principle, any person could pray and sacrifice to any god, so priests had no monopoly. They tended to be limited to particular temples and were seldom organized into bands or hierarchies. A large clan might have its own officiating priest, and the priest of a prosperous temple might make a good living from sacrifice fees. Otherwise, priesthood was not a road to status or wealth. Priests seldom gave instruction or performed divinations, though some priests in the mystery rites did both.

Many Greek religious authors were rather harsh on women. Hesiod, for instance, reported the myth of Pandora and the box of evils, which made woman the source of human woes. In other places he called woman "that beautiful evil," the "snare from which there is no escaping," and "that terrible plague."[80] Socrates, when asked about the advisibility of marriage, balanced the boon of heirs against the woes of a wife: "One quarrel after another, her dower cast in your face, the haughty disdain of her family, the garrulous tongue of your mother-in-law, the lurking paramour."[81] In Plato's *Republic*, women were to be equal to men socially and sexually, having rights to education and rule. Nonetheless, Plato tended to consider women less independent than men, in good part because of their physique: "The womb is an animal that longs to generate children." Aristotle, however, was the most unequivocal misogynist. To him women were simply inferior, both intellectually and morally. In his matter-and-form theory, women supplied only the matter for human reproduction, men supplying everything effective and active.

Women did have legal rights in Athenian society, but their lives were largely circumscribed by male control. Their basic function was to bear children. The playwright Euripides summarized the impact of this socialization, putting into the mouths of the women of his *Andromache* such self-evaluations as: "There's a touch of jealousy in the female psyche"; "For nature tempers the souls of women so they may find a pleasure in voicing their afflictions as they come"; "A woman even when married to a cad, ought to be deferential, not a squabbler"; and "And just because we women are prone to evil, what's to be gained from perverting men to match?"

On the other hand, we have seen that Greek divinity frequently was powerfully feminine. In the Minoan-Mycenaean period, a great goddess was the prime deity. In the Olympian period, Demeter, Hera, Athena, Artemis, and Aphrodite all exerted great influence. In the Hellenistic religions, Cybele and Isis more than equaled Mithra. Psychologically, then, Greek culture never doubted the divinity of the feminine. More than Israelite, Christian, or Muslim culture, Greek divinity was androgynous. Further, certain religious groups offered women escape from social oppression, such as the Eleusinian and Dionysian sects. There, in a sort of utopian free zone, women could experience equality and dignity. Although these cults never compensated for women's lack of dignity or status in ordinary life, it was an implicit admission that ordinary life was quite imperfect.

The personal side of Greek religion is perhaps most manifest in myths dealing with human creation. In the most famous collection of myths, Hesiod's *Works and Days*, ancient Greeks read that they were the last and lowest in a series of human generations. During the first ages, races of gold, silver, and bronze flourished, but they came to various bad ends. A flood intervened, followed by the age of the heroes. Finally the present iron people arose. In other words, Hesiod's myth put into Greek form the widespread belief in a golden age or a previous paradise, with the accompanying message that the present age was a low point.

Partly from this religious heritage, the prevailing mood of many Greek writers was pessimistic. As Sermonides, a writer of the seventh century B.C.E. put it, "There is no wit in man. Creatures of a day, we live like cattle, knowing nothing of how the god will bring each one to his end."[82] Others echoed Sermonides: Human beings have only a short time under the sun. Their powers fade quickly, their fortunes are uncertain. By comparison, Delphic wisdom was more positive: Gain self-knowledge and moderation. Self-knowledge, above all, was accepting one's mortality. By moderation, one could avoid hubris and tragedy. There were overtones of jealousy in this advice from Apollo, however, as though the god feared humans' yearning for immortality or resented their craving a life of passion.

Indeed, passion was ever a danger, for the Greeks were competitive and lusty. In the end, they would not give up their dreams of immortality. So becoming godlike became a central theme of philosophy and mystery religion. Empedocles, for instance, thought that his wisdom made him a god among mortals. Plato taught that the soul is divine and deathless. The common person would more likely find divinity in one of the mystery rites, through a union with Demeter or a knowledge from Isis, either of which could bring victory over death.

The personal implications of Greek religion were greatest in the philosophers'

clarification of reason, universal humanity, and the participation of divinity in human thought. As we have noted, the poets, dramatists, and early philosophers slowly clarified the nature of human reason, separating it from myth. By focusing on mind *(nous)* and its relations with being *(ousia)*, the pre-Socratics prepared the way for Plato and Aristotle, who realized how mind and being coincide. Moreover, this work did not take the Greek intellectuals away from either religion or politics. Rather, it introduced them to an order that set all the fundamentals—nature, society, self, and divinity—in harmony. In other words, it took them to the heart of what it means to be human.

Finally, the philosophers' order meant a new perspective on death. In early times, death was shadowy. For Homer, the dead had only a vague existence around their graves or in the underworld. There was no judgment or punishment for injustice towards one's fellows. Only those who had directly affronted the gods had to suffer. The mystery cults said one could conquer death by union with an immortal divinity, and their great popularity indicates the hold that death had on Greece starting in the sixth century B.C.E. The philosophers spoke of judgment and punishment because they were acutely aware that justice rules few human situations. In quite deliberate myths, Plato symbolized the inherent need we have for a final accounting. Without it, he suggested, reason would lose balance.

There is no need to review the side of divinity in the Greek world view, since we have traced its development in our history. In the eyes of many scholars, the Greeks were among the most religious of ancient peoples. From heaven to under the earth, from crude emotion to the most refined spirituality, their great culture put a religious shine on everything. Today, if we find the world "sacred" (deeply meaningful) through science or art, if we find the human being "sacred" (deeply valuable) through medicine or philosophy, if we find the political order alive with counsels both good and bad—if we ever think in these ways, it is largely because of the Greeks. They made the "transcendental" qualities—unity, truth, goodness, and beauty—part of Western religion.

SUMMARY

We have surveyed the antecedents and consequences of the rise of civilized religion. We should now reflect at least briefly on the main patterns that our survey reveals.

First, civilization—culture and social organization at a scale larger than that of the tribal village—developed on the foundations of agriculture. The increase in population, the sedentary life, and the economic and cultural specialization that farming allowed made cities and their cultural advances possible. Not surprisingly, then, many agricultural or earth-related motifs continued on in the religions of the first great civilizations. For all their moments of spiritual achievement, Egypt, Iran, and Greece all remained immersed in peasant views.

Second, the discovery of writing was essential in the advances of civilized religion. Through writing—even the hieroglyphic writing of the Egyptians—came the record that both the early civilizations themselves used and we, their latter-day students, have used to retrieve what they thought and felt. Within the early peoples' own religious horizon, the sense of history that came with writing was a significant development. Of course, oral peoples have memory and tradition, but writing makes both more precise.

Writing also raises the possibility of a new attitude toward the realities of the traditional religious world. For writing makes the realities of the traditional world *mediated*, as they previously were not. Spoken language has a holistic quality, conveying its message immediately, in a rather imperative or at least soliciting way. Written language is more detached and indirect. To the benefit of science, and perhaps the detriment of religion, it tends toward scholarship. For example, once the biblical legends were written down, scholars could dissect them at leisure. In the development of the early civilizations, we catch sizable traditions at their very revealing transition from oral to written religion.

Third, this chapter has mainly dealt with religious traditions that lasted for long stretches of time. Of course, Egypt, Iran, and Greece all changed significantly during the times that we studied. Also, Paleolithic religion probably retained its basic forms at least a dozen times longer than the religions of our three civilizations did. Nonetheless, Egypt had a quite coherent religious culture that lasted longer than Christianity has so far, and Iran and Greece both provide impressive instances of an enduring religion. Because of their duration, the world view of these religions can be reconstructed. These religions are also precious because they produced culture complex enough—theologies, arts, justifications for war, major social institutions—for us to find it familiar. Thereby, we can empathize with these civilizations more than we can with oral peoples.

Finally, we should compare the three religions here briefly. Concerning nature, they all preserved close ties with a living cosmos. In rites, myths, and popular religion, for instance, they all had strong agricultural influences. On the other hand, each separated itself from the cosmological myth somewhat. Akhenaton's reform was Egypt's most dramatic separation, but the Amon hymns and the man's dispute with his soul about suicide provide additional evidence.

Zoroaster made Iran break with the cosmological myth more sharply than Egypt did, but later Zoroastrianism retreated on this point. Greece took the only full step toward the realization of spirit. The philosophers discovered the mind; for Plato and Aristotle, what is and what can be thought coincided.

Still, none of the early civilizations broke the cosmological myth entirely. None conceived of a personal creator God. All their divinities were world forces, and all their ultimate world views tended to follow nature's rhythms.

Socially, Egypt appears as the most hierarchical and rigid civilization; its culture is remarkably static. Iran appears as a welter of ethnic influences and a welter of religious trends. It was in great turmoil, but few personalities, other than military kings, stand out. Personalities stand out most dramatically in Greece, despite its large patches of social conservatism. Especially in the Athenian golden age, tradition seemed just flexible enough. Thus, Greece fostered geniuses. In art and philosophy, we study them still. We probably know ancient Greek religion better than the other two and find it richer.

Study Questions

1. What major religious innovations did the rise of agriculture produce?
2. What was the paramount symbolization in the religion of Megalithic peoples?
3. Why was the sun so prominent in Egyptian religion?
4. Does the myth of Osiris illumine the religious significance of the pyramids?
5. In what sense did Zoroaster differentiate Iranian religious consciousness?
6. What significance do you see when you compare Ahura Mazdah and the Egyptian Amon-Re?
7. What do you make of the statement "Greek love of wisdom definitively clarified the nature of human reason"?
8. Do Dionysus and Apollo together compose a complete symbolization of divinity?
9. Is it fair to summarize the Hellenistic religions as a return to a prephilosophical emphasis on fertility, or did their "salvation" entail considerably more?

Part Two:

ASIAN RELIGIONS

Building on Part One, we may introduce the Asian religions by noting how they manifest ancient, oral, and civilized aspects. In India, for example, the ancient religious mind has long remained vital. The veneration of life forces, sex, and natural phenomena has long been popular. Similarly, a keen sense of the sacred and a rich body of rituals and mythology link Hinduism and Buddhism to oral traditions. Neither of these great Indian religions took a predominantly shamanist turn, but through the early literature of both shines the magic of the spoken word. Thus, both employ oral elements in a new synthesis rather than casting them away or leaving them behind.

From the Vedas (the Hindu scriptures) and the Tripitaka (the Buddhist scriptures), though, we can sense that Indian religion early distinguished itself from the traditions of Egypt, Iran, and Greece. Although Iranians, Greeks, and Indians share the same Indo-European ethnic and linguistic origin, only the Indians developed a strong tradition of yoga. (Whether this means that yoga first derived from the Dravidian peoples, the non-Indo-Europeans replaced by the Indo-Europe-an invaders, is not wholly certain. However, the hypothesis seems well-founded.) *"Yoga"* means "discipline," especially the interior discipline of meditation. Since prehistoric times, Indian yogis have given their culture an appreciation of spirituality and a profound hunger for peace by going deep into their own consciousnesses.

To some extent, Indian interiority paralleled that of Iran and Greece. Zoroaster and Plato, for instance, both clarified the structure and light of consciousness. However, Indian yoga took a somewhat different path. Though some Indian meditators and philosophers studied psychology and epistemology (the structure of human awareness and knowledge), most pursued wisdom lying beneath the rational mind. Sitting in a stable position, such as the lotus, most yogis tried to bring their consciousnesses to "one-pointedness"; that is, they focused on mental awareness itself rather than on its images, thoughts, or feelings. Heightening their sense of psychosomatic unity through regular breathing and other techniques, they strove for what Mircea Eliade has called *enstasis*—self-possession.

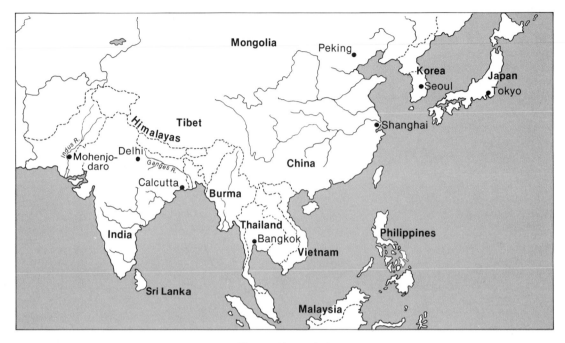

Figure 11   Asia.

Etymologically, enstasis is the opposite of ecstasis. Where ecstasis goes out, enstasis goes in. Thus, the shaman and the yogi present an extreme contrast. The former specializes in techniques that take the spirit out to travel, the latter in techniques that settle the spirit down at home. The religion of civilized India seems to have stepped away from the ancient religious mind through a disciplined search for spiritual autonomy or self-possession. Instead of wild singing and hair-raising flights of imagination, it emptied the mind of imagination to achieve tranquility and trance. Probably from these states Indians got their intuitions of Hindu *moksha* or Buddhist *nirvana*—of release from the burdensome human condition.

We will be able to justify this hypothesis in two fairly long chapters, thereby assuring that our contrast between ancient and Indian religion is not simpleminded. In its bhakti or devotional religion, for instance, India was quite ecstatic. In its mythology of the gods and heroes, it was quite imaginative. Still, you might begin your move from ancient to Indian religion by paying special attention to the yogic strain. For after all due qualification, yoga remains a distinctively Indian concept, a characteristic feature of the Hindu-Buddhist religious mind.

The chapters on Chinese and Japanese religion present an analogous situation. From prehistoric times, shamanism and a concern for the sacred prevailed in both lands. Both the Chinese and Japanese were ritualist, and both generated full mythologies. In Confucianism and Taoism, though, China discarded the ancient religious mind somewhat. By stressing ethics and nature's "Way" *(Tao)*, respectively, these two Chinese traditions forged the foundation of a vast civilized religion. (Buddhism's arrival in China strengthened this foundation.) The result was a culture that was quite formal, socially stratified, and yet aesthetic. More than Iran and Greece, China, like Egypt, developed a culture of apparent permanence, surviving numerous social upheavals through its blend of religious and ethnic spirit.

The case is somewhat different with Japan, because the native Japanese religion, Shinto, has a quite ancient point of view. In it nature bulks large, and shamanist elements are strong. However, Japan, like China, adopted Confucian, Taoist, and Buddhist strands. Together with the articulate, self-conscious Shintoism, Japan developed another civilized religion that is both formal and aesthetic. Thus, formalism and aesthetics distinguish the East Asian religions from ancient religion.

The East Asian sage is a quite elegant figure. If the shaman is an impressive ecstatic and the Indian yogi an impressive enstatic, the East Asian sage is a sober, worldly, yet graceful dancer to the *Tao*—to nature's song. That, too, is impressive.

Chapter Four

Hinduism

We have studied the ancient religious mind as evidenced among small-scale hunting peoples of both the distant and recent past and large-scale civilizations now dead. Our remaining chapters deal with living religions with long histories—the traditions and ways that organize hundreds of millions of people even today (though more and more loosely as secularism advances). These traditions and ways have existed for thousands of years, yet, through constant adaptation, they have continued to be contemporary. The present chapter deals with Hinduism, which has been central to Indian culture from prehistoric times to the present.

APPEARANCE

Imagine yourself in the departure lounge of the Tehran airport, waiting for a night flight to Delhi on Air India. Most of your fellow passengers wear turbans or saris. The plane is running on time, and after you board, you notice that the hostesses are graceful creatures wearing saris and nose rings, with spots of vermilion on their foreheads. The voice over the address system speaks colonial British with a tight Indian inflection. The food is a spicy curry, and the woman beside you tries to get it past her cranky baby, explaining that they have already been traveling two days from Washington on their way home for a visit in Bombay. The flight goes smoothly, but it is still a relief to stagger off the plane, stretch, and start the customs gauntlet. There you meet the first of dozens of bureaucratic forms, all backed by carbon paper, that will trace you across the subcontinent.

Delhi is quiet at dawn. The ancient cab careens down wide streets with wild grass growing along the edges. In the fields stand a few cows and water buffalo. The two boys sitting in the front of the cab look about fifteen. They are slight, dark, and very alert. Obviously they are used to this racing

entrance to their capital. When they have left you off at your modest hotel, you pause to test the dusty, humid air. At 6 A.M. it is 90° F.—the monsoon should arrive within the week. From experience you know that you are too keyed up to recover your lost sleep now, so you wash quickly and take to the streets. Often the first hours of immersion in a new country are the richest. It is high adventure just to walk the city.

The city is coming to life. Vendors stir by their wooden stands, where many of them have slept for the night. Cars zoom around traffic circles belching exhaust, beginning their noisy concert. Along broken sidewalks come Indians of all sizes and shapes, most in traditional garb, but a few in business suits or slacks and short-sleeved shirts. Two barefoot women kneel on the sidewalk and begin their day's work: breaking up the old brick so that the sidewalk can be rebuilt. As you approach Connaught Circus, the shops are opening—bookstores, clothing stores, restaurants. Outside these shops, under a shady portico, shoeshine men and food vendors are setting up. They smile and beckon you to inspect their goods. You smile back your "no thanks" and opt for a city tour by the government agency bus.

On the city tour your favorite stop is the Birla Temple (Figure 12), a yellow and pink sandstone enclave built by a wealthy family in the 1930s. Through the main gate pour dozens of people, mainly families with small children. The temple grounds are apparently a favorite spot for picnics and holiday outings. The first impression you have of the temple proper is "Perfect—could have been designed by Disney." It is all alcoves, extensions, niches, and wings jutting at oblique angles. In the main section, opposite the entrance, you find a cool interior. There the people wander slowly, talking and laughing but keeping a respectful atmosphere for those who bow, join their hands, and pray at one of the shrines. A priest attends the shrine for Krishna. He sits reading with head shaved and the colorful folds of his robe draping to the floor. A worshiper calls him

*Figure 12   Birla Temple, modern Hindu temple in New
Delhi, replete with statues of gods and animals. Photo by J. T. Carmody.*

and makes a contribution. The priest then sprinkles flower petals before the image of Krishna and utters low, rhythmic prayers for several minutes.

In the next chapel you read in English verses from the *Bhagavad Gita* and admire the wall murals that depict scenes from this scripture. Going outside, you wander between marble elephants into the grassy park. Behind the temple is a reflecting pool, a miniature of the famous one before the Taj Mahal, so you climb a rocky hill to see the temple mirrored in the lambent waters. The people around the park and pool are clearly very much at home. They love the cool, shady trees, the unkempt grass on which the children run barefoot.

All in all, the temple is a very colorful place: elephants and the elephant god Ganesha, Krishna, Buddha, Shiva, and numerous buxom consorts. In the monks' quarters, annexed to the temple, study is a serious business, but most of the temple has a rather light-hearted atmosphere. Overhead the sky is clear and the sun is blazing. Yet the very clarity of the air seems to intensify the murkiness of the temple's meaning. The colors and shapes of the sandstone buildings say it could only have been built in recent times, yet something prehistoric smiles from the statues in the alcoves. Verses from the *Dhammapada* that decorate the Buddha's temple blend with verses from the *Gita* singing Krishna's praise. Is it all one? To what does it tally in the mind of that small, plump woman there, lost in prayer before a statue of

Vishnu? What do her three children make of it, as they wiggle and squirm down the steps onto the grass? The only thing really clear to you is that you have no clarity. Too much runs together.

HISTORY

Pre-Vedic India

Before the first invasions of Aryans from the northwest around 2000 B.C.E., an impressive Indian culture already existed. Its beginnings stretch back to the second interglacial period (400,000–200,000 B.C.E.), and its earliest religion, on the basis of ancient peoples living in India today, was shamanist, focusing on the worship of nature—especially on the life force. In 1924 excavations at two sites along the Indus River, called Harrapa and Mohenjo-daro, furnished the first extensive evidence of a high ancient Indian culture. This culture, called the Harrapan, stretched over about 500,000 square miles[1] and was distributed in small towns between the two "capitals" of Harrapa and Mohenjo-daro. Other excavations in what is now Pakistan have disclosed cultures predating the Harrapan, but this Indus Valley culture is the largest source of information about pre-Aryan Indian ways. Carbon dating suggests that the Harrapan culture flourished about 2150–1750 B.C.E., and some evidence indicates that the culture was remarkably stable throughout that period.

Harrapa and Mohenjo-daro seem to have had populations of thirty to forty thousand. Both were about one mile square. That few weapons have been found suggests that their people were not very warlike. Outside each city was a citadel—a construction somewhat like the tiered Babylonian ziggurat—which was probably used for worship rather than for military defense. There were large granaries in the cities, two-room apartments nearby for the granary workers, and high city walls. Most building was done with kiln-dried bricks, which were standardized at 3 by 10 by 20 inches. Through the city ran an excellent sewage disposal system, with terra-cotta pipes and manholes through which workmen could enter to clean the pipes. The houses were multistoried dwellings with thick walls and flat roofs. Outside stairways to the roofs suggest that people slept there on hot nights.

The entire city plan suggests orderliness: Streets were wide and rectilinear, houses had chutes for sliding trash down into collection bins, and apartments had bathrooms and toilets. Larger buildings included a bathhouse 108 by 180 feet, with a tank 20 feet wide by 39 feet long by 8 feet deep. If this tank was used like similar ones outside Hindu temples today, its likely purpose was ritual bathing.

Some of the most significant remains from the Harrapan culture are small sandstone seals, engraved with a pictorial script and apparently used to mark property. They are decorated with various animals, both real and imaginary, and indicate a modest economic and artistic life. Other interesting finds include a small bronze statue of a dancing girl, lithe and graceful, and a red sandstone sculpture of the torso of a young man, also artistically impressive. Some scholars hypothesize that these finds indicate creative potential that was stifled by conservative forces, but others logically suggest that these artifacts are the only remains we have of a rather vigorous art whose other products perished. The first scholars, in their interpretations of pre-Aryan culture, believed that the artistry of the Harrapans was static and even monotonous, and it changed little over 400 years. The uniformity in the bricks and buildings suggests a strong deterrent to innovation, and the people were likely ruled by autocratic priests, who insisted on conformity to a theopolitical tradition based on worship at the religious citadels and lavatory tanks. Since the mid-1960s, however, this interpretation has been disputed by other artifacts and cross-cultural comparisons. Though much of what we know of the Harrapan culture does suggest stability, it probably had its ups and downs like most other cultures.

Beginnings of Hinduism

R. N. Dandekar, who refers to the Harrapan culture as "protohistoric Hinduism," has commented extensively on one religious artifact that has excited great scholarly interest—a seal depicting a three-faced nude male deity.[2] The deity has horns, sits on a stool, has an erect penis, and places his heels in a yogic position. Around him are an elephant, a tiger, a rhinoceros, a buffalo, and some antelope. He wears bangles on each arm, a chest decoration hangs round his neck, and a fan-shaped headdress rises between his horns. All these features are associated with the classical Hindu god Shiva, who rode a bull, was lord of yoga, and often appeared both nude and ithyphallic (with penis erect). This correspondence argues that the fertility associations of the classical Shiva go back to Indus Valley religious culture. Since the headdress of the sealed figure is like Shiva's hunting costume and his matted ascetic's hair, it is also likely that Indus Valley culture considered its proto-Shiva a wild yet ascetic force. Since the classical Shiva was Lord of the Animals, the representation of the animals on the seal makes the relationship almost indisputable.

A variant of this seal shows the Indus Valley god with just three symbols: a bull, a trident, and a phallus—all symbols of the classical god. Other remnants from Harrapan culture suggest that the prime aspect of the proto-Shiva was fertility, for archeologists have found a number of cylindrical cones that almost surely represent the male sexual organ (linga) as well as rings that represent the female (yoni). Fertility worship may have originally been independent of the worship of the Lord of the Animals, but by Harrapan times they clearly had joined: proto-Shiva was the god of the sexual life force. However, the yoni remains suggest that there was also a fertility cult of the mothers or of a mother goddess. Many female figurines discovered in the Indus Valley support this hypothesis. Often they carry smoke-stained cups, which suggest a practice of burning oil or incense. Other seals carry engravings of trees, animals, and water—more evidence of a sensitivity to nature's fertility.

Precisely how this fertility religion related to the apparently sedate city culture of Harrapa or Mohenjo-daro awaits explanation. The fertility emphasis continued in later religion, however, indicating that Aryans as well as the natives considered sexual powers sacred. By about 1500 B.C.E. the Harrapan culture was destroyed, after perhaps a millennium and a half of existence. (Most scholars postulate a long growth period before the 400 years of prosperity.) The destructive Aryan conquerers were a pastoral and nomadic people who loved fighting, racing, drinking, and other aspects of the warrior life. They probably came from the north, where the cooler climate favored such vigor, and they thought of themselves as the salt of the earth—their name means "from the earth" or "noble." (This name survives in *Iran* and *Eire*; in addition, all European languages save Finnish, Hungarian, and Basque are related to the Aryans' language.)

The Aryans had fair skin and pointed noses, a fact responsible for their hostile reaction to the dark, snub-nosed Dravidians. They moved by horse, ate meat, and hunted with bow and arrow. There is no evidence that they ever learned to navigate or sail, and they produced no striking art, although they did know iron and fashioned good weapons. Like many other warrior, nomadic peoples (for example, the Celts), they loved story telling and singing. Indeed, their culture and religion were highly verbal. Their society was male dominated, with a primarily patriarchal family structure, priesthood, and cast of gods.[3] Above all, they were mobile, pushing through Greece, Italy, Iran, and India. After 2000 B.C.E. they were strong enough to dominate the native Indians, but they may have started trickling into India from the northwest as much as 2000 years previously.

Troy Wilson Organ suggests that the Aryans' favorite god, Indra, whom we shall study when we turn to the *Rig-Veda*, was a projection or personification of their own sense of character.[4] He was exuberant and warlike—a boaster, a thunderbolt thrower, a big drinker, a slayer of dragons. He ruled by seizure rather than inheritance, loving action rather than stability. Indra aggressively seized the waters of heaven, released them, and fashioned the earth. Some have suggested that Indra was first a culture hero and only later a leading god, but from their earliest time in India, the Aryans undoubtedly looked to him as the source and model of their prowess in war. Even in his fondness for drinking Indra was a great model, for what hardy people has not sanctioned its love of drink?

Two peoples thus contributed to the beginnings of Indian (Hindu) culture. If the Harrapan culture was representative, the people who preexisted the Aryans in the Indus Valley were stable, even conservative city dwellers who nevertheless developed (or took from earlier peoples) fertility rites devoted to such gods as the wild proto-Shiva. The Aryans were a rough, fighting people who had a much simpler technology than the Harrapans but whose poetry and religion were more imaginative. These Aryans became the dominant force militarily and politically, imposing their will and their gods on the subjugated Dravidian natives.

However, Indian culture never lost its Dravidian features. At most they were dormant for a while. After the demise of Vedic culture, Dravidian interests in fertility reemerged (the Aryans had their own fertility interests). These interests focused on the established god Shiva, but the complex devotionalism of later Hinduism is best explained in terms of many non-Aryan factors. Since the Indians have tended to keep old practices by incorporating them into their existing ones, the persistence of the Harrapan Lord of the Animals is typically Hindu.

Vedic India

By Vedism most scholars mean the culture resulting from the mixture of Ary-ans, Harrapans, and other peoples of the Indus and Ganges valleys. This culture expressed itself in the earliest Indian writings, which are a collection of religious songs, hymns, spells, rituals, and speculations called the Vedas. It is convenient to consider them as representing the first stages of Hinduism, for although later India abandoned many of the Vedic gods and practices, the Vedas retained scriptural status throughout the later centuries, weaving themselves deeply into India's fabric.

The word *veda* means "wisdom" (cognates are the English *wit* and the German *wissen*). The Vedic pieces were originally oral. In fact, the proto-Hindus considered human speech divine, so singing and praying to the gods became sacred actions. Scholars have found that the Aryans composed some of the hymns found in the oldest Vedic literature before they entered India. The hymns honoring the sky and the dawn, for instance, are remarkably like the religious literature of other Indo-Europeans, indicating that they go back to the time before the Aryans split into the Iranian and Indian branches.

To the traditional Hindu, the Vedic literature represents the highest intuitive knowledge that the *rishis* (holy persons or seers) had attained.[5] The technical term denoting such a state of wisdom is *shruti*, which translators often render as "revelation." *Shruti* does not connote that divinities outside the human realm broke through the veil separating heaven and earth in order to impart light from above; as we shall see, Hinduism does not have such an exalted view of the gods. Rather, *shruti* implies that the eminent holy person has perceived certain things in peak experiences (often induced by the ritual drink soma). Therefore, Vedic literature, representing what the *rishis* had seen, was considered the best and holiest presentation of knowledge.

The Vedas consist of four separate collections of materials. Together, these four collections are known as the *Samhitas*. *Samhitas* therefore is a synonym for Vedas. The individual collections are called the *Rig-Veda*, *Sama-Veda*, *Yajur-Veda*, and

Atharva-Veda. The *Rig-Veda* is the oldest, largest, and most important. It contains more than a thousand *suktas*, or individual units, which are hymns to the gods, magical poems, riddles, legends, and the like. They show considerable learning and poetic skill, which argue against their being the spontaneous poetry of free-wheeling warriors or rude peasants. More likely, they represent the work of priestly leaders—the careful creation of an educated class concerned with regulating contact with the gods and maintaining its own social status.

Most of the *Rig-Veda's* hymns have two purposes. First, they praise the god being addressed; second, they ask the god for favors or benefits. For instance, the *Rig-Veda* praises Agni for deeds that show the splendor of his status as the god of fire. (These deeds appear to be not so much mythical allusions to feats that the god performed in the beginning as similes drawn from human experience. For example, Agni's flame is like the warrior's battle rush: As the warrior blazes upon the enemy, so the god of fire blazes through the brush or woods.) Then, having fattened the god's ego, the hymn singer makes his petition. In *Rig-Veda* 6 : 6 he asks for wealth: "wealth giving splendor, . . . wealth bright and vast with many heroes."

Though this praise-and-plead purpose is the most usual, the *Rig-Veda* has other functions. For instance, it includes petitions for forgiveness of sins, such as having wronged a brother, cheated at games, or abused a stranger, which indicate a developed moral sense. Although the *Rig-Veda* may not separate itself completely from an ancient world view, where being out of phase with the cosmic processes is almost physically dangerous, it provides solid evidence of religion centering on free, responsible choices made for good or evil. As well, some of the hymns of the *Rig-Veda* are philosophical, wondering about the first principle behind the many phenomena of the world. A famous philosophical text is 10 : 129, where the poet muses about the creation of the world. At the beginning there

was no being and no nonbeing, no air and no sky beyond. It was, in fact, a time before either death or immortal life had begun. Then only the One existed, drawn into being by heat that interacted with the primal waters and the void. However, from desire the One started to think and emit fertile power. Thus, impulse from above and energy from below began to make the beings of the world. But, the hymn asks in conclusion, who knows whether this speculation is valid? Even the gods were born after the world's beginning, so who can say what happened? Only one who surveys everything from the greatest high heaven knows, if indeed even that being knows.

Such deep musing, culminating in a skepticism about the human capacity to fathom creation's ways, anticipates the more philosophical portions (the Upanishads) of the Vedic literature, which we shall consider below. It is not typical of the *Samhitas*, however, for they are usually more concrete. For instance, both the tenth book of the *Rig-Veda* and the entire *Atharva-Veda* contain numerous spells and charms, indicating that the earliest Hindu mind tried to ward off forces of evil and commandeer forces of good. By contrast, the *Sama-Veda* is largely a religious songbook, while the *Yajur-Veda* is a priestly work of instructions for performing sacrifices.

In all these works, words have a more than literal intent—they have a power and force to effect what they express. Therefore, the entire Vedic literature is in a certain, modern sense magical. The *Atharva-Veda*, though, had considerable secular impact, since much of it entered Hindu medical lore, furnishing the beginnings of the extensive repertoire of incantations by which doctors tried to heal. (*Atharva* 6 : 136, for instance, has spells for growing thick hair and curing baldness.)

Ancient India assembled three other collections, which are included in what is called the Vedic literature. These are the *Brahmanas*, the *Aranyakas*, and the Upanishads. The *Brahmanas* are principally directions for sacrifice—books of ritual for priests. The *Aranyakas* are interpretations and defenses of the sacrifices—books of "theology" explaining what was done and why. The Upanishads, finally, are a collection of speculations on the ultimate order of things. They represent a departure from the magical and sacrificial mentality (though not a break). Along with the four Vedas, these three other collections also merit the rank of *shruti*. Thus, they, too, are part of the foundation of orthodox Hinduism, part of the *rishis'* legacy.

In his classical training, a noble Hindu youth memorized these four collections.[6] (However, tradition defended Vedic materials against profane use. A lower class person who even heard their reading was to have hot wax poured into his or her ears.) After memorizing them, advanced students analyzed the Vedas with the help of revered commentaries. In that way, the Vedic literature spawned philosophical and scientific discussion. Considered alone, the Vedas represent the convictions and practices of the first thousand years or so of Aryan-Hindu culture.

The Vedic Gods

A study of the Vedic gods shows what the earliest Hindus thought about the deepest forces in their world. The gods are many and complex (tradition said there were 330 million), but of course a few stand out as the most important. They are all *devas* (good divinities), as distinguished from *asuras* (evil divinities). (In Iran the terminology is just the reverse, suggesting that the Iranian-Indian split may have been theological.)[7] The Vedas cast most *devas* in human or animal form. Since the main feature of the *devas* was power, we may consider them functional forces: the warmth of the sun, the energy of the storm, and so on. To express these larger-than-life qualities, later Indian artists often gave the *devas* supernumerary bodily parts. An extra pair of arms, for instance, would indicate prowess in battle; an extra eye would indicate ability to discern events at a distance. Typically, a *deva* was a male deity associated with a female consort, who represented his energetic force *(Shakti)*. (In developed Hindu speculation, the male principle was passive, or cool.) Later Tantrist Hinduism focused on *Shakti*, often through the practice of ritual sex.

Scholars have described the worship of the many Vedic gods and *Shaktis* as *henotheism*. This word indicates that at the moment of praying or concentrating on a particular god, the worshiper tends to elevate that god to primacy without denying the existence of the other gods, who have their claims to importance. Thus, the devout Vedist placed the god he or she was addressing on center stage, but only for the moment. Psychologically, henotheism was a convenient sort of forgetting or bracketing, allowing one to elevate Agni today and Indra tomorrow, depending on whether fire or storm was more relevant. Further, the Vedic worshiper sometimes blended the attributes of one god with those of another. So a prayer for justice might address Varuna, the god of order and judgment, first, but thinking about Varuna's blazing face might bring Agni to mind. The concluding petition, then, might be to Agni.

By textual analysis, scholars have uncovered different generations of the Vedic gods. The oldest group consists of the gods of the sky and the earth that the Vedas share with other Indo-European religious texts. For instance, the Vedic Father Sky (Dyaus Pitar) is related to the Greek Zeus and the Roman Jupiter. Like them, he is the over-arching power that fertilizes the receptive earth with rain and rays of sun. The Vedic earth is the Great Mother, the fertile female.[8] These deities are not the most prominent Vedic gods, but they echo in the background as the oldest.

The second oldest group, whose age is confirmed by Iranian parallels, includes Indra, Mithra, Varuna, Agni, and Soma. We have seen that Indra was the warrior god of the storm much beloved by the Aryan conquerors. Mithra was the god of the sun. (In Iran he became the great helper of Ahura Mazdah, while in the Hellenic world he became an important mystery god.) Varuna was the god of cosmic and moral order, and Soma was the god of the exhilarating cultic drink. Known in Iran as *haoma*, soma gave visions so dazzling that it became integral to the sacramental cult (scholars dispute whether the drink was hallucinogenic). Agni, finally, was the god of fire, whose importance increased as the sacrifice focused more and more on fire. (Remember, again, the Iranian parallel: Fire became sacred to Zoroastrians and Parsis.) It is worth noting that most of the deities in this second generation represent earthly and especially heavenly forces. Perhaps the storm, the sun, and the sky were all originally joined in Dyaus Pitar, but later they became separate objects of devotion.

The third generation of gods includes Brahma, Vishnu, and Shiva, who are not true Vedic gods but rather developments of Vedic *devas* on Indian soil. In other words, they arose after the Aryans arrived in India (and so perhaps indicate Dravidian influences). We shall consider them more fully below.

Finally, the fourth generation, which comes to the fore in the Upanishads, comprises abstract deities such as One God, That One, Who, and the Father of Creation (Eka Deva, Tad Ekam, Ka, and Prajapati).[9] Upanishadic seers had become dissatisfied with the concrete, world-affirming outlook at the core of the *Rig-Veda* and searched for simpler, more spiritual notions.

The Vedic priests divided the gods according to the three realms: celestial, atmospheric, and earthly. During much of the Vedic period, the sun was the chief celestial god, Indra was the chief atmospheric god, and Agni presided over the earthly gods. Among the celestial gods, Varuna came to eclipse the sun, for his association with order attracted to him much of the awe felt for the old Dyaus Pitar.

A Dravidian god associated with Indra in the atmospheric realm was Rudra, who originally seems to have been the god of the monsoon but in Vedic times grew close to Shiva and became rather demonic.[10] As the Vedic fire sacrifice developed, Agni became more important, taking on aspects of the sun (celestial fire), lightning, and ascetic energy (inner heat). We have mentioned Soma, another earthly god. In time Indians thought that taking soma would guarantee immortality. Sarawasti, wife of Brahma, became most important in post-Vedic times, but in the scriptures she functions as the gracious goddess of music, scholarship, and speech.

Brahmanism

In the early Vedic period, the sacrifice was quite simple. It required no elaborate rituals, no temples, no images—only a field of cut grass, some ghee (clarified butter) for the fire, and some soma (some poured onto the ground for the gods and some drunk by the participants). Later the sacrifice became more elaborate, involving the chanting of magical sounds, reenacting the world's creation, and slaying a variety of animals.[11] Since this elaboration went hand in hand with the increasing importance of the priest (*brahmin*, or brahman), commentators often refer to sacrificial Vedic religion as Brahmanism.

The *Atharva-Veda* shows the magical aspects that Brahmanism developed. At their most powerful, the priests thought that their chants and sacrifices controlled the world. Whereas originally one prayed to the gods because they ran the world, in Brahmanic days the priests considered sacrificial speech and action efficacious in their own right: If one executed the ritual properly, it could not fail to obtain its object. Properly uttered, the words of prayer compelled the gods. As a result, ritual magic almost overshadowed all social life, and the cult grew more and more complicated. Not surprisingly, many people soon found this complexity intolerable. Before it lost control, however, Brahmanism made a permanent impact on Hinduism. Subsequent reinterpretations of Vedic scriptures, including that of the *Bhagavad Gita*,[12] showed great effort to retain the concept of sacrifice.

Brahmanism reached its greatest elaboration with the horse sacrifice, a ceremony that lasted more than a year. In the first step of this complicated ritual, attendants bathed a young white horse, fed it wheat cakes for three days, consecrated it by fire, and then released it and let it wander for a year. Princes and soldiers followed the horse, conquering all territory through which it traveled. After one year, servants brought the horse back to the palace. During the next new moon, the king shaved his head and beard. After an all-night vigil at the sacred fire, the queens went to the horse at dawn, anointed it, and decorated it with pearls. A sacrifice of 609 selected animals, ranging from the elephant to the bee (and sometimes a human), followed.

The sacrifice reached its climax after attendants slaughtered the horse itself and placed a blanket over it. The most important queen then slipped under the blanket to have (simulated?) sexual intercourse with the horse, while the other queens and the priests shouted obscene encouragements. After this, participants ate the horse in a ritual meal. The entire ceremony fits the pattern of ancient celebrations of the new year, which often involved sacrifices and orgies designed to renew the world's fertility.

The Upanishads

Before the end of the Vedic period, Brahmanism declined for at least two reasons. First, common sense dictated that society had more to do than listen to priests chant all day. The texts imply that even during the times of the *Rig-Veda,* people were unhappy with the priests' constant prating. A satire in 7 : 103, for instance, likens them to frogs croaking over the waters. Second, intellectuals desired something more satisfying than magic. The Upanishads reveal the intellectuals' turn to interiority, which resulted in sacrifice becoming less a matter of slaughter, ritual, and words and more a matter of soul cleansing and dedication to the divine powers.

The word *Upanishad* connotes the secret teaching that one receives at the feet of a guru. Out of hundreds of treatises (over

the period from 800 to 300 B.C.E.), a few Upanishads came to the fore.[13] They show that the intellectuals embraced a variety of styles and ideas and that their movement was poetic as much as philosophical. Whether poetic or philosophical, though, the movement's goal was quite religious: intuitive knowledge of ultimate truths.

Scholars have cited three progressions in the intellectual development of the Upanishadic movement.[14] First, belief moved the many Vedic deities into a unified conception of how the world came to order. In part, this was a shift away from the nature forces that dominated the early Vedas, a search for a single explanation for all phenomena (this search extended the idea developed in *Rig-Veda* 10 : 129). The desire for such an explanation is a spontaneous, natural urge of the human intelligence, for, given sufficient leisure and tradition, people everywhere wonder about the world's origin. In such wondering, many find a plurality of explanations to be unsatisfactory.

Thus, the writers of the Upanishads pushed beyond henotheism, which temporarily accorded an individual god such as Agni all power and might, towards monism, the notion that all entities share in and manifest a single primal reality or stuff. In the Brihad-Aranyaka Upanishad (3.9.1), for instance, a pupil asks the sage Yajnavalkya how many gods there are. Yajnavalkya begins by answering, "3,306," but the pupil keeps pushing him, and Yajnavalkya finally answers, "One." This move toward monism characterizes many Upanishads and thus much of later Hindu philosophy. Vedanta, perhaps the most famous of the orthodox philosophical schools, pushed Upanishadic monism to the point where *only* the one ultimate reality existed, everything else being illusion.

The Upanishads themselves do not agree as to whether the unity behind everything is personal, impersonal, or a mixture of the two. However, they do tend to use two words in discussing it, both of which are more impersonal than personal. The first word is *Brahman,* which generally means the first principle, cause, or stuff of the objective world. Brahman, in other words, is the final answer for the Upanishadic thinkers who wondered about how things are founded—especially things in the material world.

The second progression in Upanishadic thought shifted from concern for external matters to concern for internal matters—from objectivity to subjectivity. Whereas the Vedas resonated with the energy of storm and fire, the Upanishads discovered the world of mind and spirit. From this new world emerged the second word relating to the unity behind all things, *atman*. This word means the vital principle or deepest identity of the subject—the soul or self. Third, probing this reality by thought and meditation, the Upanishadic seers moved away from Vedic materiality to spirituality. The internal world, the world of atman and thought, was a world of *spirit*.

Combining these progressions and the new concepts of Brahman and atman, some of the Upanishadic seers found a coincidence—the basic reality within and without, of self and the world, is the same. Atman is Brahman. So in the Chandogya Upanishad (6.1.3), the father Uddalaka teaches his son Shvetaketu that Shvetaketu himself *is*, most fundamentally, Brahmanic ultimate reality: *Tat tvam asi* ("That thou art"). The soul and the stuff of the world are but two sides of the same single "be-ing" or "is-ness" that constitutes all existing things.

For the Upanishadic thinkers, this realization was liberating because it avoided the Brahmanistic multiplicity, externalism, and materialism that had sickened their souls. Though sacrifice and the gods continued to have a place in Upanishadic religion, they were quite subordinate to monism.

In addition, the Upanishadic thinkers felt an urgent need for salvation, unlike the Vedists. Perhaps echoing Buddhist beliefs, the writers of the Upanishads worked with experiences that they found more dismal, depressing, and afflicting than the first Aryans had. Whereas those vigorous warriors had fought and drunk, living for the moment, these later meditative sages examined the human condition and found it sad. To express their beliefs, they fashioned the doctrines of samsara and karma, which did not appear in the early Vedas.

Samsara (the doctrine of rebirths) implies that the given world, the world of common sense and ordinary experience, is only provisional. It is not the ultimate existence. To take it as ultimate or fully real, therefore, is to delude oneself and thus to trap oneself in a cycle of rebirths. Only when one penetrates Brahman, the truly real, can one escape this cycle. Otherwise, one must constantly travel the scale of animal life (up or down, depending on one's advances or backslidings in wisdom).

Karma is the law that governs advancement or regression in the samsaric life of deaths and rebirths. Essentially, it is the belief that all acts have unavoidable consequences. In an almost physical way, they determine one's personality. Karma also explains one's status: A person's present life is shaped by that person's past lives. The only way to escape the round of rebirths, the pain of samsara, is to advance by meritorious deeds and be saved or freed.[15] (Hinduism chooses to live with the illogic of a law both necessary and capable of being undercut by freedom.)

The Period of Native Challenge

From about 600 B.C.E. to 300 C.E. the Vedic religion, including its Upanishadic refinements, was seriously challenged by some Indians. We have already seen that the Upanishads represent an adverse reaction to sacrificial Brahmanism.[16] However, even the Upanishads themselves, the final fruits of the Vedic tradition, were eventually contested by materialist, Jain, Buddhist, devotionalist, and other religious views. As well, the entire Vedic tradition of *shruti* grew through commentaries and instructions. Hindus refer to these materials collectively as *smriti* (memory or tradition).

Some Hindus remained loyal to the

early Vedic gods and sacrifices, but the strong challenges decisively changed the religion of the majority. In fact, during the period of contest, the blend of Aryan and Dravidian traditions developed in a variety of directions. As a result, Hinduism became an umbrella religion—a shelter over India's great diversity of beliefs and customs.[17]

Materialistic, Jain, and Buddhist challenges to Vedism first arose in northeastern India, where warrior tribes were more than ready to contest the priests' pretensions to cultural control. By this time (600 B.C.E.), the Aryans had settled in villages, and India was a checkerboard of small kingdoms, each of which controlled a group of such villages. Some intellectuals, radically opposed to the Vedas, strongly attacked the Vedic belief that there is a reality other than the sensible or material. It is hard to know precisely what these materialists taught, because few of their writings have survived, but Buddhist literature reports that Ajita, a prominent materialist thinker, said that earth, air, fire, and water are the only elements—the sources of everything in the universe. According to Ajita, the differences among things just reflect different proportions of these elements. Human beings are no exception, and at death they simply dissolve back into these four elements. There is no afterlife, no reincarnation, no soul, and no Brahman. During the brief span of one's life, a person should live "realistically," enduring pain and pursuing pleasure. Nothing beyond the testimony of the senses is valid knowledge, and what the senses reveal is what is real.

Jainism was a very different challenge that grew from the struggles for enlightenment by Vardhamana, called the Jina (conqueror) or Mahavira (great man). He was born to wealth but found it unfulfilling, so he launched a life of asceticism. After gaining enlightenment by this self-denial, he successfully preached his method to others. The Jina opposed both the ritualism and the intellectualism of the Vedic tradition. The only significant sacrifice, he said, is that which conquers the self. Similarly, the only

worthy knowledge is that which enables the personality to escape karma and samsara.[18]

The Jina's followers became opponents of all forms of violence and pain. Consequently, they opposed the Vedic sacrifice of animals, calling it an assault on life that opposed true religion. Also, Jains became critical of matter. Their "karma" was a semisolid entity that attached itself to the spirit through acts involving material objects.[19] In memory of the Jina, whom they considered to be a great *tirthankara* ("crosser of the stream of sorry life"), Jains eschewed eating meat, harming anything believed to have a soul, and physical activity. Since total avoidance of these activities was practically impossible, Jains tried to balance any injury that they inflicted or bad karma that they generated by acts of self-denial or benevolence.

The popularity of Jainism and of Buddhism, which arose only slightly later, testifies to the dissatisfaction with Vedism that many Indians experienced during the sixth century B.C.E. At the time of the Mahavira's death (due to voluntary starving), his followers have been estimated at more than half a million. There were more women than men, and many more laypeople than monks and nuns. For laypeople and monks alike, however, Jainism developed guiding vows, similar to commandments, which have been a principal reason for the persistence of Jainism in India to the present.

The lay vows include commitments not to injure living beings, not to lie or steal, not to be unchaste, not to accumulate large sums of money, not to travel widely or possess more than what one needs, not to think evil of others, and not to pursue evil forms of livelihood. There are also positive vows to meditate and to support the community of ascetic monks.

Today there are about 2 million Jains in India (the largest cluster is in Calcutta), who, through their discipline and their specialization in business, have become quite prosperous. In their temples one can see pictures of nude, ascetic saints who represent an ideal of complete detachment, and the

Jain doctrine of *ahimsa* (noninjury) has made a permanent impression on Indian culture.[20]

Since we shall discuss Buddhism at length in the next chapter, we need only note here that, from a Hindu perspective, Buddhism arose, much like Jainism, as an anti-Vedic protest in the sixth century B.C.E. It was another stimulus to Hindu reform, another attack on both the Vedic sacrifices and their Brahmanistic rationale.

Bhagavata

Especially in western India, movements arose that, unlike materialism, Jainism, and Buddhism, forced changes from within Hinduism. A collective word for these movements is Bhagavata (devotionalism), which connotes an emotional attachment to personal gods such as Krishna and Shiva. Devotees *(bhaktas)* continue to claim that such devotion is a way of salvation or self-realization that is superior to sacrifice or intellectual meditation.[21]

In the central Indian city of Mathura, devotion was focused on the god Krishna. There has been much debate about the background of this god (his name means dark blue or black and was a common one). Some have claimed that Krishna originally was a solar god, others that he was a vegetative god, and still others that he was a mythical hero. Organ suggests that the Krishna cult may have appropriated five minor religions that flourished in the Mathura area.[22] All these religions related to a solar deity, whom the local people worshipped as a personal god and petitioned for gifts.

Whatever its origins, the Krishna cult became very popular, and it developed a wealth of legends about Krishna's birth and adventures that ultimately made Krishna the most beloved of the Indian deities.

In one legend, demons tried to kill the baby Krishna, but he was stronger than they. When the demoness Putana, who had taken the form of a nurse, tried to offer him a breast covered with poison, Krishna took it and sucked out all her milk and blood. When

another demon approached him, Krishna kicked the demon so hard that the demon died. Another cluster of legends describes the child Krishna's pranks (he was always stealing his mother's butter, for which he had a great appetite)[23] and the young man Krishna's affairs with young girls. Consequently, Krishna became the object of love—the love for an infant and the romantic and sexual love for a handsome young lord.[24]

The premier work of the Bhagavata tradition is the *Bhagavad Gita*, in which Krishna is the featured god. The *Gita* offers ways of salvation to all types of persons, but *bhakti* (devotional love) appears to be its highest teaching.[25] This is especially so if one reads the *Gita* as the progressive instruction of a pupil (Arjuna) by his guru god (Krishna). The *Gita* is set in the context of a great battle (the subject of the epic poem the *Mahabharata*), and it deals successively with (1) the ethical problem of war (one must do one's caste duty; there is no killing of the soul), (2) the valid ways to wisdom and realization (these are sacrifice, meditation, and action without attachment to its results), and (3) the divinity's unveiled countenance (the dazzling vision that is recounted in chap. 11). Then, in what seems to be the work's climax, Krishna tells Arjuna that the best "way" *(marga)* is love of Krishna and that he, Krishna, loves his devotee in return. In other words, there is a divine love for humanity as well as a human love for divinity (chap. 18). This final teaching, probably even more than the *Gita*'s catholic offering of many religious ways, has made it Hinduism's most influential text.

In later Hindu theology, Krishna became an avatar, or manifestation, of Vishnu, whom we shall discuss shortly. However, we should first describe the beginnings of a devotional cult to Shiva. This cult, too, was a reaction against the Vedic religion, and one of its fascinating texts is the Shvetashvatara Upanishad. For the devotees of Shiva, this text serves much as the *Bhagavad Gita* serves Krishnaites—as a gospel of the personal god's love. It is unique among the Upanishads for its theism (focus on a personal god), yet it shares with the monistic Upanishads an effort to think logically.

The author begins by asking momentous questions: What is Brahman? What causes us to be born? Then the author rejects impersonal wisdom, materialism, and pure devotion as being inadequate answers. His own answer is to interpret Brahman (the ultimate reality) as a kind of god, who may become manifest if one meditates upon him. In the Shvetashvatara Upanishad, the preferred designation for Brahman is Rudra-Shiva. Rudra probably was the Dravidian form of Indra and Shiva a god of fertility.[26] In the post-Dravidian combination of these gods, the accent was on slaying and healing, destroying and creating—the lord of the two rhythms of life.

According to this Upanishad, Shiva is in everything. He has five faces and three eyes, which show his control of all directions and all times (past, present, and future). The devotee of Shiva therefore deals with a divinity as ultimate and powerful as Krishna but whose destructive capacities are more accentuated. Rudra is a god whom one has to appease. The Vedic attitude toward him was "Go away, please." Shiva is more welcome, but his life power is nothing with which to fool. It plays when the earth quakes and when the lion tears the lamb. It weaves a net of illusion around the dance of life, making it both beguiling and dangerous.

Devotion to Krishna (Vishnu) or Shiva, then, satisfies the person who wants religious feeling and a personal god with whom to interact. Probably this sort of person predominated in Hindu history. From the legends about the gods and from the epics (especially the *Mahabharata* and the *Ramayana*), the *bhaktas* found models for religious love and for faithful living as a good child, husband, wife, and so on. Theologically, these models imply monotheism, personalism, and free self-giving rather than legalistic obligations. To the *bhaktas*, they meant finding peace by surrendering oneself in faith—making the god one's refuge and hope. In sum, bhakti was complete emotional dedication to one's god.

Smriti

During this period of challenge to Vedic authority, one other development merits attention because it was responsible for a great deal of Hindu religious literature. This movement was commentary on the Vedic literature which was intended to make it more comprehensible, practicable, and contemporary. The authority of this commentary movement is described by the word *smriti* (tradition). *Smriti* provided such diverse literatures as the *Dharma Shastras*, or law codes (of which the Laws of Manu are the most famous); the writings of the six orthodox schools of philosophy; legendary works such as the *Mahabharata* and the *Ramayana*; the *Puranas* (more legendary materials, often from folk or aboriginal sources); commentaries appended to the Vedas (for example, the *Ayur-Veda*—the "Life-Veda," devoted to systematic medicine—which tradition added to the *Atharva*); tantric writings on occult and erotic matters; writings ("Agamas") peculiar to sects such as the Vaishnavites and the Shaivites; and writings on logical or ritualistic forms of thought.

The basic form of the *smriti* was the sutra, an aphorism or short sentence designed to expose the pith of a position.[27] By the end of the third century C.E., the *smriti* tradition had developed some very important and common ways of understanding the Vedic heritage that greatly shaped Hindu social life.

For example, the *smriti* tradition developed the central trinity of Hindu gods (Trimurti) called Brahma-Vishnu-Shiva. Through history, many Hindus have believed this trinity to be an essential format of divinity. Brahma is an impersonal creator god, rather distant. Tradition depicts him as red and having four hands and four arms. He has a beard and holds a bow, a scepter, a drinking cup, and a Veda.[28] He rides on Hamsa, a white goose, and his consort is the lovely Sarawasti, whom we have mentioned as the goddess of music and scholarship.

Vishnu is a much more popular god,

whom the *Puranas* and the Vaishnavite literature consider supreme. He is associated with water, and according to tradition the Ganges flows from under his feet while he rests on the coils of the great serpent Shesha. He is a gracious god, sending many avatars of himself to help humans in need. His vehicle is the great bird/giant Garuda, and he is depicted as blue. Like an ancient monarch, he carries a conch shell, a battle discus, a club, and a lotus. He has four arms, signifying his power to fight evil, and his consort is the much beloved Lakshmi.

Shiva, as we have seen, was originally a storm and fertility god. His vehicle is the bull and he has five faces, three eyes, and four arms. His hair is matted (as befits a yogic ascetic), and his clothing is a tiger skin held by a serpent. His many consorts (*Shaktis*), which are different forms that his quiet wife Parvati assumes, are important cosmic energies. The most important ones are all menacing: Uma, an ascetic; Durga, a ten-armed demon slayer; and Kali, a black goddess who drinks blood and feeds on corpses. Shiva is the destroyer, as Brahma is the creator and Vishnu the preserver.

The commentaries also developed Vedic notions of time and extended the doctrines of karma and samsara. Time was measured in great cycles (kalpas) that stretched for 4,320,000 human (solar) years (12,000 divine years, each of which was 360 human years). Each kalpa divides into four yugas—ages having different religious qualities.[29] The krita yuga is the golden age, four times the length of the worst age (the kali yuga, which is the present time). In the golden age humans live long and happy lives that are close to perfection. In the kali yuga religion declines, sickness and sin prevail, and lives are short. After each sequence of the four ages, another kalpa begins. A thousand kalpas make a Brahma Day, the span from the universe's creation to its destruction, which is followed by a Brahma Night of the same duration. This is a period of universal rest, after which another Brahma Day follows, and so on.

Karma and samsara have enormous roles in this universal scheme. Indeed, they represent a condition of cause and effect, death and rebirth, that has antecedents and consequences without measure. As a result, *moksha* (liberation from samsara) is all the more impressive.[30] The *smriti* literature does not explain how human freedom (which it asserts) operates within karma to work *moksha,* but it does claim that one can end suffering and mortality by penetrating the veils of illusion that conceal the cosmic process.

The great social development of the *smriti* period was the caste system. The Vedas (for example, *Rig-Veda* 10:90) had spoken of the creation of humanity in terms of the four ranks: priests, warriors, merchants, and workers. In the original sacrifice Purusha, the primal man, gave his mouth, arms, thighs, and feet to make those four ranks. However, law codes such as Manu's were required to justify casteism.[31] Apparently, casteism precedes the Aryan subjugation of the native Indians, but whether it was first based on color, occupation, tribe, or religious beliefs is unclear.[32]

In practice castes subdivide into about 25,000 occupational *jatis*, which have made Hindu social life a jigsaw puzzle. These societal distinctions have spawned some social customs peculiar to the eye of the outsider. For instance, fishermen who weave their nets from right to left do not speak to fishermen who weave from left to right, and coconut harvesters do not associate with coconut cultivators. Further, members of one *jati* often cannot marry members of another. Modern India has tried to deemphasize these customs, but they remain influential. Modern India has also tried to improve the lot of the untouchables, who lie outside the caste system, but they still exist. Even now, only certain groups of people carry garbage, clean homes, work in banks, and so on.

Personal Life

During the *smriti* elaboration of Vedic tradition, another influential doctrine was that of the four legitimate life goals. These were pleasure *(kama)*, wealth *(artha)*, duty (dharma), and liberation *(moksha)*. *Kama* was the lowest goal, but it was quite legitimate. *Kama* meant sexual pleasure but also the pleasure of eating, poetry, sport, and so on. *Artha* was also a legitimate goal, and around it developed learned discussions of ethics, statecraft, manners, and the like.[33] Because the person of substance propped society, wealth had a social importance and was thus more significant than pleasure.

Dharma, or duty, was higher than pleasure or wealth. It meant principle, restraint, obligation, law, and truth—the responsible acceptance of one's social station and its implications. So in the *Bhagavad Gita*, Krishna appeals to Arjuna's dharma as a warrior: It is his duty to fight, and better one's own duty done poorly than another's done well. *Moksha* meant liberation, freedom, and escape. It was the highest goal of life, because it represented the goal of one's existence: self-realization in freedom from karma and ignorance. The concept of *moksha* meant that life is samsaric—precarious and illusory. It also meant that pleasure, wealth, and even duty all could be snares.

As a complement to its exposition of life goals, *smriti* also analyzed the stages in the ideal unfolding of a life.[34] For the upper classes (excluding the workers), the four stages, or *ashramas*, were student, householder, hermit, and wandering mendicant. In a 100-year life, each would last about 25 years. In studenthood, the young male would apprentice himself to a guru to learn the Vedic tradition and develop his character. Depending on his caste, this would last 8 to 12 years and dominate the first quarter of his life. Then he would marry, raise children, and carry out social responsibilities. Hindu society honored marriage, and the economic, political, and social responsibilities of the householder gave him considerable esteem.

When the householder saw his children's children, however, *smriti* urged him to retire from active life and start tending his soul. He could still give advice and be helpful in secular affairs, but he should increasingly detach himself from the world. Finally, free of worldly concern, seeking only *moksha*, the ideal Hindu would end his life as a poor, wandering ascetic. Thereby, he would be an object lesson in the true purpose of human life, a teacher of what mattered most.

In effect, this scheme meant an ideal development (not often realized but still influential) of learning one's tradition, gaining worldly experience, appropriating both tradition and experience by solitary reflection, and finally consummating one's time by uniting with ultimate reality. From conception to burial, numerous ceremonies paced the Hindu through this cycle. The most important were adornment with the sacred thread (signaling sufficient maturity to begin studying the Vedas), marriage, and funerary rites. Women fell outside this scheme. During most of Hindu history, their schooling, such as it was, took place at home, and they were not eligible for *moksha*.[35]

The Period of Reform

From about 300 to 1200 C.E., the various movements that criticized or amplified the Vedic heritage resulted in a full reform of Hinduism. Of course, it is difficult to distinguish additions, such as those of the *smriti* writings, from revisions, but we can see in the growth of the six orthodox philosophies (described below) and the rise of the major Hindu sects developments that effectively revamped Hinduism.

A convenient distinction in the discussion that follows is that between those who reject the Vedas (for example, materialists, Jains, and Buddhists), called *nastikas* ("those who say no"), and those who accept the Vedas, or *astikas* ("those who say yes"). The orthodox philosophies, or *darshanas*, originated with *astikas*. In other words, the orthodox philosophies were conceived as explanations of *shruti* (revelation). There are six such philosophies or schools: Mimamsa, Samkhya, Yoga, Nyaya, Vaisheshika, and

Vedanta.[36] We can content ourselves with explaining Vedanta, the most celebrated *darshana*, although we will explain some practical implications of Samkhya and Yoga.

Before reviewing Vedanta, though, we should note that none of the orthodox *darshanas* is philosophy in the modern Western sense. Rather, they are all systems of reasoning and categorizing that defend the Vedas or help bring people to *moksha* through understanding the Vedas. Thus, the soul of Vedanta is not scientific detachment or uncovering the structures of reality for their own sake—or even uncovering truth for its own sake. Rather, Vedanta brings the student to an intuitive, liberating encounter with the sacred that will validate tradition and make one wise. For that reason, Vedanta is thoroughly religious.

Shankara, the greatest of the Vedanta thinkers, was a Malabar brahmin of the ninth century who tried to systematize the Upanishads in terms of "unqualified nondualism" *(advaita)*. In other words, he tried to explain the basic Upanishadic concepts of Brahman and atman with consistency and rigor. To do this, Shankara first established that there are two kinds of knowledge, higher and lower. Lower knowledge is under the limitations of the intellect, while higher knowledge is free of such limitations.

The limitations of the intellect include its reasoning character, its dependence on the senses, and its dependence on the body to act. These limitations are all subjective, since they are limitations of the knower, or subject. The objective limitations to knowledge, due to aspects of the known thing, are space, time, change, and cause-effect relationships. Because of objective limitations, we tend not to see or grasp reality in itself.

Higher knowledge comes by a direct perception that is free of either subjective or objective limitations. In practice it is the direct vision that the seers who produced the Vedas enjoyed—*shruti*. Quite likely, therefore, Shankara assumed that the Vedanta philosopher practices a yoga like that of the ancient sages. If so, he assumed that the Vedanta philosopher experiences a removal of the veil between the self and Brahman (with which the self is actually identified).

Shankara then applied this theory of higher and lower knowledge to *hermeneutics*, the study of textual interpretation. According to Shankara, all passages of the Upanishads that treat Brahman as *one* derive from higher knowledge; all references to Brahman as *many* or dual derive from lower knowledge. We can paraphrase this by saying that Brahman in itself is one and beyond all limitations, while Brahman for us (as we perceive it through sensation and reasoning) appears to be multiple—to be both in the world and beyond it, both material cause and prime mover.

With the subtlety of a great philosopher, Shankara wove the two edges of Brahman-in-itself and Brahman-for-us into a seamless whole. With the religious hunger of a mystic, he sought to correlate within and without. (Rudolf Otto has shown the similarity of Shankara's dynamics to those of the Western mystic philosopher Meister Eckhart.)[37] Shankara's core affirmation in his philosophical construction was that reality within is identical with reality without: Atman is Brahman. In other words, when one realizes through revelation, or higher knowledge, that there is no change, no space-time limitations, no cause-effect qualifications to the real, one then discovers that there is no self. Rather, there is only the Self, the Brahman reality that one directly perceives to be the ground of internal and external being.

From the perspective of lower knowledge, there is, of course, a personal, separate, changing self (an atman, or *jiva*). In absolute terms, though, there is one indivisible reality that is both subjectivity and objectivity, that is atman-Brahman. Since we rarely perceive directly, we often live and move in maya (illusion). The world of maya is not unreal in the sense that there are no elephants in it to break your foot if you get in the way of a circus parade. The elephants in the world of maya are substantial, their dung is mighty, and their step will crush your foot. But this viewpoint has limited validity. From a higher viewpoint, all that goes on in maya has no independent existence. The elephants' movement is a "play" of the only reality that exists independently—that is uncaused, unconnected, sovereign, and fully real.[38]

Vaishnavism

In the period of reformation, then, keen speculative minds tried to rehabilitate the Vedic heritage by showing the reasonableness of *shruti*. It is doubtful that they directly converted more than a few intellectuals, but they did impressively demonstrate that orthodox Hinduism, through Vedic revelation, could enable one to make powerful interpretations of reality. The more popular reformations of Vedism were theistic movements that brought the energies of Bhagavata (devotionalism) back into the Vedic fold. Two principal such movements centered on Vishnu and Shiva. Although these two movements fought for the common person's allegiance and presented quite different versions of divinity, they both advanced Vedic tradition and made a religion that combined some intellectual clout with much emotional enthusiasm.

The theistic religion centered on Vishnu (Vaishnavism) got its impetus from the patronage of the Gupta kings in the fourth century C.E., and it depended on interpretations of the Trimurti (the Brahma-Vishnu-Shiva trinity) that placed Vishnu in the foreground. Perhaps the most winning aspect of Vaishnavite doctrine, though, was its notion that the god is concerned about human beings, fights with them against demon enemies, and sends incarnations of himself (avatars) to assist humans in troubled times. Traditionally there are ten avatars, the most important being Rama (the hero of the epic *Ramayana*), Krishna, Buddha(!), and Kalki (who is yet to come).

Vaishnavism promoted itself in several ways. Two of the most effective tied Vishnu to the bhakti cult. Between the sixth and the sixteenth centuries, the *Puranas* (legendary accounts of the exploits of gods and heroes) pushed Vishnu to the fore.[39] The *Bhagavata Purana*, perhaps the most influential, was especially successful in popularizing the avatar Krishna. In fact, the tenth book of the *Bhagavata Purana*, which celebrates Krishna's affairs with the girls who tended cows *(gopis)*, mixes erotic entertainment with symbolism of the divine-human relationship. As the cowgirls were rapt before Krishna, so could the devotee's spirit swoon before god. When one adds the stories of Krishna's extramarital affairs with Radha, his favorite *gopi*, the religious eros becomes quite intense. The *Puranas* were thus the first vehicle to elevate Vishnu and his prime avatar to the status of bhakti (devotional) gods.

The second way in which Vaishnavite bhakti was promoted occurred in southern India during the seventh and eighth centuries.[40] There Tamil-speaking troubadours called *alvars* ("persons deep in wisdom") spread devotion to Vishnu by composing religious songs. However, their wisdom was simply a deep love of Vishnu, a love that broke the bonds of caste and worldly station. The constant theme of the songs was Vishnu's own love and compassion for human beings, which moved him to send his avatars. The *alvars* were so successful that they practically ousted Buddhism from India, and they were the main reason that Vishnu-Krishna became the most attractive and influential Hindu god.

A third way that Vaishnavism prospered was more intellectual—it had the good fortune of attracting the religious philosopher Ramanuja,[41] who is now second only to Shankara in prestige. Ramanuja lived in the eleventh century, and his main accomplishment was elaborating upon the Upanishadic doctrine in a way that made divinity compatible with human love. This way goes by the name *vishishtadvaita*—"nondualism qualified by difference." It opposed the unqualified nondualism of Shankara, whom Ramanuja regarded as his philosophical enemy. For Ramanuja, Brahman consisted of three realities: the unconscious universe of matter, the conscious community of finite selves, and the transcendent lord Ishvara.

Further, Ramanuja held that the Upanishadic formula "This thou art" meant not absolute identity between atman and Brahman but a relationship: the psychological oneness that love produces. The highest way to liberation was therefore loving devotion to the highest lord who represented Brahman. Knowledge and pure action were good paths, but love was better. By substituting Vishnu or Krishna for Brahman or Ishvara, the Vaishnavites made Ramanuja a philosophical defender of their bhakti. For those who wanted to reformulate revealed doctrine through love, Ramanuja was the man.

Shaivism

Contending with Vaishnavism was Shaivism—devotion to Shiva. Shankara had been a Shaivite, but his intellectualism hardly satisfied the common person's desires for an emotional relationship with divinity. As we have seen, Shiva was a somewhat wild god of fertility and destruction. He was the Lord of the Dance of Life and the destroyer who terminated each kalpa of cosmic time. From the earliest available evidence, Shaivism was a response to this wild god. It was frequently a source of emotional excesses, and its tone always mixed love with more fear and awe than Vaishnavism did.[42]

For example, one of the earliest Shaivite sects, which the *Mahabharata* calls Pashupati, taught that in order to end human misery and transcend the material world, one had to engage in such rituals as smearing the body with cremation ashes; eating excrement, carrion, or human flesh; drinking from human skulls; simulating sexual intercourse; and frenzied dancing. Members of other sects, such as the eleventh-century Kalamukha (named for the black mark they wore on their foreheads), became notorious as drug addicts, drunkards, and even murderers.[43] Even when Shaivites were thoroughly

respectable, their religion was more fiery and zealous in its asceticism than that of the love-struck but more refined Vaishnavites. Shaivite priests tended to come from the lower, non-Brahmin classes, and Shaivite followers often regarded the *lingam* (phallus) as Shiva's main emblem. Parallel to the Vaishnavite *alvars* were the Shaivite *adiyars*, whose poetry and hymns were a principal factor in Shiva's rise to prominence, especially in southern India.

The Shaivite movement also received royal patronage in southern India from the fifth to the tenth centuries. During those centuries the Shaivites waged war against both the Buddhists and the Jains. After winning that fight they turned on the Vaishnavites, singing of Shiva's superiority to Vishnu. In their theology they stressed not only the Lord of the Cosmic Dance and the god of fertility and destruction but also the hidden god. Even the worship of the phallus they enshrouded in mystery by placing it behind a veil. In addition, they often substituted representations of Nandi, Shiva's bull, or one of his *Shaktis* for the god Shiva himself.

Thus, the worshiper of Shiva grew conscious that he or she was a sinner through the mysterious ritual and Shiva's own symbols of fire and a skull. As a result, there was little equality, little of the lover-beloved relationship, between the devotee and Shiva. The Shaivite deprecatingly referred to himself or herself as a cur. That the god would come to such a person was pure grace. Worship, then, was essentially gratitude that the tempestuous god chose to forgive rather than destroy.

Shaktism

A last reformulation of the Hindu tradition came through movements that scholars group as Shaktism or Tantrism.[44] This sort of Hinduism focused on secret lore whose prime objective was to liberate the energies of sex and magic. Insofar as Shiva's *Shaktis* represented the energy of female divinity, they exemplified Tantrist powers.

It is hard to know exactly what *Shakti* sects believed and practiced, because most of their rites were secret, but one of their main beliefs was that the union of coitus is the best analogy for the relationship between the cosmos and its energy flow. This belief seems to have spawned a theory of parallels or dualisms, in which male-female, right-left, and positive-negative pairings all had magical aspects. (In this belief Tantrism resembles Chinese yin-yang theory, which we will consider in Chapter 6.)

One of the many Tantrist rituals for gaining *moksha* was called *chakrapuja* (circle worship). In it men and women (Tantrist groups tended to admit members without regard for sex or caste) used a series of elements (all having Sanskrit names beginning with the letter *m*) that might facilitate union with Shakti: wine, meat, fish, parched rice, and copulation. In right-hand Tantrism these elements were symbols. Left-hand Tantrism used the actual elements (not hedonistically but with ritual discipline, to participate in *lila* [reality's play]). Other Tantrist practices involved meditation to arouse the *kundalini*—the snake of energy lying dormant at the base of the spine.[45]

Overall, then, the reformation of the Vedic tradition meant expanded roles for the Vedic gods and a shift of popular religion from sacrifice to devotional, theistic worship. The reformers tried to defend and extend their ancient heritage, allowing people to respond to any part of it that they found attractive. In this way, the reformers created an eclectic religion that is very tolerant of diversity in religious doctrine and practice.

The Period of Foreign Challenge

From about 1200 C.E. on, Hinduism increasingly contended with foreign cultures, rulers, and religions. Islam and Christianity both made serious impacts on Indian life, and their presence is felt to this day. Islam, a factor in India from the eighth century on, first affected Indians of the Sind and Punjab regions in the northwestern part of ancient India, where Muslims traded and made military conquests. Invasions in the eleventh century put much of the Indus Valley region under Muslim control, and by 1206 Islam had conquered most of northern India. By 1335 Muslims controlled the south as well, and their final dynasty, the Mogul, did not end until 1858.

The policies of Muslim leaders toward Hinduism varied. Many were tolerant and allowed the Indians freedom to practice their traditional ways. Others, such as the Mogul zealot Aurangzeb (ruled 1658–1707), attempted to establish a thoroughly Muslim state and so tried to stop drinking, gambling, prostitution, the use of narcotics, and other practices that were prohibited by Islamic doctrine. Aurangzeb destroyed over 200 Hindu temples in 1679 alone, and he discriminated against Hindus in the collection of taxes and custom duties and in various other ways.

The permanent changes that Islam made in Hinduism and that Hinduism made in Indian Islam are hard to determine because the two faiths are intertwined. Islamic architecture and learning influenced Hinduism deeply, while Hindu casteism affected Indian Muslims as well. Muslim fundamentalism, based on the belief that the Qur'an is God's final word, probably upgraded the status of the Hindu Vedas, and many Hindus found *Sufism*, the devotional branch of Islam, quite compatible with their native bhakti practices.

One definite result of Islam's presence in India was a new, syncretistic religion, Sikhism. Traces of it were found among Hindus who considered aspects of Islam very attractive, but it actually began as a result of the revelations of the prophet Nanak, a Punjabi born in 1469. Nanak's visions prompted him to sing the praise of a divinity that blended elements of the Muslim Allah and the Hindu Trimurti. This God he called the True Name. The religious prescriptions for serving the True Name that he set for his followers were rather severe and anticeremonial, steering away from Hindu pilgrimages and devotions and favoring compassion and neighborly good deeds. The Sikhs developed into a small but hardy religious band,

and on numerous occasions they proved to be excellent warriors. They number about 6 million in India today, and their great shrine remains in Amritsar in the northwest. Many of the other holy Sikh sites, however, are now in Pakistan because of the 1947 partition.[46]

Christianity has been present in India since the first century C.E. according to stories about the apostle Thomas's adventures there. It is more certain that a bishop of Alexandria sent a delegation to India in 189 C.E. and that an Indian representative attended the Council of Nicaea (325 C.E.). Only in the sixteenth century, however, did the Christian missionary presence become strong, in the wake of Portuguese (and later Dutch and English) traders. The British East India Company, founded in 1600, increasingly controlled the Indian economy and trade, and after the Sepoy Mutiny in 1857 the company, which had become a sort of government, gave way to direct colonial rule. When India became independent in 1947, after almost a century of British colonial rule, it had some experience with the political ideas and social institutions of the modern West.

The Christian impact, as distinguished from the Western impact, has not been impressive statistically. According to 1964 census figures, only 2.4 percent of all Indians considered themselves Christians. Nevertheless, Christians opened hundreds of charitable institutions, especially schools, and were responsible for the first leprosaria. They also promoted hospital care for the tuberculous and the insane. In fact, Christianity's greatest impact was probably the rousing of the Hindu social conscience. The tradition of dharma as social responsibility had not resulted in the establishment of institutions for the poor and sickly. While Western culture opened India to modern science, technology, and democratic political theory, Western religion drove home the ideal of social concern. Mother Teresa of Calcutta continues that tradition today.

The native Hindu movements during the past seven centuries have not been particularly social.[47] After the reformation of the ancient tradition, Hinduism directed itself toward the further development of bhakti. Islamic Sufism stimulated this tendency, as we suggested above. In the religious poetry of Kabir, a forerunner of the Sikh founder Nanak, the love of God became the heart of a religion that ignored distinctions between Muslims and Hindus, priests and workers.[48] For Kabir this love correlated with a pure heart only.

For Ramananda, a follower of the philosopher Ramanuja, the important thing was to adore God, whom Ramananda called Rama, with fervent devotion. Rama considered all persons equal. In southern India, especially among the people who spoke Tamil, the Lord Vishnu increasingly appeared as a god of pure grace. Self-concern is useless and distracting, the Tamils told their Sanskrit Vaishnavite brethren. Not works but love is redeeming.

In west central India, from the thirteenth to the seventeenth centuries, a poetic movement called the Maratha renaissance carried the message of bhakti. Tukaram, the greatest poet of this movement, stressed God's otherness and the sinfulness of human beings. His god was not the Brahman who was identical with one's innermost self but a free agent and lover whose goodness in saving sinners was the more impressive because of their distance from him.

Modern Bhakti

In these and other movements, modern Hinduism increasingly focused on bhakti, moving away from Vedic orthodoxy. The singers of bhakti cared little whether their doctrines squared with the Upanishads or the great commentators. The notions of *shruti* or *smriti*, in fact, meant little to them. They thought that the love they had found undercut traditional views of social classes, sex, and even religions. The god of love was no creator of castes, no despiser of women, no pawn of Hindus against Muslims. With little concern for intellectual or social implications, the singers and seers who dominated modern bhakti gave themselves over to ecstatic love.

Perhaps the greatest representative of

bhakti was Chaitanya, a sixteenth-century Bengali saint whom his followers worship as an avatar of Krishna.[49] Chaitanya, originally a brahmin, converted to Vaishnavism and spent his days worshipping Lord Krishna in the great Bengali temple of Puri. Increasingly his devotions became emotional, involving singing, weeping, dancing, and epileptic fits. He died in delirium in the surf off Puri, where he was bathing. Somewhat typically for modern bhakti, Chaitanya repudiated the Vedas and nondualistic Vedanta philosophy as opposing a gracious god. All were welcome in his sect, regardless of caste, and he even sanctioned worship of a black stone, thinking that it might help some followers' devotion. He stressed the followers' assimilation with Radha, Krishna's lover, arguing that the soul's relation to God is always female to male.

Yet Chaitanya also stressed the necessity to toil at religious love and opposed those who argued that grace was attained without effort. His followers deified him, seeing his unbounded religious ecstasy as the ideal communion of divinity and humanity. He was the major figure in the devotional surge toward Lord Krishna that produced some remarkable Bengali love poetry during the sixteenth and seventeenth centuries.[50] His movement continues, with a rather high profile, in the United States through the work of Swami Prabhupada, founder of the International Society for Krishna Consciousness and of the Bhaktivedanta Book Trust. The swami's monks in saffron robes who chant on street corners and his numerous publications[51] have made "Hare Krishna" part of our religious vocabulary.

Partly in opposition to the excesses of bhakti and partly because of the influence of Western culture, a group of Bengali intellectuals in the early nineteenth century began to "purify" Hinduism by bringing it up to the standards that they saw in Christianity. The first such effort was the founding of the group Brahmo Samaj by Rammohan Roy in 1828. Roy was a well-educated brahmin whose contacts with Islam and Christianity led him to think that there should be only one God for all persons, who should inspire social concern.

God should, for example, oppose such barbarism as suttee (*sati*), the Hindu practice in which a widow climbed on her husband's funeral pyre and burned with him.[52] In 1811 Roy had witnessed the suttee of his sister-in-law, whom relatives kept on the pyre even though she was screaming and struggling to escape. He knew that in Calcutta alone there were over 1,500 such immolations between 1815 and 1818. Roy pressured the British to outlaw the practice, and in 1829 a declaration was issued that forbade it (though it did not completely stamp it out). Members of the Brahmo Samaj thought this sort of social concern was essential to pure religion.[53]

Another movement to modernize Hinduism that originated in Bengal in the nineteenth century was the Ramakrishna Mission. Its founder, Ramakrishna, was an uneducated brahmin who became a mystic devotee of the goddess Kali, a *Shakti* of Shiva, whom he worshipped as a divine Mother. After visions of Kali and then of Rama, the epic hero, Ramakrishna progressed through the Tantrist, Vaishnavite, and Vedanta disciplines, having the ecstatic experiences associated with the traditions of each. He even lived as a Muslim and a Christian, learning the mystic teachings of those traditions. From such eclectic experience he developed the joyous doctrine that we can find God everywhere: Divinity beats in each human heart. Ramakrishna's teachings achieved worldwide publicity through his disciple Vivekananda, who stressed the theme of worshipping God by serving human beings. The Ramakrishna Mission has sponsored hospitals, schools, and cultural centers, and it keeps an American presence through the Vedanta Society, which has chapters in many American cities.[54]

Tagore and Gandhi

In the twentieth century, these currents of domestic and foreign stimuli to reli-

*Figure 13   Raj-ghat, memorial to M. K. Gandhi in Delhi.
Photo by J. T. Carmody.*

gious and social reform inevitably affected the controversies over Indian nationalism and independence. The controversies themselves largely turned on the assets and liabilities of the British and Indian cultures. Not all Indians opposed the British, largely because they did not have a single national tradition themselves. Rather, Indians tended to think of themselves as Bengalis or Gujaratis or Punjabis—natives of their own district, with its own language and traditions. What the Indian tradition meant, therefore, was far from clear. This fact emerges in the lives of two of the most intriguing modern-day personalities, Tagore and Gandhi.

Rabindranath Tagore (1861–1941), modern India's most illustrious writer, won the Nobel Prize for literature in 1913. His life's work was a search for artistic and educational forms that would instill Indians with a broad humanism. For this reason, he was leery of nationalism, fearing that it would crush individual creativity and blind Indians to values outside their own country. In the West, Tagore found a salutary energy, a concern for the material world, which seemed to him precisely the cure for India's deep cultural ills. However, he despised the Western industrial nations' stress on machinery, power politics, and democracy. In Tagore's renewed Hinduism, India would give and receive—give resources for individual creativity and receive Western energies for using that creativity to improve society.

Mohandas Gandhi (1869–1948) was a political genius who made some of Tagore's vision practical. He trained as a lawyer in England and found his vocation as an advocate of the masses in South Africa, where he represented "colored" minorities. In India Gandhi drew in part on a Western idealism that he culled from such diverse sources as the New Testament, Tolstoy's writings on Christian socialism, Ruskin's writings on the dignity of work, and Thoreau's writings on civil disobedience. He joined this Western idealism with a shrewd political pragmatism of his own and Indian religious notions, including the *Bhagavad Gita's* doctrine of karma-yoga (work as a spiritual discipline) and the Jain-Hindu notion of *ahimsa* (noninjury). Gandhi's synthesis of these ideas resulted in what he called *satyagraha* (truth force). To oppose the might of Britain he used the shaming power of a simple truth: Indians, like all human beings, deserve the right to control their own destinies.

Gandhi was a genius at symbolizing truth force. In Joan Bondurant's study,[55] one can see how he worked out *satyagraha* campaigns of civil disobedience, striking, marshaling public support, and so on. In Erik Erikson's study of Gandhi at middle age,[56] one can see the psychological roots of *satyagraha* and something of its promise as an instrument for sociopolitical change in the nuclear age. In Gandhi himself one can see the conflicts, confusions, and riches of the Hindu tradition in the mid-twentieth century, for he called himself just a seeker of *moksha*, just a servant of the one God found whenever we harken to truth.[57]

STRUCTURAL ANALYSIS

Nature

For the most part, Hinduism considers nature (the physical cosmos) to be real, knowable, and orderly. The cosmos is a continuum of lives; consequently, human life is seen as an ongoing interaction with the lives of creatures above and below it. Finally, most Hindus consider divinity to be more than physical nature and human self-realization (*moksha*) to entail release from the laws of karma. Let us develop these ideas.

The statement that the physical cosmos is real requires some qualification. Through history, the average Hindu, concerned with making a living and caring for a family, has had little doubt that the fields, flocks, and other physical phenomena are real. Also, the hymns of the Veda that revere the sun and the storm express a vivid appreciation of nature. Even many of the philosophers spoke of the world as *sat*—having being or reality. Only the idealistic thought of the Upanishads, as the Vedanta developed and somewhat organized it, called the physical world into question.

Furthermore, because of the Vedic notion of *rita* (order, duty, or ritual) and the later notion of karma, Hinduism found the natural world quite orderly. *Rita* presided over such phenomena as sunrise and sunset and the seasons. Karma expressed the Hindu belief that all acts in the cosmos result from previous causes or choices and produce inevitable effects. To be sure, there are various religious paths (*margas*) for escaping karmic inevitability, and we shall discuss those paths below. Nonetheless, *rita* and karma suggest that the world is patterned, regular, and dependable. This does not mean that flood, famine, earthquake, sickness, or war cannot occur, but it does mean that none of these calamities makes the world absurd.

Karma, as we have seen, was connected with the notion of transmigration and rebirth. *Rita* is involved with the vast space-time dimensions in which Hindu cosmology delights. Together these concepts give nature a gigantic expanse that is replete with connections. The connections that most interested the average Hindu linked the myriad living things. Astrology and astronomy brought some people in contact with planetary forces, but the average Indian was more interested in other people and animals. Shaivites expressed this interest by venerating the powers of fertility. Ancient rites honoring the Great Mother and other rites stressing Shaktism reveal other Hindu responses to the wonders of life. The symbolism surrounding Shiva and his consorts (such as Kali) explicitly links life with death.

At a level above the ancient mentality's concerns with the vegetative cycle of death and rebirth and the taking of life by life, Hinduism placed the connection between death and life in the context of the great cycles of creation and destruction: the Brahma Day and Brahma Night, Shiva's dance of life and death, and the sportive play of *lila* or *maya*.

The Jain notion of *ahimsa*, which many Hindus adopted to varying degrees, implied the connectedness of all lives through its practice of not harming any living thing. Many Indians refused to eat meat out of the desire not to harm animals. Nonviolence toward the cow, which one might not kill even to help the starving (but which might itself starve), epitomized for many Hindus a necessary reverence for life. Taking karma and transmigration (the passing of the life force from one entity to another) seriously, the Hindu thought that life, including one's own, was constantly recasting itself into new vegetative and animal forms. Such life was not an evolutionary accident or something that ended at the grave. The inmost life principle continued on.

Hinduism had negative as well as positive aspects. Certainly maya and samsara can carry negative overtones. In fact, the whole thrust toward *moksha* suggests that the natural sphere is of limited value. For more than a few Indians, the natural sphere has been a prison or place of suffering. Yogis of different schools, for instance, have tried to withdraw from materiality in order to cultivate enstasis.[58] Other Hindu mystics have sensed that there was something more ultimate than the ritual sacrifice, the play of natural processes, and even the emotions of the devout worshiper of the bhakti god.[59] In this sense samsara opposed the freedom suggested by *moksha*, which meant exit from what one had known as natural conditions.

Another negative view of the natural world results from Hinduism's relative disregard for social improvements. However, it is misleading to label Hinduism as world denying or life denying, since India's culture has produced warriors, merchants, artists,

and scientists—a full citizenry who took secular life seriously.[60] Nonetheless, Hindu culture was seldom secular or materialistic in our modern senses, usually stabilizing society by referring to a god or Brahman transcending human space and time. (We may say the same of traditional premodern societies generally.) In addition, Hinduism's reference to metaphysical concepts retarded its concern with health care, education, and economic prosperity for the masses. (Again, we could say this of many other traditional cultures.) When he argued for a secular state and a turn to science rather than religion, Nehru spoke for many modern, educated Indians. Even today, the religion of the villages, which is often quite primitive, hinders the improvement of agriculture, family planning, housing, and health care.

Thus, Hinduism's Aryan beginnings, which were so bursting with love of physical life, and Dravidian beginnings, which were tantamount to nature and fertility worship, were negated over time. The most serious blows came from intellectual Hinduism and bhakti, which found life good by spiritual exercises and thus were not concerned with transforming nature or social justice.

In Eric Voegelin's terms, neither the early Hinduism that began close to nature nor that which withdrew from nature to human spirit escaped the cosmological myth. In Israel, Greece, and European Christian culture, such a withdrawal made nature less than divine. Unlike the religions of these Western cultures and the prophetic theology of Islam, Hinduism tended to keep gods and humans within the cosmic milieu. *Moksha* is an exception, but *moksha* was seldom articulated clearly. It primarily proposed that human self-realization comes by escaping the given world.

One confirmation of the view that Hinduism did not differentiate the realms of nature, divinity, and society is that the concept of creation from nothingness never became a dominant Hindu belief. In Hindu cosmology the universe goes its rhythmic way of Brahma Days and Brahma Nights; it has always existed and always will. Insofar as the concept of *moksha* suggests that we may transcend this cosmic rhythm, it carried seeds of a doctrine of creation from nothingness. However, the Hindu explanation of creation involves gods molding the world from preexisting stuff.[61] Thus Hinduism differs from Western religion by considering the world divine. It always remained somewhat under the cosmological myth.

Society

As we have seen, Hinduism structured society by caste and numerous occupational subclasses. In addition, families traced themselves back through their departed ancestors.[62] Outside the four castes were the untouchables, and there were also occasional instances of slavery. The basic structure of the four castes received religious sanction in the *Rig-Veda* (10 : 90), where the priests, warriors, merchants, and workers emerged from the Great Man's body after he was sacrificed.

The Laws of Manu, expanding the doctrine of casteism, specified the castes' social duties. The brahmin, for instance, had six required acts: teaching, studying, sacrificing for himself, sacrificing for others, making gifts, and receiving gifts. Brahmins also were to avoid working at agriculture and selling certain foods (such as flesh and salt). Were they to do these things, they would assume the character of the persons of the other castes. In a similar way, Manu set duties and prohibitions for the warriors, merchants, and workers, giving the entire society a comprehensive dharma. As a result, Hindus considered their dharma to be a given rather than a matter of debate or free choice. Indeed, it was the basic cement of Hindu society.[63]

Nonetheless, various religious inspirations and movements introduced some flexibility. Many of the bhakti cults rejected caste distinctions, contending that all persons are equal in the god's sight. The possibility of stepping outside the ordinary organization of things in order to become a full-time ascetic or seeker of liberation loosened the stranglehold of both dharma and caste. Throughout history, the patchwork organization of the Indian nation also added to social flexibility. Since most of the people lived in villages, and most of the administrative units were local rather than national, local customs were very strong.

Thus, Hindu society was remarkably diverse and tolerant despite its official rigidity. The complexity of social stations and religious allegiances meant that there were many legitimate ways through life. In the family, which was usually quite large, or extended, the chief figure was the father. Family organization was usually patriarchal, as was property administration. Women had some property rights, according to some legal schools, but their position was generally inferior. In fact, the place of women in Hindu society illustrates well the overall Hindu social and religious outlooks.

Women's Status

We know little about the earliest Indian women's social status. There is evidence of fertility rites among the pre-Aryans, as we have seen, suggesting a cult of a mother goddess or a matriarchal social structure. In Vedic times women clearly were subordinate to men, but in earlier times they may have held important cultic offices, created canonical hymns, and been scholars, poets, and teachers.[64] In the Brihad-Aranyaka Upanishad, the woman Gargi questions the sage Yajnavalkya, indicating that wisdom was not exclusively a male concern. It therefore seems likely that in early India at least some girls of the upper castes received religious training like the boys'.

However, between the first Vedas (1500 B.C.E.) and the first codes of law (100 C.E.), women's religious role steadily declined. A major reason for this was the lowering of the marriage age from fifteen or sixteen to ten and even five. This both removed the possibility of education (and consequently religious office) and fixed women's role to being wife and mother. In fact, in later Hinduism being a wife was so important that a widow was prohibited from mentioning any man's name but that of her deceased husband. Even if she had been a child bride or had never consummated her marriage, the widow was not to violate her duty to her deceased husband and remarry. If she did, she would bring disgrace on herself in the present life and enter the womb of a jackal for her next rebirth.

Thus, the widow was the most forlorn of Hindu women. Without a husband, she was a financial liability to those who supported her. If menstruating, she could be a source of ritual pollution. If barren, she was useless to a society that considered women essentially as child producers. In such a social position, many widows must have felt that they had little to lose by throwing themselves on their husband's funeral pyre.[65] (Even suttee, though, was not simple. If the widow did not burn herself out of pure conjugal love, her act was without merit.)

Women were sometimes admitted as equals into the bhakti and Tantrist sects. However, two circumstances in Tantrism minimized the social liberation that the open admission might have effected. First, the Tantrist sects tended to be esoteric, or secret, which made their public impact minor. Second, the Tantrist interest in tapping *shakti* energies often led to the exploitation of women by men. Thus, the males tried to gain powers of liberation *(moksha)* by symbolic or actual sexual intercourse, with the result that the females became instruments rather than equal partners. Nevertheless, the Tantrist image of perfection as being androgynous tended to boost the value of femaleness. How much this ideal actually benefited Indian women is difficult to say, but it probably did very little. In Hindu society, women were not generally eligible for *moksha;* the best that a woman could hope for was to be reborn as a man. There is little evidence that Tantrism eliminated this belief.

In fact, the overall status of women in Hinduism was that of wards. They were subject, successively, to fathers, husbands, and elder sons. As soon as they approached puberty, their fathers hastened to marry them off, and during their wedded lives they were to honor their husbands without reservation. According to the *Padmapurana,* an influential text, this held true even if their husbands were deformed, aged, debauched, lived openly with other women, or showed them no affection. To ritualize this attitude of devotion, orthodox Hindu authors counseled wives to adore the big toe of their husband's right foot, bathing it as they would an idol, and offering incense before it as they would to a great god.[66]

Worse than ward status, however, was the strain of misogyny (hatred of women) running through Hindu culture. The birth of a girl was not an occasion for joy. Hindus attributed it to bad karma in a previous life and frequently announced the event by saying, "Nothing was born." A girl was a financial burden, for unless her parents arranged a dowry there was small chance that she would marry, and the Vedic notion that women are necessary if men are to be complete (which the gods' consorts evidence) lost out to Manu's view that women are as impure as falsehood itself. In fact, Manu counseled "the wise" never to sit with a woman in a lonely place, even if that woman be one's mother, sister, or daughter.[67]

Consequently, Hindu religious texts frequently imagine a woman as a snake, hell's entrance, death, a prostitute, or an adulteress. In Manu's code, slaying a woman was one of the minor offenses. In the Hindu family, the basic unit of society, woman was therefore the negative charge. The high status of the householder did not extend to his wife or female children. India only honored women for giving birth and slavishly serving their husbands. (In a study of the emotional attitudes that this pattern has inculcated in modern India, Aileen Ross found the following intensity ratings for the listed relationships [the higher the number, the more intense the relationship]: mother-son, 115; brother-sister, 90; brother-brother, 75; father-son, 74; husband-wife, 16; sister-sister, 5. She gives no rating for the mother-daughter relationship.)[68]

Conclusion

The rewards of Hindu religion were in the hands of a relative few. By excluding women, untouchables, and workers, Hinduism told well more than half the population that their best hope was rebirth in a better station sometime in the future. (For the most part, only a member of a high caste could reach *moksha.*) However, in the family and the different trades, dharma gave all castes some legitimacy. Nonetheless, if the fundamental belief of Hinduism is considered to be the struggle for self-realization, these honors were rather tainted. For instance, in the ideal life cycle men of the upper three castes were to leave their families in middle age and retire from social life. A husband might take his wife into retirement with him, but he had no obligation to do so. If anything, tradition probably encouraged him to go off alone. What a person intent on self-realization did for children, servants, or the lower classes in his city was secondary to what he did for his own atman. In the Brihad-Aranyaka Upanishad (2.4.5), Yajnavalkya praised his wife Maitreyi for wanting his help in gaining immortality rather than in gaining wealth. This made her dear to him, not because he loved her earthly self but because he loved her atman.

The smaller units of Hindu society were less honored religiously than they were in other cultures. For instance, although Hindu marriage involved a sacramental rite, it was not regarded as highly as Jewish marriage, which is one of life's three great blessings (the Torah, good deeds, and marriage). The larger social organizations in India never approached the unity of a nation or empire, so one does not find the analogies between earth and heaven that one finds in Mesopotamia or Egypt, where the king was the mediator of divine substance, or *maat*—the mediator between the above of the gods and the below of the human realm. Indians may have sometimes pictured the realm of the many gods as a sort of government with superiors and subordinates, but this imagery is not so strong as it was in Greece or China.

Indian society was simply too diverse and too fragmented to reflect the macrocosm.

Thus, Hindu society is very complex. Dharma meant that religion supported a responsible attitude toward society, and the law treatises specified these responsibilities. On the other hand, *moksha* and bhakti militated against taking worldly life too seriously. For those absorbed in religious liberation or religious love, political, economic, and even family structures must have seemed of negligible importance.

Understandably, many of the great religious figures of Indian history left the social scheme. The Mahavira and the Buddha both left high-caste homes (the Buddha, in fact, left a wife and small child). Shankara urged celibacy and skipping the two middle stages of the life cycle so that one could pursue liberation wholeheartedly. The wandering minstrels of bhakti clearly did little for their families' or towns' social stability. Since pleasure and wealth meant less than duty and liberation, they were less effective ties to temporal pursuits than they have been in other cultures. Thus, Hindu society was remarkably "unhistorical"—not simply in the sense that it kept relatively few records of temporal affairs but in the deeper sense that it defined itself by a striving for something that was not temporal.

Self

Obviously, the average Hindu did not think about the self in isolation from nature and society. The social caste-system and the cosmic samsara-transmigration system were the framework of any studious self-examination. Within this framework, however, an individual might set about the task of trying to attain *atmansiddhi*, the perfecting of human nature. This was another way, more concrete perhaps, of posing what *moksha* or the *mahatma* (the "great soul") meant.

In the *Rig-Veda, atmansiddhi* was the pious man who faithfully recited the hymns and made sacrifices to the gods.[69] The *Brahmanas* changed the ideal to the priest who could faultlessly conduct the expanded ritual. The Upanishads shifted perfection toward the acquisition of secret knowledge about reality. The *smriti* literature valued more worldly achievement. There the most excellent man was he who could rule public affairs and lead in community matters. The *Bhagavad Gita* spoke of love as the highest attainment, but it described the realized human personality as being stable in wisdom and having overcome the desires of both the flesh and ambition. Recently Indian saints such as Ramakrishna and Gandhi have stressed, respectively, the mystic loss of self in God and the service of Truth. Clearly, therefore, Hindu tradition allows the self many forms. Generally speaking, though, the ideal implies emotional, intellectual, and spiritual maturity and honors the social side of human being as well as the solitary.

Hinduism's ideal self can also be analyzed by reviewing the stages of the life cycle. Studentship was a time for learning both tradition and self-mastery. From the guru the student learned what the scriptures and classics *meant*—how one could take them to heart and practice them. As well, living in poverty and practicing celibacy and obedience were intended to develop self-control, so that in later life one could do what one should and be master of one's passions.

The householder applied this education in experience and assumed responsibilities. Many Hindus have complained bitterly about child marriage,[70] arguing that it inhibited their ability to mature in a healthy fashion. This is certainly true for girls, and most boys as well. When they married at sensible ages, however, Indians had the chance to assume the responsibilities of being spouses, parents, and contributing members to society. They could pursue the lower goods, pleasure and prosperity, but within the higher dharma of their caste. If the emotional intensity profile of the family described earlier held true throughout history, the husband and wife were evidently not the prime relationship in the Hindu household. Rath-

er, marriage was intended more for raising children, continuing the family line, providing a place for the aged, and revering the departed ancestors than for the romantic fulfillment of the man and woman.

In the third stage of the life cycle, occurring after about twenty years of householdership, the self was to step away and reflect on what it had experienced. This custom reminds one of the Chinese saying "In office a Confucian, in retirement a Taoist." The "Confucian" mentality of the householder, concerned with practicalities, ought in the third *ashrama* (stage) to slowly yield to the "Taoist" mentality of contemplating nature's ways and nourishing one's poetic spirit. This corresponds to psychologist C. G. Jung's view that in the second half of life the personality tends to grow more reflective as it prepares for death and tries to accept what its life has amounted to thus far. In such reflection the lessons of youth are reviewed. As a youth one could hear the guru and try to take his teaching to heart, but that effort was bound to be shallow, because one did not have enough experience to know what the superficially simple precepts really meant. By the age of retirement, though, the reflective person could see that dharma really was necessary for personal and social order, because he had witnessed the chaos that follows when people do not fulfill their responsibilities.

However, we can only fully analyze the ultimate point to "forest dwelling," as the third stage was often called, by linking it with the final stage. The lessons of reflection were not part of an abstract or objective science of human behavior. Rather, one retired in order to care for the personal soul—to gain deliverance. Indians pictured the sage that emerged in the fourth stage, at the end of life, as a wandering ascetic. Stripped of goods and concerns, he moved freely in pursuit of *moksha* (or demonstrating its achievement). If, as a beggar, he was a social burden, he more than recompensed society by his example and teaching.

As we mentioned earlier, this final stress on *moksha* made Indian society "unhistorical." For more so than the West, India placed religion before all else. To be sure, *moksha* has parallels with the Western "unitive way," which ideally followed periods of penance and intellectual awakening. (And, to be sure, not all Indians were wholeheartedly religious.) But this Western scheme was intended primarily for monks and priests, not for laypersons as the four Hindu stages were.

The Upanishads jostled the classical life cycle for many. As we have seen, the Upanishadic self was the atman identified with Brahman. For this revered part of the Hindu tradition, then, the most important aspect of the self was the spiritual core. Less than the body, this spiritual core was the key to escaping rebirth. If one was serious about escaping rebirth, why wait for the final stages of the life cycle? Why not cultivate the atman full-time? Some such reasoning surely prompted those who became wanderers long before old age. Whether through study or meditation, they pursued a way that implied that the self's needs or aspirations could outweigh social responsibilities.

To be sure, the sage or liberated person ultimately was a boon to society, which recognized this through its support of beggars and yogis. Still, there was a conflict between the freedom to pursue *moksha* full-time and the social expectancies of marriage and procreation. The Buddha's "great renunciation" crystallizes this tension. He wanted to pursue enlightenment, but his father wanted him to continue the family rule. So he had to sneak away in the night, renouncing social obligations.

Bhakti, too, jostled the serene four-stage life cycle in its assertion that love of the god was the ultimate value. Such love was apparently available to women and outcastes, as well as to men of high social status. The conceptions of heaven and hell of the bhakti sects varied and were often unclear, but the love of the personal god definitely became the way to both his grace and a happy afterlife. However, how this meshed with the traditional view of reincarnation is rather obscure.

For our interests, however, it seems clear that the bhakti movement indicated to individuals that the most important thing in their lives was not an ascetic withdrawal to achieve *moksha* but a passionate immersion in emotional love. Often this must have seemed like recompense to women for their having been left outside the official structure of the life cycle. By fasting, pilgrimages, prayers, and the performance of devotion *(puja)* in the home, women and others outside the structure could accomplish the essence of *moksha*—uniting themselves with a reality beyond samsara. When they took up bhakti, then, many Indians had good reason to reject the traditional ways. Their new treasure more than cast the elitist *moksha* in the shade.

In the last thousand years or so, the individual Hindu has therefore had a variety of ways of viewing his or her life journey. The four stages, the Upanishadic or bhakti wandering, the household devotions—any of these concepts could give their lives meaning. Hinduism explicitly recognized that people's needs differed by speaking of four *margas* that could lead to fulfillment and liberation. Among intellectuals, the way of knowledge was prestigious. In this *marga* one studied the classical texts, the Vedic *shruti* and commentators' *smriti*, pursuing an intuitive insight into reality. Shankara's higher knowledge is one version of this ideal. If one could gain the viewpoint where Brahman was the reality of everything, one had gained redeeming wisdom.

The Samkhya philosophical tradition had a dualistic viewpoint. By its elaboration of matter *(prakriti)* and spirit *(purusha)*, Samkhya gave sense experience more validity than Vedanta did. The reality of matter meant highlighting the three *gunas*, or constituent qualities, that comprise everything.[71] *Sattva, rajas,* and *tamas* tended toward virtue, passion, and dullness, respectively. The self was thus to strive for *sattva's* rule.

But philosophy patently did not attract everyone, and many whom it did attract could not spare the time to study.

Figure 14   Dancing Krishna (Krishnagopal), thirteenth century, Chola period. Nelson Gallery–Atkins Museum, Kansas City, Missouri (Nelson Fund).

taken with this teaching of the *Gita,* used spinning as an example of *karma-marga* or *karma-yoga* (work discipline). One just let the wheel turn, trying to join one's spirit to its revolutions and paying the quantity of production little heed. When *karma-yoga* was joined to the notion that one's work was a matter of caste obligation, or dharma, it became another powerful message that the status quo was holy and meaningful.

A third *marga* was meditation *(dhyana),* which meant some variant of the practices that Patanjali's *Yoga Sutras* sketch.[72] Contrasted with the way of knowledge, the way of meditation did not directly imply study and did not directly pursue intuitive vision. Rather, it was usually based on the conviction that one can reach the real self by quieting the senses and mental activity in order to descend without thinking to the personality's depths. In this progression, one approached a state of deep sleep and then went beyond it to nondualism. "Seedless *samadhi*" (pure consciousness) was the highest of the eight branches of yogic progress, but to enter *moksha* one had to leave even it behind. Along the way to *samadhi* one might acquire various paranormal powers (such as clairvoyance or telepathy), but these were of little account. Below even the subconscious one wished to rest without desire on the bottom of pure spirit. For the many who meditated, the way of *dhyana* usually meant peace, a great sensitivity to body-spirit relationships (through, for example, posture and breath control), and a deepening sense of the oneness of all reality.

Finally, bhakti had the status of a *marga,* and, according to the *Bhagavad Gita,* it could be a very high way. Of course, *bhaktas* ran the gamut from emotional hysteria to lofty mysticism. The *Gita* qualified the self-assertiveness justified by bhakti, however, by making its final revelation not human love of divinity but Krishna's love for humans. On the basis of such revelation, the *bhakta* was responding to divinity as divinity had shown itself to be. In other words, the *bhakta* was realizing human fulfillment by

Therefore, the way of *karma* (here understood as meaning works or action) better served many people. The *Bhagavad Gita* more than sanctioned this way, which amounted to a discipline of detachment. If one did one's daily affairs peacefully and with equanimity of spirit, then one would not be tied to the world of samsara. Doing just the work, without concern for its "fruits" (success or failure), one gave *karma* (here meaning the law of cause and effect) nothing to grasp. Gandhi, who was much imitating God. (That was true of the yogi as well, which suggests that in India, as in other religious cultures, the self was finally an image of divinity.)

Divinity

Our final consideration is how Hinduism experienced and conceptualized divinity. This is no less complex than the dimensions of nature, society, and the self. In the early Vedic literature, the gods are principally natural phenomena. It is the wondrous qualities of the storm or fire that elevate Indra and Agni to prominence. By the time that the Brahmanic emphasis on sacrificial ritual dominated, the gods had come under human control. The final stage of Brahmanism was the view that the ritual, if properly performed, inevitably attains its goal—it compels the gods to obey. When we couple this subordinating view of the gods with the notion of samsara, the gods become less venerable than human beings. Human beings have the potential to break with samsara and to transcend the transmigratory realm in *moksha*. The gods, despite their heavenly estate, are still within the transmigratory realm and cannot escape into *moksha*.

The Upanishads, as we saw, moved away from the plurality of gods toward monism. One can debate whether this view is atheistic or religious, but the debate turns on semantics. However, both the Upanishads and the Vedanta philosophers stated that the knowledge of Brahman or atman is redemptive. Such knowledge, in other words, is not simply factual or scientific but has the power to transform one's life—it is light out of existential darkness. Therefore, from the side of the one who experiences Brahman's dominance, we can surely speak of "religious" (ultimately concerned) overtones.

As well, the place that Brahman has in the world view of the Upanishads and the Vedanta correlates with the place that God has in monotheism. Brahman is the basis of everything, if not the creator. It is the

supreme value, because nothing is worth more than the ultimate being, which, once seen, sets all in light and order.

The two aspects of Brahman, finally, approximate what monotheistic religions have made of their God. Being beyond the human realm *(nirguna)*, Brahman recedes into mystery. This parallels the Christian God's quality of always being ineffable and inconceivable. But being within the human realm *(saguna)*, Brahman is the basis of nature and culture. In this way it approximates the Christian conception of the Logos, in whom all creation holds together.

Brahman, of course, is impersonal, whereas most monotheistic religions conceive their deities on the model of the human personality. If we free personality of its human limitations, however, Brahman might qualify as personal. Either way, it is the functional equivalent of the most comprehensive realities of other religions. Like the *Tao* it cannot be named, yet it mothers the ten thousand things. Like the Buddhist Suchness or Buddha-nature, it must be described in both absolute and relative terms.

The bhakti cults revered still another form of Hindu divinity. For the followers of Vishnu-Krishna or Shiva, the older type of henotheism (elevating one god to primacy of place) returns with a vengeance. Vaishnavites do not strictly deny the reality of Shiva or Brahma, nor do followers of these other gods deny the reality of Vishnu or Krishna. The mere fact that bhakti sects devoted to different gods contend among themselves shows that they take the other gods seriously. But the emotional ardor of the devoted *bhaktas* suggests that they grant their gods the ultimate value of a monotheistic God. The same holds for devotees of goddesses, who may actually outnumber devotees of the male gods. The Devi-mahatmya writings, for instance, have fashioned a warrior queen who is the equal of Vishnu.[73]

In Krishna's manifestation to Arjuna in the *Bhagavad Gita*, we can see how this monotheistic value took symbolic form. Krishna becomes the explosive energy of all reality. In the *Gita*, his theophany (manifestation of divinity) is the ultimate revelation of how divinity assumes many masks in space and time. Whatever reality is, Krishna is its dynamic source. Much like the Upanishadic Brahman, he is the one source capable of manifesting itself in many forms. But whereas the atmosphere of Brahman is serene and cool, the bhakti-prone Krishna is turbulent and hot. When J. Robert Oppenheimer, one of the developers of the American atom bomb, saw the first nuclear explosion, Krishna's dazzling self-revelation came to his mind. Thus, the Hindu divinity, like the Hebrew divinity of the chariot or the Zoroastrian divinity of the sacrifice, could be a refining fire.

This refining fire makes the world rise from and fall back into formlessness. As we have seen, the Trimurti of Brahma, Vishnu, and Shiva stands for creation, preservation, and destruction. Shiva himself, however, presides over life and death as the Lord of the Dance of Creation. The Shaivites, in this belief, indicate more clearly than the Vaishnavites how many Hindus retain a quite ancient notion of divinity.[74] Shiva is a complex reality, to be sure, but his ascetic and destructive aspects reflect quite ancient encounters with spiritual forces.

Through his *Shaktis* Kali and Durga, Shiva relates to grisly cults trafficking in corpses and skulls. Through his association with basic life forces, he is a link between *bhaktas* and the rude snake worshipers who still populate rural India. There is manifest in this wild god, therefore, another version of divinity's energy. In contrast to the Vedantic Brahman, Shiva is turbulent and hot, and his energy is as concrete and intrusive as its symbolic phallus. (There are equally concrete female deities, but, unfortunately, scholars have not studied them as thoroughly.)[75]

Indian divinity thus has many levels and many facets. It follows that Hinduism

itself has many forms and many values, since the concept of divinity is the heart of any religion. In our opinion, the dimensions of nature, society, and the self are subordinate to the dimension of divinity, since the last determines the places of the first three. In other words, Hindus arrange nature, society, and the self in view of the Agni, Brahma, or Krishna who centers their lives in mystery. If Brahma is the divinity, then nature, society, and the self are all versions of maya, are all illusion and play. If Agni, the god to whom one directs the fire sacrifice, is the divinity, then nature stands by divine heat, society stands by priestly sacrificers, and the self strives after *tapas* (ascetic heat) or lives by ritual mantras (verbal formulas for controlling the divine forces). Finally, if Shiva is the divinity, then divinity destroys castes, is the arbiter of life and death, and reduces the self to a beggar for grace.

Nevertheless, one could begin with the view of nature, society, or the self and develop what divinity and the other two subordinate dimensions meant. In other words, cosmology, sociology, and psychology have their legitimate places in religious analysis.

However, historians of religion believe that no system of interpretation can truly substitute for the system that the religion itself implicitly uses. In other words, we cannot reduce the religions to their cosmological, sociological, or psychological factors. They must remain essentially what they claim to be: ways emanating from and leading to the divine. For this reason, the concept of divinity in a religion will always be the most crucial concept. God or ultimate reality is by definition the ultimate shaper of a world view, because divinity determines the placement of the other dimensions and thus the world view. Having had many forms of divinity, Hinduism has had many world views.

Study Questions

1. What does the Harrapan proto-Shiva suggest about pre-Vedic Indian religion?
2. Why did Vedic religion come to stress sacrifice?
3. How could Upanishadic knowledge bring salvation?
4. Can you translate *moksha* into terms that your contemporaries would find attractive?
5. In what sense did *bhakti* personalize Hindu divinity?
6. Does the status of Indian women through the ages wholly discredit Hinduism?
7. To what extent could we adapt the classical Hindu life cycle to the needs of Americans today?
8. Does Indian religion show that ultimate reality is at least as much impersonal as personal?

Chapter Five

BUDDHISM: TWENTY-FIVE KEY DATES

536–476 B.C.E.	BUDDHA
519	GAUTAMA'S ENLIGHTENMENT
473	FIRST BUDDHIST CONGRESS
363	SECOND BUDDHIST CONGRESS
273–236	REIGN OF BUDDHIST EMPEROR ASOKA
236	RISE OF MAHAYANA TRADITION
160	*PRAJNA-PARAMITA* LITERATURE
80	LOTUS SUTRA; BUDDHIST DECLINE IN INDIA
CA. 200 C.E.	NAGARJUNA, LEADING PHILOSOPHER
220–552	MISSIONS TO VIETNAM, CHINA, KOREA, BURMA, JAVA, SUMATRA, JAPAN
430	BUDDHAGHOSA, LEADING PHILOSOPHER
594	BUDDHISM PROCLAIMED JAPANESE STATE RELIGION

Buddhism

Buddhism arose in India when a strong, enlightened personality, Siddhartha Gautama, persuasively proposed a better way to structure individual and social life than did contemporary Brahmanistic Hinduism. Moreover, his contemporaries were sufficiently impressed to institutionalize his teaching and assure its survival. Where Buddhism survived and most prospered, however, was not the Enlightened One's native land; in India Hindu devotionalism and then Islam proved more powerful than Gautama's "middle way." Missionary Buddhism kept the Way alive and developing. Consequently, we will begin with a description of Buddhism in Thailand and Japan today.

APPEARANCE

Bangkok is a lovely city of Buddhist temples. Both its past history and its present culture reflect the deep influence of the Buddha. Similarly Kyoto, the ancient Japanese capital, is still a living example of Buddhist culture.

Were you to visit the Imperial Compound in Bangkok (Figure 15), you might well consider your air fare a bargain. The vivid blue sky sets off a complex of shrines and government buildings whose beauty is so overwhelming that one can only call the compound a jewel. First of all, it is brilliantly colorful. The slanted roofs of the buildings, which seem midway between Indian and Chinese styles, are of orange, blue, and green enamel tile. Their sharply angled gold peaks and corners represent Garuda, the giant bird who flies Buddhas and emperors on their celestial journeys. In some portions of the compound many small shrines run together, connected by porticoes. The shrines contain relics of holy persons or worthy benefactors. At their entrances, two fierce protector spirits usually stand guard; they can be ten feet tall and have the bulging eyes and ready swords of folk mythology. They are at once amusing and instructive, three-dimensional cartoons and object lessons in religious imagination.

In other corners of the compound delicate spires curlicue skyward, like gold-dipped cones of soft ice cream. Within the most celebrated Thai shrine, that of the Emerald Buddha, dozens of monks, devout laity, and slightly confused tourists kneel or pad softly in stocking feet. The Emerald Buddha is perhaps four feet high and carved in jade. He is dressed according to the season, being naked in the summer and covered with a little shawl when the weather is cool. The devotion to him is a mixture of aesthetic appreciation for his artistic rendering in precious stone and genuine religious veneration of the light and fulfillment that he represents.

In Kyoto many temples vie for the tourist's favor. The Moss Temple first beckons as a respite from the summer heat and city turmoil. Many shades of green vegetation slow one's pace, encouraging a return to the simple beauties of natural growth. Passing the small tea cottage near the first bend in the green stream prompts one to think of the exquisite ceremonies that Buddhism nurtured. Taking tea in a disciplined, simple ceremony acts out the immediacy and the flow of the world made apparent through enlightenment. Delighting in bamboo and rough stones, Japanese have venerated nature since prehistoric times, joining this attitude to their Buddhist sense for the unity of life, the cycles of the samsaric wheel.

Kyoto's Zen Rock Garden is likewise an education in Buddhism. The empty space around the rocks (the expanse of raked sand) teaches as much about emptiness as most sutras can. Indeed, even Westerners contemplating the angular rocks learn of the relation between the bare and the penetrating. Such contemplation recalls Zen master Ikkyu's response to a layperson who asked him how to make progress: "Attention."[1] Close attention to the sand and the rocks works a peculiar purification.

The rival for the Rock Garden's preeminence in Kyoto is probably the Golden Pavilion Temple (Figure 16). There the pond

Figure 15   Temples of the Imperial Compound, Bangkok.
Photo by J. T. Carmody.

characteristic of Buddhist temple grounds perfectly mirrors a three-story frame structure gilded with gold. On a clear day it produces a double image of peaceful beauty. Perhaps recalling Hua-yen Buddhism's use of mirror imagery to show the connectedness of all things, the visitor at the Golden Pavilion starts to wonder about image and reality, about how things appear and what they really are. The pond is so pleasing yet varies so with the seasons that it joins beauty and change in a yearly ballet. When the cherry blossoms bloom around the pagoda, Buddha-nature (ultimate reality) dons pale pink. When the snow settles on the frozen pond, Buddha-nature is pure white. Gardeners can manipulate the blossoms and the snow, but much in the present is out of human hands. The Golden Pavilion teaches this lesson very gently.

HISTORY

The Buddha

The Buddha was born about 560 B.C.E. in the town of Kapilavastu in what is now a part of Nepal just below the Himalayan foothills. His people were a warrior tribe called Sakyas and his clan name was Gautama. The religious climate in which he grew up was quite heated. Some objectors were challenging the dominance of the priestly brahmin class. As we saw in the last chapter, the writers of the early Upanishads reveal the dissatisfaction with sacrifice that was burning among intellectuals, while the accounts of the Mahavira are evidence of the ascetic movement that also challenged the priestly religion of sacrifice. In secular culture, the sixth century B.C.E. saw a movement from

*Figure 16   The Golden Pavilion Temple, Kyoto.
Photo by J. T. Carmody.*

tribal rule toward small-scale monarchy, a growth in urban populations, the beginnings of money-based economies, the beginnings of government bureaucracies, and the rise of a wealthy merchant class.[2] Thus, the Buddha grew up in a time of rapid change, when people were in turmoil over religion and open to new teachings.

Pious myth heavily embellishes the accounts of the Buddha's birth and early life, so it is difficult to describe this period of his life accurately. Legend has it that his father, Suddhodana, was a king, and that he received a revelation that his child would be a world ruler if the child stayed at home but a spiritual saviour if the child left home. According to other legends, the Buddha passed from his mother's side without causing her any pain, stood up, strode seven paces, and announced, "No more births for me!"[3] In other words, the child would be a spiritual conquerer—an Enlightened One.

As the Buddha grew, his father surrounded him with pleasures and distractions in order to keep him in the palace and away from the sights of ordinary life. When the Buddha came of age, the father married him to a lovely woman named Yasodhara. So Sakyamuni ("sage of the Sakyas") lived in relative contentment until his late twenties. By the time of his own son's birth, however, the Buddha was restless. (He named the child Rahula [fetter].)

What really precipitated Sakyamuni's religious crisis, though, was an experience he had outside the palace. On several outings he met people who were aged, diseased, or dead. They shocked him severely, and he became anxiety ridden. How could anyone take life lightly if these were its constant dangers? Meditating on age, disease, and death, the young prince decided to cast away his round of pleasures and solve the riddle of life's meaning by becoming a wandering beggar. Renouncing his wife, child, father, and goods, he set off to answer his soul's yearning.

The teachers to whom the Buddha first apprenticed himself specialized in meditation and asceticism. Their meditation, it appears, was a yogic pursuit of enlightenment through *samadhi* (trance). From them the Buddha learned much about the levels of consciousness but was not fully satisfied. The teachers could not bring him to dispassion, tranquillity, enlightenment, or nirvana (a state of liberation beyond samsara). In other words, the Buddha wanted a direct perception of how things are and a complete break with the realm of space, time, and rebirth.

To attain these goals, Sakyamuni turned to asceticism to such a degree that he almost starved himself. The texts claim that when he touched his navel, he could feel his backbone. In any event, asceticism did not bring what Sakyamuni sought either. (Because of this, he and his followers have always urged moderation in fasting and bodily disciplines. Theirs, they like to say, is a middle way between indulgence and severity that strives to keep the body healthy, as a valuable ally should be, and to keep the personality from excessive self-concern.)

What liberated the Buddha, apparently, was recalling moments of peace and joy from his childhood, when he had sat in calm but perceptive contemplation. According to the traditional accounts, Mara, the personification of evil or death, tried to tempt Buddha (who sat meditating under a fig tree) away from this pursuit.[4] First, he sent a host of demons, but the Buddha's merit and love protected him. Then, with increased fear that this contemplator might escape his realm, the evil one invoked his own power. However, when Mara called on his retinue of demons to witness his power, the Buddha, who was alone, called on mother earth, which quaked in acknowledgement. As a

last ploy, Mara commissioned his three daughters (Discontent, Delight, and Desire) to seduce the sage. But they, too, failed, and Mara withdrew. (Psychological interpretation can illuminate the details of this legend when they are considered as symbols of dramatic changes in the personality—the challenges, fears, resistance, and final breakthrough.)

Enlightenment

The *enlightenment* (realization of the truth) itself occurred on a night of the full moon. According to tradition, Buddha ascended the four stages of trance. In later times these four stages were considered as a progressive clarification of consciousness: (1) detachment from sense objects and calming the passions; (2) nonreasoning and "simple" concentration; (3) dispassionate mindfulness and consciousness with bodily bliss; and (4) pure awareness and peace without pain, elation, or depression.[5]

According to tradition, then, one progressed in a contemplative sitting by moving from confusion and sense knowledge to pure, unemotional awareness. The assumption was that this progress facilitated direct perception of reality—seeing things as they really are. It might bring in its train magical powers (the ability to walk on water, to know others' minds, or to remember one's previous lives, for instance), but its most important achievement was to eliminate desire, wrong views, and ignorance, which are the bonds that tie one to samsara. To break them is therefore to free consciousness for nirvana.

Another traditional way of describing the Buddha's enlightenment is to trace his progress through the night. During the first watch (evening), he acquired knowledge of his previous lives. This is a power that some shamans claim, so it is not Buddha's distinguishing achievement. During the second watch (midnight), he acquired the "divine eye" with which he surveyed the karmic state of all beings—the dying and rebirth cycle that is their destiny. With this vision

The Eightfold Path outlines the life-style that Buddha developed for people who accepted his teaching and wanted to pursue nirvana. As such, it is more detailed than a description of what Buddha directly experienced in enlightenment—something that he probably elaborated on later. The explanation of reality that Buddha developed out of enlightenment, which became known as the doctrine of dependent coarising, also came later. It explains the causal connections that link all beings.

Enlightenment seems to have been the dramatic experience of vividly perceiving that life, which Sakyamuni had found to consist of suffering, had a solution. One could escape the terror of aging, sickness, and death by withdrawing one's concerns for or anxieties about them—by no longer desiring youth, health, or even life itself. By withdrawing in this manner, one gave karma nothing to which to cling, for desire was the means by which karma kept the personality on the wheel of dying and rebirth. Removing desire therefore took away karma's hold. To destroy desire for karmic existence, though, one had to penetrate the illusion of its goodness. That is, one had to remove the ignorance that makes sensual pleasures, financial success, prestige, and so on, seem good. Buddha designed the Eightfold Path and the doctrine of dependent coarising in order to remove ignorance and rout desire.

Figure 17   Head of Buddha, third to fifth century, C.E. Nelson Gallery–Atkins Museum, Kansas City, Missouri (Nelson Fund).

he realized that good deeds beget good karma and a move toward freedom from this destiny, while bad deeds beget bad karma and a deeper entrenchment in samsara. The second achievement made Buddha a moralistic philosopher, insofar as he saw the condition of all beings as a function of their ethical or unethical behavior.

During the third watch (late night), the Buddha reached the peak of perception, attaining "the extinction of the outflows" (the stopping of desire for samsaric existence) and grasping the essence of what became the Four Noble Truths: (1) All life is suffering; (2) the cause of suffering is desire; (3) stopping desire will stop suffering; and (4) the Eightfold Path (explained below) is the best way to stop desire.

Dependent Coarising and the Eightfold Path

Often Buddhists picture dependent coarising as a wheel with twelve sections or a chain with twelve links (the first and the last are joined to make a circuit).[6] These twelve links explain the round of samsaric existence. They are not an abstract teaching for the edification of the philosophical mind, but an extension of the essentially therapeutic analysis that the Buddha thought would cure people of their basic illness.

The wheel of dependent coarising turns in this way: (1) Aging and dying depend on rebirth; (2) rebirth depends on becoming;

(3) becoming depends on the appropriation of certain necessary materials; (4) appropriation depends on desire for such materials; (5) desire depends upon feeling; (6) feeling depends upon contact with material reality; (7) contact depends on the senses; (8) the senses depend on "name" (the mind) and "form" (the body); (9) name and form depend on consciousness (the spark of sentient life); (10) consciousness shapes itself by karma; (11) the karma causing rebirth depends on ignorance of the Four Noble Truths; and (12) therefore, the basic cause of samsara is ignorance.

One can run this series forward and back, but the important concept is that ignorance (of the Four Noble Truths) is the cause of painful human existence, and that aging and dying are its final overwhelming effects and the most vivid aspects of samsara. Thus, the chain of dependent coarising is a sort of practical analysis of human existence. It mingles concepts of physical phenomena (for example, aging and dying depend on rebirth) and concepts of psychological phenomena (for example, appropriation depends on desire). The result is called *dependent coarising* (or origination) because it is a doctrine of mutual causality.

In the Buddha's enlightenment, as he and his followers elaborated upon it, there is no single cause of the way things are. Rather, all things are continually rotating in this twelve-stage wheel of existence. Each stage of the wheel passes the power of movement along to the next. The only way to step off the wheel, to break the chain, is to gain enlightenment and so detach the stage of ignorance. If we do detach ignorance, we stand free of karma, karmic consciousness, and so on, all the way to aging and rebirth.

The result of enlightenment, then, is no rebirth, which is the implication of nirvana. Nirvana is the state in which the chain of existence does not obtain—in which desire is "blown out" and one escapes karma and samsara. Thus, nirvana begins with enlightenment and becomes definitive with death. By his enlightenment, for instance, the Buddha had broken the chain of dependent co-

arising; at his death his nirvana freed him from rebirths.

The Eightfold Path (which is the Fourth Noble Truth) details how we may dispel ignorance and gain nirvana[7] by describing a middle way between sensuality and extreme asceticism that consists of (1) right views, (2) right intention, (3) right speech, (4) right action, (5) right livelihood, (6) right effort, (7) right mindfulness, and (8) right concentration. "Right views" means knowledge of the Four Noble Truths. "Right intention" means dispassion, benevolence, and refusal to injure others. "Right speech" means no lying, slander, abuse, or idle talk. "Right action" means not taking life, stealing, or being sexually disordered. "Right livelihood" is an occupation that does not harm living things; thus, butchers, hunters, fishers, and sellers of weapons or liquor are proscribed. "Right effort" avoids the arising of evil thoughts. In "right mindfulness," awareness is disciplined so that it focuses on an object or idea to know its essential reality. "Right concentration" focuses on a worthy object of meditation.

The first two aspects of the Eightfold Path, right views and right intention, comprise the wisdom portion of the Buddhist program. If we know the Four Noble Truths and if we orient ourselves toward them with the right spiritual disposition, then we are wise and come to religious peace. Tradition groups aspects three, four, and five under morality.[8] To speak, to act, and to make one's living in wise ways amount to an ethics for nirvana, a morality that will liberate one from suffering. Finally, aspects six, seven, and eight entail meditation. By setting consciousness correctly through right effort, mindfulness, and concentration, one can perceive the structures of reality and thus personally validate the Buddha's enlightened understanding.[9]

The three divisions of the Eightfold Path compose a single entity, a program in which each of the three parts reinforces the other two. Wisdom sets up the game plan, the basic theory of what the human condition is and how one is to cope with it. Morality applies wisdom to daily life by specifying how one should speak, act, and support oneself. Regular meditation focuses one on the primary truths and the reality to which they apply. In meditation the Buddhist personally appropriates the official wisdom, personally examines the ethical life. As a result, meditation builds up the Buddhist's spiritual force, encouraging the peaceful disposition necessary for a person to be nonviolent and kindly.[10]

The Dharma

Buddhists have seen in Sakyamuni's enlightenment the great act founding their religion. The Buddha is worthy of following because in enlightenment he became flooded with knowledge *(bodhi)*. What he saw under the Bodhi Tree in the third watch was nothing less than the formula for measuring life and curing its mortal illness. The Four Noble Truths and dependent coarising are two favorite ways of presenting the essential truths of Buddha's knowledge.

Buddha himself apparently debated what to do after achieving enlightenment. On the one hand, he had this dazzling light, this potent medicine, to dispense. On the other hand, there was dreary evidence that humanity, mired in its attachments, would find his teaching hard to comprehend and accept.[11] Legend says that the god Brahma appeared to the Buddha and pleaded that the Enlightened One teach what he had seen for the sake of wayward humanity. Out of compassion (which became the premier Buddhist virtue), the Enlightened One finally agreed to Brahma's request.

According to tradition, his first sermon occurred in Deer Park near Benares, about five days' walk from Gaya, where enlightenment took place. He preached first to some former ascetic companions who had rejected him when he turned away from their harsh mortification, and his calm bearing won them over. What Buddha first preached was the Four Noble Truths, but he apparently prefaced his preaching with a solemn declaration of his authority as an immortal enlightened one. From this preface Buddhists have concluded that one must have faith in the authority behind the *dharma* (the teaching) if the dharma is to have its intended effect.

The Buddha's preaching won him innumerable converts, men and women alike, many of whom decided to dedicate their lives to following him and his way. A great number entered the *sangha*, or monastic order, assuming a life of celibacy, poverty, and submission to rules of discipline.[12] Other followers decided to practice the dharma while remaining in their lay state, and they frequently gave the Buddha and the Buddhist community land and money.[13] In both cases people became Buddhists by taking "refuge" in the three "jewels" of the Enlightened One's religion: the Buddha himself, the teaching (dharma), and the community (*sangha* can mean either the monastic community or the entire community of Buddhists, lay and monastic, past and present).[14]

By uttering three times the vow of taking refuge, one became a follower in a strict, official sense. (This act reflects the special, almost magical effect that words had in ancient India. When the Buddha preached, just as when the Vedic priests uttered sacrificial formulas, an active force was believed to be activated. When one took refuge, the words effected a binding to the Buddha, the teaching, and the community.)

In time a catechism developed to explain the Buddha's teaching. One of the catechism's most important notions was the "three marks" of reality. Together with the Four Noble Truths and dependent coarising, the three marks have helped countless Buddhists hold the dharma clearly in mind. According to this conception, all reality is painful, fleeting, and selfless. This formula adds something to the insights of the Four Noble Truths. That all life or reality is painful is the first truth: the reality of suffering. By this Buddhists do not mean that one never experiences pleasant things or that one has no joy. Rather, they mean that no matter how pleasant or joyous one's life, it is bound to include disappointment, sickness, misunderstanding, and finally death. Since the joyous things do not last, even they have an aspect of painfulness.

Second, all life is fleeting, or passing. Everything changes—nothing stays the same. Therefore, realistically there is nothing to which we can cling, nothing that we can rely on absolutely. In fact, even our own realities (our "selves") change. On one level, we move through the life cycle from youth to old age. On a more subtle level, our thoughts, our convictions, and our emotions change.

Third, there is no self. For Buddhists, the fleetingness of our own consciousness proves that there is no atman—no solid soul or self. In this the Buddhists directly opposed Hinduism as well as common belief. All people, it seems, naturally think that they have personal identities. Buddhists claim that personalities consist of nothing solid or permanent. We are but packages of physical and mental stuff that is temporarily bound together in our present proportions.

The tradition calls the component parts of all things *skandhas* (heaps), which number five: body, feeling, conception, karmic disposition, and consciousness. Together the *skandhas* make the world and the person of appearances, and they also constitute the basis for clinging to existence and rebirth. To cut through the illusion of a self is therefore the most important blow that one can strike against ignorance. This is done by being open to the flowing character of all life and decisively pursuing nirvana.

The three marks of reality summarize why the wise person does not desire sentient existence, which is the cloth of which nightmares are made. The Buddha's own teaching once likened the nightmare of desire to a raging fire. In his Fire Sermon,[15] the Buddha told his monks that all things are on fire: The eyes are on fire with the forms they perceive, the passions with hatred and infatua-

tion, the ears with sounds, the nose with smells, the tongue with tastes, and the mind with ideas. This fiery desire produces birth, old age, death, sorrow, misery, lamentation, grief, and despair. Therefore, the learned and the noble are averse to the works of the senses and the mind, and turn toward what cools the body and the consciousness. In so doing they become free from this painful world. Like the Enlightened One himself, they move with the grace of detachment, the serenity of one who possesses peace.

The early teachers described the realms of rebirth to which humans were subject and in so doing developed a Buddhist version of the Indian cosmic powers and zones of the afterlife. Essentially, the Buddhist wheel of rebirth can occupy any of six realms or destinies. Three are lower realms (hells), which are karmic punishment for bad deeds. The other three are higher realms (heavens) in which good deeds are rewarded. The lowest hell is for punishing the wicked by means befitting their particular crimes. However, these punishments are not eternal; after individuals have paid their karmic debt, they can reenter the human realm by rebirth. Above the lowest hell is the station of the "hungry ghosts," who wander the earth's surface begging for food. The third and least severe realm of the wicked is that of animals. If one is reborn in that realm, one suffers the abuses endured by dumb beasts.

The fortunate destinies reward good karma. The human realm is the first, and in it one can perform meritorious deeds. Since one can only earn merit as a human being, this realm is the most decisive for one's destiny. Even entering nirvana from a heavenly realm above the human is made possible through merit developed in a previous existence as a human.

The two final realms are those of the demigods (Titans) and the gods proper. Both include a variety of beings, all of whom are subject to rebirth. Since even the Buddhist gods are subject to rebirth, their happiness is not at all comparable to the final bliss of nirvana. Better to be a human being advancing toward enlightenment than a divinity liable to the pains of another transmigratory cycle. Perhaps for that reason, the Buddhist spirits and divinities, as well as the Buddhist ghosts and demons, seem inferior to the human being. Apparently Buddhism adopted wicked and good spirits from Indian culture without much thought. In subjecting these spirits to the powers of an *arhat* (one who achieves nirvana), however, Buddhists minimized their fearsomeness.

Despite its sometimes lurid description of the six realms, the dharma basically stated that each individual is responsible for his or her own destiny. The future is neither accidental, fated, nor determined by the gods. If one has a strong will to achieve salvation, a day of final triumph will surely come. As a result, karma is less an enslavement than an encouragement. If one strives to do good deeds (to live by the dharma in wisdom-morality-meditation), one cannot fail to progress toward freedom. At the least, one will come to life again in more favorable circumstances. Thus, Buddhism ousts the gods and the fates from control over human destiny. This is interesting sociologically, because Buddhism has been most appealing to people who have wanted control over their own lives, such as warriors and merchants.

The simpler folk, who might have to spur themselves to such a sober and confident state of mind, drew encouragement from Buddhist art, which illustrates the delights of heaven and the torments of hell. Many renditions of the wheel of life, for instance, show Mara (Death) devouring the material world and those who cling to it. In the center of the wheel are such symbolic animals as the cock (desire), the snake (hatred), and the pig (delusion), who work to keep the wheel turning.[16] "Break with these," the art shouts. "Rise up. You have nothing to lose but your chains."

The dharma, therefore, began as a proclamation of diagnosis and cure. Likening himself to a doctor, the Buddha told his followers not to lose themselves in extraneous questions about where karma or ignorance comes from. Furthermore, he told them not to concentrate on whether the world is eternal or how to conceive of nirvana. To ponder such issues, said the Buddha, would be like a man severely wounded with an arrow who refuses treatment until he knows the caste and character of the man who shot him. The point is to get the arrow out. Similarly, the point to human existence is to break the wheel of rebirth, to slay the monstrous round of suffering, fleetingness, and emptiness.

For about forty-five years after his enlightenment, the Buddha preached variants on his basic themes: the Four Noble Truths, dependent coarising, and the three marks. His sangha grew, as monks, nuns, and laypersons responded to his simple, clear message. At his death he had laid the essential foundation of Buddhism—its basic doctrine and way of life. Thus, his death (*parinirvana*) came in the peace of trance. The physical cause of his death was either pork or mushrooms (depending on which commentator one reads), but in the Buddhist view the more profound cause was the Buddha's sense of completeness. When he asked his followers for the last time whether they had any questions, all stood silent. So he passed into trance and out of this painful realm. According to legend, the earth quaked and the sky thundered in final tribute.

Early Buddhism

After the Buddha's death his followers gathered to codify the dharma, which he had said should be their leader after him. According to tradition, they held a council at Rajagraha during the first monsoon season after the *parinirvana* to settle both the dharma and the Vinaya (the monastic rules). The canon of Buddhist scriptures that we now possess supposedly is the fruit of this council. However, textual analysis suggests that the dharma was transmitted orally for perhaps three centuries. Today the Pali canon (the authoritative collection of materials in the Indian vernacular that the Theravadins use) consists of five *nikayas*, which are collections of discourses (sutras), that the Buddha supposedly preached. Just one of these collections, the middle-length *Majjhima Nikaya*, runs to 1100 pages in modern printing.

In addition to these sutras and the monastic rules, early Buddhists added to the canon the *Abhidhamma* treatises of the early philosophers, who tried to analyze reality by correlating the Buddha's teaching with the experiences of meditation. Therefore, the Buddhist tendency in forming a canon (etymologically, a ruler) by which to measure faith and doctrine was to be as comprehensive as possible.

However, within 100 years of the Buddha's death, dissensions (primarily over doctrine) split the sangha.[17] These were the precursors of the major division of Buddhism into the Theravadan and Mahayana schools, which we shall consider below. The apparent forerunners of the Mahayana schools were the Mahasanghikas, who seem to have favored the laity's interests, while the Sthaviras (Elders), the precursors of the Theravadins, stressed the authority of the monks. About 200 years after the Buddha's death the Pudgalavadins branched off of the Sthaviras; they taught that there is a person or self (neither identical with the *skandhas* nor separate from them) that is the basis of knowledge, transmigration, and entrance into nirvana.

These first schisms prefigured later Buddhist history. New schools have constantly arisen as new insights or problems made old views unacceptable. As a result, the sangha has not been an effective centralized authority or a successful source of unity. Nonetheless, it has given all Buddhists certain essential teachings (almost all sects would agree to what we have expounded of dharma so far). Also, it has fostered a fairly uniform monastic life, for sects have tended to follow the Vinaya even when they held different doctrines. The monastic order, which has always been the heart of Buddhism (monks have tended to take precedence over laity as an almost unquestioned law of nature), has been a source of stability in Buddhism. We should therefore describe the lives of Buddhist monks and nuns.

Monasticism

A major influence on the Buddhist monastic routine has been Buddha's own life. According to Buddhaghosa, a Ceylonese commentator in the fifth century C.E., the Buddha used to rise at daybreak, wash, and then sit in meditation until it was time to go begging for food. He stayed close enough to a village (wandering from one to another) to obtain food, but far enough away to obtain quiet. Usually devout laity would invite him in, and after eating lightly he would teach them the dharma. Then he would return to his residence, wash, and rest. After this he would preach to the monks and respond to their requests for individual guidance. After another rest he would preach to the laity and then take a cool bath. His evening would consist of more individual conferences, after which, Buddhaghosa claims, he would receive any deities who came for instruction.[18]

The Vinaya established rules that would promote such a steady life of meditation, begging, preaching, and counsel. Originally the monks always wandered except during the rainy season, but later they assumed a more stable setting with quiet lands and a few simple buildings. From the Vinaya's list of capital offenses, though, we can see that a monk's robe did not necessarily make him a saint.

The four misdeeds that merited expulsion from the order were fornication, theft, killing, and "falsely claiming spiritual attainments." Committing any of thirteen lesser misdeeds led to a group meeting of the sangha and probation. They included sexual offenses (intentional ejaculation, touching a woman, speaking suggestively to a woman, urging a woman to gain merit by submitting to a "man of religion," and serving as a procurer), violating the rules that limited the size and specified the site of a monk's dwelling, falsely accusing other monks of grievous violations of the rule, fomenting discord among the monks, or espousing schismatic positions. With appropriate changes, similar rules governed the nuns' lives.

There were hundreds of other things that monks and nuns could not do, and all of them suggest something about the ideals of the sangha. Prohibitions from lying, slander, stealing another's sleeping space, and "sporting in the water" testify to an ideal of honest and direct speech, mutual consideration, and grave decorum. Similarly, prohibitions from digging in the ground and practicing agriculture reflect the ideals of not taking other creatures' lives and of begging one's food. Rules for good posture and table manners indicate that an ideal monk stood erect, kept his eyes downcast, refrained from loud laughter, and did not smack his lips, talk with his mouth full, or throw food into his mouth. The refined *bhiksu* (monk) also could not excrete while standing up or excrete onto growing grass or into the water. Finally, he was not supposed to preach the dharma to monks or laypersons carrying parasols, staffs, swords, or other weapons, or wearing slippers, sandals, turbans, or other head coverings.

The sangha accepted recruits from all social classes, and many of them were youths. From this circumstance and a familiarity with Indian toilet customs, one can understand the concern for the rights of the growing grass and the water. In addition, historians regularly note that the Vinaya is remarkably free from taboos (irrational proscriptions of contact with certain items labeled dangerous, such as menstrual blood, corpses, hair, or fingernails), although Buddhism developed its share of irrationalities. Monks often carried their two principal fears (of taking life or being sexually incontinent) to unjustifiable extremes. Especially regarding matters of sex, the monastic legislation was not always reasonable. (This is also true of Christian monastic legislation.)

The Laity

From earliest times, Buddhism encouraged its laity to pursue an arduous religious life. Though his or her white robe never merited the honor that a monk's colored robe received, a layperson who had taken refuge in the three jewels and contributed to the sangha's support was an honorable follower. Early Buddhism specified morality *(sila)* for the laity in five precepts. The first of these was to refrain from killing living beings. (Unintentional killing was not an offense, and agriculturalists only had to minimize their damage to life.) The second was to refrain from stealing. The third precept dealt with sexual matters. It forbade intercourse with another person's wife, a nun, or a woman betrothed to another man. It also urged restraint with a wife who was pregnant, nursing, or under a religious vow of sexual abstinence. Apparently relations with courtesans were licit, and the commentators' explanation of this precept assumes that it is the male's duty to provide control in sexual matters (because females are by nature wanton). The fourth precept imposed restraint from lying, and the fifth precept forbade drinking alcoholic beverages.

This ethical code was the layperson's chief focus. Occasionally he or she received instruction in meditation or the doctrine of wisdom, and later Mahayana sects considered the laity fully capable of reaching nirvana (in the beginning only monks were so considered). (Nuns never had the status of monks, in part because of legends that the Buddha established nunneries only reluctantly.) The principal lay virtues were to be generous in supporting monks and to witness to Buddhist values in the world. The financial support, obviously enough, was a two-edged sword. Monks who put on spiritual airs would annoy the laity who were sweating to support them. On the other hand, monks constantly faced a temptation to tailor their doctrine to please the laity and so boost their financial contributions. The best defenses against such abuses were monasteries in which the monks lived very simple, poor lives and worked hard at manual tasks.

Other practices that devout laity might take up included regular fasting, days of retreat for reading the scriptures, praying, hearing sermons, giving up luxurious furniture and housing, abstaining from singing, dancing, and theater, and decreasing their sexual activity. Clearly, such practices further advanced the pious layperson toward a monastic sort of regime and often smacked of puritanism.

Scholars suggest that early Buddhism did not develop many new ceremonies or rites of passage; instead it integrated local celebrations and customs into its practices. To this day, birth and wedding ceremonies do not involve Buddhist priests very much, but funeral services do. In early times, the Indian Buddhists likely celebrated the New Year and a day of offering to the ancestors, both of which were probably adopted from Hinduism. In addition, Indian Buddhists commemorated the Buddha's birthday and the day of his enlightenment. Robinson and Johnson suggest that cults of trees, tree spirits, serpents, fertility goddesses, and funeral mounds all came from preexisting Indian religious customs.[19] However, the Bodhi Tree under which the Buddha came to enlightenment prompted many Buddhists to revere trees. Such trees, along with *stupas* (burial mounds) of holy persons, were popular places of devotion.

The worship of statues of the Buddha grew popular only under the influence of Mahayana theology after 100 C.E., but an earlier veneration of certain symbols of the Buddha (an empty throne, a pair of footprints, a wheel or lotus, or a bodhi tree) paved the way. These symbols signified such things as Buddha's presence in the world, his royal renunciation, and the dharma he preached. The lotus became an especially popular symbol, since it stood for the growth of pure enlightenment from the mud of worldly life.

Meditation

A central aspect of early Buddhist life was meditation, which has remained a primary way to realize the wisdom and to inspire the practice that lead to nirvana. Meditation *(dhyana)* designated mental discipline. For instance, one could meditate by practicing certain devotional exercises that focused attention on one of the three jewels—the Buddha, the dharma, or the sangha. These would be recalled as the refuges under which one had taken shelter, and the meditator's sense of wonder and gratitude for protection would increase his or her emotional attachment. Thus, such meditative exercises were a sort of bhakti.

Indeed, both the saints *(bodhisattvas)* and the Buddha could become objects of loving concentration. However, such devotion was not meditation proper, for *dhyana* was a discipline of consciousness similar to yoga. As is clear from the story of his own life, Buddha's enlightenment came after he had experienced various methods of "mindfulness" and trance. It is proper, then, to consider Buddhist meditation a species of yoga.[20]

The mindfulness of Buddhists was usually a control of the senses and imagination geared to bringing "one-pointed mental consciousness" to bear on the truths of the dharma. For instance, one fixed on mental processes to become aware of their stream and the *skandhas* and to focus on the belief that all is fleeting, painful, and selfless. In addition, meditation masters encouraged monks to bolster their flight from the world by contemplating the contemptibleness of the body and its pleasures.

Buddhaghosa, for example, proposed lengthy exercises concerning the repulsiveness of food. To help monks eschew it, he suggested that they consider (1) that they have to go get food and thus leave their solitude; (2) that they have to search it out through muddy streets and often suffer abuse from villagers; (3) that chewing food crushes it to a state of repulsiveness, "like a dog's vomit in a dog's trough"; (4) that the four effluvia (bile, phlegm, blood, and pus) go to work on the ingested food; (5) that the food goes into the stomach, which "resembles a cesspool that has not been washed for a long time"; (6) that the food has to pass through this cesspool and its malodorous regions, which are traversed by the stomach's winds; (7) that digested food is not like gold or silver but gives off foam and bubbles, becoming excrement and filling the abdomen like yellow loam in a tube; (8) that digested food brings forth various "putridities," such as hair and nails, and that poorly digested food produces ringworm, itching, leprosy, eczema, and dysentery; (9) that excreted food is offensive and a cause of sadness; and (10) that eating and excreting soil the body.[21]

This master has similarly attractive proposals for meditations on corpses and even beautiful women. A beautiful woman, for instance, is really a bag of bones and foul odors. In a few years she will be a corpse, and like all dead corpses she will be full of worms and maggots. Only a fool would risk nirvana for illusory pleasure with her.

However, wisdom was more than just attacks on hindrances to freedom and nirvana. In careful meditations, Buddhist adepts tried to replicate the Enlightened One's experience during the night of vision, cultivating first his one-pointedness of mind and then his dispassionate heightening of awareness. Adepts also composed meditations focusing on doctrinal points such as the Four Noble Truths or the three marks in order to see their reality directly. This was similar to the insight practices or the way of knowledge (jnana-marga) that Hinduism offered, though of course Buddhist beliefs often differed from Hindu.

Mahayana

This last type of meditation clearly brought dhyana and wisdom (prajna) close together. In the development of Buddhist sects, which reached its most important

point in the years 100 B.C.E. to 100 C.E. with the rise of the Mahayana, the wisdom-meditation beliefs were more important than the disputes about morality. The Vinaya was similarly observed by all sects. Also, the laity in the different sects followed the same general precepts. However, the saintly ideal and the place of the laity differed among Theravadins and Mahayanists. Even more, the notion of the Buddha and the range of metaphysics varied considerably. The rise of Mahayana was the first major change in Buddhism.[22] Before its emergence, early Buddhism was fairly uniform in its understanding of Buddha-dharma-sangha and wisdom-morality-meditation. (Theravada has essentially kept early Buddhist beliefs, so the description of Buddhism thus far characterizes Theravada.)

Of course, Mahayana was not without forerunners. We have indicated the lay orientation of the Mahasanghikas, and also the split among the Sthaviras that occurred when the Pudgalavadins advocated the reality of the person. However, the hallmark of Mahayana was its literature, which placed in the mouth of the Buddha sutras describing a new ideal and a new version of wisdom. Mahayana means "great vehicle," symbolizing a large raft able to carry multitudes across the stream of samsara to nirvana. Hinayana is the term of reproach that Mahayanists used to characterize those who rejected their literature and views. It means "lesser vehicle," symbolizing a small raft able to carry only a few persons across the samsaric stream. Members of the non-Mahayana schools refer to themselves not as Hinayanists but as Theravadins, pointing with pride to the antiquity of their traditions and claiming to have preserved the original spirit of Buddhism better than the innovating Mahayanists. Today Theravada Buddhism dominates Sri Lanka, Thailand, Burma, the Khmer Republic (Cambodia), and Laos. Other Asian countries are dominated by Mahayana Buddhism.

Let us deal first with two innovative teachings of the Mahayana schools, emptiness and mind-only, and then consider the

Mahayana views of the Buddhist ideal and of the Buddha himself.

Emptiness

Emptiness *(sunyata)* is a hallmark of Mahayana teaching. In fact, the Mahayana sutras known as the *Prajna-paramita* ("wisdom-that-has-gone-beyond") center on this notion. By the end of the Mahayana development, emptiness had in effect become a fourth mark of all reality. Besides being painful, fleeting, and selfless, all reality was empty. Thus, further rumination on the three marks led Mahayana philosophers to consider a fourth mark, emptiness, as the most significant mark of all reality. No reality was a substance, having an "own-being." Obviously, therefore, none could be an atman, be constant, or be fully satisfying.

The Heart Sutra, a short specimen of the *Prajna-paramita*, exemplifies the dialectical reasoning with which Mahayana worked on emptiness. We can also perceive the paradoxical result of this reasoning: Nirvana and samsara are one. The sutra begins with an act of reverence (which reminds us that this is religious wisdom, not arid speculation): "Homage to the Perfection of Wisdom, the Lovely, the Holy."[23] "The Lovely" *(Bhagavati)* is feminine, indicating that Buddhism conceives of wisdom as a goddess or maternal figure, out of whom issues the light of knowledge.[24] Next the sutra speaks of the bodhisattva (saint) Avalokitesvara (who in East Asia became Kuan-yin) moving in the course of the wisdom that has gone beyond (that has reached the shore of nirvana) and looking down compassionately on our world. He beheld but five heaps (the *skandhas*), and he saw that they were in their own-being (their substance) empty *(sunya)*.

The word *sunya*, Conze tells us, conveys the idea that something that looks like much is really nothing. Etymologically it relates to the word *swelled*. As a swelled head is much ado about nothing, so things that are *sunya* appear to be full, solid, or substantial but actually are not. The spiritual implication of emptiness *(sunyata)* is that

the world around us should not put us in bondage, for it has nothing of substance with which to tie us. Philosophically the word implies *anatman* (no-self), that there is nothing independent of other existents. For the Mahayana, all dharmas (here meaning items of existence) are correlated, and any one dharma is a void.

Dialectics

Having recalled these staples of Mahayana tradition, the Heart Sutra then employs dialectics (the act of playing both sides of an issue) in analyzing the five *skandhas:* Form is emptiness, and this very emptiness is form. Feeling, perception, impulse, and consciousness are all emptiness, and emptiness is feeling, perception, impulse, and consciousness. This identification, the sutra emphasizes, can be seen by anyone "here"—from the viewpoint of the wisdom that has gone beyond. Therefore, reminiscent of Shankara's two levels of knowing Brahman, the *Prajna-paramita* says that there are two ways of looking at ordinary reality. From the lower point of view, feeling, perception, impulse, consciousness, and form are all "something." From the higher viewpoint of enlightenment or perfect wisdom, however, these terms all designate something that is empty, that has no solid core or own-being.

To deal with any dharma as though it were full, therefore, would be to deal with it at least erroneously and possibly desirously—thus, karmically. If, however, we see that *nothing* is pleasant, stable, or full, then we will deal with all things in detachment, moving through them toward nirvana. So, according to the sutra, a bodhisattva sees things without "thought coverings," does not tremble at the emptiness that this attitude reveals, and thereby attains nirvana. That is what all Buddhas (Gautama is not the only one) have done, and it shows that the *Prajna-paramita* is a great spell of knowledge (the sutra concludes with a mantra, a chanting of a wisdom spell: "Gone, gone, gone beyond, gone altogether beyond,

O what an awakening, all-hail—this completes the Heart of perfect wisdom").[25]

In some of its literature, then, the Indian Mahayana equated the perception of emptiness with the wisdom that makes a bodhisattva. To realize fully how all things are empty was to dispel the spontaneous but illusory view of things that ties one to samsara and rebirth. If things are really empty, then there is nothing to cling to. Then things can move in the coordinated "dance," the flow, that nature invites us to join. Emptiness does not mean that realities have no value, that they do not impinge on our senses, or that we cannot reason over them in the laboratory or excise them with a surgeon's scalpel. For Mahayanists, emptiness means that we should use all realities freely without clinging, letting them go their dancing way. Because nirvana so impressed them, the Mahayana philosophers saw that nothing that is not nirvana is real, is independently existent. In this sense that which is not nirvana is empty, and they would wean us from our naive impression that it is full.

Such weaning, however, is only the first phase of a two-phase task, according to philosophers such as Nagarjuna (around 200 C.E.). The first move in the dialectics of wisdom, described above, is to realize that things are not what they appear to be, and so to distinguish between lower knowledge and higher, between apparent reality (samsara) and full reality (nirvana). However, we must further understand the concepts of emptiness and nirvana themselves. Emptiness is not another kind of thing or quality, and it is thus not full. Nirvana is neither a void nor a plenum (fullness) like Brahman. Rather, it is the ultimate reality present in the relative realities of the samsaric world. Nirvana and samsara thus are one, because neither is a something opposed to other things. Both are qualities (the absolute quality that everything has insofar as it has being, and the relative quality that everything of our direct experience has insofar as its being is always painful, fleeting, selfless, and empty).

All this is very hard to grasp, and Nagarjuna spent much energy reducing all reifying (treating as a thing) language to absurdity.[26] Perhaps we can best understand what the Mahayana philosophers of emptiness were saying through a Zen notion. Before enlightenment, mountains are mountains, rivers are rivers, and trees are trees. When enlightenment starts to dawn, the world turns over, and mountains, rivers, and trees are no longer what they seemed to be. After enlightenment, though, when we are stable in wisdom, mountains are again mountains, rivers are again rivers, and trees are again trees.

In other words, before one starts out for enlightenment (starts out to imitate the Buddha), one has commonsensical perceptions of things: Mountains are mountains. Then, after one has studied things, meditated somewhat, and purified one's moral habits, things look quite different. One cannot take the mountain for granted. There is a wonder, a mystery in its being. Even though it seems permanent, analysis shows that the mountain is fleeting (for example, it wears away), painful, and without self. It is empty; it is not nirvana. With full illumination, however, the world again turns right side up. The mountain is just a mountain. One is not back at the beginning, however, for the enlightened view of the mountain is different from the commonsensical view. For the enlightened person the mountain is just there, playing its part in the fleeting dance of dharmas, which are all empty in themselves but which combine to give us this world of appearances. In other words, the mountain is nirvana in the midst of samsara, being in the midst of becoming. That is its grandeur and its poverty.

Mind-only

Emptiness was the special concern of the Madhyamika Mahayana school.[27] The second major Mahayana school, the Yogacara, which became influential from about 300 C.E. on, proposed another influential teaching on ultimate reality, mind-only.[28] Like the teaching on emptiness, it went beyond early Buddhist teaching, and the Theravadins rejected the sutras that attributed this teaching to the Buddha. The teaching of mind-only held that all realities are finally products of the cosmic mind. There were antecedents to this viewpoint in the morality literature that Mahayana shared with the Theravadins, such as the *Dhammapada*, and the proponents of emptiness implied it in their belief that all phenomena are illusory (maya), because we do not grasp them in their ultimately empty reality. The *Dhammapada*'s interest, however, was practical, not speculative: "What we are today comes from our thoughts of yesterday, and our present thoughts build our life of tomorrow: our life is the creation of our mind."[29] The Yogacarins wanted a fuller explanation of mental reality, probably because their intuitions grew out of meditational or yogic practices (whence their name).

One of the principal Yogacarin sutras, the *Lankavatara*,[30] described a tier of consciousnesses in the individual culminating in a "storehouse" consciousness *(alayavijnana)* that is the base of the individual's deepest awareness, the individual's tie to the cosmic. The storehouse consciousness is itself unconscious and inactive, but it is the repository of the "seeds" that ripen into human deeds and awareness. Further, Yogacarins sometimes called the storehouse consciousness the Buddha's womb. Thereby, they made the Buddha or Tathagata (Enlightened Being) a metaphysical principle—a foundation of all reality.

From the womb of the Buddha issued the purified thoughts and beings of enlightenment. The symbolism is often garbled (and interestingly feminine, suggesting a Buddhist version of androgyny or primal wholeness). Its main point, though, is clear: The womb of the Buddha *(Tathagata-garbha)* is present in all living beings, irradiating them with enlightenment. Like the feminine *Prajna-paramita*, then, the ultimate reality of the Yogacarins "mothers" the many individual things (that are themselves empty). It is the great mental storehouse from which they issue, the matrix that holds them all in being. It stimulates their dancing flux.

This view has interesting parallels with the Chinese philosophy of the *Tao* that mothers the ten thousand things. For the Yogacarins, though, the dharmas that dance and the *Tathagata-garbha* from which they issue are all mental. There is only mind— material reality is an illusion. When one reaches wisdom and leaves lower knowledge behind, material reality will become almost uninteresting.

Mahayana Devotion

Both major Mahayana schools developed sophisticated philosophies to correlate the many beings of experience with the simple finality of nirvana. It was not philosophy that brought Mahayana popular influence, though, but its openness to the laity's spiritual needs, its devotional theology. Early Buddhism held monks in greater regard, considering them the only true followers of Buddha. They were the teachers, the determiners of doctrine, and the guardians of morality. They were the stewards of tradition who made the sangha a jewel alongside the Buddha and the dharma. Consequently, the laity considered themselves to be working out a better karma, so that in their next lives they might be monks (or, if they were women, so that they might be men). The central lay virtue, as we have seen, was giving financial support to the monasteries, and the sangha seldom admitted laity to the higher occupations of philosophy or meditation.

Mahayana changed this view of the laity. Stressing the Buddha's compassion and his resourcefulness in saving all living creatures, it gradually qualified the Theravadin ideal of the arhat (saint) and fashioned a new, more socially oriented ideal. Mahayana thereby prepared the way for later schools that were in effect Buddhist bhakti sects, such as the Pure Land sect. Such sects believed that through graceful compassion, a Buddha or bodhisattva only required that one devoutly repeat his name and place full trust in him for salvation. In this "degenerate age," the difficult paths of wisdom and meditation were open only to the few. Therefore, the Enlightened One had opened a broader path of devotion, so that laity as well as monks might reach paradise and then nirvana.

Mahayana did not attack monastic dignity. Rather, it just stressed the social side of the ideal. The Mahayanists saw the Hinayana arhat as too individualistic. To pursue one's own enlightenment and salvation, apart from those of all living creatures, seemed selfish. So the Mahayanists began to talk of a bodhisattva, who postpones entrance into nirvana in order to labor for the salvation of all living things. Out of great compassion *(mahakaruna)*, he would remain in the samsaric world for eons if need be, content to put off final bliss so as to help save everything that exists in the cycle of life: humans, birds, plants, and trees.

In Mahayana Buddhism, then, one would finally take a bodhisattva vow, making one's goal not just gaining nirvana for oneself but for all one's fellow creatures. Mahayanists stressed six great "perfections" *(paramitas)* in becoming a bodhisattva, which effectively summarize Mahayana religious living. First was the perfection of giving: giving material things to those in need, but also giving spiritual instructions, one's own body and life, or even one's own karmic merit. In a life of compassionate generosity, everything could be given over to others. Mahayanists understood the perfections of morality, patience, vigor, meditation, and wisdom in a similarly broad fashion. Thus, they applied the traditional triad of wisdom-morality-meditation in more social ways. Giving, patience, and vigor meant that one became selfless in more than a metaphysical way. For the love of others, for the grand vision of a totally perfected world, the saint would cheerfully donate his goods and talents, suffer abuses, and labor ceaselessly.

Finally, Mahayanists moved away from the early Buddhist view that Sakyamuni was just a man who gained enlightenment. Instead, they began to contemplate his preexistence and the status he had gained as a knowledge being. In this contemplation, his earthly life receded in importance, so much that some Mahayanists began to say that he had only apparently assumed a human body. Then, linking this stress on the Buddha's metaphysical essence with the Indian doctrine of endless kalpas of cosmic time and endless stretches of cosmic space, Mahayanists spoke of many Buddhas who had existed before Sakyamuni and of many Buddhas who presided in other cosmic realms.

In this way the notion of Buddhahood greatly expanded. First it was the quality shared by many cosmic beings of wisdom and realization. Later, in East Asian Mahayana, Buddhahood became the metaphysical notion that *all* beings are in essence enlightenment beings. Enlightenment, therefore, is just realizing one's Buddha-nature. It is the beginning of nirvana, the break with samsara, and the achievement of perfect wisdom all in one.

Buddhahood thus became complex and many-sided. The Buddha came to have three bodies: an apparition body, in which he appeared to perceivers; a dharma body, in which he was the principle of reality or the cosmic presence of nirvana; and a glorification body, in which he manifested his bliss to the heavenly beings. Moreover, the distinction between Buddhas and great bodhisattvas blurred and largely dissolved in the popular mind, giving Buddhist "divinity" a full spectrum of holy beings. Citing the Mahayana understanding of divinity, therefore, is the surest way to refute claims that Buddhism is not a religion. Whatever merit the position that Buddhism is not a religion has rests in the strictly human experiences that *may* have been the core of the historical Buddha's enlightenment. By the fifth or sixth century after the Buddha's death, the hills were alive with chants to a variety of divine figures.

Tantrism

We have seen the Hindu mixture of occult and erotic practices called Tantrism or Shaktism. Indian Buddhism helped create this trend and incorporated many of its notions. Buddhist Tantrism in India seems to have originated around the sixth century C.E., flourishing first in the northwest. From the eighth century on it prospered around Bengal, combining with *Prajna-paramita* philosophy and native magical practices. It later reached Sri Lanka, Burma, and Indonesia.[31] Often it merged with Shaivism, but in Tibet it combined with native Bon (shamanist) practices and became the dominant Buddhist faith.[32]

Tantrism had antecedents in both Buddha's teaching and in the surrounding Hindu Brahmanism. Buddha appears to have allowed magical spells, and the canon contains reputed cures for snakebite and other dangers. *Prajna-paramita* sutras such as the Heart often ended with spells, transferring certain key ideas and words from strictly intellectual notions to mantras. In Brahmanic sacrifices, as we noted, the prayers were understood so literally that they became mantras; if a priest recited a prayer properly, it was sure to accomplish its end.

Buddhist Tantrists took over such sacred sounds as "om," as well as esoteric yogic systems, such as *kundalini*, which associated sacred syllables with force centers *(chakras)* in the body. They also used mandalas (magic figures, such as circles and squares) and even *stupas* (shrines). The Buddhist Tantrists were thus hardly bizarre or innovative, mainly developing ancient Hindu esoteric practices in a new setting.

What novelty the Tantrists did introduce into Buddhism came from their creative use of rites that acted out mandalas and esoteric doctrines about bodily forces. Perhaps under the influence of Yogacara meditation, which induced states of trance, the Tantrists developed rituals in which participants identified with particular deities. If it is true that many meditation schools, such as the Yogacara, employed mandalas for the early stages of trance in order to focus consciousness, then the Tantrists probably built on well-established practices. In their theoretical elaboration, however, they retrieved

certain cosmological notions that we saw in our study of the ancient religious mind.

For instance, they came to see the *stupas* as replicas of the cosmos. The railings that separated the *stupa* precinct from secular ground divided the sacred from the profane. The edge of the moving mandala that the Tantrist troupe would dance or act out had a function similar to that of the railings. Often Tantrism strove to symbolize the entire cosmic plan. Indeed, the Tantrists tried to draw heavenly worlds (bodhisattva realms) and gods into their meditations and rituals.

A principal metaphysical support of Tantrism was the Madhyamika doctrine of emptiness, which the Tantrists interpreted to mean that all beings are intrinsically pure. Consequently, they used odd elements in their rituals, especially erotic ones, in order to drive home the truths of emptiness, purity, and freedom. For the most part, these ways did not become public, since the Tantrists went to considerable pains to keep their rites and teachings secret. In fact, they developed a cryptic language that they called "twilight speech," in which sexual references were abundant.[33] For instance, they called the male and female organs "thunderbolt" and "lotus," respectively. As with Hindu Tantrism, it is not always possible to tell whether such speech is symbolic or literal. Some defenders of Tantrism claim that it tamed sexual energy in the Indian tradition by subjecting it to symbolization, meditative discipline, and moral restraints. Other critics, however, view Buddhist Tantrism as a corruption of a tradition originally quite intolerant of libidinal practices. For them the Tantrist explanation that, since everything is mind-only, the practice of erotic rites means little is simply a rationalization.

In a typical Tantrist meditation, the meditator would begin with traditional preliminaries such as seeking refuge in the three jewels, cleansing himself of sins (by confession or bathing), praying to past masters, or drawing a mandala to define the sacred space of the extraordinary reality that his rite was going to involve. Then the meditator would take on the identity of a deity and disperse all appearances of the world into emptiness. Next, using his imagination, the meditator would picture himself as the god whose identity he was projecting.

So pictured, he and his consort would sit on the central throne of the mandala space and engage in sexual union. Then he would imagine various Buddhas parading into the sacred space of the mandala and assimilate them into his body and senses. In that assimilation, his speech would become divine, he could receive offerings as a god, and he could perform any of the deity's functions. So charged with divinity, he would then return to the ordinary world, bringing back to it the great power of a Buddha's divine understanding.[34]

Dialectics

Tantrism adopted the Mahayana notion that nirvana and samsara are one and interpreted it to mean that the things of the world of appearances are not ultimate. Thus, classifying them as good or bad or in any other way can prevent one from appreciating their truly empty character. Sutras favored by the Tantrists portrayed the Buddha as having told only "conceited" people that fleeing lewdness, anger, and folly produces liberation. He did not necessarily forbid these things to bodhisattvas. A bodhisattva, then, may appear to be breaking precepts and sinning, but since he is pure of heart, these outward appearances are misleading.

For instance, he may seem to have five wives and concubines yet actually keep his passions free of lust. Like the lotus flowering from the mire, he is purity rising above anything degraded or stained. Working off this model, Tantrists spoke of fighting fire with fire, destroying vice by practicing it with discipline, and rendering poison harmless by small, steady ingestions of it. Using profiles of different character types, the Tantrist masters would also prescribe exercises for different character types, such as the irascible, the timid, or the lusty.

Much in this dialectical development probably was a mixture of self-deception and fascination with the power of imagination and sexual energy. Commenting on the traditional Tibetan texts about the saint Naropa, Herbert Guenther has sketched Tibetan dialectical thought about reality.[35] It moves through the field of the emotions and passions, much as Nagarjuna's dialectic moves through the field of thoughts and judgments, leaving little ordinary understanding upright. For if one seriously considers emptiness and the equation of nirvana and samsara, then everything does indeed overturn for a while. As a result, it is not surprising that the ancient equating of the real with the vividly experienced returns to power. Because imaginative trance can be quite vivid (as can dreams and hallucinations), the space of its mandalas may seem quite real. Then, one can indeed become the god that one's meditation has invoked.

Similarly, the forces of such a god's interactions with a divine spouse, or with alcohol, or with such tabooed objects as skulls can convince the Tantrist that through his rites he is truly tapping divine powers. Mesmerizing themselves in these ways, the Tantrists attributed great religious significance to inner light flashes, heat flashes, and orgasm. They tended to see such events as physical and psychological movements of mystic forces through special bodily columns and centers. All these experiences served enlightenment. If you saw vibrantly colorful images, felt pulsations and rushes, you were approaching success. Of course, meditation masters warned of illusion, but in the jungle of Tantrism, reality and illusion are difficult to differentiate.

The relation of the master (guru) and the disciple was central in Tantrism, because the master represented the tradition. (Zen has maintained this stress on the master but not the Tantrist eroticism.) The Tantrist gurus forced their pupils to engage in quite bizarre and painful practices to teach them to examine the mirror of their minds, to learn the illusory character of all phenomena, and to stop the cravings and jealousies that clouded their mirror.[36] Often pronouncing the death of old judgments and the birth of new ones of enlightenment, the guru confused the pupil, punished him, and pushed him to break with convention and ordinary vision. When Buddhism had become vegetarian, Tantrist masters urged eating flesh. When Buddhism advocated teetotalism, they urged intoxicating spirits. In such ways, Tantrist wisdom became paradoxical and eccentric.[37] To illustrate the fundamental truths of mind-only and emptiness, the Tantrists would take up each of society's most strongly held prohibitions and violate them. Incest, drinking blood from emptied skulls—every taboo could become a gateway to wisdom. In fact, the stronger the taboo, the more psychic energy it offered.

Tibet

Tantrism was welcomed in Tibet and came to dominate in the region between India and China. Our first historical records date from only the seventh century C.E., when Chinese historians started mentioning it. Under King Srongsten Gampo in 632, Tibet borrowed both writing and Buddhism from Kashmir. Toward the end of the eighth century, two notable Indian figures came to Tibet, Santaraskita and Padmasambhava, who founded a lasting Tibetan sangha. Tradition credits Padmasambhava with inaugurating the influential Nying-ma-pas Tantrist sect, while Santaraskita apparently was responsible for the triumph of Indian traditions over challenges from Chinese schools (especially Ch'an). Since that triumph, Tibet has owed more to Indian scholarship and philosophy than to Chinese.

Stephan Beyer emphasizes that Indian academic structures greatly influenced Tibetan Buddhism.[38] During the Indian Gupta dynasty (320–540 C.E.), great monastic universities became the pillars of Buddhism. The "curricular Buddhism" of these schools encompassed all the arts and sciences. Further, meditation integrated with scholasticism, which assured that the academic efforts to correlate Buddhist beliefs with existing knowledge never divorced themselves from practical religion. The Tibetan adoption of an Indian rather than a Chinese religious style correlated with this union of study and meditation, for the Indian schools favored a gradual penetration of enlightenment, in which study could play an important role.

One characteristic of Tibetan Buddhism has therefore been its line of scholars based in monastic universities. They have produced voluminous translations and commentaries for the canonical scriptures, as well as a tradition that learning should inform ritualist life. Learning and ritual, in fact, became the primary foci of the Tibetan monastic life. The king and the common people looked to the monastery for magical protection through ritual against evil powers, while individual monks utilized both meditation and ritual in their pursuit of enlightenment.

The typical day of a traditional Tibetan monk began with a private ritual contemplation (Tantrist) before dawn for an hour and a half. During the morning, the monk regularly participated in the community's prayers for two hours and then worked in the monastic library. He devoted the afternoon to more work and public ceremony and again meditated in the evening.

Many monks spent a lifetime in this regime, coming to the monastery at the age of nine or ten and receiving a thorough training in the scriptures, meditation techniques, and ceremonial details. As suggested above, the king supported this life-style, because ritual could prop his authority. (Pre-Buddhist Tibetan culture thought of the king in ancient sacred terms, as the tie between heaven and earth. Something of this ancient view continued when monks prayed and conducted rituals for the king's good health.) The common people, whose shamanist heritage emphasized many malevolent spirits of sickness and death, saw in the ritual spells and ceremonies a powerful defense. As a result, the monasteries were quite practical institutions for them, too.

By emphasizing ritual in both public ceremonies and private meditations, Tibetan Buddhism created its own version of the Tantrist belief that the imagination, senses, and psychological and bodily powers are all potential sources of energy for enlightenment and wisdom. When we discussed Indian Tantrism, we considered how the adept tried to identify with divine forces and gain control over a *cosmion*—a "little world" that represented universal space and time. The Tibetan Tantrist cult acted out many such identifications, so that the common people could indwell something comfortingly universal. The worship of the goddess Tara, for instance, which monasteries and popular festivals promoted, gave the world a motherly and protecting aspect. Monks and laity both prayed personally to Tara for help, while many of Tibet's musical and dancing arts developed through festivals devoted to her.

The success that Buddhism enjoyed in Tibet may also be linked to its ability to capitalize on native shamanist themes and political institutions. The ancient Tibetan Bon ("he who invokes the gods") was a shaman very like the Siberian shaman. Beating his drum, whirling in dance, weaving his spells, he fought against the demons of sickness and death.[39] In addition to developing its own Tantrist rituals to cover these interests of the older religion, Tibetan Buddhism also produced a type of wandering, "crazy" saint who evinced much of the awe and respect that the older shamans had.

The prototype of this ascetic, visionary holy man in Tibet was the much beloved Milarepa (1040–1123).[40] After a harsh initiation by family suffering and a cruel guru, he took to the mountain slopes and gained a reputation for working wonders. In his songs he poetically expressed profound insights into both the nature of dharma reality and the psychology of the ascetic life. Other famous Tibetan saints, such as Tilopa and Naropa, were similarly poetic. They show that for personal religious life, Tantrism could cast all conventional values and

assumptions in doubt so that it could relentlessly pursue enlightenment.

Buddhism capitalized on the demise of the kingship in Tibet in the ninth century to establish a theocratic regime with the monastery at its heart. Despite early persecutions during a period of kings' intrigues and assassinations, by the eleventh century the monasteries were strong. Until the recent Communist takeover, in fact, the monasteries and the Dalai Lamas (religious leaders) dominated Tibetan politics (often with much intrigue and sectarian strife).[41] The Mongol emperor Kublai Khan granted the abbot 'Phags-pa (1235–1280) temporal power over all Tibet, firmly establishing a theocratic rule. By the fourteenth century, however, Tibet was a cauldron of various Buddhist sects vying for power. The Nyingma-pas sect that Padmasambhava founded claimed a certain primacy because of its antiquity, and it also kept close ties with the ancient shamanist loyalties.

Of the sects that developed after the demise of the Chinese T'ang dynasty in the ninth century, the most important was the Ge-lug, which shrewdly employed the idea of reincarnation. Consequently, the Mongols both recognized the Dalai Lama as a spiritual leader and considered him a grandson of the Mongol chief. From the sixteenth century onwards, the Ge-lug wielded great political clout. The Dalai Lamas, for the most part, have been men of considerable spiritual and political acumen, and their rule has meant a vigorous sangha. Presently, the fourteenth Dalai Lama (b. 1935) is in exile from the Chinese Communists, but he is still the spiritual leader of tens of thousands of Tibetan refugees.

Tibetan Buddhism thus stands out for its Tantrist bent and its especially knotted political history. Few cultures have so absorbed one version of Buddhism as Tibet has absorbed the "thunderbolt vehicle" (Tantrism). Perhaps the most famous Tibetan religious text to reach the West is the *Tibetan Book of the Dead*,[42] which purportedly describes the experiences of the deceased during the forty-nine days between physical death and entry into a new karmic state. By employing vivid imagery and specifying rituals designed to help the deceased to achieve nirvana, the *Book of the Dead* exemplifies the Tantrist mentality well. It is a journey through the imagination and unconscious that severely challenges most notions of reality, since it maintains that the period right after death is the most opportune time for liberation.

The Demise of Indian Buddhism

Buddhism declined in India after the seventh century, only in part because of Tantrist emphases. Invaders such as the White Huns and the Muslims wrecked many Buddhist strongholds, while the revival of Hinduism, especially of Hindu bhakti sects of Vishnu and Shiva, undermined Buddhism. Mahayana fought theistic Hinduism quite fiercely, not at all seeing it as equivalent to the Buddhist theology of bodhisattvas and Buddhas, but Hinduism ultimately prevailed due to its great ability to incorporate other movements. Indeed, Buddha became one of the Vaishnavite avatars.

By the seventh century the sangha had grown wealthy and held much land—facts that contributed to a decline in religious fervor and to antipathy among the laity. From the time of its first patronage under Asoka (around 260 B.C.E.), Buddhism enjoyed occasional support from princes and kings, and its ability to preach the dharma, to enjoy favor at court, and to influence culture depended on this support. The Kusana dynasty (ca. 78–320 C.E.), for instance, was a good time for Buddhists, while the Gupta age (320–540 C.E.) revived Hinduism. When the Muslims finally established control in India, Buddhism suffered accordingly. Early missionary activity had exported it, however, and Buddhism proved to be hardier on foreign soil than on Indian. So Hinduism, which has largely been confined to India, became the native tradition that opposed the

Muslims, while Buddhism became an internationalized brand of Indian culture.[43]

China

Buddhism may have entered China as early as the beginning of the first century B.C.E. and almost certainly established itself by the middle of the second century C.E.[44] Buddhist missionaries traveled along the trade routes that linked northeastern India and China, probably entering at Tun-huang in the west. By 148 C.E., monks such as An Shih-kao had settled at Lo-yang, considerably to the east, and begun translating Buddhist texts. The first interests of these translators and their audiences appear to have been meditation and philosophy, which suggests that the Chinese first considered Buddhism similar to Taoism. However, as the translating progressed through the Han dynasty (ended 220 C.E.), sutras on morality and the Western Paradise of the Buddha became popular, too.

From this beginning, Buddhism slowly adapted to Chinese ways. Most of the preachers and translators who worked from the third to the fifth centuries C.E. favored Taoist terminology. This was especially true in the south, where the intelligentsia created a market for philosophy. In the less cultured north, Buddhism made progress by being presented as a powerful magic.[45] By the middle of the fifth century, China had its own sectarian schools, comparable to those that had developed in India. Thus, by that time most of the major Buddhist philosophies and devotional practices had assumed a Chinese style, including the *Abhidhamma*, which was a system that employed erudite philosophy and psychology in interpreting the scriptures, and the Indian Madhyamika and Yogacara schools. In general, Mahayana attracted the Chinese more than Theravada, and so the native schools that prospered developed Mahayana positions.

The Chinese brought to Buddhism an interest in bridging the gap between the present age and the age of the Buddha by constructing a line of masters along which the dharma passed intact. The master was more historical than timeless scriptural texts were, and the authority-minded Chinese were more concerned about history than the Indians had been.

Indeed, conflicts over the sutras were a sore problem for the Chinese, and in trying to reconcile seemingly contradictory positions, they frequently considered one scripture as being authoritative. A principal basis for the differences among the burgeoning Chinese Buddhist sects, therefore, lay in which scripture the sect's founder had chosen as most authoritative. (The notion of sects is distinctly Chinese, since it is based on the old concept of the clan. Chinese culture venerated its ancestors, and each Chinese Buddhist school accordingly had its dharma founder or patriarchal teacher.)

The most popular sects were the Ch'an and Ching-t'u, which devoted themselves to meditation and the Pure Land (a Buddhist heaven), respectively. As we mentioned earlier, the Chinese took to meditation from the beginning of their encounter with Buddhism. There are evidences of yogic practices in the Taoist works attributed to Lao-tzu and Chuang-tzu, and certainly Taoist imagery of what the sage who knows the "inside" can accomplish had made many Chinese eager to tap interior powers. Ch'an

capitalized on this interest, working out a simple regime and theory that focused on meditation.[46] (Ch'an is the translation of the Indian *dhyana*; the Japanese translation is Zen.) Its principal text was the *Lankavatara Sutra*, which the Yogacarins also much revered, because that text stressed the mentality of all reality.

According to legend, Bodhidharma, an Indian meditation master devoted to the *Lankavatara*, founded Ch'an in the fifth century C.E. Paintings portray Bodhidharma as a fierce champion of single-mindedness, and he valued neither pious works nor recitations of the sutras. Only insight into one's own nature, which was identical with the dharma-nature of all reality, was of significance; only enlightenment justified the Buddhist life. Tradition credits Bodhidharma with developing the technique of "wall gazing," which was a kind of peaceful meditation—what the Japanese later called "just sitting" *(shikan-taza)*.

Probably the most eminent of the Ch'an patriarchs who succeeded Bodhidharma was the sixth patriarch, Hui-neng. According to the *Platform Sutra*, which purports to present his teachings, Hui-neng gained his predecessor's mantle of authority by surpassing his rival, Shen-hsiu, in a demonstration of dharma insight. To express his understanding, Shen-hsiu wrote:

The body is the Bodhi Tree
The mind is like a bright mirror and stand.
At all times wipe it diligently,
Don't let there be any dust.

Hui-neng responded:

Bodhi really has no tree;
The bright mirror also has no stand.
Buddha-nature is forever pure;
Where is there room for dust?[47]

This juxtaposition of the masters' verses reflects the beliefs of the southern Ch'an school, which looked to Hui-neng as the authoritative spokesman for its position that enlightenment comes suddenly. Because all Buddha-nature is intrinsically pure, one need only let it manifest itself. The northern school held that enlightenment comes gradually and thus counseled regular meditation. (Hui-neng himself probably would have fought any sharp distinction between meditation and the rest of life. In wisdom all things are one and pure.) The southern school finally took precedence.[48]

Pure Land Buddhism (Ching-t'u) derived from T'an-luan (476–542). He sought religious solace from a grave illness, and after trying several systems, he came to the doctrine of Amitabha Buddha and the Pure Land. Amitabha is the Buddha of Light, devotion to whom supposedly assures one a place in the Western Paradise. T'an-luan stressed faith in Amitabha and the recitation of Amitabha's name as ways to achieve such salvation. This, he and his successors reasoned, was a doctrine both possible and appropriate in the difficult present age. The Pure Land sect greatly appealed to the laity, and it developed hymns and graphic representations of paradise to focus its imagination. In stressing love or emotional attachment to Amitabha (called Amida in China), it amounted to a Chinese Buddhist bhakti. By chanting "na-mo a-mi-t'o-fo" ("greetings to Amida Buddha"), millions of Chinese found a simple way to fulfill their religious needs and made Amida the most popular god of Chinese history.[49]

These schools dominated Buddhism's rise in China, and during the peak of their influence (900–1300), they shaped the best minds, the art, and much of the imperial policy. Despite periods of persecution, Buddhism held spiritual sway until the fourteenth century. After that time each generation had its eminent monks, but neo-Confucian thought was the prevailing doctrine. Today, under the Communists, the Buddhist physical holdings seem quite devastated. Officially all religion is opposed, but some accommodation may permit Chinese Buddhism to survive.[50]

Japan

Buddhism infiltrated Japan by way of Korea during the second half of the sixth century c.e. It first appealed to members of the royal court as a possible source of blessing and good fortune. Also, it carried overtones of Chinese culture, which had great prestige. The Japanese rulers, in the midst of trying to solidify their country, thought of the new religion as a possible means, along with Confucian ethics, for unifying social life. So, during the seventh century, emperors built shrines and monasteries as part of the state apparatus. In the eighth century, when the capital was at Nara, the Hua-yen (called Kegon in Japan) school established itself and began to exert great influence. The government ideologues expediently equated the emperor with the Hua-yen Buddha Vairocana, and they made the Hua-yen realm of "dharmas not impeding one another"[51] a model for Japanese society. Kegon has survived in Japan to the present day, and it now has about 500 clergy and 125 temples.

At Nara, Buddhism had considerable influence on the arts and crafts, but when the imperial seat moved to Kyoto, it had even more. In the early ninth century, under the monk Saicho, Mount Hiei became an immensely successful center of T'ien-t'ai (Japanese "Tendai"). In its heyday this center had over 3,000 buildings and 30,000 monks.[52] Also in the ninth century the religious genius Kobo Daishi established a school (Shingon) that eventually overtook Tendai in popularity. It was a form of Tantrism that focused on Vairocana as the cosmic Buddha, and it won great favor because of its colorful rituals and Kobo Daishi's political flair.[53] Buddhism of the Heian period (794–1185) finally grew rather corrupt, however, because of the collusion between the monks and the ruling families. When power passed to the military and the court moved to Kamakura, the time was ripe for more popular and native forms of Japanese Buddhism.

Primary among them were the sects of Pure Land Buddhism. As in China, these were devotional schools dedicated to Amitabha. Other sects, such as Tendai, tried in their syntheses to provide for the laity's needs by sanctioning such practices as the chanting of Amitabha's name. However, the Pure Land sects made this practice central. Two great champions of Pure Land were Honen (1133–1212) and Shinran (1173–1262). Honen had considerable success in gaining imperial support for his movement because of his manifest humility and faith. His pupil Shinran felt that the goddess Kwannon (the Indian Avalokitesvara and Chinese Kuan-yin) inspired him to marry, and he received Honen's approval. By this move Shinran made his branch of Pure Land both closer to the laity and a champion of family life. He pushed the chanting of Amitabha's name, the necessity of faith for salvation, and the presence of the gracious Buddha-nature in all living beings.

Still another branch of popular Japanese Buddhism was founded by Nichiren (1222–1282). After considerable time in the Tendai monastery on Mount Hiei, Nichiren became convinced of the need for a purer religion. Tendai at that time had become so diffuse in its efforts to embrace all movements that Nichiren found it hopelessly unclear. So he settled on simply preaching the Lotus Sutra; however, he innovated by chanting a salutation to the sutra that was similar to Pure Land's salutation to Amitabha. By this chanting, one could attain moral virtue, Buddhahood, and paradise. Nichiren was a rather rabid religionist, convinced that other sects were grievously misleading, so he condemned Shingon and Pure Land for neglecting the historical Buddha Sakyamuni in favor of Vairocana. As well, he castigated *Zen* (the Japanese Ch'an sect stressing meditation) for neglecting the eternal Buddha of the Lotus Sutra. For this harshness he narrowly escaped a prophet's reward (martyrdom).

Zen

The Chinese Ch'an sect was present in Japan from the seventh century, but it only gained popularity during the Kamakura period (1185–1333). While the court was in Kamakura, eclecticism fell out of favor and pure single-mindedness was in style. Eisai (1141–1215) was an early Zen master. He began his religious career as a Tendai monk but, dissatisfied, went to China for training in the Lin-chi (Japanese "Rinzai") school of Ch'an. Returning to Japan, he convinced the now influential military class to accept Zen, and he adroitly avoided destructive conflicts with Tendai and Shingon. The link between Zen and the military class has been a hallmark of this school (especially of the Rinzai branch). As a result, Zen has furnished the martial arts and swordsmanship with most of their spiritual rationale. In addition, the Rinzai monk pursues a spartan regime of simplicity and self-discipline, which makes him the most austere of the Japanese warriors of the spirit. Japan also remembers Eisai as the father of tea, for when he returned from China, Eisai brought back some tea seeds and encouraged their planting around Zen monasteries.

A second great figure in the history of Zen is Dogen (1200–1253), who founded the Soto school. After an unsatisfying stay on Mount Hiei, he, too, left in search of a more satisfying regime. Coming under Eisai's influence, he went to China to study and then returned to live a very simple life based on *zazen*—sitting meditation. Zen reveres Dogen as a penetrating thinker who furnished it with some of its deepest metaphysical bases. Analyzing the experiences of *zazen*, Dogen produced a Japanese version of the dialectics of Buddha-nature that we associate with Nagarjuna in India. From experiencing the oneness of all things as it shines forth in enlightenment, Dogen was able to clarify the nature of consciousness and the wonder of simple "is-ness." Contemporary Zen masters such as Yasutani-roshi and Philip Kapleau esteem him most highly.[54]

The fall of the Kamakura rule in the

fourteenth century led to great civil strife. The Zen sects were the only ones that held themselves aloof from the fray, their monasteries becoming havens of peace and respite for intellectuals and artists. These monasteries were enterprising and self-sustaining, and often centers of education and culture. During the Tokugawa regime (1600–1867), Buddhism became a bureau of the state.[55] The ethical code (Bushido) that governed both warriors and merchants owed a great deal to Zen discipline, while the devotional sects continued to provide outlets for Buddhist religious emotions. The state kept a close eye on the clergy, tending to tie them to the care of temples, and the general atmosphere was one of stability and stagnation.

Modern Times

Under the Meiji restoration of the emperor, Shinto forces attacked Buddhism. A principal part of the attack was nationalistic: Shinto claimed to be the more ancient and truly Japanese religion. The Buddhists rose to the challenge, however, and modernized considerably. They tried to educate their clergy better for the new times, and they often opened schools for the laity. In fact, Buddhist centers in modern times have taken on many of the features of a Western parish, with organizations for children, small publications, Sunday school, meditation groups, charitable ventures, and so on. Some of the most beautiful Japanese shrines continue to be under Buddhist administration, and Japanese Buddhism has a healthy scholarly life. Along with Tibetan Tantrism, Zen has had considerable success in the West. In California, for instance, groups of meditators and several monasteries are flourishing.[56]

Two Zen teachers, D. T. Suzuki and Shunryu Suzuki (no relation), have played a large role in this journey of Japanese Buddhism to the West. D. T. Suzuki was a prolific author, who commented especially on the place of Zen in the history of Japanese culture.[57] Since he was fluent in Indian and Western languages, he became the prime ambassador to Western intellectuals of the importance of mind, enlightenment, and nature's oneness. Shunryu Suzuki was a Soto master who wrote only one book but whose personality and simple style have captivated Americans interested in Buddhism.[58] His teaching clarifies the difference between Soto and Rinzai: Where Rinzai tends to strive for enlightenment (satori) directly, trying to break the dualistic mind through intense meditation on koans (paradoxical sayings such as "the sound of one hand clapping"), Soto is more relaxed. It believes that "just sitting" *(shikan-taza)* is an exercise of one's Buddha-nature and so more important than the peak experience of satori. So Shunryu Suzuki's brief addresses to his meditation groups stress the value of being attentive to each moment of the here and now.

STRUCTURAL ANALYSIS

Nature

Stepping back from the historical view of Buddhism, we find that Buddhist attitudes toward nature do not fit together neatly. From its Indian origins, Buddhism assumed much of Hinduism's cosmological complexity. That meant taking up not only a world that stretched for vast distances and existed for immense eons (kalpas) but also the Aryan materialism and yogic spiritualism that lay behind such a cosmology. However, Buddhism came to contribute its own world views. Its numerous "Buddha-fields," for instance, are heavenly realms with which our earthly space-time system shares the boundless universe.

Buddhism has had few equivalents to Vedic materialism, but Buddhism used the doctrine of samsara early in its history to justify acceptance of one's worldly situation and working only to improve it (rather than to escape it for nirvana). On the other hand, the ancient Indian yogic practices impressed the Buddha and his followers deeply. Since Gautama had in fact become enlightened through meditation, and since this enlightenment expressed itself in terms of the antimaterial Four Noble Truths, Buddhism could never settle comfortably in the given world of the senses and pleasure.

Initially, therefore, Buddhism looked on nature or physical reality as much less than the most real or valuable portion of existence. Certainly the belief that all life is suffering reflects a rather negative attitude toward nature, and it indicates that what the eyes see and the ears hear is not the realm of true reality or true fulfillment. Also, to analyze physical reality in terms of three negative "marks" (pain, fleetingness, and selflessness) further devalues nature. At the least, one is not to desire sensory contacts with the world, because such desire binds one to illusory reality and produces only pain. Thus, Indian Buddhists separated themselves from nature (and society and self).

Because the great interest of early Buddhist philosophy was an analysis of dharmas based on probings of consciousness sharpened by intense meditation, the material aspects of the natural realm fell by the way. At best they were background realities and values. The scholastic Abhidhammists did not deny nature, for they were acutely aware of the senses, but they did deflect religious consciousness away from it.[59] Far more impressive than natural phenomena were the states of consciousness that seemed to go below the sensible flux to pure spirituality. They were the places where the Indian Buddhists preferred to linger.

In considering the Buddhist view of nature, we must distinguish between the inclinations of the meditators and scholars, who were interested in nonphysical states of consciousness, and the inclinations of the laity, who saw the world more concretely and less analytically. As we might expect, the laity was more worldly than the monks. When they heard that all life is suffering, they thought of their family burdens, their vulnerability to sickness, and the many ways in which nature and time seemed out

of their control. The comforts that they received from Buddhist preaching, therefore, lay in the promise that right living would take them a step closer to the kind of existence where their pain would be less and their enjoyment greater.[60]

Thus, it is no surprise that the most popular Buddhist movements were built on the Indian traditions of bhakti. Just as popular Hinduism fixed on Vishnu, Krishna, and Shiva, popular Buddhism fixed on Amitabha, Avalokitesvara, and Vairocana. These celestial Buddhas or bodhisattvas drew the popular religious imagination away from the historical Buddha and the commonplace world of the here and now to the realm of future fulfillment. In that way, popular Buddhism lay between the deemphasis of the physical realm that the monks and scholars practiced and the simple acceptance of physical life that a worldly or naturalist outlook (such as that of the early Vedas) produced. Emotional Buddhism influenced the sense perceptions of the laity so that this world became just the preliminary to the Western Paradise.[61]

Samsara and Nirvana

As the intellectuals and contemplatives worked further with immaterial consciousness and its philosophical consequences, they changed the relationships between samsara and nirvana. In the beginning, Buddhism thought of samsara as the imperfect, illusory realm of given, sense-bound existence. The Buddha himself exemplified this view when he urged his followers to escape the world that is "burning" to achieve nirvana. His original message regularly said that spontaneous experience makes one ill, and that health lies in rejecting attachments to spontaneous experience. With time, however, the philosophers, especially the Mahayanists, came to consider the relations between nirvana and samsara as being more complex. From analyzing the implications of these concepts, the philosophers determined that nirvana is not a thing or a place. The Buddha realized this, for he consistently refused to describe nirvana in detail. But while the Buddha's refusal was practical (such a description would not help solve the existential problems of being in pain), the refusal of the later philosophers, such as Nagarjuna, was largely epistemological and metaphysical. That is, they thought that we cannot think of such a concept as nirvana without reifying it (making it a thing), and that the reality of nirvana must completely transcend the realm of things.

From the viewpoint of the wisdom that has gone beyond (has assumed a transcendent, or epistemologically and metaphysically adequate, point of view), nirvana is the basis and the inmost reality of samsara, so we cannot finally separate nirvana and samsara. They are one, because all the reality of samsara (even the reality of appearances) is grounded in the ultimate reality that we call nirvana.

To follow this line of thought is no easy task, so only the elite grasped the philosophy of the *Prajna-paramita*, with its concepts of emptiness and transcendence. That philosophy influenced the devotional life of Mahayana and the ritual life of Tantrism, however, because even the simple people could grasp its positive implications as presented by the preachers. These positive implications, which blossomed most fully in the East Asian cultures, reduced to seeing that all reality is one. The other side of saying that all dharmas are empty is to say that the Buddha-nature (or nirvana, or the other ways of expressing the ultimate totality) is present everywhere. This belief gave religion a very positive tone. For instance, if all things contain the Buddha-nature, then our world will become glowingly fresh and beautiful as we realize who and what we are.

East Asia

When the message about Buddha-nature came to China and Japan, it was a spark meeting ready tinder. The native traditions of those cultures stressed an ideal har-mony of all nature's elements. In fact, both Taoism and Shinto set the individual in a natural whole or pattern (gestalt), inculcating a great reverence for nature and a special sensitivity to natural rhythms (the annual seasons, for instance). Especially in China, the tradition counseled the individual in the landscape of nature to find peace by attunement to the cosmic music, the universal way. Because Buddhism had better techniques (primarily meditative) for sharpening a sense of the oneness of things and their flow, and because it also had a more highly developed system for explaining reality's interconnectedness, serious Chinese and Japanese took it to heart. They could satisfy their native hunger to be at one with nature by following the new wisdom's way. More profoundly and intensely than with their native religious systems, they could enjoy the beauty of emptiness, of fullness, and of Buddha-nature's endlessly creative overflow into trees, mountains, streams, and people.

The East Asian forms of Buddhism, of course, also developed an imaginative or devotional religion for the common people, such as the Pure Land sects. They developed festivals, ceremonies, mythologies of ghosts and helping spirits, and amalgamations of Buddhist lore and native magic.[62] At the heart of the most intense East Asian Buddhist efforts, however, we find that the concept of nature emerges differently than in India. In Hua-yen or Ch'an Buddhism, for instance, aesthetics seem more important than in Indian Madhyamika or Yogacara. That is, the Chinese love of natural beauty makes a stronger impression.

Whereas Indian philosophers love the subtlety of conceptual analysis, Chinese philosophers love the oneness and beauty of the concrete, here-and-now world. Consequently, when the circle of samsara-nirvana relations turns in East Asia, it seems to come back close to a naive starting point. In the beginning, mountains are mountains, and trees are trees. The Chinese and Japanese thinkers accept turning away from this naive starting point, as done by Buddha and then by the Indian philosophers, but they finally bend back to it. For their enlightenment, nature or physical reality just *is*, and such is-ness applies to mountains and trees as much as it applies to the transcendent quality in them that the mind can discern. In other words, after its discernment of nirvana and then its mental reconstitution of nirvana with samsara, East Asian Buddhism placed the ultimate realities and values right back in concrete, here-and-now, visible and audible nature. The landscape paintings, moss and rock gardens, tea ceremonies, and the like exemplify this attitude, as does *shikan-taza*.[63]

Tantrist Buddhism, finally, shares with East Asian schools the belief in the oneness of samsara and nirvana that Indian Mahayana developed but differs in its expression of this belief through ritual magic and imagination. Tibetan practices, for example, are neither intellectual like Indian Buddhism nor nature based and contemplative like East Asian Buddhism. Rather, they play with the world, both loving nature and kicking it away, through sights (mandalas), sounds (mantras), and ceremonies (symbolic intercourse) that engage the participant both psychologically and physically. Insofar as physical nature reaches into the human being through the subconscious and unconscious, Tantrism has most successfully honored and provided for nature's "depth psychology."

Society

The Indian society of the Buddha was divided into castes, which were religiously sanctioned as a way of maintaining social order. Moreover, casteism was part of Vedic India's cosmological myth, since human society's order resulted from the sacrifice of Purusha, according to legend. In Brahmanism, the priests merited their primary status because they derived from Purusha's head.

Buddha, himself a member of the warrior class, brought a message that clashed with this hierarchy. His dharma taught that beings are to free themselves from painful worldly life. Since this invitation was from nature, from what we are, it was more compelling than the call to accept the caste tradition. At least Buddhists could strongly refute the cosmological myth that legitimated casteism. Many warriors and merchants no doubt found Buddhism a convenient weapon in their struggles with the brahmins for power. So they and others who wanted to change the status quo gave Buddhism a close hearing.

There was great liberation potential in the Buddha's message. Indeed, there was considerable radicalism. Buddha did not concern himself very much with politics as such, but his stress on enlightenment, nirvana, and the human calling to conquer karma and samsara, challenged the politics of his day, as did the decision to admit persons of all castes into the sangha, including women. This decision was only a logical application of the belief that all humans were in misery.

In application, of course, Buddhism never fully realized these ideals of liberation and radical equality. Caste was too much a part of Indian society to be exorcised without great difficulty. For instance, the *Dhammapada* (vv. 383–423) uses the brahmin as a figure of perfection. The "true Brahmin," it is at pains to show, is not he who is born into a priestly bloodline but he who gains a noble character through morality, meditation, and wisdom. Nonetheless, the *Dhammapada* does not choose to reinterpret the Sudra (lowest class worker). It is the brahmin who continues to denote nobility.

Women's Status

Buddhism offered Indian females considerably more than had been available to them previously.[64] Women were capable of enlightenment and could join the monastic community as nuns. This was in stark contrast to the classical Hindu view, which held that women had to be reborn as men to be eligible for *moksha.* By opening religious life to Indian women, Buddhists gave them an option besides marriage and motherhood—a sort of career and chance for independence. No longer did a girl and her family have to concentrate single-mindedly on gathering a dowry and arranging a wedding. Indeed, Buddhists viewed Hindu child marriage darkly, and they thought it more than fitting that women should travel to hear the Buddha preach. In later times, women could preach themselves, but from the beginning they could give time and money to the new cause.

Moreover, by offering an alternative to marriage, Buddhism inevitably gave women more voice in their marriage decisions and then in their conjugal lives. In fact, Buddhism viewed spouses as near equals. The husband was to give the wife respect, courtesy, faithfulness, and authority, while the wife was to give the husband duties well done, hospitality to their parents, faithfulness, watchfulness over his earnings, skill, and industry. One concrete way in which a Buddhist wife shared authority was in choosing their children's careers. For instance, to enter a monastery, a child needed both parents' consent. Married women could inherit and manage property without interference. Buddhism did not require or even expect that widows be recluses, while suttee was abhorrent to a religion that condemned animal sacrifice, murder, and suicide. Finally, Buddhist widows could enter the sangha, where they might find religious companionship, or they could stay in the world, remarry, inherit, and manage their own affairs.

Still, Buddhism never treated women as full equals of men. Though the logic of equal existential pain and equal possession of the Buddha-nature could have run to equal political and educational opportunities, it seldom did. Nuns had varying degrees of freedom to run their own affairs in the monasteries, but they were regularly subject to monks. Women never gained regular access to power over males, either in Buddhism's conception of the religious community or in its conception of marriage. Insofar as celibacy became part of the Buddhist ideal, marriage became a second-class vocation and women became a religious danger.[65]

Politics

In its relations with secular political powers, Buddhism had varying fortunes. The Buddha seems to have concerned himself little with pleasing public authorities or worrying how his spiritual realm related to the temporal. By the time of Asoka, however, the importance of royal patronage became clear. Much of Buddhism's influence outside India began when Asoka dispatched missionaries to foreign lands, and his efforts to instill Buddhist norms of ethics and nonviolence in his government became a model for later ages. As Christianity rethought Jesus' dictum about rendering unto Caesar the things that are Caesar's when it found a potentially Christian Caesar in Constantine, so Buddhism after Asoka longed for a union of dharma and kingly authority in the hope that such a union could beget a religious society.

Historically Buddhists tried to gain favor at court.[66] In Sri Lanka, Burma, Thailand, and the rest of Southeast Asia, this effort succeeded, and temporal rulers played a large role in Theravada's victory over Mahayana and Hinduism. In China, Buddhism's fortunes depended on whether it fared better or worse than Confucianism in getting the emperor's ear. During the worse periods, it became the object of imperial persecution. The same was true in Japan, where such persecution had much the same rationale: Buddhism was not the native tradition. Overall, however, Buddhism fared well in East Asia. It had to coexist with Confucian and Taoist cultural forces there, but it regularly dominated philosophy, funeral rites, and art.

For instance, as we have seen, Zen's favor with the ruling classes in Japan after the fall of the Heian dynasty made that sect tremendously influential. Indeed, so long as

Japan favored the samurai or warrior ideal, Zen was close to the corridors of power. Finally, Tibet realized the theocratic ideals that Asoka had sparked, for throughout most of its history religious leaders doubled as temporal powers. However, the intrigue, murder, and moral laxity that this binding of the two powers produced during certain periods of Tibetan history necessitated rethinking the relation between the religious and the secular powers.

As with Christianity, a tension is built in between the Buddhist religious community and any temporal state. The sangha and the church both make claims upon their followers that can bring them into conflict with secular powers. Since these claims are made in the name of dharma or God, they carry an aura of sacredness or of coming from a higher authority. To be sure, Buddhism took pains to establish an ethics that urged peaceful citizenship.[67] But the proviso always lurking behind these sincere efforts was that secular rulers not order things unjust, evil, or irreligious. The things that rightly are Caesar's are limited. So long as there is a Christ or a Buddha, a God or a nirvana, Caesar cannot claim everything.

One ploy that Caesar can develop, however, is to claim that he, rather than the priests or monks, is the representative of God or dharma. In other words, employing the aspect of the cosmological myth by which the human ruler is the link between heaven and earth, the king can claim a sacredness of his own. Many Christian successors to Constantine claimed this, and in effect many Buddhist rulers after Asoka did also. Voegelin has sketched the preparation for this sort of claim that a society such as the Mongol had; according to this hypothesis, Kublai Khan gave the Dalai Lama authority over Tibet as an administrative extension of his own sacred power.[68]

Despite its focus on otherworldly matters, then, Buddhism remained knotted in secular-religious controversies. Since it did not clearly establish an authority outside the cosmos (for instance, by coming to a doctrine of creation from nothingness), it was always theoretically liable to attack from kingly Buddhists who wanted to make dharma serve the state.

The Sangha

The sangha alternately raised and dashed hopes for humans living together in harmony and peace. Energetic monasteries, run by learned and holy monks or nuns, were models of what human society could be. Living simply, obeying a common rule and a common authority, such Buddhist professionals acted out a vision of equality and cooperation. When a monastery was in good spiritual fettle, one survived there only if one's motivation was religious. Meditation, hard work, austerity in diet and clothing, long periods of silence, celibacy—these staples of Zen monastic life offered little to the worldling. Monasteries of the devotional sects were quite different. People entered them rather grudgingly and briefly in order to learn the minimal ritual and doctrine necessary to function at the inherited family temple. Early Buddhist monasteries also differed from the pampered, court-favored centers of learning, art, and intrigue that were frequently spawned by Far Eastern Buddhism. So long as the genuine articles existed, Buddhism was alive and well.

The life of Buddhist laity has always reflected the state of the monastic sangha. When the monasteries were spiritually active, the laity tended to support them generously. In return, the monks usually served the laity spiritually. During these periods, the notion that the layperson's vocational obligation was primarily to support the monks evoked no cynicism. On the other hand, when the monks were lax, the reaction of the laity was ambivalent. The laity enjoyed seeing clay feet under yellow robes, but they missed the examples and teachings that might have dissolved some of their own clay. Ideally, then, the monks and nuns and the laity have provided mutual support.[69] Mahayana and Tantra have acted on this ideal by equating nirvana and samsara in such a way that vocational differences between the laity and the clergy were lessened. Even for these schools, however, the monasteries have symbolized places of retreat, meditation, study, and ritual devotion.

The Buddhist thought that most affected society, though, was that the Buddha-nature exists in all beings and makes them worthy of respect and holy living. The bodhisattva vow that Mahayana developed gave this belief solid form, insofar as one aspired to earn the salvation of all living beings. Buddhism has often failed to practice the bodhisattva vow in terms of establishing hospitals, schools, and other charitable institutions as Western religion would do, but the Buddhist record in performing good deeds is not negligible. Buddhist monasteries have not been exclusively places of spiritual retreat, and the bodhisattva's "great compassion" has touched other beings' bodies as well as souls.

Still, the social vision of Buddhism has remained quite spiritual. The bodhisattva's compassion has primarily been directed toward what Buddhism considers the deeper portion of human misery, namely, our living apart from enlightenment in karmic distress. So the ideal society spawned by the Four Noble Truths became similar to the Christian Communion of Saints in that it stretched beyond the temporal world to heaven (the Western Paradise). There all Buddhists might experience how oneness is social.

Self

The practical accent of Buddha's original preaching made the issues related to self paramount. Yet, paradoxically, a capital thesis in that preaching was that self is an illusion, "the most pernicious of errors, the most deceitful of illusions."[70] Consequently, Buddhist religious experience and doctrine concerning the self have been complex. On the one hand, Buddhism has directly addressed individuals, insisting that only the individual can change his or her life. On the other hand, Buddhism has counseled that in order to escape samsara and achieve nirvana,

we have to rid ourselves of the notion that we have or are an atman, a soul, or self. This belief has prompted some of Buddhism's central meditation practices and philosophical doctrines.

Historically, the teaching of no-self most distinguished the Buddha's way from that of his Hindu predecessors. As we have seen, a staple of Upanishadic wisdom was that the self is part of the great Atman (the interior aspect of Brahman). In yogic meditation, the Hindu tried to realize this ultimate identity, to experience the oneness of everything in Atman. When Buddha turned away from this teaching, calling human identity just a bundle of elements *(skandhas)* temporarily fused, he laid down a philosophical challenge that Hindu and Buddhist philosophers seldom neglected in later centuries. What motivated this new conception of the human being?

The principal motive, it appears, was Buddha's conviction that the key to human problems is desire. If pain expresses the problem ("All life is painful"), then desire expresses its cause ("The cause of suffering is desire"). These, we have seen, are the first two Noble Truths. The Third Noble Truth ("The removal of desire leads to the removal of suffering") extends the first two, and when Buddhists pondered its meaning and implications, they came to the doctrine of no-self.

The Third Noble Truth itself is psychological. For instance, we may analyze the suffering in human relations in terms of desire. Parents desire their children's success and love. When the children choose paths other than what the parents have dreamed, or when the children demand distance in order to grow into their own separate identities, the parents suffer pain. They feel disappointed or rejected, or that their toil and anxiety have gone for naught. Buddhists would tell such parents that their relations with their children have been unwise or impure. Because they have desired success and love, instead of remaining calm and free, they have set karmic bonds that were sure to cause pain.

But to cut the karmic bonds, the Third Noble Truth implies, one must get to the root of the desire. At this point one must turn psychology into metaphysics—one must realize that the self from which desires emanate is neither stable, fixed, permanent, or, ultimately, real. In our distraction and illusion, we gladly accept the fiction that we have stable selves. Under the prod of analysis and meditation, however, we start to see what Alfred North Whitehead (the Western philosopher currently touted as the most "Buddhist" of our metaphysicians)[71] called the "fallacy of misplaced concreteness."

In simple terms, the prime reality in our interior lives is flux. At each moment we are different "selves." True, some continuity exists in that we remember past events and project future ones. But this continuity hardly justifies the clinging reliance on a permanent self, which is the substance of desire.

What Buddhists stressed, therefore, was the change and coordination of the "self's" components, just as they stressed the interconnectedness and flux of the entire world (through dependent coarising). They developed a view of both the interior realm of consciousness and the exterior realm of nature that became quite relational. Their metaphysics focused on nature's coordinated interdependencies, its continual movement. The self could not be the exception to such a world view. Humans were too clearly a part of the total natural process to violate the process's fundamental laws. And just as analysis showed all the natural elements to be empty, so, too, analysis showed the self to be empty.

Therefore, Buddhists directly denied what Western philosophers such as Aristotle called a "substance." To live religiously, in accordance with the facts of consciousness, one had to cast off the naive assumption that the human person is a solid something—one had to slide into the flux. In so doing, one could both remove the basis for desire and open up the possibility for union with the rest of coordinated reality.

This movement toward union with the rest of reality became the positive counterweight to the Buddhist negative view of the self. That is, as people advanced in their meditation and understanding, they started to glimpse what Mahayana saw in enlightenment: the realization that all Buddha-nature is one. According to the *Prajna-paramita*, ultimately only Buddha-nature (or Suchness) existed. All multiplicity or discreteness resulted from a less than ultimate viewpoint. Yogacara texts such as the Chinese *Awakening of Faith*[72] explicitly correlated this viewpoint of ultimate wisdom with meditation. Stressing the centrality of mind, the *Awakening of Faith* tried to lead the reader toward the realization that his or her own consciousness reflected the ultimate oneness. Such a realization, of course, meant the death of the illusion that one was an independent atman.

We have belabored this teaching of no-self because it seems most important to the Buddhist attitude toward the individual. It is also the key to the Buddhist view that nature flows to oneness and that society should strive for ultimate reality by means of enlightenment. Because of *anatman* (no-self), the individual could move toward greater intimacy with nature. There were no barriers of separate identity, no walls making him or her isolated. For those who attained enlightenment through the dharma, this oneness of self, nature, and society was a personal experience. As a contemporary account of enlightenment puts it, "The big clock chimes—not the clock but Mind chimes. The universe itself chimes. There is neither Mind nor universe. Dong, dong, dong! I've totally disappeared. Buddha is!"[73]

Buddhism regularly counseled the individual to regard the body, the family, society, and even a spouse or a child with detachment. One was to revere and discipline the body according to the middle way. Clearly, though, the body was a temporary station on the way to nirvana or one's next incarnation. Wealth and pleasure were not, as they were for Hinduism, worthy life goals.

The family was a necessary unit, biologically and socially, but frequently it was also an impediment to spiritual advancement, as the Buddha's own life showed. Society would ideally be a context for mutual support in realizing enlightenment. Personal bonds, therefore, could not be passionate and karmic, and even a spouse or a child came under this law.

The love proper to a Buddhist was therefore "great compassion"—desire for the other's good in nirvana. This became no-desire in worldly terms. So alcohol, sex, clothing, and other items affecting the body were governed by the ethical rule of detachment (and came under the "Buddhist economics" that E. F. Schumacher made a cornerstone of his book *Small Is Beautiful*).[74] So business, politics, and art ideally sprang from a free spirit. East Asian painting, poetry, and calligraphy, for instance, ideally occurred in a state of no-mind.[75] Contrary to the regular Western view of the artist, in which the person agonizes through his or her work to produce a vision (and a self), the East Asian artist was to let art flow out of a meditative experience. Its hallmark was to be spontaneity, and the major stumbling block to spontaneity was self-concern.

Tantrism seems to qualify the Buddhist view of the self, since it allowed a more intense connection with food, alcohol, sex, and material ritual items. However, according to its own masters, the watchword in Tantrist rituals was still discipline and detachment. To use alcohol or sex licentiously was just a quick way to attachment and bad karma. The point to Tantrist ritual was to master these items and to retain the energies that would have flowed out to them. In Tantrist sexual yoga, for instance, the male was supposed to discipline himself in order to gain the female *Shakti* power. (That this abused women by making them means to men's ends seems to have been acceptable. Perhaps equal detachment on the females' part was supposed to make the rite equally efficacious for them.) The Tantrists argued that such a detachment "reversed" the spontaneous eroticism of desire, capturing its energy for enlightenment more effectively than avoidance would have.

There were, of course, varying degrees of commitment to the doctrine of no-self and varying understandings of it. The Pudgalavadins, as we noted, produced a doctrine of the person that returned the atman.[76] Many Buddhists, laity and monks alike, were strong personalities and so did not take no-self to mean a loss of decisiveness. The Buddhists who settled for improving their karma by meritorious deeds (and who frequently kept close records to detail their progress) must have been hard put not to be intensely self-conscious. The artists who worked in no-mind, overspilling with enlightened union with Buddha-nature, must have numbered relatively few. Therefore, there is substantial historical evidence that no-self was a hard doctrine to live. Like the Christian doctrine of selfless, suffering love *(agape)*, it was not realized just by vowing.

Even if not carried out, the doctrine of no-self shaped Buddhist culture. Wherever Buddhist religion was vigorous, the doctrine of no-self was influential. In fact, we often can sense its effects in the peace and humor of Buddhist texts. Many texts, of course, are complicated and complex. However, some raise serenity, irony, paradox, and wit to a high religious art. For instance, in one story two monks meet a fetching damsel by a rushing river. One charitably hoists her and carries her across. Later the second monk chastises the first for such sensual contact. The first monk replies, "I let the girl down when we crossed the river. Why are you still carrying her?" The Buddhist ideal was to carry nothing, to be utterly free.[77]

Divinity

Debate has raged over the question of whether Buddhism is a theistic religion. For instance, Chogyam Trungpa, a Tibetan master now living in the United States, has complained, "It is especially unfortunate that Buddhism has been presented as a theistic religion, whereas in fact it is a non-theistic spiritual philosophy, psychology, and way of life."[78] On the other hand, there is a good reason why scholars have frequently presented Buddhism as a theistic religion: It has frequently been such.[79] Devotional Buddhism has venerated a variety of Buddhas and bodhisattvas, treating them as other religions treat gods and saints. Also, the Buddhist concepts of nirvana, Buddha-nature, and emptiness have on occasion evinced the sacred aura of divinity, generating language that can only be called, by its difference from ordinary language, religious. Therefore, Buddhism frequently has been both theistic and religious.

To be sure, the Buddha himself does not appear to have claimed divinity. For example, he cast no speeches in the "I am" form that the Jesus of John's Gospel assumed. Rather, Gautama seems to have been a human being who thought that he had found the key to living well. The key was enlightenment, whose expression was the Four Noble Truths. In the enlightenment experience, Gautama encountered ultimate reality. The overtones to this encounter gleaned from the texts are not those of meeting a personal God. Whether that differentiates Gautama's ultimate reality from the God of Western religion is another question, whose answer depends on careful analysis of peak experiences and conceptions of ultimate reality. The personal character of the Western God is not so simple as many Westerners assume, and the impersonal quality of Gautama's encounter with nirvana is less absolute than many assume.[80]

Nonetheless, let us grant that Buddha's enlightenment and preaching do not posit a God. In this we would be agreeing with humanistic interpreters such as Trungpa, dismissing theories (such as Paul Tillich's) which state that one's ultimate concern (in this case nirvana) is one's de facto god. More problematic for the strictly humanistic interpreter of Buddhism is the popular reception that Gautama himself has received through the centuries. First, all

Buddhists grant Gautama a special authority in interpreting what human life is. Otherwise, there would be no sense in calling someone a Buddhist.[81]

Second, however, Buddha is divine and is related to ultimate reality in less sophisticated, more obvious ways. In Mahayana, the doctrine of Buddha's three bodies has led to the belief that Gautama was a historical form or manifestation of Suchness—the ultimate stuff.[82] In popular Buddhism the faith in the power of the various Buddhas to save, as well as to perform miracles, has been clear evidence that Buddhism for many has been not only a religion but a personal religion. To save, in any profound sense, is to heal and protect life from evil, which only a transcendent being can do. Insofar as Buddhas gave transcendent being personal form, they encouraged people to treat them religiously. For religion is the response to mystery that goes beyond humanistic or scientific resources and reaches out to something more.

When Pure Land founders urged the recitation of Amitabha's name, when Nichiren urged the salutation of the Lotus Sutra, when monks lighted incense and chanted hymns of praise, when the laity prayed for prosperity and against sickness—when Buddhists did any of these things, they engaged in religion.[83] Further, when they gave personal names, faces, and attributes to the objects that their salutations, chantings, or prayers addressed, they evidenced aspects of theistic religion. They put gods, if not God, as partners to their action and petition. It simply ignores or distorts what Buddhists have done through history to claim that Buddhism has not been a theistic religion.

Where Buddhism does have a distinctive divinity or ultimate reality is in the identification of nature with nirvana that Mahayana and Tantrism developed. Hinduism, of course, had yogic and philosophical strains that approached this identification. On the whole, though, Indian thought maintained for Brahman a certain otherness. The *nirguna* (unmanifest) Brahman probably did not break the cosmological myth, but it did separate ultimate reality from the here and now.

In East Asian Buddhism, the love of nature native to the civilizations there reduced this separation. While nirvana or the Buddha-nature could have ontological (metaphysical) differences from physical nature, the oneness of that ultimate reality was manifested in rock gardens, in valleys hung with mist, and in floral arrangements. The emptiness and transcendental wisdom related to a solid here and now, for dualistic thinking went against the East Asian grain by frustrating its meditation's quests for unity with Buddha-nature. Even today, a master such as Shunryu Suzuki does not seek the Buddha-nature by flight to a transcendent realm—Buddha-nature is within each moment. Suzuki, however, can speak of God.[84] Whether he equates God with Buddha-nature is not clear, but his regime is sufficiently religious to honor the word *God* and sympathize with its denotations.

The concept of ultimate reality, then, is susceptible to theistic interpretation at most points in Buddhism's history. For Trungpa's own tradition, Tibetan Tantrism, this is also the case. Imaginative identification with deities in meditational exercises, popular celebrations of festivals to the goddess Tara, prayers and spells to deities and such saints as Milarepa and Naropa—these clearly indicate that Tibetan Buddhism has been a religion consorting with gods. Whether by devotion, imagination, meditation, or philosophical exercise, the state to which Buddhism has aspired transcends irreligious, secular reality. It has an aura of the holy, and it has frequently produced holy persons.

Another interesting aspect of Buddhist divinity is its feminine overtones. We have already noted that the *Prajna-paramita* was in effect a mother goddess and that the Yogacara storehouse consciousness was linked with a cosmic Buddhist womb *(Tathagata-garbha)*. Much more influential than these rather abstruse aspects of divinity, however, were the bodhisattva Kuan-yin

Figure 18   Kuan-yin seated in the "royal ease" position. Courtesy Museum of Fine Arts, Boston, Harvey Edward Wetzel Fund.

and the goddess Tara. As Tay's study suggests,[85] Kuan-yin (Figure 18) has been a "goddess of mercy" or a "Buddhist madonna" of a cult occupying half of Asia. In most East Asian homes, a shrine to Kuan-yin focuses the family's desire, even in this life, to rise above karma through the help of a motherly deity who could empathize with human need. In any event, it is clear that very many Buddhists faced life crises by depending on this figure wholeheartedly.

Nirvana has been a help to Buddhists in ages past, it will likely be their hope for years to come, and the careful observer also sees in it aspects of divinity. As a symbol of what life should be, of how human consciousness ought to find fulfillment, it has protected Buddhists against absurdity. In doing so, nirvana has functioned precisely as divinity must. For divinity must be the beyond, the really real. Human beings have a concern for that kind of divinity in their consciousnesses. They are all apt to seek the center, as well as the beginning and the end. When Yeats wrote that the center does not hold, he exposed a horror latent in the modern world. To be without anchors of meaning, cast adrift in a flux going nowhere for no reason, would be the denial of Yeats's very constitution.

Few religions have probed the paradoxes of the center, of empty fullness, more acutely than Buddhism. Few have so focused life on the pursuit of enlightenment. One way, in fact, of interpreting how nirvana conquers karma is to say that it transforms the personality by substituting ultimate concerns for nonultimate ones—that it makes the Buddhist's treasure mystery rather than food, sex, money, or prestige. Nirvana itself is the extinguishing of karmic desire. It is the state of the human flame when it has burned away its oxygen and gone on to purer fuel. Though most of the descriptions of nirvana are in this negative style,[86] Buddhists have added that nirvana is not a void in the sense of a simple nothingness. Rather, it is a source of perfection, fulfillment, and bliss.

To say, then, that nirvana is present in, or even identical with, samsara is to say that present life may carry perfection, fulfillment, and bliss. When Buddhism accents this positive language, it becomes a humanistic religion, correlating divinity with the other three dimensions of reality. For nirvana in the present is what the selfless person seeks in communion, what a dharma-guided society seeks as its preservation from distraction, what nature grasped in enlightenment playfully dances. Thus, Buddhism's negative ultimate can become a center that holds very powerfully, that assures questioners of answers, that tells lovers there *are* objects worthy of their love.

In its own way, therefore, Buddhism has brought home to its adherents one of the final curiosities that human consciousness must admit: We must lose life to find it, we must place meaning in mystery if we are to make it secure.[87] As a result, Buddhism knows that to liberate speech for truth we must go into silence, to gain freedom we must renounce desire, to enhance samsara we must open to nirvana. Each of these religious paradoxes depends on the holding of the Buddhist center. Were there no nirvana, no realm of the really real or holy, none of the paradoxes would make any sense. Insofar as Buddhism does make sense, enlightening minds and enhancing lives, it at least intimates its central force. In sutras, statues of bodhisattvas, lonely mountain retreats, artistic rituals, and ethical codes, that central force is clearly suggested. Empty and gone beyond, as the Heart Sutra says, yet everything's oneness, it has been the treasure behind the three treasures. The Buddha, the dharma, and the sangha—they all live from and for nirvana, from and for Buddhist ultimate reality.

Study Questions

1. What was the essence of Gautama's enlightenment?
2. Is wisdom-morality-meditation a comprehensive, fully adequate religious regime?
3. In what sense was Mahayana both more popular and more speculative than Theravada?
4. How did Tantrist Buddhism concretize the notion that nirvana and samsara are one?
5. What is the relation between Ch'an Buddhism and Pure Land Buddhism?
6. Does Buddhism merge nature and divinity?
7. How would you try to persuade your best friend that he or she has no self?
8. Can you explain the Buddhist symbols of the wheel and the lotus?

Chapter Six

CHINESE RELIGION: TWENTY-FIVE KEY DATES

CA. 3500 B.C.E.   EARLIEST CHINESE CITY

CA. 1600   SHANG BRONZE AGE CULTURE

551–479   CONFUCIUS

520   TRADITIONAL DATE FOR DEATH OF LAO-TZU

403–221   WARRING STATES PERIOD

206   HAN DYNASTY REUNITES CHINA

CA. 200   RISE OF RELIGIOUS TAOISM

CA. 112   OPENING OF "SILK ROAD" LINKS CHINA WITH WEST

CA. 150 C.E.   BUDDHISM REACHES CHINA

304–589   HUNS FRAGMENT CHINA

607   BEGINNING OF CHINESE CULTURAL INFLUENCE IN JAPAN

658   HEIGHT OF CHINESE POWER IN CENTRAL ASIA

Chinese Religion

Buddhism made a permanent impact on Chinese culture,[1] but native Chinese religion always had at least equal influence. In this chapter we consider the history of native Chinese religion and its contributions to the Chinese world view. To begin, we observe Chinese life today in Hong Kong.

APPEARANCE

Most Chinese people today, of course, are behind the "bamboo curtain" that surrounds the People's Republic of China. A few scholars have studied portions of religious life there, but access to the common people and unhindered observation of their daily lives have only become possible since the death of Mao. The studies so far indicate that Mao's campaign against religion and the older, Confucian-based culture was relatively successful. Temples and shrines now have an insignificant role in Chinese life. Still, there is evidence that the older beliefs and customs have not completely died. In rural areas peasants still view the land as being filled with spirits. At times of sickness and death, many people still reach out to unseen powers. Even within the government bureaucracy, Confucian hierarchical thinking, as well as a veneration for leaders that can border on worship, suggest that the Communist Chinese personality has yet to distinguish itself.[2]

In Hong Kong, despite British and Western influences, one can see traditional funeral processions, worship in temples, fortune tellers, and more. Dragon parades wind through the streets on holidays, complete with firecrackers, tumblers, and colored lanterns. They recall the "diffused" operation of religious magic that C. K. Yang found characteristic of Chinese religion.[3] In Hong Kong this mixes curiously with a more apparent dedication to business. The visitor landing at the airport at Kowloon wonders first at the daring of jets dropping between the mountains and the sea dozens of times each day to land on a thin strip of tarmac. Inside the airport terminal, a most efficient hotel service secures for visitors whatever sort of accommodation they desire, and they are then whisked off in trucklike limousines.

As the limousines hurtle through the hilly and crowded streets, stores and signs assault the passengers. Hong Kong is not a Delhi or a Cairo, in which modern building and commerce perch precariously on a poor and ancient physical and human base. It has bicycles and rickshas, but few beasts of burden. Its cars are modern, its people in a hurry. Clothing, electronics, jewelry, and souvenirs are staples. As one gazes across the narrow strait to Hong Kong proper while waiting for the Red Star ferry, the high-rise hotels and banks gleam in the sunlight. On foggy days their tops are obscured by the low-hanging mist. A lot of energy and money went into building them, and a lot of energy and money crackles in the streets. The business of Hong Kong is business.

When one starts to study Hong Kong, though, its Western facade begins to blur. It is not just that tailors work twelve hours a day, seven days a week. Nor is it just that modern containerized shipping goes on in the midst of little junks and sampans. Rather, it is that the emporiums allow aisle space for robed counselors and fortune-tellers, who do a thriving business. It is that behind the Hiltons and Intercontinentals is a temple, dark and smoky, with food offerings, burning tapers, and statues of Buddha, Confucius, and Taoist saints. Tablets revealing family lines suggest a long history of ancestor veneration. Fortune slips suggest a continuing interest in divination. In the dark, perfumed air, very old traditions run together. The back streets of Hong Kong are a step back into the millennia of Chinese tradition.

HISTORY

Preaxial Chinese Religion

Philosopher Karl Jaspers has spoken of an "axial period" of human civilization, during which the essential insights arose that spawned the great cultures.[4] In China the axial period was the sixth and fifth centuries B.C.E., and the two most important figures were Confucius and Lao-tzu, whose Confucianism and Taoism, respectively, formed the basis for all subsequent Chinese culture. Before them, however, were centuries, perhaps even millennia, of nature- and ancestor-oriented responses to the sacred, when the ancient mind dominated the Chinese people. As we suggested in our discussion of the ancient mind, some of its oldest features persisted through periods of "higher" culture. In China, for instance, divination mixed with the Confucian ethical code, so that the prime divinatory text, the *I Ching*, became one of the Confucian classics. As the popular Chinese folk novel *Monkey* shows,[5] other ancient attitudes were alive well into the sixteenth century C.E. So the preaxial world view that we now sketch was a constant feature throughout Chinese religious history.

First, though, we must qualify the concept of Chinese religion. China, like most ancient cultures, did not develop religion as a separate realm of human concern. The rites, sacred mythology, ethics, and the like that bound the Chinese peoples were simply their culture. These cultural phenomena were not distinguished from the daily routine. So, what we underscore here for our purposes is not necessarily what the Chinese underscored. Second, the Chinese attitude toward ultimate reality stressed nature—the physical world. Nature was the (sacred) essential context of human existence, and there was no clear creator outside nature.

Of course, nature appeared to be both constant and changing. The cosmos was always there, but it had seasons and rhythms, as well as unexpected activities such as storms and earthquakes. To explain this tension between stability and change, the Chinese thought in terms of a union of opposing basic forces. Yang was the force of light, heat, and maleness. Yin was the balancing force of darkness, cold, and female-

ness. The changes in the relations between yang and yin accounted for the seasons, the moon's phases, and the tides.

Another aspect of nature was the mixture or proportions of the five vital forces (water, fire, wood, metal, and earth) at any given time. They were the qualities that activated nature—that gave particular things and events their character. Together, the yin-yang theory and the theory of the five vital forces formed the first Chinese explanation of nature.[6]

Above the system, not as its creator from nothingness but as its semipersonal overlord, was the heavenly ruler. His domain was human and natural behavior. The heavenly ruler probably was the first ancestor of the ruling dynasty. That is, the Chinese first conceived him as the clan head of the ancient ruling house of Shang.[7] Later they modified this anthropomorphic conception to heaven, a largely impersonal force. Then the emperor became the "Son of Heaven," not in the sense that he was the descendant of the first ancestral leader of the ruling clan but in the sense that he represented the force that governed the world.[8]

Another name for the director of the natural system was *Tao*. Essentially, *Tao* meant "way" or "path." The Confucians spoke of the *Tao* of the ancients—the customs or ethos that prevailed in the golden beginning times. Similarly, the Chinese Buddhists described their tradition as the "Way of the Buddha." However, the Taoists most directly appropriated the naturalistic overtones to *Tao* and focused on nature's directing path. For them the *Tao* was an ultimate reality, both within the system and beyond it.

We shall see below how the *Tao* was characteristic of the different Chinese religious traditions. The point here is that they all assumed the ancient view that nature is sufficiently orderly to suggest an overseer and a path. Within the natural system, however, the prehistoric Chinese stressed harmony. That is, they tended to think that trees, rivers, clouds, animals, and humans some qualifications that we shall mention, the Chinese have favored long life rather than immortality, enlightenment that polishes worldly vision rather than enlightenment that draws one out of the world. Ch'an's transformation of the Mahayana philosophy of nirvana owed much to Taoist philosophy and this ancient worldliness.

The Peasant Heritage

The preaxial views of nature, therefore, provided the axial thinkers with basic beliefs about nature's patterns, elements, and the consubstantiality (of the same substance) of humans with other forms of life. From these beliefs, the axial thinkers developed prescriptions for both social and individual life. In that way, ancient reflection helped form the rational framework of classical Chinese culture. More influential, though, was the nonrational heritage of the preaxial days. The vast majority of China's billions have been peasants, who, with relatively few changes, continued to stress magic, animistic forces, amulets, and divination rites up to the beginning of the twentieth century (if not right up to the present).

Folk religion is always an effort to explain nature, but it employs a logic that is more symbolic than that of yin-yang, the five dynamic qualities, or *Tao*. Rather, it emphasizes similarities and differences, whether in shapes, sizes, or names. As close to dreaming as to science, folk religion easily allows the subconscious great influence. So, for instance, diviners thought they had a key to nature in the cracks of a baked tortoise shell, or the flight patterns of birds, or the broken and unbroken lines that the *I Ching* interpreted as ratios of yin and yang. It was but a small step to use these interpretational techniques to control nature—to use them as magic.

One functionary who specialized in this symbolic magic was the practitioner of *feng-shui*.[10] *Feng-shui* was the study of winds and water, or geomancy. Essentially, it involved how to position a building most auspiciously. In a convoluted symbolism

Figure 19 Zoomorphic spiral, western Chou dynasty, probably early ninth century B.C.E. Nelson Gallery–Atkins Museum, Kansas City, Missouri (Nelson Fund).

compose something whole. As a result, natural phenomena could be portents, while human actions, whether good or evil, influenced both heaven and earth. As the Native Americans identified closely with their forests, so the oldest Chinese were citizens of nature, not a species standing outside and apart from it. Consequently, they did not consider human beings as superior to the other creatures of the cosmos.

When Chuang-tzu spoke of reentering the Great Clod,[9] he spoke from this ancient conviction. To die and return to the material world, perhaps to be a tree or a fish in the next round, was natural and right. With pertaining to dragons and tigers, it tried to make the living forces of nature yield good fortune by figuring out the spiritual lay of the land. What nature disposed, according to *feng-shui*, architecture could oppose or exploit. For instance, straight lines were believed to be evil influences, but trees or a fresh pond could ward them off. Consequently, the basic design of Chinese villages included trees and ponds for protection. Similarly, a winding approach to a house diverted evil forces. The *feng-shui* diviner plotted all the forces, good and evil, with a sort of compass that marked the different circles of power of these forces. *Feng-shui* has prevailed well into modern times, a fact attesting to its perceived importance.

Other important ancient functionaries were the mediums and the shamans. As Waley's translations suggest,[11] the shaman's song frequently called on a personal spirit to come down and enlighten him. Perhaps, then, the Chinese shaman (or shamaness) was less ecstatic than the Siberian, more a subject of possession or a medium than a traveler to the gods.[12] More importantly, the existence of the shaman shows that ancient China believed in a realm of personified spirits.[13] These spirits could come to susceptible individuals with lights and messages or be the spirits of departed ancestors speaking through a medium who was in trance. If one did not revere them, speak well of them, and give them gifts of food, the ancestor spirits could turn nasty.

In later times, ordinary people thought that the ancestor spirits lived in a spiritual equivalent of the human world, where they needed such things as food, clothing, and money. Thus, pious children would burn paper money to send assistance to their departed parents.[14] In fact, one's primary obligation of a religious sort was just such acts of commemoration, reverence, and help. This ancestor veneration so impressed Western missionaries that they fought bitterly among themselves about its meaning. Some missionaries found ancestor rites idolatrous, while others found them praiseworthy expressions of familial love.[15]

Exorcism

Another feature of ancient Chinese religion was the personification and exorcism of evil. In historical times, the Taoist priesthood dominated exorcism, but the roots of exorcism go further back. Peter Goullart has given an eyewitness account of a modern Taoist exorcism,[16] complete with descriptions of weird phenomena like those enacted in the American film *The Exorcist*. The assumption behind exorcism, of course, is that evil forces invade and possess a person. In part, this assumption is just the logical conclusion of a thought world in which shamanism is possible. If the Chinese shaman could be invaded by his helping spirit, and if evil spirits existed, then other persons could be invaded by evil spirits. If we follow another line of logic, demon possession is just the development of ancient fears of evil, while exorcism is just the development of ancient ways of combating such fear.

Goullart's description of the "energumen" (demoniac), however, renders the evil most concrete. The possessing power curses, threatens, and pours out hate (in a terrifying distortion of the demoniac's own voice). It bloats the demoniac's body, pushing the bedspring on which he rests down to the floor. The demoniac howls like an animal, gives off horrid smells, and empties his bladder and bowels repeatedly. Onlookers are terrified, and the Taoist priest strains to the utmost in his spiritual struggles with the evil one. The reader senses something absolutely primitive: human shock before the possibility of naked evil.

In his summary of the religious beliefs of the Chinese Neolithic age,[17] Mircea Eliade sketches the general context for such shock, as well as for shamanism, divination, and other ancient features that we have discussed. There was from earliest times a connection between life, fertility, death, and afterlife that took the form of a regular cosmic cycle and gave rise to annual religious rites. Further, the ancestors were a source of magical and religious power, and all natural forces had an aura of mystery—the mystery of the conjunction of opposites: of life and death, good and evil, rational and irrational. Possession and exorcism, then, are but vivid instances of a generally volatile mix. The ancient Chinese world was thoroughly alive, and one never knew precisely where its power would go.

Confucianism

Confucius (551–479 B.C.E.) becam the father of Chinese culture by transforming the ancient traditions into at least the beginnings of a code for directing social life. More than two centuries passed before his doctrine became the state orthodoxy (during the Han dynasty, 206 B.C.E.–220 C.E.), but from the outset it had a healing effect on Chinese society. Confucius lived during a warring period of Chinese history, an epoch of nearly constant social disorder. For Master Kung (another name for Confucius), the way from such disorder toward peace was obtained from the ancients—the venerable ancestors who were closer to the beginning and wiser than the people of the present age. What the ancestors knew, what made them wise, were the decrees of heaven. As we have seen, heaven meant nature's overlord. Thus, Confucius accepted the ancient, preaxial notion that nature has some order. In his view, the way to a peaceful and prosperous society was to adapt to that order. People could do that externally through sacrificial rites and hierarchical social relationships. Internally, one had to know the human mind, and the human mind had to be set in *jen* (fellow feeling or love).[18]

For external order, the emperor was paramount. As the Son of Heaven, he conveyed heaven's will to earth. In other words, the China of Confucius's time held to the cosmological myth. With many other ancient societies, it shared the notion that the king was the sacred intermediary between the realm of heaven and the realm modeled upon it, earth. What the king did for human society, then, was both priestly and exemplary. By officiating at the most important rites, through which his people tried to achieve harmony with heaven, the king represented society before the ultimate judge of society's fate. By the example that he set at court and by the way that he directed imperial policy, the king not only served as a good or bad model for his followers but also led the state in following or defying heaven's intent. The king achieved his power simply through his close connection to heaven.[19]

Confucius approved of the model leadership of the legendary kings, and he also approved of the notion that ritual makes a sacrament of the vital flow between heaven and earth. One focus of his teaching, then, was historical: He concentrated on how the ancients reportedly acted. Another focus was liturgical. He was himself a master of court ritual, and he thought that proper sacrifice and etiquette were very important. Probably Confucius's most profound impact on Chinese culture, though, was his clarification of human virtues, or spiritual qualities.

Having had little success in public affairs (he never obtained high office or found a ruler willing to hire his counsel), he turned to teaching young men wise politics and the way to private virtue. In other words, he became the center of an academic circle, like that of Plato, which had ongoing dialogues about the good life, political science, private and public morality, and so on. Confucius consistently stressed practicality in his tutoring. The wisdom that he loved intended the good society, the commonweal. It was not a yogic or shamanic regime dedicated to a single individual's spiritual development.

The *Analects* are a collection of fragments from the Master. In them we can see why Confucius impressed his followers, who finally made him the model wise man. (After his death, Confucius gained semidivine status and became the center of a religious cult.)[20] Especially in the third through ninth books, the Confucians preserved sayings that seem to be original, although Confucius himself claimed no originality. In fact, he did not even claim divine inspiration. His way was nothing novel; he only studied the past and then transmitted the ancients' customs. But when Confucius speaks of hearing the way in the morning and dying content in the evening, we sense how thoroughly he had embraced *Tao*. When he says that at seventy he could do whatever his instincts prompted, we sense that he felt a mystic union with the Way and that the Way dominated his entire personality.

For Confucius, the Way manifests itself as a golden mean. It opens a path between punctiliousness and irregularity, between submissiveness and independence. Most situations are governed by a protocol that will yield graceful interactions if it is followed wholeheartedly. The task of the gentleman is to know that protocol, intuit how it applies in particular cases, and have the discipline to carry it out. The death of a parent, for instance, is a prime occasion for a gentleman to express his love and respect for that parent. According to the rites of mourning, he should retire from public affairs, simplify his living arrangements, and devote himself to grieving (for as long as three years).

As that example suggests, filial piety was a cornerstone of Confucianism. If the relations at home were correct, other social relationships would likely fall in line. The Confucian classic *The Great Learning*[21] spells out this theory, linking the individual in the family to the order of both the state and the cosmos. Moreover, the family circle was the training ground for a gentleman's lifelong dedication to humanity *(jen)* and ritual propriety *(li)*. When a man developed a sincere love for his parents and carried out his filial duties, he rooted himself firmly in both *jen* and *li*. (We consider the place of women below in the section on society.) Confucius's own teaching, therefore, called for a balance between interior goodness and exterior grace. He thought that if people knew their inner minds (grasped at "inwit," in Ezra Pound's translation)[22] and manifested their knowledge through social decorum,

then society would have both the substance and the appearance of humanity.

Different followers developed different aspects of Confucius's teaching. Mencius, for instance, changed the Master's view of *jen*, drawing it down from the almost divine status accorded it by Confucius and making it a real possibility for everyman.[23] For Mencius human nature was innately good. We are only evil or disordered because we forget our original nature. Like the deforested local hill, the typical human mind is so abused that we cannot see its spontaneous tendency toward altruism and justice. If we would stop deforesting it with vice, we would realize that virtue is instinctive. Just as anyone who sees a child at the edge of a well rushes to save the youth, so anyone educated in gentlemanliness will rush to solve civic problems.

Thus, Mencius centered Confucius's teaching on the goodness of human nature. Living two centuries after the Master, Mencius tried to repeat Confucius's way of life. So, he searched for an ideal king who would take his counsel, but he had to be satisfied in having a circle of young students. Mencius, though, somewhat lacked Confucius's restraint in discussing heavenly things (Confucius considered the human realm more than enough to master). According to Lee Yearley,[24] Mencius practiced a disciplined religion to increase physical vigor by acting with purity of heart, and he was willing to die for certain things such as justice and goodness. So, just as one can consider some of Confucius's sayings as quite religious (for example, "It is not better to pay court to the stove than to heaven"), one can view Mencius as having transcendent beliefs. Both Confucian thinkers, we believe, appealed to more than human prudence.

Mencius also proposed an ultimately religious theory that history moves in cycles, depending upon how a given ruling family handles the *te* (the power to govern well) that heaven dispenses.[25] The sharpest implication of this theory was that an unjust ruler might lose the mandate of heaven—

that a revolutionary might properly receive it. Further, Mencius advanced the view that the king only brought prosperity when he convinced the people that the things of the state were their own. This view was in part shrewd psychology: A people who have access to the royal park will think it small even if it is 100 miles square; a people denied access to a royal park one mile square will complain that it is far too vast. As well, however, it brought Confucius's stress on leadership by example and virtue up-to-date: Only if the king demonstrates virtue can he expect the people to be virtuous.

A legalistic wing among Confucius's later followers, led by Hsun-tzu, opposed both Mencius's teaching that human nature is essentially good and the non-Confucian Mo-tzu's doctrine of universal love.[26] Hsun-tzu taught that only strong law can confine human nature to right action; for that reason so many mountains remain bald. Further, Hsun-tzu connected this belief with Confucius's own stress on ritual, arguing that law and etiquette have the pedagogical function of showing the inner spirit what goodness and justice really mean. Unfortunately, later apologists for the state took some of Hsun-tzu's ideas as a warrant for government by compulsion. In themselves, however, his ideas perhaps complemented Mencius's program as much as they opposed it, by clarifying the place for external codes. Arthur Waley, at least, has tried to show that Hsun-tzu mainly reacted against possible abuses of Mencius's views on human nature.[27]

In summary, then, the hallmarks of the original Confucians were a reliance on ancient models, a concern for the golden mean between externalism and internalism, a stress on filial piety, and a deep respect for the ruler's connection with heaven. These socially oriented thinkers emphasized breeding, grace, and public service. Their goal was harmony and balance through a hierarchical social order.[28] They gave little attention to the rights of peasants or women, but they did prize ethical integrity, compassion, and learning. Against the blood and violence of their times, they called for a rule through moral force. This was their permanent legacy: Humanity is fidelity to virtue.

Taoism

The classical, axial-period Taoists responded to the troubled warring period quite differently than the Confucians did. They agreed that the times were disordered and that the way to set them straight was by means of the ancients' *Tao*. But the great Taoist thinkers, such as Chuang-tzu and Lao-tzu, were more imaginative and mystical than the Confucians. In their broad speculation, they probed not only the natural functions of the Way and the interior exercises that could align one with it but also the revolt against conventional values that union with *Tao* seemed to imply. Of the two great Taoists, Chuang-tzu is the more poetic and paradoxical. His stories stress the personal effects of living with *Tao*. Lao-tzu's orientation is more political. For him *Tao* gives a model for civil rule, lessons in what succeeds and what brings grief. Insofar as Chuang-tzu is more theoretical and less concerned with political applications, he enjoys a certain logical priority over Lao-tzu.[29]

Chuang-tzu

What impressed Chuang-tzu most was the influence of one's viewpoint. The common person, for example, can make little of the ancients' communion with nature, unconcern for human opinion, and freedom. Such things are like the great bird flying off where the sparrow has never been. Yet if one advances in the "fasting of the spirit" that the ancients practiced, their behavior starts to make sense. Apparently such "fasting of the spirit" was a meditative regime in which one lay aside distractions and let simple, deep powers of spiritual consciousness issue forth.

Chuang-tzu pictured those powers rather dramatically: They can send the sage flying on the clouds or riding on the winds, for they free the soul so that it can be directed by *Tao* itself. *Tao* is the wind blowing on the ten thousand things, the music of the spheres. With little regard for petty humankind, it works nature's rhythms. The way to peace, spiritual ecstasy, and long life is to join nature's rhythms. But by joining nature's rhythms, one abandons social conventions. *Tao* throws off our human judgments of good and bad, right and wrong. Thus, the true Taoist becomes eccentric with respect to the rest of society, for he (or she, though women seldom participated in Chinese society) prefers obscure peace to troubled power, leisurely contemplation to hectic productivity.

In rather technical terms, Chuang-tzu attacked those who thought they could tie language directly to thought and so clarify all discourse. If *Tao* touches language and thought, he showed, they become highly symbolic. Moreover, Chuang-tzu made his attack on conventional values and language into simple good sense. It is the worthless, cast-off, unpopular trees and people that survive. Those who would be prominent, who would shine in public, often end up without a limb (as punishment for crime or disfavor). When he was asked to join the government, Chuang-tzu said he would rather drag his tail in the mud like a turtle. When his wife died, he sang and drummed instead of mourning: She was just following *Tao*, just taking another turn. Puncturing cant, deflating pomposity, excoriating our tendency to trade interior freedom for exterior position, Chuang-tzu ridiculed the sober Confucians. They, like other prosaic realists, seemed too dull to be borne—too dull for a life of spiritual adventure, for a *Tao* as magnificent as the heavens and as close as the dung.

Lao-tzu

Thomas Merton has published a delightful interpretation of Chuang-tzu that relates him to the contemplative spirit of Western poets and monks.[30] No one has done quite the same thing for Lao-tzu or the *Tao Te Ching*, perhaps because Lao-tzu's style is more impersonal. The *Tao Te Ching* (*The Way and Its Power*),[31] like the *Chuang-*

tzu (the book left by Chuang-tzu and his school), is of undetermined origin. Its author's existence is more uncertain than that of the *Analects*. But the book itself has become a world classic, in good measure because of its mystic depth (and vagueness). In it a very original mind meditates on *Tao's* paradoxical qualities to glean lessons about human society. Interpreters vary in the weight they give to the mystical aspects of the *Tao Te Ching*,[32] but in any interpretation Lao-tzu thought that *Tao* holds the secret to good life.

Consequently, a major concern of the *Tao Te Ching* is to elucidate just how nature does operate and how society should imitate it. Its basic conclusion, presented in a series of striking images, is that *Tao* moves nature through *wu-wei* (active not-doing). Three of the principal images are the valley, the female, and the uncarved block. Together, they indicate *Tao's* distance from most human expectations. The valley symbolizes *Tao's* inclination toward the lowly, the underlying, rather than the prominent or impressive. Lao-tzu's female is a lesson in the power of passivity, of yielding and adaptability. She influences not by assault but by indirection, by nuance and suggestion. The uncarved block is human nature before society limits it. These images all show *wu-wei*.

Wu-wei is also shown in the power of the infant, whose helplessness can dominate an entire family. It is in the power of water, which patiently wears away rock. Wryly Lao-tzu reminds us of the obvious: A valley resists storms better than a mountain, a female tends to outlive a male, an infant is freer than a king, and a house is valuable for the space inside it. Such lessons underscore a reality that common sense tends to ignore because it tends to notice only what is prominent. In contrast, *Tao* moves nature by a subtle, elastic power. Were rulers to imitate *Tao*, moving others by *wu-wei* rather than *pa* (violent force), society might prosper.

Wu-wei, it follows, tries to short-circuit the law of the human jungle, the round after round of tit for tat.[33] But to gain *wu-wei*, human nature must become like an uncarved block, which is perhaps the most important of Lao-tzu's symbols. (Holmes Welch, who argues that we can read the *Tao Te Ching* on several levels, makes the uncarved block its key.)[34] It symbolizes the priority of natural simplicity over social adornment. A block of wood or jade, before it is carved, has infinite potential, but once we have made it into a table or a piece of jewelry, its use is fixed and limited.

Impressed by the limitless creativity of nature, Lao-tzu wanted to recover human nature's originality. In his eyes, the Confucians tended to overspecialize human nature. A society with fewer "modern" advances, less technology, and more spontaneous interaction with nature and fellow humans would be much richer than the Confucians'.[35] The Taoists, who took their lead from Lao-tzu and Chuang-tzu, tried to show how less could be more, how neglect could be cultivation. If people would shut the doors of their senses and thus cut off distractions, how less can be more would be obvious. The good life is not found in having but in being. By being simple, whole, alert, and sensitive in feeling, one finds joy.

Throughout history, many commentators have criticized Lao-tzu and his followers for both naiveté and obscurantism. They have especially jumped on the Taoist precept that a good way to promote peace and simplicity is to keep the people ignorant. Taoists believed that by not knowing and therefore not having many desires, a populace is quite docile. Critics maintain that it is but a short step from such docility to sheephood and being at the mercy of evil rulers. The commentators have a point: The ideas expressed in some of Lao-tzu's sayings invite easy abuse. For instance:

Heaven and Earth are ruthless;
To them the ten thousand things are but as straw dogs.
The sage too is ruthless;
To him the people are but as straw dogs.[36]

However, a close reading of the *Tao Te Ching* shows that *wu-wei* is quite different from mindless docility or even complete pacifism. Rather, it includes the regretful use of force in order to cut short greater evil. As well, *wu-wei* is not sentimental, which further distinguishes it from most Westerners' views of "the people." As easily as nature itself, *wu-wei* discards what is outworn, alternating life with death. Because of this objectivity, Taoism can seem inhumane. For a people close to nature, though, humaneness is a less anthropocentric virtue than it is for ourselves. It is less personal and more influenced by the belief that self-concern is folly.

Religious Taoism and Aesthetics

Two great consequences of the school founded by Chuang-tzu and Lao-tzu had considerable influence through subsequent Chinese history. One consequence was religious Taoism, which was considerably different from the philosophical Taoism of the founding fathers in that it employed their symbolism literally and turned to quests for magical powers and immortality.[37] A second consequence was aesthetic: Chinese art became heavily Taoist.

The religious Taoists formed a "church," generated a massive literature complete with ritualistic and alchemical lore, and earned the wrath of modern educated Chinese, who considered religious Taoism a bastion of superstition. Also, religious Taoists became embroiled in politics and sponsored violent revolutionary groups.[38] Their magic and revolutionary politics went together, because from their magic they derived utopian visions of what human society ought to become.

The religious Taoists sought physical immortality by diverse routes.[39] Some sponsored voyages to the magical islands in the East, where the immortals were thought to dwell. (Sad to say, none of the voyagers ever came back to describe the immortals or their fountain of youth.) Others pursued alchemy, not to turn base metal into gold but to find the elixir of immortality. At one point they thought they had found this elixir in cinnabar (mercuric sulfide), which they persuaded emperors to imbibe so that the rulers could thwart death. On another sad day the religious Taoists discovered that cinnabar is a poison—a powerful elixir of mortality.

A third Taoist interest was hygiene. The two favorite regimes were breathing air and practicing a quasi-Tantric sexual yoga. Along with some dietary oddities, some religious Taoists counseled trying to breathe like an infant in the womb, so as to use up the vital force as slowly as possible. Adepts would lie in bed all day, trying to hold their breath for at first a hundred and eventually a thousand counts. Perhaps some became euphoric through carbon dioxide intoxication. Others went to their reward more quickly than their meat-eating fellows. The yogis of sex practiced retention of the semen during intercourse, thinking that this vital substance could be rechanneled to the brain and thereby enhance one's powers and longevity. Modern physiology says that the semen goes to the bladder, striking another blow against religious Taoism.

Religious Taoism also developed regimes of meditation, which it coupled with a complicated roster of gods. The basic assumption behind this venture was that the human body is a microcosm—a miniature world.[40] Within it, certain gods preside over particular organs and functions. By visualizing one of these gods, Taoists thought, one could identify with its powers of immortality.[41]

Taoism had as strong an impact on Chinese aesthetics as it did on Chinese popular religion.[42] As a guide to creativity, it stressed spontaneity and flow. Largely due to Taoist inspiration, calligraphy, painting, poetry, and music ideally issued from a meditative communion with the nature of things. In what Ch'an popularized as "no-mind," artists worked spontaneously, without calculation or design. Their products were the outflow of a fullness far more comprehensive than logic or method. In fact, the artists were supposed to render both the stream of nature and the way that particular items suddenly focus that stream. So a bird alighting on a tree, a rush of wind, the striking colors of persimmons at daybreak—these were typical themes of poetry and art. Taoist artists owed a great deal to the "retirement" that Taoism advocated as a respite and counterpoint to Confucian "office."[43] Mixed with Buddhist aesthetics, Taoism provided China with most of its artistic depth. Nature, art, and the spirit so came together for the traditional Chinese that they considered their Way superior to that of the rest of the world.

The Popular Amalgamation

By around 350 B.C.E. preaxial folk religion, Confucianism, and Taoism had come together, along with lesser philosophical movements. The major developments from that time until the Christian era were the establishment by the Han emperors of Confucian ideas as a sort of state orthodoxy, the flowering of religious Taoism, and the beginnings of Chinese Buddhism. With influence shifting among the movements, the mixture bubbled and boiled until neo-Confucianism emerged preeminent in the late Sung dynasty (twelfth century C.E.). In this section we try to analyze the effects of the different traditions in the daily life of the Chinese. Since this long stretch of history dominates Chinese culture, we are in effect trying to describe its most representative consciousness.

The Preeminence of Confucianism

In the typical Chinese family religious attention focused on ancestors. The family gained its identity from its clan, so by venerating its dead it constantly reaffirmed who it was. Because Confucianism emphasized filial piety, it suited this clan pattern quite nicely. The most devout thing one could do was to honor one's predecessors. In addition, familial piety involved a broad set of clan obligations whose guiding maxim was "Never bring dishonor on your lineage." Because the Confucians specialized in rites, protocol, gentlemanly bearing, and the like, which gave form to honor, they prescribed most clearly what the typical family wanted to know.

Confucianism was equally important in helping the public articulate the larger, state-centered concern for identity and honor. The emperor was the latest descendant of a most honorable clan, and the emperor's veneration of his ancestors had almost cosmic implications. In addition, the emperor wanted to justify the obedience of and respect from his subordinates. With its sensitivity to rank and its emphasis on a hierarchical social structure to maintain social order, Confucianism buttressed the status quo, which most rulers desired. Thus, the Confucian writings, first informally and later formally, became the basis of a gentleman's education. Further, because gentlemen were obviously the best civil servants, mastering the Confucian writings became a prerequisite to a career in government. As Lawrence Thompson notes, from the middle of the second century B.C.E. to the twentieth century C.E., the canon of Confucian writings influenced the minds of all educated Chinese.[44]

The Non-Confucian Opposition

Thus, Confucianism was the most influential religious tradition for the public functions of the family and the state, and in that sense the most official. For private worship, philosophy, and art, however, Buddhism and Taoism were quite influential. Buddhism and Taoism contended for influence at court and sometimes gained dominance. After the fall of the Han dynasty

(third century C.E.), for instance, Confucian influence waned, and Buddhism gained great influence that lasted well into the ninth century. Nonetheless, in most periods the state bureaucracy hewed to the Confucian line.

Buddhism's major impact in the public sphere was its control of burial rites. In time, China associated funerals with monks. Partly out of envy at such influence and partly out of its own searches for enlightenment, Taoism established monastic communities in the fourth century C.E. Along with the rituals of the Taoist priesthood and the Taoist political parties, these communities were strong sources of Taoist public influence.

However, in their struggles against Confucian dominance, Buddhism and Taoism primarily depended upon their greater appeal to individualist and artistic sentiments. In comparison, the sober Confucians offered little to nourish a private, meditative, philosophical, or aesthetic life, although they were not completely lacking resources for nurturing private satisfactions. The Master's love of music, for instance, though he set it in a traditional and public context, could have inspired personal creativity in the arts. However, such inspiration tended to fall to Buddhists and Taoists.

In addition, the Buddhist and Taoist texts seemed richer and more mysterious to middle-aged people seeking meaning in their existence. Few Chinese could live fifty years and not suffer some surfeit from rules, laws, ceremonies, or traditions. At such a point, the lean paradoxes of Chuang-tzu, Lao-tzu, the *Prajna-paramita*, and Ch'an grew very attractive. So did the *Tao* that could not be named, the Buddhist emptiness that one had to attend in silence.

Only the educated upper classes, of course, had the opportunity to immerse themselves in any of the three traditions. For the majority of the population, the influence of these traditions only vaguely affected a world dominated by family loyalties and naturalistic animism, largely because the Chinese population was always overwhelmingly comprised of peasants. Close to nature, these people filtered Buddhist and Taoist ideas through a primal reverence and fear for nature's powers.

For instance, the Chinese peasants incorporated Buddhist demonology, Taoist demonology, and both traditions' concern with saints into their ancient world of ghosts and helpers, which was home to the ancestors. This world was real because it affected the peasants each day, as the family sacrificed or tried to avert bad luck. The magical world of the spirits was alive. Daily the phenomena of the sky and the fields expressed that world's mysteries, and the wind and the sea carried great swans and dragons. The cities and the imperial court had their influence on the hamlets, but real life there confronted nature with little polish or form. What we might call an instinctive Confucianism about family relations blended with an instinctive Taoism about nature and human destiny to produce a curious mixture of formality and magic.

Moreover, the peasants had not separated, either through study or deep meditation, rationality from mythical or pragmatic hopes and fears. Getting enough food, sheltering one's family, warding off sickness, continuing the family line—those were the concerns of the villagers. To meet them, different gods were honored at festivals for the new year and for the changing seasons. As well, the Buddhist Goddess of mercy drew those seeking easy births and strong children, and the Taoist cult of the immortals attracted a few who wanted longevity or knowledge of the rulers of their bodily organs. Tradition sanctioned these quests for meaning, but it was a tradition with many cracks. Daily life was largely a fearful effort to avoid the wrath of the ancestors or the evil spirits.

Mercantile Religion

By the fourteenth century C.E., guilds of artisans and businessmen had developed and folk religiosity in China had become more mercantile. The guild became a sort of

family or clan and had its patron gods and rituals. People now invoked the spirits who were the patrons of good selling, and a folk mentality affected the examinations that were part of the way to civil office. For instance, masters of the Confucian classics who did well in the examinations and secured good jobs took on an aura of religious power. As well, numerous stories were told of scholars who received miraculous help from a patron deity, and these scholars gave the Confucians their own measure of magic and mystery.[45]

The common people also went to a great variety of shrines and temples to find out their futures. In addition, students prayed for success in their examinations, travelers prayed for safe journeys, and young people prayed for good marriages. Popular Chinese religion thus became almost economic. Gods and powers were the foci of business—a business of getting along well with an unseen world of fate and fortune. Confucianism, Taoism, and Buddhism all were mixed into this economic popular religion, but its base was preaxial superstition. Few Chinese were so far from nature or so safe from adverse fortune that "secularism" was a live option. The state somewhat controlled religion by keeping the Buddhist and Taoist clergy in check, but the religious life of the family and the individual ran all the traditions together in a form that was largely outside the government's control.

Neo-Confucianism

During the Sung dynasty (960–1279 C.E.), the axial Confucian thought that lay in the teachings of Confucius, Mencius, and Hsun-tzu grew into a full-fledged philosophy that included metaphysical interpretations of nature and humanity. That was largely in response to the impressive systems that Buddhism, with its Mahayana doctrines of emptiness and the Buddha's cosmic body (*dharmakaya*), and to a lesser extent Taoism had developed. To Confucius's ethics the neo-Confucians added an explanation of all reality. They accepted the ancient world view, granting an important place to sacrifices for the state and the family. As well, they accepted the moral supremacy of the sage, whose virtuous power might move society or even nature. But they went on and reasoned the sort of reality that nature must be if the sacrifices or the sages were to be efficacious. This neo-Confucian development gave the Sung rulers and their successors a doctrine that buttressed their practical preference for Confucian ethics.

The neo-Confucian philosophy of nature that gained the most adherents involved the interaction of two elements, principle and ether. Ether, or breath, was the basis of the material universe. All solid things condensed out of ether and eventually dissolved back into it.[46] In the dynamic phases of this cycle, ether was an ultimate form of yang. In the still phases, it was the ultimate form of yin. The neo-Confucian view of material nature therefore preserved the tension of dualities—of hot and cold, male and female, light and dark—that had always fascinated the Chinese. One reason for the acceptance of neo-Confucianism, in fact, was that it appeared as just a modern version of the ancient patrimony. The second element in nature's dualism, principle, etymologically related to the veins in jade or the grain in wood. It was the *pattern* running through all material things, their direction and purpose. If you opposed principle (went against the grain), all things became difficult. In terms of cognitional theory, the neo-Confucians invoked principle to explain the mind's ability to move from the known to the unknown. They also used it to ground the mind's appreciation of the connectedness of things. Principle was considered to be innate in human beings—it was nature's inborn guidance. The main task of human maturation and education was to remove the impediments that kept people from perceiving their principle. This task implied a sort of asceticism or moral diligence, sometimes involving meditation and self-denial.

Finally, the neo-Confucians tried to assimilate the folk aspect of Confucianism by finding a place for the spirits. They preferred not to venerate the ancestors' ghosts, but they allowed that *shen* and *kuei* (the two traditional kinds of spirits) could be the stretching and contracting of ether. In that way, they could let the spirits work the planets, the stars, the mountains, the rivers, and so on. Once again, neo-Confucianism was less personal than the earlier traditions, but its new, rather rationalistic system stayed in touch with the old roots.

Chu Hsi (1130–1200 C.E.) was the master thinker who systematized these neo-Confucian ideas.[47] His predilection was sober analysis, a sort of scientific philosophy, and he concentrated on physical nature. Another more idealistic wing of the neo-Confucians took to the Ch'an stress on mind and tended to place principle in the context of a meditative, as well as an analytic, cultivation of reason. Because Chu Hsi's ideas became authoritative in such government-controlled areas as the civil service examinations, neo-Confucianism inculcated in the educated classes a realistic, affirmative view of material nature. However, it accepted meditation enough to stay competitive with Ch'an,[48] and it tried to stay open to such artistic movements as the magnificent Sung dynasty landscape painting.

Despite these metaphysical developments, neo-Confucianism retained a commitment to the traditional Confucian virtues associated with character building. The paramount virtue continued to be *jen.* The ideogram for *jen* represented a human being: *jen* is humaneness—what makes us human. We are not fully human simply by receiving life in a human form. Rather, our humanity depends upon community, human reciprocity.[49] *Jen* pointed in that direction. It connected with the Confucian golden rule of not doing to others what you would not want them to do to you. Against individualism, it implied that people have to live together helpfully, even lovingly. People have to cultivate their instinctive benevolence, their instinctive ability to put themselves in another's shoes. That cultivation was the primary educational task of Confucius and Mencius.

The neo-Confucians also kept the four other traditional virtues: *yi, li, chih,* and *hsin. Yi* meant duty or justice, and it signified what is right, what law and custom prescribe. Its context, therefore, was the Chinese culture's detailed specification of rights and obligations. Where *jen* undercut such formalities, giving justice its heart, *yi* took care of contractual exactitudes.

Li, which meant manners or propriety, was less exact than *yi.* To some extent it depended on learning, so Confucius tried to teach by word and example what a gentleman would do in various circumstances, but it also required instinct, breeding, or intuition. Handling authority over household servants, men in the fields, or subordinates in the civil service involved *li.* So, too, did deference to superiors, avoidance of ostentation, and a generally graceful style. *Li* therefore was the unguent that soothed all social friction. In a society that prohibited the display of hostile emotion, that insisted on a good "face," *li* was very important.

Chih (wisdom) was not a deep penetration of ultimate reality like the Buddhist *Prajna-paramita*; it depended on neither enlightenment nor mystical union with *Tao.* Rather, it was a prudent sense of right and wrong, decent and indecent, profitable and unprofitable that one could hope to gain by revering the ancients and attentive living. *Hsin* meant trustworthiness or good faith. It was related to *jen* insofar as what one trusts in another is his or her decency or humanity, but it pertained more to a person's reliability or dependability. A person of *hsin* was not flighty or capricious.

Some commentators consider these Confucian virtues moralistic or humanistic rather than religious. The virtues amounted to a secular sketch of what right living, living according to *Tao,* entailed. It is true that in neo-Confucian times *Tao,* the Way of Heaven, involved the ancestral clan leader or the overarching seer less than it had in pre-

axial or axial times; by the Sung dynasty, *Tao* was for many Confucians just a name for nature's rationality. Still, the difficulty of fully realizing the five virtues remained. So, too, did the character of the Way, if only because Taoists and Buddhists considered the Way sacred. Given our assumption that all ultimate concerns entail religion, neo-Confucian meditation and invocation of the Way and its argument that the five virtues expressed the Way suggest religion.

In summary, neo-Confucianism tried to update the Master's teaching for less anthropomorphic, more rational times. (Until the early twentieth century, though, the neo-Confucians honored Master Kung as a patron saint and endorsed a certain amount of popular ritual.) By acknowledging the power of the Buddhist and Taoist philosophies and incorporating some of their elements into neo-Confucian beliefs, the neo-Confucians expanded what had largely been an ethical code into a full philosophy of nature and humanity.[50]

The Communist Era

For over two millennia, the axial ideas and beliefs that we have described prevailed in China with amazing stability and consistency. (Indeed, Hans Steininger has said of Confucianism, "It is these ethics which even today we meet all over East Asia.")[51] Despite new dynasties, wars, changing artistic styles, and even dramatic new religions such as Buddhism and Christianity, the general culture perdured. In the family, the government bureaucracy, and the villages, the folk/Confucian tradition was especially solid.

However, that changed in the early twentieth century. From without, Western science and Western sociopolitical thought dealt it heavy blows; from within, the decay of the imperial government led to the birth of the republic in 1912. Belatedly, China entered the modern world. In the twentieth century, its ancient culture showed cracks and strains everywhere. As a result, Chinese religious traditions, especially Confucianism, came under strong attack. Identified with the old culture, they seemed out of place in the modern world. Since the "cultural renaissance" of 1917, China has tried to cast off its Confucian shackles; since the Communist takeover of 1949, China has espoused a program of ongoing revolution.[52]

The paramount figure in this program, of course, was Mao Tse-tung. Mao was born in 1893 in Hunan (a south-central province) of a "middle" peasant family (that is, not one of abject poverty). His father had little culture or education, and his mother was a devout Buddhist. Mao himself received a traditional primary school education, whose core was memorizing the Confucian classics. (As a result, he developed a profound distaste for Confucius.) He had to leave school when he was thirteen to work the land, but prompted by his desire for more education, he ran away and enrolled in a modern high school. There he first encountered Western authors who challenged traditional Chinese culture. (At that time many educated Chinese felt humiliated by their defeat by the British in the Opium War of 1839–42, their defeat by the Japanese in 1895, and the repression of their Boxer Uprising in 1900 by a coalition of mainly Western powers. In the opinion of biographer Stuart Shram, Mao probably saw China's need to gain respect in the international community more clearly than he saw its internal needs.)[53]

During his student days in Hunan, Mao gradually came under the influence of socialist and revolutionary writers. He was at Changsha during the revolutionary battles of 1911, but his military participation there was probably slight. In school, though, he had to confront the intellectual turmoil of a country that had abolished its traditional examination system (the backbone of its educational structure) in 1905. Perhaps as a result, from 1913 to 1918 he apparently studied mainly on his own. He read Western authors, did some teaching, and edged toward a career of political activism.

The May 4, 1919, demonstrations against the Japanese intensified his commitment to Chinese self-determination, and the news coming out of now-Communist Russia began to color his thought. By 1920 he was a dedicated political activist, engaged in publishing and organizing, although what he was against was clearer than what he was for. He was against a class structure that oppressed peasants, workers, and women and against Chinese lowliness in the world of nations. He was vaguely for a revolution or new regime that would remove these evils.

Slowly Mao adopted a more positive program due to increased engagement with the developing Chinese Communist party, increased knowledge of developments in Russia, and then years as a guerrilla soldier. Before long, Mao was a convert to Marxism-Leninism. He joined the Chinese Communist party in 1921, took part in the Communist collaboration with Chiang Kai-shek's Kuomintang party until 1926, and then led Communist forces that opposed Chiang. By 1935 Mao was in charge of the Communist party and engaged in what became his legendary "long march." Through World War II the Communists and the Kuomintang collaborated uneasily against the Japanese; after the war the final conflict with Chiang led to the Communist takeover in 1949. Throughout this period Mao pursued the twofold career of military general and political theoretician. While gaining power he collaborated with the Russians, but he eventually decided that China had to go its own way. The result was a massive experiment in agrarian reform, enfranchising the lower classes, and trying to control economics by Marxist-Leninist and Maoist dogma.

The reason for this brief biographical sketch of Mao is that he was the most important figure in China's break with tradition and plunge into modernity. Influenced by the Confucian classics and Buddhism, he nevertheless repudiated them both. On the surface at least, Maoism took shape as a secular humanism—a system that referred to nothing more absolute than "the people." Some of its doctrines and programs dramatically changed the life of the people. The women's movement, for instance, and the related changes in the marriage law raised an entire segment of the population from subjection to near equality.[54] By stressing agricultural production, local health care, and "cellular" local government, Chinese Communism has become an even more grandiose socialist experiment than the Russian.

As part of the program instituting these changes, Mao's party denounced religion. Instead of gods and sacrifices, it offered self-reliance, hard work, and the mystique that the people united are invincible. Temples became government property, religious professionals were persecuted, and religious literature was derided or proscribed. The party likewise attacked the Confucian classics, virtues, and traditions. Throughout, its goal was to destroy the old class society and make a new people with one will and one future.

However, as one might expect, religion and tradition died harder than the Communists had hoped. In the rural regions, peasant traditions continued to have great influence. Among the intellectuals, conforming to the party line resulted in rather wooden, if not second-class, philosophy, science, and art. According to R. J. Lifton,[55] Mao himself ruminated on immortality in his last years, for he saw the problem of keeping the revolution "green"—retrieving for a new generation the experiences of the long march and the other peak events that had united the wills of the founding generation.

Something of that concern comes through in the last of Mao's poems.[56] "Two Birds," supposedly written in 1965, contrasts a sparrow, concerned only with beef-filled goulash, with a soaring roc that sees how the world is turning upside down. The options, Mao seems to say, are settling down in material comfort and keeping the revolution green. Many commentators have seen in Mao's sporadic activism (periods of stability followed by upheavals such as the Cultural Revolution) an effort to ward off stagnation.

Whether the constant call to renew revolutionary fervor will continue now that Mao has died is hard to predict. Likely the cult of the leader, which reached impressive proportions under Mao, will diminish. This cult developed prayers and hymns that treated Mao not only as a military and political leader and a great father figure but also as a sort of saviour. Individual needs, nationalistic pride, and other psychic forces can combine to surprising effect. At least, they suggest that religious fires still burn at the Chinese foundation.

STRUCTURAL ANALYSIS

Nature

All ancient societies lived deep in what we have called the cosmological myth, and China was no exception.[57] However, China did not have India's tendency to call sensory experience into question. Throughout its axial period, China's attitude was that nature is utterly real—more primordial than human beings. After the axial period, when Buddhism had a deep effect, native Chinese thought and the dharma were joined in more than a marriage of convenience. For instance, the Ch'an and Hua-yen schools translated the Mahayana philosophy of emptiness into a Chinese version of the theory that nirvana is identical with samsara. Furthermore, although Buddhist devotional sects among the masses drew attention to the heavenly Pure Land, they also described the Pure Land as a present reality. Overall, then, nature bulked large and unquestioned. The vast majority of Chinese doubted neither its reality nor its ultimacy. If there had been a question of subordinating one of the four dimensions of reality (nature, society, self, and divinity), nature would have been the last to go.

Physical reality took form through

Tao. Tao was the most basic force holding nature together. To be sure, the *Tao* most to the fore here is that which humans can name. The nameless *Tao* (which to Lao-tzu was the more real) was too vast, too primordial, too womblike for humans to grasp. It was so unlimited as to be somewhat beyond the world, so full or complete as to be beyond our comprehension.

So, it was the worldly Way—the cause of the seasons, the peculiarities of history, the laws of gravity and the tides—that dominated most Chinese reflection on nature. Most Chinese reflection on nature concerned manifest entities, patterns and forces that affected human beings. The other latent *Tao* was only the intuition of an intellectual, indeed of a mystical, elite. Not only could that *Tao* not be named, it could not be brought under human control. Consequently, it was the best candidate in pre-Buddhist Chinese thought for the mystery whose uncontrollability is our primary indication that something more powerful and basic than what we see is at the origin of things.

Tao, it follows, was both Logos and mother. As Logos, it was the reasonable pattern, the intelligence running through nature. As mother, it was the source of all things. Neither being nor nonbeing, the maternal *Tao* existed in a realm of its own. Yet this transcendent realm was also the basis for all the other realms of nature. The fish, waters, clouds, trees, mud, dung, and other elements of observable reality existed by *Tao*. Both the manner in which they existed and the fact that they existed implied this ultimate. So *Tao* functioned as the within and the without. Not many Chinese reasoned in this somewhat relentless way, but their more poetic and circular descriptions take us to such conclusions. Nature had a sense and a mystery, and this sense finally owed to its mystery. The pregnant word *Tao* signified both.

Throughout Chinese history, *Tao* retained this richness. Confucians and Buddhists used it to express their understanding of nature, as did Taoists themselves. Frequently *Tao* was associated with heaven

(t'ien), which often gave it a sacred aspect. Originally heaven was the overseer (a notion that the Chinese shared with Indians and Near Easterners). There was nothing that heaven did not notice and record. Heaven itself, though, never took on personal features among the Chinese. No father with a white beard, no Apollo with a dashing chariot became its emblem. Neither the sun nor the moon solicited reverence as the primary form of heaven. If anything, the sky itself, broad and indistinct, was the focus of Chinese devotion.

Opposite to the sky was the earth. Yet the earth seldom was viewed maternally, as it was by many ancient peoples. The Chinese acknowledged the mysteries of vegetation, seasonal changes, the fallow and the productive, and they touched their newborns to the earth in recognition of their origin. But the maternal aspect of nature's bounty they attributed more to *Tao* than to the earth. Perhaps they were more attuned to pattern and flow than to dirt-bound production. (Or perhaps we are speaking mainly about the beliefs of poets and intellectuals, whose writings shape our impressions overmuch.)

In any event, Lao-tzu, Chuang-tzu, and the Buddhists consistently invested nature with an aura of ultimacy and preferred to bow before *Tao*. For instance, Chuang-tzu's Great Clod is more than mother earth. Returning to the Clod at death keeps one in a universal rhythm. The Great Clod is the material system, the massive lump, that *Tao* turns. Similarly, Buddhist landscapers and gardeners went beyond mother earth to Suchness, Buddha-nature, or emptiness for their inspiration. Although the Japanese developed the aesthetic resulting from this inspiration more fully, it first came from China.

Folk Views

More mundane matters—such as yin and yang, the five dynamic qualities, and the ghosts and helping spirits—absorbed the masses. These concepts rendered Chinese nature lively.[58] Of course, virtually all ancient peoples thought of nature as alive. Although the Chinese stressed the cult of ancestor spirits more than comparable peoples, such veneration was yet present among other peoples. Indian Buddhists, for instance, thought that the dead would turn malevolent unless the living venerated them.

Chinese folk religion is also distinctive (although, again, not unique) in its concern for the compass directions. The geomancy of *feng-shui* is a clear expression of Chinese emphasis on nature's four directions. Of course, other peoples were concerned with directions; Native Americans made a great deal of the four geographic directions, while early civilized peoples such as the Egyptians built their temples with great concern for their orientation toward the sun. However, China carried this concern to a high art. Even for the average person, the angle of the wind or the shape of the terrain was magically influential.

Chinese divination expressed another set of naturalistic assumptions. The *I Ching*, for instance, elaborated upon the belief that yin-yang components shape human participation in nature's course of events. Like the African diviner who studied the patterns of chits in a magical basket, the Chinese fortune-teller believed that numbers and designs expressed nature's coherence. In popular Chinese religion, then, there was a primal sense that nature coordinates with mind. That sense did not develop to the point of control over nature as it would have in science, but for Chinese diviners, astrologers, and even fortune-tellers, this sense had great mythic power.

Such a mythic mentality may largely derive from a deep appreciation of what might be. Anything that is not contradictory might be. Therefore, anything noncontradictory can, under the pressure of imaginative suggestion, be accepted as something that is or that soon will be. From Laetrile to the stock market, we can see the same dynamics at work in late twentieth-century America.

In the *I Ching's* patterns of broken and unbroken lines, Chinese diviners were moved by the powerful human tendency to blur the distinction between what might be and what is, between the imaginable and the real. The interest motivating mathematicians, physicists, novelists, and theologians is little different from this tendency. The creative imagination uncovers realities much better than the imagination of the marketplace. The diviners were better in that they made both natural and human events coherent, even elegant.[59]

The place of human beings in Chinese nature, despite the diviners' claims that humans can read the signs of nature's processes, was rather humble. China was not a land where conquerors of heaven were exalted or where intellectuals identified the human spirit with an absolute spirit (exceptions might have existed among the Taoists and Buddhists). Throughout Chinese history humans have been considered rather insignificant compared with nature.

We can feel this mood in Chinese art. The tiny human figures in landscape paintings, for instance, contrast markedly with Western portraiture. In much Western religious art, even when divinity is clearly the paramount power, divinity gathers a people or incarnates a word. When Taoists or Buddhists correlated human beings with *Tao* or Buddha-nature, human beings came out small. The way of the wise, therefore, was indirect and nonassertive. Enlightenment involved losing the self, recognizing the fallacy of "I." In addition to the social forces that predominated over the self, there was a more comprehensive dominance by nature. Whether through Taoist return to the elements or Buddhist transmigration, the self was ever on the verge of slipping back into an unconscious, purely natural process. Since natural processes were the action on center stage, human figures were bound to be of marginal significance.

Nature in Buddhism

Richard Mather has shown that the concept of nirvana only won acceptance in

China after the Buddhists modified it considerably.[60] At the outset, ultimate Buddhist reality seemed wholly contradictory to Chinese concreteness. Thus, Chinese Buddhists accomplished a rather thorough cross-cultural translation. They had predecessors in the Indian Mahayanists, who identified samsara with nirvana, but the Mahayanists were far more abstract than the Chinese. Indeed, Ch'an probably became the most successful of the sects rooted in Mahayana metaphysics because it most thoroughly domesticated nirvana. Little interested in words or speculations, Ch'an focused on meditation, by which one might experience nirvana. It also stressed physical work, art, and ritual that deemphasized dualistic thinking. This deemphasis is more familiar to Western readers in its Japanese form, but it had a Chinese beginning.[61]

So the radical Buddha-nature (whether as emptiness or as mind-only) found in Ch'an a natural form. It could be the essence of all physical things, so present that one need not flee the world nor even close one's eyes to experience it. Since meditation expresses this conviction through the bodily postures that one assumes, one has only to sit squarely in the midst of natural reality and focus on its is-ness. (Not incidentally, one does not close one's eyes. The proper focus is neither a direction within nor a withdrawal to fix on the passing mental stream. In Ch'an it is a gaze with eyes open toward the end of one's nose.) The objective is to see without reasoning the reality that is right here. Such seeing should not focus on particulars, or concern itself with colors and forms. Rather, it should appreciate reality's simple oneness by not making distinctions. When such appreciation flowers, there is enlightenment: "I came to realize clearly that Mind is no other than mountains and rivers and the great wide earth, the sun and the moon and the stars."[62]

Society

Historically, China used Confucianism as its binding social force, and Confucianism thoroughly subordinated individuals to the community. Consequently, the Chinese individual felt inserted not only into a nature more impressive than the self but also into a society greater than its parts. Further, the great Confucian thinkers based their theory of ideal social relationships on legendary rulers of the past. Such rulers embodied the social *Tao*. Their way, then, was a paradigm that ordered society by exemplary morality. Somewhat magically, the virtue *(te)* that went out from the legendary kings and dukes brought those it touched into harmony, at least according to Confucianism.

The Confucian mythic history evidences the common ancient notion of sacred kingship. Because the ruler stands at the peak of the human pyramid, he can conduct heaven's governing power to earth. The Chinese king manifested this holy mediating role by offering sacrifices to the gods of heaven and earth. On occasion, he sacrificed human beings.[63]

The imperial cult, consequently, was the keystone in the Chinese social edifice, and the Confucian notion of *li* (propriety) applied especially to the punctilious execution of its ceremonies. To know the music and ritual appropriate to different occasions was the mark of a high gentleman. In fact, from this cultic center radiated something religious that touched all social relationships. Since human activities related to heaven, they partook of cultic propriety. By maintaining a harmonious family, for instance, individuals contributed to the most important order, that between natural divinity and humanity.

The harmony that the Confucians encouraged, though it extended to all aspects of social life,[64] expressed itself most importantly in its rating of key human relationships. It rated men over women (and so pictured marriage not as a partnership but as the wife's servitude to the husband). It rated children (among whom the eldest son was the plum) distinctly inferior to the parents—so much so that obedience and service toward the parents (most importantly toward the father) dominated the lives of children. Likewise, rulers were rated over subjects, masters over peasants, and, to a lesser extent, elder brothers over younger brothers.

In logical extension of their veneration of the past, the Chinese honored ancient ancestors more than more recent ones, and they rated children according to the order of their birth. Surely some parents loved a younger son more than an elder son or a gracious girl more than a mulish boy, but in determining the important matter of inheritance, age was the sole standard. In these and many other ways, Chinese society looked backwards. The past was the age of paradigms; the elderly were the fonts of wisdom. The axial masters of Chinese political thought give little evidence of celebrating youth or brave new worlds.

Social space was similarly static. From the ruler's key connection to heaven, the social classes descended in clearly defined ranks with little egalitarian or democratic moderation. The Confucians especially felt that the rank of a person was important. One said quite different things to a fellow noble riding in a hunting carriage than to the carriage driver. A person of breeding knew and respected such differences. If Confucius and Mencius themselves are representative, such a person was almost prickly about his social rights.

For example, the master would not visit just anyone, and for a pupil to come into town and not quickly pay a visit of homage was a serious slight. Somewhat like Plato, the Confucian master protected his dignity and honor. Perhaps surprisingly, the Confucians turned their insistence on moral worth into a partial break with the cosmological myth (and with sacred kingship). Implicit in their exaltation of virtue over external station was a turn to the wisdom of the sage—a turn from cosmology to anthropology.[65]

Women's Status

Among the Confucians, a peasant or a woman was unlikely to find honor simply through interior excellence. In fact, of the three Chinese traditions, Confucianism was the most misogynistic. The woman's role in Confucianism was to obey and serve her parents, husband, and husband's parents. She was useless until she produced a male heir, and her premarital chastity and marital fidelity were more important than a man's. In some periods, obsession with female chastity became so great that society insisted upon total sexual segregation.[66]

Since a Chinese woman's destiny was early marriage, childbearing, and household duties, her education was minimal. She was not necessarily her husband's friend, confidante, or lover—males and courtesans could fulfill these roles. A Chinese woman was primarily her husband's source of sons. They were the reason for her marriage—indeed, for her sex. As a result, the ideal Chinese woman was retiring, silent, and fertile. Custom severely curtailed her freedoms, but never more cruelly than through foot binding. Mary Daly recently described this custom in graphic terms: "The Chinese ritual of footbinding was a thousand-year-old horror show in which women were grotesquely crippled from very early childhood. As Andrea Dworkin so vividly demonstrates, the hideous three-inch-long 'lotus' hooks—which in reality were odiferous, useless stumps—were the means by which the Chinese patriarchs saw to it that their girls and women would never 'run around.' "[67] However, there is anthropological evidence that many Chinese women overcame their submissive role by cleverly manipulating gossip so that abusive husbands or mothers-in-law would lose face.[68] Still, until the Communist takeover, women had no place in the political system and did very well if they merely outwitted it.

The Taoists were kinder to women and to the socially downtrodden generally. They were responsible for curtailing the murder of female infants by exposure, and their more positive regard for female symbols as examples of how the *Tao* worked upgraded femininity.[69] This was not an unmixed blessing, since it involved the "strength" of the one who was submissive and the manipulative power of the one who got herself mounted. Still, by bestowing feminine or maternal attributes on the *Tao* itself, the Taoists made femininity intrinsic to ultimate reality.[70]

Further, the Taoist political system, based on *wu-wei*, did not value force. In this Taoists were like the Confucians, agreeing that virtue and example produce social prosperity. (Radical philosophical Taoists, though, challenged the notion of virtue.) Also, the Taoists kept alive the paradox that is important to spiritual vitality. Chuang-tzu observed that many members of the upper class were miserable. By comparison, some poor people lived wholesome lives close to *Tao*. By such an awareness of the paradox of riches and poverty, Taoists prevented Confucian formalism from paralyzing Chinese society. So long as China honored Taoist poetry and Taoist retirement, *life* and *death* remained ambivalent terms.

Buddhist Social Influence

Buddhism downplayed social differences in another way. By teaching that the Buddha-nature is present in all reality, it said that equality is more basic than social differentiation. The monastic sangha institutionalized this equality. It would be naive to think that background or wealth played no part in monks' evaluations of one another, but the sangha was governed by a monastic code that underplayed wealth and severely limited monks' possessions.

Furthermore, during many periods in Chinese history, the sangha was genuinely spiritual. That is, its actual raison d'être was religious growth. In such times, the only "aristocracy" was determined by spiritual insight. For instance, though Hui-neng, who became the sixth Ch'an patriarch, was born poor (and, according to legend, brought up illiterate), his spiritual gifts mattered far more. Because he was religiously apt, a reading of the Diamond Sutra opened his mind to

Buddha's light. After enlightenment, his peasant origins became insignificant.

The Buddhist sangha also improved the lot of women. It offered an alternative to early marriage and the strict confinement of the woman's family role. In the sangha a woman did not have full control of her life, but she did often have more peer support and female friendship than she could have in the outside world. In fact, Confucian traditionalists hated Buddhist nuns for their influence on other women. By telling women there were alternatives to wifely subjection, the nuns supposedly sowed seeds of discontent. Besides the jealousy of their Confucian and Taoist rivals, then, and the sometimes warranted outrage at their extensive landholdings, the Buddhists suffered persecution because they offered attractive alternatives to traditional Chinese family and social structures. The government frequently forced monks and nuns back into lay life during a time of purge to force them back into traditional social patterns.

Thus, although persecution was not the norm, Buddhists and other effective religionists often felt the controlling hands of the state. Formally, there was little independent religious authority. In times of peace, Buddhists and Taoists were left to go their own ways. When they perceived any threat, however, the rulers clamped down and made it clear that religion was a function of an integrated Chinese culture, not something outside of the culture that could set itself up as the critic of culture. As the Taoist revolutionary sects showed, the rulers had good grounds for their fears.

Thus, Chinese religion was what Yang has called "diffused."[71] Stronger by far than any institutional achievements was a pervasive sense of the supernatural. In good part because it propped the state against the potential rebellion that Taoism and Buddhism housed, Confucianism became the state orthodoxy. Taoism and Buddhism, by contrast, were always somewhat heterodox.[72]

Among the common people, an important function of religion was to shore up received culture and authority. Apart from advanced positions in Taoist and Buddhist thought, religion did not liberate the individual. In this sense, Chinese religion broke neither the cosmological myth nor what we might call the social myth (conceiving of the political community as being divine). Both nature and the state (or the local duchy during the many periods of fragmentation) preexisted the individual and predominated over him or her.

As a result, China had little sense that the human mind makes its own reality—little enlightenment, in the European sense. Neither by revelation nor by reason did Chinese culture gain a sophisticated sense of history (the one human spirit's unfolding through time) or philosophy (life arranged around this spirit's eros). Consequently, it remained closer to nature and more socially unified than later Western religious society did. The Chinese defined themselves by their land and their group. Happy to be the center of the earth, the Chinese empire regarded all outsiders as barbarians and as less than fully human. This attitude resulted because millennia of living within a shared myth of nature and society had wrought a very strong cultural identity. That was both Confucianism's triumph and its limitation.

Self

The Chinese view of the self has been indirectly indicated by our stress on the primacy of nature and society. Nevertheless, the Chinese experimented with various conceptions of the self, just as they experimented with gunpowder, acupuncture, and pottery. As Donald Munro has shown,[73] axial Chinese thought, both Confucian and Taoist, wrestled with the possibility that human beings are essentially equal (at least male human beings). The effect of this belief on the hierarchical structure of Confucianism is complex, but the Chinese concepts of *jen* and *li* (goodness and propriety) indicate that the Chinese sensed that all persons have something to share as a basis for mutual respect.

In the structure of society, then, the self had some right to acknowledgement. Despite one's subordination to the whole (or, in many cases, one's near slavery), the common person found in such an author as Mencius a champion of the self's essential goodness. Mencius counseled princes to take their people's welfare to heart; his counsel was clearly more than a pragmatic bit of advice about how to avoid rebellions.

Further, the Confucians exercised considerable care on the self's education, at least for the middle and upper classes. Their major motivation seems to have been societal needs (as opposed to the self's intrinsic dignity), but by stressing character formation, the Confucians had to probe what the self's substance and dignity were. They decided, with considerable prodding from Confucius himself, that the paramount human faculty was the inner mind. If one could act from this inner mind with clarity and dispassion, one could act humanely and civilly. The core of the Confucian view of the self, therefore, was a certain rationalism. Confucianism did not stress speculative reason (that which gives rise to abstract theory), since Confucianism was not concerned with the human capacity to illumine or be illumined by the Logos of nature, but it did stress practical reason or prudence. Laying aside passion and prejudice (which required self-control), the good Confucian could hope with experience to discern the appropriate and harmonizing course of action.

Either through reflection on history or further rumination on the mind, the Confucians eventually linked practical reason with the ancients' *Tao*. It is clear from the myths handed down that the foremost ancestors were persons of composed, effective good sense, which enhanced their people's common good and even prosperity. Because they were not venal or petty, the ancestors were able to lead by example—by radiating the power of *jen*.

On further reflection, the Confucians confirmed that the zenith of human achievement (which Confucius himself later came to epitomize) was such inner-directed action. In other words, the magisterial spirit feared no outer laws or sanctions. It was autonomous—it delighted in the good for its own sake. Though Confucius and Mencius both longed for public office, a major reason that neither ever achieved it was that neither would compromise his standards. Their uncompromising integrity became a lesson to disciples for centuries. When a devout Confucian observed an inhumane ruler, he felt more pity than envy.

The Taoist Self

The Taoists, who paid greater attention to the relationship between human consciousness and the cosmic *Tao*, produced a more paradoxical view of the self. They went against the Confucian standards of sagehood. Their masters were either cryptic eccentrics such as Chuang-tzu or magical "immortals" possessing paranormal powers. The cryptics' suspicion of human reason developed into a strong attack on logic and Confucian prudence. Logically, the *Chuang-tzu's* chapter on seeing things as equal suggests that the philosophical Taoists found conventional language and morality both arbitrary and relative.[74] Standard terms in Confucian discourse such as *great* and *small*, *good* and *bad* (which were also used in the Chinese linguistic analysis contemporary with Chuang-tzu) turned out to be wholly relative. In fact, the Taoists cast doubt on the entire realm of discursive reason, which plods along from premise to premise and often misses the whole. If one could argue either side of a proposition, as lawyers always have tended to do, one clearly was not in the realm of ultimate concern.

For the philosophical Taoists, the realm of ultimate concern pivoted on *Tao*. They attempted to reach that realm by meditation and *wu-wei*. Consequently, they individualized the self more than the Confucians did. The Confucians, of course, realized that the talents of people differ, including the talent to reach the still inner reason from which humane action emanates. But the Taoists went beyond reason

itself, encouraging each person to write his or her own script. What was important was that one write to the tune of the *Tao*. What the specific story was, how one chose to enact *Tao's* inspiration, was secondary.

One of Taoism's greatest influences on Buddhism shows in Ch'an's acceptance of this individualism. Placing little stock in doctrines or formulas, the master determined enlightenment by the pupil's whole bearing. The flash of an eye, the slash of a sword—a single gesture could indicate an enlightened being. One could even "slay the Buddha"—throw off all traditional guidance—if one had reached the goal. To the unenlightened majority, one's actions and life would be strange. Quite literally, one would be eccentric. But if the *Tao* or Buddhanature really became the self's treasure, such eccentricity was but the near side of freedom.

The religious Taoists saw the self as a mortal physical body. Therefore, by the several "hygienic" regimes mentioned, they tried to prolong physical life. As a result, religious Taoists experimented with yogic practices, many of them in the vein of Indian *kundalini* or Tibetan Tantrism, both of which viewed the body as a repository of energy centers.[75] Depending on the particular interest of a religious Taoist group, the self might focus on breath or semen or some other quintessence.

Further, most Taoists regarded the body as a warehouse of tiny gods, each in charge of a particular bodily part. In yogic exercise the adept was to visualize the god in charge of the spleen or the heart, and so gain health or blessing there. By their quests for immortality (in the sense of continued physical existence), then, the religious Taoists simultaneously underscored mortality and suggested that humans can defeat death. They did not distinguish an immaterial part of the self as candidate for such survival, but they did probe the relations between contemplative ecstasy and nature's apparent immortality.[76]

In such magical concerns, which show numerous shamanist motifs, the religious Taoists exhibited aspects of ancient folk religion. Their "immortals" owed a good deal to the revered ancestors of the clans, who continued on in a real and effective, if indistinct, existence after death. Also, the religious Taoists exploited the folk aspects in the theory of yin and yang (which worked out to a doctrine of two souls—*p'o* and *hun*). Much of the rationale for the ancient burial rites lay in efforts to assure that the yin soul not become an avenging ghost. The yang soul, if survivors treated it well, would become a heavenly source of blessings. In that way, the folk view of the self involved a certain dualism, and when the Taoists spoke of immortality, many of the common people probably understood them as trying to maximize the happiness of the yang soul.

Karma and No-Self

Through Buddhism, China received a heavy dose of belief in karma. That was most effective in the popular Buddhist sects, among which Pure Land headed the list, but it entered the general religious stream, influencing even those who rarely participated in Buddhist rites. Karma, of course, meant that the self was immersed in a system of rewards and punishments. All its actions, good or bad, had their inevitable effects. Past lives pressed upon the present, and the present was but a prelude to a future life. In popular Buddhism, this doctrine encouraged a sort of bookkeeping. Sometimes quite formally, with ledgers and numbers, Buddhists tried to calculate their karmic situation and plan out a better destiny. More generally, the concept of karma prompted the belief that the self's present existence was a trial that would be evaluated at death. How heavily this sense of trial pressed on the average person is hard to say. Combined with the rather lurid popular pictures of the several hells awaiting the wicked, though, karma probably sparked its share of nightmares.

The philosophical and meditative Chinese Buddhist sects accepted the traditional doctrine of no-self. So, the Chinese thinkers who followed Madhyamika or Yogacara speculation agreed that emptiness or mind-only implied an effort to rout the illusion of a permanent personal identity. To become part of the oneness of Buddha-nature and join the dance of the dharmas, the individual had to annihilate samsaric misconceptions about the substantiality of the self. The Chinese appear to have been more concrete than the Indians in such efforts. That is, where the Indians often reasoned over the self very closely, trying by dialectics to understand the illusion of selfhood, the Chinese tried to get the self to see reality's totality. Such seems to be the intent of pictures that T'ien-t'ai and Hua-yen masters drew, as well as the intent of the more radical techniques of Ch'an. Bodhidharma's "just sitting" and "wall gazing," for example, were exercises designed to make clear that only Buddha-nature is real.

Overall, these various Chinese religious views of the self made for considerable confusion and complexity. Despite Buddhist philosophical influence, the average person through Chinese history apparently did not doubt the reality of his or her self. The educational and governmental establishments in most periods were shaped by the Confucian ideal of a sober, restrained, altruistic personality. One aimed at discipline and grace, at becoming a source of wisdom. The force that shaped the Confucian self was political in the sense that living together with family members and fellow citizens rather than in isolation was the norm. Only the few artistic and religious professionals seem to have broken this pattern. For them Taoist or Buddhist contemplative solitude stressed the mystery of the self insofar as the self was where the *Tao* or Buddha-nature most directly manifested itself. According to Lao-tzu, one would find *Tao* by shutting the "doors" (the senses) and going within.

The conceptions of the self that were presented in the three high traditions blurred when they entered the common culture. Most of the people came to Confucianism, Buddhism, or Taoism from its superstitious or magical side. So the Confucian scholar became a sort of wonder worker, the Buddhist bodhisattva glamorized holiness, and the Taoist "immortal" represented victory over death. From the ancient spirit world, ancestors and ghosts said that being conscious meant participating in a cosmos that was alive, a system of heavens and hells that impinged on the present.

Divinity

China was only vaguely aware of sacred powers and ultimate reality, lacking a monotheistic or even a henotheistic tradition. At most, certain high points of Buddhist and Taoist speculation, and to a lesser extent of Confucian speculation, indicated a monism—a single, impersonal principle that is the inmost reality of all beings. As we have seen, the first stirrings of religious consciousness probably apotheosized (deified) the clan founder, making him the "face" of over-watching Heaven. As nature became better understood, however, heaven became less personal as the general symbol of the vast sky. Earth, in association with a maternal *Tao*, took on overtones of a Great Mother, but with less of the humanity and intimacy that other cultures developed.

For most Chinese throughout history, nature has been the effective divinity. In other words, nature and divinity ran together. The physical world itself was something sacred and mysterious. This world intimated something beyond itself that was grasped by those who saw nature with mystic clarity, but the majority at best sensed this something beyond only vaguely. To sense clearly the *Tao* that cannot be named, one must reject the adequacy of all things nameable. Realizing that water, air, fire, wood, earth, yang, yin, and so on do not explain the totality of heaven and earth, the mind senses that the ultimate is of a different order. It is without the limitations that characterize all the primal elements. As such, it must dwell in obscurity, too full or great or bright for mere human intelligence. Philosophical Taoism and Buddhism but intimate that line of thought.

A muted reference to ultimacy probably plays in Confucius's laconic references to heaven. For the most part, the Master refrained from speculating about heavenly things. Like Alexander Pope, he believed that "the proper study of man is man." But Confucius's reverence toward the sacrifice to heaven suggests that, had such a modern Western notion been available to him, he would not have explained the sacrifice as a humanistic means of social bonding. Rather, he probably saw a link between the ancients' *Tao* and the way of sacred nature, and so viewed the sacrifice as humanity's chance to align itself with the power that most mattered, the power behind all life and all things.

Confucius made heaven the ultimate sanction for his ethical program. He believed that those who pay full court to the stove have no recourse when they fail. The true judge of success and failure must be more stable than a human creation. Against the Taoist belief that heaven treats all creatures as straw dogs, Confucius believed that heaven is the great champion of *yi* (justice). We go well beyond Confucius himself if we work this commitment to heaven into a theology or a theodicy (a vindication of God's justice). Clearly, however, the Confucians justified their calls to virtue by appealing to suprahuman standards.

Buddhism, of course, addressed ultimacy more squarely. In the philosophical mainstream, an impersonal ultimate (whether nirvana, Buddha-nature, Suchness, or emptiness) held sway. This mainstream tended to be monistic. That is, it suggested that the ultimate is the single, really real existent. For the idealists, the accent was on the mentality of the ultimate. In their view, the many things that we perceive by sense are fraudulent because only spirit or mind finally makes something be. For the less idealistic schools, material things and ideas were equally fraudulent. To accept the apparent plurality of either physical nature or consciousness was the folly of an unenlightened mind. The idealists were less concerned with physical nature than the

Figure 20   Lohan (arhat), Liao-Chin dynasty, tenth to thirteenth century, C.E. Nelson Gallery–Atkins Museum, Kansas City, Missouri (Nelson Fund).

its "otherness," even when they loved that otherness as something near and dear. Because of its great value, nirvana functioned as the philosophical Buddhists' divinity. Mainstream philosophy did not conceptualize it as a God or as something personal, although it did relate it to the holy power that makes things be. That power, Van der Leeuw has shown, is a constant in human conceptions of divinity.[77]

Buddhism also tends to speak of ultimacy as the Buddha's "body." In addition to the body of Sakyamuni, there were the dharma-body and the bliss-body. The dharma-body was an equivalent of Suchness, or the final metaphysical principle. It connoted a teaching (dharma) prescriptive of all reality itself—a sort of cosmic Logos. However, because this dharma-body had some connection with the physical body and the teaching of Sakyamuni, it somewhat personalized the Buddhist divinity. That did not make it a God, but it does indicate that Buddhism is not a strictly impersonal monism (let alone an antireligious humanism) as many interpreters conclude.

In popular Buddhism, such as Pure Land, some divinities had quite precise features. The Buddha of Light, Amitabha, had a "personality" rather like that of an Apollo or a Krishna. The reliance on such Buddhas as Amitabha, like the reliance on bodhisattvas or the goddess of mercy Kuan-yin, was definitely a theistic bhakti. Between devotee and divinity a personal bond of love grew up. Just as the goddess Tara personalized Tibetan Buddhist divinity, Kuan-yin gave Chinese Buddhists a motherly figure of comfort and mercy. (C. N. Tay, as we noted in the previous chapter, has described Kuan-yin as the cult of half Asia.)[78]

But if people rely on a mother goddess, they have a theistic deity at hand, even if they do not clearly distinguish it from other deities or from an impersonal natural force. In its popular religion, then, Chinese Buddhism offered an access to aspects of ultimate reality that Confucianism barely indicated. (Taoism is more complicated: The *Tao* was a mother, and religious sects made

nonidealists. By calling all dharmas empty, the followers of Madhyamika went directly to the rather worldly point of the wisdom-that-has-gone-beyond. By contrast, those who followed Yogacara idealism stayed apart from the physical world mentally.

All Buddhist schools, however, characterized ultimate reality indirectly. By the Buddha's own teaching, talk about the nature of nirvana was useless. Nirvana was not a void, not a nothingness. Chinese Buddhists could equal Hindus in calling nirvana being, bliss, and awareness. But they stressed

Lao-tzu into a cosmic principle.) The cult of Confucius himself qualifies this judgment somewhat, but overall the Buddhists offered the most personal concepts of divinity.

The beliefs of philosophical and religious Taoists, of course, must be distinguished. As we have seen, the philosophical Taoists, following Chuang-tzu and Lao-tzu, fixed on the cosmic Way. Often they seem to have invested it with divine attributes. For the philosophers, *Tao* was the source, the ultimate power, the model, and the prime value of the world. Inspiration from it, communion with it, and direction by it were the ways to wisdom, wholeness, and fulfillment.

Nonetheless, despite intuitions in Lao-tzu that *Tao* is beyond the physical world, philosophers tended to equate *Tao* with nature. The naturalistic symbolism they preferred suggests this, as does their unconcern with immortality or an afterlife. If *Tao* had been independent of nature, union with *Tao* should have generated thoughts about escaping the cycle of birth and death. In India, for instance, the *nirguna* (unmanifest) Brahman and the Buddhist ultimate led to doctrines of *moksha* and *nirvana* as human release. For Chuang-tzu and Lao-tzu, natural harmony in the present was all-important, and they paid little heed to future enjoyment of some otherworldly states. Consequently, the divinity of *Tao* was preeminently the undergirding and direction it gave cosmic nature.

Reaching back to prehistory, the religious Taoists conceived of a pantheon of divine forces, often giving them picturesque names and features. Furthermore, the goal of religious Taoist practices was to prolong life, and so religious Taoists ventured into alchemy and yoga, as well as voyages to the Lands of the Blessed (the Immortals). What they shared with their philosophical counterparts, however, was a characteristically Chinese concern with the body. Their ideal was

not an extinction of suffering humanity in nirvana, not a release in *moksha*, but a consolidation of vital powers so as to resist death. Their divinities, consequently, were gods who could help this process, or "immortals" (who probably spanned the often narrow gap between saints and gods) who had successfully accomplished such consolidation. In either case, they offered followers encouragement and models.

How did Chinese divinity appear in the popular amalgamation? Through ritualistic, emotional, and shamanic points of entry.[79] The prevailing magic in the popular mind, which was primarily interested in warding off evil fortune and attracting good, and the great importance of ancestor veneration gave ultimate reality a rainbow of colors. Ceremonies at the family hearth reaffirmed the clan by acknowledging the reality of its ancestors. Ceremonies in the fields, for building a new dwelling, or for curing someone seriously ill brought people face to face with spooky forces of life, luck, and disease. Shamans and mediums were the key figures, contacting spirits and ancestral souls. Diviners gave advice and told fortunes. The average person gathered talismans and totems, but also Buddhist and Taoist saints. The educated people patronized Confucius, but even they were open to other sacred figures who offered help. To say the least, then, the Chinese religious mind was syncretistic, and the study of folk religion, as recent studies suggest,[80] has to be very comprehensive.

However, most characteristic of China is its commitment to physical nature. It shares this with Japan and with many ancient peoples, but China most directed its various intimations of divinity toward nature. The *Tao*, the Chinese Buddha-nature, the field of spirits—these far outweighed personal qualities. At least as much as the American Indian Wakan Tanka, the Chinese divinity was the arc of the sky, the pulse of the earth, the life-force itself.

Study Questions

1. Can one sketch the outline of axial Chinese religion in terms of *Tao*?
2. What are the positive aspects of Chinese ritual propriety *(li)*?
3. What are the negative aspects of *wu-wei*?
4. Why were the ancestors such a potent symbol in popular Chinese religion?
5. Explain some of the likely assumptions and dynamics in Chinese divination.
6. If you meditate on the practice of foot binding, how do you picture Chinese social arrangements?
7. Why did philosophical Taoism long exist alongside religious Taoism, and how can one reconcile their different views of immortality?

Chapter Seven

JAPANESE RELIGION: TWENTY-FIVE KEY DATES

CA. 4500–250 B.C.E.	JOMON PERIOD: HUNTING AND GATHERING
CA. 660	JIMMU, TRADITIONAL FIRST EMPEROR
CA. 250 B.C.E.–250 C.E.	YAYOI PERIOD: BLENDING OF ETHNIC GROUPS
5 C.E.	BUILDING OF NATIONAL SHRINE AT ISE
285	CONFUCIANISM INTRODUCED
CA. 550	BUDDHISM INTRODUCED
594	BUDDHISM PROCLAIMED STATE RELIGION
645	TAIKA REFORM REMODELS JAPAN ON CHINESE LINES
712–720	COMPLETION OF SHINTO CHRONICLES
805–806	INTRODUCTION OF TENDAI AND SHINGON BUDDHIST SECTS
890	CULTURAL RENAISSANCE: NOVELS, LANDSCAPE PAINTING, POETRY
1175–1253	INTRODUCTION OF PURE LAND, ZEN, AND NICHIREN BUDDHIST SECTS

Japanese Religion

1333   CIVIL WAR

1549   FRANCIS XAVIER ARRIVES IN JAPAN

1600–1867   TOKUGAWA ERA: CONFUCIANISM PROSPERS, BUDDHISM CONTROLLED BY STATE

1646–1694   BASHO, LEADING BUDDHIST POET

1650   BEGINNING OF POPULAR LITERARY CULTURE

1730–1801   MOTOORI NORINAGA, LEADER OF SHINTO RENAISSANCE

1850   NEW RELIGIONS EMERGE

1854   ADMIRAL PERRY FORCES TRADE WITH WEST

1868–1871   MEIJI PERSECUTION OF BUDDHISM; SHINTO BROUGHT UNDER STATE CONTROL

1894–1905   SUCCESSFUL WARS WITH CHINA AND RUSSIA

1899   RELIGION FORBIDDEN IN PUBLIC SCHOOLS

1939   DEPARTMENT OF EDUCATION CONTROLS ALL RELIGIOUS BODIES

1945   JAPAN SURRENDERS IN WORLD WAR II; SHINTO DISESTABLISHED

To complete our survey of religions in East Asia, we move from China to Japan. Actually, much of what we have seen in China appears in Japan. We have already noted this, for instance, regarding Buddhism. In the main, the schools that the Chinese developed took root in Japan; furthermore, Confucianism had a strong impact. Nonetheless, Japan was never a passive recipient of Chinese culture. In religion, as in other spheres, it adapted the imported ideas so that they could grow on Japanese soil.

The major influence in the native Japanese tradition that forced such adaptations was Shinto, which was an aboriginal nature religion that became more clearly defined under the impact of Buddhism. Consequently, our historical survey focuses on Shinto and indicates how the traditions imported from China and later from the West transformed the Shinto tradition into the syncretistic religion that has characterized Japan through most of its history. In reviewing Japan's history, we will divide it into the major periods delineated by H. Byron Earhart: the ancient-formative, the medieval-elaborative, and the modern-reformative.[1]

APPEARANCE

In steamy mid-July we were sitting on a park bench in Tokyo, reflecting on how the Meiji shrine there compared with the Shinto shrines we had seen in Kyoto and Ise, when an elderly man, dressed in a kimono, approached to chat. He was a retired businessman come for his daily walk and swim in a pool near the shrine. We offered a chance for him to indulge his curiosity, practice his English, test Japanese-American relations (he had been in World War II), and, as it turned out, inform us what the Japanese way in religion really is. "You have one God," he rather incautiously pronounced. "We have thousands—eight hundred thousand, according to tradition. In this park many gods dwell. We come to enjoy the beauty and honor them." With much warmth and good cheer, he questioned us about our trip, and

then rambled off for his swim. Had we met a living Shintoist?

Perhaps, but answering this question exactly would require defining some terms. The man had not called himself or his people Shintoists, Buddhists, or anything else. He just used the pronoun *we*. The *we* indicates an ethnic solidarity which even traveling Japanese manifest. Despite the evidence that today's Japanese people are comprised of at least three racial strains, there has been enough time and isolation for those strains to merge into something distinctive. What these people hold in common overshadows their sects and individual religious traditions.

The 800 thousand gods conjure the Shinto *kami* (spirits or gods), but through history the Japanese have also honored a plethora of Buddhist divinities. Perhaps the most significant line in the man's little speech was: "We come to enjoy the beauty." In counterpoint to its industrial development, Japan retains a great love of natural beauty. Its gardens, parks, and pools are not merely props to sanity in the midst of bustle and smog. As places for aesthetic, religious, and recreational experience, they remain central in the people's spiritual life. At the Shinto (and Buddhist) shrines one glimpses the earliest Japanese Way that even today has its effect.

HISTORY

The Ancient-Formative Period

According to ethnologists, the people we now call the Japanese are a mixture of an indigenous people (the Ainu) and peoples from the Asiatic mainland and the southern islands. This mixture is one clue to the composite character of Japanese religion as well as to the general tolerance that has historically marked Japanese culture. The native religion goes back to the Japanese prehistoric period, which lasted until the early centuries C.E. Clay figurines that archeologists have excavated from this earliest Jomon period indicate a special concern with fertility.[2] As the hunting and gathering culture of the earliest period gave way to agriculture and village settlement, religious practices came to focus on agricultural festivals, revering the dead, and honoring the leaders of the ruling clans. According to the primitive mythology, which existed long before the written versions that date from the eighth century, such leaders were descendants of the deity—once again a version of sacred kingship.

However, the mythology and cult surrounding the ruling family were but part of the earliest Japanese religion. Research suggests that in the villages outside the leading families' influence, people probably conceived of a world similar to that of Siberian shamanists. That world has three layers. The middle is the realm of humans, where we have a measure of control, but the realms above and below, which spirit beings control, are far larger. The kami dwell in the high plain of heaven and are the objects of cultic worship; the spirits of the dead live below, condemned to a filthy region called Yomi.[3] (In some versions, the dead go to a land beyond the sea.) Apparently Yomi was especially important for the aristocrats' cult, which suggests not only a connection between folk and imperial religion but also the reason why Shinto came to stress ritual purification, especially from polluting contacts with the dead.

The Kami

The kami represented the sacred power involved in the principal concerns of prehistoric Japanese religion (kingship, burial of the dead, and ritual purification).[4] They were rather shadowy figures or spiritual forces who were wiser and more powerful than humans. From time to time, kami would descend to earth, especially if a human called them down and helped them assume a shape (in their own world the kami were shapeless). They were called down by means of *yorishiro*—tall, thin objects that attracted the kami. Pine trees and elongated rocks were typical *yorishiro*, and they suggest that the kami had phallic connotations. To a lesser extent, rocks of female shape also attracted the kami, and relics from the great

tombs of the third and fourth centuries—a profusion of mirrors, swords, and curved jewels—suggest that these artifacts also drew the kami. (Such objects became part of the imperial regalia.)

Because the kami held key information about human destiny, it was important to call them down into human consciousness. That occurred through the kami's possession of shamans or mediums. Most of the early shamans *(miko)* were women, and they functioned in both the aristocratic and the popular cults. Ichiro Hori has shown that female shamans persisted throughout Japanese history.[5] The *miko* were quite important to society. They tended to band together and travel a circuit of villages, primarily to act as mediums for contact with the dead but also to serve as diviners and oracles. They also ministered to spiritual and physical ills, which popular culture largely attributed to malign spirits. As a result, the *miko* developed both a poetic and a pharmacological lore. In composing songs and dances to accompany their ministrations, they contributed a great deal to the formation of traditional Japanese dance, theater, balladry, and puppetry.

Essentially, the kami were the forces of nature. They impressed the Japanese ancient mind, as they impressed the ancient mind elsewhere, by their striking power. Sensitive individuals could contact them, but the kami remained rather wild and unpredictable. Later, Shinto shrines stressed natural groves of tall trees and founders of religious cults were often possessed by spirits. As the early mythology shows, however, the kami remained in charge.

As the eighth-century chronicles, the *Kojiki* and *Nihon-shoki*, have preserved it, Japanese mythology adapted to Chinese influences early on. For example, redactors regularly changed the Japanese sacred number 8 to the Chinese sacred number 9,[6] and they were influenced by the Chinese cosmogonic myths. The result was a creation account in which the world began as a fusion of heaven and earth in an unformed, egg-shaped mass that contained all the forces of life. Gradually the purer parts separated and ascended to heaven, while the grosser portions descended and became the earth.

Shinto Mythology

Chinese influence disappears when the chronicles come to the myths of the kami's origin and to the related question of how the Japanese islands came to be. The first kami god was a reed shoot that formed between heaven and earth; he established the first land. Six generations later, the divine creator couple, Izanagi and Izanami, arose by spontaneous generation. They married and produced the creations that followed.

For instance, heaven commanded Izanagi and Izanami to solidify the earth, which hitherto had been only a mass of brine. Standing on a bridge between heaven and the briny mass, they lowered a jeweled spear and churned the brine. When they lifted the spear, drops fell, solidified, and became the first island. The couple descended to this island, erected a heavenly pillar (the typical shamanistic connector to heaven), and proceeded to procreate. The account of their interaction is both amusing and revealing:

Now the male deity turning by the left, and the female deity by the right, they went around the pillar of the land separately. When they met together on one side, the female deity spoke first and said: "How delightful! I have met with a lovely youth." The male deity was displeased, and said: "I am a man, and by right should have spoken first. How is it that on the contrary thou, a woman, should have been the first to speak? This was unlucky. Let us go round again." Upon this the two deities went back, and having met anew, this time the male deity spoke first, and said: "How delightful! I have met a lovely maiden."[7]

In tortuous logic, the myth describes the fate of the first two. Izanami died giving birth to fire, and Izanagi followed her to the underworld. Izanagi then produced many deities in an effort to purify himself of the pollution of the underworld. By washing his left eye he produced the sun-goddess Amaterasu, and by washing his right eye he produced the moon-god. When he washed his nose he produced the wind-god Susanoo. In this story of descent to the underworld and divine creation, scholars see an expression of the aboriginal Japanese fears of death and rites of purification. The sun-goddess, who became the supreme being of the Yamato clan, a powerful Japanese family, and the focus of the clan's cultic center at Ise, presided over the land of fertility and life. Opposing her was the domain of darkness and death. Rituals were performed to keep darkness and death from afflicting sunny fertility—harvests, human procreation, and so on. As Izanagi purified himself of death by plunging into the sea, the Japanese throughout their history have used salt as a prophylactic. People still scatter it around the house after a funeral, place it at the edge of a well, set a little cake of it by a door jamb, and even scatter it before the bulging sumo wrestler as he advances toward his opponent.[8]

In subsequent myths, Amaterasu and Susanoo have numerous adventures arising from the antagonism between the life-giving sun and the withering wind. These figures also demonstrate the trickster and noble sides of natural divinity. Susanoo, the trickster, committed "heavenly offenses" that later became a focus of ritual purification: He broke the irrigation channels for the imperial rice field that Amaterasu had set up; he flayed a piebald colt and flung it into the imperial hall; and, worst of all, he excreted on the goddess's imperial throne. Unaware, she "went straight there and took her seat. Accordingly, the Sun Goddess drew herself up and was sickened."[9] These offenses reflect practical problems of an agricultural society (respecting others' fields), cultic problems (a sacrificial colt was probably supposed to be of a single color and not be flayed), and speculation on the tension between divine forces of nature.

From these and other materials in the earliest chronicles, it is clear that the ancient-formative period of Japanese history centered on natural forces, some of which were anthropomorphized. In the background were the kami, whom we may consider as foci of divine power. Anything striking or powerful could be a kami. To relate themselves to the natural world, the early Japanese told stories of their love for their beautiful islands (worthy of being the center of creation) and of the divine descent of their rulers. The fact that Amaterasu is a sun-goddess suggests an early matriarchy, as does the fact that kingship only came with the Taika reforms of 645C.E. Shinto maintained the divinity of the emperor until the mid-twentieth century, when the victorious allies forced the emperor to renounce his claims.

Buddhism sometimes eclipsed Shinto, but the native tradition always lay ready to reassert itself. Whenever there was a stimulus to depreciate foreign influences and exalt native ones, Shinto quickly bounced back. Also, Shinto only defined itself in the seventh century, when Buddhism, Confucianism, and Taoism started to predominate. In crystallizing, it acquired Buddhist philosophy, Confucian ethics, and Taoist naturalism. The result was a nature-oriented worship with special emphasis on averting pollution. Shinto domesticated Buddhism as a religion of kami-bodhisattvas, and it topped Confucian social thought with the emperor's divine right.

The Medieval-Elaborative Period

During the Taika period (645–710), Japan experienced its first extensive contact with a literate, highly organized foreign culture—China's.[10] It quickly took up Chinese writing and Confucian bureaucracy. As well, it accepted the influence of the Buddhist,

Confucian, and Taoist religious figures who accompanied the Chinese traders and politicians. Reacting to those influences, the native religion strove to assert itself. Hitherto, it had been diffuse and unstructured. As *Shinto* ("the way of the kami"), it began to compete with the ways of the Buddha, the Tao, and Confucius. However, at this early period and throughout subsequent times, such competition produced more syncretism than warfare.

By the end of the Nara period (710–784), Japan had a fairly elaborate court life. A class of nobles emerged that was distinct from the common farmers, and a native literature arose, which identified a Japanese culture. Buddhism had established its major schools, and the government loosely organized the many religious temples. By such organizing, the government in effect proclaimed a state Buddhism, but the common people cottoned to the new religion less than the emperor and the nobles did. Nonetheless, Buddhism quickly started to affect Japanese culture, offering it a philosophy far more penetrating than the native tradition. Japanese political thinkers accepted Confucianism as the rationale for good government, and Confucian formality encroached on social interactions. Religious Taoism had its biggest impact on Japanese rituals and folk beliefs. It impressed the common people as a source of blessings, and they took to its immortals and gods of the body.

Earhart defines the medieval-elaborative period of Japanese history, when these religious traditions were adopted, as being the years 794 through 1600.[11] This stretches from the Heian era, when the court at Kyoto had a glorious culture, through the Kamakura and Muromachi eras, and ends with the fall of the Momoyama dynasty. During the Heian era, court life developed a sophisticated aesthetic sense; by the Kamakura era the warrior estates had assumed power and made the emperor merely a puppet. As we noted earlier, the Buddhist sects of Shingon and Tendai, which dominated the Heian era, were esoteric, comprehensive systems that tried to accommodate a variety of interests. Though they later lost influence to Zen and

Pure Land, they began Buddhism's penetration of the lower classes. For its own part, Shinto kept pace with Buddhism by organizing itself.

In the Kamakura period (1185–1333), Buddhism responded to the increasing importance of the warrior class. Zen especially became a central part of the warrior's discipline, furnishing spiritual resources for his ideal of fearlessness and spontaneous action. Among the common people, devotional Buddhism—Pure Land and Nichiren—gained favor. They effected the final domestication of Buddhism, making it serve the lower classes in their search for prosperity and a good afterlife. In this period Shinto became highly eclectic, as we shall see more fully below, for by then it had fully combined with popular Buddhism.

The Muromachi (1333–1568) and Momoyama (1568–1600) eras were periods of great civil strife. Agriculture developed, towns and marketing grew, and military rulers (shoguns) gained power. Japan was first exposed to Western religion in the sixteenth century, at which time its own religious traditions were tightly controlled by the government. Shinto experienced a considerable revival, as the government used it to buttress the imperial family line. Overall, the religious situation was confused.

Japanese Buddhism

Francis Cook has summarized the Japanese innovations of traditional Buddhism.[12] First, the Japanese tended not to adhere to traditional codes of conduct, whether for laity *(sila)* or for monks *(vinaya)*. Eventually, priests were able to marry, eating meat and drinking alcoholic beverages were allowed, and monks could have more than a spare wardrobe. Second, Japanese Buddhism tended to move religious activity from the temple to the home. As a result, emphasis was shifted to the laity, and monks or priests were relegated to the care of temples and the performance of ceremonies (especially funerals). Caring for temples frequently came to be a family affair, as fathers passed a priesthood on to their sons.

Third, after the Kamakura period several sects promulgated the notion that one practice summarized Buddhism. In that they were to a degree reacting against the syncretism of the Shingon and Tendai sects. For instance, Honen made chanting Amida's name (a practice known as *nembutsu*) the only way to be reborn in the Pure Land. Dogen, the founder of Soto Zen, thought that *zazen* (meditative sitting) summarized everything essential. Nichiren, finally, insisted that chanting "homage to the Sutra of the Lotus of the True Law" was the way to identify with the Buddha. What these sects shared was a strong stress on faith. The personality would only come to enlightenment, they argued, if one engaged all of one's will and emotion.

Overall, the Japanese gave Buddhism a strong aesthetic aspect. This ranged from a general emphasis on a simple, direct style in speech and bearing to haiku (seventeen-syllable poems calculated to give a fleeting glimpse of reality), the martial arts (swordsmanship and archery), and the use of incense, flowers, candles, and music. The tea ceremony, which concerned not only the tea itself but also the architecture of the teahouse and the style of the utensils, became a religious and aesthetic way of life. In the twelfth century, the monk Saigyo fused nature, religion, and art through his exquisite poetry.[13] In the seventeenth century, the poet Basho wrote such haiku as the following:

April's air stirs in	*White cloud of mist*
Willow-leaves . . .	*Above white*
A butterfly	*Cherry-blossoms . . .*
Floats and balances[14]	*Dawn-shining mountains*[15]

Even recent literature, such as that by the Nobel laureate Yasunari Kawabata, employs this aesthetic. The tea ceremony has a central place in his *Thousand Cranes*;[16] his *The Master of Go*[17] shows how a game can symbolize existence and be the basis of an entire life-style; and *The Sound of the Mountain*[18] pivots on nature symbolism.

Shinto and Christianity

While Japan worked its changes on Buddhism, Shinto was liberally borrowing from the foreign traditions. Since it represented the oldest native traditions, the result was a great enrichment, or at least a great complication, of what constituted Shinto. From Buddhism, Shintoists developed the notion that the kami were traces of the original substances of particular Buddhas and bodhisattvas. As a result, Buddhist deities were enshrined by Shintoists (and kami by Buddhists). So thoroughly did Buddhism and Shinto combine that Dengyo Daishi and Kobo Daishi, the founders of Tendai and Shingon, thought it natural to erect shrines to honor the kami of the mountains of their monastic retreats.

From Shingon, Shintoists absorbed certain esoteric practices, such as using mandalas to represent the basic dualities of mind-matter, male-female, and dynamic-static.[19] Because of such dualism, people began to call Shinto "Ryobu," which means "two parts" or "dual." In one of its most dramatic actions, dualistic Shinto gave the Ise shrine an inner and outer precinct to make two mandalas that would represent the two sides of Amaterasu. She was the sun-goddess of the ancient traditions, but she was also Vairocana, the shining Buddha of Heaven.

Later in the medieval period, a number of Shinto scholars took issue with syncretism.[20] Some of them just wanted to upset the evenhandedness that had developed, so that the kami would predominate over the bodhisattvas or so that Amaterasu would predominate over Vairocana. Others wanted to rid Shinto of its syncretions and return it to its original form. The most

important of these medieval Shinto reformers were Kitabatake and Yoshida, who worked in the fourteenth and fifteenth centuries. They drew from writings of Ise priests, who wanted to give Shinto a scripture comparable to that of the Buddhists. Another step in the consolidation of Shinto's position was the organizing of its shrines, which began in the tenth century and continued through to the twentieth. The resulting network provided every clan and village with a shrine to represent its ties with the kami.

In the mid-sixteenth century Christianity came to Japan in the person of the charismatic Jesuit missionary Francis Xavier. It flourished for about a century, until the Tokugawa rulers first proscribed it and then bitterly persecuted it. The first Western missionaries made a great impact because Japan was used to religions of salvation. Pure Land Buddhism, for instance, was then popular among the common people. By impressing the local warrior rulers (often by holding out prospects of trade with the West), the Christians gained the right to missionize much of Japan and made some lasting converts. Western artifacts fascinated the Japanese as well, and for a while things Western were the vogue.

However, before the missionaries could completely adapt Christianity to Japanese ways, the shoguns became suspicious that they had political and economic designs. The shogun Ieyasu (1542–1616) killed many who had converted to Christianity, and after his death Christianity's brief chapter in Japanese history came to a bloody close. Shusaku Endo's recent novel about the Christians' persecution, *Silence*,[21] caused a stir among the contemporary Japanese Christian community because of its vivid description of the trials (in faith as well as body) that the missionaries underwent.

At the end of the medieval period of elaboration (around 1600), then, five traditions were interacting. Buddhism brought Japan a profound philosophy that stressed the flux of human experience, the foundation of is-ness, and death. In return, it was revamped to suit Japanese tastes. Confucianism furnished a rationale for the state bureaucracy and for social relationships. It stressed formality and inner control, which especially suited merchants and government officials, and one can see its imprint in the Bushido Code, which prevailed during the Tokugawa period.[22] Taoism most influenced folk religion, while, as we have seen, Shinto developed a rationale for the kami and a strong shrine system. Christianity came to represent foreign intrusion, but since it converted perhaps 500,000 Japanese, it also satisfied a hunger for other ways to salvation. Probably the average person mixed elements from these traditions with folk superstitions in order to fashion a family-centered religion that would harmonize human beings with the forces—kami, bodhisattvas, and evil spirits—that presided over good fortune and bad.

The Modern-Reformative Period

During the Tokugawa shogunate (military dictatorship), which lasted from 1600 to 1867, Japan experienced peace and stability. The Tokugawa rulers expelled the Christian missionaries and severely limited contacts with the West. The biggest shift in the social structure was the rise of the merchant class, which went hand in hand with the growth of cities.

Regarding religion, the Tokugawa shoguns made sure that all traditions served the state's goals of stability. In the beginning of the seventeenth century those goals had popular support because the preceding dynasties had allowed great civil strife. Buddhists had to submit to being an arm of the state. Neo-Confucianism eclipsed Buddhism in state influence, largely because it was less likely to stir thoughts of independence or individualism. Shinto suffered some decline in popular influence but retained a base in folk religion. As well, Shinto generated a clearer rationale for separating from Buddhism.

Finally, during the Tokugawa period the first new religions arose. They were eclectic packagings of the previous, medieval elements, and they drew their success by contrasting favorably with the highly formal, even static, culture that prevailed in the early nineteenth century. The new religions usually sprang from a charismatic leader who furnished a connection with the kami—indeed, whom his or her followers took to be a kami. By personalizing religion and addressing individual faith, the new religions stood out from the dominant formalism and offered something attractively dynamic.

The Bushido Code provides a good summary of the religious and ethical values that formed the Japanese character through the late medieval and early modern period. John Noss says of Bushido:

Bushido did not consist of finally fixed rules. It was a convention; more accurately, it was a system of propriety, preserved in unwritten law and expressing a spirit, an ideal of behavior. As such, it owed something to all the cultural and spiritual forces of the feudal era. Shinto supplied it the spirit of devotion to country and overlord, Confucianism provided its ethical substance, Zen Buddhism its method of private self-discipline, and the feudal habit of life contributed to it the spirit of unquestioning obedience to superiors and a sense of honor that was never to be compromised.[23]

Bushido was the "way of the warrior," whether he be a samurai (warrior) in fact or only in spirit. For Japanese women, the Bushido concern for honor focused on chastity. Manuals instructed young girls who had been compromised how to commit suicide (with the dagger each girl received when she came of age), including details of how, after plunging in the blade, she should tie her lower limbs together so as to secure modesty even in death. When a powerful lord would not stop his advances, the noble Lady Kesa promised to submit if he would kill her samurai husband first. The lord agreed, and she told him to come to her bedroom after midnight and kill the sleeper with wet hair. Then she got her husband drunk, so that he would sleep soundly, washed her hair, and crept under the covers to await her fate.[24]

From the close of the Tokugawa period in 1867 to World War II, Japan was in transit to modernity. It abolished the military dictatorship and restored the emperor. It also changed from a largely decentralized feudal society into a modern nation organized from Tokyo. Japan made astonishing strides in education and culture, assimilating Western science and again opening itself to the outside world (at first under duress, due to Admiral Perry and the U.S. gunboats during 1853 and 1854, then voluntarily). Success in two major wars with China and Russia between 1895 and 1905 gave the Japanese great confidence, and the first third of the twentieth century was a time of increasingly strident nationalism.

During this period Buddhism lost its official status as a branch of the government, Shinto was established as the state religion, and Christianity was reintroduced. In addition, more new religions appeared, which, like Buddhism and Shinto, took on nationalistic overtones.

For our interests, the modern period, beginning with the Meiji Restoration (of the emperor) in 1868, is most significant because of the revival of Shinto. This was largely a political operation, designed to glorify the imperial family and to unify the country around its oldest traditions. Edwin Reis-

chauer has described the widespread changes in secular life that the Meiji leaders introduced.[25] Japanese cities were revamped, and Western ideas of individual rights and responsibilities that are part of a modern state were brought in. H. B. Earhart provides documents of the propaganda that Meiji leaders generated to link the nation with religion and reestablish Japan's sense of divine mission.[26] "The Imperial Rescript on Education" (1890),[27] for instance, explicitly linked the imperial throne ("coeval with heaven and earth") with filial piety to make nationalism the supreme personal virtue. To bring their tradition up-to-date and do what their revered ancestors had done, the modern Japanese had only to be utterly loyal to the emperor. In fact, Joseph Kitagawa has argued that the Japanese notion of national community *(kokutai)* "incorporates all the major thrusts of individual and corporate orientation of the Japanese people to a sacral order of reality."[28]

The New Religions

Since the government was pushing Shinto, the new religions tended to join the nationalistic trend. Tenrikyo and Soka Gakkai both owe as much to Buddhist as to Shinto inspiration, but other new religions found it useful to shelter under the nationalistic umbrella. Tenrikyo sprang from a revelation that its founder, Nakayama Miki, had in 1838.[29] She had been a devout Pure Land Buddhist, but while serving as a medium in a healing ceremony for her son, she felt a kami possess her—the "true, original kami Tenri O no Mikoto" ("God the Parent"). Miki embarked on a mission to spread her good news, healing sick people and promulgating the recitation of "I put my faith in Tenri O no Mikoto." The Tokugawa authorities harassed her somewhat, but in time a large number of followers accepted her as a living kami. Her writings became the Tenrikyo scripture, her songs became its hymns, and her dances shaped its liturgy. Recalling the creation myth of Izanagi and Izanami, she built a shrine "at the center of the world," where the first parents had brought forth the land. The shrine had a square opening in its roof and a tall wooden column—ancient symbolism for the connection to heaven.

Miki's teachings stress joyous living. In the beginning God the Parent made humans for happiness, but we became self-willed and gloomy. By returning to God the Parent and dropping self-concern, we can restore our original joy. The way to return is faith in God the Parent and participation in Tenrikyo worship. Earhart has suggested that Tenrikyo's success comes in part from its return to peasant values.[30] By stressing gratitude for (sacred) creation, social rather than individual good, hard manual work, and the like, this sect has generated great popular enthusiasm. By the end of the nineteenth century, Tenrikyo claimed over two million members, testifying to the power of combining old, shamanistic elements with new organizational forms and liturgies. Tenrikyo even revived the ancient Shinto concern for purification by focusing on an interior cleansing of doubts and untoward desires.

Soka Gakkai derives from Makiguichi Tsunesaburo (1871–1944), who preached a new social ethic based on three virtues: beauty, gain, and goodness.[31] Makiguichi found Nichiren Buddhism attractive, so he worked out his ethics in terms of the Lotus Sutra: Beauty, gain, and goodness came from faith in the Lotus. During World War II the leaders of Soka Gakkai refused the government's request that all religionists support the military effort, arguing that compliance would compromise the truth of the Lotus Sutra (by associating Soka Gakkai with other Buddhist sects and with Shintoists). For this they went to prison. Makiguichi died in prison, but his movement revived after the war through the efforts of Toda Josei. By 1957 Toda had reached his goal of enrolling 750,000 families, largely through his fine organizational abilities and his shrewd use of enthusiastic youths. As well, Soka Gakkai capitalized on the frustration of Buddhists committed to the Lotus Sutra but alienated by the bickering among the various Nichiren groups. In a time of national confusion, Soka Gakkai's absolutism (all other religious options were held to be false) held great appeal. According to Soka Gakkai, commitment to the Lotus Sutra (and to itself) would dissolve all ambiguities.

Many observers have criticized Soka Gakkai for its vehement missionizing and its political involvement. It offers a "cellular" structure like that of communists, a simple program for daily devotion, pilgrimages to the National Central Temple near Mount Fuji, and an extensive educational program. Under the name Nichiren Shosu, it has exported itself to the West, and though Soka Gakkai has separated from its political arm (Komeito), the party continues to have considerable political effect.

Recent History

Japan's defeat in World War II produced great national trauma, prompting the success of hundreds of new religions. Culturally, defeat meant a shattering of national pride; religiously, it meant a body blow to state Shinto. The Western conquerors, led by Douglas MacArthur, force-fed the Japanese democracy and the concept of individual liberties. On its own, Japan rebuilt with incredible speed, soon becoming the economic giant of Asia. The new constitution disestablished Shinto and allowed complete individual religious freedom. The older traditions, which people identified with the national self-consciousness of prewar times, were shattered, and the new religions rushed in to fill the void. In the past fifteen years or so, the older traditions have regrouped, especially Buddhism, but the dominant trend has been secularism. Caught up in its technological spurt, Japan has seemingly put aside nationalistic and cultural issues, preferring to let the traumas of the war heal by benign neglect.

Today the Japanese religious picture is quite complicated. The culture is secular-

Figure 21   Moss Temple grounds, Kyoto. Photo by J. T. Carmody.

istic, at least outwardly, but in the alleyways Buddhism and Christianity struggle to revive themselves. Confucian and Taoist elements remain part of the Japanese psyche, but in rather muted voice. Strangely, perhaps, it is Shinto—the ancient version rather than the state—that is the strongest religious presence. Divinity in nature, which Japanese religion has always stressed, continues in the shrines that connect present times to the aboriginal kami.

STRUCTURAL ANALYSIS

Nature

From its earliest beginnings, Japanese religion has been enraptured by nature. Y. T. Hosoi has detailed prehistoric Japan's focus on the sacred tree;[32] Waida has described the rich mythology that surrounded the moon;[33] and ancient mythology, as we have seen, featured the sun-goddess Amaterasu and the wind-god Susanoo. Further, we best describe the kami as nature forces (though they could also possess human beings), and the Japanese Buddhists' love for nature, which poets such as Saigyo and Basho dramatize, developed from a pre-Buddhist base. A closeness to nature, a love of natural beauty, an aesthetic geared to flowers and trees, seasons and vistas—these have been Japanese characteristics.

Japanese folk religion, which exerted a hardy influence, viewed nature with a peasant's eye. Nature was fertile and fickle, nourishing and devastating. The early myths reflect this paradoxical quality. The sun-goddess was benevolent—a source of warmth, light, and the power to make things grow. The wind-god was unpredictable, often destructive. Susanoo's punishment for his misdeeds belies a peasant hope that nature's order and benevolence will prevail. However, Susanoo and his like might have destructive outbreaks at any time: Japan has been a land of earthquakes, volcanoes, floods, and typhoons. Japan is a very beautiful land, but rugged and not easily tamed, and controlling the effects of nature has been a herculean task. Perhaps that accounts for the Japanese delight in gardens and groves—places where they have brought peace to nature.

As we noted in describing the Japanese innovations of Buddhism, this sort of delight showed in the Japanese embellishment of religious ceremonies. Not only do most temples have some sort of grounds, often quite lovely, but their liturgies employ flowers, incense, candles, and other adornments. Along with the Japanese stress on order and cleanliness, which goes back to ancient concerns for purification, a desire has grown to make living graceful. Buddhism has benefited from this desire, as the breathtaking Moss Temple and the Rock Garden Temple grounds show. In Shinto shrines, such as Ise, Heian, and Meiji, gardens, pools, fields of flowers, and lofty trees also reflect this desire.

The mode in which the Japanese have received these nature lessons, we suggest, has been "religio-aesthetic." Japan is not very concerned with a philosophy of nature in the Western sense. It does not analyze "prime matter" or the nature of nuclear particles. Its religion appears to move by a sense of harmony. If the folk interest is nature's agricultural energies (and the powers responsible for sickness), the higher-class interest is nature's ability to soothe. Sensing that the groves and gardens represent something primal, the warrior, merchant, and bureaucrat have returned to it to escape the human concerns that threaten to swamp them. By communion with nature, the samurai warrior could collect his spirit for a single-minded attack. By slipping away from his accounting, the merchant could anticipate a "retirement," which, in Japan as well as China, allowed more poetic, Taoist preoccupations. The same applies to the bureaucrat. Even today's emperor, who is merely a figurehead, specializes in marine biology. Somewhat inept in social situations, he comes alive in his pools and gardens.

This interest in nature is religious in the sense that nature has regularly represented to the Japanese something ultimate. Thus, concern for nature has often been an ultimate concern—a stance before the holy. This stance seldom involved violent beliefs. The major prophetic figures do not tell tales of burning bushes or theologize out of mysteriously parted seas. Rather, the predominant mood has been peaceful and unitive.[34] Japanese religion tries to gain access to the core of the personality, where the personality touches nature's flow. It tries, probably semiconsciously, to let the moss and rocks work their influence. These objects can summarize existence, giving messages from mind-only. Such Buddhist ideas suggest emptiness—the strangely satisfying "nothing-ness" that the spirit disgusted with ideas, the spirit more holistically inclined, often finds in open space or the sea.

The religious veneration of nature, or even the religio-aesthetic use of nature for soothing the soul, implies an impersonal ultimacy. Further, it implies that humanity, as well as divinity, is more at one with nature than over or against it. Religion based on nature, in fact, tends to collapse humans and gods into nature's forces or nature's flows. As a result, Japan has not seen the world as created by a transcendent force. Rather, Japan has let nature somewhat suppress knowledge and love of divinity, subordinating them to energy and flow. Human beings have been encouraged not to exploit nature (though recent technological changes qualify this statement). Through most of Japanese history, one would prune or rake nature rather than lay waste to it, at least in part because human beings did not have a biblical writ to fill the earth and subdue it.[35] Rather, they had a call to live with nature. Today we might hear that as a call to be ecological, grateful, and thus graceful.

This emphasis on nature relegated intellectual concerns to second place. Many monks have lived in mountain fastnesses, while relatively few have been theoreticians of divinity's word. The reasoning of theoreticians tends to be sharp, attacking, and dialectical. The reasoning of contemplative monks tends to be poetic, symbolic, and expressive. Those who ponder the "feminine" intelligence of Eastern cultures come upon this contemplative mind. Generally, Japan has sought the whole rather than the part, the movement rather than the arrest, the beauty as well as the utility. These are feminine characteristics only if *masculine* refers to only one sort of logic (the shortest distance between two points). If a culture moves more circuitously, Western men will likely call it feminine. We are fortunate to live in a time that challenges such stereotypes.

Society

Women's Status

It is ironic that a culture that has been considered feminine has been almost oppressively male dominated. Although there are traces of an early matriarchy and strong influences from female shamans and their successors in the new religions, women have regularly occupied a low position in Japanese society. Of course, women's influence in the traditional home and even the modern office is stronger than superficial sociology suggests.[36] Expert in the very refined Japanese tact, wives and mothers have found ways of influence despite their institutionalized powerlessness. Officially, however, Japan accepted Confucian notions of social relationships (no doubt because they fit traditional predilections), so the female was almost always designated as the underling.

The important religious roles played by females in Japanese history should be further discussed. Perhaps their phallic overtones made it fitting that the kami should possess females. Or perhaps shamanism offered the powerless a chance to gain attention and influence. Whatever the reasons, women were the prime contact with divinity in folk Shinto, despite strong menstrual taboos. As well, they were the prime contact with the spirits of the dead and so were central in maintaining the clan. The figurines from the prehistoric Jomon period suggest that women were originally considered awesome because of their power to give birth. The almost complete failure of the women's liberation movement in contemporary Japan suggests that the powers of women represented by these former roles have long been suppressed.

For reasons of psychological convenience as well as self-interest, the men dominating Japanese society have found it advantageous to place religion and femininity in opposition to warfare and business. As the recourse to nature (retirement) has been in contrast to things official, so the recourse to monasteries, female shamans, and even geishas has been in contrast to workaday life. In part, of course, this contrast links religion with recreation, art, and family life. (In modern Japan a man identifies as much with his job and company as with his family.) Thus, nature, religion, and women are considered surplus commodities and yet especially valuable ones: surplus in that they do not figure much in modern work, but valuable in that work alone does not constitute a complete existence.

Clan Emphasis

The modern stress on a man's work, identifying him with his corporation, is the result of the group structure of Japanese business. Consequently, the typical businessman takes much of his recreation with his fellow workers apart from his family.

Considered in the context of Japanese religious history, this situation is somewhat anomalous. Earhart, for instance, has gathered documents that testify to the religious significance of family life,[37] showing the sense of clan that has predominated. (In fact, the modern corporation exploits this sense of clan loyalty.)

Moreover, a characteristic of the traditional family was concern with the dead. As in China, ancestor veneration was a significant portion of the average person's religious contacts with ultimate powers. Originally, the Japanese probably believed that the departed continued to hover around the places where they had lived. The Japanese tended to associate their ancestors with kami and bodhisattvas after these figures were introduced by Shinto and Buddhism. Therefore, in its petitions and venerations, the clan reminded itself of its own identity (the function that some sociologists, such as Durkheim, have considered the main rationale for religion) and kept attuned to the natural forces of life and death.

Thus, the family tended to be the locus of daily worship, and the family shrine tended to predominate over the village or national shrine. Still, there was not a sharp division between the family clan and the national clan. The emperor was often considered the head not only of his own line but also of the entire Japanese people; the gods of Shinto mythology were the gods of the collective Japanese group; and national shrines such as Ise were the site of ceremonies performed on behalf of the entire nation. Kitagawa's study,[38] referred to above, underscores the Japanese idea of a national community. Alan Miller has shown that in some periods the state functioned as a liturgical community.[39] Waida augments these studies with data suggesting that both the national community and the national liturgy are rooted in the concept of a sacred kingship,[40] while Davis has recently detailed the complicated dynamics of myth and ritual that bind a typical new religious community.[41]

These studies all spotlight the manifold cohesiveness of Japanese religious society. Japan is not a place where Whitehead's definition of religion (what a person does with his or her solitude) is very helpful.[42] Although standing alone before the Golden Pavilion has shaped for many Japanese a sense of ultimacy,[43] group activities—at home, in war, or at work—have been the crucial factors in developing such a sense.

Ethics

This historical sense of clan was accompanied by certain ethical assumptions that were immensely influential in shaping the Japanese conscience. The small boy trudging off to school would hear his mother call after him, "Don't come home if you disgrace us by failing your examination." The medieval samurai felt that his life belonged to his feudal lord. If he failed his lord, by being defeated or less than fully successful, he was expected to offer to commit ritual suicide—to petition his lord for this "favor," so that he might mend the honor he had violated. In contemporary Japan, the individual worker is supposed to promote the honor of his bosses above all. He is to assume any failures by his group and to attribute any successes to the group's leader. Thus, the boss (or at most the group as a whole) always gets credit for a bright idea or increased productivity. If the worker does not rock the boat, the corporation will take care of all his needs until he dies.

Buddhism offered an alternative to the Japanese group orientation. Though the Buddha's own thought was quite social, as manifested by the sangha, his original message stressed the uniqueness of each individual's situation. It is true that each being possessed the Buddha-nature (at least according to Mahayana Buddhism, which introduced the Buddha to Japan), and that this belief coupled with the doctrine of no-self led to a conception of the oneness of reality. Practically, however, the Buddha made the existential personality the religious battleground. Only the individual could remove the poison of karma and rebirth; only the individual could pronounce the Buddhist vows for himself or herself, let alone live them out. So, at the beginning, Buddhism offered little to a clan or state seeking to make itself the center of the world.

In Japan Buddhism both kept some of its individualism and suffered a socialization. As Zen perhaps best shows, the sangha could gear itself to making free spirits. Its discipline could be odd, even cranky. At least, the Zen masters brim with spontaneity, venerating their tradition but often in iconoclastic ways. Yet Japan acculturated Buddhism. Indeed, Buddhism became a government agency, propping war lords and nationalistic ideology. Ultimately, Japan decided that Shinto served nationalism better than Buddhism, but that was not for Buddhism's lack of trying.

Self

Theoretically in Buddhism there was no self and so no barrier (for the enlightened) to union with nature or the group. Shinto defined the self less clearly than it defined nature or the group. Thus, when Confucianism brought an elaborate social protocol, the sense of self in Japanese religious consciousness was bound to be deemphasized.

In fact, Japanese religion does not emerge as a champion of freethinking. Compared with religion elsewhere, Japanese religion does not support individual initiative or responsibility to a significant degree. Except for Zen, Japan has told the individual that fulfillment is a matter of harmonizing with nature and society. For instance, the traditional Japanese artist did not agonize in the creative process like Western artists do. Japanese art has not been primarily for working out a self. We may doubt, therefore, that many Japanese artists have thought of their lives or work in terms of Patrick White's "vivisection" (of experience).[44]

More prominent has been the Taoist notion that the artist goes to the center of nature, where the Way rules, and from union with the Way spontaneously expresses a fleeting glimpse of reality.[45] The fall of a cherry blossom, the pattern of a scarf, the rumble of a mountain—those are the subjects that seize a Basho or a Kawabata. In the tea ceremony, the No play, archery, or swordsmanship, the ideal is selflessness. Such activities, in fact, are but active forms of what the meditator pursues in *zazen*. Cast off the dichotomizing mind, the culture has said. Distinguish no more between your self and the world. Distinguishing makes for multiplicity and illusion. Buddha-nature is one. Full attainment, in the Japanese aesthetic religion, is the unitive mind, the mind lost in Mind.

As a consequence of selflessness, the individual Japanese may appear ethically underdeveloped to the Westerner. Such a description can provoke confusion, as well as misperception and offense. Still, a Western student has to begin with existing Western categories, even if they prove inappropriate. In Western ethics, the individual person judges right and wrong, largely because Greek philosophy and Israelite religion, the bases for Western culture, made the individual an intellectual and moral subject of revelation—in the Greek case, revelation from a logical being; in the Israelite, revelation from a willful God. By the time of the Enlightenment (the eighteenth century), the West had developed this patrimony to the point that the individual could be autonomous and ethics a matter of individual reasoning. Even though recent thought has found this view to be inadequate, it remains influential and at least partially true.

For instance, Western scholars of Shinto such as Bownas[46] and Blacker[47] go out of their way to underscore that its persistent concern with pollution had little to do with morality. Pollution did not pertain to the intentions of the actor, and no distinctions were made between accidental and deliberate violations. Merely to shed blood or encounter death was polluting. Consequently, the polluted person did not have to assume responsibility, to repent, or to renew the self morally. Essentially, both the pollution and the purification were external to the violator and amoral. Polluting acts occurred in the context of rather physical forces, akin to electricity or the shark's response to blood.

In the medieval period, the warrior or serf let his master be his will. The master held the power of life and death over the servant; morality was more a matter of loyalty to the master than loyalty to conscience. This deemphasis on conscience in personal life has persisted even in the modern period. As the honor accorded ritual suicide suggests, the individual has been subject to the social code in nearly all matters.

The corporation dominates modern Japanese life. The individual favors working in a group, where both responsibility and success are shared. The worst thing that can befall an individual is the need to step out of the group and speak up in his own name. Shame is the force that sustains the Japanese social code. Whether an act is right or wrong is not as important as whether it will bring shame to the family, the company, or the country. Thus, the uproar over the disclosures of widespread bribery among government officials doing business with American aircraft companies, as reported in the Japanese press in 1976, centered less on dishonesty than on disgrace. These officials tarnished the good name of the government and of the Japanese people in the world community. That the actions were instances of gross self-aggrandizement—or simply modern theft—was secondary. Similarly, when the Japanese retreated from Hong Kong at the end of World War II, the emperor's statements contained no acknowledgement of defeat, let alone any indication of wrong in Japan's original aggression. They read like a communique from a bureaucratic agency announcing a change from the use of green memo paper to blue.

Of course, the Japanese ways have a logic and a morality of their own. We are not concerned here with the difficult, though crucial, business of working out a transcultural ethics, rooted in the essential human drives to know and love, that would apply everywhere.[48] Rather, the present purpose is descriptive: trying to characterize for a Western audience the Japanese sense of self. The Japanese self appears unwilling to stand up and take personal responsibility as well as uncommonly polite and helpful. Further, what Japanese may lack as individuals they compensate for as groups. Japanese groups are quiet, clean, helpful, and cooperative; indeed, as their productivity shows, few peoples can match their discipline and output.

From medieval times, as we suggested earlier, an individual's proper bearing toward the group was loosely codified in Bushido, the warrior's way. Bushido was a sort of chivalry, expressing how the gentleman or person of honor would act. It smacked of Shinto devotion to country, Confucian propriety, and Zen self-discipline, rounding these concepts together to create a spirit of obedience and loyalty. The loyalty was primarily to the emperor and secondarily to one's immediate overlord. However, there were other Bushido virtues, and describing them will flesh out the Japanese sense of ethics.

For instance, the honorable person was grateful: for goods that others (especially parents and superiors) gave him or her, for life, for the beautiful Japanese land, and for all the boons of the kami. Another Bushido virtue was courage. The Japanese gymnast in the 1976 Olympics who did his routine with a broken leg (finishing with a ten-foot somersault from the rings) demonstrated Bushido courage to millions of homes the world over. In the warrior ideal, life itself was secondary to loyalty or honor. As Ignatius Loyola described Christian commitment to Christ in terms of a Spanish hidalgo's willingness to die for his commander, Bushido held as virtuous the courage to die for one's military leader or emperor.

Justice, truthfulness, politeness, and reserve were other Bushido values, inspiring the young person to develop a stern self-discipline. Most of all, he or she was to keep emotion in check, never revealing anger or small-mindedness. Robert Bellah's study of Tokugawa religion suggests that Bushido discipline is largely the basis for the vitality of the modern Japanese economy, serving a similar purpose as Protestant worldliness did to Western capitalism.[49]

The watchwords for the individual in Japanese religious history, then, were discipline and self-effacement. Fulfillment would come from submission to nature and service to the group, not from self-development or personal contact with God. The religious traditions, consequently, tended to help satisfy society's need for good workers and compliant citizens. Although this is true of religious traditions in most places, it stands out in Japan. The happy life that a new religion such as Tenrikyo holds out to its faithful is the result of reviving ancient concepts, including the submersion of the individual in the group; Soka Gakkai and other politically active religions stress service to the group.

Just as radical and Marxist political groups in the West offer their faithful a cause in which to lose themselves, the Japanese new religions have capitalized on the security that an individual feels in being part of a large group. In the clan, the nation, or the religious group, the Japanese individual has felt secure—safe from meaninglessness and partner to something large and compelling. All the beauty in Japanese culture, all the intelligence in Japanese technology, ought to incline us to study such "belonging" carefully.

Divinity

Japanese divinity, though complex, is essentially an impersonal collectivity of natural forces. Although devotion to a particular kami, Buddha, or Taoist god qualifies this assertion somewhat (the people who place offerings at the "baby shrine" of the Goddess of Mercy in Tokyo no doubt pray to an individual figure), the sharply defined personage

that we associate with the God of Western religion hardly appears in Japan. The gods of Shinto mythology, for instance, have a quite finite knowledge, love, and power; they have not separated from the cosmos to make particular demands. (Particular kami do take over individuals such as Miki, the foundress of Tenrikyo, so we must qualify that statement, too.)

In the course of Japanese history, there have been personal claims to divinity such as Miki's. In the thirteenth century, Nichiren was confident enough of his success in propagating Buddhist dharma to proclaim himself "Bodhisattva of Superb Action."[50] In his case, a strong imagination took advantage of the common doctrine about the Buddha-nature residing in all living things. For the common populace, though, divinity did not reflect individual humanity. Its best representations were nature or the clan. Yet insofar as people always conceive of divinity through their sense of perfection or power (and through their revelatory experiences), even impersonal Japanese divinity occasionally touched the human qualities of knowledge and love.

The Buddhists best showed divine knowledge to Japan—the ultimate reality that shone in enlightenment. Insofar as Japan deified the Buddha, it deified glorious understanding. From enlightenment, further, one could reason that the Buddha-nature was the basis for the world's intelligibility. It was what makes things be and what gives things meaning. It was also an active source, issuing all things from its womb. The generation of all things from Buddha-nature was not the same as the "logical" creation that Hellenized Western religion developed, but it did equate Buddhist ultimate reality with mind and understanding.

Love was another matter. The bodhisattva vow, of course, included great compassion, and all East Asia best loved the bodhisattva Kuan-yin, the goddess of mercy, to whom it looked for motherly care. In keeping with the injunction to stop craving, though, love or compassion was not to stir

Figure 22   *Torii (sacred gateway) to National Shinto Shrine at Ise.*
Photo by J. T. Carmody.

desire, however noble. So one could work for the salvation of all beings in good cheer, believing that their present sufferings were no cause for raging against divinity's or even society's injustices. So the love of the bodhisattva, even when it entailed suffering, was of a different sort than the redemptive love (agape) in Western religion.[51] For Japan evil is more an illusion than a disordered love or an idolatry. In the eons of time, in the vastness of *ku* (emptiness), present problems are but fleeting. If we abandon thinking about them and loose our attachment to them, we can meld into the One. Then death loses its sting and suffering has no fangs.[52]

The Buddhists were by far the most acute Japanese philosophers; the conceptions of divinity in the other traditions were far less generalized. For Japanese folk religion, which touched all but the most intellectual, divinity was quite piecemeal. Its representation was the local shrine or the house altar; neither negated the other, and neither denied the divinity of the shrines in the neighboring villages or of the altars in the next block. Folk religiosity therefore was quite tolerant—and quite confusing. It was relatively happy to multiply divinities without seeming necessity. A Shinto wedding, a Buddhist funeral, and a good many charms in between were the common custom. The gods of Shinto mythology, Taoist magic, and popular Buddhism but varied a sacredness felt to be quite near. For the few who hungered after simplicity, nature or the Buddhist void sufficed. Either could anchor spirituality in the present. Either could rouse wonder and make any time or space profound.

The times and spaces that were most wonderful, though, were the folk festivals and the popular pilgrim shrines. As the diary of a pilgrim to Ise puts it: "One does not feel like an ordinary person any longer but as though reborn in another world."[53] At special festivals or shrines, one passed a threshold *(limen)* and went from the ordinary to the sacred world. The diary of the Ise pilgrim describes this liminal experience in the aesthetic manner noted above: The pine groves have an unearthly shadow; the rare flowers that survived the frost carry a delicate pathos; most of the adornments in the shrine recall the ancient days, when religious life was honest, simple, and rough. The pilgrim notes the spray over the hills, the solitary woods that beckon to the meditative. He washes in the sea to gain outer purity and strives for a clean Shinto worship (with no Buddhist interference) to gain inner purity. Throughout, the physical beauty of Ise engrosses him.

There is something fresh and clean in such Japanese perceptions of divinity. Scholars of Shinto stress that most of the kami were forces of good, but Japanese cleanliness and goodness were astringent, dealing more with mountain streams than with human persons. Indeed, the Japanese divinity differs from ordinary persons by assuming the simplicity of streams and rocks. Far from the madding crowd, it booms in the surf, arches in the pines. As we may analyze Indian yoga in terms of a desire to return to a primal state below busy consciousness, so we may analyze Japanese naturalism as a search for relief from social complication, individual tension, and even the busy world of blessings and spells. Probably this search was seldom fully conscious, but it breathes in the pilgrim's account. He feels released into a new world, reborn, because the Ise grove dwarfs him with the peace that nature had before humans arrived.

If so, the divinity that Japan called upon to sanction its special place in the sun was beyond all social arrangements. The pilgrim in the grove does not concern himself with his clan. His country and people are present indirectly (Ise is their national holy place), but something else is to the fore—the mystery behind or in the is-ness of things.

Study Questions

1. In what sense is Shinto a fertility religion?

2. Can you explain the Buddhist philosophy behind the two Basho poems given in the text?

3. What seem to have been the primary psychodynamics of the new religions?

4. Analyze the feminine and masculine components in native Japanese culture.

5. How does the Japanese sense of shame differ from the Western sense of sin?

6. Does Japan make any hard distinctions between aesthetics and religion?

Part Three:

NEAR EASTERN RELIGIONS

You now know a fair amount about how Asian religion has regarded nature, society, the self, and ultimate reality or divinity. The religions that arose in the Near East (Judaism, Christianity, and Islam) differ notably on these points.

First, Near Eastern religion is more realistic about the natural world than Asian religion is. By *realistic* we mean "undoubting": Judaism, Christianity, and Islam show little of the Hindu or Buddhist inclination to consider physical phenomena illusory (as evidenced in maya or samsara). As you know, India has doubted the physical world more than East Asia, but East Asian Buddhism brought samsara to China and Japan. In contrast, the Near Eastern religions were tutored by the Bible and the Qur'an to consider nature as God's creation. That somewhat relativized nature—nature did not exist independently—but more importantly, it verified the reports of the senses and prevented any concept like samsara.

Second, the Near Eastern religions have generally been more cohesive (at least in their theory) and action oriented than Asian religions have been. Hinduism was part of Indian culture, which it considerably informed, but through most of its history India was a rather loose collection of quite disparate kingdoms. Buddhism became a multiethnic religion, and perhaps for that reason its key social concept, the sangha, was more inclusive than anything comparable in Hinduism. (Indeed, the sangha is quite parallel to the Church or the Muslim *Ummah*.) However, neither China nor Japan developed a religious collectivity (apart from the sangha) that stood out from existing ethnic or cultural groupings.

Further, none of the Asian religions strike the Western reader as passionate for social justice, corporal works of mercy, or institutionalized charity. Hindu dharma, Buddhist morality, and Confucian ethics had many lofty social ideals, but they did not produce the drive toward democracy and equal sharing that their Western counterparts did. They did not, for instance, make as much of popular education, nursing, or almsgiving (though Buddhists were supposed to support mendicant [begging] monks). Similarly, their castes, peasantry, and poor seem more tolerated, more condoned or even

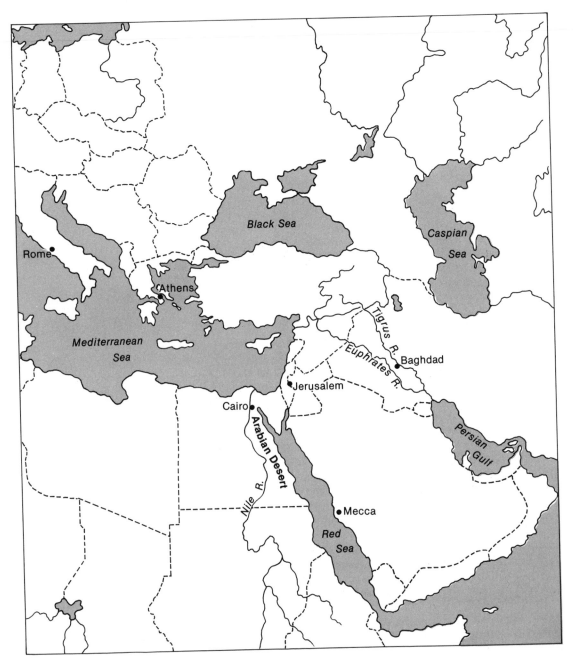

Figure 23   The Near East.

sponsored, than Western slaves, peasantry, and poor are. We do not make this observation judgmentally (the Asian religions have their own basis for judgment), and we make it with all due qualification and certainly with no boosterism for the West.

Third, the Near Eastern religions differ from the Asian religions in several ways concerning the self. The Asian religions (more so in India than in East Asia) focus on the human spirit in such a way that the human body is perceived as less real than it is in the West. The mature self of wisdom or enlightenment in Asian religions differs from the West's prophet, as elaborated below. The Near Eastern scriptures clearly refuse to dichotomize the personality—to split body and spirit apart. For them the human person is a unity, and the reality of the body and the spirit is never doubted. Thus, Near Eastern religions show neither a great urge to leave the body nor a doctrine of no-self *(anatman).* (Greek and Gnostic thought accounts for the dualism that sometimes shows in Christianity; such dualism is hardly apparent in either Judaism or Islam.)

The wise person in India or the Far East is enlightened. As the word *Buddhism* suggests (from *bodhi* meaning "knowledge"), Asia seeks light for the mind and clarity for the spirit. The West does not dispute this quest, especially when it turns toward secular education (which narrows the meaning of *knowledge*). However, the West uses a different metaphor. While Eastern "light" or wisdom is associated with seeing, prophecy is associated with hearing. In part because many influential Near Eastern religious personalities came from the desert, where the eye has little food, aural imagery prevails in the Bible and the Qur'an. (Greek thought, however, was oriented toward seeing and light.) The word of God, spoken to the heart (of the faithful listener), is the foundation of the Near Eastern religious program. The prophet, then, is not so much enlightened as inspired—addressed and directed by a spirit that uses him or her as a mouthpiece.

Fourth, these models for the religious self clearly correlate with the different conceptions of ultimate reality or God. The Asian conception is of an impersonal entity, while the Near Eastern conception is of a personal one. The Hindu *Brahman*, Buddhist *Nirvana,* and Chinese *Tao* were all more coextensive with nature than beyond it. Further, none was a superperson prone to uttering a directive word. Thus, neither India nor the Far East broke with the cosmological myth by proposing a doctrine of creation from nothingness. In the following chapters, we will also maintain that the God of the Bible and the Qur'an, although the Near Eastern religions sense the dangers of anthropomorphism, knows and loves in such a way that Western religion becomes fundamentally interpersonal. To be sure, Asian divinities took on human features and solicited not just meditation but petitionary prayer. To be sure, no one has ever seen the biblical God's face, and the Qur'anic God is not a person with whom you casually chat. Nonetheless, India senses an impersonal foundation for the world and East Asia glides towards Tao in ways that the Near Eastern religions do not.

Last, if India is meditative and East Asia is aesthetic, then the Near East and West are ethical. India stresses rational spirit, East Asia stresses harmony, and the three Near Eastern religions, at their foundations, stress will. Greek thought does give the West, especially the Christian West, a charge of speculative intellectualism. Nevertheless, love (the primary act of the will) is the greatest Christian virtue, and both Jews and Muslims prize deeds over thoughts. "Ethical monotheism" is a phrase that scholars sometimes use to describe biblical religion; with some elaboration it will serve you well in Part Three.

Chapter Eight

JUDAISM: TWENTY-FIVE KEY DATES

CA. 1200 B.C.E.	EXODUS FROM EGYPT
CA. 1013–973	DAVID
722	FALL OF NORTHERN KINGDOM TO ASSYRIA
586	FALL OF SOUTHERN KINGDOM TO BABYLON
331	ALEXANDER CONQUERS PALESTINE
168	MACCABEAN REVOLT
63	ROMANS CONQUER JERUSALEM
70 C.E.	ROMANS DESTROY JERUSALEM
80–110	CANONIZATION OF HEBREW SCRIPTURES
CA. 200	PROMULGATION OF MISHNAH
CA. 500	BABYLONIAN TALMUD COMPLETE IN ROUGH FORM
640	MUSLIM CONQUEST OF MIDDLE EAST

Judaism

J udaism is the oldest of the three major prophetic religions. The founding and development of Christianity and Islam could not have occurred without the preexistence of Judaism. (Zoroastrianism can claim some prophetic equality with Judaism, but its prophecies never became dominant in Near Eastern and Western beliefs. Zoroastrianism's major influence in the West was its eschatology—its ideas of death, judgment, resurrection, punishment, the warfare between good and evil, and so on.) Abraham, Moses, David, Elijah, Isaiah—they are the personalities that dominated the Near Eastern beginning.

APPEARANCE

In recent times, to arrive at Ben-Gurion Airport outside Tel Aviv has been to enter a climate of tension. Because of terrorist incidents the whole airport is fraught with caution. Security measures for departing passengers are the most severe in the world. As if to downplay the dangers, though, the authorities expedite the entry of new arrivals, rushing them through to the money changers and taxis. That rush adds a touch of Europe to the normally languid Middle East, as do the fields made green through irrigation. The land has bloomed, the trees, once destroyed, have returned. Just the hour's drive from the airport to Jerusalem tells the new arrival that in contemporary Israel the Middle East has a Western will and a technological mind.

Jerusalem is the spiritual heart of modern Israel, as it has been the Jews' spiritual center through nineteen centuries of Diaspora (dispersal).[1] Christians and Muslims revere it as a holy city, but it is absolutely pivotal for Jews. The new city blares with taxis, gleams with white high rises. From any of its several hills you see overgrown lots and new constructions juxtaposed—an aggressively expanding city. The old city bustles with tourists and is more multilingual. Jews share it with Muslims and Christians of various denominations. It is a blend of churches and bazaars, piety and merchandising.

Often, in fact, it merchandises piety, for the traffic is heavy in pieces of the "true" cross, tours of the tomb of David, slides of the Dome of the Rock. You can walk along walls that go back to the time of Herod, if not to David himself, yet on either side of the Western Wall modernity intrudes. To the west is the showplace of new Jerusalem, the modern apartments of which the mayor is so proud. To the east, in the precinct of the mosques, are soldiers dressed in olive drab who check all parcels and handbags. Their authority derives from their small machine guns.

At the Western Wall, Judaism's most revered memorial, men don prayer shawls and join women in weeping. The wall is steeped in history. Its sheer presence occasions great joy: For centuries Jews had little access to this remnant of the Temple. To approach it and pray, then, fulfills the dreams of generations. On the other hand, those dreams were so often nightmares that the wall is also a pillar of sorrow. Those praying may feel, "Why should we be so fortunate? What of the centuries when 'next year in Jerusalem' was but an illusion? What of the millions who perished without a sign of God's care?" The prayers at the wall, like Jewish prayer generally, are more for the collectivity than for the individual. They praise God for his steadfastness, ask God for his protection, and wonder why human history involves so much suffering.

Complementary to the ancient memorial of the Western Wall is a new memorial at Yad Vashem. Yad Vashem lies outside Jerusalem, on a high hill from which the land stretches forth. It has a pillar, a museum, and an undying flame—all to commemorate the Holocaust. The Holocaust, of course, is the "burnt offering" of six million Jews in the concentration camps of World War II. The Holocaust gave Zionism—the movement to return to the ancient land—much greater impetus than it had before the war.[2] Opposite Yad Vashem, on Mount

Herzl, lie buried the founder of Zionism, Theodor Herzl, and other Zionist heroes.

Outside Munich, at the remains of the Dachau death camp, is confirmation of the documentation found in the Yad Vashem museum. Though not everyone who died in the Nazi concentration camps was a Jew, the desire to achieve a "final solution" to the "Jewish question" was a major reason for building the camps. When the cantor sings his haunting song before the undying flame at Yad Vashem, the shivers run to Dachau. They touch the Western Wall, the garrisons on the West Bank, even the menorahs (Jewish candelabra) in the Jewish Museum. The past life on the holy land, the present militarism, and the traditional faith—they all pour into the lament.

These psychic currents run in other national waters, too. As of 1970, about 44 percent of the world's 14 million Jews lived in the United States.[3] Only 24 percent lived in Israel, so the United States had almost twice as many Jews as Judaism's own nation. Eighteen percent resided in the Soviet Union, which gives weight to Soviet Jews' struggle for the right to emigrate. Because of its internationalism, then, Judaism is a religious and historical question for all the Western world. Its history in Europe, as well as its current situation in the world's economic trouble spot, gives Judaism a far more international presence than its tiny population would indicate. Whether and how Israel survives are questions that make the Western Wall a major symbol of humanity's current spiritual drama.

HISTORY

The Biblical Period

"From the point of view of the Jew, Judaism and the Religion of Israel are the same, and what is called the religion of [biblical] Israel is but one chapter of a long and variegated historical continuum."[4] We accept this point of view, avoiding the Christian tendency to distinguish biblical Judaism from Judaism in the common era. In the beginning, the Jews were most likely a loose collection of seminomadic tribes that wandered in what is today Israel, Jordan, Lebanon, and Syria. They may have cultivated some crops, but their self-designation was "wandering Aramaeans" (Deut. 26 : 5). Thus, when scouts returned from Canaan (present-day Western Israel) with grapes, pomegranates, and figs (products of settled cultivators), they caused quite a stir.[5]

Members of an extended family tended to worship their particular "god of the father," defining themselves largely in terms of their patriarch and his god. The cult therefore centered on clan remembrance of this god, who wandered with the tribe in its nomadic life. The common name for such a clan divinity was *el.* Before their settlement in Canaan, the people seem to have worshipped a variety of *els:* the god of the mountain, the god of seeing, the god of eternity, and so on. Usually they worshipped at altars constructed of unhewn stones, which they considered the god's house. In addition to the *els* were household deities and minor divinities and demons of the desert. In later orthodox Jewish interpretation, Abraham drew on whatever sense there was of a unity among these *els* or of a supreme *el* over the others to dedicate himself to a God who was beyond nature. That God, the creator of the world, Abraham called Yahweh.[6]

For later orthodoxy, Abraham became the "Father" of the Jews and his God Yahweh became their God. In that sense, Judaism began with Abraham. Abraham lived around 1800 B.C.E. From about 1650 to 1280, the people of Abraham, then known as Hebrews, were in Egypt, subjects of the Egyptian kingdom.[7] Their leader at the end of their stay in Egypt was Moses. In later Jewish theology, Moses functioned as the founder of the Jewish people, because God revealed through Moses his will to strike a covenant and fashion himself a people. In the incident at the burning bush, Jewish faith said, Moses experienced God's self-revelation. God commissioned Moses to lead the people out of Egypt, giving as His authoritative name only "I am who I am" (or "I am whatever I want to be").

Moses then led an exodus from Egypt; in the most significant episode in that exodus, Egyptian pursuers drowned in the sea. Free of them, the Israelites (the descendants of Jacob, Abraham's grandson) wandered in the desert until they entered the homeland that God had promised them. The deliverance from Egypt through the unexpected event at the Reed Sea (not the present-day Red Sea) marked all subsequent Jewish faith. Looking back to this event, later generations clung to the belief that their God ruled history and would continue to liberate them from oppression.

In the desert, Moses and the people tested the meaning of their exodus experience. They came to believe, through what the Bible pictures as God's miraculous speaking to them, that they were bound to God by a covenant.[8] In this compact, based on the relation between an overlord and a vassal, God pledged care and the people pledged fidelity. The commandments accompanying this covenant gave the binding relationship (which the Bible saw as prefigured in Adam, Noah, and Abraham) an ethics. They became the basis of the Law and the revelation that bound the people together.

When the Israelites finally settled in Canaan (in the latter half of the thirteenth century B.C.E. under Moses' successor Joshua),[9] they changed from a nomadic to an agricultural people. They were still a group of confederated tribes, but in settlement their bonds tended to loosen, as each group kept to its own area and developed its own ways. Only in times of common danger would the groups weld together. Settlement also meant religious changes, as local sanctuaries replaced the wandering ark of the covenant as the house of God. A somewhat professional priesthood apparently developed around these sanctuaries, and as the Israelites conquered Canaanite temples, they took over the scribal schools attached to the temples. These schools were probably the first sources of written Hebrew religious literature. In addition, the Canaanite religion itself was a great influence on the Israelites. Before long it produced a conflict between Israelites who favored the older God Yahweh—the God of Abraham, Moses, and the covenant—and those who favored the agricultural gods (baals) of the Canaanites.

Kings and Prophets

From about 1200 to 1000 B.C.E., the Israelites had a government by "judges"—charismatic leaders who took command in times of common danger. However, they eventually adopted monarchical rule, organizing a sturdy little kingdom under David at a new capital: Jerusalem. This kingdom unified the tribes of both north and south, and under Solomon, David's son, it had a brief but golden age of culture and empire. Some of the most striking narratives of the Hebrew Bible (Old Testament) derive from this period, including the brilliant memoir we find in 2 Samuel, chapters 13–20.[10]

In these narratives, David is portrayed as the ideal king and yet a man undeniably human—lustful for Bathsheba, tragically at odds with his son Absalom. Much later, David's achievements in war and his fashioning a kingdom for peace made him the focus of messianic hopes—hopes for a king anointed by God who would usher in a new age of prosperity and peace. David, then, was the Jewish prototype for sacred kingship. Similarly, David's son Solomon became the prototype for wisdom; just as many pious Jews attributed the Psalms to David, so they attributed much of the Bible's wisdom literature to Solomon.

Following Solomon's death, the northern and southern portions of the kingdom split apart. The north (Israel) lasted from 922 to 722 B.C.E, when it fell to Assyria. The south (Judah) lasted until 586, when it fell to Babylon. (Both Assyria and Babylon lay to the northeast.) These were centuries of great political strife. They also spawned a series of important religious "prophets," who dominate the next phase of biblical history. Greatest of the early prophets was Elijah, who preached in the north against the corrupt kings Ahab and Ahaziah and the queen Jezebel. The legendary stories about Elijah portray him as a champion of Yahweh and of true prophecy against the false prophets of the Canaanite baals. What is clear from these stories is the influence at that time of charismatic personalities who felt that God inspired them to stand up for the old religious ways—even if doing so infuriated the establishment.

Around 750 B.C.E. the northern prophet Amos, who was the first of the writing prophets, issued a clarion call for justice. Changing the notion that Yahweh was simply Israel's protector, Amos made his divine blessings dependent on repentance from sin. His God was clearly in charge of nature, but the key access to him was social justice. In other words, he was a God of people and history, especially concerned that humans deal with one another fairly and compassionately.

Hosea, another northern prophet, also spoke up for mercy and justice (and for nonidolatrous cult), but he expressed God's attitude as that of a spouse willing to suffer infidelity, unable to cast off his beloved (the people covenanted to him). In the south, the successors to these northern prophets were Isaiah, Jeremiah, and "Second Isaiah" (the source of Isaiah, chapters 40–55). They made the same demands, but with greater stress on punishment by foreign powers. Reading the signs of the times, they thought that God would subject his people to captivity because they had not relied upon him in pure faith. However, both Jeremiah and Second Isaiah held out hope for a new beginning, assuring Judah that a remnant of the people would keep faith.

During the reign of the southern king Josiah (640–609 B.C.E.), there was a religious reform that scripture scholars see as the source of the "Deuteronomic" recasting of the early Jewish tradition. It shaped not only the book of Deuteronomy but other historical writings as well. Among the influential ideas were that Yahweh had elected Israel to be his people; that observing the covenant laws was necessary for religious prosperity;

that Jews ought to repudiate contacts with foreigners and foreign gods; that the cult should be consolidated in Jerusalem; and that Israel ought to rely only on Yahweh, since he controls history and oversees nature.

Both the prophets and the Deuteronomic historian-theologians, therefore, testify to the dangers to survival that Jews of that time felt. Political subjugation by the much larger neighboring powers was ever a possibility, but it was less ominous than cultural assimilation. To preserve their identity, these religious spokesmen felt, Jews would have to keep clear of their neighbors' fertility religion. Only an adherence to a quite different god—to the single divinity Yahweh, the God of Moses and Abraham—could keep the people true to themselves.

Thus, the stress on nonidolatrous cult and on detailed religious law was most likely a reaction to the threat of adopting non-Hebrew influences. For instance, both adopting kingship and holding agricultural celebrations could be false steps, because they could take the Israelites away from Yahweh. When the Israelites were dispersed into Babylon, Jews of the southern kingdom tested the prophets' theology. A few realized what they had lost by playing power politics and relying on new gods. When the Persians gained control of the region from the Babylonians, Artaxerxes (464–424 B.C.E.) allowed Jews to return to Jerusalem. The relatively small number who did return under Nehemiah and Ezra chose to rebuild the Temple and reestablish themselves on the basis of a strict adherence to the covenant law. Marriage to foreigners was interdicted, and priests strictly controlled the new Temple.

Covenantal Theology

From their exile to Babylon, Jews thought they had learned a capital lesson. They now viewed their history as one of wavering fidelity to the covenant, and this view suggested to them that infidelity to religious law led to national disaster. God had chosen them by covenanting with them in a special way, and unless they responded with signal fidelity, they would reap not blessing but judgment. Consequently, the returnees stressed their isolation and uniqueness. Still, historical experience also suggested, at least to some prophets and religious thinkers, that God himself was universal, Lord of all peoples. His dominion included the foreign nations, for they had obviously served as his instruments for chastening Israel. He had punished through the Babylonians and freed through the Persians.

As a result, exile and return made Jews focus more and more on Jerusalem and its cult as the source of their identity. At the same time, they clarified their ideas about God's worldwide outreach, finally realizing that God had to be the creator of all things. Views of the covenant changed somewhat, but the predominant view was that God would punish Israel for infidelity and reward it for standing firm. However, God was not bound to be merciful. Mercy, rather, was an outflow of his unpredictable, unmeasurable goodness. Somehow, despite all human weakness, God would give a new future. Often the Jews envisioned this future as messianic—coming through a holy ruler anointed by God.

The stress on covenant by the Deuteronomic and postexilic leaders exalted Moses as the religious figure par excellence. However much David stood for kingly success, indeed for the very establishment of Jerusalem, Moses stood for the Torah—revelation, teaching, law. The Torah was a much more solid foundation than either kingship or Jerusalem. By the words of God's mouth, the heavens were made. By the words God spoke through Moses' mouth, the Jews were made a people. If the people kept to those words, they would choose life. If they forgot them or put them aside, they would choose death. Thus, Moses said: "I call heaven and earth to witness against you this day, that I have set before you life and death, blessing and curse; therefore, choose life, that you and your descendants may live, loving the Lord your God, obeying his voice, and clinging to him"

(Deut. 30 : 19–20). In the sober climate that followed the return from exile, the wise way for Jews seemed to be to keep to themselves and their own special laws.

Wisdom and Apocalypse

Two other movements marked the Jewish biblical period. The first is found in the wisdom literature of the Hebrew Bible. As many commentators point out,[11] Ecclesiastes and Proverbs bear the marks of the prudential, reflective thought expressed in maxims that was available from Egypt. Somewhat incongruously, it grafted itself onto Jewish speculation about God's action, which suggests that postexilic Judaism found its times rather trying. At least, the wisdom literature is dour and sober compared with the historical and prophetic sections of the Bible. It retains a faith that God still has his hand on the tiller but it finds the seas gray and choppy. The fire in the Jewish soul for poetry and prophecy had been tempered.

The Book of Job, however, is an exception. Job probes the problem of suffering, which surely is a wisdom concern, but it reaches poetic depths. Job reveals that the innocent do suffer mysteriously—that we cannot understand our fate, because all human life unfolds by the plan of a God whose mind we cannot know. This God set the boundaries of the seas, made the different species of all living things. He is not someone we can take to court, not someone who has to account to us. Rather, we can only cling to him in darkness and in trust. Because Job does not profess the older theology, in which punishment was in response to sin, instead proposing a mystery beyond legalistic logic, it brings the postexilic centuries some religious distinction. Against the tendency to a rather arid adherence to the covenant code, Job indicated a contemplative mind that knew how all law falls away when the spirit faces God directly.

By the end of the third century B.C.E., however, the constraints on Jewish national life brought about another reaction to the problems of suffering and providence. Job refers to Satan, a force of evil that opposes God (though God controls him), and, perhaps due to Iranian influences, in the last years of the pre–common era a dualistic concern with good and evil came to the fore. God and his supporting angels fought against Satan and his minions. The world, in fact, was conceived of as a cosmic battlefield, with God and the forces of light against the forces of darkness. For the first time, Jewish religion started to focus on an afterlife. Pressed by the problem that the good do not necessarily meet with reward nor the evil with punishment, Jewish religion raised the notion that a divine judgment would mete out proper justice. Correspondingly, it started to imagine heavenly places for the good who pass judgment and infernal places for the wicked who fail.

The Book of Daniel expresses these concerns through what scholars call "apocalyptic" imagination.[12] This imagination purports to be a revelation *(apocalypsis)* from God about how the future will unfold. Psychologically, it is an effort to comfort people who are under stress with promises that they will find vindication. Theologically, it puts a sharp edge on the question of whether God controls history. Daniel joins apocalyptic concern with the older prophetic concern with a messiah, casting the future vindication of the Jews in terms of a supernal being (the "Son of Man") who will come on the clouds. His coming is the dramatic climax in the eschatological scenario that Jews developed in postexilic times. Thus, the Son of Man came to figure in many apocalyptic writings (most of them not included in the Bible), and among apocalyptic believers he was the preferred version of the messianic king. (Christians seized on this figure as a principal explanation of Jesus.)

Hellenism

From the end of the fourth century B.C.E., the political fate of the Jews lay in the hands first of the Greeks and then of the Romans. Thus, Greek and Roman influences mixed with Israel's wisdom and apocalyptic concerns. The ideals that the Jews derived from Alexander the Great are commonly labeled "Hellenistic." They included the notion that all persons have a basis for community *(koinonia)* in human reason and so can share an inhabited world *(ecumene)*.[13] Contact with Hellenism divided the Jewish community. Some priests and intellectuals took to the notion of a common humanity, as well as to Greek science, philosophy, and drama, but the majority of the people, sensing a threat to their identity, reacted adversely. By the time that Antiochus IV tried to enforce pagan Hellenism and destroy traditional Judaism, most Jews supported the (successful) revolt that the Maccabees led in 168 B.C.E.[14]

Nonetheless, Hellenism influenced the Jewish conception of law, and it sparked the first strictly philosophical efforts to make the Torah appear reasonable to any clear-thinking person. Philo, a contemporary of Jesus, and Maimonides, a thinker of the twelfth century C.E., were the great expositors of this sort of philosophy. In the final decades of the biblical period, however, political and religious differences (largely about how to respond to Roman rule and to Greek intellectualism) divided the Jewish communities. Some people, called the Zealots, urged political action, in the spirit of the Maccabean rebellion. These Zealots opposed those (such as the Essenes of the Qumran community around the Dead Sea) who urged a withdrawal from political life and a purification for the coming of the Messiah. The Pharisees and Sadducees, lay and priestly groups, adopted centrist positions, urging both a political accommodation and a reliance on the Torah.

Rabbinic Judaism

The forces who urged revolt against the Romans suffered a crushing defeat in 70 C.E., when Titus destroyed the Temple in Jerusalem and cast out most of the Jews into the Diaspora (in this context, *Diaspora* refers to the settlement of Jews outside of Pales-

*Figure 24   Jerusalem: The Western Wall, with the Dome of
the Rock in the background. Photo by J. T. Carmody.*

tine). The Pharisees and their successors, the doctors of the law, picked up the pieces. They originated with the lay scribes (lawyers) who arose in the postexilic Hellenistic period, but they did not organize themselves as a distinct party until the Maccabean revolt.[15] The Pharisees stood for a close observance of the covenant law, applying it in all aspects of daily life. This belief had come to dominate the scribes who preceded the Pharisees, and it dominated the rabbis (teachers) who came after them.

In the Diaspora these rabbis became the center of communal life. The Temple had fallen and with it the cultic priesthood. So the alternative to cultic sacrifice—an alternative that had begun in Babylonian exile, when Jerusalem and the Temple were far away—filled the religious void. This alternative was the synagogue—the gathering place where the community could pray and hear expositions of the Torah. The synagogue became the central institution of Judaism in exile, and the study necessary to expose the Torah well made Judaism an intellectual powerhouse.

What we call rabbinic Judaism focuses on the synagogue, legal exposition, and study that emphasize the teacher (the rabbi). Increasingly, the teachers wanted to base their expositions on the teachings of their eminent predecessors, so they gathered a great collection of commentaries. Eventually, this collection became the Talmud ("the Learning"), a vast collection of the oral law that was composed of the Mishnah (itself a collection of interpretations of biblical legal materials) and the Gemara (commentaries on the Mishnah).[16]

The Mishnah arose at the end of the

first century B.C.E. from the new practice of settling legal disputes by a systematized appeal to recognized authorities. This practice prompted a conflict between the Sadducees and the Pharisees. The Mishnah represented a Pharisaic effort to outflank the Sadducees, who denied the binding character of the oral law and relied on the literal biblical text alone. After the Temple fell in 70 C.E. and times became tumultuous, a written record of all the great teachers' legal opinions became highly desirable. The recording took place in Jabneh, a town on the coast west of Jerusalem. Many teachers moved to Jabneh, among them the great Rabbi Akiba (50–135), who later set up his own influential academy at Bene-Berak to the north. They began the real systematization of the Mishnah (the word implies repetition). The Mishnah continued and even intensified the scrutiny of every scriptural jot and tittle, but it went hand in hand with more pastoral activities.

Under the emperor Hadrian, Jews felt so oppressed, especially by his decision to build a temple to Jupiter on the site of the great Jewish Temple in Jerusalem, that they mounted the short-lived revolt led by Bar Kokhba. The Romans crushed it in 135 C.E., and thenceforth Jews could enter Jerusalem only on the anniversary of the destruction of the Temple, when they might weep at the wall (Figure 24).

In Babylon, to which many of the teachers fled, the talmudic work went on. When Hadrian died in 138, Palestinian Jews' fortunes rose, and a new intellectual center soon was established in Galilee. There, under Rabbi Judah, the Mishnah was elaborated to the point where it could be both a code and a digest of the oral law. It consisted of six parts, whose subject matter reveals a great deal about the rabbis' conception of religious life.[17] The first Order (part) deals with the biblical precepts concerning the rights of the poor, the rights of priests, the fruits of the harvest, and other agricultural matters. The second Order deals with the Sabbath, festivals, fasts, and the calendar. The third Order (entitled "Women") contains laws of marriage and divorce and other laws governing the relations between the sexes. The section entitled "Damages" addresses civil and criminal law. The fifth Order deals with cultic matters and the slaughtering of animals, and the final Order concerns ritual cleanliness.

Law and Lore

Perhaps the best-known portion of the Talmud is the *Pirke Avot* ("Sayings of the Fathers"), the last tractate of the fourth Order.[18] It contains opinions of some of the oldest and most influential rabbis, but it is especially valuable for the spirit, the animating love, with which it infuses both the study of the Torah and the ethical life that the Torah should inspire. Often commentators on Judaism state that the Talmud represents a psychology of defense. It is a "fence" for Torah—a protective device to keep people from violating the Law on which their identity and survival depend.

But the religious spirit of the Fathers forces us to analyze this interpretation. The Fathers built an ethics and religion that are, if not offensive, at least positive and constructive. On first reading, the *Pirke Avot* suggests the thought of sober, disciplined, studious minds—minds not unlike that of Ecclesiastes and the other wisdom writers. However, further study shows that the Fathers' sobriety encourages a study that reaches the heart. This is explicit in Johanan ben Zacchai (2:13), but surely it is implicit in Hillel (1:12), Simeon the Just (1:2), and many others.

The rabbis called the legal portion of the Talmud *halakah*. Through reason, analogies, and deep thought, it made the most minute applications of the Torah. For instance, halakah concerned itself with the dietary laws intended to keep the Jews' eating practices clean or fitting *(kosher)*. It also went deeply into the laws for the observance of the Sabbath. For centuries such laws, in their biblical forms (for example, Leviticus and Numbers), had kept the Jews separate from their neighbors. As the scribes,

Pharisees, and then the Diaspora rabbis concentrated their legal expertise, however, halakah became very complex. Certainly in the Roman Empire, non-Jews strongly associated the Jews with their laws. Thus, halakah partly contributed to anti-Semitism, insofar as it stressed the sense of "otherness" that often is used to justify bigotry.

Balancing the strictly legal teaching and lore, however, was the looser, more folkloric *haggadah*. This was a treasury of exegetical and homiletic (preaching) stories that applied biblical passages to a congregation's present circumstances.[19] Where halakah reasoned closely, haggadah was apt to employ mythic devices, including paradigmatic figures and symbols. Haggadah drew much of its authority from the fact that Jewish theology had always held (at least in the ultimately dominant Pharisaic opinion) that an oral Torah accompanied the written Law of Moses (the Pentateuch, or first five books of the Bible) and the other books of the Hebrew Bible. Haggadah shows unscientific but pious reflection over traditional passages, especially those of scripture, that pictured God in His holy freedom—God at work creating this world in which we live.

Thus, tradition relates Rabbi Hanina bar Pappa's teaching on how God guides conception: "The name of the angel appointed over conception is Night. He takes the seed and lays it before the Holy One, blessed be he, and says to him: Master of the universe, what is this seed to be—mighty or weak, wise or foolish, rich or poor? But he does not say 'wicked' or 'righteous.' So according to Rabbi Hanina. For Rabbi Hanina said: 'All is in the hands of heaven, except the fear of heaven.' " In other words, the haggadah tried to explain how a phenomenon (such as conception) was under God's control. It also urged certain attitudes (such as fear of heaven) to make faith consonant with such control. This method probably began with Ezra in the postexilic period, and it dominated what Jewish historians call the Soferic period, when the scribes came to dominate the reassembled community's spiritual life. Haggadah continued to develop side by side

with halakah for at least a millennium, ministering to the needs that common folk had for a teaching that was vivid and exemplary.

In Babylon, under the rule of the Exilarch (as the head of the Diaspora community was known in the common era), scholars collected the fruits resulting from discussions of Rabbi Judah's Mishnah which were conducted at various academies. In addition, they immersed themselves in the ideas and *responsa* (masters' answers to questions about the Law's application) that flowed between Babylon and Palestine. Both halakah and haggadah contributed to this broad collection of legal materials, and the final redaction of the Babylonian Talmud, written early in the fifth century, amounted to an encyclopedia of scholarly opinion not only on the law but also on much of the learning of the day, including biology, medicine, and astronomy, that formed the background for many of the discussions.

Talmudic Religion

In terms of theology proper, the Talmud (whether the Palestinian or the more influential Babylonian version) clung to scriptural faith.[20] Its central pillar was the Shema (Deut. 6 : 4): "Hear, O Israel, the Lord is our God, the Lord is One." (A second pillar was the biblical notion of election.) The Talmudic view of the Shema was practical rather than speculative. That is, the rabbis did not spend much energy probing the unity of God, the confluence of the divine attributes, or the like. The oneness of God meant to them God's sole dominion over life. He was the Lord of all peoples, the world's only source and guide.[21] The most practical of God's attributes were his justice and his mercy, but how they correlated was not obvious. Clear enough, though, were the implications for ethics and piety: A person ought to reckon with God's justice by acting righteously and avoiding condemnation. A person also ought to rely on God's mercy, remembering that he is slow to anger and quick to forgive.

Through such righteous living, a person could look forward to God's kingdom, which would come through the Messiah. The Messiah would rejuvenate or transform this earthly realm, which is so often a source of suffering. Of the Messiah Isadore Epstein says, "At the highest the Messiah is but a moral leader who will be instrumental in fully rehabilitating Israel in its ancient homeland, and through a restored Israel bring about the moral and spiritual regeneration of the whole of humanity, making all mankind fit citizens of the Kingdom."[22] This description rejects the Christian tendency to equate the Messiah with a divine son and also provides a foundation for the Zionistic fervor to return to the land. The concept of God's kingdom eventually included a supernatural dimension (heaven), but Judaism rather distinctively emphasizes that personal fulfillment comes through daily life.

The thrust of the Talmud, therefore, is not so much theological as ethical. The rabbis were more interested in what one did than in how one spoke or thought. So they balanced considerable theological leeway with detailed expectations of behavior. One could hold any opinion about the subtleties of God's nature, but how one observed the Sabbath was clearly specified.[23] A major effect of this ethical concern was the refinement of the already quite sensitive morality of the Hebrew Bible. For instance, the rabbis wanted to safeguard the body against even the threat of mortal injury, so they called wicked the mere raising of a hand against a person.

Similarly, since the right to life entailed the right to a livelihood, the rabbis concerned themselves with economic justice, proscribing once accepted business practices such as cornering a market, misrepresenting a product, trading on a customer's ignorance, and so on. In the same spirit, they pondered a person's rights to honor and reputation. To slander another obviously was forbidden, but they reprehended even putting another to shame, likening the blush of the shamed to the red of bloodshed.

Despite the caricature that they were concerned only with legalistic niceties, their writings show that the rabbis were very sensitive to social interaction. Lying, hatred, infringement on others' liberty—all these were targets of their teachings. The rabbis held that the goods of the earth, which prompt so much human contentiousness, were to be for all persons. Thus, after a harvest, the owner should leave his field open for the public to glean; the wealthy are obligated to help the poor; and no bread should ever go to waste. Moreover, the rabbis did not limit their lofty social ideals to the Jewish community. Glossing the injunction of Lev. 19:34 to love the stranger "who sojourns with you . . . as yourself," the Talmudists made little political or social distinction between Jew and non-Jew. Human rights applied to all.

The spirit of talmudic ethics, thus, is both precise and broad. The Talmud goes to extreme detail, but it applies to all humanity. According to the Talmud, the great vices are envy, greed, and pride, for they destroy the social fabric. Anger is also socially destructive, so the rabbis lay great stress on self-control. On the other hand, self-control should not become gloomy asceticism. Generally speaking, the Talmud views the goods of the earth as being for our enjoyment. We should fear neither the body nor the world.

In fact, God, who gives us both the body and the world, obliges us to keep them healthy and fruitful. To spurn bodily or material goods without great reason, then, would be to show ingratitude to God—to withdraw from the order God has chosen to create. Wealth and marriage, for instance, should be viewed as great blessings that should be accepted with simple thankfulness. For the truest wealth, finally, is to be content with one's lot. In faith, the pious Jew tried to raise his sights beyond everyday worries to the master of the universe, from whom so many good things flow. The ultimate purpose of religious life was to sanctify this master's name—to live in such love of God that his praise was always on one's lips.

Hallowing Time

Through religious observances the Talmudists set the social program for inculcating their ethical ideals. In practice, every day was to be hallowed from its beginning. At rising the faithful Jew would thank God for the night's rest, affirm God's unity, and dedicate the coming hours to God's praise. He was supposed to pray at least three times each day: upon rising, in mid-afternoon, and in the evening. Ritual washings, as well as the kosher diet, reminded the faithful of the cleanliness that dedication to God required. Prayer garments such as the fringed prayer shawl; the phylacteries, or *tefellin* (scriptural texts worn on the head and the arm); and the head covering reinforced this cleanliness. The mezuzah (container of scriptural texts urging wholehearted love of God) over the door was a reminder to the entire home to adopt this attitude. Home was to be a place of law-abiding love. When possible, Jews would say their daily prayers together in the synagogue.

The synagogue, of course, was also the site of congregational worship on the Sabbath and on the great feasts that punctuated the year. Primary among them were (and still are) Passover, a spring festival that celebrates the exodus of Israelites from Egypt; Shavuot, a wheat harvest festival occurring seven weeks after Passover; Booths (Sukkoth), a fall harvest festival whose special feature is the erection of branch or straw booths that commemorate God's care of the Israelites while they were in the wilderness; New Year's; and the Day of Atonement *(Yom Kippur).*

The last is the most somber and solemn of the celebrations: the day on which one fasts and prays forgiveness of sins. It is a time when estranged members of the community should make efforts to reconcile their differences, and when all persons should rededicate themselves to the holiness that God's covenant demands. There are other holidays through the year, most of them joyous, and collectively they serve the several purposes of a theistic cult: recalling God's great favors (anamnesis), binding the community in common faith, and expiating offenses and restoring hopes.

In the home celebration of the Sabbath did for the week what the annual feasts did for the year. It gave time a cycle with a peak that had special meaning. From midweek all looked forward to the Sabbath joy, preparing the house and the food for God's bride. When the mother lit the candles and the Sabbath drew near, even the poorest Jew could feel that life was good. Special hospitality was the Sabbath rule; rest and spiritual regeneration were the Sabbath order. Regretful as all were to see the Sabbath end, a glow lingered that strengthened them so that they could return to the workaday world.[24]

The principal rites of passage were circumcision, through which males entered the covenant community on their eighth day; bar mitzvah, to celebrate the coming of age; marriage; and burial. Through communal celebration, these rites reenforced the faith that life is good, the Torah is life's crown, marriage is a human's natural estate, and death is not the final word.

The Medieval Period

From the seventh century on, this talmudic religious program structured the lives of Jews who were mainly under Muslim rule.[25] Muhammad himself took rather kindly to Judaism, because he thought that his own revelation was rooted in biblical thought. "Hence his uncompromising monotheistic doctrine, his insistence on formal prayers, fasting and almsgiving, his adoption of the Day of Atonement, his introduction of dietary laws (such as the prohibition of swine's flesh), and his requirement that his followers turn towards Jerusalem in prayer."[26] However, things grew more complicated when the Jews refused to convert to Islam, and under Muhammad and his successors the Jews had to endure not a little trouble. Nonetheless, Muslims frequently found Jews useful as translators or businessmen, and Muslim countries were generally tolerant. So long as non-Muslim religious groups posed no threat to security or ortho-doxy, they could have a decent, if second-rate, civil status.[27]

During the first centuries of Muslim power, the Jewish community's prestigious center of learning was at the heart of its Diaspora in Baghdad (in Babylonia). Accord-ing to talmudic tradition, the leaders of the Baghdad schools gave *responsa* to points of law and held sway over community religion. They also fixed the pattern of communal worship, which hitherto had been a source of confusion and controversy. During the ninth and tenth centuries, the scholars of the Bab-ylonian schools also standardized the pro-nunciation for the Hebrew Bible. These scholars (Masoretes) supplied the vowel points, accents, and other signs necessary to make readable a text that had consisted only of consonants. (Pronunciation, conse-quently, had been a matter of oral tradi-tion.) The same work went on in Palestine, and eventually the version of a Palestinian author named Ben Asher won acceptance as the canonical text.

At the end of the first millennium of the common era, Jews emigrated to Europe, North Africa, and Egypt, taking with them the scholarship of the talmudic school to which they felt the closest ties. The Babylo-nian traditions were more popular, but in countries such as Italy, which had close ties with Palestine, Palestinian influence was great. In Europe, of course, the Jews were largely under Christian rule, although south-ern Spain and southern France were under Muslim rule.

The two great Jewish traditions, the Sephardic (Spanish) and the Ashkenazic (German), can be characterized by their sub-jugation under either Muslim or Christian rule, respectively. The two traditions shared more than they held separately because of the Talmudists, and their different styles in intellectual matters and in piety largely derive from the different cultures in which they evolved. In the tenth and eleventh cen-turies, the Sephardim in Spain developed a golden culture, with philosophy, exegesis, poetry, and scientific learning at their peak.

Toledo and Cordoba were great centers of learning, but so were Cairo, Avila, and Lis-bon.

The major internal problem during this period was the Karaite heresy, which began under the leadership of Anan ben David in the eighth century. This movement rejected the Talmud and based its beliefs on a literal reading of the scriptures. For instance, Karaite Sabbath law forbade wash-ing, leaving the house, carrying anything from one room to another, wearing anything except a shirt, making a bed, or any other activity construed as work. Karaites inter-preted the injunction of Exod. 35 : 3, to kin-dle no fires on the Sabbath, to mean that one had to spend Friday night and Saturday in darkness and cold. They were so scrupulous about incest laws that finding an acceptable marriage partner was difficult.

Because Karaism appealed to individ-ual conscience and had some master propa-gandists, it mustered considerable support. Anan withdrew from Babylonia to Jerusa-lem, where he set up a community, and he pushed for a complete break with talmudic Jews (called Rabbanites). In the ninth and tenth centuries Karaism spread to Persia, Egypt, Spain, and parts of Asia and seemed to be on the verge of replacing Judaism. When we add to its appeal the confusion that the Muslim recovery of Greek learning was pro-ducing in scholarly circles, we can under-stand the complexity of the Jewish religious situation and why it came close to crisis. With literalist Karaites on their right and rationalistic Hellenists on their left, the Tal-mudists felt besieged.

The Talmudists responded to the Karaites with an intensive campaign of bib-lical study, which included exegesis, He-brew grammar, philology, and the other learning necessary to defend their own inter-pretations of the sacred text. Against the rationalists they took up the tools of philos-ophy, logic, and physical science in an effort to show the compatibility of reason and faith. The great champion in this talmudic or Rabbanite counterattack was Saadya ben Joseph (892–942), who lived in upper Egypt.

He combined Hebrew and Arabic learning, biblical scholarship, and philosophical erudition. In addition, he wrote halakic *responsa*, codified rules of talmudic logic, resolved problems with the calendar, and composed an order for public worship.[28] The counterattack that he spearheaded was successful, and when the Jews fled from Babylonia at the breakup of the Muslim empire into the eastern and western caliphates, they took with them at least the beginnings of a renewed talmudic tradition. The golden age in Spain was in no small measure possible because of this renewal.

Philosophy

The early medieval period thus saw a ferment in talmudic learning. As well, a Jewish philosophical theology arose.[29] While Philo, in the first century of the common era, worked at what could be called philosophical theology, trying to reconcile Hellenistic thought with biblical thought, the medieval thinkers, especially Maimonides, brought philosophy into the Jewish mainstream.

Philo, whose strong point had been what he called *allegoresis* (a reading of scripture on several levels, so as to remove the problems that the philosophical mind might have with anthropomorphism), never exerted a decisive influence on his contemporaries. Maimonides did. He was the response that made Judaism competitive in the new arena opened by the Muslim retrieval of Aristotelian logic and science. As such, his work was apologetic, making Judaism a strong contender in the debates that were being conducted by the Western religions on the supposedly common ground of rational analysis. However, Maimonides' work was also constructive, setting talmudic and traditional learning in the context of a philosophical system. Finally, the philosophical services of thinkers such as Maimonides were very useful in internal fights with literalists such as the Karaites, who (despite their literalism about points of biblical law) mocked both biblical anthropomorphism and much of haggadah (because it was poetic and symbolic).

The great questions of this period of philosophical debate were the criteria of biblical exegesis, the relation of faith to reason, the nature of the human personality and its relation to God, God's existence and attributes, the creation of the world, and providence and theodicy (God's justice). In debating these questions, the philosophers based their work on the Greek view that contemplation *(theoria)* is the most noble human work. Thus, the Jewish philosophers made rationality the source of human imaging of God. From that they derived an obligation (they would have called it a religious obligation) to develop one's reason—to explore God and his world.

Whereas for the Talmudist study of the Torah was the highest activity, many of the medieval philosophers considered the contemplation of God's eternal forms (through which he had created the world) as such. Maimonides became the prince of Jewish philosophers largely because he was also learned in the talmudic tradition and so could reconcile the old with the new. For him philosophical contemplation did not take one away from the Torah, because the proper object of philosophical contemplation is the one Law we find in both scripture and nature.

A key teaching in Maimonides' system was divine incorporeality. God had to be one, which he could not be if he occupied a body, since matter is a principle of multiplicity. To rationalize the anthropomorphic biblical descriptions of God, where he has bodily emotions if not form, Maimonides allegorized as Philo had done. The dynamic to his system, however, was the conviction that philosophical reason can provide the key to scripture. As his own *Guide for the Perplexed* puts it, "This book will then be a key admitting to places the gates of which would otherwise be closed. When the gates are opened and men enter, their souls will enjoy repose, their eyes will be gratified, and even their bodies, after all toil and labor, will be refreshed."[30]

Maimonides has probably been most influential through the thirteen articles in which he summarized Jewish faith, and which even today are listed in the standard prayer book. They are: (1) the existence of God, (2) God's unity, (3) God's incorporeality, (4) God's eternity, (5) the obligation to worship God alone, (6) prophecy, (7) the superiority of the prophecy of Moses, (8) the Torah as God's revelation to Moses, (9) the Torah's immutability, (10) God's omniscience, (11) reward and punishment, (12) the coming of the Messiah, and (13) the resurrection of the dead.[31] In this summary a philosopher gave the key headings under which reason and biblical revelation could be reconciled.

However, Jewish philosophy before Maimonides expressed a somewhat contrary position. The lyrical writer Judah Halevi (ca. 1086–1145), for instance, insisted that the God of Aristotle is not the God of Abraham and the biblical Fathers. Halevi's position is reminiscent of the later Christian philosopher Blaise Pascal, and it draws on the same sort of religious experience that made Pascal visualize God as a consuming fire—no Aristotelian "prime mover" but a vortex of personal love. Halevi did not despise reason, but he insisted that it is less than full religious experience, faith, or love. Moreover, he was concerned that Judaism remember where it had found God in the past—that it not lose itself in supposedly timeless philosophical truths. Concrete historical acts had furnished the Jews their election and destiny as God's covenanted people, not eternal forms ever available for human contemplation.

Mysticism

The devotional current in influential philosophers shows that the appropriation of Greek rationality did not extinguish Jewish mystical life, any more than it extinguished talmudic preoccupation with law. Law, in the sense of guidance for a daily practice of faith and ethics, certainly predominated over philosophy in the popular religious mind, but both philosophy and mysticism

colored its interpretation. Gershom Scholem has treated the major trends in Jewish mysticism admirably,[32] tracing them back to biblical origins. The major influence, discernible even in Maimonides' doctrine of God, was Ezekiel's vision of the divine chariot *(merkabah)*. Philosophers and mystics alike agreed that under this symbolism lay the most profound mysteries of the divine nature. The Talmudists tended to stay away from the subject, lest they fall into impious speculation, but the mystics, even though they cautioned about dangers, repeatedly went back to it.

In medieval Germany a movement arose among people called the Hasidim, who upheld a relatively new spiritual ideal. Biblical religion had spoken of the poor of God *(anawim)*, and from early times a *hasid* was one who piously devoted himself to God. The medieval expression of this piety, in which intellectualism was subordinate to devotion, contested rabbinic learning. What characterized the truly pious person, this movement argued, was serenity of mind, altruism, and renunciation of worldly things. The asceticism, especially, ran counter to traditional Judaism, for it seemed to entail turning away from the world. Indeed, Hasidic speech relates to the reality that has always drawn mystics and caused them to neglect the world—the reality of glimpsing the divine being itself, of experiencing the biblical "goodness of the Lord." This divine love exalts the soul and seems far more precious than anything the world can offer.

Hasidism in its medieval, Germanic form is not the direct ancestor of the modern pietism that goes by this name. Intervening between Hasidism's two phases was a most influential Jewish mysticism, that of the Cabala. *Cabala* means "tradition," and the Cabalists sought to legitimize their movement by tracing it back to secret teachings of the patriarchs and Moses.

Such secret or esoteric overtones stamp Cabalism as a sort of Jewish Gnosticism (secret knowledge); indeed, several Cabalistic doctrines smack of the Gnostic concerns with the divine *pleroma* (fullness), the emanations of different divine aspects, and secret doctrines explaining how divinity intends to redeem the wicked fallen world.[33] Thus, R.J.Z. Werblowsky characterizes Cabalism as a "theosophical" (concerning wisdom about God) movement especially concerned with the *pleroma*.[34] This fullness, which the prophets glimpsed in their ecstatic visions, humans can only conceive symbolically. Hence, Cabalists engaged in their own brand of allegorical exegesis of scripture, trying to decode secret symbols about divinity that the Hebrew Bible couched in deceptively simple language.

For Cabalistic thought, the divine and the human spheres are interdependent. The fallen state of the world (most acutely manifested in the suffering of the Jews, God's chosen people) signals a disruption within the divine essence itself. Human sinfulness, it follows, reflects this divine wounding. On the other hand, human holiness contributes to God's repair, and so every human act takes on cosmic significance. In fact, human life can become a sort of mystery play or theurgy (divine work), in which the significant aspect of its actions is their wounding or repairing of the divine life.

When the Spaniards expelled the Jews from the Iberian Peninsula at the end of the fifteenth century, the Cabalists had the perfect crisis on which to focus their somewhat fevered imaginations. Isaac Luria, who taught in Jerusalem in the sixteenth century, and Sabbatai Zevi, the "false messiah" of the seventeenth century, interpreted the expulsion as an effect of a cosmic disaster that actually occurred before Adam's fall. They had great popular impact.

The paramount book of the Cabalistic movement, and the most representative of its symbolism, was the *Zohar*—the "Book of Splendor." From 1500 to 1800, the *Zohar* exerted an influence equal to that of the Bible and the Talmud. Analysis of the work suggests that it was written in Spain at the end of the thirteenth century, most likely by Moses de León.[35] The *Zohar* is similar to haggadic materials in that it interprets scrip-

tural texts symbolically and in pietistic fashion rather than in the legal manner of halakah. What distinguishes the *Zohar* from traditional haggadah is its suffusion with the Gnostic ideas mentioned above. For instance, its commentary on the first verse of the Hebrew Bible, Gen. 1:1, goes immediately to what the divine nature was really like "in the beginning": Within the most hidden recess of the infinite *eyn sof*, the divine essence, a dark flame went forth, issuing in the *sefiroth*. The *sefiroth* were what the philosophers called the realm of divine attributes, but the mystics saw them as the emanations of God's own being. Such a view makes the world alive with divinity. It gives history and human experience eternal implications, because the emanations move through our time, our flesh, our blood.

The *Zohar* turns over each word of Genesis, searching for hidden clues to the divine plan. It concerns itself with the numerical value of the words' letters (for example, a = 1) and correlates clues in Genesis with clues from other visionary parts of the Hebrew Bible, such as Ezekiel, chapter 1, and Isaiah, chapter 6. To align its interpretation with respectable past commentary, it cites traditional rabbis, but the *Zohar*'s immediate concern is not the rabbis' interest in ethics but an imaginative contemplation of divinity and the divine plan.

In other words, the *Zohar* draws persons with the splendor of its vision, its graphic display of divinity. With its beauty, the *Zohar* can move the spirit to ecstatic joy. No doubt the Cabalists devoutly hoped that such an imaginative and contemplative experience would build up faith and inspire good works. However, they differed from the Talmudists (some of whom had secret sympathy for Cabalism) in their predilection for visionary appreciation of the Law's source rather than a sober perusal of the Law's applications.

The Modern Period

If the mark of modernity is a turn from rather mythical religious authority to human authority and self-reliance, modernity did not begin for Judaism until the end of the eighteenth century. In fact, thorough exposure to a secularized, technological culture did not come to most of the rural population of the eastern European *shtetls* (villages) until close to World War II. Until that time enlightenment and reform made little impact, for talmudic and Hasidic orthodoxy kept the traditions basically unchanged.[36]

Cecil Roth[37] and Leon Poliakov[38] have described the constant repression and persecution that Jews endured in medieval and early modern times. What Roth calls "the crowning tragedy" was the Jews' expulsion from the Iberian Peninsula in 1492, since that devastated what had been Jewry's greatest cultural achievement. In its aftermath, the eastern European ghetto became home to most Jews, and the false messiah Sabbatai Zevi, who finally apostatized to Islam, shows the intensity that Jewish messianic yearning reached by the mid-seventeenth century. Part of the success of Israel Baal-Shem-Tov (1700–1760), the father of modern Hasidism, resulted from the effects of Sabbatai Zevi. There was a void into which apostasy, nihilism, and antinomianism (lawlessness) threatened to rush.

Baal-Shem-Tov and his followers taught a religious inwardness, a joyous communion with God.[39] They sought to restore the traditional faith, which they saw as endangered by false messianism, arid intellectualism, and talmudic legalism. Hasidism did not attack the law and traditional practice itself. Rather, it shifted Jewish religious focus from the "scientific" rabbinic leader to the gifted Hasid or holy person, who manifested divine wisdom and joy. The movement quickly caught fire in eastern Europe, and thousands rushed to the Hasidic "courts." In their vivid portrait of *shtetl* life, Zborowski and Herzog[40] have shown the attraction that the Hasidim exerted in the typical village. Many of the villagers (usually men) yearned to go off to the courts for spiritual refreshment, and many would leave their families for substantial periods of time.

Hasidism tended toward irrationalism and an intolerance of anything modern, but for discerning contemporary Jews such as Martin Buber[41] and Abraham Heschel,[42] it became a valuable resource. Although large portions of the educated, who were desirous of a Jewish enlightenment and a Jewish emancipation from Christian discrimination, strongly opposed Hasidic piety, it remained vigorous in the villages well into the twentieth century. There it tended to commingle with talmudic faith, blending legal observance with emotional fervor. Jewish village life hinged on the Sabbath (in the time-organizing way described above) and on three blessings: the Torah, marriage, and good deeds.

The Torah meant God's revelation and Law. In practice, it meant the exaltation of learning. *Shtetl* parents hoped that they would have learned sons, well versed in the Law, who would bring glory to the family. Thus, the ideal son was thin and pale, a martyr to his books. From age five or so he marched off to a long day of study, beginning his education by memorizing a Hebrew that he did not understand and then progressing to subtle talmudic commentaries. The Torah shaped the economic and family lives of *shtetl* Jews, because men tried to free themselves for study, placing the financial burdens on women. The poor scholar, revered in the *shul* (synagogue school) but master of a threadbare family, exemplified the choices and values that the Torah inspired.

Many men did work in trades (the state usually prevented Jews from owning land and farming), but even they would try to gain dignity by devoting their spare time to learning. Glory for women came from caring for the home, the children, and often a little shop. So much were those responsibilities part of religion for women that no commandments prescribed for them exact times for prayer, fasting, synagogue attendance, charitable works, or the like. Women's 3 principal *mitzvah* (duties) out of the traditional 613 were to bake the Sabbath bread, light the Sabbath candles, and visit the ritual bath *(mikvah)* after menstruation.

In the *shtetl*, marriage was the natural human situation and children were its crown. Father and mother were obligated to create a home steeped in Torah and good deeds (fulfillment of the *mitzvah* and acts of charity). In semiserious popular humor, nothing was worse than an old maid, while an unmarried man was pitied as being incomplete. Of course, kosher rules and keen legal observance marked the devout home, which was but a cell of the organic community. That community supported needy individual members with material goods, sympathy in times of trouble, and unanimity in religious ideals. One had to share one's wealth there, whether wealth of money or wealth of mind, and the seats of honor in the synagogue went to the learned and to the community's financial benefactors.

Tribulations

The community exacted quite a toll through the pressure it exerted to conform with its ideals and through the gossip and judgment that ever circulated. Nevertheless, most Jews gladly accepted being bound by the common laws and custom, and few Jews could avoid being bound by the equally overt and common suffering. The urban populations in the Russian and Polish ghettos shared an almost paranoid spiritual life, with pogroms (persecutions) a constant specter, while the rural populations of eastern Europe never knew when some new discrimination or purge would break out. In both situations, Jews' mainstay was their solidarity in faith. Consequently, we can understand how threatening movements to change the faith, such as the Reform or Enlightenment (described below), must have been. The old ways had been the foundation of Jewish sanity. New conditions, as in Germany and the United States, seemed much less solid than long familiar suffering and endurance.

The bulk of the Jewish population in the late 1700s was in eastern Europe: the pale of the Russian empire, Austria, and Prussia. Their life was rather precarious, and attacks by Russians and Ukranians produced a stream of emigrants to the New World. Yet European Jews contributed to the formation of the notion of the modern, secular state, probably because they hoped that it would offer them greater religious freedom. The Jewish philosopher Spinoza (1632–1672) suggested such a political arrangement, and Moses Mendelssohn (1729–1786), a German man of letters, plumped for a secular state prior to the French Revolution. Generally, Jews' civil status seemed to prosper in countries or under regimes that were open to the new, liberal ideas of equality. However, when nationalism prevailed, the Jews tended to experience more anti-Semitism, since non-Jews considered them outsiders at such times.

Jacob A. Argus has noted three principal Jewish reactions to modern nationalism.[43] First, many Jews identified themselves with the people among whom they lived. For instance, German Jews became great supporters of German culture, which was enjoying a golden age in music and philosophy. Second, some of the Jewish intelligentsia embraced the new universalist philosophies that downplayed race or ethnicity and that stressed the common humanity all persons share through their reason. Third, some Jews incorporated nationalistic feelings into their own group consciousness by thinking of the cohesiveness of the "nation" of Israel. Argus sees these reactions working, respectively, in the time of Emancipation in France (see below), the socialist movements in Europe and Russia (which led to the formation of the *Bund* [party], influential in Poland during the two world wars, and also to the Reform movements in Germany and the Anglo-American world), and the Zionist movement, which he conceives of as a Jewish nationalistic renaissance.

Dissolution of Traditional Judaism

Jacob Neusner attributes the breakup of traditional Judaism in the modern period to two factors, the Enlightenment and Hasidism.[44] The Enlightenment, whose main feature according to Kant was the realization that humanity should be guided by its own reason and not by institutional authorities, in effect attacked the legal and philosophical underpinnings of traditional Judaism. By extending political rights to Jews ("Emancipation"), the Gentile thinkers of the Enlightenment took away the basis of the Jewish community—it was no longer a ghetto or a world set apart from the national mainstream.

By its philosophical turn to individual reason, the Enlightenment attacked the talmudic assumption that traditional law and its interpretation by the Fathers are the best guides for life. Thus, intellectual Jews who accepted the ideals of the Enlightenment tended to abandon talmudic scholarship (or at least deny that it was the most important learning) and devote themselves to secular learning. This movement spawned the distinguished line of Jewish scientists, social thinkers, and humanists, but it meant that the Jewish community lost some of its best talent. It also meant intellectual warfare between the advocates of the new learning and the defenders of the old.

The relation of Hasidism to traditional, talmudic Judaism is more complex. On the one hand, as we have seen, Hasidism accepted traditional assumptions about the Law, the specialness of the people, the coming of the Messiah, and the reality of God's reign over the world. On the other hand, Hasidism set the charismatic holy man rather than the learned rabbi at the center of the community.[45] This new figure, the *tzaddik* (righteous one), Hasidim revered for his intimacy with God, his ability to pray evocatively, and his gifts as a storyteller. (As a storyteller he was an updated version of the ancient haggadist.) But the simple faithful held the *tzaddik* to be a wonder worker.

Thus, the Hasidim abound with stories of God's coming to the aid of his oppressed people through the special interventions of the *tzaddik*.[46] The story with which Elie Wiesel prefaces his novel *The Gates of the Forest* epitomizes the impact of Hasidic faith in the masters' powers:

When the great Rabbi Israel Ba'al Shem-Tov saw misfortune threatening the Jews it was his custom to go into a certain part of the forest to meditate. There he would light a fire, say a special prayer, and the miracle would be accomplished and the misfortune averted. Later, when his disciple, the celebrated Magid of Mezritch, had occasion, for the same reason, to intercede with heaven, he would go to the same place in the forest and say: "Master of the Universe, listen! I do not know how to light the fire, but I am still able to say the prayer" and again the miracle would be accomplished. . . . Then it fell to Rabbi Israel of Rizhyn to overcome misfortune. Sitting in his armchair, his head in his hands, he spoke to God: "I am unable to light the fire and I do not know the prayer; I cannot even find the place in the forest. All I can do is to tell the story, and this must be sufficient." And it was sufficient. God made man because he loves stories.[47]

Reform

Thus, the traditional legal authority crumbled because of the new secular learning. From within, Judaism succumbed to a desire for more emotionally or spiritually satisfying evidence of God's helpfulness. In response to this crisis of the tradition came a "Reform" of orthodox conceptions. On a popular level (though we are still speaking of the relatively educated), Reform meant an effort to accept modern culture and still remain a Jew. In other words, it meant searching for new definitions of Jewishness that would not necessitate alienation from the intellectual and political life of Gentile fellow nationalists.

Among the "virtuosi," as Neusner calls the important personalities of the Reform movement, the effort was not just accommodation but rethinking the tradition to bring it up-to-date with integrity. A good part of the virtuosi's effort emphasized the Jewish philosophical and ethical beliefs that seemed eminently rational (and so applicable to all persons). In effect, emphasis shifted from what was distinctive in Judaism, what gave Jews their unique status as God's chosen ones, to what Judaism could offer to all humanity.

The stress of Reform was ethical. Reform Jews saw their tradition as offering all peoples a moral sensitivity, a concern for the rights of conscience and social justice, which derived from the prophets and the great rabbis but that could serve the dawning future age of equality, political freedom, and mutual respect. In part, this ethical stress was the result of wishful thinking. Reform Jews tended to be talented people who were either formally or informally excluded from national and university life. As a result, their visions of a new day led them to stress what in their own religious past might abet equal opportunity.

A response to Reform within Judaism was a self-conscious "Orthodoxy." It tended to recruit those who shared many of the Reformers' perceptions but who disagreed with their reinterpretation of the tradition. Instead, Orthodoxy insisted that the Torah be the judge of modernity and not vice versa. Positively, however, the Orthodox conceded the possibility that living with Gentiles might be a good, God-intended arrangement. No doubt, the breakup of Christian control over culture that marked the Western shift from medieval to modern times played a strong role in this reevaluation. That is, the Orthodox realized that, despite its evident dangers to faith, living among Gentiles might free Jews of the prejudice endemic in medieval Christian faith. (In its most viru-

lent form, that prejudice branded all Jews as "Christ killers.")

In their contests with the Reformers, the Orthodox could draw on factors that tradition had driven deep into the Jewish psyche. First, there was the conservatism that was almost intrinsic to a faith built on teaching "fathers" and the father-figure of the family. Such conservatism made it difficult for the younger generation to convince the older. Second, the Orthodox could claim, much more plausibly than the Reformed, that they represented the wisdom and experience of the past by which the people had survived. Third, the Orthodox were more genuinely religious than the Reformed; although the virtuosi wanted to develop faith, the majority of reformers were secularly minded, drawn by goods outside the traditional culture. Last, the combination of these factors gave Orthodoxy the advantage of appearing safer and surer than Reform.[48]

Zionism

The movement most responsible for the establishment of the state of Israel is Zionism. Most of the medieval piety movements anticipated Zionism insofar as their messianism regularly involved the notion of returning to the ancestral land (and to the holiest of cities, Jerusalem). Thus, the Karaites of eighth-century Iraq (Babylonia) emigrated to Israel, and some of the Cabalists took up residence in Galilee. In the eighteenth and nineteenth centuries, Hasidim in Poland sent many people to the Holy Land, with the result that there were circles of devout Jews in Jerusalem, Tiberias, and Safed.[49] The upsurge of nationalism in modern Europe tended to make Jews consider their own national roots, while new movements of social thought, including those led by Marx and Tolstoy, caused many Jews to dream about a new society based on the *kibbutz* (collective).

The greatest impetus to Zionism, however, was the persecutions that convinced European Jews they were in peril on

Figure 25   Infamous gate at Dachau concentration camp, outside Munich, reading "Work Frees." Photo by J. T. Carmody.

the Continent: pogroms in Russia from 1880 to 1905, Ukranian massacres from 1917 to 1922, persecutions in Poland between 1922 and 1939, and, above all, the Nazi persecution that began in 1933. By 1948 about 650,000 Jews lived within the British mandate of Palestine, and at the birth of Israel many hundreds of thousands more emigrated from Europe and from Arab lands (where, after the 1948 war, conditions were difficult). The main ideologist for the movement was a Viennese named Theodor Herzl. His witness of anti-Semitism during the Dreyfus case in France at the end of the nineteenth century convinced him and many other Jews that only by having their own nation could Jews be free of constant persecution.

Today Judaism is most vital in Israel and the United States, and in both places the battles over what it means to be a Jew in the modern world continue unabated. Israel has become the spiritual center of Judaism, and what faith can mean after Auschwitz and the Holocaust has become the prime topic of theological discussion.[50] Because of its vigorous intellectual tradition, Judaism disproportionately contributes to the debates about the value of modernity, and its voice is now influencing many Christian thinkers.[51]

STRUCTURAL ANALYSIS
Nature

Generally speaking, nature has not been an important concept in Judaism. For example, Maimonides did not refer to it in his thirteen articles of faith, and scholars dealing with the biblical period,[52] a historical perspective,[53] or even Jewish values[54] do not focus on nature. That does not mean, of course, that Jews had no consciousness of their land or that the physical world played no part in their religion.

In the biblical period nature was quite important, because the earliest "Jews" were shepherds or farmers. The earliest theology appears to have been a veneration of different *els* (gods) related to natural powers, and the constant lament of the prophets and other biblical theologians that the gods of the neighboring peoples (the Canaanites especially) were seducing the people away from true religion is testimony that the cosmological myth held considerable attraction.

Still, contesting the cosmological myth (in which divinity is immanent to the world and natural processes are divinity's most intimate operations) were the "great acts" of Yahweh in his people's time. Eric Voegelin has argued that "history" itself (our human conception of time) is substantially the product of Israelite theology.[55] For Voegelin, history gets periodicity from the revelations of a God outside the world, and it is those revelations that decisively shaped the Jewish people. So Yahweh, the most transcendent of Gods, was also the most interactive. He was the God of the Fathers, Abraham, Isaac, and Jacob. He was the one who led the ancestors out of Egypt, struck the covenant on Sinai, and ushered the people into the promised land.

From the beginning, the Jewish conception of God, coupled with the Jewish ethnic memory and sense of identification through religious history, combined to deemphasize nature as a religious focus. As the Psalms show, Yahweh was the lord of nature as well as of time. He was the creator of the physical world, the benefactor of good harvests, a God who could appear with clouds and lightning. What made him special in Jewish eyes, though, was his redemptive activity and covenanting—actions in which he stepped out of natural phenomena and acted on a personal basis.

For instance, the liturgical feasts, though they began as nature festivals, ran through the agricultural year, and were expressions of gratitude for harvests, reached their peak at Passover and Yom Kippur—celebrations of historical events and of a moral requirement based on the covenant. Further, the sacrificial aspect of early Jewish worship was replaced by the sermonizing and Bible reading of the synagogue. In fact, as the Torah grew in influence, the human qualities of law, reason, study, and ethics came to the fore. Celebrations still involved food, drink, and dance, but they were probably due more to a social sense, from a desire to affirm a common identity, than from a close connection with Mother Earth or Father Sky. (Interestingly, though, in their elaboration of the Torah, the rabbis were remarkably sensitive to animals' welfare. They glossed the biblical injunction not to muzzle the grinding ox, and they demanded that ritual slaughtering be as painless as possible.)

Urban Values

Many of the countries in which Jews lived, as a distinct and often inhibited minority, forbade them ownership of land, while their tradition of study tended to lead them into intellectual occupations and business. The tensions between *shtetl* Jews and *goyim* (Gentiles) in eastern Europe, for instance, were due as much to different occupations as to different theologies. The Gentile peasants worked the land and valued rather brutish strength. The *shtetl* Jews did not farm, engaging themselves in small businesses and study.

As a result, the qualities valued by the Jews were not the goyish qualities of strength and violence. Jews were not to fight, engage in hard labor, drink, or carouse. They were to be disciplined, cultured, and family and community oriented. Because few Jews lived on farms, they had to concentrate on living in densely populated areas. The Gentile peasants needed customers for their goods, middlemen for their trades, craftsmen, and doctors, and Jews tended to fill these roles. Thus, they clearly stood at some remove from nature.

Women's Status

The Jews, then, focused more on culture than on nature.[56] Anthropologists sometimes use these two concepts as opposing points on a spectrum to determine a people's attitudes toward itself and cosmological processes. For instance, anthropologists have used this spectrum to study sex roles.[57] Women have generally been associated with nature, because of menstruation, childbirth, nursing, and—to male eyes—more instinctive, less cerebral behavior. Men have been associated with culture: craft, art, literature, and politics. It does not take a great deal of research to dispute this construct, but many societies have used it, more or less consciously, to characterize sex roles. Therefore, the construct is useful in analyzing how societies view the play of physical nature in human nature.

This sexual stereotype is somewhat applicable among Jews. As we noted, during many periods of Jewish history women worked or ran the home while the men studied. The biblical portrait of women,[58] and the portrait of women in the Talmud [59] and in the *responsa*,[60] reflect a traditional view that placed women away from law and the mind and towards nature and the body. Separating the patriarchal structure of Middle Eastern society, the Jewish religious conception of God (usually as a husband or father, seldom as a wife or mother), and the Jewish perception of nature is almost impossible. The facts, however, are that women and nature went together and that they were subordinate to men and culture.

For instance, women did not read the Torah in the synagogue (usually they could not read Hebrew), did not have many legal obligations (only three *mitzvah* pertaining only to them), could not be priests or rabbis, were tabooed during menstruation, and were both indulged and criticized for their "flightiness." Under biblical law, Jewish women were essentially considered as property—akin to animals and goods. For instance, the laws concerning adultery and rape were principally intended to protect the rights of the male—the injured husband or father. The principal value of women throughout Jewish history was motherhood—a quite "natural" function. They seldom could have careers and had difficulty obtaining the education that would have enabled them to be their husbands' best friends. They were the source of the family line and of emotional support, not leaders. In good measure because he enjoyed being less natural, the male Jew prayed thanks to God for not having created him a woman.[61]

Zionism

With Zionism and the return to the holy land, Judaism has brought back to center stage a theme that was prominent in premodern times—the predilection for Israel and Jerusalem as the most religious places, favoring the prosperity of Jewish faith. In the centuries of Diaspora, the typical Jew felt something of what the first biblical exiles lamented—the inability to sing and rejoice in a foreign land. No doubt that feeling did not afflict the descendants of the actual exiles as intensely, for few of them returned from Babylon when they had the opportunity, but it mixed a certain nature orientation with Jews' desire to have a place of their own. Consequently, Israel became not just a venerable place but also a beautiful, fruitful, arable, desirable land. Thus, the biblical theme of a promised land joined with messianic hopes to link the new age that the Messiah would usher in and the people's return to a place flowing with milk and honey. Zionism drew on these traditional themes, joining them to socialistic (if not utopian) theories of working the land and living together in close cooperation.

Though few American Jews farm or do their religious thinking along cosmological lines, quite a few Israelis live in a kibbutz and work the land (and quite a few American Jewish youths join them for a summer or a year). The land, if not nature, is most important to kibbutzniks. Because of Israel's ancient history and Jews' present need to have their own place in the sun, the Israelis are more agrarian than their recent predecessors were. How that affects their religious consciousness is hard to determine. Many do not consider themselves religious, and they often view their life on the land, even though it brings them close to nature, in sociological terms. Frequently, then, they resemble other idealistic groups who form communes and farm in order to augment their freedom (and often to "purify" their lives). On the other hand, those who do form kibbutzim out of religious motivations are often fundamentalists who are trying to regain their biblical heritage. That heritage is not so much harvesting God's earth as living where God made the Jews his special people.

Thus, Judaism views nature much differently than the Eastern religions do. To be sure, some Jews have farmed, and some nonfarming Jews have found religious significance in seasons, sunsets, flowers, and stocks of grain. However, the Hebrew Bible, the Talmud, and other products of the mind have been more central to the tradition.

Society

Few religions are as community minded as Judaism. Even when we consider that modern individualism is a historical novelty, the fact remains that the Jews were the chosen *people*—chosen as a group or line rather than as individuals. From tribal beginnings, through kingdom, Diaspora, and ethnic diversification, Jewish religion has always been a group affair. Of course, the Torah is inseparable from this phenomenon, for it is a special law designed expressly for the chosen, covenanted people. It sprang from a group sense that life must flow to "our" God, who led us out of captivity to be his own people. The Torah also specified the theological direction of Jews by giving election and covenant the forms by which they shaped social life.

Thus, the synagogue has been a popular gathering place, uniting the action of the people. The Christian *ecclesia* ("church") has a similar etymological meaning, but the building it names has been almost as much a place for private prayer as for public. Perhaps the relative smallness of the Jewish population has helped it to gain a more worldwide sense of community than Christians have. Perhaps, as well, the relative mildness of its sectarian divisions has helped to keep Judaism a family affair. In any event, Muslims, despite their democratic worship and pilgrimage, have been less united than Jews have been, and Christians, despite their lofty theology of the Church, have been more individual oriented and divided. Finally, nothing in Hinduism or Buddhism prompts a different judgment: Judaism is unified and social to an incomparable degree.

A Jew has always prayed in the plural, for the sake of the many. When a student or scholar devoted himself to Torah, it was usually in common. In the *shtetl*, one clearly lived very much with people—at times oppressively so. As we noted, wealth was for the common good and study had teaching as its goal. Moreover, unlike in Indian society, the Jewish life cycle did not include withdrawal into the forest, and no honor was accorded the individual who dropped out of the group to pursue individual salvation. Unlike Christian society, Jewish society had no monastic alternative (neither solitary nor communitarian) to marriage and family life.[62] (The Essene community at Qumran, if it was an exception to this rule, was short-lived.)

The rabbinic mind uncompromisingly intended that all the people live socially. The scholar pondered a law incumbent on all; the working person normally was in business rather than in the solitude of the fields or the forests; in the home, which was largely the woman's province, feelings were gotten "out," almost compulsively expressed. In fact, silence was considered antisocial and even cruel behavior. The two things that a child could do to punish its mother were not to eat and not to speak. Finally, community conversation buzzed with a detailed analysis of each member's learning, wealth, and family lineage. Small wonder, then, that being called forth to read the Torah before the community was an honor, placing one among the *sheyneh yidn*, the "beautiful Jews."

As we have seen, this communitarian consciousness is rooted in patriarchal times. Jews first identified themselves by their tribal origins, which they tied together under the concept of "the twelve tribes." They attributed their sense of commonness to fatherly figures: Abraham, Moses, and David. Abraham was the source of the seed. To him had been the promise of a progeny as numerous as the stars in the heavens or the grains of sand along the sea. Moses was the founding father, in the sense of being the lawgiver. David was the sacred king, the mediator between heaven and earth, the top of the human pyramid. From his line would spring the Messiah. In a special way, the capital city of Jerusalem was the city of David.

Prophecy and the Chosen People

Of the three key figures, Moses predominated, because the Law that came through him was the backbone of Jewish religious life. As different cultures were assimilated by Judaism, Abraham's lineage became less important than his exemplary faith. Similarly, as political sovereignty became a dim memory, David's kingship became more metaphorical, propping future hopes rather than guiding present living. Moses, however, stayed wholly relevant: He authored the code that kept Jews united; he

was the mediator of the covenant into which the community circumcised each male. When prophecy had become central to Jewish religion, Moses became the prophet par excellence.

Prophecy, which often distinguishes Western religion from Eastern wisdom religion, is not so much the predictions that appear in today's tabloids as a discernment of what the divine spirit is saying to the people of God. The great biblical prophets analyzed the state of faith and, from that analysis, shrewdly estimated political or military fortunes. A goodly portion of such recorded prophecy was, of course, written after the fact. No portion of respectable prophecy, though, pries into the divine mystery. God remains God; the prophet has only the word that God deigns to speak. The establishment of Moses as the supreme prophet testifies to the social utility that Jews have expected communication with God to bear. They expected such communication to result in communal renovation, strengthening, and redirection. Prophecy was not a display of individual virtuosity or a matter involving crystal balls.

As prophecy intimates, the ultimate bonding agent of Jewish society has been God; only the atypical, modern secular Jew would dispute this. Through history the master of the universe, the Adonai that all prayers bless, has bound Jews together as his people. Physically and legally one is a Jew if one is born of a Jewish mother; spiritually one is a Jew if one identifies oneself with the people fashioned at Sinai, framed by the Torah, and covenanted to God. To be sure, many problems attend election as God's people, and Jews have not been unmindful of them. Indeed, the relation between the chosen people and the Gentile nations has been a constant topic for Jewish meditation. In good times, such meditation has turned over history's mysteries gratefully: Why were we chosen when we show no special merits? What are our obligations to the nations?

Indubitably, the Gentile nations were under God's direction, too. It could not be that God had no fulfillment in store for them. So Jewish thinkers worked out the notion of the Noachian covenant: God made a pact with the Gentile nations modeled after the promise he made to Noah, in which he stressed the need for human beings to respect life, especially by avoiding bloodshed. The Bible sees the rainbow as a symbol of God's fidelity to this pact: He will never destroy humanity, never again allow it to suffer as it did in the flood. Yet God could well have more in store for the nations than this Noachian covenant, and Israel's vocation was to be a light unto the nations—to provide them with a greater knowledge of God. In that way, being the chosen people became less a matter of honor than of responsibility.

In bad times, however, reflection on being chosen by God had to probe darker mysteries. For instance, the prophets almost fixated on the horror that Israelites refused their election. Such people wanted kings like the nations had, cults like those to Baal, fertility from the land rather than from the covenant. With some deliberateness, many Jews turned their backs on God because they could not endure living in faith; "I am whatever I want to be" was too much for them. For the prophets, this was the deepest sickness of the soul, the most debilitating sin, as well as a rejection of Israel's better self. The worst of biblical times, then, occurred when people left the covenantal faith.

At such times, the prophets brought the whole question of what the Jewish people at core were into paradox. They spoke of a remnant, of an Israel within Israel that was composed of the few who did keep faith. A major Jewish-Christian controversy has hung on this point, for Christians have claimed to succeed Israel by accepting God's later revelation (specifically, his revelation in Jesus the Christ). Within the Jewish community, prophetic religious leaders have worried about the correlation between bad faith and loss of membership.

The Law

For rabbinic Judaism, the law helped to ease the problem of bad faith. Without

abandoning their ideal of the perfect faith outlined in Maimonides' thirteen articles, the rabbis focused more on performance than on motivation or thought. What one believed about God, within broad limits, was less important than keeping the Sabbath and fulfilling one's communal obligations. This attitude encouraged considerable intellectual freedom, including lively debate, tolerance, and theological ambiguity. As well, it prevented the establishment of a clear-cut religious authority and dogma, such as that encountered by Roman Catholicism in the magisterium of its councils and popes. The law, which seemed so specific, had dozens of interpreters. On and on the Talmud grew, because most interpreters had insights worth preserving.

The result was a subtle but significant shift in the notion of the faith requisite for community membership. It was expressed in action, not in speculation or confession. How one used one's body, money, and time was more important than how one used one's mind or tongue. Such a practical view of faith meant that the community could bind itself through rituals, ethics, and laws without excessive concern about their meaning (although the rabbis did not ignore their meaning or the proper motivation behind actions).

This emphasis on action relates to the Jewish refusal to separate mind and body and to the Jewish commitment to hallowing life. One obeyed the law to express and learn that God, who is holy, wants holy people. Through the quite overt keeping of the law, Jews reminded themselves that they were the people called to sanctify God's name. A Jew knew that his neighbor accepted this identity because he could see that his neighbor obeyed the law. Not accidentally, withdrawal from the law and from the traditional God whom the law hallowed have gone hand in hand in modern times.

The Holocaust

Lastly, contemporary Jewish identity has been annealed as a result of the Holocaust. While exodus and entry into the promised land characterized Jews in biblical times, suffering and persecution have characterized Jews recently. Jewish commentators have no consensus on what recent history means. For Richard Rubenstein, it means the death of the traditional God.[63] For Emil Fackenheim, it means a call to hold together both evil and divine providence.[64] For Hanna Arendt, it shows that history can make evil utterly commonplace or banal.[65] Such commentators do agree that we must not ignore, deny, or explain away the evil of the Holocaust. As Elie Wiesel has said, it is better to keep silent than to depreciate the suffering of so many innocent victims with "explanations."[66] Thus, Jewish identity, the theme of so many American novels, has yet to be fully resolved.

Self

An intense community, such as Judaism's, can heighten individualism. One can prize the individual because the richer the individual, the richer the group. Judaism appears to have appreciated this proposition.

For example, after the prophets (such as Ezekiel and Jeremiah), individual responsibility separated from collective responsibility. No longer could one hold, rather magically, that the fathers had eaten sour grapes and so set the children's teeth on edge. Further, both Hellenization and internal legal development set apart individual reason. For instance, Jewish thinkers in Alexandria reflected Platonic, Aristotelian, Epicurean, and Stoic interests in mind and reason. Philo, the luminary of these thinkers, tried to correlate Mosaic teaching with a cosmic law. In the medieval period, Maimonides, Halevi, and others tried to square the Torah with rational demands for a less mythic, more analytic explanation of faith. Since the individual soul is the site of reason, such concerns inevitably clarified the personality's partial independence of group thought. That is, it underscored that any particular person might grasp or miss the divine Law.

Moreover, the Torah and the Talmud themselves inculcated something of this sensitivity. As a scriptural religion, Judaism demanded literacy and encouraged learning. But, literature and learning are obviously cultural developments deriving from a common human nature that tend to distinguish people according to their talent. Thus, the bright little boy may distinguish himself by the age of ten. Through his unique gifts he may stand out from the crowd, and even increase regard for his family. If he develops into a sage, he will join the line of masters whose commentaries on the Law are the classics. So, by stressing personal insight, legal study encouraged individuation.

To a lesser degree, Jewish mysticism and Jewish attitudes towards wealth also encouraged individuation. Mysticism, like study, is a personal inward phenomenon. Despite its debt to tradition and its occurrence within a community of faith, mysticism is a solitary pursuit involving an "I-Thou" relation. When mysticism flowered in Judaism, it produced revered personalities, such as the Baal-Shem-Tov and the Maggid of Mezritch. To their disciples, these *tzaddikim* were stunning demonstrations of the ardor which divinity could inspire. Their personalities were special, set apart, distinguished. Despite the threats that mysticism posed for the traditional rabbinic authority, the mystics were precious for strengthening the common people's faith. Thus, one could aspire to Hasidic distinction, as one could aspire to rabbinic distinction. Because mystical prowess edified the community, it was a worthy ambition.

Analogously, one could aspire to the (lesser) distinction that came with wealth. Judaism is not, comparatively speaking, an ascetic religion. As much as Hinduism, it views wealth or prosperity as a legitimate life goal. For his good fortune and financial talent, as well as for his philanthropy, a successful Jew could win recognition. True, with success he was sure to gain a host of petitioners, but their attestation to his generosity somewhat offset the burden that they imposed.

This description of the self must be

qualified in discussing women. Since their vocation was marriage and practicality, their distinction was basically reflected—that of being a rich man's wife or a scholar's mother. Nevertheless, women had rights to self-expression, at least regarding nonscriptural matters. The tradition that a woman had no soul did not mean that she had no say. In matters of the home or the shop, she probably had the dominant say. In matters of affection or emotion, she surely did. Thus, few distinguished Jews were not first signalized by women, and most *shtetl* neighborhoods recognized certain girls as being especially nubile and certain mothers as being especially benevolent.

Mind-Body Unity

Judaism stressed the unity of mind and body, eschewing a body-soul or matter-spirit duality. Scholars usually contrast biblical Jewish notions of personhood and contemporary Greek notions. This contrast can illumine the tendency of Judaism towards an existential concreteness that most of Western culture has been struggling for centuries to recapture.

For instance, Descartes, the father of modern European philosophy, worked hard to reconcile the opposition within the human being between its *res cogitans* (thinking part) and its *res extensa* (material part). In contrast, the "soul" *(nepes)* of Hebrew biblical thought was a unity of mind and body that could not be divided into thinking and material parts. So the heart rather than the head stood for the center of thought and emotion. Out of the fullness of the heart the mouth would speak. This conviction fought against the Hellenization of Jewish theology, which would have made the mouth speak what reason dictated. It fought against the aridity latent in rabbinic theology, keeping space for haggadic tales whose appeal was more than mental. The earthiness that one finds in Hebrew literature, from biblical times to the present,[67] reflects these convictions about the heart and body.

Further, through his or her body, the Jewish personality maintained contact with the natural world. In the beginning, God had formed human beings from the earth, breathing into them a living spirit. Various biblical figures, such as Job, acknowledge this connection with the earth when they humble themselves before God and say, "We are but dust and ashes." The connection with the earth is more intense in the command to be fruitful and multiply, for the command implies that living things have an inbuilt drive to survive and grow. Biblical notions of stewardship over the earth found an evolutionary aspect in the command to be fruitful and multiply. (They also subordinated nature to human need.)

The command to be fruitful and multiply also influenced Jewish attitudes toward marriage. The fulfillment of the spouses was a value, at least in talmudic times, but a strong focus was always kept on procreation. As many commentators point out, the late development of the notion of personal immortality in Judaism is due not only to the lack of a clear sense of a spiritual (immaterial) soul, but also to the tendency to think that one continued to exist through one's offspring. In other words, the family line was a sort of concrete immortality.

Thus, marriage was a treasure of Jewish faith in part because it prevented the individual from being totally lost in the abyss of death. From this and other benefits attributed to marriage, sexual activity derived a certain dignity, even a certain obligation. It is true that in rabbinic Judaism prudery seemed to offset the high evaluation of sexual love. The rabbis counseled against raising one's eyes to a woman's face, and they desired that the sexes be segregated as much as possible. They laid on women the heavy burden of the temptress that we have seen in other religions. Indeed, in Judaism, unchastity was not only sinful but also deplorable because it drew the mind down from the (masculine) heights of the Torah and prayer.

In most orthodox homes (which for the poor often had only one or two rooms), husband and wife did not sleep in the same bed. Tradition encouraged them to have relations except during the menstrual flow but to keep the sexual appetite in check. One of the nice customs of the Sabbath, however, was that in its leisure spouses should make love. As the Cabalists stressed, the Sabbath was the bride of God. Consequently, they found in the coexistence of man and woman a supplement to the notion that human reason is an image of God. Humanity also images God through sexual love, acting in accordance with the Genesis line "male and female he created them."

The Human Spirit

In prophecy Jewish religion found understandings of God's relationship to the human spirit new to human history. That is, the ecstatic experience of the prophets, who seem to have begun as wandering bands of exultants *(nebi'im)*, evolved into something other than ordinary shamanism (which we may take as the typical model of ancient ecstasy). For where shamanism usually kept the world divine and usually confused the relations between imagination and reason in the ecstatic experience (though some shamans were well aware of the divine incomprehensibility), the prophets had experiences that burned below imagination to the base of the spirit. The burning bush, for instance, occasioned the realization that we only know of God what the divine mystery shows in time. Elijah's small, still voice suggested that God comes more through spiritual recollection than through natural storms. Jeremiah, finally, went to the core of the matter: Divine creativity best expresses itself by writing its law upon the human heart.

That does not mean that the prophetic, or later the mystical, Jews did not mix myth, symbol, and imagination. The *merkabah* (chariot) imagery, as we mentioned, dominated even the philosophers' ruminations about God, while the Cabalists' bliss was to imagine the divine emanations. Still, the union of the entire numinous experience (the entire experience of divinity) with ethical demands refined what it means to be religious by communion with a transcendent God. Implicit in the prophetic and talmudic program is that true religion is doing justice and worshipping purely. It is the twofold commandment of loving God (who is one) and loving one's neighbor (who is another self). This maxim developed into the powerful concept of individual conscience: One only is the mystery that dominates and constitutes the human person in its being and its morality alike. Realizing such monotheism was a deathblow to all idolatry, an emancipation of the Jewish spirit. History continues to unfold the implications of this ethical monotheism. From biblical times, then, the Jews have cast the self, as well as the people, in partnership with a single God.

Divinity

The question of the place of divinity in Judaism is difficult for Westerners, because the Jewish God is inseparable from Western culture. We can no more filter out Israelite ethical monotheism from the Western world view than we can filter out Greek reason. It requires considerable imaginative energy, therefore, to grasp the origins of Jewish divinity and trace how those beginnings developed into theological conceptualizations.

The biblical beginnings were extremely novel, constituting a "leap in being" rivaled only by the Greek clarification of reason. The biblical beginnings were deep spiritual experiences: irruptions of divinity that seized and formed the soul (more than they clarified reason). The God who was revealed was lively, personal, and free.

Perhaps because the genius of Israelite religion was not reason but spirit, the biblical Jews expressed this God's character as the world's origin and destiny in myths. That is, they expressed the truth of order, of humanity's proper place in and with nature and God, symbolically, from the "dead spot," the bottom of the soul, which revelation seizes. Moreover, having expressed its order mythologically, the Israelite religious genius hardly criticized its symbols, making little effort to interpret them in clearer, if less complete, conceptual terms. In other words, it did not attack the problems of inner coherence that today's analytic philosophy associates with meaning.[68] So the God of Moses "is" only what time shows him to be; the God of Genesis makes the world "in the beginning" from primal chaos, the status of which is quite unclear; and the God of Isaiah (chapter 6) is placed beyond the world by a dazzling cluster of symbols.

Christian Contrast

The development from these biblical beginnings followed a somewhat different course in Jewish theology than in Christian theology. Christian theology, Eastern and Western alike, structured itself through Hellenistic philosophy. Origen, Arius, Athanasius, the Cappadocians, Augustine—these great speculators utilized the Greek discovery of mind. No less, the architects of doctrinal theology that succeeded them (Nestorius, Cyril, Boethius, Anselm, and Aquinas) designed with Greek intellectual tools. Jewish theology for the most part bypassed Hellenism. As we have seen, Philo and Maimonides appropriated Greek logic, Greek epistemology (theory of knowledge), and Greek metaphysics. The mainline, talmudic development of the Torah, though, contained Hellenism's impact.

The overall result was a theological predominance of law over philosophy. The infrastructure of Jewish belief appears less, or at least quite differently, defined than the Christian. It did not try to ground itself in reflective reason as Christian scholasticism did. At its core, Jewish theology was a symbolic, ethical, and mystical movement, if not flux. It was more imaginative and less controlled and clarified by philosophy than Christian theology was. As well, it was more historical—more concerned with honoring the covenantal mystery and keeping the teachers' traditions.

Christians could reply that they tried hard to honor the new covenant and that their doctrine of apostolic succession was an effort to keep their teachers' traditions. True enough, but the increasingly speculative emphasis of Christian theology made its

consciousness of history less effective and tangible than that of Jewish theology. As well, Christianity spread to many ethnic groups, among whom unity was hard to maintain. Last, in Jewish theology one did not have a metaphysics of God developed from the psychology of His human image, as one did in Augustine and Aquinas. Rather, one had amazing refinements of the behavior that living with God demanded.

The impact of this difference is perhaps clearest in the two religions' doctrines of God's relation to the world. Working from a similar literature (the Hebrew Bible was the Christians' Old Testament), the two theologies went quite different ways. Christian scholasticism developed the position that God has no "real" relations with the world or with human beings. Rather, all God's relations with the world are simply "rational" *(entia rationis* ["clarifications that have no foundation in the divine being itself"]).

The consequence of this Hellenistically based conceptualization is that God does not change, suffer, move, or develop in his relations with creatures. This makes for a theology that is at variance with the biblical picture (and, according to contemporary "process theology," at variance with intuitions of "perfection" that challenge the intuitions of Hellenistic thought).[69] Except perhaps for the Jewish philosophers, Jewish theology kept God "really" related to the world—the God of refined Jewish reflection was held accountable for history and thought capable of change and movement.

The differences in this aspect of God's conception in popular Judaism and Christianity are less pronounced, because popular Christian faith seems to have imagined God more on the model of biblical anthropomorphism than on the model of the philosophical theologians' "Pure Act" of being. In terms of prayer (which Friedrich Heiler has suggested is the most central religious activity),[70] the average Jew and Christian likely thought about God in the same way: God is interested in us, loves us, listens to our petitions, and controls the world in such a way that our prayers can make a difference. If this popular equivalence is valid, Jewish "professional" theology kept closer ties to its faithful than Christian "professional" theology did.

Thus far, our comparison of Christian and Jewish conceptions of divinity has bracketed the question of Jesus' divinity. Clearly, however, the Christian development of Jesus as the Messiah into the union of his humanity with God differentiates Christian theology from Jewish. In fact, it even separates Christians from those Jews who view Jesus as a remarkable expression of Jewish religion. Moreover, when Jesus' divinity produces the Christian conception of God as the Trinity (Father, Son, and Spirit), the difference becomes extreme. At that point, the two prophetic religions become different faiths.

Contrast with Other Religions

The divinity in the Hindu consciousness is substantially impersonal. Hindus did personify divinity through the Trimurti (Vishnu and Shiva especially) and through their avatars (Krishna especially), but not to the extent of the Jewish God. Similarly, Buddhist consciousness requires considerable reworking (of nirvana, Buddha-nature, or emptiness) to become theological, and even if we can thereby establish a Buddhist divinity (beyond the numerous buddhas and bodhisattvas), its main face is impersonal. Chinese religion offers divinity in the modes of heaven or *Tao*, both of which underscore

the personal aspect of Judaism's divinity. The kami of Japan are essentially nature forces, and the divinities such as Kuan-yin, who exerted great popular influence because they did have a personal face, were never the *sole* God.

The case is different with Islam, because (largely through borrowings from biblical thought) Allah is personal, one, and in charge of the world. Conceptually, therefore, Islamic theology changed less of what it received from Jewish tradition about God than Christian theology did. In popular religion, however, Islam appears more fatalistic than Judaism. Consequently, its God appears less involved, less changeable than the Jewish God. Alternatively, Muslims so stressed Allah's power that they somewhat suppressed human freedom (though officially they affirmed it). Nonetheless, Allah is as near as the pulse at one's throat, and he is merciful, compassionate, willing to forgive the sinner, and an intervener for Muslims in holy war. Thus, the Muslim God can make a difference in a believer's life.

Because of its strict monotheism, Islam probably has a doctrine of God that is closest to that of Judaism. Thus, Islam has multiplied the effects of Jewish revelation. However, the ripple of monotheism through Islamic cultures produced quite a different law, tradition of scholarship, and piety. In terms of practice, then, the two theologies are quite distinct.

Study Questions

1. Why was David's kingship an ambiguous symbol?
2. What is the main theme of the history that the Hebrew Bible writes?
3. In what ways does rabbinic or talmudic religion differ from biblical religion?
4. How would you summarize the religious mentality expressed in Maimonides' thirteen articles of faith?
5. In what ways has Judaism focused more on culture than on nature?
6. Discuss the significance of celebrating a Sabbath each week.
7. Can you define exactly the senses in which the Jewish God is *creator* and *redeemer*?

Chapter Nine

CHRISTIANITY: TWENTY-FIVE KEY DATES

CA. 30 C.E.	DEATH OF JESUS OF NAZARETH
CA. 65	DEATH OF APOSTLE PAUL
CA. 95	LAST OF NEW TESTAMENT WRITINGS
CA. 100–165	JUSTIN MARTYR, LEADING APOLOGIST
CA. 185–254	ORIGEN, LEADING THEOLOGIAN
313	CHRISTIANS FREED OF LEGAL PERSECUTION
325	FIRST COUNCIL OF NICAEA
354–430	AUGUSTINE, LEADING THEOLOGIAN
451	COUNCIL OF CHALCEDON
CA. 480–550	BENEDICT, FOUNDER OF WESTERN MONASTICISM
CA. 540–604	POPE GREGORY I, FOUNDER OF MEDIEVAL PAPACY
787	SECOND COUNCIL OF NICAEA (LAST ONE THAT THE ORTHODOX CHURCH CONSIDERS ECUMENICAL)

Christianity

If we gather all its parts, Christianity is the largest religion in the world. What began as a Jewish sect has carried its version of the Torah and prophecy around the globe.[1] We begin our study of Christianity by describing its appearance in several different countries.

APPEARANCE

We have tried to indicate something of what Jerusalem means to Jews. To a lesser but still significant extent, Jerusalem is for Christians as well as Muslims the "Holy City." Christians venerate Jerusalem because of its significance for Jesus and the early Church. It is the place where Jesus died and the Church was born. Today the different groups of Jesus' followers preserve, even hawk, this memory. Franciscan priests in brown robes lead pilgrims through the narrow streets of the Old City, along the *via dolorosa*—the path down which Jesus carried the cross according to tradition. Behind high walls are numerous churches dedicated to events in Jesus' life. For instance, a church lies near a grove of olive trees where the Gospels say Jesus prayed after the Last Supper.

In Bethlehem, a few miles south of Jerusalem, a church sits at the spot where tradition says Jesus was born. One corner of it belongs to Eastern Orthodox Christians, who celebrate their solemn liturgy in flowing robes and conical hats and with clouds of incense. In another corner Catholics stand watch at a grotto they venerate as the birthplace.

Christianity is simpler—theologically and culturally—in Rome than in Jerusalem. Despite its historical riches of a pre-Christian culture, Rome clearly is a Catholic capital today. Even many Italian Communists marry, baptize their children, and are buried in Catholic ceremonies. St. Peter's and the Vatican, as well as the art of Florence and Venice, are unthinkable apart from Italy's Catholic history.

St. Peter's disappoints few visitors. Its sheer size is impressive, but it is more than a giant. Michelangelo's *Pietà*, for instance, is exquisite. Bernini's columns around the main altar also deserve their fame. The whole basilica, in fact, recalls the age when Christ's vicars patronized art to make Catholic religion stream forth in crimson, azure, ermine, and gold.

Eastern Orthodoxy has no capital, but you can feel its pulse in Athens. The humble cathedral, for example, shows some of the differences between Eastern Christendom and Western. First, its layout is not the long rectangle of St. Peter's but a more intimate square. People stand close together before the icons. Second, Orthodox devotion to Mary is different from what the *Pietà* suggests. For the East, Mary is the *theotokos* (the God-bearer). Portraits of her show a queen of heaven with crown and mantle. Her infant is a princely teacher, his hand raised for blessing. In the cathedral people pause before an icon or Bible, cross themselves from right to left, and end their prayers with a kiss. On the Greek islands are tiny churches, whitewashed and onion spired. Their people project a tough, deep-burning faith that dresses widows in black for the rest of their lives and disciplines the flesh. The Orthodox priests, too, seem fierce. Their full beards, bushy brows, and black robes pay the world and the body little homage.

Dourness winds through the streets of Geneva, where John Calvin's spirit lives. Though Lake Leman (Geneva) sparkles with Gallic charm, the stony streets are all Protestant discipline. Geneva is the peak of Swiss neutrality, and the World Council of Churches there tries to keep the Christian peace. It is open to Catholics and Orthodox, but their participation has been limited. In recent years the World Council has supported third world movements, calling for a new economic order. That has not sat well with conservative brethren, who used to hesitate to mix religion and politics. For progressives, the World Council's internationalism has made Geneva the center of a new reformation. While the old Reformation was a matter of returning to scripture, the new reform would increase bread for the world.

The art, spirit, and politics of Christianity clearly vary among the three major traditions, yet their common heritage still shapes the West. Even though Western culture proclaims itself secular, it originates from a Christian past. Without its Christian heritage, Western secularism would have few of its analytic tools—and fewer of its enemies. If this state of affairs seems asleep in the frame churches of rural America, it is fully alert in the centers of culture. Detroit and Wall Street, for instance, are brazen in their contempt of biblical justice. If it is easier for a camel to pass through the eye of the needle than for a rich person to enter the Kingdom of God, Detroit, Wall Street, Madison Avenue, and America's other centers of affluence are home to many who stand outside the kingdom.

HISTORY

Jesus

Christianity developed from the life and work of Jesus of Nazareth,[2] as Buddhism developed from the life and work of Gautama. Jesus (whose historical reality is attested to by such non-Christian authors as Josephus, Tacitus, Suetonius, and Pliny the Younger) was born about 4 B.C.E. (by current calendars) in Palestine. We know little about his youth except through Gospel stories, such as those of his circumcision and his dialogues with religious teachers. (The stories of his birth are legendary, in the service of the various New Testament authors' theologies.)[3] We assume that he grew up as a Jewish youth of his times. About the year 27 C.E. he started from his native Galilee on a career as an itinerant preacher. Geza Vermes has described the contemporary political and religious context, suggesting that Jesus was a preacher and healer on the model of the *hasid* (pious one) familiar to his time and locale.[4]

While Jesus' message has been inter-preted in very different ways, certain essentials seem quite clear. Joachim Jeremias's careful study argues that Jesus' own voice echoes in the New Testament parables, riddles, discussions of the reign of God, the peculiar use of *amen*, and the peculiar use of *Abba* (Father) for God.[5] On etymological and historical grounds, these are the safest leads to how Jesus himself preached (with concrete, lively language) and to what he had to say (that a new time was dawning and that God is intimately parental). In their admirable digest of Christian theology, Rahner and Vorgrimler state that Jesus' main theme was an announcement that the reign of God is at hand in his (Jesus') own person.[6] That reign or kingdom was a new beginning, a time of justice and holiness.

According to the New Testament writers, this theme meant that Jesus had fulfilled Jewish religion and superseded it. Jesus himself solicited a radical commitment to the new opportunities that God's reign offered, which included intimacy with God and friendship with other persons. The morality that Jesus anticipated in the kingdom[7] is most graphic in his Sermon on the Mount. There the evangelists have him bless those who are poor, gentle, mourning, hungry and thirsty for what is right, merciful, pure in heart, peacemaking, and suffering for the cause of justice. They are the citizens of the kingdom; dispositions or circumstances like theirs render human beings open to divine love. The gist of Jesus' own life, according to the New Testament, was just such love.

Information on Jesus' public life and ministry remains imprecise (because of the limited sources). Apparently he linked his work with that of John the Baptist, his message raised opposition from the religious establishment, he worked out only some of the particulars for living in the kingdom, and he predicted woe to those who rejected his program. Further, he planted at least the seeds of the Christian Church by gathering disciples and co-workers, and he gained a reputation as a healer. His death came by order of the Roman procurator Pontius Pilate on the dubious grounds that he threatened the peace.

Interpretations

Beyond this bare outline, historical and theological interpretations diverge. According to the New Testament and the orthodox faith of later centuries, the old reign of Satan and sin died with Jesus. Further, after death Jesus was raised (resurrected) and was disclosed to be "Lord" or ruler of humanity. More tersely, Jesus was the divine Son whose dying and rising brought the world salvation. This interpretation thus stresses a twofold quality in Jesus: He was both human and divine. The councils that specifically discussed and defined Jesus' being found this interpretation to be the intent of the Gospel and Epistle writers.

Another interpretation of the New Testament is that Jesus was the Messiah— the anointed king of the age of grace, where *grace* came to mean not just peace and material plenty but intimacy with God and sharing in divine life. From the titles that the New Testament gives to Jesus, his own reported claims, and the miracles (healings, raisings from the dead, and so on) that the New Testament attributes to Jesus, we can conclude that the New Testament writers found him most remarkable—so remarkable that he had to be more than human. For them he was the bringer of salvation,[8] God's Word incarnate, the Christ (Messiah), and the divine Son.

In the earliest portions of the New Testament, the Epistles, Jesus is a living spiritual reality. The assumption behind Paul's directions for Church life, for instance, is that "the Lord" lives in Christians' midst. After Jesus' death, his followers apparently thought that his movement was finished, but the events of the Resurrection convinced them that he had assumed a new form of existence. They stayed together in Jerusalem; at Pentecost (seven weeks after Passover, when Jesus had died), they experienced what they called the Holy Spirit,

whom they thought Jesus and the Father had sent. The Spirit charged them to go out and preach about Jesus. Thus, the early Christians proclaimed that Jesus' life and death were the definitive act of salvation. The disciples also preached that Jesus was the Messiah. As such he was in accordance with Jewish tradition and yet responsible for its transformation. From a historical perspective, then, the first Christians appear as sectarian Jews—Jews with a new interpretation of messianism.

It took some time for the first interpretations of Jesus to sift out and clarify, and a principal catalyst in that process was Paul. From the accounts in Acts and his own writings, Paul was a Pharisaic Jew whose conversion on the road to Damascus (Acts 9 : 3–9) was quite dramatic. After his conversion he tried to show his fellow Jews that Jesus was their Messiah, but their opposition to his preaching, plus his own further reflection on Jesus' life and death, led Paul to think that in Jesus God had opened the covenant to all persons—Gentiles as well as Jews.

Consequently, Paul made the gospel (good news) about Jesus a transformation of the Torah. Because God had fulfilled in Jesus the intent of the Law, the Law's many detailed prescriptions were passé. Adherence to an external code could not make one righteous (on even terms with God). Only by opening to God's love and healing could one stand before Him acceptably. Paul called that opening "faith." For him Jesus was the agent of a shift from the Torah to the gospel, from works to faith. The way to become right with God was to commit oneself to Jesus. Thus, for Paul, Jesus represented the kingdom, embodied God's grace. As Paul's vision spread, he saw Jesus' transition from death to life as the climax of salvation history. Jesus the Christ was a new Adam, a new beginning for the human race. All who clung to him, who used him to interpret their lives, became members of his "body." Christ and the Church formed a living entity.

Paul's interpretation of Jesus was the key to early Christianity developing into a universal religion. By dropping the requirements of the Jewish Law and extending membership to all who would base their lives on Jesus, the early Church broke with Judaism irreparably. The Torah had been the cornerstone of covenantal life. Most Jews, understandably, were not willing to throw the Torah over or enter a new covenant. Some who had seen Jesus heal or heard him preach joined his cause; the apostles who began the Church after Jesus' death, for instance, were Jews who journeyed from the Torah to the gospel. However, most Jews had not heard or seen Jesus, and for historical, psychological, political, and religious reasons they could not accept the claims about him.

The Gentiles who warmed to the gospel lived in a Hellenistic milieu that was ripe for salvation.[9] Just as Judaism was in turmoil, with Zealots, Pharisees, Sadducees, and Essenes all urging different reactions to Roman rule, so, too, were the belief systems of the Gentiles. Through the mystery religions, Gnosticism, and philosophy, a large number of Gentiles were pursuing salvation avidly. Jesus as a savior figure fit many of their needs. In a short while, Christianity established itself as a new wisdom or gnosis (secret knowledge), too. It offered fulfillment in this life, immortality in a world to come.

A New World View

As a result of the gospel and Paul's theology, within a generation of Jesus' death Jewish and Greek thought had combined into a powerful new world view.[10] From Judaism came the concepts of prophet and messiah. From Hellenism came the notions of savior and god. In the Church's hands, they all were underscored. Jesus was the successor to Moses, the giver of a new Law, Daniel's Son of man come to inaugurate the messianic age, the conqueror of death and disorder, and the Logos (Word) of eternal divinity come into time. He was alpha and omega—the beginning and the end. All past history, from the first parent Adam, had been but a preparation for his coming. All of the future would unfold his implications, climaxing in a final judgment and a fulfillment in heaven.

At first the Christians expected the future to be short. Jesus would soon return in power and glory to consummate his work. As the years went by, the beliefs shifted. Jesus had accomplished the essentials of salvation through his death and resurrection. However long it took in God's dispensation for Jesus' salvation to work itself out, there was no doubt of the final success. The faithful would just have to endure. Living in faith and hope, they were to preach the good news to all whom they could reach.

In that way—first with a sense that the time was short and then with a sense that Jesus was life's best interpretation—Christianity began its missionary career, preaching the gospel to the ends of the earth. In that, too, it differed from Judaism, which little proselytized. The next chapters in the Christian story concern the effects of moving the gospel into different cultures.[11]

The Apostolic Age

The Gospel writers—Mark, Matthew, Luke, and John—also interpreted the life of Jesus.[12] Even in the most journalistic portions of the New Testament, they have cast Jesus' sayings and doings in terms of their own theologies. Matthew, for instance, works largely with Jewish notions, trying to show that Jesus is the successor to Moses, the gospel is the successor to the Torah, and so on. The other Gospels, as well as Hebrews and Revelation, are similarly theological. John arranges Jesus' public life around a series of signs giving him a sacramental glow and making him a thaumaturgist (wonder worker). The second half of John's Gospel concentrates on Jesus' "glory": his intimacy with the heavenly Father and his victorious death and resurrection. Hebrews tries to show that Jesus fulfilled Jewish types of sacrifice, while Revelation is a Christian apocalypse (disclosure) designed to shore up faith against Roman persecution.

By the end of the first century, then,

the Church had a variety of theologies. The majority were extensions of Jewish religion in the light of Jesus as the Messiah. The "apostolic age" is the period of elaboration of what Jesus meant and how the Church was to organize itself. It embraces roughly the first three centuries, and a central concern was authority. For the early Church, an *apostolos* was a person to whom God delegated Church authority. It depended on the Jewish notion of *saliah*—a Hebrew legal term that meant "the authoritative representation of an individual or group in juridical or legal matters."[13]

During Jesus' ministry, his twelve intimates were the apostles par excellence, since they had received their commission from Jesus himself. Clearly the Twelve formed a collegial group with Peter as their head,[14] and the Church accepted their authority. However, balancing this apostolic, "official" authority was a looser, charismatic leadership expressed through prophecy, teaching, speaking in tongues, and so on.

The earliest Church preaching was intended to show that Jesus fulfilled the promises of Jewish scripture. In their teaching, the apostles relied on oral tradition about Jesus' person and words. The first great problem in the apostolic age, as we saw, was the Pauline (pertaining to Paul) problem of opening the Church to the Gentiles.

During the second century the leadership of the Church passed from those who had seen Jesus themselves to those who had received the gospel from eyewitnesses but had not themselves known the Lord. The "Fathers" who led the second-century Church are therefore apostolic in the sense that they had direct contact with the Twelve. One of the apostolic fathers was Clement of Rome, whom tradition calls the successor to Peter as leader of the Christian community in Rome. Clement wrote an epistle in the style of Paul that called for Church unity. Hermas wrote a pastoral piece that called for tight moral discipline. Igna-

tius of Antioch wrote several letters about keeping faith in the face of martyrdom. These three apostolic writers and other writers from the early second century[15] reveal something of the young Church's internal and external problems. Internally, keeping discipline was obviously a major difficulty. As Christ's return was delayed, human weaknesses and individualism asserted themselves. Externally, from the time of Nero (54–68), the Church was ever liable to persecution by the Roman authorities.

A celebrated non-Christian source describing the situation early in the second century is a letter written by Pliny the Younger, governor of Bithynia on the Black Sea, to the emperor Trajan about 112. Romans had executed some Christians (their faith seemed incompatible with the pledge of loyalty to Caesar that Rome required), and Pliny described the Christians' religious activities in order to give the emperor the information necessary to ascertain what sort of a threat they really were. According to the letter, the Christians would gather before dawn one day a week, sing hymns to a certain "Chrestus" whom they treated as a god, and take an oath to abstain from crime. Then they would end their meeting with a common meal. Trajan answered that if other Christians would recant and "worship our gods," Pliny might pardon them. Clearly the Roman authorities of the time worried about secret societies that might sow seeds of revolution. Since the Romans looked on religion as the bond of their realm, they were especially sensitive to groups who did not seem to worship the traditional Roman deities.

Christians expanded throughout the Roman Empire during the second and third centuries. By 300 they probably constituted the majority population in Asia Minor and Carthage, and they were at least a noticeable fraction of the population along the northern shore of the Mediterranean. Their major political problem, gaining sufferance from the Roman authorities, was not solved until Constantine came to power early in the fourth century.

Gnosticism

More potentially destructive than Rome were the Gnostic heresies. Their teachings varied considerably, but their common element was heterodox Judaism under the influence of Hellenistic and Iranian thought. In essence most Gnosticism involved a dualistic mythology. Matter, the negative principle, came from a Demiurge— a subordinate divinity whom the Father God begot as Wisdom but who fell from grace. Divinity itself was a *pleroma* (fullness) of times and levels. Gnosticism offered a revelation to certain "elect" persons: If they would hate this lower world of material creation (which was under the fallen Demiurge) and believe in a higher spiritual and divine realm, they might return to glory with God.

To explain their revelation, the Gnostics taught that each of the elect had a hidden spark from God's eternal world. The sparks fell into matter because of a heavenly war between darkness and light (or, in other versions, because of an accident during the production of the divine emanations). The jealous, inferior god who clumsily fashioned the material realm, which is subject to time and fate, was born in the same accidental process. He was the author of carnal humanity, in which the divine spark was a prisoner. Higher beings would one day dissolve this fallen world, but in the meantime they call to our hidden sparks by means of saviours, revelations, and rites of baptism.[16]

Gnosticism blended the Hellenistic notion of divine emanation, mystery religion notions about salvation through sacramental rites, and Jewish notions of sin and redemption. It stressed the division between this world and heaven, the evil of matter and the flesh, and the need for asceticism (celibacy and bodily discipline) to gain freedom from matter. Valentinus is the most celebrated Gnostic teacher, but we know his system largely through the apostolic father Irenaeus, whose influential *Against Heresies* attacked it harshly.

Other threats to Christianity during the early period included the prophecies of Marcion, Montanus, and Mani.[17] Marcion was a Christian excommunicate who maintained that the Christian gospel is wholly a matter of love rather than a matter of law. On that account, he completely rejected the Old Testament (Jewish scripture), finding the God of Genesis incompatible with the God of Jesus. Montanus led a heretical apocalyptic movement based on the primacy of the Holy Spirit. His followers expected the outpouring of the Holy Spirit on the Church. In its own prophets, Montanism saw the beginnings of the bestowal of the Spirit. Montanism developed an impressive asceticism, and it captured the estimable African thinker Tertullian, who found it more spiritual than Christianity under the discipline of Rome.

Mani lived from about 215 to 275 in Persia and India (to which he fled from Zoroastrian persecution). His system supposed a primeval conflict between light and darkness, and it, too, stressed asceticism. The object of Manichaeanism was to release the particles of light that Satan had stolen and placed in the human brain. Buddha, the Israelite prophets, Jesus, and Mani himself were the messengers whom God had sent to teach human beings the way to salvation. Manichaeanism spread to Egypt, Africa, and even Rome. During the early years of his adult life, the great Christian thinker Augustine was a Manichaean.

The apostolic period, then, was a time of missionary expansion, the development of Christian doctrine (largely through opposition to Gnostic rivals), and persecution. The Roman emperors Decius (249–251) and Diocletian (284–305) made enough martyrs to make professing Christian faith a serious matter. Christians had to meet secretly in catacombs (caves) or private homes, and their organization had to be informal. Their leaders (bishops and elders) were indistinguishable from ordinary people, and their teaching had a *disciplina arcani*—a strict code of secrecy. Those who died giving testimony to their faith (martyrs, etymologically meaning "witnesses") were great heroes, whom heaven would greet with open arms. One of the greatest early controversies, in fact, concerned the status of those who had recanted their faith to avoid martyrdom and then, in a period of calm, asked readmission to the Christian community. Donatus led a party of rigorists who insisted that traitors had no place in the Church and that any sacraments (holy rites) that they administered would be invalid. Augustine successfully opposed Donatus, arguing for greater clemency and for Christ's decisive role in the inner administration of the sacraments.

Only a thin line separates the apostolic fathers from the conciliar fathers and the great theologians of the "patristic" age (age of the Fathers), for the three centuries after the deaths of the Twelve were characterized by a continuity of theological themes. First, there was the task of defending Church discipline and morality against both laxness and rigorism. Second, Church leaders had to walk a middle way between inspiration through charismata and institutional authority. Against Gnostics, the Church had to affirm the goodness of material creation. Against those who denied Jesus' humanity (the Docetists), it had to maintain that he was fully human and had really suffered and died. The Christian Church had little power in the secular world until the conversion of Constantine (312), so even when it was not suffering active persecution, it was not very influential. Church leaders continued to reflect on the relation between Jesus and Judaism, as well as on conceptions of Jesus and God that would make most sense to educated Hellenists.

The apostolic Church developed a rule by local bishops. They became the primary teachers of doctrine, the primary defenders of orthodox (straight) belief. The bishops led the common worship, settled community disputes, and, to the extent that their talents allowed, fought heresies through sermons and writings. They were the main line of Fathers around whom the early Church arranged itself. The great heroes, as we mentioned, were the martyrs, and the life of the community took its liturgical pattern from the Eucharist (communal meal) and baptism (rite of entry into the Church). Forgiving sins raised questions of moral theology, for after baptism all were supposed to keep their faith pure, but gradually the Church allowed sinners to return to the community after they did penance. In the first three centuries, then, the Church established elements of the character that it has borne ever since.

The Conciliar Age

During the fourth and fifth centuries, a number of meetings (councils) of Church leaders were held that formally established the discipline and official doctrine (dogma) that any group in union with the apostolic Church had to adopt.[18] From those meetings came the name for the next period of Christian history. Above all, the meetings dealt with the central issues of the Christian creed, hammering out the dogmas about God, Jesus, salvation, and the like that became the backbone of Christian theology. Various controversies made Church leaders realize that it was imperative to determine which apostolic sources were genuine expressions of faith and which were not. That imperative resulted in the establishment of a Christian scriptural canon.

Three main factors determined the final canon: whether the writing in question came from an apostle or a close associate of an apostle, whether it was accepted by the Church at large, and whether its contents were edifying for faith.[19] As early as 170, leaders in Rome had determined a canon of authoritative books in response to the canon drawn up by the heretic Marcion. Yet for many decades no list was agreed upon by the entire Church because local traditions varied.

For instance, the East long hesitated to accept Revelation, while the West was chary about Hebrews. In the early decades of the fourth century, Bishop Eusebius of Caesarea (perhaps the first significant Church historian) divided candidate books into three categories: acknowledged, disputed, and spurious. The acknowledged and the disputed books constitute the twenty-seven books of today's New Testament. In 367 Athanasius of Alexandria published a "Festal Letter" that listed these twenty-seven books, which earned the approval of Fathers such as Jerome and Augustine and the endorsements of synods (councils) at Hippo (393) and Carthage (397 and 419).

The first great dogmatic council occurred at Nicaea in Bithynia (south of the Black Sea) in 325. It produced the Nicene Creed (statement of belief) that was especially important for clarifying Jesus' divine status as Logos or Son. Prior to Nicaea, most churches had been content to repeat what scripture (Jewish and Christian both) said about God and Jesus. However, Church theologians did not know how to respond to questions that scripture did not address. One such question came from Arius, a priest of Antioch, who proposed that Jesus, as the Logos of God (the divine Son), is subordinate to the Father. In short, Arius' proposition was that if one drew a line between created beings and the uncreated divine substance, the Logos would fall on the side of created beings, because "there was a then when he was not." Arius' principal opponent was Athanasius.

Arius represented the Syrian theological tradition that centered at Antioch, while Athanasius represented the theologians of Alexandria, who descended from Clement of Alexandria (ca. 150–215), one of the first Christian theologians to cast faith as a philosophy that might persuade educated Hellenists, and Origen (ca. 185–254), the first great Christian speculator. Working with Platonic philosophy, Origen wrote immensely influential commentaries on scripture and expositions of Christian doctrine.

Athanasius, drawing on the Alexandrian tradition, assaulted Arius' argument. Speaking for what he held to be orthodoxy, he said that the Logos was of the same substance as the Father, possessing the single divine nature. Nicaea agreed with Athanasius, making his position dogma. There were many political machinations, as different factions chose different theological sides, and Arianism thrived among Germanic tribes well into the sixth century. However, the Nicene Creed, which codified Athanasius' position, came into common use, with the result that the divinity of the Logos became common faith.

Trinitarian Doctrine

Athanasius also perceived that the canonical literature gave the Holy Spirit divinity equal to that of the Father and the Son. Therefore, he extended the meaning of his word *homoousion* (of one stuff) to include the Holy Spirit and so set the lines of what would become, at the Council of Constantinople in 381, the doctrine of the Spirit's divinity. That completed the doctrine of the Trinity: one God who is three equal "persons," each of whom fully possesses the single divine nature.

Augustine, bishop of Hippo in Africa, expressed this doctrine in terms of a psychological analogy that shaped Western Christian speculation. He proposed that as memory, understanding, and love are all mind, so (but without human imperfections) are Father, Son, and Holy Spirit all divinity. The Father is as an inexhaustible memory (from which all creation comes), the Logos is as the Father's self-awareness, and the Spirit is as their boundless love.

In the Trinitarian controversies (and perhaps even more in the subsequent Christological controversies [controversies about Jesus Christ]), the terminology that eventually became fixed was still quite fluid.[20] Bernard Lonergan has argued that the Church's decision to respond to Arius and so coin new language for new problems (problems not resolved by scripture) was a decisive advance in its self-understanding.[21] It would have been obscurantism, or anti-intellectualism, to refuse to grapple with questions as serious and legitimate as Arius'. (Indeed, it would have been the sort of "interdict" on the mind's drive to understand for which Eric

Voegelin has severely criticized Karl Marx.)[22] By responding to Arius' challenge, the Church affirmed its ability to determine the meaning of scripture and to develop doctrine as new situations required.

Politics

The conciliar definitions gave Christian faith considerably more precision and at least tacitly encouraged theologians to study and speculate further on the doctrinal tracts that they had laid out. The conciliar age was also fraught with the intrusions of secular leaders, for after Constantine and his successors made Christianity the favored imperial religion, the emperors assumed that they had the right, even the pious duty, to intervene in Church affairs. Thus, the tension between Church and state, as we now call it, started its long and tangled history in the conciliar age. Whether this led to the Caesaropapism (domination of the Church by the emperor) that afflicted the Eastern portions of Christianity before the schism of 1054 is a matter for learned historians to decide. We need only point out here that, because of Christianity's official status, the councils became a matter of imperial interest.

In fact, the councils were the spearhead of the advances that the Church and state made into one another's affairs.[23] No longer were Christians under the constant threat of persecution and martyrdom. They could enter worldly occupations, including government service—a situation that both weakened their faith and made it more realistic. As a result, the original feeling of urgency gave way to the realization that the Lord's return might be far down the road. Thus, Christianity had to become a faith that was viable in the world.

Monasticism

Such worldliness stimulated new religious movements within the Church that opposed the laxness or "accommodation" that worldly success easily begot. The most important reforms generated interest in monasticism and virginity (which overlapped,

insofar as monks took vows of celibacy). Both males and females found a monastic life of dedication to prayer and charitable works a way of maintaining their martyrlike intensity of faith. Theirs was a "white" martyrdom, not the red one of blood, and many found that it led them to the desert for solitude and asceticism. The great hero of the day, in fact, was the desert father Antony, who made a great impression on Athanasius. Thomas Merton has gathered a good selection of the desert fathers' sayings.[24] In it one sees both a bare faith and considerable shrewdness about what happens to people when they set out to meet God.

Partly because of the dangers of desert solitude, many monks soon formed communities, and before long these communities admitted women (nuns). In the East, communal (cenobitic) monasticism took form under the guidance of Basil, bishop of Caesarea. His rule (which owed much to Pachomius, the founder of communal monasticism) became the common law. In the West the rule of Benedict predominated. So the dedication that had previously been an informal option (largely in terms of virginity or widowhood) took institutional form. Thenceforth monasteries were powerhouses of Christian faith that laity and clerics alike viewed as centers of holiness. That, too, was an innovation added to New Testament religion, which had no monastic life. The Church's decision that monastic life was truly in keeping with New Testament religion was analogous to the decision to coin new doctrinal concepts. Quite consistently, the Protestant Reformers of the sixteenth century opposed the development of monasticism (as being unbiblical), just as they opposed the development of the Catholic notion of authority.

Christology

The councils not only set the pattern of Trinitarian faith that dominated the following centuries but also dealt with a host of problems that arose when people started to think about Jesus as the divine Word. Nestorius, from Antioch, and Cyril, from Alexandria, squared off in Christological controversy, and again Alexandria won. Nestorius stressed the unity of the Christian God, though he affirmed Christ's two natures (human and divine). Cyril thought that Nestorius' affirmation was not strong enough to safeguard the singleness of Jesus Christ the God-man, so he pressed for a "hypostatic" (personal) union of the two natures. Councils of Ephesus (431) and Chalcedon (451) affirmed Cyril's doctrine of one "person" and two "natures." Later Christological development affirmed that Jesus had a rational soul, two wills, and two sets of operations. This orthodox Christology resulted from trying to systematize the scriptural teaching about God and Jesus. Orthodoxy cast many groups in the shade, branding their positions as heretical, but it also developed Christ's meaning considerably.

Orthodoxy

Orthodoxy has two principal meanings. It may refer to the Eastern churches that separated from Rome in 1054 or to the "right belief" established by scripture, tradition, and the councils. In this section we address the first concept, describing the growth of Eastern Christianity after the conciliar age (most of the great councils took place in the East). The term *Orthodox* was adopted for two reasons: The Orthodox church thought of itself as keeping the traditional faith, especially regarding the episcopal (pertaining to bishops) focus of Church authority; *orthodoxy* has also meant, especially in the East, "right praise." As "right praise" the term links the Orthodox conception of faith to the glorious Orthodox liturgy (which primarily is a praise of God).

Western theologians, many of whom were monks dedicated to a rich communal worship, coined the expression "Lex orandi, lex credendi"—the law of prayer is the law of faith. Similarly, Eastern theologians felt that the Church expresses itself most fully in the liturgy. This communal worship *(liturgy* means "the work of the people") had developed a sacramental system in which

baptism and the Eucharist ("the Lord's Supper") were especially important in the apostolic age. In the early medieval period, when Orthodoxy took form, the liturgy flowered. The result was a calendar of holy days, a full ritual that involved music, art, incense, iconography, and more. Thus, communal worship became the dramatic center of Eastern Church life.

As we have noted, the councils of the fourth and fifth centuries occasioned theological division as well as theological clarification. In the fifth century, during the Christological controversies, more deviant versions of faith arose—Nestorian, Monophysite (one nature in Christ), and others—because as the councils established accepted beliefs, they excluded other options. Often the deviant minority party continued a church life, with the result that there were large numbers of heterodox Christians in the East. As Arianism remained robust even after its rejection by the Council of Nicaea, so the Christologically heterodox groups did not simply recant or go back into the woodwork. Thus, the major split between East and West that occurred in 1054 was not without Eastern forerunners.[25]

From the ninth to the fifteenth centuries, a complicated, still quite obscure process of alienation between Byzantine (Eastern) Christianity and Roman Christianity resulted in their separation. Each group finally rejected the other, charging it with having broken the traditional faith. Some of the factors in the separation were the fall of the eastern Roman Empire, the failure of the Crusades, the growing antagonism of Islam, the growth of the papacy, the stirrings of Protestant reactions against the papacy, and the rivalry between Russia and western Europe.[26] These factors take us to the beginning of modernity in Eastern Christendom, explaining why East and West have remained divided to the present.

Religious Issues

Thus, the break between Eastern and Western Christianity owed a great deal to political and cultural conflicts. Although

Figure 26   Christ in Majesty, northeast Spain, twelfth century. Courtesy Museum of Fine Arts, Boston, Marie Antoinette Evans Fund.

have serious theological implications (for instance, on the structure of the church and its authority), but they do not affect the cardinal doctrines of the Christian faith: Trinity, grace, and incarnation, except for Photius' last point on false teaching about the Holy Spirit.

The most acute point of theological difference between the East and the West was what came to be known as the *Filioque.* According to the Nicene Creed, within the life of the Trinity the Holy Spirit proceeds from the Father. The Western Council of Toledo (589) made an addition to the Nicene Creed: The Holy Spirit proceeds not just from the Father but also from the Son (*Filioque* means "And from the Son"). Each tradition became attached to its Trinitarian formula, and so the *Filioque* became a sharp bone of contention. The East claimed that it was heretical; the West claimed it merely articulated a tacit understanding of traditional faith that Nicaea had assumed. The practical significance of the difference is not clear, but it probably shows the East's tendency to appreciate the Father's primal mystery—the Father's status as a fathomless source from which *everything* issues.

In response to Photius, Latin theologians composed their own list. In their view the Eastern discipline that allowed clerics to marry, that baptized by immersion, that celebrated the Eucharist with leavened bread, and that had different rules for fasting deviated from tradition. The debate even descended to such details as whether bishops should wear rings, whether clergy should wear beards, and whether instrumental music was valid at the liturgy. However, the main theological issue continued to be the *Filioque,* while the main political issue emerged as the difference in the churches' understanding of authority. The Eastern church's tradition was a loose federation of bishops, all of whom were considered successors of the apostles. The Eastern church also stressed the rights of individual churches and ethnic groups. The Western tradition was a "monarchical" leadership by the bishop of Rome. As successor to Peter,

separating these conflicts from theological differences is virtually impossible, we can delineate some of the more clearly religious issues. For instance, the patriarch Photius, who presided at Constantinople from 858 to 886, drew up a list of what Byzantines considered to be Latin (Western) errors in faith. This list reveals how the two portions of Christendom had developed different understandings of orthodoxy. In this list Photius cited irregularities in the observance of Lent (the period of penance before Easter), compulsory celibacy for the clergy, denying priests the power to administer confirmation (the Christian sacrament of adulthood), and false teaching about the Holy Spirit. Clearly, the list concentrates on points of church discipline and administration. They he claimed primacy over the other churches.

When the Byzantine empire was about to fall to the Turks, the Eastern and Western factions met for the last time at the Council of Florence (1439). That was long after the mutual anathemas of 1054 (described below), but the East hoped to secure both Church unification and Western help against Islam. On the agenda were only four points (the other disagreements having fallen away as trivial). They were the prerogatives of the bishop of Rome, the *Filioque* clause, the doctrine of purgatory (the teaching that there is an intermediate state between heaven and hell, which the Orthodox condemned as unbiblical), and whether to use leavened or unleavened bread in the Eucharist. In retrospect, theologians have judged the last two items as relatively inconsequential. The first two were interrelated, because the Council of Florence came to focus on the question of whether the pope had the right to alter an ecumenical creed (that is, add *Filioque* to the Nicene Creed). Due to their political problems (the menace of the Turks), the Greeks (Easterners) accepted the *Filioque* and agreed to certain papal prerogatives. The union was confined to paper, though, because back at home Orthodox synods refused to ratify the agreements signed by their delegates.

Separation

The pivotal moment in the East-West division was the mutual excommunications of 1054, which were due more to politics (or to snappish personalities) than to theology. Pope Leo IX had sent a Western delegation to Constantinople headed by one Cardinal Humbert. The Normans were menacing Leo and also the Emperor Constantine Monomachus, so a major goal was to unite the churches to oppose a common foe. Humbert seems to have been a narrow, contentious type, as was his Eastern counterpart, the patriarch Michael Cerularius. When Pope Leo died in 1054, Cerularius held that Hum-

bert's credentials were void. Humbert responded by laying on the altar of St. Sophia in Constantinople a letter that excommunicated the patriarch and all his associates. The patriarch then assembled his own council, which excommunicated Humbert in return. The emperor dispatched the cardinal back to Rome with presents, hoping that the next pope would appoint a new legate who could heal the breach. But the Normans prevented the popes from resuming negotiations, so the mutual excommunications stood until after the Second Vatican Council in the early 1960s.

Basically, the division between the Eastern and Western branches of the Church was a tragic accident. (Historians now say much the same of the sixteenth-century Reformation split in Europe.) Political circumstances, differences in traditional ways of celebrating faith, and, above all, differences in temperament and cultural backgrounds were more decisive than hard theological differences. What Orthodox and Catholics (and Protestants and Catholics) held in common was far more significant than what they held apart. It took centuries for Christians to realize that millions of people (for example, Asians) knew nothing about their God, let alone their Christ—centuries for them to realize their own solidarity and so begin an "ecumenical (worldwide) movement" for Church unification. The sticking point through those centuries was a main factor in the East-West division—papal authority. Today there are creative approaches by which Protestant and Orthodox Churches might acknowledge certain papal powers, but full accord remains quite distant.

Thus, the Orthodox church represents an understanding of Christianity somewhat different than that of Western Christianity.[27] It numbers perhaps 70 million persons, depending on the estimates used for Russia, and within the family of Christian churches it stresses the conciliar tradition, the federation of local churches in geographical families, and a lofty theology of the Trinity, Christology, and grace. As we noted, the liturgy is its center, and it has a rich sacramental life.[28]

At the Orthodox liturgy, one feels a Christian "pneumaticism": The Holy Spirit is dramatically present to effect the sacraments. In the invocation made over the eucharistic gifts (the *epiclesis*), Orthodoxy stresses the Holy Spirit's role in transforming the bread and wine into Christ's substance. In its baptism and confession of sins, Orthodoxy's accent is sharing God's life—beginning divine life in baptism or repairing it in penance. Overall, Orthodoxy places the mystery of the Christian God to the fore. For the East, God is less a lawgiver or a judge than a spiritual power operating through creation. Creation ought to respond to God's power and beauty, so the Divine Liturgy becomes a song of praise, a hymn to the goodness and love that pour forth from the Father of Lights. Orthodoxy especially venerates Mary, the Mother of God, for her share in the "economy" of salvation—her share in the design of grace that raises humans to participate in the divine immortality. Bernhard Schultze offers a full sketch of Orthodox doctrines and a full listing of its different family members.[29] He shows that, through many political troubles, Orthodoxy has kept faith with Jesus and the Christian beginnings.

The Medieval Period

In discussing the medieval period of Christianity, we shift focus from the East, where Orthodox faith took shape, to the European West. Evangelization (missionizing) of Europe progressed steadily from the time of the councils, most of it presuming somewhat vaguely that the bishop of Rome was preeminent among the Church's episcopal leaders. During the fifth and sixth centuries, Christian missionaries made considerable inroads among the Germanic tribes. Frequently they would convert tribal leaders from paganism or Arianism, and then the entire tribe would convert. However, Western state leaders tended to think that the Church was something for them to control. That tendency, plus problems of Church discipline, made the Western situation confusing. From the tenth century, however, there were efforts to reform the Church and increase its spiritual vitality. In the eleventh and twelfth centuries, such efforts —especially those that originated at the Abbey of Cluny in Burgundy—were fairly successful.

As well, individual church leaders found that they could increase their freedom from local secular rulers by increasing their allegiance to the bishop of Rome. The friction between Church and state therefore shifted to the interaction between the pope and the Germanic emperor. A key issue was who should appoint local bishops. The investiture controversy, as it is called, was solved in a compromise in the Concordat of Worms (1122). Secular rulers had to recognize the independence of the local bishop by virtue of his loyalty to the pope, and the pope had to consult the emperor and appoint bishops acceptable to him.[30]

During the twelfth century the Crusades to the holy sites in Palestine riveted the Christian imagination, but they tended to increase the alienation between Eastern and Western Christendom. When the Fourth Crusade (1204) conquered Constantinople, set up a Western prince, and tried to Latinize the Eastern church, relations deteriorated to their lowest point. By 1453, after the Councils of Lyon and Florence had done little to heal the wounds of division, and after Easterners had suffered centuries of Western domination, a popular slogan circulated stating that Turks would be better rulers than Western Christians.

During the twelfth century, Europe developed strong cities, with a concomitant shift of economic and political power. This development slowly transformed the feudal system of which the Church had been an intimate part. As a result, considerable resistance to the established Church power and faith arose among some groups, such as the Waldenses, who urged a return to apostolic simplicity and poverty. Groups that owed a debt to the East, such as the French Albigensians, pushed Manichaean values in their war on the flesh and their contempt for the material world.

To meet the challenge of such reformers, the Roman church developed new orders of priests and monks, the most important of which were the Dominicans and the Franciscans. Saint Dominic (1170–1221) organized his group to preach against the heretics, and one of the devotions it added was the rosary—a string of beads for counting prayers to the Virgin Mary. The Franciscans stemmed from the charismatic *poverello* (pauper) Francis of Assisi (1181–1226), who dedicated himself to simple living. His angelic love of nature and of the infant Jesus made a deep impression on subsequent generations of Christians. Both Dominicans and Franciscans were innovations on the established (largely Benedictine) model of Western monasticism. Principally, they had more freedom than Benedictines to move out of the cloister and its settled, agricultural rhythms. They were mobile, and therefore quite effective in responding to different religious trouble spots.

Scholasticism

The thirteenth century was the high point of medieval intellectual life, and the movement known as Scholasticism reached its peak then. The Scholastics systematized the conciliar and patristic (the Fathers') theological doctrines.[31] Augustine was their great master, but where Augustine worked with neo-Platonic thought categories (developed by thinkers, such as Plotinus, who developed Plato's ideas), Thomas Aquinas (1225–1274), the greatest of the medievals, worked with Aristotelian categories. Between Augustine and Aquinas lived Anselm (1033–1109), who developed the notion that theology is "faith seeking understanding." That is, on the basis of a firm Christian commitment (rooted in scriptural, conciliar, and patristic doctrine), the theologian ought to learn as much as the divine mysteries allowed.

Anselm's definition was a writ of intellectual emancipation. Though they accepted the disciplines of tradition and the Church's teaching office, the medieval theologians seized the right to develop reason and use it to illumine the realities of faith. Consequently, teachers such as Peter Lombard and Peter Abelard prepared lists of patristic opinions on different theological topics and started to reason them through dialectically. Franciscan theologians, such as Alexander of Hales and Bonaventure, and Dominican theologians, such as Albert the Great and Thomas Aquinas, developed this dialectics, writing voluminously on philosophical and theological topics.

After a great struggle, the position of Aquinas, who most carefully related reason and faith, gained the greatest following. Just as conciliar theology had moved beyond scriptural ideas (in order to illumine scripture), so Aquinas' Scholastic theology moved beyond conciliar theology in order to illumine it through Greek philosophy. For Aquinas, philosophy was the wisdom available to reason. It was a universal basis for discussion, regardless of religious allegiance. Jews, Muslims, Christians, and pagans all had reason, and so all could philosophize. Theology, which rested on divine revelation, perfected philosophy, taking it into realms that it could not penetrate on its own. (For instance, without revelation philosophy would not know of the Trinity or the Incarnation [the Word made flesh].) Aquinas developed a powerful system of philosophical theology, but he was by no means the only impressive medieval thinker. His school, Thomism, trusted in reason, had a hopeful view of the world, thoroughly analyzed the Trinity, Christology, and grace, made a careful analysis of human virtues and vices, and viewed the world as a hierarchy of levels of being, with matter on the bottom, humans in the middle, and God at the top.[32]

Hierarchy

Aquinas' hierarchy had counterparts in the medieval church structure. The clergy had separated themselves from the laity, and within the clerical order there were numerous ranks: monks, priests, canons, bishops, abbots, archbishops, cardinals, and more. The papacy had a considerable bureaucracy and wielded great secular power. Because the general culture had a Christian world view, heaven and hell had a vivid reality. Thus, the papal power to bar persons from church membership and so from heaven made people fear the pope greatly. Considerable worldliness entered into the papal use of excommunication, interdict, and the like, because by medieval times the church had forgotten the *parousia* (second coming of Christ) and was concentrating on shaping daily life.

The unsurpassed literary rendition of medieval Christianity is Dante's *Divine Comedy*. It shows the medievals' hierarchical thinking, their concern with heaven, hell, and purgatory, the venality of many medieval clergy, the infusion of pagan learning into medieval culture, and the sophistication of medieval moral theology, which catalogued virtues and vices quite precisely. Another wonderful source of insight into medieval Christianity is Chaucer's *Canterbury Tales*, which describes the daily habits of representative social types and the unconscious ways in which faith wove through medieval culture. From Dante and Chaucer one gathers that intellectuals of the late medieval period, especially nonclerical intellectuals, found many defects in the hierarchical church, yet they basically accepted the terms of Christian faith. Their criticism focused on the discrepancy between the values that the church professed and the all-too-human way in which it conducted itself.

The medieval cathedrals also exhibited hierarchy through their stretching from earth toward heaven. They instruct us about medieval faith, for towns built them to be a means of indoctrination. You can see this today in the Gothic masterpieces of Notre Dame de Chartres and Notre Dame de Paris. The basic architectural thrust is towards heaven, as all commentators point out, yet within the cathedrals are windows and stat-

ues that bring God down into daily life. Most cathedrals were built over centuries, and sometimes the townspeople contributed free labor, as if they wanted the cathedral to praise God doubly. Significantly, Chartres and Notre Dame de Paris both bear Mary's name. As the Virgin Mother of God, Queen of Heaven, and recourse of weak human beings, Mary was a mainstay of medieval faith.

In their battles with the Arians during the fifth and sixth centuries, Church leaders had necessarily stressed Jesus' divinity, which the Arians denied. Consequently, the Roman liturgy had come to place Christ and the action of the Mass apart from the people (as befit Christ-God). The size of the cathedrals, the inability of many people to see the ceremonies, the inability of many people to understand the Latin in which the ceremonies were conducted—all these factors prompted devotion to Mary and the infant Jesus, which brought God closer and made faith more human. Divinity was not fearsome if one could shelter behind a young mother's kindness, a baby's vulnerability. So such devotions balanced the rather stern official cult.

Around the cathedral walls, in wonderful stained glass, were biblical scenes, pictures of saints, and the like that told even the illiterate what faith meant. With the statues of the Virgin and Jesus, they gave comfort to the person who slipped into the cathedral's darkness to pray. In its majestic space, one gained a proper perspective on one's problems. At a time when hard work, early death, and many sufferings were the rule, the cathedrals were for many a great support.

Monastic life progressed during the Middle Ages, though new orders such as the Franciscans and Dominicans neither completely replaced the more stable Benedictines nor completely abandoned their regimes. The great work of the monastic community was to celebrate the divine "office": liturgical prayers throughout the day and a communal Mass. By the thirteenth century, the Eucharist involved a rather

solemn moments, such as the celebration of Christ's Passion, chant could express deep sorrow, prefiguring, for instance, the music of Johann Sebastian Bach.

As it developed, the Mass increasingly tended to represent Christ's sacrificial death. That did not deny the motif of a common meal, but it shifted emphasis to the consecration of the elements (bread and wine), because in the theologians' interpretations, the separation of the bread and wine stood for the sundering of Jesus' body on the cross. As a prayer (the "sequence") for the feast of Corpus Christi (attributed to Thomas Aquinas) shows, the consecrated host (bread) came to epitomize God's presence and redemptive action. The consecration was a miracle that the liturgy enacted each day. Paradoxically, the host defied the senses and nourished the soul. Because Jesus' body remained in church, the church was indeed God's house. Indeed, in the host, Jesus made himself available for reverence and prayer. Along with the cult of the Virgin (see Figure 27) and the cults of the many medieval saints, the cult of the Eucharist gave people at the bottom of the Church pyramid another source of comfort.

Thus, the average person went through a harsh medieval life in fear and trembling but with many sources of hope that such a life would lead to heaven. The worldliness of much church life was balanced by the sacramental ceremonies that stressed the primacy of heaven. Rather clearly, the faithful knew that they stood between heaven and earth. They were citizens of two worlds, and the best medieval theology and religious art counseled them to live their dual citizenship gracefully. For instance, the cathedral and monastic schools joined piety to learning. The mystery plays and even the *danse macabre* (dance of death) brought home to the common people that death levels pope and pauper to strict equality. In fact, "Momento mori" ("Remember death") was a pietistic watchword. Since death was a gateway to eternal life, "*momento mori*" had more than negative overtones.

Figure 27   Madonna with the Child Jesus, *late fifteenth century. Nelson Gallery–Atkins Museum, Kansas City, Missouri (Nelson Fund).*

complex ceremony, with choral music, gorgeous vestments, and precious vessels for the bread and wine. Gregorian chants best represent the music, which was lively and alert, giving many psalms a joyous lilt. For

The Period of Reform

In the piety that dominated the period between the high Middle Ages and the sixteenth-century Protestant Reformation, the most influential work was the *Imitation of Christ* by Thomas a Kempis (1380–1471).[33] The book evidences a sober awareness of death and a general view that life is a vale of tears. Both reflect a medieval heritage. Some church historians have called the *Imitation* the second most influential book in Christian history, second only to the New Testament. It breathes a certain air of discontent—the mood of the Netherlands, where it arose. It also breathes a desire to experience religious consolation—the same desire that figured prominently in Martin Luther's spiritual biography.[34] However, the *Imitation* represents only one aspect of the period before the Reformation. Political factors certainly were a dominant influence, as was the fourteenth-century plague, which killed perhaps three-fourths of the population of Europe and Asia,[35] excited a great fear of devils and witches,[36] and made clear humanity's impotence and mortality.

During the late fourteenth and the fifteenth centuries, the papacy was in great disarray. At one point there were two claimants to the chair in Rome, one in Rome and one in Avignon. In the East the Muslims held Asia Minor and Greece, their most dramatic victory being at Constantinople in 1453. Well into the fifteenth century, southern Spain was under Muslim control, while in Italy the spirit of the Renaissance seemed stronger than conciliar attempts to reform the papacy. In addition, there were frictions among local rulers within the Italian, French, and German realms; the middle classes emerged as a result of city life and economic changes; and the pre-Lutheran attacks on church corruption of the Lollards (followers of John Wycliffe in England) and the Hussites (followers of John Huss in Bohemia) took place.

The spark that set the Reformation blazing was Martin Luther (1483–1546), an Augustinian monk whose study and spiritual searches had convinced him that the heart of the gospel is the Pauline justification by faith (the belief that only faith makes one right with God). Only by reviving this Pauline theme could Christianity regain its pure beginnings. As John Kent has shown, there is a link between this central Lutheran idea and the themes of religious freedom and religious certainty that preoccupied later Protestants.[37] Justification by faith meant the fall of a whole system of "works" that the Catholic church had developed by late medieval times—the Mass, the sacraments, the rosary, and so forth.

Luther was prompted by the prevailing practice of indulgences (papal remissions of purgatorial punishment due for sins), which one could obtain for various good deeds, including almsgiving. Behind this practice lay some simple economics. The popes had spent lavishly in their Renaissance enthusiasm for art and culture. Leo X, for instance, was perhaps 125,000 ducats in debt at the time that he endorsed the preaching of Johann Tetzel, Luther's first adversary,[38] which endorsed granting an indulgence for a contribution to the building of St. Peter's in Rome. To Luther the whole system—the pope's extravagance, his pretension to control a treasury of merits generated by the saints, out of which he might draw "credits" to cover sinner's debts, and his focusing this economics on the Mass—was blasphemous. On October 31, 1517, Luther nailed his Ninety-five Theses to the door of the castle church at Wittenberg, which amounted to a formal challenge to the system.

Many Germans who for political or religious reasons had grievances against Rome supported Luther. As his thought expanded, he made scripture the sole arbiter of Christian faith, declared the primacy of individual conscience, upgraded the status of the layperson, and urged the use of the vernacular rather than Latin. Luther also stressed the uniqueness of Christ's death on the cross and so taught that the Eucharist principally commemorates the Last Supper, rather than representing Christ's sacrificial death. On the basis of scripture, he judged the doctrine of purgatory unfounded and the practice of monastic life an aberration. Because Luther was a fine preacher, he made these ideas matters for discussion in the marketplace. By translating the Bible into German, he put the central basis for his reform within reach of all literate people (and just about standardized High German in the process). Finally, Luther's departure from monastic life and subsequent marriage led thousands more to leave their monasteries and convents.

The Spread of Reformation

Luther's reform in Germany quickly generated uprisings elsewhere. In Switzerland, Ulrich Zwingli (among the German speaking) and John Calvin (among the French speaking) led movements with similar themes. In England, Henry VIII and Thomas Cranmer separated their church from Rome. Generally, these reformers' writings show the influence of humanistic movements, from the Renaissance on, that had undermined the Scholastic framework.[39] As well, they show a link to the spiritualist movements that were in search of a more emotionally satisfying faith. As the Reformation worked out, Lutheranism took root in countries with a primarily agrarian economy, such as Germany and Scandinavia, while Calvinism took root in countries with a commercial economy, such as French Switzerland, France, Flanders, and the Netherlands.[40]

Calvin had the greatest influence, however, on America, since France and Flanders largely returned to Catholicism, while Dutch Calvinism mixed with both the older piety espoused by the *Imitation of Christ* and the humanism of Desiderius Erasmus. In America, the Puritans from England were inspired by Calvin's desire to honor God by consecrating all of life to his kingship. Consequently, they tried to develop a theocratic state. Calvin's notions of God's sovereignty guided Jonathan Edwards, the first major American theologian,[41] and through Ed-

wards much of the "Great Awakening" (the revivalist movement that Edwards sparked in New England from 1740 to 1743) and subsequent American religious life bore a Calvinist imprint.

From the middle of the sixteenth to the middle of the seventeenth century, religious wars ravaged much of Europe. In France they subserved civil frictions. The Edict of Nantes (1598) preserved the status quo: Protestant areas would remain Protestant, Catholic areas (the majority) would remain Catholic. In the Netherlands the wars had the character of a rebellion against Spain. The northern Netherlands became largely Protestant, while the southern Netherlands remained under Spanish power and so Catholic. Germany was the most furious battlefield. Until the Peace of Münster (1648) there was constant carnage. The upshot in Germany was the famous dictum *"Cujus regio, ejus religio"*: Each area would follow the religion of its prince.

In England, Henry VIII found the Reformation currents useful in his struggle with the papacy to have his marriage to Catherine of Aragon annulled. Henry declared the king supreme in all matters that touched the church in England, and he eagerly took monastic lands and income to finance his war against France. In 1571, under Henry's daughter Elizabeth I, the English bishops published their Thirty-nine Articles of Faith, which formalized their special blend of Protestantism and Catholicism.

Catholic Reform

The Catholic response to the Protestant Reformation took place at the Council of Trent (1545–1563). Trent affirmed the reliance of the church on both scripture and tradition, the effective power of the sacraments, the need for humans to cooperate in the work of justification (that is, no justification by faith alone), and the possibility of sin after justification. It also provided for reforms in clerical education and a general housecleaning to remove the laxness and venality that had made the Reformers' charges more than credible. Probably the most powerful single agent of the Catholic Reformation was the Society of Jesus (the Jesuits), which Pope Paul III approved in 1540. Its founder was Ignatius of Loyola, a Basque.

Ignatius' companions quickly proved themselves the best combination of learning and zealous faith. Therefore, they were assigned many of the tasks of teaching and missionizing that were central to Catholic renewal. Peter Canisius in Germany, Robert Bellarmine in Italy, and Francisco Suárez in Spain were intellectuals and educators (the first two also became prelates) who had a great deal to do with revitalizing Catholicism in their countries. Jesuit missionaries to Asia such as Francis Xavier, Matteo Ricci, and Robert di Nobili, also had great success. Xavier was a charismatic figure of the first order, able to stir crowds without even knowing their language. Ricci and di Nobili took on the customs of the people with whom they worked (Chinese and Indians) and confronted the vast task of forming native versions of Christianity. Jesuits also ministered underground to Catholics in England (several lost their lives in the effort), and they went to the New World to missionize Canada, the American Southwest, and Latin America.[42]

Further Developments

A century after Luther's Ninety-five Theses, Europe washed in waves of Reformation and Counter Reformation (the Catholic Reformation). In England, the alternation of Catholic and Protestant monarchs led to a series of repressive measures, while the Calvinism first of the Scot John Knox and then of the Puritans made great gains. The Spanish and Portuguese were exporting Catholicism through their great trading ventures, while the Dutch and English were exporting Protestantism. Consequently, Christian division became a worldwide affair.

Seventeenth-century America became a refuge for Protestants who opposed what they considered oppressive practices in their native lands and who stressed individual rights of conscience. The Church of England was strong in Virginia, Georgia, and the Carolinas. The Dutch Reformed Church dominated New York and New Jersey. Germans and Dutch flocked to Pennsylvania, while Congregationalists dominated New England. As the Reformation principle of individual conscience worked its influence, more and more groups splintered off to search out places where they could live their convictions in peace. According to Sidney Mead, the unique character of American religion has been that it formed a national culture and law on the basis of its pluralism.[43]

In its Reformation, Catholicism set new standards for its popes and clergy. It also obtained a new spirituality (largely Jesuit) that tried to adapt traditional piety to the new age of individual conscience. Commentators have nominated Loyola's *Spiritual Exercises* as the third most influential Christian book. If we substitute *Catholic* for *Christian*, they are likely correct. The work is in the form of meditations on different gospel scenes, but Ignatius designed them to bring about a "discernment of spirits" and a choice of a way of life. Some commentators point out that the mysticism of the exercises is a shift to the interior in keeping with the shift of the great Spanish mystics Teresa of Avila and John of the Cross, and that the exercises bring the medieval mystical tradition up-to-date by tailoring it to a more active life. Other commentators have shown Ignatius' anticipation of a modern "mystagogy" (exercise in the experience of God) and mystical dialectics.[44] From the *Spiritual Exercises* and other works of the Catholic Reformation, the Roman church learned how persons might work in the world with the hope of finding God in all things. That made it easier for Rome to bless new active orders of priests, brothers, and nuns.

As Robert McAfee Brown has shown,[45] the spirit of Protestantism that has come down from the sixteenth century stresses, first, the notion of reform itself—of always having to renew one's faith because of one's sure distance from God's holy will. Second, it stresses God's sovereignty, the authority of scripture, the priesthood of all believers, and the vocation of the laity to exercise their faith in the midst of the secular world. Ever since Luther and Calvin, the Bible has been the great text for both Protestant worship and Protestant theology, while, as historical sociologists such as Max Weber have suggested,[46] Protestant discipline has been a main ingredient in the rise of capitalistic culture.

The Reformation left Protestants and Catholics at odds, and the conflict has abated only in recent years. Today they seem to agree (despite such throwbacks as Northern Ireland) that the Reformers had legitimate grievances and that the Reformers' return to scripture renewed faith. On the other hand, Protestant and Catholic scholars also agree that many of the defects in modern Christianity result from its lacking the sense of a catholic tradition and common authority. The ecumenical task for the future is for Christians to put their humpty-dumpty together again.

Modernity

In this section we concentrate on the eighteenth and nineteenth centuries, though aspects of modernity clearly are found in the seventeenth century and still persist today. From the myriad events and thinkers who shaped the eighteenth and nineteenth centuries we must select the most crucial. Clearly the Enlightenment was crucial, as were the revolutions in France and America, which were related to it. Of the thinkers, the line from Descartes to Marx that passes through Hume, Kant, and Hegel is perhaps the most significant.

The religious life of the West changed dramatically in the modern period. It had to contend with new political, philosophical, and scientific thought. More profoundly, for the first time it met a passionate counter-faith, for modernity opposed deep commitment to humanity's own powers to reliance on God.

Heribert Raab has written, "The Enlightenment denotes the most revolutionary of all movements which the Occident has undergone in the course of history."[47] He makes reference to Protestant historian Ernst Troeltsch's view that the Enlightenment marks the beginning of the modern period of European culture, ending the previous theological or ecclesiastical culture.

The Enlightenment began in the Netherlands and England in the mid-seventeenth century, but its most outstanding expressions arose in France and Germany. French rationalistic and materialistic philosophy (such as that of Voltaire, Helvétius, and Comte) and French revolutionary political action both derived from the Enlightenment. In Germany, Leibniz, Lessing, and Kant were its first philosophical offspring, while the "enlightened despotism" of Frederick the Great and Joseph II was a political result.

The Enlightenment thinkers saw themselves as part of a movement for progress, the watchword of which was criticism. They took as their enemy ignorance, intolerance, and repression, vowing to attack all their manifestations in national culture. To power this critical warfare they drew on the model of the new physical science (especially that of Newton). That meant setting goals of clarity, precision, and rational order. Thus, the Enlightenment was a tremendous affirmation of humanity's rational capacities. Further, it assumed that both creation and human nature were essentially good, thus producing an expectation of great progress. Things would improve and freedom would increase as trustworthy critical reason expressed trustworthy human nature in a quite trustworthy natural order.

Quite obviously, the Enlightenment view of human nature clashed with that of traditional Christianity. Although reason held an important place in the medieval Scholastic synthesis, the medieval mind never doubted that human nature is only perfectible through divine grace. In Reformation thought, Protestant and Catholic alike, both human reason and human love suffer the effects of sin, with the result that only God can give the fulfillment they seek. The Enlightenment contested the beliefs of both periods.

In fact, Alexander Pope (1688–1744) epitomized his era when he said that the proper concern of man is man. Drawing on Renaissance humanism as well as on Reformation individualism, the Enlightenment thinkers concluded that things outside the province of human experience are of marginal concern. How we define human experience, of course, is a capital question. Enlightenment leaders tended to distrust both mystical experience and systematic reason (Hegel was an exception), preferring empiricism instead. Thus, Hume made a deep impression by limiting human thought to what sensation can verify. In the political sphere, the new thinkers sought to establish empirical laws of human nature that might help provide liberty, fraternity, and equality. Even when such philosophy or political science grew quite abstract (as in the case of the French revolutionary philosophies), there was agreement that theology and revelation were irrelevant.

For Kant and Hegel, the great innovators in the philosophy of consciousness, the reason that was to secure "the system" would not be subordinate to traditional faith. Thus, biblical, conciliar, and even Reformation notions of how things are in the world were rejected during the Enlightenment. By a turn to the thinking subject, reality became the domain that we now call the secular world. The transcendent domain, the holy world that past ages had called the most objective, had no place in the new world view. Only as a manifestation of human self-expression, individual or social, did religion merit attention.

A great many factors were at work in this subjective turn, of course, and not all of them rooted in human pride. A general disgust with religion—well deserved after a century of religious wars—certainly made a new, humanistic beginning attractive. The overbearing weight of ecclesiastical institu-

tions, which regularly stomped on individual rights and opposed free scientific inquiry, made anticlericalism rather healthy. (The Inquisition is a heinous instance of religion used to trample human dignity.)

In the sciences, the excitement of empirical discoveries and the slow differentiation of canons of critical judgment were forces that seemed to oppose faith. Under the banner of religion huddled so much superstition and antiintellectualism that simple integrity drove many educated people away from the church. The best and the brightest frequently found themselves forced to choose between their love of human culture (intelligence, sober judgment, and compassionate love that represent humanity at its best) and religion, Christianity, or even God.

However, applying Enlightenment beliefs to philosophy and politics did not prove to be an unqualified boon to humanity. Unfettered reason and humanism produced horrors that quite challenged those of the religious witch hunts and inquisitions. For instance, the bloodbaths of the French Revolution differed little from those of the religious wars, showing that not all fanaticism trumpeted about God. The American Constitution, despite its debt to Enlightenment humanism and its expression of democratic freedoms, was the framework of a culture that often considered nonwhites and women less than human.[48] The Marxist-Leninist-Maoist brand of political religion, which is largely indebted to Hegel, produced inhuman totalitarian regimes. Small wonder, then, that Eric Voegelin found the path from Enlightenment to revolution to be a way of self-deification—a vicious way of placing selected human beings in the seat of divine mystery at the expense of others.[49]

Those who defended the pre-Enlightenment order argued that the fallacies in the new order were both subtle and patent. On the subtle side, a thorough critical analysis of experience showed that there is more to reality than what Enlightenment philosophy acknowledged. For instance, mystical, mythical, poetic, romantic, and even creatively scientific thought all stand outside of Enlightenment epistemology (theory of knowledge). On the patent side, observation of human behavior showed that reason seldom guides public affairs. Putting these objections to Enlightenment together, Christian apologists argued that an experience of God can take one beyond empirical reason and a human irrationality exists that is well labeled "sin." The legacy of modernity is the continuing Western debate over the assets and liabilities of critical reason.

The Contemporary Situation

The principles of Reformation and modernity have worked for more than four and a half centuries since Martin Luther. The reforming spirit continued both within and without Lutheranism and Calvinism, simplifying Christianity to yield a stark biblical faith and worship. Thus, Puritanism, Methodism, and Baptist religion moved Protestantism farther from Catholic dogmatic and sacramental theology. In reacting to this trend, Anglo-Catholicism tried to mediate between the ancient Catholic tradition and the Protestant instinct for the new religious needs of post-Renaissance society. However, the tide of the Protestant sectarians brought waves of individual, enthusiastic experience, which in turn promoted preaching, revivalism, and biblical literalism. Meanwhile, traditional Catholic authority fought modernity tooth and nail, only accepting modern scholarship and modern conceptions of human rights in the twentieth century.

During the nineteenth century, the Enlightenment meant liberalism in religious matters. Christianity was adapted to the needs of the day, which liberals thought were primarily humanistic in character. Adolf Harnack's slogan that the Christian essence is "the fatherhood of God and the brotherhood of man" encapsules much of the liberal spirit.

On occasion, both liberals and evangelicals (people rooted in the gospel) pressed for social change. The industrial revolution produced some abysmal working conditions, and Christian exponents of the "social gospel" agreed with Karl Marx that such conditions destroyed human dignity. In the "liberation theology" of recent years, this kinship has become explicit, and many liberation theologians are combining Marxist economic analyses with Christian beliefs. The most eloquent are Latin Americans,[50] but thought like theirs has penetrated the counsels of both Geneva and Rome. Recently Latinos, blacks, Asians, and feminists in North America who want to promote social change through radical Christian faith have rallied around liberation theology.[51]

In American religious history, a central theme has been what Martin Marty calls "righteous empire."[52] With this phrase Marty tries to summarize the Protestant experience in the New World. It entailed divine errands in the wilderness, the sacred tasks of making God's new Israel, and a manifest destiny to show the world a truly Christian society. There was some breakup of the empire on the divisions among the many American Christian churches, and so there was a rather reluctant settling for a civic code that granted *all* persons religious liberty, freedom of conscience, and separation of Church and state.

The effort of Enlightenment figures such as Jefferson and Franklin to make a state that was both humanistic and Christian has been a striking experiment. However, American civil religion has been neither fully Christian nor fully human as measured by Christian dogma or post-Enlightenment criticism.[53]

Puritanism, liberalism, and Marxism have all emerged as forms of Gnosticism.[54] Although these three viewpoints relate to the Enlightenment (and contribute to U.S. history) in quite different ways, they all depart from the classical political theory that developed from Greek reason and Jewish-Christian revelation. In other words, the majority movements in modern politics have not been concerned with maintaining a balance between divinity and humanity, faith and reason, transcendent reality and the world at hand. For the most part, they have concentrated on the second terms in these pairings or even tried to convert the first terms into the second.

The result has been an apotheosis (divinization) of humanity, a hearty optimism and faith in human reason, and a nearly mystical commitment to political action—with little feel for the irony involved. In the domain of scholarship, the historian has wielded more power than the theologian. In the domain of popular Christian religion, there has been considerable defense of the secular. Only after Vietnam, Watergate, and a proliferation of crises (ecological, nuclear, and economic), whose interrelationships challenge our cultural values, did Americans begin to suspect that modern Gnosticism had led them far astray. Within Christianity, these crises have become a common challenge. Only people who ignore reality do not feel their impact. They require a thorough rethinking of the faith handed down as well as a thorough critique of the gospel as lived by Wall Street.[55]

Furthermore, Christians have had to rethink their assumptions about revelation, salvation, the centrality of Christ, and the position of "pagans" as they have learned about other religions. Because of both secular and religious developments, then, the current Christian situation is complex and demanding. Science, technology, politics, and history (in other cultures as well as those that derive from Christianity) all demand reconciliation with traditional faith.

These concerns of current Western theologians press in upon even an introductory text in world religions. First, we cannot separate them from the assumptions with which scholarship approaches any religious tradition today. That is, we cannot cite religious phenomena, separate central ones from peripheral ones, and compose historical or comparative analyses without understanding just what religious phenomena are and why some are central. Even a student or scholar with no express theory about such things has a tacit theory about them.

For instance, some people think of religion in terms of social ceremonies. For them a person who does not attend church or synagogue regularly is not religious. Other people define religion as the urge to know and love that opens onto mystery. For them the irreligious person blocks off contemplative love. We favor the second interpretation.

Second, the concerns that modernity generated often spark a quarrel between scholarship and faith. Persons committed to religious traditions may feel that detached, critical, scientific treatment of their beliefs and worship distorts them. American Indians, for instance, have said that anthropologists' comments on their sacred dances are usually trivial.[56] Without the experience of being lost in communion with the Great Spirit, the anthropologist can only ruminate about group contagion or the therapies of rhythm. There are analogies in every religion. At the heart of the effort to describe the reality of religious experience lie the unavoidable issues of critical reason and experiential faith.

As a result of the Enlightenment, contemporary scholars test every observation, every statement, every memory—they accept nothing uncritically. From traditional faith comes the axiom that one must believe in order to understand, love in order to see. That axiom finally implies that faith is an act greater and more comprehensive than reason.

Third, these interpretational issues are especially acute in contemporary Western culture because they arose due to the effects of Christianity. Indeed, the Christian blend of Israelite revelation and Greek reason may have carried their seeds from the beginning. By the happenstance (or providence) that Christianity became the dominant European world view, and the happenstance that European culture developed science, history, and philosophy into the massive critical apparatus that we possess today, these issues are fundamental to both contemporary Western culture and contemporary Christian faith. The result is a constant, if frequently subtle, interplay.

For instance, religion does not go

away just because critical reason argues it off the property. Usually, it simply takes another form—the scientist or historian whose life turns on research becomes "religious" about his or her work. Indeed, the more creative such a historian or scientist is, the more passionate, even lyric and reverent, he or she will be about the commitment to truth and objectivity that the work demands. Similarly, the devoted social activist, whether Marxist or not, tends to survive through a largely unprovable faith that history has a meaningful direction or that giving one's life to improve other people's lot makes sense. Even the typical citizen who goes along without much reflection or passion hears a few whispers of God.[57]

STRUCTURAL ANALYSIS

Nature

Theologians who treat the meaning of nature in Christianity show that nature has usually signified human essence.[58] That does not mean that Christianity has denied the reality of the physical world. On the contrary, its Greek and Israelite sources both gave Christianity a realistic orientation toward the world, in contrast to the idealism of Indian (many Hindu and Buddhist) views of nature. Moreover, the body of Jesus, insofar as Christian faith made him the Logos incarnate, was an anchor to realism. Against the Gnostics, who were their foremost adversaries, the early Christian writers insisted on the reality and goodness of matter. If God himself had made the world, and God's own Son had assumed flesh, both the world and human flesh had to be good.

Nonetheless, because of the early controversies about the being of God and Christ, the word *physis* (nature) connoted divine and human "whatness" more than it connoted external reality. During the early controversies about free will and sin, Christian speculation finally concluded that the redemption and salvation that Christ had worked were beyond that to which human beings have any right. Thus, they were supernatural gifts

that come only by grace. Grace, it followed, is a generosity that God does not owe us. Further, redemption and salvation so transform human nature that it can share in God's own divine nature (2 Pet. 1 : 4). By itself, apart from grace, nature is unredeemed, unsaved, something far from the glory of divinity. These beliefs dominated classical Christian theology (Catholic, Orthodox, and Protestant alike).

In discussing creation we find more extensive Christian considerations of the physical world.[59] God stands to the world as its independent, uncaused source, who made it from nothing by his simple free choice. As we have noted previously, creation distinguishes the Western God from the Eastern ultimate, since the Eastern ultimate generally does not transcend the physical world and make it from nothing. The first mark of the natural world for the Christian, then, has been its subordination to divine creativity. Considerable time passed before the full conceptualization of creation was developed (from a combination of biblical and philosophical sources), but from the beginning the God of the burning bush was not a Brahman or a Tao.

Somewhat relatedly, in Western religion the human being has not been the tiny figure found in East Asian landscape painting. In most periods of Christian history, nature was considered mysterious and overpowering, but the Genesis story that God gave human beings dominion over nature shaped a belief that the physical world exists for humanity's sake. Christianity has taught its faithful to husband the physical world and use it. Little in the Christian message proposed that humans should ravage the world, but equally little proposed integrating human life with nature's ecology or preserving nature's gifts through frugality and reverence. In most periods Christians found nature abundant and generous, so conservation was not a major concern.

Further, the biblical fear of nature gods contributed to a semiconscious Christian effort to make nature undivine. In rural places (among European peasants, for instance), this effort succeeded only partially.

Overall, though, it was quite central to the Christian theology of creation. Coming from God, the world was good. But since it came from God by his free choice, springing from nothingness, the world was definitely not divine. Thus, the Christian interest in transforming human nature combined with a continuance of the biblical prophets' objection to the nature gods; thus, the physical world was made a subordinate, even somewhat ambivalent, concept.

Nature as Profane

The relative profanity (nonsacredness) that Christians attributed to nature played a rather complex role in the rise of Western science. When the Greek protoscientists, or early natural philosophers, developed a rude demythologizing of nature, they established the principle that the physical world is open to rational investigation. Thus, it was not blasphemous to pry into nature's secrets, and it could be profitable: Nature yields valuable information to those who pry well.

In Christian hands this demythologizing went several steps further. Pre-Renaissance scholars (many of them monks) worked at what we would call physics or biology, although such work was subordinated to theology. In other words, the basically religious culture preceding the Renaissance determined that theology would be the queen of the sciences. At best philosophy was this queen's handmaid, and natural philosophy (science and philosophy had not yet become clearly separated) was a legitimate but not very pressing task. That the handmaid might pursue this task with enthusiasm was a sign that God has made us by nature Aristotelians (Aristotle said that all persons by nature desire to know), but surely theology was a nobler call.

The phenomenon of Christian alchemy, which scholars do not yet fully understand, suggests an underground resistance to the neat official hierarchy. Psychological studies, such as C. G. Jung's, and studies by historians of religion, such as Mir-

cea Eliade's, suggest that European alchemy was religiously motivated. The Catholic church recognized this, for it associated alchemists with wizards, witches, astrologers, magicians, and sorcerers, tabooing them all as persons who probably were consorting with Satan. In other words, the veneration of nature posed a definite threat to the church. Church powers thought it incompatible with orthodox faith that Christ had subordinated the psychic or parapsychic powers of "this age" and freed human beings for genuine religion: love of a nature-transcending God and love of fellow humans.

Science

Thus, prior to the Renaissance, the Catholic church kept physical science on a rather short leash. The controversy that the new theories of Galileo Galilei (1564–1642) raised shows the church attitude that still prevailed in the seventeenth century: Faith had to predominate over the evidence of the senses. Shoring up theological notions (that the earth was the center of the universe was a theological axiom) was more important than allowing intelligence the freedom to investigate nature as it would.

Enlightenment thinkers were reacting to that sort of dogmatism and theological control when they attacked Christian faith. Almost in the name of a higher religion (fidelity to conscience), they attacked theology as dishonest. Since the scientific method, as we now call it, that was disengaging itself from theology (despite the church's protests) brought tangible results, it drove the ecclesiastical authorities deeper and deeper into their indefensible corner. Still, the passion of their faith made the authorities fly their flag decades after it was in tatters. Long after the Galileo disgrace, when even the Roman Holy Office allowed the sun to be the center of the universe, the church opposed new scientific theories on theological grounds. Thus, many Christian leaders denounced Darwin and Freud, because evolution and psychoanalysis seemed to refute the image of human nature that religious tradition had developed. The creature who was little less than an angel, the creature for whom Christ had shed his blood, the creature who was the very image of God could not have descended from an ape or have unconscious lust for its parents.

Thus, one can appreciate the modern intellectuals' alienation from the church. From the Renaissance to the quite recent past, Christian leadership has often opposed free scientific inquiry. As late as 1950, Pope Pius XII blasted polygenism (the anthropological theory that the human race arose from several different protohuman genetic pools) on the grounds that Adam and Eve had to be the original progenitors of all human beings. As well, he blasted existentialism. Even today debates about creation (the Genesis account versus the big bang theory) continue a warfare between theology and science. Literalism, to say nothing of the desire to control other persons' minds and morals, is far from dead in Christian circles.

Regarding the investigation of nature, therefore, the Christian legacy has been mixed. At first Christianity supported reason, the reality and goodness of the world, and the value of scientific contemplation. When investigation seemed to threaten faith, Christian orthodoxy tried to check the scientific mind. In elitist circles today things are much better, for theologians now analyze the implications of scientific findings for ethics and faith. For instance, they discuss genetic engineering, nuclear research, the medical definition of death, and the like from a belief in the Christian concept of human dignity. Some confusion still remains about the line between religion and science, but history has chastened theologians considerably, and they are now slow to condemn scientific research.

On the other side, at least a few scientists doubt that the scientific method alone is a comprehensive way of life. Not only does scientific research tend to ignore ethical questions about the social applications of its findings (for example, its findings about nuclear energy), it also finds itself more and more appreciative of nature's complexity—indeed, of nature's mystery. Every scientific discovery raises many more questions, whether in the realm of atomic particles, the realm of life, or the realm of the stars. Nature itself, we are finding, is a collection of mysteries.[60] Thus, nature commands respect, even awe, that is quite different from the arrogance with which earlier, mechanistic scientists attacked it. In fact, for some philosophers of science, such as Whitehead,[61] nature is the concrete form of divinity.

Sacramentalism and Mysticism

Christian sacramentalism has somewhat closed the gap between the place of nature in Christian religion and that in Eastern traditions that was opened by the Western separation of reason from myth. As well, Christian mystics who have sensed a divine presence in woods and birds have been rather Taoist in their style. In its worship and sacramental theology, Christian religion expressed the belief that God called creation good. Often, it applied a mythic and poetic intelligence that made the world mysterious, awesome, and alive. Baptismal water, eucharistic bread and wine, wax, incense, flowers, salt, oil—they have all enriched the liturgy. On the most solemn feast of Easter, the liturgy spoke as though all of creation got into the act, joining in the *Exultet*—the song of great rejoicing. In the liturgy of Good Friday, which commemorates Christ's death, the tree of the cross (the holy rood) became a new *axis mundi*—a new cosmic pillar linking heaven and earth. Taking over Psalm 150, Christians praised God in his firmament. Taking over other psalms, they made the mountains and the beasts coconspirators to God's praise. All creation, then, should resound to the music of the spheres. All creation should sing as it labors for redemption. Nature was part of a divine drama, part of a cosmic play of sin and grace.

Partly from such liturgical encouragement, Christian mystics have often shown a delight in nature like that of their East Asian counterparts. The accents have been different, since the Christian God is not the impersonal Buddha-nature, but they have not been contradictory. For instance, Francis of Assisi felt free to praise God as manifested in nature. Francis composed famous canticles to brother sun and sister moon, and the legends about his intimacy with animals are a sort of Christian prefiguring of the messianic age of fulfillment. It recalls Isaiah's figures of the child playing at the asp's hole and the lion lying down with the lamb. In the messianic age men and women will once more be intimate with nature, as they were when God made them "in the beginning."

For the early desert fathers, the wilderness was a place to become sanctified. For many Puritans and early Americans, the wilderness brought to mind Israel's wanderings in the desert—the place where its religion was pure. Thus, a romantic strain of Christian thought kept nature close to God. Sometimes it made the city less desirable for religious life than the country. Often it made solitude close to the elements a privileged place for prayer. As a result, the Christian God was strong as the seas, everlasting as the hills, lovely as the lilies of the field.

Society

Central to the Christian notion of society is the Church. It could oppose the state, standing as the religious collectivity against the secular. It was also the place where Christian life was supposed to show itself as something mysteriously organic—as the "body" of Christ. In the earliest periods of Church history, before Theodosius established Christianity as the official Roman faith, church leaders led quite unpretentious lives. Meetings of the community tended to be small gatherings in members' homes, and the bishop who led the liturgy might earn his bread as a cobbler or a craftsman. New Testament models suggested that carpentry (the occupation of Jesus) and tentmaking (the occupation of Paul) were more than honorable occupations. To those who waited idly for the *parousia*, the Church said, "Work—or no community support." In fact, most Christians in the beginning were nondescript working people. The *Epistle to Diognetius*[62] portrays a Christian existence in the world whereby faith made one a solid citizen.

Nonetheless, from early times Christians also felt that preaching the gospel was an especially honorable work and that some community leaders ought to be free to labor at it full-time. The decision to have deacons care for temporal affairs (Acts 6 : 1–6) suggests that Christians quickly established a hierarchy of tasks parallel to the hierarchy of Christian authorities. The work that preoccupied Church leaders and that later theology regarded as the Church's basic duty was a ministry or service in terms of "Word and Sacrament."[63] "Word" was, in the first instance, the scriptures. From the outset, they guided worship, theology, and private reflection. Ministry of the Word included commenting on scripture to edify the assembly and preaching to the outside world (missionizing).

The Word itself was the gospel, but also the Logos. Thus, it implied reciting the dramatic story of what God, out of his love, had chosen to do for humanity. The decisive episode in that story was Jesus' death and resurrection. And Jesus—the Christ, the Logos—became present in a special way through the preaching of the gospel. Faith in Jesus was the "entry" to the gospel view or "economy" of salvation, and faith demanded "hearing."

Developing biblical categories, today's theologians have shown that Jesus himself is the Church's primal sacrament;[64] his flesh is the greatest sign of God's nature and God's love. The Johannine writings contain the richest New Testament sacramental theology, but all the early literature makes clear that sacramental life is a life of union with Jesus. Sacramental life continued the incarnation of divinity; through its cyclical recall of the mysteries of Jesus' life, it led Church members ever deeper into God's love.

The sacraments, then, became Christian rites of passage.[65] Baptism, which faith experienced as a going down with Jesus in death and a coming up with him in resurrection, was the rite of entry or initiation. In the early centuries it was principally for adults, who received it only after a period of intense instruction. Catechumens (those under instruction) had to leave the Mass at the end of the liturgy of the Word. To witness the sacred actions that followed, one had to be a full member, well initiated in the symbolic language of meal and sacrifice.

Through history Christians developed other rites of passage. After infant baptism had become common, confirmation marked the transition to adulthood. Marriage solemnized the joining of woman and man in a common life. Ordination solemnized the election and dedication of Church leaders. Through sacred anointing, Christians prepared the sick for death. Through penance they ritualized contrition for and absolution of sin. Finally, the Eucharist, or Lord's Supper, memorialized Jesus' last meal and his death and resurrection.

The Catholic church celebrated all of these sacraments; the Orthodox church had a rich liturgy that distinguished between two primary sacraments (baptism and the Eucharist) and the rest; and the Protestant church reacted against the excesses in the Catholic system, opting for a more severe worship that stressed the liturgy of the Word. Protestants tended to regard only baptism and the Eucharist as sacraments based on scripture, downplaying the other five.

Polity

Christian society centered on worship through Word and Sacrament. Its structural organization was rather fluid at first and varied from place to place. In that early arrangement we can discern elements of all three of the later church polities: the episcopal, presbyterial (of the elders), and congregational. With time, though, came the monarchical structure of Roman Catholicism, the collegial model of Orthodoxy, and the government by elders that characterized much of Protestantism.

In the West before the Reformation, the structure of the Catholic church was pyramidal. At the top was the pope, along the bottom were the laity. In between, in descending order, were cardinals, bishops, and priests. The "religious" (those who had taken vows of poverty, chastity, and obedience, usually in the context of a communal life) were in the middle, though technically most religious groups had both clerical and lay members. Status, naturally and unbiblically enough, was accorded those at the top. Thus, the Council of Trent, reacting against Reformation notions that all Christians are "saints," denounced any diminution of virginity in favor of marriage. As a result, for many Roman Catholics the Church meant the clergy. That was less true for Protestants and Orthodox, because their theologies stressed, respectively, the priesthood of all believers and the mystical union of all believers with Christ as the head. As well, the Protestant churches had a strong theory, if not always a strong practice, that ministry is honorable in the measure that it is a service.

Women's Status

In principle, the Christian Church was democratic in that all persons, regardless of sex, race, or background, were welcome. Each Church member had her or his own gift from God, and each was a unique reflection of God. Thus, there was the Pauline dictum (Gal. 3 : 28) that in Christ there is neither Jew nor Greek, male nor female, slave nor free. In practice, however, women have been second-rate citizens in all branches of Christianity. Neither the Catholic nor the Orthodox churches would ordain women (that remains true today), nor would many Protestant churches. By associating women with Eve, the cause of Adam's fall (1 Tim. 2 : 14), the church suggested that they were responsible for human misery and sin. Thus, the fulminations of ascetics (usually celibate males) against women's wiles were a staple of the literature on how to avoid sin.

From the New Testament, men could

buttress their supremacy by citing Pauline texts (Eph. 5 : 22–23, 1 Tim. 2 : 11–12) stating that wives were subordinate to their husbands and ought to keep silent in church. From the patristic age they could draw on what we can only call the misogyny of Jerome, Chrysostom, Tertullian, and others who portrayed woman as the gateway to hell. Augustine, perhaps from his personal experience of concubinage, made sexual congress the channel of original sin. Medieval theologians, such as the Dominican authors of the *Malleus Maleficarum (Hammer of Witches)* cited witches as being the cause of much psychological imbalance. In the name of preserving true faith, church authorities tortured and killed thousands of witches.[66] Moreover, the Reformation did not relieve women's plight. Luther thought that woman's vocation was to "bear herself out" with children, while John Knox trumpeted against "petticoat" power in the church. Reformation biblicism, then, meant merely a return to the patriarchy of the scriptures.

With a patriarchal God and an ambivalent role model in Mary the Virgin Mother, Christian women for the most part heard and obeyed. They had some measure of religious self-expression in their convents, and some of them gained leadership roles in the Protestant sects, but from the standpoint of today's egalitarian sentiments, their fate through Christian history was uniformly dismal.[67]

Church and State

The Christian view of society outside the Church varied over time. According to the New Testament Revelation, Roman society was a beast that the coming Messiah had to slay if the earth were to be fair. During the persecutions, which some recent scholarship has downplayed, this view was influential. As a result, earthly life was held cheap compared to heavenly life. When the Church gained security with Constantine, it changed its tune. Eusebius, for instance, practically ranked Constantine with the twelve apostles. In reaction to this secularization, as we noted, the monastic movement restored the tension between time and eternity. The Western father Tertullian, for instance, cast doubt on the worth of secular culture, asking what Athens had to do with Jerusalem. However, other patristic figures, such as Clement of Alexandria and Augustine, recognized that Christianity needed an intellectual respectability if it were to prosper, so they started to give their theology an infrastructure of Greek philosophy.

By the medieval period, a certain harmony obtained, as most of the culture was formed in accordance with Christian ideals (if not practice). There was a balance between reason and revelation, between emperor and pope. In practice, however, the competition between the emperor and the pope was fierce, for each tended to claim ascendancy over the other. Consequently, Church leaders such as Ambrose and Hildebrand, who stood up to kings or even brought them to heel, were great heroes.

The Reformation depended in good measure on the political power plays of its day; through application of the principle that a region would follow the religion of its ruler, a great deal of religious power returned to the local prince. Theologically, Luther tended towards a dualism of powers, religious and secular, while Calvin promoted a theocratic state in which citizens would live under Christian law. Thus, the Reformation did not initially encourage the modern pluralistic state. In America the religious communities of the colonial period had to legalize pluralism if the colonies were to be united. With great reluctance on the part of many, the united colonies disestablished religion, and their act had enormous implications.

Since about the time of Voltaire (1694–1778), American pluralism has become something of a model for world government. Other nations have not formalized that model, with the slight exception of the United Nations, but its spirit has been at least a small counterweight to their nationalism. The model says that to live together well, human beings must find nondogmatic principles that can be common to all and that will generate the basic cooperation necessary for peace.

Through most of Christian history, though, the ideal society has been one that at worst allowed Christians freedom to exercise their religious convictions and at best institutionalized a Christian regimen. For instance, only recently has Roman Catholicism backed off its teaching that it ought to be the established religion in any country with a Catholic majority. By its decree on religious liberty, the Second Vatican Council made an unprecedented acknowledgment of the rights of other religious communities. Orthodoxy has had difficulty with secular rulers through most of its history,[68] in part because of its organization as a cluster of national churches. To this day Russian Orthodoxy, the largest group, is shackled by its country's secular rulers. Protestantism has been more secular than Catholicism or Orthodoxy, so its ideas on the relations between church and state have been the most advanced.

What the Church ought to do for secular society, in contrast to what it has asked of secular society, has also varied historically. Generally, the Church has thought it should be a city on the hilltop—a witness to the commonweal that comes from mutual support and love. In other words, the Church ought to be the place where society can see human community in action—can see love, cooperation, and mutual support. All human groups seek such community, and they have greater difficulty when they are large or their members have different values. The Church ought to manifest this community. In what Karl Rahner has called today's diaspora situation,[69] in which Christians are losing members, it becomes crucial that this concept of witness replace the ambition to rule over secular society that has dominated many periods of the Christian past. Many contemporary theologians want the Church to be with the poor, the oppressed, the people whom Jesus names in the beatitudes, for that is where its witness would be most vivid.

Self

The conceptions of nature and society that we have sketched above suggest the Christian view of the self. The biblical teaching that God placed human beings over nature has meant to Christians that the human person is of much greater value than the plants and animals.

Furthermore, as Christian social theory interacted with the secular elaboration of human nature through Western history, the individual acquired greater stature than in the East. In the East, as in ancient societies, the group predominated over the individual. One was most importantly a member of a tribe and only secondarily a unique person. As an image of God, the individual was more significant under Christianity. Of course, at times both secular and religious authorities crushed individuals ruthlessly. Nonetheless, because he bore the life of Christ, the individual person commanded respect. In matters of ethics, for instance, the notion of individual conscience counterbalanced the finespun codes of the canon lawyers and the moral theologians. The sacrament of penance epitomized this, for penance was essentially a self-accusation in which the individual, helped by the church's representative, passed judgment on his or her standing before God.

By standing out from nature and having personal rights, the Christian individual was conscious of being a unique self. Historically, the Church did not lay great emphasis on fulfilling one's unique self by communing with nature, but it did lay great emphasis on fitting into the social body of Christ. In fact, the charity of the community united was to be the primary sign of God's presence. Beyond social fulfillment, however, Christian theology encouraged the self to commune with divinity itself—with the Father, Son, and Holy Spirit. During the biblical period that meant putting on the "mind of Christ." During the patristic age it meant that grace is a share in divine nature and that religion is a process of divinization. Since the Hellenistic divinity was above all immortal, religion was a process of immortalization.

In medieval speculation, the self's fulfillment was the "beatific vision." By directly perceiving God's essence, our human drives to know and love (Augustine's famous "restless heart") would find a restful bliss. For the Thomists, participation in the divine nature through grace meant sharing in the "missions" of the Son and Holy Spirit. Thus, one's contemplation, knowing, and loving flowed into and out from the dynamic relations that characterized God's own inner life. The Reformation returned to biblical emphases, sending persons to study the Word and to work in the world. For Orthodoxy the Divine Liturgy, with special accents on the Holy Spirit and the Mother of God, nourished one throughout life.[70]

In many periods, Christians never quite found the balance between life in the world and life that looked to heaven as its true home. Prior to the Reformation, Christians probably gave greater emphasis to the latter. Since the Reformation and the Enlightenment, they have emphasized worldliness, for the world has become much more important than heaven.

Religious Development

Stressing communion with God, traditional Christian spiritual masters developed certain models of what happens in the life of the religious person. One of the most influential traditions involved the "three ways" that the self would travel. First, one had to walk the "purgative" way, which meant purging oneself of sin and developing virtuous habits. Then one would enter the long way of "illumination," by which the Christian truths of Word and Sacrament would slowly become one's own. No longer would they be external concepts—in time they would become inner principles of judgment and action. Finally, consummating the spiritual life was the "unitive" way, by which the self would unite with God as in a deep friendship or even a marriage. Occasionally such union would produce experiences of rapture, and one could speak of mysticism strictly so called ("infused contemplation"). Clearly, then, the paradigm of the three ways depended on the notion that final fulfillment is communion with God.

The saints who modeled Christian selfhood tended to be wholeheartedly given to communion with God. They also had to manifest charity for their fellows, but the spotlight was on their love of God. Because solitude or monastic withdrawal seemed to foster love of God, by allowing the freedom for deep, leisurely prayer, most saints went outside of family or civic life to lose themselves in devotion. That was the pattern up to the Reformation, and it took Christian selfhood some distance from the New Testament's view that prayer is important but not dominant.[71] Still, as the world became more important, the concept of saintliness expanded to include the service of other human beings. The Church had always honored certain holy married persons, certain holy civic leaders, but by late medieval times it had to contend with a more dynamic society.

Consequently, the Protestant emphasis on holy worldliness found a ready audience among many postmedievals. This emphasis did not remove the notion that one is a pilgrim trying to make progress through time towards a more lasting city. However, it did upgrade the status of family life, business, and government. Indeed, by the nineteenth century, tracts appeared with the theme that Jesus was the greatest salesman of all time. As well, one could hear Andrew Carnegie defend capitalistic wealth as God's way of keeping the poor from squandering his gifts.

Sin

Related to the capital question of what the self should most value is the complicated Christian teaching about original sin. At its crudest, the teaching said that all persons not baptized were bound to Satan and on the road to hell. Hell was essentially the deprivation of God (the loss of the beatific vision), but because of a gruesome imagery of fire and brimstone, it was popularly conceived of as a place of physical suffering. The ceremony for infant baptism, then, contained an exorcism of Satan—to save the little one from evil and make it pure for God. (Unbaptized babies who died before reaching the age of responsibility, and so before the possibility of personal sin, went to "Limbo," a state of "natural" happiness without beatific vision.)

A key moment in the development of the doctrine of original sin was Augustine's reading of the fall as a social act. Adam's sin alienated all human beings from God, for Adam was the head of the entire race. Augustine took the seeds of this view from Paul (for instance, Rom. 5:12–14). It suggested that Christ is the head of a now holy race, but those not baptized into Christ belong to an old human nature destined for punishment.

The classical Protestant thinkers owed a great deal to Augustine, whom they much preferred to Aquinas; thus, their reform of theology emphasized original sin. Like Augustine, they interpreted Genesis and Paul rather literally, thinking in terms of corporate sinners and saints. The famous double predestination of Calvinism was an attempt to explain human beings' different fates (going to hell or heaven) as members of Adam or members of Christ without removing the mystery of God's creative vision and providence. Whom God has destined for heaven will surely end up there. Likewise, whom He has set for hell will fall into the flame.

In a fateful development of Calvinistic predestination, the signs of election to heaven became outward decorum and even material prosperity. That meant the double burden of being both poor and damned and the double blessing of being both rich and saved. Eventually more careful Bible readers recognized that this correspondence contradicted the Sermon on the Mount, but a lot of Calvinists thoroughly enjoyed storing up plenty in their barns and letting their souls wax fat.

How inherently wicked or good the self is was an important question in the Reformation debates between Protestants and Catholics. Protestants, following Luther's stress on justification by faith and Calvin's stress on God's sovereignty, tended to emphasize the corruption of human nature through sin. Catholics, partly in reaction to that Protestant position and partly from their own emphasis on the sacraments and the Incarnation, saw an essential goodness in human nature (though they spoke of sin as darkening the mind and weakening the will). Clearly, though, Christianity made the West suspicious of human instincts. Many Christians were indoctrinated with the belief that they were wicked sinners. Often that led them to oscillate between self-punishment and, in compensation, self-indulgence. However, through penance one could experience God's mercy—the almost delicious sense of being loved gratuitously. Then the Johannine promise (1 John 3 : 20) that even when our hearts condemn us God is greater than our hearts could burst into joyous effect.

The Pauline discussion of sin and grace in terms of "flesh" and "spirit" focused Christian discussion of the self as embodied. That Paul's original language did not intend a matter-spirit dualism was almost forgotten after Christianity took up Greek thought. As a result, extremists tended to deprecate the body, marriage, and the world of human affairs as fleshly pursuits. In response to the Manichaean and Albigensian heresies, the Catholic church affirmed the goodness of the body, but the church's general orientation toward heaven, its introduction of celibacy for holders of high church offices, and its preference for ascetic saints tended to make the average person regret his or her flesh. For women this caused considerable suffering, because the male church teachers often projected their sexual problems onto women. In that case, women became wanton, seductive, and dangerous.

On the other hand, a certain realism about worldly life, in which imperfection if not sin was inevitable, tended to soften this rigorism. Christian moral theologians have usually taught that sins of the flesh are less grievous than sins of the spirit (such as pride, anger, or hatred). Although at one point Roman Catholic moralists classified all sexual offenses as serious ("mortal" as opposed to "venial" sins), there were effective if unauthorized counterforces in the bawdiness of Chaucer and Boccaccio and the frequent concubinage of members of the clergy.

Image of God

The self was an image of God, principally because of its reason and free will. The intellectual light that Augustine, in good neo-Platonic style, saw as a participation in eternal light was concrete evidence that God is more intimate to his images than they are to themselves. Most forms of Christianity held the freedom to love or not to love God to be beyond question. How to reconcile this freedom with God's omniscience was a thorny issue, but the idea of freedom was seldom abandoned. Augustine's theories, which tied into his stress on omniscience (as opposed to the Pelagian stress on human freedom), gave ammunition to those who wanted to downplay human works or goodness. Thus, they attracted Luther and others enamored of justification by faith. Aquinas' rather complex position strove for a balance by carefully distinguishing the realms of divine infinitude and human finitude.[72] Jesuits and Dominicans engaged in a tedious debate over this issue at the end of the sixteenth century, and, partly out of exhaustion, most theologians have since been quick to stress the mystery in any relation that involves the incomprehensible divine nature. In practice, then, Christianity has held human beings liable for their acts but has left final judgment to God.

Thus, the Christian concept of self has been complex. Christianity has never had a significant no-self doctrine like Buddhism, but where the self does gravitate—to society, sin, grace, reason, love, God, or something else—has not been clear. The tendency has been to place the self in the mystery of God—to make divinity the beginning and the end of this little consciousness that we carry so fleetingly.

Divinity

God is the heart of Christian religion, as God is the heart of any theistic religion. The first Christian conception of God was Jewish. Jesus himself accepted the God of the Fathers—Abraham, Isaac, and Jacob. This God, as we have seen, interacted with human beings and was personal. His guidance of humanity peaked in his liberation of Israel from Egypt and his covenanting with Israel on Mount Sinai. As numerous theologians have pointed out, it was difficult for Jesus to designate himself as divine, because to do so would have confused his identity with that of his "Father." In other words, the God of Jewish faith was Jesus' Father, his source.

Christians have waged fiery debates about the places of reason and revelation in developing Jesus' notion of God. A generation ago, the Protestant theologians Karl Barth and Paul Tillich presented radically different approaches. Barth insisted on the primacy of revelation, while Tillich began with reason and an existential analysis of the human situation.[73] Barth's position was that we can only know who and what God is through the self-expression that he has made in Jesus Christ. Apart from this primary revelation, Barth said, all reasoning about divinity is a matter of human pride, and the philosophies and religions are enemies of true Christian theology. Tillich argued that no revelation stands apart from human minds and historical circumstances. Jesus himself spoke in the language of his people; the circumstances of his time and place qualified what he could think and say. Indeed, all theology reflects the prevailing understanding. For that reason, we never finally penetrate revelation. The "deposit of faith" that tradition said finished with the death of the last apostle paid such interest through later time that theology kept changing.

Implicit in these two positions is the dialectic between above and below that marks all religion. The conciliar age and the medieval period developed both revelation (considered to be from above) and reason (from below) to interpret the biblical word. One result of this balance was a discussion of God in terms of the (Aristotelian) doctrine of causality, which fascinated the medieval mind. God was the font of being, the prime mover behind the entire creational chain, and the final cause that lures all creation toward its fulfillment. By inference from the contingent (nonnecessary) nature of human experience, the philosophers concluded that God had to be a necessary fullness of existence. According to Etienne Gilson, perhaps the most distinguished Catholic historian of Christian philosophy, this position amounted to a philosophical elaboration of the self-designation God gave in Exodus 3 : 14—"I am what I am."[74]

In medieval Christian thought, human beings could reason that God exists but not reach what God is. Essentially, God was a mysterious fullness of being too rich or too bright for the human mind to grasp. The less sophisticated thinkers often thought that revelation had removed this mystery. Deeper thinkers, however, realized that, if anything, the Incarnation of the divine Logos (the heart of Christian revelation) compounded the mystery, adding the question of how divinity can express itself in another form—the infinite Son or Holy Spirit, but also, more pressingly, the finite God-man.

What the deep thinkers realized was that they could only propose analogies from human experience. Accepting the fact of revelation in Jesus Christ, which led to the facts of the Incarnation, the Trinity, grace, and creation from nothingness, they had to propose the most astute hypotheses they could. Such hypotheses were precious if they explained at all what the traditional faith, as expressed in the Bible and the councils, said. Nonetheless, no hypothesis gave one a direct vision of God.

God as the Trinity

In dealing with the revealed God's inner nature, the concept of the Trinity was paramount. Orthodox catholic (universal) faith held that Father–Son–Holy Spirit was attested by the scriptures and defined by the councils. As we indicated, the psychological analogy that Augustine and Aquinas developed gained great respect, the West considering it the "purest" (the least material) analogy. Thus, the God of Christian speculation was a fullness of intelligence and love. He was perfection, in need of nothing outside himself. He was the creator and redeemer, moved only by his own goodness. The Incarnation was the main instance of his outpouring, but glimpses of God abounded everywhere. Subhuman creatures were his "vestiges" (footprints); human beings were his images. Christians were images of his great image, for they reflected the eternal icon, the Logos-Son.

Regarding the Trinity, Christians stood in the Son's position, receiving their likeness to God from the Father and expressing it through Spirit-carried love. The similitude broke down, however, because the divine persons were only relationally distinct (that is, Son and Father differed only as begotten and begetter), while humans remained creatures distinct from God. Still, the consummation of faith, whether occurring in worldly mystical experience or in the beatific vision,[75] meant knowing with something of divinity's own knowledge, loving with something of divinity's own love.

Biblical Renewal

When Reformation thought returned to biblical conceptions, because it found the medieval synthesis too abstract and unhistorical, it revived the notion that faith is a living interpersonal relation to God. This contrasted somewhat with the position of most Scholasticism, which stressed the propositional knowledge (the information) that faith provides. As well, the Reformers revived the twin notions of God's judgment and his merciful love. By faith, God became one's "rock and salvation"—the one on whom to rely. Between the times of Luther and Kierkegaard, such faith became paradoxical—a leap. In the face of the "impossibility" of the Incarnation, Kierkegaard jumped into the intellectual abyss, proposing that what reason could not fathom divinity could yet do, because it moved by reasons the mind knew not, by reasons of the heart.

The Hebrew notion of *hesed* (steadfast, merciful love), which kept God to his freely chosen covenant, encouraged believers to trust that no situation in their lives was hopeless. If Ezekiel's God could raise dry bone back to fleshly life, Jesus' God could use even suffering and evil to his own inscrutable ends. Was not God's chosen way of salvation, the death of his only begotten Son, the surest sign that no one had ever understood him? As the heavens are above the earth, so were God's ways above the ways of human beings. For that reason, the Reformers wanted only a Pauline faith: God's power and wisdom are Christ crucified.

Did this finally mean a justification of God by surrender? For the deeper theologians, who had frequently wrestled with unbelief personally, the answer was yes. With Job and Paul, they said that the pot cannot tell the potter how to fashion. For the sake of their sanity, they had to affirm that God is wise and just (and even loving) in all his doings. How this worked out, however, they often could not say. Surrender was finally a matter of trust, a matter of unexpectedly feeling God's love. As the mistranslation of Job put it, "Though he slay me, yet will I trust him." The farthest reach of the Christian conception of God was an intimate marriage of lives and fortunes. What the prophet Hosea had written of God's constancy, even his vulnerability, the new biblical theologians found in New Testament *agape* (love).

The Johannine epistles say God is this *agape*. The Pauline epistles say *agape* is the greatest of God's gifts. The biblical theologians translated *agape* as self-sacrificing love. Beyond *eros* (self-fulfilling love) or *philia* (the love of friendship), it worked through God's use of the cross. Thus, it was an attack on evil, on lovelessness. Thus, it broke the circle of tit for tat, of sin and retribution. God the judge finally yielded to God the lov-

er. In Jesus he suffered evil to undo evil, thereby making a new creation. The lamb who was slain for this new creation is worthy of all glory and honor, because his sacrifice shows a divinity greater than one could ever imagine. Only the nursing mother who could never abandon her child, the Lucan (pertaining to Luke) prodigal father, or the lover to whom the beloved is more than another self could glimpse this *mysterion*— this plan of God's love, hidden from all ages.

In contrast to other religions' versions of divinity, Christian theology stressed the personal, loving character of God that Jesus' flesh disclosed. Jesus was God in human terms. (He was also humanity fulfilled by union with divinity.) As a result, Christianity did not appreciate the impersonal divinity of nature so dear to East Asian and Indian thought. This divinity was implicit in Christian theology, but the personalistic emphasis placed it in the shade.

At its better moments, Christianity was grateful to Judaism, since it had adopted most of Judaism's doctrine of God. As well, it was mindful of the continuing election of Israel that Paul had proclaimed (Romans, chapters 9–11). At its worst, Christianity condemned Jews as Christ killers and spoke of their responsibility for his blood. Islam confronted Christianity with claims of a later, perfected revelation and prophecy, and with an adamant insistence on God's unity. For Islam, and for Judaism, the Christian doctrine of the Trinity violated monotheism. Christian claims that God is both one and three seemed to Muslims and Jews incoherent, while Christian allegiance to Jesus clashed with Muslim allegiance to the Qur'an and Jewish allegiance to the Torah. Those clashes remain with us yet.

As the center of the Christian world view, God in Christ dominated Christian conceptions of nature, society, and self. Nature was but God's cloak. It was a lovely gift, but it sprang from nothingness and was wholly under God's control. With each extension of space and time by science, the awe of sophisticated believers increased: A more complex nature only magnified their God all the more.

Similarly, God was the norm and goal of Christian society, because his law was the source of all natural law and because eternal life with God in heaven was the goal of all persons. God wanted human beings to form a community. Christ showed them the love that could bring that about. Thus, the vocation of the self was to obey the great twofold command: to love God with whole mind, heart, soul, and strength and to love neighbor as itself.

Study Questions

1. Why is it easier for a camel to pass through the eye of a needle than for a rich person to enter the kingdom of God?

2. Contrast Jesus with the Buddha.

3. Elaborate on the following extract: "From Judaism came the concepts of prophet and messiah. From Hellenism came the notions of saviour and god. In the Church's hands, they were all underscored."

4. Why were the Councils of Nicaea and Chalcedon portentous?

5. How did the Mass summarize medieval Christian symbolism?

6. Describe the spirit of Protestantism.

7. How does the eighteenth-century Enlightenment contrast with faith, mysticism, and symbolism?

8. Has Christianity both spawned physical science and frustrated it?

9. Compose a brief rite for Christian baptism, stressing the Orthodox reliance on the Holy Spirit.

Chapter Ten

ISLAM: TWENTY-FIVE KEY DATES

570 C.E.	BIRTH OF MUHAMMAD
609–610	FIRST QUR'ANIC REVELATIONS
622	HEJIRA (FLIGHT TO MEDINA)
630	CONQUEST OF MECCA
632	DEATH OF MUHAMMAD
636–640	CONQUEST OF DAMASCUS, JERUSALEM, EGYPT, PERSIA
CA. 650	ESTABLISHMENT OF THE CANON OF THE QUR'AN
661–750	UMAYYAD CALIPHATE
680	MURDER OF HUSAIN, SHIITE SAINT
711	MUSLIM ENTRY INTO SPAIN
713	MUSLIM ENTRY INTO INDUS VALLEY
750–1258	ABBASID CALIPHATE

Islam

The prophetic religion that began with Israel and took a new turn in Christianity gained a further career in Islam. Islam, which is the world's fastest-growing religion today, arose from the visions of the prophet Muhammad. At its height, Islam stretched from India to western Spain.[1] Today it is a great force in Africa, a middling presence in China and the Soviet Union, a shareholder in the petropolitics of the Middle East, a huge presence in Indonesia, and the religion of more than 6 million North Americans. To study the religion behind the crescent flag, we begin by describing its traces in several different locations.

APPEARANCE

A likely first encounter with Islam is in southern Spain, which has a proud Moorish (Spanish Muslim) heritage. Toledo city walls date back to the Arab conquest, and the art of El Greco reflects a culture that mixed Jews, Muslims, and Christians with few problems. Farther south, the Muslim traces are stronger, as evidenced by the great mosque in Cordoba. Although Christians remade it into a cathedral, Islamic art still shines in the beautiful *mihrab*—the niche in the wall (gilded in blue and gold) that directs the worshiper towards Mecca. At Granada the Alhambra that faces the snow-capped Sierra Nevada mountains demonstrates the architecture that thirteenth- and fourteenth-century Muslim rulers could command. Fernando Diaz-Plaja's study of Spanish character[2] shows that Islam left its effects on the population, too. Something of today's Castilian pride came from Andalusian Moors, who felt that their scimitar contained the courage of Muhammad's original holy warriors and that their mathematics and medicine extended the Greek golden age.

In Cairo all evidence of Islam is current. Though the Pyramids and the Nile conjure images of the pharaohs, the dusty main streets feature flowing garments and tapered minarets. In the train terminal, prayer mats come out when the call to prayer sounds. The Westernized businessmen in the air-conditioned, first-class coaches seem to pay the haunting verses little heed, but the verses clearly move the workers outside. On a Friday, the Muslim holy day, what look like middle-class families picnic at the fine Cairo zoo. The university nearby closes on Friday, so students hoist small children to see the lions. In Cairo's back streets, where thousands live five and six to a room, the small children run around in pajamas or run into the streets to play amidst the buses and taxis. The poverty of the back streets suggests a certain fatalism. Just as dozens of children die each year in the traffic, so thousands, perhaps millions, suffer from malnutrition.

In Jerusalem the Islamic presence may seem surprising, if one expects to find only a Jewish capital.[3] But Jerusalem is the third holiest Muslim city, ranking behind only Mecca and Medina. Abraham and Jesus are Muslim prophets, and the Qur'an extols Mary. The mosque at the Dome of the Rock (Figure 28), behind the Western Wall, is a gorgeous tribute to Muhammad's night flight to heaven and to Abraham's faith in being willing to sacrifice Ishmael (in the Muslim version of the story).

The Dome of the Rock is stunning. Its blue, green, red, and gold somehow never clash. The rock itself, around which lushly carpeted corridors wind, is but a mass of stone, but the beauty of its surroundings transforms it into a pillar of faith. In a small chamber under the rock, devout Muslims kneel, lost in obeisance and prayer. Upstairs Israeli guards prod an Arab who has stretched out behind a pillar to enjoy the carpet's softness and steal a mid-morning nap. They are another reminder that the Middle East is very complex.

Northeast of Jerusalem the volatile Shia Islam of Iran presents yet new images. Two-thirds of the women of Tehran are veiled, although they may wear blue jeans under their black draping and their dark eyes may flash contemporary signals. With the ouster of the shah in 1979, Iran became the

Figure 28   Dome of the Rock. Photo by J. T. Carmody.

most visible example of Islam's moves to restore traditional culture. The passions responsible for the headlines showed that submission (the root meaning of *Islam*) was potent indeed. Iran today hardly acknowledges that Zoroaster once inspired its people and little doubts that the Prophet (Muhammad) laid out its way. Everywhere, there is oil, religion, and emotion. How they will mix in the Iranian future will be a prime indicator of what other Muslim states will attempt.

In India, Delhi reveals much more than a Hindu heritage. From 1200 to 1857 Delhi was the center of a Muslim empire. The great mosque of the old city, as well as the Mogul monuments on the outskirts, speak of that empire's splendor. The city of Agra is the most eloquent witness, though, because it is the home of the Taj Mahal. The symmetry of this wonder of the world makes

the golden age of Islamic culture appear quite contemporary. Forget that the ruler who built it wanted to memorialize his wife; forget that he was slain before he could build a matching black mausoleum for himself. Simply enjoy the minarets at the corners, the graceful swell of the domes. It is as though the reflecting pool and the gardens mirror the Qur'an's picture of Paradise. Agra's heat is more humid than that of the Arabian desert, and it inspires a longing for cool, shade, and flowing waters.

Behind the Taj Mahal, water buffalo that hulk in the Jumna river flats temper the paradisal daydream, reminding the visitor that this is Indian Islam—Islam that contended with Hinduism, influenced Hindu bhakti through its Sufis, begot syncretistic Sikhism, and led, rather inevitably, to partition and the creation of Pakistan. Indian Islam was the faith of conquerors, of outsiders, that gathered millions of disciples but never won the subcontinent's soul. So the water buffalo, though not quite sacred cows, have Hindu rights to life. It would be aesthetically more pleasing were they not squatting behind the Taj Mahal, but Hindu *ahimsa* (noninjury) says let them be.

HISTORY

Muhammad

Islam stems directly from the two precepts contained in the profession of faith: "There is no God but God, and Muhammad is his Prophet." Allah (God) is the ultimate agent of Islamic revelation and religion, but he chose to work through Muhammad. Thus, Muhammad was the spokesman, the medium, of a definitive message and book (the Qur'an). Through it God expressed once and for all the divine mercy and judgment.

Muhammad was born in 570 C.E. in Mecca, which is in present-day Saudi Arabia. Around 610, he began to receive revelations. At that time, the religious milieu of the Arabian Peninsula was "a rather primitive polydemonism and worship of stones, stars, caves and trees."[4] Most of the people identified with one of the nomadic tribes that lived in the area. Mecca was a religious and commercial center, where people came to venerate the Black Stone, set in what is known as the Kaaba. Today scholars surmise that the stone was a meteorite. Whatever its origin, it served as a rallying point for local soothsayers and poets, who dominated the Arabic religion that Muhammad witnessed as a youth. The likeliest forerunners of Muhammad's strict monotheism were the *hanifs*, who took offense at the polydemonism and sought a purer faith, although to what extent they inspired Muhammad is not known.

W. Montgomery Watt has stressed the commercial strife that divided the people of Mecca during Muhammad's early years.[5] The conflict between the Byzantine and Persian empires affected Mecca, because traders from those realms passed through it. Among the Arabs there, a difficult social transition was under way from a nomadic society, in which loyalty was to one's clan, to a mercantile society, in which loyalty was to one's business partners (or simply to profit). The result was considerable upheaval. Before that time persons such as orphans and widows, who fell outside of nuclear families and trading groups, could find support in their larger clans, but the social change destroyed this support. Muhammad grew up as an orphan, so he must have felt some of the suffering experienced by such persons. Indeed, much of the social reform in his early message was to provide a religious basis for a unity extending beyond the clan that would prompt concern for orphans, widows, and the poor.

Muhammad grew up in a branch of the ruling Kuraish family under the care of his uncle, and he probably entered his family's caravan trade as a youth. In adulthood he married a wealthy widow, Khadija, who was some years older than he and who had been his employer. They had six children, of whom four daughters survived. Whether from personal troubles, challenges in the social situation, or a positive desire to understand the world more deeply, Muhammad developed the habit of going off to the hills nearby. There, in a cave, he enjoyed meditative solitude and began to have visions. His first visions, according to the Qur'an (53 : 1–18, 81:15–25) were of someone "terrible in power, very strong."[6] That personage hovered near him on the horizon and imparted a revelation. It and subsequent revelations finally convinced Muhammad that God was choosing him to be a messenger.

At first, he wondered if he was going crazy. However, Khadija encouraged him to believe in the revelations, and as his thought clarified, he attributed them to the angel Gabriel. Muhammad continued to receive revelations for the rest of his life (over twenty years), and these messages, which either he or early disciples wrote down on "pieces of paper, stones, palm-leaves, shoulder-blades, ribs and bits of leather,"[7] formed the basis of the Qur'an.

From what scholars conjecture to be the early revelations, five major themes emerge: God's goodness and power, the need to return to God for judgment, gratitude and worship in response to God's goodness and pending judgment, generosity toward one's fellow human beings, and Muhammad's own vocation of proclaiming the message of goodness and judgment.

Muhammad's proclamation met with considerable resistance, principally because it threatened some powerful vested interests. First, the absoluteness of Allah threatened the traditional polytheism. However, it was much more than a challenge to custom and traditional religion—it was a challenge to the commerce that had grown up around the Kaaba. The livelihoods of the merchants who sold amulets, the soothsayers who sold fortunes, and the semiecstatic poets who lyricized the old gods were all imperiled.[8] Second, Muhammad's call for social justice implied a revolution—if not in contemporary financial arrangements, at least in contemporary attitudes. Third, the message of judgment was hardly welcome, for no age likes to find itself set before divine justice, hell fire, or the sword of retribution. Last, many Meccans ridiculed Muhammad's notion of the resurrection of the body.

Rise to Power

Initially rejected, Muhammad drew consolation from the fate of prophets who had preceded him. Increasingly, it appears, he learned about Judaism and Christianity from believers of those traditions who either lived in the area or traveled it for trade. The first converts to Muhammad's revelations came from within his own family. When he started to preach publicly, around 613, the leaders of the most powerful clans opposed him vigorously. He thus tended to be most successful among the low-ranking clans and those with young leaders ripe for a new order. Also, those who were considered "weak" (without strong clan protection) found the new prophecy attractive. Muhammad was proposing a religious association based on faith in Allah that transcended clan allegiances and so might make them stronger.

In 619 Muhammad suffered a personal crisis. His wife and uncle, who had been his foremost supporters, both died. Muslims ("submitters" to his God) were slowly increasing in number, but the future was very uncertain. In 622 he left Mecca and went to Yathrib, to the north, to arbitrate a long-standing dispute between two leading tribes. He settled there, and the town became Medina, the town of the Prophet. Muslims call Muhammad's departure or flight from Mecca the *Hejira*, and they view it as the turning point in the history of early Islam. Annemarie Schimmel interprets the Hejira as the complete breakup of Muhammad's relations with his own tribe—a definitive break with the old order,[9] which was a virtually unheard-of act in the clan-based society of the time.

Al Faruqi emphasizes the positive work that went on in Medina: the "promulgation of a constitution and the launching of the Islamic polity on its universal mission."[10] Muhammad proved to be a good politician, able to organize the Meccan emigrants and the Medina clans into a single group.

One problem for Muhammad in Medina was the local Jewish community, who refused to accept him as a genuine prophet and ridiculed his interpretation of Jewish scripture. Apparently Muhammad either drove them out of Medina or had them killed or sold into slavery.[11] After consolidating his power base and building support among the neighboring bedouin tribes, Muhammad started to challenge the Meccans. He disrupted their trade in an effort to overthrow the city's commercial base, and in 624 his vastly outnumbered troops won a surprising victory at Badr. Finally, after several further skirmishes, Muhammad won a decisive victory at the Battle of the Ditch.

Muhammad's greatest triumphs came through diplomacy among the tribes, however. Mecca finally fell in 630 without the stroke of a single sword. In control, Muhammad cleansed the Kaaba of pagan idols. He then consolidated his victory by a final military triumph over resistant Meccans at Hunayn. This settled the matter for most onlookers, and thenceforth the surrounding tribes were in Muhammad's hands.

In the two remaining years of his life, Muhammad further developed the educational program that he had set up in Medina. "The centre of all his preoccupations was the training, educating, and disciplining of his community. They were to be the leaven to leaven the whole lump—for he had no illusions about the Arab character and realized that any genuine conversion of the majority could only be the end of a long process extending far beyond his own lifetime."[12] Muhammad soon became the focus of Arab solidarity, and just before his death, he apparently contemplated action against the Byzantine powers in the north, perhaps because Muslim nationalism meant a growing hostility toward Greeks and their Christian Arab allies. The quick military victories of his successor Abu Bakr make most sense on the assumption that he simply executed plans that Muhammad himself had formulated.

Personality

Muhammad demonstrated an abundant humanity. In addition to his religious sensitivity and his political and military skills, Muhammad manifested a notable sympathy for the weak, a gentleness, a slowness to anger, some shyness in social relations, and a sense of humor.[13] According to the *Hadith* (tradition), for instance, the Prophet's second in command, Abu Bakr, started to beat a pilgrim for letting a camel stray. Muhammad began to smile and then indicated to Abu Bakr the irony that a pilgrim like Bakr (a pilgrim through life) should beat a pilgrim to Mecca.

In glimpses obtained from the Qur'an and the earliest levels of the tradition, Muhammad seems to have been an ordinary man whom God singled out to receive revelations. Muhammad's virtue was to accept his commission and keep faith with it until death. The emphasis in the Prophet's own preaching on the sovereignty of God and on the divine authority for the Qur'anic mes-

sage led him to stress his own ordinariness, his liability to error, and the like. He made no claim to miraculous power. The central miracle was the Qur'an itself—a message of such sublimity and eloquence that it testified beyond doubt to a divine source. In keeping with Muhammad's own humility, orthodox Islam has condemned any move to exalt Muhammad above ordinary humanity or worship him.

Nonetheless, popular Muslim religion sometimes seized on hints in the Qur'an and made Muhammad superhuman. The most famous of its images is Muhammad's "night journey" to Jerusalem, after which he ascended to Paradise, talked with the prophets who preceded him, and experienced an ineffable vision of God. This story became so popular that it finally entered orthodox faith. Later religious faith also elaborated on Muhammad's preaching of the coming Last Judgment and tended to think of the Prophet as its shield and intercessor on the Last Day.

Sufis (devotional Muslims) and other mystics elaborated a view of Muhammad as the supreme saint and mystic, while some Muslims given to cosmological speculation gave Muhammad an eternal preexistence, which related to the eternal preexistence of the Qur'an. This belief gave Muhammad a role in creation as the intermediary between God and humanity. The mystic al-Hallaj, whom Islamic authorities killed because he claimed oneness with the deity, saw Muhammad as the first of the prophets—as the Light that was the source of all their lights: "He was before all, his name the first in the Book of Fate; he was known before all things and all being, and will endure after the end of all."[14] In such understandings, the Prophet became the supreme exemplar, the mediator, something close to the Word of creation.

Qur'anic Religion

After Muhammad's death, his followers collected the texts of his revelations and established the orthodox version during the rule of Othman (644–656). "To this day this version remains as the authoritative word of God. But, owing to the fact that the kufic script in which the Koran was originally written contained no indication of vowels or diacritical points, variant readings are recognized by Muslims as of equal authority."[15]

The present version of the collection follows the editorial principle that the chapters (suras) should be ordered in decreasing length. The result is that the present text tells the reader nothing about the chronology of the revelations. While scholars have attempted to distinguish the Meccan utterances from the Medinan, their work is often so tedious (distinguishing separate verses within a sura) that no one theory of the chronology has won universal acceptance. Therefore, it is more expeditious simply to accept the fact that Muhammad's revelations were written down and that he used them as the basis of the program that he urged on his listeners. Among the earliest themes of his preaching were the sovereignty of God, the imminence of judgment, and the need for fraternal charity.

Cragg and other commentators insist on the importance of the Qur'anic Arabic.[16] Muslims consider the Qur'an to be written in the purest Arabic. Its style, as well as its message, prove to them that it must have come directly from God. Jeffrey and al Faruqi have both given thematic presentations of the Qur'an's religious materials.[17] They organize the Qur'an's seemingly repetitious or circular presentations, and by following them we may get a sense of how Islamic revelation developed.

An early Meccan passage (96 : 1–5) emphasizes that Muhammad experienced his call as a command to *recite*, although his recitations only became clear as time passed. Sura 53, lines 1–18, richly symbolizes how Muhammad experienced his call. Because of Muhammad's vision of the angel Gabriel, the Muslim theology of revelation granted Gabriel an important role as the mediator in transmitting the Qur'an. In Sura 81, lines 15–29, are suggestions that Muhammad's early preaching met with disbelief and even

contempt. Indeed, the Prophet seems to have had to defend himself against the charge of jinn (demon) possession.

Suras 73 and 74 buttress the tradition that Muhammad regularly used to go off to a cave to pray. Wrapped in a mantle against the night cold, he would seek God's comfort. This image has been a model for countless Sufis and ascetics as they have sought an experiential knowledge of Allah. Other Qur'anic passages that are considered reflections of Muhammad's early concerns boom forth a praise of God, a sense of God's overwhelming majesty, that suggests Rudolf Otto's classic definition of the holy: the mystery that is both alluring and threatening.

The later passages of the Qur'an, those that likely were written in Medina, concern more practical affairs. As the head of an established political and religious community, Muhammad had to deal with questions of law and order. Thus, we can find the seeds of later Islamic law on inheritance, women, divorce, warfare, and the like. These seeds, plus the *Hadith*, which contains what the Prophet himself taught and judged,[18] are the primary sources of Islamic law. Generally, Muhammad's law and social teaching were advances on the prevailing mores. They improved the lot of the downtrodden and humanized both business and war. For instance, Muhammad made widows and orphans the prime beneficiaries of the *zakat* (almsgiving) required of all the faithful. Two points on which outsiders frequently fault Muhammad and the Qur'an are the doctrines of holy war (jihad) and polygamy. Nevertheless, they were improvements on the pre-Muslim practices and improved treatment of both women and prisoners of war.

On the basis of the Qur'an's prescriptions for a true Islam, a true religion of submission to the will of Allah, Muslims have elaborated five cardinal duties known as the "pillars" of true faith. They are: witnessing to faith (proclaiming the Creed), ritual prayer, fasting during the lunar month of Ramadan, almsgiving, and pilgrimage to Mecca. The witness to faith epitomizes the

Muslim's orientation in the universe: There is no God but God, and Muhammad is his Prophet. Allah is the only fit object of worship, and Muhammad is the last of the prophets—the "seal."

What a comparativist might call the rigorous monotheism of Islam has both negative and positive aspects. Negatively, in what amounts to an attack on false religion, Islam makes idolatry (associating anything with Allah) the capital sin. At the outset, then, Muhammad's revelation implied an attack on the prevailing Arab religion. Later it led to a polemic against Christian Trinitarianism and a check on worldly pride or mammon that might diminish God's sovereignty. Positively, Islamic monotheism generated great praise for the "Lord of the Worlds"[19]—the Creator who guides all things, who is the beauty and power by which the world moves. For the Muslim mystics, the words of the Creed swelled with hidden meaning. Like the Cabalists, some Muslim mystics assigned each letter a numerical value and then composed numerological accounts of how the world hangs together. Many Muslim mystics pushed the concept of divine sovereignty so far that they denied the existence of anything apart from Allah. Not only was there no God beside him, there was no being apart from his Being. While the orthodox Muslims found such pantheism blasphemous, the mystics tended to stress the oneness of the Lord's domain.[20] Last, rigorous monotheism implied that Muhammad himself was not divine. His high status was to be the *rasul*—the prophetic mouthpiece. (In later devotion, as we have seen, there was a tendency to exalt Muhammad, and later theology often viewed the Qur'an as coeternal with God, much as rabbinic theology saw the Torah as coeternal with God.)

The second pillar of faith is prayer, which has worked out as an obligation to pray five times daily. Authoritative authors such as al-Ghazali went to great lengths to specify the postures, words, number of bows, and proper places and times for prayer,[21] but the primary effect of the second pillar on the common people was to pace them through the day in the great Muslim practice of remembrance *(dhikr)*. At each call from the minaret, they were to remember the one God whom they serve—remember his compassion, his mercy, and his justice. Ideally, by praying fervently at the appointed hours, one can forge a chain that links together more and more moments of remembrance, so that God progressively comes to dominate all one's thought, action, and emotion. Experiencing Muslim prayer is impressive. The slow chant of the Qur'anic words becomes haunting, stirring even the non-Arabist. The voice (usually recorded today) is passionate—a lover's near sob, a tremulous witness to God's grandeur.

Third, what the prayer times are to the day, the holy month of Ramadan is to the year. Ramadan is the month of fasting and (interestingly enough) of celebration. Through all the hours of daylight (from the time that one can distinguish a black thread from a white), no food or drink is to pass the lips. Thereby, the Muslim learns discipline, sacrifice, and the price that divine treasures cost.[22] Against the secular succession of months, in which no time is more significant than any other, the religionist erects special times like Ramadan. These times oppose the flux, fence off a portion of time as sacred.

Fourth, Islam develops a similar paradigm for space by praying toward Mecca and by the obligation to make a pilgrimage to Mecca at least once in one's lifetime. For Muslims, Mecca is the center, the *omphalos* (navel) where the world was born. It is the holy city where Qur'anic revelation was disclosed to the world. Thus, the psychodynamics of the pilgrimage run deep. Without doubt, devout pilgrims feel that they are going to the holiest spot in creation.

On pilgrimage, Muslims dress alike, go through the same traditional actions, and often experience an exhilarating sense of community. The fifth pillar, almsgiving, focuses this sense of community in a practical, economic way. By insisting that all contribute to the support of the poor (often one-fortieth of their wealth annually), Qur'anic religion gives its community *(Ummah)*[23] food and clothing. The Muslim alms, then, is more than a tiny dole or act of charity—it is an act of social, corporate responsibility. Further, it reminds the advantaged that they are one family with the disadvantaged and that the stern Judge will demand a strict account of what they have done with his gifts.

Sura 4, lines 134–137, gathers the pillars together and shows their common foundation: faith in God, in his Word, in his coming judgment:

O believers, be you securers of justice, witnesses for God, even though it be against yourselves, or your parents and kinsmen, whether the man be rich or poor; God stands close to either. Then follow not caprice, so as to swerve. For if you twist or turn, God is aware of the things you do. O Believers, believe in God and His Messenger and the Book He sent down on His messenger and the Book which He sent down before [the Bible]. Whoso disbelieves in God and His Angels and His Books, and His Messengers, and the Last Day, has surely gone astray into far error. Those who believe, and then disbelieve, and then believe, and then disbelieve, and then increase in unbelief—God is not likely to forgive them, neither to guide them on any way.

That strong commitment to the Prophet and to the Qur'an founded Islam. Muhammad's prophecy became the basis of Islam's external missionizing and internal religious development. Praise belongs only to God. God is the Lord of all beings. He is the all-merciful, the compassionate, the Master of the Day of Judgment and Resurrection. Blessing is to serve God, to pray to God, to have God guide one on the straight path (Qur'an 1:5). Burning with this conviction, Muslims poured out of Mecca to conquer the world.

The Age of Conquest

At Muhammad's death in 632 most of Arabia had accepted Islam, though often the allegiance was superficial. Some tribes took the occasion of the Prophet's death to attempt a revolt. General Khalid al-Walid, who served the first caliph (leader) Abu Bakr, crushed them within a year. Thus, when Abu Bakr died in 636, Arabia was united and poised for adventure. The obvious foes were Byzantium and Persia, which threatened Arabian prosperity and were ripe for religious and military conquest. The Muslim armies were amazingly effective. By 636 they controlled both Damascus and Jerusalem. As important in this lightning conquest as their military skill, though, was the unrest of the peoples they conquered. Those peoples "welcomed the Muslims as kin-liberators from Byzantine politics, economic exploitation, Church persecution, and social tyranny."[24] On the eastern frontier, Muslim armies spread into Persian territory, and by 649 all of Persia was in Arab hands.

The quick conquest of Syria released men for further expeditions in the West; by 640 there were conquests in Egypt. Cairo and Alexandria soon fell, and despite resistance from the Roman emperor Constans, the Arabs established themselves as a marine power operating from the southeastern Mediterranean. By 648 they had conquered Cyprus; by 655 they were in charge of the waters around Greece and Sicily. On land in North Africa, the Muslims conquered the Berber region of Tripoli in 643 and then proceeded to Carthage and to the Nubian regions along the Nile, conquering the Nubian capital city of Dongola. When the Umayyad caliphate established itself in 661, the ventures became even more far-reaching. Soon Muslims were as far away as China, India, and western Europe. By 699 Islam occupied Afghanistan, while various campaigns south of the Caspian and Aral seas brought Armenia, Iraq, Iran, and eastern India into the Muslim fold by 800.

At the beginning of the ninth century, Arab rule along the southern Mediterranean stretched from Palestine to the Atlantic. Muslims controlled three-quarters of the Iberian Peninsula, and most Mediterranean traffic had to reckon with Muslim sallies. European campaigns had brought Arab soldiers as far north as Orleans, and they strongly influenced the southern portions of the Frankish kingdom. In 732 Muslims had taken Toulouse and then the whole of Aquitaine, moving into Bordeaux and Tours. Charles Martel stopped them at Poitiers, but in 734 they crossed the Rhone and captured Arles, Saint-Remy, and Avignon. Then they fortified Languedoc and recaptured Lyons and Burgundy. In the ninth century, from their positions in southeastern France, they pushed northeast as far as Switzerland. By daring naval raids, they harassed such ports as Marseilles and even Oye on the coast of Brittany.

Toward the end of the ninth century, Islam controlled most of western Switzerland and ruled many of the Alpine passes. In the mid-tenth century Muslims were at Lake Geneva, taking Neuchâtel and Saint Gall. Only the attacks of the Huns and the Hungarians from the north and northeast and the deterioration of the Spain-based Umayyad caliphate kept them from ruling all of southern Europe. However, Muslim expansion ended after 1050, for the Normans pushed Islam out of southern France, southern Italy, Corsica, Sardinia, and Sicily.

By 1250, Islam's European presence had weakened considerably. Only southern-most Spain and eastern Anatolia held secure. However, Islam had spread through all of Persia, crossed northern India, and reached the western Chinese border. In East Asia, it had a discernible presence in Sumatra, Borneo, and Java. All of North Africa was securely Muslim, while down the East African coast as far as Madagascar it exerted a strong influence. In many of these regions, of course, substantial portions of the populations remained non-Muslim. For instance, in Egypt many Monophysite and Coptic Christians remained loyal to their own traditions, as did many Christians in Anatolia and Syria. Nestorian Christians in Iraq north of Baghdad held out, while portions of southern Persia remained Zoroastrian strongholds. In India the majority remained Hindu, especially in the central and southern regions.

Motivations

Through this age of conquest and expansion, the basic Muslim strategy revolved around the use of the desert.[25] Just as modern empires, such as the British, made great use of naval power, so the Arabs exploited their experience with the desert, using it for communication, transferring supplies, and retreating safely in time of emergency. In their spread through North Africa, they established main towns at the edge of the desert. In Syria they employed such conquered cities as Damascus to the extent that they lay close to the desert. Through the Umayyad period (to 750), these garrison towns at the edge of the desert were the centers of Arab government. By dominating them and by introducing Arabic as the language of government, the conquerors exerted a disproportionate influence (they usually remained a minority of the total population). The towns served as the chief markets for the agricultural produce of the neighboring areas, and around their markets clusters of artisan quarters developed. By imposing discriminatory taxes on the outlying populations, the Arabs encouraged the citizenry to congregate in the cities, making their control easier.

Historians debate the motivation for

all this expansion, and we can safely say that it was complex. The Arabs were likely suffering from population pressures on the Arabian Peninsula, which incited many of them to search for more land. Precedents for such an outflow occurred in the fifth and sixth centuries, prior to Islam, and apparently from even earlier times the land to the northeast, especially the Fertile Crescent, served as a safety valve for overpopulation. Bernard Lewis has suggested that older historians overestimated the role of religion in the Islamic conquests and that more recent historians have underestimated it. In his own view, "its [religion's] importance lies in the temporary psychological change which it wrought in a people who were naturally excitable and temperamental, unaccustomed to any sort of discipline, willing to be persuaded, but never to be commanded. It made them for a time more self-confident and more amenable to control."[26]

Symbolically, religion served as a rallying point for the Arab cause. It stressed common bondage to a single Lord, and it dignified the Arab movement with a sort of manifest destiny. Certainly the generals who dominated the era of conquest were as accomplished in worldly affairs as they were in religious. For Khalid and Amr, two of the most outstanding, the utilitarian values of religion seem to have been clear.

The Islamic administration of the conquered territories was also quite pragmatic. Rather understandably, the interests served were not those of the conquered subjects but those of the aristocracy that conquest created—the interests of the Arab rulers. Thus, the temper of the Arab military commanders and then of the quasi-military Arab governors most determined how Islam treated its new peoples. At the beginning of the conquest in Byzantium and Persia, Muslims kept the old administrative structures. In the 640s, though, they shifted to a new format, through which the caliphs could impress their will more directly.

However, at first there was no unified imperial law. The conquerors struck different bargains with different peoples, and some stipulated that local customs or laws remain in force. The Arabs tended to take only the property of the state (and that of the new regime's enemies); other landowners who were willing to recognize the new regime could keep their holdings provided they paid a sizable tax. Nevertheless, there were opportunities for Muslim "speculators," as we might call them, to gain lands outside the garrison center on which they would have to pay only light levies.

At first, the conquered peoples were allowed to retain most of their traditional civil and religious rights. The Muslims grouped most of the conquered non-Muslims together as *Dhimmis*—members of religions that Arab law tolerated. As "peoples of the book," Jews and Christians had title to special respect. There were nevertheless frictions, especially if subjects were blatantly derogatory of the Prophet and his Book, but usually people were not compelled to convert to Islam. Because Arab rule regularly promised to be more just than Byzantine rule, many Jews and Christians are on record as having welcomed the change. For example, in Palestine the Samaritans actively assisted the invaders. The Arabs were not always sure how to handle such complicity, especially when it developed into a desire to convert to Islam. Islam and Arabism were so synonymous that the first converts had to become *Mawali*—clients of one of the Arab tribes. In fact, converts seldom gained equal status, especially regarding such material benefits as the booty that warriors received after a conquest.

Internal Strife

Despite its enormous outward success in the age of conquest, the Islamic community suffered notable internal divisions. With the exception of Abu Bakr, the first caliphs, known as the *Rashidun* (rightly guided), all left office by murder. (Despite that fact, modern Islam has considered their time the golden age.)[27] Ali, the fourth caliph, was the center of a fierce struggle for control. His main opponent was Muawiya, the head of a unified stronghold in Syria. Muawiya maneuvered to have the legitimacy of Ali's caliphate called into question. As a result, Ali lost support in his own group, and dissidents called Kharijites appeared who had a hand in many later conflicts. A Kharijite killed Ali in 661, and the caliphate passed to the Umayyad dynasty—the followers of Muawiya.

However, Ali's influence did not end with his assassination. In fact, his assassination became part of Islam's deepest division, the one between the Shia (party), who were loyalists to Ali, and the Sunni (traditionalists). The "party" supporting Ali believed that the successors to Muhammad ought to come from Muhammad's family—in other words, that Islamic leadership should be hereditary. This conviction was supported by certain verses of the Qur'an, in which the Prophet supposedly indicated that Ali would be his successor. The Shia therefore consider the first three caliphs, who preceded Ali, as having been usurpers. After Ali's death, they took up the cause of his sons, Hasan and Husain.

The word that the Shia gave to the power that descended through Muhammad's family line was *imamah* (leadership). Through its history, the Shia has made it a cardinal doctrine that Muhammad's bloodline has an exclusive right to *imamah*. The slaughter of Husain in Iraq in 680 was an especially tragic event, and the Shiites have come to commemorate it as the greatest of their annual festivals. It gives their Islam a strong emphasis on sorrow, suffering, and emotion that quite distinguish it from Sunni piety.[28]

Of course, our brief summary has presented only a slice of the dense military, political, and religious history that shaped the first unfolding of Qur'anic faith. Externally, Islam's quick successes testified as much to the political vacuum within which the conquered peoples lived and to their oppression as it did to Arab military genius. Internally, Islam's great energy made for considerable strife. However, during the following centuries, religion and culture caught up with the military wildfire, consolidating the empire and making it much more than just a far-flung envelopment.

The Golden Civilization

In his history of science, Stephen Mason states that Muslim scientific culture began in the era of the Umayyads.[29] The Umayyads had been auxiliaries of the Romans in Syria, so when they established the caliphate in Damascus in 661, they brought an enthusiasm for Hellenistic culture. In particular, they became patrons of the sciences. For example, in 700 they founded an astronomical observatory at Damascus. However, the Umayyads fell to the Abbasids in 749. The Abbasids set their caliphate in Baghdad and turned to Persian rather than Hellenistic culture, supporting the Persian specialities of medicine and astronomy. Al-Mansur, the second Abbasid caliph, was also devoted to learning, bringing Indian astronomers and doctors to Baghdad and having many Indian scientific treatises translated. Under his successors, translation continued to be a major project. As a result, many Greek treatises (for example, those of Galen and Ptolemy) became available to Muslims. Partly because of Babylonian and Zoroastrian influences, the Baghdad caliphs deemed astronomy especially important. They imported Indian mathematicians to help in astronomical calculations and made Baghdad a center of astronomical learning.

Al-Razi (865–925) collected voluminous lore on medicine from Greek, Indian, and Middle Eastern sources. Indeed, he may even have drawn on Chinese sources, for there is a story that he entertained a Chinese scholar who learned to speak Arabic, and his successors' works include what seems to be the Chinese doctrine of the pulses. A Muslim alchemy arose in the ninth century with Jabir ibn-Hayyar, but in Islam alchemy remained somewhat suspect because the authorities linked it with mystical religion. Some radical Sufis became deeply involved in alchemy, but orthodox Sunni had the works of at least one such group, the "Brethren of Purity," declared heretical and burned. Principally, the orthodox favored the rational geometry and deductive science of the Greeks.

From 970, the Spanish branch of the

Muslim empire had a distinguished scientific center in Cordoba. Similarly, the religious authorities patronized science, especially medicine and astronomy, at Toledo from the early eleventh century. The Spanish Muslims tended to be critical of Ptolemy and to favor Aristotelian doctrines. Averroës (1126–1198) was a great Aristotelian synthesizer who composed a full philosophical corpus.

By conquering the territory between the Muslim East and the kingdom of Sung China, the Mongols expedited trade and the flow of learned information between East and West. Marco Polo (1254–1324) was able to travel to the East because of Mongol rule, which also enabled the Chinese Mar Jaballaha (1244–1317) to come West and become the Nestorian Christian patriarch. When the Mongols conquered China they left its bureaucratic structure intact. They set up an observatory in Peking and staffed it with Muslims. In the West they conquered the Abbasid capital of Baghdad in 1258, where they continued to support astronomical studies.

Albert Moore has shown the effects of Islam's monotheism in the field of art, arguing that it led to a classical concentration on the architecture and ornamentation of the mosque.[30] This art reached its peak in the sixteenth and seventeenth centuries, leaving impressive monuments in Ottoman Turkey, Safavid Persia, and Mughal India. Schuyler Cammann[31] has shown exceptions to the generally nonrepresentational character of Islamic art in Persian works, and Moore indicates that paintings of hunting and of love scenes were permitted in private Muslim homes. Nonetheless, the preponderance of Muslim art during the golden age was nonpictorial, including rugs, vases, lamps, and mosques.

A distinctively Islamic calligraphy developed from the trend to decorate pages from the Qur'an. The Qur'an itself praises the art of writing (96 : 4), and speaks of being written on a heavenly tablet (85 : 21–22). The favorite script was Kufic, which originated in the new Islamic town of Kufa near Babylon, and it was the standard script model from about the seventh to eleventh centuries. It is vertical, massive, and angular, while its prime alternate, the Naskhi script, is horizontal, flowing, and rounded. A favorite subject for embellishment has been the *Bismallah*, the prefix to the Qur'anic suras ("In the name of God"). Through an extension of calligraphic swirls and loops, Muslims developed an ingenious ability to suggest flowers, birds, lions, and so on. The Sufi interest in numerology also encouraged artistic work.

Architecture and Poetry

As we suggested, Islam also influenced architecture. The mosque was a sort of theology in the concrete. Muslim architects tried to embody the faith and conviction that all of life stands subject to Allah, that no great distinction should be made between sacred dwellings and profane. The guiding idea in the construction of a mosque was simply to house a space for prayer and prostration. The *Hadith* reported that the Prophet led his first companions outside the city, so that they could pray together in an open space. At Medina, the usual place for prayer was the open courtyard of Muhammad's own house. For convenience, the architects tried to construct a churchlike building that had the character of an open space where many faithful might go through the same rhythmic motions of bowing, kneeling, prostrating, and praying together.

The representative mosque, such as the great Mosque of Cordoba or the al-Aqsa mosque of Jerusalem, is spacious and beautifully but simply adorned. It has rugs (often very beautiful) on the floors and numerous pillars for support, but no furniture—no pews, chairs, or altars. Often there is a pulpit (in some cases two, one for reading the Qur'an and one for preaching), and the most impressive ornamentation is the tile or gold leaf that decorates the ceiling or the *mihrab*.

Significantly, mosque art is not radically different from that of Muslim palaces—for example, that of the Alhambra. In the Alhambra gardens and pools suggest sec-

*Figure 29   Courtyard of Cairo Mosque, with purification fountain.
Photo by J. T. Carmody.*

ular pleasure, but they also remind one of the Qur'anic descriptions of Paradise. The ornamentation of the ceilings and walls of the Alhambra is indistinguishable from that found in many mosques. The basic ornamental motif is repetition, seemingly endless patterns, whether representational (roses and leaves), semiabstract (vine tendrils and rosettes), or completely abstract (geometric patterns). This motif is known as the infinite pattern, and some suggest that it has theological significance: It does not want to rival God by creating anything fixed or permanent. Popular art often violates this pattern, suggesting that it most applied to mosques and official constructions. For instance, a Persian manuscript painting of the sixteenth century portrays Muhammad's ascent to Paradise, complete with winged angels,

dishes of fruit, showers of pearls, and rubies.

A. J. Arberry has translated a representative collection of Islamic writings,[32] and it suggests a great breadth and lyricism. Poetry always held a place of honor among Arabs, for eloquence had always been considered a trait of a great man, even before the advent of Islam. Much as the Greeks valued military prowess and the ability to persuade others, so the Arabs made their mother tongue a prime object of artistic devotion.

The ancient poetry was born in the desert, so it was replete with desert images and themes. With expansion and conquest, however, Islam became largely an urban culture,[33] so there was need to reshape its poetry. Meter, rhyme, and new imagery became the chief tools. The result was a very complex style: "We have called this poetry arabesque, and indeed it is fully as exquisitely and delicately ornamented as the finest Saracenic architecture."[34] The thirteenth-century poet Ibn al-Khabbaza fashioned an elegy that epitomized Arab eloquence: "Your life was of the order true of Arab eloquence; the tale was brief, the words were few, the meaning was immense."[35]

The themes that dominate Arberry's poetic selections are not especially religious: the beauty of a beloved, trees, battle, and, for humor, the flanks and shanks of an ant. Still, some of the religious mystics, such as Junaid, Rumi, and the woman Rabia, gained fame for their poetic skills. Most were Sufis—devotees of religious emotion and feeling. Among the religious poets of Islam, the Persians were most eminent. Their themes and images center on the Sufi goal of self-effacement in the divine immensity. For instance, Rumi often portrayed the soul's sense of abandonment in moments of trial when it could not feel the divine embrace: "Hearken to this Reed forlorn, Breathing ever since 'twas torn from its rushy bed, a strain of impassioned love and pain."[36] In this way, the talented Sufi writers won considerable respect from the cultured. To be able to express their religious vision with eloquence made them seem less eccentric, more representative of traditional Arab cultural ideals.

Law

Within the inner precincts of Islam, neither science nor art constituted the main cultural development. Rather, the most important flowering of Qur'anic faith was the law *(sharia)*.[37] As the opening verses of the Qur'an suggest, a fundamental concern in Islam is guidance, and Islam went to lawyers, not to scientists, poets, or even mystics, for its most trustworthy guidance. In fact, Islam obtained little guidance from philosophical theology, which began a most promising career but foundered on the shoals of sectarian controversy and debates about the relation of reason to faith. Although numerous schools of law developed, the differences among them were relatively slight, and they usually left little place for innovative reason. Thus, the authorities accounted them more trustworthy than philosophical theology—better cement for Muslim society.

The early theological discussions dealt with the nature of faith. Idolatry and unbelief were the major evils for the Qur'an, so it was important to understand them well. The types of sins were also an important early theological focus. Later debates focused on the unity of God (in the context of discussing the divine attributes) and on the relation of the divine sovereignty to human freedom. While there was a full spectrum of opinions, in Sunni quarters the more moderate positions tended to win favor. Before long, however, Islam effectively curtailed speculation, favoring instead careful efforts to ascertain what legal precedents any *practical* problem had in the *Hadith* of the Prophet, the Qur'an, community consensus, or analogous situations.

To be sure, Muslims did not view religious law as a human creation. Rather, it was divine guidance, the expression of God's own will. The goal of the lawyers was to offer comprehensive guidance for all of life—much as the rabbis' goal was to apply the Torah to all of life. In practice, the lawyers tended to divide their subject matter into obligations to God (for example, profession of faith and performance of prayer) and obligations to other human beings (for example, individual and social morality, such as not lying and not stealing). The lawyers classified theology under the first set of obligations, for theology was the science of right belief, and right belief was primary among the things that human beings owed to God. As they refined their science, the lawyers also distinguished all human actions according to five headings: obligatory, recommended, permitted, disapproved, and forbidden. Thus, one had to confess the unity of God and the Prophethood of Muhammad, one was counseled to avoid divorce, and one was forbidden to eat pork. Since

Muslim society was a theocracy, *sharia* was the code of the land. While that made for a certain unity and order, it also prepared the way for the Sufi emphasis on personal devotion.

Division

A minor source of division within the Muslim community was the differences in law developed by the various schools. The Hanafite school came to dominate Muslim countries north and east of the Arabian Peninsula. Within Arabia itself the dominant school was founded by ibn-Hanbal. Northeast Africa was under Shafite and Hanafite lawyers, while Malikite opinions were the most prestigious in northwestern Africa. In Persia the Shia sect had its own law. On the whole, that distribution still holds today.

Given the four recognized legal codes of Sunni, the large Shia minority, and the division of the Islamic empire into eastern and western parts centered at Baghdad and Cordoba, respectively, one can see that religious and political unity was less than perfect. Still, Muslims holding to the five pillars and the Qur'an had more in common with one another than they had with any non-Muslim peoples. Thus, legal or creedal differences did not divide Muslim religion severely. In contrast, different devotional styles, such as Sufism, caused considerable hubbub.

Sufism

Opinions about the merits of Sufism differ. Fazlur Rahman, commenting especially on the work of al-Ghazali (1058–1111), speaks of the "fresh vitality" that al-Ghazali's devotionalism infused into the Muslim community.[38] Isma'il al Faruqi, on the contrary, cites Sufism as the first step in Islam's decline from its golden civilization.[39] It is true that al-Ghazali was not a typical Sufi (he had great learning as well as great piety), and that al Faruqi's sympathies lie with the reforming Wahabis (see below), for whom Sufism was an abomination. Still,

a survey of studies shows quite mixed reactions to Sufism. Most commentators agree that its initial centuries (the ninth through thirteenth) were more creative and positive than its later ones.

At the outset, Sufism (the name likely comes from the Arabic word for wool, which Sufis wore as a gesture of simplicity)[40] stood for reform and personal piety. In a time when political and military success tempted Islam to worldliness, and when the rise of the law brought the dangers of legalism, the Sufis looked to the model of Muhammad at prayer, communing with God. For them the heart of Islam was personal submission to Allah, personal guidance along the straight path. In later centuries, through its brotherhoods and saints, Sufism set a great deal of the emotional, anti-intellectual, and anti-progressive tone of an Islam that had lost its status as a world power.

Several cultural streams ran together to form the Sufi movement. First was the ascetic current from traditional desert life, which was basic and simple—a daily call for endurance. Out of a keen sense of the religious values in such a harsh life, Abu Dharr al-Ghifari, a companion of the Prophet, chastised the early leaders who wanted to lead a sumptuous court life after their conquests. Second, many of the Sufi ecstatics, as we mentioned, drew on the Arab love of poetry. Their lyric depictions of the love of God, coupled with the Qur'an's eloquence, drew sensitive persons to the side of a living, personal faith that might realize the beauties of Islam.

Third, the more speculative Sufis drew on Gnostic ideas that floated in from Egypt and the Fertile Crescent. By the ninth century, Sufi contemplatives (especially the Persian Illuminationists) were utilizing those ideas to analyze the relations between divinity and the world. (The Sufis seem to have found the emanational ideas—the theories of how the world flowed out of the divine essence—rather than the dualistic theories of good and evil most attractive.) This kind of understanding, along with the alchemical interests noted previously, was the beginning of the esoteric and sometimes magical lore for which the orthodox theologians and lawyers held Sufis suspect. Lastly, Indian (especially Buddhist) thought apparently influenced the eastern portions of the Muslim realm, and it perhaps was a source of the tendencies toward self-annihilation that became important in Sufi mystical doctrine.

Taken at their own word, the Sufis desired to be faithful followers of Muhammad and the Qur'an. The more honored among them never intended any schismatic or heretical movements. Rather, they resembled spiritual writers of other traditions, such as the Christian Thomas a Kempis, in that they wanted to "feel compunction rather than know its definition." The most famous statement of this desire occurs in al-Ghazali's description of his withdrawal from his prestigious teaching post in Baghdad in order to settle the conflicts in his soul: "I was continuously tossed about between the attractions of worldly desire and the impulses towards eternal life."[41] Upon retiring into solitude to purify his soul, he found the peace he had sought. From being a learned philosopher, theologian, and lawyer, he became a follower of the mystical way, which the Sufis represented: "I learnt with certainty that it is above all the mystics who walk on the road of God; their life is the best life, their method the soundest method, their character the purest character; indeed, were the intellect of the intellectuals and the learning of the learned and the scholarship of the scholars, who are versed in the profundities of revealed truth, brought together in the attempt to improve the life and character of the mystics, they would find no way of doing so."[42]

In Idries Shah's collection of Sufi sayings,[43] one catches overtones of the pedagogical genius that the spiritual masters developed. Much like the Hasidim, they fashioned stories to carry their messages about the paradoxes of the spiritual life, the need for being focused and wholehearted, the way that God comes in the midst of everyday life. In these stories, the poor man turns out to be rich; the fool turns out to be truly wise. Like their counterparts in other traditions, the Sufis left no doubt that riches and prestige tend to be obstacles to spirituality. As well, they questioned the rational, "right-handed" portions of the personality, arguing that the more intuitive, "left-handed" portions (what the Chinese called "yin") must have their due if one is to achieve balance and fullness.

Predictably, this challenge to the expectations of society, of the religious authorities, and of the literally minded won the Sufis no love. Perhaps to intensify their opposition, some Sufis became even more poetic, challenging the establishment and suggesting that its religion was little more than dead convention. For instance, when Hasan of Basra was asked what Islam was and who were Muslims, he replied, "Islam is in the books and Muslims are in the tomb."[44] This oracular reply could mean that the Qur'an holds the secrets to true submission and that the earth holds the bodies of the great exemplars of the past. However, it could also mean that what people take to be Islam (the official version) is actually a dead letter, something buried and forgotten, because no one lives it anymore. Along similar lines is a story of a dervish who meets the devil. The devil is just sitting patiently, so the dervish asks him why he is not out making mischief. The devil replies, "Since the theoreticians and would-be teachers of the Path have appeared in such numbers, there is nothing left for me to do."[45]

Decline

By the beginning of the fourteenth century, the age of some of the greatest Sufi figures was over; Sufism started to decline, and with it much of Islam's religious vitality. The orders continued to multiply, and many princes and sultans continued to patronize them, but abuse, scandal, and superstition became more and more common. In Arberry's view, "It was inevitable, as soon as legends of miracles became attached to the names of the great mystics, that the credulous masses should applaud imposture more than true devotion; the cult of the saints against which orthodox Islam ineffectually protested, promoted ignorance and superstition, and confounded charlatanry with lofty speculation. To live scandalously, to act impudently, to speak unintelligibly—this was the easy highroad to fame, wealth, and power."[46] Much as the Buddhist eccentrics in Tibet became rather complex models of saintliness, so eccentrics made Sufism quite ambiguous.

Still, the Sufis played a considerable role in the expansion of Islam, largely by serving as models of piety for the common people and giving them hopes of wonder working. For instance, Sufi folk literature played an important role in the expansion of Indian Islam during the fifteenth through seventeenth centuries,[47] while genuine Sufi spirituality aroused strong devotion in North Africa well into the twentieth century.[48] The organizations of Sufi influence were the Sufi orders, or brotherhoods. The first seems to date from the twelfth century. Abd al-Qadir, who began his religious career in Baghdad as a student of Hanbalite law, converted to Sufism and became a preacher on the holy life. The many converts and followers that he gathered came to call themselves Qadiris, and historians often regard their association as the first brotherhood. It has been especially influential in India, where it has a presence even today. Al-Qadir was a traditionalist who called for strict adherence to the Qur'an and condemned any antinomian (lawless) tendencies. No doubt this helped his group become acceptable.

A second great order, also influential in India, derived from al-Suhrawardi (1144–1234), a moderate. Other orders of significant number and influence were the Shadhiliya, who were especially successful in Egypt, North Africa, Arabia, and Syria, and the Turkish order of the Mevleviya, which derived from the renowned Persian poet Rumi.

Typically, at the order's local lodge, a small number of professionals resided to teach and lead worship. Most members were (and are) lay adherents who came for instruc-tion when they could and who supported the lodge by contributing money, manual labor, and so on. Each order tended to have its own distinctive ritual, whose purpose was usually to attain ecstatic experience. The ritual was the group's interpretation of the general virtue of *dhikr* (remembrance) that all Muslims seek. For instance, whirling dances characterized many of the Mevlevi dervish meetings, while Saadeeyeh Sufis developed a ceremony in which the head of the order rode over prone devotees on horseback.

The writings of the theosophist Gurdjieff have introduced a number of Sufi ideas into contemporary American consciousness. Overall, however, Islam has been making its greatest strides among Africans who have found that it suits their traditional tribal structure and their nationalistic mood better than Christianity.[49] The divisions and declines that sundered Islam before this modern resurgence were largely due to a combination of Sufi magic and orthodox rigidity, which undermined the fusion of piety and order that any vital religion has to have.

Islam also suffered from a counterattack by the countries that it had conquered. For instance, the European countries who supported the Crusades sharply contracted the empire that Islam had forged in its golden age. Historians date the point of decline differently. Bernard Lewis, for instance, holds that by the eleventh century Islam was in "manifest decay."[50] In addition to what they suffered at the hands of the Crusaders in the Holy Land and from the Europeans' counterattack in southern Europe, the Arabs found themselves superseded in the East by the Turks, who became Muslims, and by the Mongols, who at first showed no interest in Islam. The latter conquered both Persia and Iraq, causing a breakdown of Muslim power.

The Turkish Mamluks established themselves in Cairo by the mid-thirteenth century, ruling Egypt and Syria until 1517. When Vasco da Gama circumnavigated Africa in 1498, much of the Muslim economic and political power, which derived from Muslim control of the trade with India, quickly faded. The Ottoman Turks replaced the Mamluks in the early sixteenth century and ruled Middle Eastern Islam for almost 400 years.[51] Only in southern Arabia (Yemen) did Arab speakers remain largely free of foreign domination.

Late Empire and Modernity

During the period of empire (the Ottoman Empire of Turkey and the Middle East, the Safavid dynasty in Persia,[52] and the Mogul dynasty in India),[53] at least three general changes occurred in Muslim society. The first was the transformation of the Islamic Near East from a commercial economy based on money to a feudal economy based on subsistence farming. The second was the replacement in positions of authority of Arabic-speaking peoples by Turks. The Arab tribes retained their independence in the desert regions, where they held out quite well against Turkish rule. In the cities and cultivated valleys (the plains of Iraq, Syria, and Egypt), however, the Arabs became completely subjected, and the glorious language that had been the pride of Islam became the argot of an enslaved population. Psychologically, the Turks grew accustomed to taking the initiative and commanding, and the Arabs grew accustomed to passivity and subjection. The third change was the transfer of the seat of Islam from Iraq to Egypt. Iraq was too remote from Turkey and the Mediterranean to be the base for the eastern wing of Islam, so Egypt—which was on the other principal trade route and which was the most unified area geographically—became the new center.[54]

As a result of this shift, Turkish and to a lesser degree Persian became the languages of Islam. At first many of the subject peoples welcomed the Ottoman takeover from the Mamluks as a return to political order. By the eighteenth century, however, the Ottoman Empire was in decay—corrupt, anarchic, and stagnant. The principal religious form of revolt during this period was Sufism. At first Sufism was mainly an escape for oppressed individuals, but with the organization of more brotherhoods, it became a

social movement that was especially powerful among the artisan class. The long centuries of stagnation finally ended, however, with increased contact with the West. From the beginning of the sixteenth century, European expansion brought some of the new learning of the Renaissance and the Reformation. The French in particular had considerable influence in the Middle East, and Napoleon's easy conquest of the Ottoman Mamluks at the end of the eighteenth century was the final blow to Islamic military glory.

The Wahabis

Also during the time of Napoleon arose an Islamic reform that was designed to check the infection of Sufism.[55] One of the first leaders in this reform was a stern traditionalist named Muhammad ibn Abd al-Wahab, whose followers came to be known as Wahabis. They called for a return to the doctrines and practices of the early generations, of the ancestors whom they venerated.

In law, the Wahabis favored the rigorous interpretations of the Hanbalite school, and they abhorred the veneration of saints, which they considered superstitious. Thus, they inveighed against supposed holy personages, living or dead, and went out of their way to destroy the shrines that had become places of popular piety or pilgrimage. They further objected that the worship of saints presumed "partners" of God and so was idolatrous. The punishment due such idolatry was death. Some of the more rabid Wahabis went so far as to classify the more lenient lawyers and schools as being guilty of idolatry (and so punishable by death). The Wahabis were based in Arabia, whence they waged war on their dissenting neighbors. They went down to military defeat in their 1818 Turco-Egyptian campaign, but their puritanical reform had much ideological success and spread to other parts of the Islamic world.

An immediate effect of the Wahabi movement was great hostility toward the Sufi brotherhoods. In fact, Muslims interested in renovating orthodoxy singled out the Sufis as their great enemies, although they also attacked the scholasticism of such theological centers as al-Azhar in Cairo. One of the leaders of the nineteenth-century reform was the apostle of Pan-Islam, Jamal al-Din al-Afghani, who proposed the political unification of all Muslim countries under the caliphate of the Ottoman sultans. While Pan-Islam has never been realized, it stimulated the widespread search for an effective Muslim response to modernity. In India and Egypt, conservative groups arose that gravitated toward the Wahabi position. Many of the Sufi organizations lost their strength, and those that survived tended to back away from gnosis and return to a more traditional theology.

Even before this conservative threat, however, the Sufis had reformed on their own, sponsoring a number of missions in Africa, India, and Indonesia. For the most part these were peaceful, but occasionally they involved military ventures. In fact, some groups quite consciously took up the Qur'anic tradition of holy war, including the "Indian Wahabis" and the Mahdists in the Sudan. However, even in decline the Sufi brotherhoods kept dear to Islam the notion of bonding together for mutual support in faith.

The organizations that have grown up in recent times, such as the Association for Muslim Youth and the Muslim Brotherhood, seem in good measure an effort to fill the void created by the demise of the brotherhoods. The new groups differ by operating primarily in pluralistic cultures, while the Sufi orders drew on the ardor of a homogeneous culture that was secure in its unchallenged faith.

Western Influence

A characteristic of Islamic modernity was the invasion of Western secular ideas. These ideas came on the heels of modern Western takeovers in the Middle East, at first through the administrations of the Europeans who governed the newly acquired territories and then through the educational systems, which were Westernized. The new classes of native professionals—doctors, lawyers, and journalists—frequently trained abroad or in native schools run by Westerners. One political effect of such training was to raise Muslim feelings of nationalism and to provoke cries for Westernized systems of government. The new ideas challenged the *madrasas,* or religious schools, too, for it was not immediately apparent that these new ideas could be taught along with traditional theories of revelation and Qur'anic inspiration.

From the nineteenth century on, the economics, politics, education, social habits, and even religion of Muslims were increasingly affected by the upheaval that resulted from the European Renaissance and Enlightenment. Some countries remained largely insulated from Western notions, but they tended to be backward portions of the old empire with little political impact. As we might expect, the cities bore the brunt of the challenge. In theology the outward Muslim reaction was to close ranks. Still, even in the most fiercely traditionalist schools, modern notions—such as the freedom of human beings to shape their own destinies—softened the old propositions about providence and predestination.

Indeed, when it was convenient, theologians incorporated modern science into their argumentation. For instance, some Muslim theologians justified the doctrine that God creates the world continuously by citing atomic theory. The less theologically inclined among the modern educated classes contented themselves by asserting that Islam, as submission to the Master of Truth, in principle cannot conflict with modern science or with any empirically verified truths.

Controversy over societal matters has been more heated than that over theology because the guidance provided by the traditional legal schools diverged more sharply from Western mores than Muslim theology diverged from Western theology. Slowly Islamic countries have developed civil codes and separated civil courts from religious courts. In the mid-nineteenth century, the Turkish Republic breached the wall of tradition when it abolished the authority of the *sharia* in civil matters. In other countries the *sharia* has remained the outer form, but new legislative codes direct the interpretations. The tactic has been to invoke the Qur'an, the Hadith, and the traditions of the schools but to leave the legislators and judges free to choose the authority that is most appropriate. Specifically, the legal reforms have applied primarily to marriage contracts (protecting girls against child marriage), divorce proceedings, and polygamy—central factors in the traditional family structure.

What new theology will emerge from the dynamics of these changes remains to be seen. H. A. R. Gibb has pointed out that by granting jurists freedom to interpret the traditional opinions and by departing from the old norm that there had to be a uniformity of interpretation throughout the Islamic community, the reformers have introduced a "Protestant principle" into the previously "Catholic" social consciousness.[56] Indeed, through its fairly rigid law, Islam had reified (made objective) its community more thoroughly than the other religions had.[57] Whether the demise of the former practice will result in a Protestant splintering of Islam is difficult to predict. On the one hand, it is difficult to recall the critical or independent spirit once it has broken loose. On the other hand, there are signs of a growing Islamic fundamentalism similar to the fundamentalism by which some Protestant Christians are battling the spirit of criticism.

Relatedly, liberal Muslim reformers attracted to Marxist thought seem to bypass the socialist call for a new order and to desire, rather nostalgically, the old ideological uniformity. The traditionalists, such as the Saudis, find Marxism completely repulsive because of its atheism. Whether they can progress satisfactorily by means of a capitalistic economy and technology, though, is far from certain. Critical-mindedness in the laboratory and simple faith in religion are

not impossible, but few people in any faith manage them without a kind of schizophrenia.

Publications of the American Academic Association for Peace in the Middle East suggest that the recent history of such countries ("confrontation states") as Syria and Jordan explains much of the current turmoil in the Middle East.[58] These countries have been trying to adapt their economics, their politics, and their religion to the modern world. On the one hand, their models for this transition have been the Western nations, who produced modernity. On the other hand, Western nationalism has taught them to insist on their right to a nationalistic expression of their ethnicity, their history, and their religious cohesiveness. The current catalysts for this process are Israel and oil.

Finally, Islamic secularism is less advanced than Western secularism. True, fundamentalism attracts a noteworthy number of Christians and Jews, but their cultures more clearly differentiate the civic realm, the realm shared with citizens of other religious convictions (or of none), than Islamic countries do. Conversely, Islam has kept the sacred and the secular more tightly conjoined than Christianity or Judaism has. It professes that there is no secular realm—that everything lives by the will and touch of Allah, who is as near as the pulse at one's throat.

STRUCTURAL ANALYSIS

Nature

The key to the Muslim notion of nature is its concept of creation. As much as the biblical religion on which it built, Islam sees God as the maker of all that is. Several Qur'anic passages establish this doctrine. For instance, Sura 10 describes the Lord as "God, who created the heavens and the earth in six days, then sat Himself upon the Throne directing the affair." This is the biblical imagery of creation: Genesis spreading

God's work over six days. Moreover, the Qur'an finds significance in this creation in that through creation God has given God-fearing people signs of his dominion. By making the sun a radiance and the moon a light, by giving them "stations" so that astronomers can calculate time, and by alternating night and day, God has set over humankind a heaven full of signs. Just as Immanuel Kant spoke of the starry heavens above as a wonder that can incite a true grasp of the human condition, so Muhammad unselfconsciously expressed the sovereignty of his God by referring to the divine guidance of the stars, the heavenly circuits by which the Creator periodizes our time.

Sura 13 repeats this theme, adding earthly phenomena: It is He who stretched out the earth, set firm mountains and rivers, and placed two kinds of every fruit. The abundance of nature testifies to the abundance of nature's source and ought to remind human beings of God's power and provision. Thus, the Creator is not only strong but also admirable in his design of the world and praiseworthy in his concern for human welfare as evidenced by his bounty. In this way the best features of nature become analogies for God in the Qur'an. The "Light-Verse" of Sura 24 gives one of the most famous of these analogies: God is the Light of the heavens and the earth. His light is as a niche where there is a lamp. The lamp is in a glass, the glass is like a glittering star. The lamp is kindled from a Blessed Tree, an olive neither of the East nor of the West, whose oil would shine even if no fire touched it. Light upon light, God guides to the Light whom he will.

Religiously, then, nature is replete with signs in which wise persons discern God's creative presence. However, nature is not itself a divinity or a form of God's presence. Unlike East Asian thought, Islamic thought does not mix divinity with the cosmos. Islam separated from the ancient cosmological myth, in that Allah transcends the world. One may say that the biblical prophets' critique of nature gods combined with Muhammad's negative reaction to the polytheism of his times to correlate transcendence and anti-idolatry. So the signs that nature gives to the God-fearing are not themselves sacraments. They point beyond themselves; the divinity does not come in them. Water, oil, bread, wine—they are not miniature incarnations of divinity. The God of Islam has no incarnation, no personal or material forms by which he becomes present.

Isma'il al Faruqi tries to establish that Islam is rationalistic, meaning that Islam's highest religious certainty *(iman)* is not merely an act of believing, an "act of faith," but "a state in which religious knowledge produces an intuition of its certainty as a result of the consideration and weighing of all possible alternatives."[59] Then, in treating what he considers Islam's second essential quality (that it is "transcendentalist"), al Faruqi argues that Islam rejects all forms of immanentism for the divine. In other words, Creator is Creator, creature is creature, and never the twain shall meet. This transcendentalism provides the context for al Faruqi's discussion of the Muslim view of nature, the lead sentence of which is "Nature is not transcendent and constitutes an autonomous realm."[60] From this it follows that nature contains no divinity in its materials or its forces. It is totally real, wholly created. It is actual and objective, and "it contains no mystery."[61]

Thus, for al Faruqi, Islamic nature is utterly profane, in no way sacred (since nothing is sacred without mystery). That interpretation seems considerably more rationalistic than what most Muslims themselves have thought, for, as we suggested above, most Muslims have not followed Western Enlightenment by separating the sacred from the secular. When al Faruqi says that nature must be unmysterious to be autonomous, regular, and knowable, we are tempted to say that he protests overmuch. The mechanistic scientist of the nineteenth century could write such a description of nature, but few contemporary scientists and few traditional Muslims would do so.

Some Muslim thinkers might have

lost contact with nature's mystery, but they were not in the majority, for that would have made Islam a comparative anomaly. For example, Jews and Christians, despite sharing the notion of a transcendent Creator, used psalms that glorified God's provision of food in due season. With Job, they found that the world and its train of strange animals were marvelous indeed. The Hasidim looked to the world for divine sparks, and the Christian poets drew on the sacraments and on the model of saints such as Francis of Assisi to consider the world pregnant with God's power. Both of Islam's sister faiths did develop nature less than the Eastern religions did, and they did fear the forces of fertility, the polytheism, that afflicted the lands of their origin. But in the actual exercise of their faiths, nature was alive with the mystery of God and was neither profane nor autonomous.

Still, al Faruqi is right in implying that nature never dominated Islam or Arab culture. For instance, the earliest poetry deals more with war and nomadic life than with Father Sky and Mother Earth. Pre-Muslim Arabia worshipped natural and agricultural forces, but Qur'anic monotheism attacked them harshly. In religious art, as we have seen, the prohibition on images was not absolute, although religious art tended to avoid representations of natural scenes, let alone representations of God.

Still, the prime material for worship, the Qur'an itself, contained natural figures and not merely in the context of creation. Thus, it embellished its theme of judgment and recompense with naturalistic imagery. For instance, if one denied God's bounties—did not live the truth that God ever labors creatively for human benefit—then "against you shall be loosed a flame of fire, and molten brass" (55 : 35). Judgment is a day when "heaven is split asunder and turns crimson like red leather" (55 : 37), when sinners will go to Gehenna and hot boiling water. However, those who fear God will enter Paradise. The main image for Paradise is the Garden. There the virtuous will find two fountains running with water, fruits of all kinds, virgin maidens lovely as rubies and coral. Paradise has green pastures, gushing water, fruits, palm trees, pomegranates, and cool pavilions. (55 : 50–70).

Thus, the Qur'an considered nature a factor in the mysteries of judgment, punishment, and reward as the images of Fire and Garden clearly show. Moreover, mythological elaboration of these themes in popular religion was quite unrestrained. "Hell, sometimes imagined as a terrible monster, is described as filled with fire and stinking water, and awful trees with poisonous fruits grow there."[62] In the popular conception, angels presided over Hell, meting out punishments, while Heaven became a place for enjoying fruit, wine, and the charming black-eyed virgins.

Like other religions, Islam maintained that justice would be served in the afterlife through reward for the pious faithful and punishment for the unbelievers. Sex was high on the list of pleasures, so Paradise was rich with sex. Islam depicted sex from the male point of view, with details of "maidens restraining their glances, untouched before them by any man or jinn" (55 : 55). As we shall see below, Islam did not declare the goodness of sex so loudly and clearly for women. In fact, there has been ambiguity, puritanism, and a double standard concerning sex in Muslim society. Still, the basic fact that Islam does not paint heaven as an ethereal, wholly spiritual realm shows that it blesses human nature.

In summary, nature for Islam is one locus of God's signs to humanity. Nature is less prominent than in East Asian or ancient religion. Rather, Islam configures itself socially and theologically, focusing on the community and the sovereign Lord.

Muslim spirituality manifests something of this emphasis, in that one of its interests is to keep nature under control. By fasting, a Muslim tames the nature closest to the self. By confessing that there is no God but God, a Muslim clears the world of competitors to the Creator and Judge. That means that many devout Muslims' ideal is a bare vista. The Sufis manifested this ideal most fully, for many of them saw life as a pilgrimage to union with a God much more valuable than anything worldly. In less deliberate but still consoling ways, the poor merchant or soldier learns from misfortune how precarious a worldly vista is. Although the physical world is definitely real and on occasion quite good, the human's role is to observe it closely enough so that it serves as a guidepost to Heaven. A Muslim can be comfortable in the natural world but only as a visitor. Life in the natural world soon passes, and Judgment depends on higher things, such as one's faith, one's prayer, and one's generosity in giving alms. The tradition does not teach people that the Judge will ask them how they treated the environment or whether they tore the bosom of mother earth. Those issues are far less important than whether they remembered Allah and his Prophet.

Society

Estimates of the social innovations that Islam introduced and the degree of social perfection that it achieved vary considerably. In this section we present a positive opinion, a negative opinion, a view on Islamic ethics, and a short essay on women under Islam.

A Positive View

The proponent of Islam, Isma'il al Faruqi, begins with the thesis that Muslim society existed so that human beings might realize the "divine pattern." Elemental in that pattern was the family. Marriage was a civil contract, not a sacrament, and a man could marry more than one wife so long as he provided justice, equity, and loving care. Private property and the pursuit of wealth were inviolate rights, but wealth brought the obligation to care for the deprived. Concerning the right to life: "The life of one's fellowman is inviolate, except by due process of law. Nothing may henceforth be decided by force or violence. Such recourse is legitimate only in self-defense and in the safeguarding of the

security of missionaries. For the Muslim is duty-bound to bring his faith to the knowledge of mankind with sound preaching and wise counsel, to convey the warning and command of his Lord."[63]

The Muslim political unit was the *Ummah*, which was as comprehensive as the broadest notions of church or sangha. Tradition says that the Qur'an teaches that the Prophet and his successors bore a theocratic power. That is, they had authority in both the religious and the secular spheres, because Islam does not distinguish the two. Due to the concept of the Ummah, Muslims had to fight for brethren in other places who suffered tyranny (Qur'an 4 : 75). For Muslim leaders, the consensus of the community was an important goal, for they wanted a single divine rope to bind the Ummah together. Strong faith was to create an equality among all believers, and God would reward every man and woman who was faithful through difficulties and trials. Muslims were to bring their disputes to the Prophet or his successors, and they all had a common duty to worship God, to obey God's commands, and to do good and avoid evil.

Members were to be to one another as brothers and mutual guardians (9 : 71), respecting life and enjoying its good things. Woman came from the soul of man (4 : 1). Both men and women had the right to what they had earned, and both could enter Paradise, although "men have priority over women, by virtue of what God has endowed to them and by what they spend on women of their wealth" (4 : 34). Men were to provide their women tenderness and affluence if they could. Marriage was the usual state, and Islam did not support celibacy. Almsgiving was a primary obligation, and one was to go beyond justice to charity and forgiveness. From the call that God gave the Prophet, ideally all human beings would come to reason and felicity. Since God clearly did not compel non-Muslims to believe, Muslims themselves had no right to force others to believe (10 : 99, 108). However, the Qur'an regards balefully non-Muslims who contract with Islam and renege: "Lesser than the beasts in the eye of God are the unbelievers for they have covenanted with you and violated their covenant shamelessly in every case. If you lay hold of them in war, make of them a lesson to the others" (8 : 55).

The covenant of Medina that Muhammad composed gave Jews explicit rights: "To the Jews who follow us belong assistance and equal treatment from us without either injustice or discrimination."[64] The basic status of non-Muslims within the state that Muhammad envisioned was what might be called "colleagueship"—peaceful cooperation. The democratic principles applying to Muslim citizenship were individual responsibility, equality, the leaders' responsibility to run the government, and the mutual security of all citizens. In its law the state was to regard itself as a replica of the cosmic state that God runs by strict and unalterable laws. In effect, this meant buttressing Islamic convictions with a sure faith in divine justice on Judgment Day. The imam, or leader, led the community in upholding the law. This was the basis for his quasi-contractual relationship with the Ummah.

The Islamic state made a threefold division of humanity: Muslims, covenanters, and enemies. The Muslim peoples who constituted the *Dar al-Islam* (House of Islam) could not legitimately resort to war against one another. Covenanters were non-Muslims who had made compacts of peace, and their rights and duties were the same as those of Muslims. Al Faruqi does not specify the fate of enemies, although he notes the Qur'anic teaching that Muslims are to preach to them but not force them to convert. Presumably, holy war only resulted when enemies rejected both conversion and covenant. If an enemy responded with hostility, Muslim security necessitated war. What happened when the enemy simply wanted to be left alone or considered a Muslim takeover of its area unacceptable is not clear. However, it was clearly not blameworthy for Islam "to combat with the sword the sword which stands between it and man, preventing Islam from conveying its call and man from listening to or receiving it."[65]

A Negative View

Evaluating Muhammad and Islam in the context of the ecumenic age, Eric Voegelin enters a more critical opinion: "Islam was primarily an ecumenic religion and only secondarily an empire. Hence it reveals in its extreme form the danger which beset all of the religions of the Ecumenic Age, the danger of impairing their universality by letting their ecumenic mission slide over into the acquisition of world-immanent, pragmatic power."[66]

On occasion, the Arab militancy of Muhammad's ancestors shaped the Qur'anic conception of religious mission itself (for example, 21 : 16–18). In Sura 8, this leads to counsel that is easily abused: "The infidels must desist from their unbelief or the tension between truth and falsehood in the world will be removed by energetic action (VIII, 40–41). . . . For 'surely the worst beasts in the sight of God are the ingrate who will not believe' (VIII, 57)."[67] Although Voegelin does not consider the Qur'anic precepts on respecting non-Muslims' consciences, al Faruqi does not mention the counsel to slaughter (8 : 68).

Ethics

Annemarie Schimmel has sketched Muslim ethics, which presumably directed Muslim actions.[68] The guiding principle was to serve God as though you saw him in front of you. In other words, belief in Allah, Judgment, and the necessity of right deeds were the bases of Islamic ethics. Religious bonds rather than blood bonds, pure faith rather than idolatry, and sexual restraint rather than indecency—these were notable advances made by the Qur'an over Arab paganism. In addition to the exhortations to justice and charity found in the Meccan suras and the detailed legislation of the Medinan suras, those who survived Muhammad looked back on the Prophet's own life as the key to how a Muslim ought to live.

The early disputes about the fate of a sinner and the place of good works, which divided the theological and legal schools, suggest that human beings were considered free and responsible. As we noted, the law distinguishes five kinds of actions, from the commanded to the forbidden. The Qur'an deals with adultery, murder, and theft, prescribing stern punishments for them. Women had the right to refuse a proposed marriage, but men had greater rights than women in divorce. The wife had to obey her husband, who could punish her, and she always had to be at his disposal. "If a husband kills his wife and her lover *in flagrante delicto* [in the act of adultery itself] he is not punishable. Sodomy is likewise forbidden (though often practised in a society which excluded women largely from daily life. The object of Persian and Turkish love poetry is generally masculine)."[69]

The Qur'an takes slavery for granted, but it recommends humane treatment and commends freeing slaves. Only non-Muslim prisoners of war could legally become slaves. Discrimination because of color and race was unlawful, though some racial prejudice mars Islamic history. When the law reached its final stage of development around 1000, its detailed specifications tended to become mechanical. The mystics therefore tried to make ethics spring from a deeper relationship with God. The first virtue they taught was *wara*—abstention from everything unlawful or dubious. In other words, one was not to nitpick but to act from the heart and turn away from anything that might displease God. Masters such as al-Ghazali developed a shrewd psychology of virtue and vice, which they deployed in order to bring about the highest perfection. That perfection was living every moment in the presence of God. Finally, the general effect of Muslim ethics was to heighten awareness of one's distance from the divine purity and so lead one to beg God's mercy and forgiveness.

Women's Status

The status of women in Islam says a great deal about Muslim society.[70] In the Qur'an there is some basis for sexual equality: reward and punishment in the afterlife depend on deeds, not gender; marriage and conjugal life are precious; women have dowry rights in some divorces, inheritance rights, rights to remarry, and rights to protection in time of pregnancy and nursing. However, women's rights were not equal to those that the Qur'an gave males in either divorce or inheritance. Moreover, the Qur'an does not even consider the possibility that women might assume leadership roles in the community, receive an education equal to that of males, teach law or theology, or engage in polygamy (as males could).

Further, the misogyny latent in most patriarchal religions had dark effects in Muslim society. As late as 1970, an Arab sheik offered the opinion that "educated or not a woman is a woman and the Prophet—God's prayers and peace on him—had said that women are lacking in mind and religion."[71] The tradition placed more women in the Fire than in the Garden, and the prime determinant of their destiny was their treatment of their husbands. In legend Muhammad virtually despised female nature as stupid and irreligious. Its specific defects were menstruation, which interfered with prayer and fasting, and unreliability, which made a woman's witness worth only half a man's in court. Obedience to her husband was the woman's first duty; failure to do so can still get her killed today.[72]

The Muslim woman was considered erotic and empty-headed. Thus she was subject to purdah (seclusion and veiling), polygyny, concubinage, and the harem. Women were not to be taught to read and write ("a great calamity"), and they were morally "bent" because they came from Adam's bent rib. Thus, in many men's eyes, they had a dismal existence: "It were best for a girl not to come into existence, but being born she had better be married or buried."[73] Recent Muslims, especially Africans, have defended clitoridectomy and kindred operations, frequently with the following sort of rationale: "Circumcision of women releases them from their bondage to sex, and enables them to fulfill their real destiny as mother."[74] As she has done in the cases of suttee, foot binding, and witch burning, Mary Daly has vividly described African genital mutilation, eschewing defused scholarly speech.[75]

Another revealing view of women in Islamic society comes from the imagery of the Garden.[76] For many men, the best part of the heavenly Garden was the *hur:* dark-eyed, buxom virgins. In addition to his earthly wife, each male in Heaven could expect to have seventy *hur.* They would never be sick, menstruating, pregnant (unless he wished), bad-tempered, or jealous. He would be able to deflower a thousand each month and find them all intact when he returned to them. In descriptions of the Judgment scene, one sees the reverse of this fantasy: Women are in charge of men, which is a sure sign of disorder.

In fairness, Islam improved the lot of Arab women considerably, and certain parts of the community allowed women a function in the Hadith,[77] in scholarship, and in saintliness.[78] Also, many modern Muslims deplore the injustices that women have suffered in the past, interpret Qur'anic religion in a way that gives women great dignity, and bitterly oppose the drive of fundamentalists to return to such traditions as marrying girls off when they reach thirteen.

Divisions

The different Islamic cultures were bonded by the Qur'an despite their geographical, linguistic, ethnic, and even theological differences. The principal theological division, as we noted, has been between the Shiites and the Sunnis. However, as W. Montgomery Watt has shown, the formative period of Islamic thought saw a variety of controversies and then "heterodoxies."[79]

In India Islamic elements fused with Hindu elements to create Sikhism, and Islam was also the inspiration behind Baha'i. Baha'i is a universalist religion that stresses the unity of all traditions and the basic oneness of the human race. It arose in nineteenth-century Persia when a Shiite Muslim, Sayyid Ali Muhammad, declared that he was the twelfth imam—the last, messianic leader whom the Shia awaits. Sayyid took the designation *Bab* ("gate"), and his follower Baha'Ullah produced writings that became classic works of Baha'i faith. Today Baha'i has about 5 million adherents. Its world center is on Mount Carmel in Haifa, Israel, where there is a lovely garden and shrine to the Bab (Figure 30).[80]

Self

The strong control of the Ummah by religious law had two primary effects on the individual or self. First, the common code that governed external behavior shaped and constrained the majority. In other words, most Muslims accepted the ethics sketched above. Second, the Sufis and mystics drew a substantial minority to a more internal doctrine of the self shaped by personal devotion. Such devotion sought to unite the individual with God experientially. Thus, the first lesson that it taught was that the human person has a spiritual substance or capacity that can unite with God.

These two effects on selfhood produced a balance in Muslim religion: The self learned that membership in the House of Islam depended on observing the common law, which led to merit and the Garden, and that it could anticipate the Garden and taste God's joy in the present life.

The orthodox conception of the self began with the notion of creation. In Sura 96 the self is described essentially as a small thing that God made from a blood clot or a drop of sperm. The essence of Islam and of being a Muslim was to recognize the creator-creature relation: a sovereign God who is completely the Lord of a very insignificant vassal. The basic scriptural message of Islamic anthropology is submission, even a certain holy slavery.

This attitude was no false humility. Rather, it was the bare truth of the human condition. Human beings came from God, and their destiny depended on living out the pattern that God had in making them. Thus, they had no basis for self-glorification. Thus,

Figure 30   Shrine to the Bab, Haifa. Photo by J. T. Carmody.

the exclamations of an al-Hallaj, who claimed identification with God (through mystical union), could only sound blasphemous to the majority, who were immersed in the literal text. Between the divine Lord and the human vassal there stretched an impassable gulf. However much genuine love might have drawn the spirit up to God, however much God's intimate mercy might have descended toward human flesh, the essential difference in their states remained.

From other Qur'anic accounts of creation one can gather the impression that, despite their lowliness, human beings have a special status among all creatures. Al Faruqi calls this status being God's "vicegerent" on earth.[81] The word *lakum* ("for you") appears in the stories of how God made the earth to produce herbs, crops, and animals and of how God made the sea to carry ships and the camels and sheep to bring forth their offspring.[82] In the stories of Adam's creation (for instance, 2 : 28, 15 : 29, 32 : 8), the angels object to God's making human beings, but God forms this first man from clay and water, gives him a most beautiful form, and breathes his spirit into him. Then he makes the angels bow before Adam, for Adam is to be the *khalifa* (vicegerent) on earth, having in this capacity the right and duty to carry out God's orders. Echoing Genesis, Sura 2 : 31 speaks of God's teaching Adam the names of all things, which means giving him power over all things, since to control a being's name was to have power over it. The end God had in mind for such a creature, the recompense that He expected, was adoration:

"We have created men and jinn only for adoration" (51 : 51).

We can see, therefore, the basis for the Islamic view that God made the earth subject to human control. Along with the doctrine of God's transcendence, this anthropocentricity in creation helped to deemphasize nature. As we argued above, naming and ruling the world did not remove nature's mystery. Even with nature's mystery, however, the Muslim felt that the earth had been given into his (and to a lesser extent her) control. Nonetheless, Muslim teachings about human nature honored its ties with the earth, its creation from clay and water.

Anthropology

In traditional Muslim anthropology (view of human nature) the spiritual faculties had several names. The *nafs* was essentially the animal soul, the source of concupiscence (desire). It had the connotation of belonging to the lower part of the personality—to the flesh that incites evil. (Sometimes, though, it just means "self.") The *ruh* was the spirit, come from Allah, that animates the human body. Muslims often pictured it as a subtle matter that permeates the human body. Reason *(aql)* was the spiritual faculty by which human beings discern right and wrong. Finally, the mystics spoke of the *qalb*—the heart that is the faculty by which one obtains direct knowledge of God.

For some of the Sufis, the doctrine of creation in God's image was crucial. On occasion, neo-Platonic or Gnostic notions colored this doctrine to mean that the soul wanders in exile. It can return to its home, though, if it appropriates secret teaching or learns certain meditative techniques. From the notion of creation in God's image, the Sufis also developed their concept of the *insan kamil*, the perfect man. Usually they applied it to Muhammad, who contained all the divine attributes and who served as a microcosm of divinity.

The destiny of the human being, as we have seen, was either the Fire or the Garden.

Islam did not consider man and woman to be laboring under a "fallen" human nature, for Muslims did not regard the sin of Adam and Eve as being contagious or passed on to their offspring. Thus, Islam did not speak of redemption. The Prophet was a revealer or a medium of revelation; he was not a ransom, a victim, or a suffering servant. Instead of sin (in the deep sense of alienation from God by irrational actions), Islam tended to stress human forgetfulness (of God's goodness). Human nature was weak—prone to a kind of religious amnesia. In the Prophet's own conception of human destiny, men and women have a common responsibility to remember God's goodness and to respond by fulfilling his will. Originally, both men and women were to offer prayer and alms; however, in later times women's status deteriorated, and they did not have this obligation.

The self that was faithful to the identity set by the community could expect to gain Paradise. God would forgive sins (violations of religious law), so they did not mean a loss of community membership. (However, the dissident Kharijites said that every Muslim who committed a grave sin was an unbeliever.) What separated one from the Ummah in the orthodox view was to deny that the injunctions of the Qur'an came from God and thus were eternally binding. Among the Shia, who predominate in Iran, faith also included acknowledging the mystical imam of the time—the hidden successor to Ali whom the Shiites expect to come as the messiah. By uniting with this hidden imam, one partook of salvation.

Historically, the major theoretical question concerning the self was the relation of human freedom to divine will. At least in the Meccan sections, the Qur'an takes human freedom for granted. Muhammad's call and his preaching make no sense without a capacity to respond. Similarly, the scenes of Judgment Day assume that human beings have been responsible for their actions—that they could have done otherwise than they did. However, later Qur'anic passages emphasize God's omnipotence. As a result, the question arises, Does God lead some persons astray—or at least leave them in error?

In the Umayyad period a group of strict predestinarians (the Jabriya) stressed God's complete control. Opposing them were the Qasriya, who defended human responsibility. The Mutazilites defended both human freedom and God's perfect justice. Still another position, that of al-Ashari, satisfied many people with the following formula: "God creates in man the will to act and the act, and man acquires the act by performing it." To say the least, the issue vexed Islam. In later times the common person frequently felt that life was fated—that it was out of his or her hands. Among the few monistic mystics, human freedom was lost in the divine nature.

In summary, Islam has given the self rather complex directives. The core message is that membership in the Prophet's community and submission to God fulfill the human duties. The way to realize oneself is to follow the community law. In the present, such self-realization means spiritual security; in the future, it will mean Paradise. While waiting for Paradise, one can work the earth, trade, fight, or enjoy the pleasures of the senses, so long as the chosen activity does not divert one from the ultimate reality of God. If one is submissive to God, most things are licit. More things are licit for men than for women, as we have seen, but the Qur'an did improve the Arab woman's lot considerably.

Still, the popular image of Muhammad as a man who could satisfy nine wives and still receive revelations greater than those of Jesus inculcated a certain bravado in all but the most ascetic males. Since Islamic education deals primarily with religious lore, it does not necessarily demythologize Muhammad's popular image. As well, education is largely denied women. Therefore, tradition tends to describe sexuality mainly from a male point of view. That point of view tends to meld with the patterns set forth in the eternal Qur'an. Following these patterns, one lets God more and more dominate the entire self.

Divinity

Islam is perhaps the most theocentric of the major religions.[83] In Muhammad's revelation, Allah emerged to become the sovereign Lord. Before Muhammad, some Arabs had spoken of a high god "Allah" who was above the numerous idols. The divine name itself seems to fuse two words: al-Ilah ("the God"). It was an attempt to designate an ultimate divinity, a God who was beyond all demigods. From his visionary experience, Muhammad recognized that Allah is the only divinity, and that his primary designations are "Creator" and "Judge." As such, Allah leaves no place for other deities to function in either the world's creation or in the destiny of humankind.

Islam polished its theocentricity through controversy with polytheistic Arabs and then with Christians committed to the Incarnation and the Trinity. Sura 112, which Schimmel calls the logical end of the Qur'an,[84] puts the matter succinctly: "Say: He is Allah, One; Allah, the Eternal; He brought not forth nor hath He been brought forth; Coequal with Him there hath never been anyone."

The Creator made the world in six days (or in a single moment, according to Sura 54 : 50). Muslims trusted that he guides the world wisely and unfailingly. God's knowledge of all creatures is total, and his mercy extends to all who acknowledge him. It is God in whose name every work is being begun and upon whose will every future action depends. Thus, one had to add "insha Allah" ("if God wills") to every sentence that refers to a future act or a new direction of thought. To try to indicate God's fullness, the Qur'an encircles him with "most beautiful names." He is the First and the Last, the Inward and the Outward. Above all, he is Merciful and Compassionate. He is the All-Holy, the Peace, the Light of Heaven and Earth. Transcendent though he be, he is also as near as the jugular pulse. Wherever one turns, there is his Face (the Qur'anic expression for God's essence).

Many scholars find the negative portion of the Creed ("no God but Allah") very important, since it unequivocally rejects other peoples' gods. As well, it determined that the greatest sin in the Muslim code would be *shirk*—idolatry or "association" (of other objects of worship with God). The mystics sometimes took this to mean that nothing but God exists—that God alone is real. Among modern Muslims, anti-idolatry on occasion has worked against ideologies such as Marxism, capitalism, and nationalism, which some orthodox Muslims find incompatible with pure monotheism. Insofar as such ideologies enlist the ultimate concern of many human beings, they amount to new kinds of paganism.

However, the theology of the Qur'an itself is not without ambiguity. After Muhammad's death, debates arose about God's nature. At the beginning, the orthodox clung to the letter and imagery of the received text. That meant accepting descriptions of God that gave him a face, hands, and the like. The Mutazilites, who had contact with Hellenistic rationalism, pointed out the dangers latent in such anthropomorphism: When we think of God in human terms, we think of him as finite.[85] Thus, the Mutazilites clung to the absolute unity of God, accepting as a consequence that God cannot be imagined. In other words, they prized God's difference—the gulf that lies between the Creator and everything created. In Western terms, that made them "negative" theologians. Indeed, to safeguard God's unity, the Mutazilites even questioned the doctrine of the divine attributes (that God has speech, sight, and so on). For that reason, the orthodox described the Mutazilites as "those who deny the attributes," a charge of heresy.

In these debates, Muslims shared with Jews and Christians the consequences of an exposure to Greek reason. They had to ask whether their descriptions of God could be reconciled with what they could infer from the divine transcendence. For instance, they could infer that a Creator would be independent of the world, unlimited, unimaginable in created terms. From that it followed that any picture of God would be at best a happy convenience—a more or less useful fiction that might help some people's faith. As a further extension of such rationalism, the Mutazilites denied that the Qur'an is God's uncreated word. To them that would have made it a coeternal attribute, something ever existent with God. However, calling the Qur'an "created" deeply offended the orthodox, for whom the Arabic text expressed a heavenly prototype. The human Qur'an was unalterable (which led the orthodox to resist all attempts to translate it from Arabic), because it derived from eternity. Thus, the Mutazilites and the orthodox clashed in their theologies of revelation.

Further, the Mutazilites insisted that God has to be just and true. For the divine will to be arbitrary would violate God's own inner consistency. Consequently, God has to reward the just with Heaven and punish the evil with Hell. As well, God cannot be the author of sin, so human beings must have free will. To the less intellectual Muslim majority, this logic seemed rarefied, and they could not follow its deductive chain. "Limiting" God's freedom jarred with their sense of the divine sovereignty. Indeed, popular orthodoxy never fully accepted either human freedom or the notion that God had to obey rules for creation, even if they were his own. Popular orthodoxy preferred to leave all things in God's hands and saw little reason to puzzle over human freedom, God's noncontradiction, or the other problems that vexed the Mutazilites.

Al-Ashari, who had mediated the debate on the question of divine providence and human freedom, also mediated the question of the divine attributes. To the Mutazilites, he insisted that God has attributes (thereby saving the picture in the Qur'an). To the traditionalists, he insisted that we cannot say precisely how God has his attributes. In al-Ashari's eyes, both anthropomorphism and the denial of attributes were grave sins.

Among the Arab philosophers,[86] such as Avicenna, Greek doctrines stimulated the conception of God as a first cause whose being is pure existence. In contrast, the Sufis forwent philosophical speculation, favoring instead a personal experience of the divine. For them the profitable way was not reasoning but intuition. Further, the Sufis opposed Qur'anic fundamentalists by proposing that we should obey God out of love. To the fundamentalists, such a personal relationship seemed novel, for they admitted only a relationship of obedience: The Creator commanded and the creature obeyed. Because the Sufis were more ecstatic than either the fundamentalists or the philosophers, they are a richer source for ascertaining the beauty of the Islamic God—the allure of Allah's mystery and its fearsomeness.

The basic Islamic program for worshipping God has always been the five pillars. In the daily prayer *(salat),* one expressed one's submission to God and so one's faith in God's Lordship. Historically, men attended the Friday common worship in the mosque, while women prayed at home. Sufi circles developed unstructured prayer, which frequently involved a repetition of God's holy names. On the folk level, magical practices mixed with worship. The Qur'an gives them some foundation by saying that the (bad) angels Harut and Marut taught the Babylonians magic (2 : 96). Ordinarily, the magician knew formulas that could conjure the jinns or the angels. This has led to an expansion of the ways in which one can imagine the spirits and call them to one's aid. Amulets, reproductions of verses from the Qur'an, reproductions of God's names, and so on, are popular expressions of Muslim (magical) interest in attaining good luck. Similarly, Muslims continue to dread the "evil eye." To ward off its malignant influence, people constantly intersperse their conversation with "as God wills." As well, they wear amulets or give their children ugly names to keep the evil ones away.

Popular religion also retains a considerable interest in astrology, prophecy, and fortune-telling. A favorite technique for divining the future is to open the Qur'an at random and take the first verse that one's eye falls on as a cipher for what is to come.

Other popular methods are reading palms or coffee grounds.

Sacrifice also has a place in Muslim worship. Those who can afford it immolate a sheep on the Day of Slaughtering during the annual pilgrimage to Mecca. This sacrifice is in memory of Abraham, who was willing to sacrifice his son Ishmael. People also make votive offerings—cocks, sheep, and so on— at holy places such as the tombs of saints. The animal should be slaughtered ritually, by cutting its jugular and trachea in one stroke; tradition recommends giving it to the poor. Finally, sacrifice is appropriate on almost any important occasion, such as starting construction of a house, celebrating a child's birthday, or expiating an offense.

Although Islam places no mediators between God and human beings, it has made both Muhammad and many saints quite important objects of devotion. The members of Muhammad's family enjoyed special privileges, and Ali, his cousin and son-in-law, became a cult figure while still alive to those who considered him to be Muhammad's legitimate heir. The Shia expanded the Creed to include the words "Ali is the Friend of God." The Shia also venerated the line of imams, with special emphasis upon the currently hidden imam. He is the ruler of the age, and he will return at the end of the world to fill the world with justice. In Iran this imam's name accompanies the promulgation of laws, and he is for true Shiites an object of intense personal devotion.[87] Ali's son Husain also plays an important role, for the celebration of his assassination is a day of deep mourning.[88] Among the Sufis, the leaders of the orders were venerated, as were holy persons who gained a reputation for miracles. The latter often received special tombs to which the faithful would go for cures and favors.[89]

Angels are also essential objects of Muslim faith. According to tradition, God created them from light. The Qur'an stresses that they are neither children of Allah nor female beings. They are intelligent and can become visible. From the Qur'an, Muslims know Gabriel as the angel of revelation. Israfil will blow the trumpet at Doomsday, and Azrael is the angel of death. Iblis is the fallen angel. Like Harut and Marut, he is a source of evil. Harut and Marut taught humankind witchcraft, but a beautiful woman seduced them and then imprisoned them in a well in Babylonia.[90] Thus, the sacred space between the creature and the Creator has been abuzz with personages of interest.

The Islamic divinity is similar to that of the other theistic religions. Though its official doctrine insists on God's uniqueness, the comparativist finds that its popular practice deviates from its doctrine. Muslims perhaps have read the Qur'an more literally than other religionists have read their respective scriptures, since Islamic orthodoxy reified it into God's eternal Word, but there are analogies in Judaism, Christianity, and Hinduism. Clearly, though, Muslim faith aspired to make things simple: a black-and-white doctrine of God, Muhammad, and Judgment; a program of genius (the five pillars) for reducing this faith to practice; a single community of believers dedicated to filling the earth with true religion—with submission to the Grand Lord of the Worlds.

As events in Iran and Afghanistan in early 1980 showed, this aspiration toward simplicity has often had quite complicated effects. The condition of human beings—their space, time, and imperfection—renders pure submission to the Lord of the Worlds more an ideal than a fact.

Study Questions

1. Contrast Muhammad with the Buddha and with Jesus.
2. In what sense is Islam the preeminent religion of the book?
3. Do the five pillars make a comprehensive, fully adequate religious program?
4. Explain briefly how Qur'anic religion could inspire the golden age of Arabic civilization.
5. What does Sufism contribute to the family of Islam?
6. Compare the position of women in Islam, Judaism, and Christianity.
7. How well does submission describe the relation between the Muslim and Allah?

Conclusion

AMERICAN RELIGIOUS HISTORY: TWENTY-FIVE KEY DATES

1492	ABOUT 10 MILLION AMERICAN INDIANS LIVING NORTH OF RIO GRANDE
1565	ROMAN CATHOLIC COLONY AT ST. AUGUSTINE
1619	BEGINNING OF BLACK SLAVERY
1620	MAYFLOWER COMPACT
1654	FIRST JEWISH SETTLEMENT IN NEW AMSTERDAM
1683	WILLIAM PENN FOUNDS PHILADELPHIA
1734	GREAT AWAKENING IN NEW ENGLAND
1776	DECLARATION OF INDEPENDENCE EXPRESSES NONCONFORMIST, ENLIGHTENMENT-INFLUENCED RELIGIOUS OUTLOOK
1784	DEATH OF SHAKER LEADER ANNE LEE
1799	CREATION OF RUSSIAN ORTHODOX DIOCESE IN ALASKA
1801	BEGINNINGS OF WESTERN REVIVALISM
1836	FOUNDING OF TRANSCENDENTALIST CLUB IN CONCORD, MASS.

Summary Reflections

At the outset, we postulated that the religious life of humanity is a vast and diversified spectacle. Perhaps you now find that postulate only too well verified. The ancient religious mind, the wisdom religions of the East, the prophetic religions of the West all combine to make a tapestry of unmanageable proportions. We have tried to discern some of this tapestry's principal patterns. We have tried to present the information and the themes that might make such terms as *Hinduism* or *Islam* intelligible. Our final task is to review the whole and suggest its implications.

UNITY AND DIVERSITY

The unity of the phenomena we have studied is religion—the common quest for a way to the center. The diversity of the phenomena makes the religions—the distinctive traditional ways in which sizable numbers of people have worked at this quest together. Specifically, we have studied the ancient, the Indian, the East Asian, and the originally Near Eastern traditional ways.

The quests are all deeply humanistic. For instance, according to C. G. Jung,[1] the American Indian or African who greets the sun as a daily miracle performs deep psychic work. The Hindu who makes *puja* (worship) or whom bhakti carries to Krishna constructs a world that makes sense and provides emotional comfort. The same is true of Buddhists who ponder koans, Taoists who try to confect the elixir of immortality, and Hasidic Jews who learn diamond cutting to preserve what they can of the old *shtetl* life. In most times and places, the religions have supported or developed meaning unpretentiously, unobtrusively. For most people the traditions have worked subtly as sets of largely unquestioned assumptions.

Still, the traditions have varied in their subtleness. People who ate bean curd sensed the world differently than people who ate roasted lamb. The Prophet who recited, "There is no God but God," oriented Arabs away from the world that the Greek philosopher Thales saw ("The world is full of gods"). The recent introduction of social scientific and critical historical methods has made religious studies more empirically minded and so more sensitive to such variety. Thus, the differences among the religions have been in the spotlight.

Quite properly, we have seen that Hinduism and Islam are vast concepts. Indeed, they are quite abstract, for Hindus and Muslims have lived out their dharma and Qur'an very differently depending on time, place, and station. Therefore, to talk about Hinduism or Islam requires finding common qualities among great diversity, such as a regard for the Vedas or the Prophet, for karma or the Garden. Increasingly scholars debate whether there is a common quality among all the traditions, a common religion at the traditions' cores.

We believe that there is such a common quality or unity, and at various points we have described it as a common attraction toward mystery. Relatedly, we believe that the empiricism that misses such unity and mystery is at least an unwitting reductionism—an insistence that humanity is no more than as it behaves. Usually, that insistence indicates an impoverished imagination and interiority—an inability to intuit how two different behaviors (for example, shamanic ecstasy and yogic enstasis) might be directed toward the same goal: sacredness, the really real.[2]

The tricky thing about meaning, which extroverted observers tend to miss, is that ultimacy or mystery is always but a step away. Still, distraction and lack of reflection on the part of either the people under scrutiny or the scholars who are scrutinizing are defenses that mystery easily breaks down. As Wakan Tanka, Brahman, nirvana, Tao, the Torah, God, and Allah, ultimacy broke down the defenses against deep meaning in the peoples we have studied. Whether they wanted it or not (and usually they did), sacred mystery defined their world.

Figure 31   Taj Mahal: Islam on Hindu soil. Photo by J. T. Carmody.

If one can see the sacred, it breaks through the Iron, Bamboo, and other curtains that divide our world today. Perhaps the only traces of the sacred we can see are the anxieties on which the aspirin industry trades. Or perhaps we are able to appreciate it in the Nobel Prize–winning efforts of outstanding scientists and writers. Either way, with or without overt theology, ultimacy is always at hand. We may choose not to embrace it, not to call mystery our inmost vocation. However, as surely as we suffer and die, it will embrace us. All people by nature desire to know, Aristotle declared. Our mortal condition makes Aristotle's dogma existential: All people by nature desire to know the mystery from which they come and to which they go. All people are by nature set for religion.

Religion

The word *religion* refers to the inmost human vocation. By empirical fact as well as theoretical interpretation, *religion* pertains to all life that is reflective, that heads into mystery. Largely for that reason, the word *religion* was seldom uttered by the great teachers.[3] They rather spoke of meaning, the way to "walk," the traditional wisdom, the balance called justice, and the fire called love. Because they were embodied spirits speaking to other embodied spirits, they used familiar figures: mountains, rivers, widows giving alms. Further, their speech led to common action: rhythmic prostrations, gutsy resistance to the emperor, dancing with the Torah, helping a friend. All of these actions, though, were religious.

People organized communities around the great teachers' speech and actions. The communities expressed their religion (their venture after meaning into mystery) in ways that Joachim Wach has labeled theoretical, social, and active.[4] That is, they made theologies, brotherhoods and sisterhoods, and liturgies and laws. Regularly, the communities lost the spirit of their founders, as succeeding generations regularly prized order more than charisma, control more than inspiration, and orthodoxy more than creativity. Just as regularly, reformers tried to find their way back to the original vision. In China it was "Back to the ancients." In the West it was "Back to the Word."

The various traditions have shaped their peoples in endless ways. Some have spoken rather simply—Judaism and Islam, for instance. Others have made strange bedfellows and cultures more complex, such as the religions of China and Japan. Still, all traditions have used the past to decipher the present and to prepare for the future. All have received and handed on.

That handing on is what we mean by *tradition.*[5] None of us fashions meaning free of external influences. All of us receive a cultural inheritance, meager or rich, to which we add. We do this willy-nilly—by having children, teaching students, working with colleagues, supporting friends. Original sin is the dark side of such a sense of tradition. According to this concept, we all take our first breath in air that is polluted, in a game that is tilted against us. How polluted or tilted the world is has been a matter of vigorous debate. The only consensus seems to be that evil is a sad fact and that there is sufficient good to justify hope. The handing on therefore leads all the religions to revile evil and to buttress hope—a process that can be called a concern for salvation.

For instance, ancient peoples banded together for evolutionary salvation—against the evil of extinction and in hope that the race would go on. Close to the earth, they thought in concrete terms, undifferentiatingly, telling stories of life and death. Life came from the fatherly sky and the motherly earth. Life was as possible, as renewable, as heavenly water and productive dirt. Death was breathtakingly near, but perhaps the dead were as seed falling in the ground. Perhaps they were but a link in the chain of generations. Or, maybe they passed to a new form of life. As smoke passes from burning wood, so perhaps the subtle part of a human, the part that thinks and travels in dreams, could pass to a new state. In those ways, perhaps, ancient peoples fought for hope, tried to block out absurdity.

To suffer, lose, rejoice, or trust—such acts know no religious, ethnic, or national bounds. We all walk a way (if only a way to death) that we cannot name. We all seek (if only covertly) a path that is straight, a path that mystery blesses. If some of our predecessors have been Nordic berserks, who heated up to feel mystery boil, others have been Eastern yogis, who so slowed themselves that they could be buried alive. If some of our predecessors have been erotics, convinced that the force of the way is sexual *shakti*, others have been lonely ascetics, convinced that meat clouds the spirit. There are few roads that no one has taken, few options that no one has tried. Though the options make all the difference for the individual, we can see from others where we might have gone. Indeed, that is a major reason why we study the humanities. There would be no basis for studying the humanities were there no unity called human nature. Likewise, there would be no religious studies were there no unity called religion.

Contending with nature, society, the self, and whatever ultimacy they have known, all human beings have mused about their sunrise and sunset. For all of them, the cosmos and the group have had effects, the self and ultimacy have beguiled. Without and within each person, the world has taken shape, changed, occasionally threatened to slip away. Since we are "synthetic" beings, whose incarnate spirits include the lowest matter and the heights of thought, we cannot escape religion's full span. Madness comes when the span tilts and the synthesis comes unglued. Boredom comes when we lose the span's tension, when imagination goes stale. In health, we find nature, society, and the self fascinating. In health, science, politics, and art are all essential, all deeply humanistic. If they become so specialized, so arcane, that their essential humanity is not apparent, we must speak of disease—of dysfunction, pathology, alienation.

Though disease has terrible power in our time, as the arms race and the prison systems show, it has always written arguments for despair. Parents who wept over dead children heard despair at Stonehenge, Gettysburg, and My Lai. Every woman raped, every man tortured, has heard counsel to abandon hope. Amazingly, though, human beings will not live by despair alone. Their very sense that the times are out of joint is a cry that there ought to be health.

Until we give up completely, we label health as normal. Disease, we say, is the lack of health. Evil, we say, is the lack of good—of proper order, right being, justice, and love. Indeed, so deep is our drive toward health that we cannot think of nonbeing and evil directly. They are irrational, absurd, and void. In their hope, then, the religions uncover more religion. In their hope, Marxists and Christians can dialogue.

Meaning and Idiosyncrasy

The themes above are some of the constants that all the traditions carry. If they are general, it is because they pertain to all of humanity. In religious perspective, our human characteristics comprise a common condemnation (or consecration) to meaning. Thus, the differences among traditions are simply *how* their peoples have sought, conceived, and enacted meaning. That affirms, of course, that differences do differentiate.[6] It affirms that a Buddhist is not a Hindu and a Christian is not a Jew.

Because he or she is always dealing both with religion as a whole and with the individual religions, the student of religion must develop a peculiar balance. If she or he

is blind to the unity behind all religions, the student will miss the deep humanity that the traditions can offer us. On the other hand, if the student sweeps all the information together, making all Buddhists anonymous Christians or all Christians renegade Jews, he or she will miss the texture that religion always has in people's lives. As is often the case, the ideal involves a duality: *both* cutting to the heart of the matter, where all humans are siblings, *and* respecting the idiosyncrasies that differentiate people as nations, tribes, sexes, individuals, and traditional religionists.

The idiosyncrasies are mysterious. Why should the Buddha have proposed noself? A first answer might be because no-self answered the question of suffering that Buddha's personal life and the life of his Indian culture posed. Fine, but this is hardly an end to the matter. Why should death, disease, and putrefaction have troubled this particular prince so deeply? Presumably many other princes saw corpses without deciding to leave their palaces, wives, and children to adopt a life of asceticism; similarly, many other cultures experienced suffering. Why, then, did the Indians penetrate the psychology of suffering so profoundly? Why not the Babylonians, Chinese, Aztecs, or Mayans?

As those questions show, there is a limit to historical analysis. It can explain some of the differences among individuals or cultures, but their real origin lies beyond it. For the real origin of differences is the incomprehensible world order[7]–Paul's *mysterion*. We did not set the cosmic dust spinning. We don't know why it wove the combinations it did. Therefore, when we respect differences, we respect the totality of history and its mystery. We respect the ultimacy behind the facts, the often very brutal facts, that just this universal drama has played and no other.

Let us again try to be concrete. The Australian dream world, as scholars imperfectly reconstruct it from artifacts and interviews, reflects the peculiar landscape of the Australian continent. The aboriginal myths are similar to those of other areas that explain how the ancestors or demiurges fashioned the world, yet the aboriginal world is unique. The Australian use of the *tjurunga*, the sacred wooden boards, for instance, is distinctive. Other ancient peoples painted and carved, but none (that we know) with just the Australian concern for totemic ancestors. Or consider African peoples' use of masks. That, too, has analogies—with the American Indian use of *kachinas* and even the Greek use of theater masks. Yet in Africa masks relate to thought, such as Ogotemmeli's Dogon thought,[8] that speaks of man and woman, fox and anthill, smithy and granary as the people of no other continent do. Again, the Chinese divination practice of *feng-shui* (geomancy) is like the complex basket divination of the Africans, yet they differ greatly. The two types of divination have the same purpose (to determine what will happen in nature and time), but they express it differently. *Feng-shui* would not seem appropriate in the Congo.

Differences also appear among religions about which we have more historical information. For instance, Judaism memorialized the Exodus (flight from Egypt) in a Passover ritual. Something happened to get the people out of Egypt, and Jewish religious memory attributed it to God and Moses. In time the happening became a paradigm for interpreting Jewish history. Because of what happened in the past, faithful Jews endured their trials with hope. God would deliver them again somehow. That sort of historical memory, that "anamnesis," gave Jews an identity different than that of the Canaanites, Egyptians, Romans, or Germans. Indeed, without their religious memory, Jews today would have little identity crisis. It is the Exodus that makes the Holocaust so shattering. It is the Exodus and the Holocaust together that make the current state of Israel so tense.

For Christians, the Exodus was a prefiguration of the liberation that Jesus' death and resurrection worked. In their eyes, Jesus' "passover" made a new creation, Jesus' spirit formed a new Israel, Jesus' teaching estab-

lished a new covenant. The lamb of the old Passover was a figure of Jesus the victim and conqueror. In the heavenly Jerusalem, Jesus the lamb receives all power, glory, and honor. In fact, the lamb has married the heavenly Jerusalem. Further, the heavenly Jerusalem has no temple, because "the Lord God Almighty and the Lamb were themselves the temple, and the city did not need the sun or the moon for light, since it was lit by the radiant glory of God and the Lamb was a lighted torch for it" (Rev. 21 : 22–23). This imagery—this radical interpretation of Exodus and Passover—developed within a century of Jesus' death. By then Christians and Jews had irrevocably separated. For nineteen centuries, they have identified themselves through mutual opposition.

For Muslims, Muhammad makes a reality different from the reality that Moses makes for Jews or Jesus for Christians. The difference is rooted in pre-Islamic Arab culture and took form in Muhammad's own psyche, where he received visions not of a burning bush or a dove descending from heaven but of the angel Gabriel. This difference flowered in Islamic conquest, which made the Prophet's people imperial in ways that Jews and Christians never were. Muslims swept across the Mediterranean world as Jews never thought to do, and they rejected priests, monks, and sacraments. Even their abuse of women was distinctive: a blend of polygyny, purdah, the harem, clitoridectomy, and *hur*.

A mosque, a synagogue, and a church all show likenesses to a Hindu or a Buddhist temple. All five enclose sacred space. But the first three have a family likeness that separates them from the latter two. Principally their space reverberates with the Word of a creator God. Still, one is not likely to confuse a mosque with a church or a synagogue. The Word takes a different form in St. Peter's than it does in a synagogue in Skokie, Illinois, or a mosque in Cairo.

Differences, then, are real. We could develop that theme for Hinduism contrasted with Jainism or Buddhism, for Catholics contrasted with Orthodox or Protestants. How great differences are, how divergent they make their adherents' realities, is difficult to determine. Often it seems as much a matter of the analyst's temperament as of the adherents' realities. In the terms of a recent debate,[9] the analyst who has an "esoteric" (inner) personality tends to stress the unity in the traditions, while the "exoteric" (outer) personality tends to stress the diversity.

Esoteric types respond to innermost notions and innermost realities. For them, a common mystery is as real as distinctive facts, even more real. Therefore, esoteric types tend to the negative way—the Hindu *"neti, neti"* ("not this, not that"). They may downplay or even disparage the diverse ways that people have chosen to pursue the supreme value. In contrast, exoteric types respond to outer phenomena—to the actual births, hungers, murders, orgasms, and deaths that make people's lives colorful, intense, palpably real. They fear that moving away from such realities ignores the way things are.

Beside exoteric blood, sweat, and tears, God does seem esoteric, pale and abstract. Looking closely, though, we find that esoterica have given religions most of their life. For instance, what would American Indian ceremonies—the Sun Dance, the vision quest, the potlatch (gift-giving feast)—have been without Wakan Tanka, without the Great Spirit? What would the Egyptian pyramids have been without Osiris and Re? Those pale gods gave the ceremonies and massive stones their meaning. Apart from such meaning, exoterica are mute. The same applies in other traditions. Hindu bhakti festivals make no sense without a Krishna to play the flute, a Kali to wield the sword. Buddhist meditation depends completely on karma and nirvana. In the West, circumcision, the Eucharist, and the Muslim *hajj* (pilgrimage to Mecca) depend on the covenant, the redemption, and the eternal Word. In the lives of religious people, the exoteric is a body for the esoteric. It should be the same in the writings of religion scholars.

THE USES OF RELIGION

Our discussion so far suggests that religion has served several uses. Historically, most people have groped after meaning through a religious tradition. Even when they came to conclusions that differed from those of fellow traditionists (fellow Jews or fellow Christians, for instance), a tradition set before them their major questions. For example, Maimonides and Halevi evaluated reason differently, but their common Jewish tradition set them the question, How does reason relate to faith? Similarly, Aquinas and Bonaventure evaluated love differently, but their common Christian tradition set them Paul's dictum that love is the greatest of God's gifts. In those cases, unity probably predominated over difference, though when partisanship flamed, the difference generated great heat.

Jews, Christians, Hindus, and Buddhists also tried to be faithful to the unity that they glimpsed in diverse peoples. They all met peoples who did not accept their tradition—did not accept the Torah, Jesus, the Vedas, or Buddha. Such peoples sought a living, wept when they were in pain, and hoped for a happy future. They might have had funny customs, but they, too, worried about doing what was right. Sometimes they even came through with a surprising act of kindness. Even when they did not—when they were abrupt traders or harsh rulers—they expressed qualities one already knew from home: fellow Hindus profiteered, fellow Christians kicked the dog.

Thus, the fact that people were members of particular religions and members of the human race made people aware that their cultures were both many and one. The notion of a universal humanity[10] may only have come to consciousness clearly in the ecumenical age, but people knew it instinctively long before that time. When sexual relations with a foreign slave begot a half-breed, people instinctively knew the falsity of racist biology. When a foreigner performed an act of kindness, prejudice had to loosen.

Because religion has been at the historical center of people's meaning systems, religion has played a key role in this dialectic of unity and difference, and this dialectic has played a key role in religion. When Francis Xavier met the Japanese, he thought that they were the most moral people in the world. As a result, his notions of sin, grace, paganism, and hell were challenged. Centuries later, his fellow Jesuit Karl Rahner, building on experiences such as Xavier's, developed a theory he called the "supernatural existential."[11] Simply, it meant that no people live apart from grace.

A first value of religion, then, is that it prompts people to broaden their horizons. When it deals with a genuinely mysterious ultimate, religion makes all fellow humans brothers and sisters. (When it does not deal with a genuinely mysterious ultimate, we may infer, religion makes fellow humans slaves, victims, and enemies.)

A second value of religion is education. From its station at the core of people's quests for meaning, religion can teach students of human behavior that reality can be both/and. For instance, religious wars have shown that faith can be *both* demonic *and* sanctifying. In Jewish, Christian, and Muslim faith, it has made for demonic faith a special symbol: holy war. Thus, Psalm 137 told Israelite soldiers to smash the heads of enemy babies against the wall. Thus, the Qur'an (8 : 68) instructed Muslim soldiers to slaughter and reap booty. Thus, American "'Christian'" soldiers found it fitting to destroy Vietnamese towns in order to save them. Muhammad, David, Saint Louis—they are all ambiguous warrior saints.

To be sure, religious battle is not monochromatic. In its time, the theory of a just war made much sense. There is an ambiguity about war, as there is an ambiguity about pacifism. Sensing the latter, Gandhi gave the opinion that it was better to fight than to choose pacifism out of cowardice. Films of British and Indian soldiers felling Gandhi's *satyagrahis* with clubs and rifle butts show that his opinion came from experience.

A similar both/and attends marriage, celibacy, the treatment of women, and the treatment of slaves. For instance, though slavery is almost wholly a stigma, some Muslim and Christian owners treated their slaves compassionately. The same is true of polygamous husbands—traditional African, Muslim, and Mormon alike. For example, as Islam improved the lot of slaves at its outset, so it improved the general lot of wives.

Thus, a knowledge of religion stimulates a respect for human variety—for the wide spectrum between good and evil. As the religious philosophers who reflect on ultimate mystery find human beings quite alike, so the religious historians find that religious peoples are nearly equal in their diversity and complexity.

Let us again try to concretize our hypotheses by citing familiar examples. Eskimos, for instance, have had limited chances to develop wisdom about human unity and difference; their religion has usually served a more basic usefulness. Through their shamanistic world view, Eskimos have endured nearly unbelievable cold and darkness for sheer survival and sanity. In fact, early observers attributed Eskimo shamanism to a nervous pathology brought on by their environment. Specifically, those observers spoke of visions that "arctic hysteria" induced. However, later and more sophisticated scholars, such as Mircea Eliade, argue that shamanism is so widespread that climatic conditions alone could hardly account for it. Further, they show that shamans are often their tribes' most intelligent and stable persons. Precisely by bearing the tribe's fears, a shaman's ecstasy is a source of order and hope. From deep within themselves, shamans have formed traditions that hold at bay the chaos threatened by disease, death, cold, or the absence of game.

The utility of a religious venerable

such as Black Elk was much the same. Clearly, his vision that the Sioux nation's hoop would be restored did not come to reality in his lifetime, but that did not make his vision without value. The core of religion is mystery-held meaning. Black Elk's vision illumined the Sioux condition and nursed the Sioux with meaning. Just by occurring, then, it was beneficial. To be sure, it would have been better had mundane improvements in the Sioux condition been made. To be sure, the tribe ought to regain its freedom to revere its holy land. Core meaning, in Black Elk's vision or any other religious benefaction, does not take care of all worldly needs. Nonetheless, shamanism is finally useful because of meanings we cannot touch or see. It is finally useful because of its spiritual intuition, its "faith."

Were shamanistic dance only a choreography, not a matter of faith, we could reproduce it off Broadway. Because it makes sacred the four compass directions, giving them mystery-held meaning, shamanistic dance is more than entertainment. The four directions are symbols of the one force of creation; they are points at which the Great Spirit can enter the world. Because the human spirit has, in Aquinas' term, a quasi-infinity, it can reach up to the Great Spirit. Because it has, in Augustine's term, a restless heart, fair maidens, fair lads, precious metals, and abundant crops all fail to satisfy it. The human spirit must intend the All.

Still, our reflection turns again. The All must touch fair maidens and rich crops. It must shine and blow in a world of particulars, a world firm under moccasined feet. Thus, north, south, east, and west are the gates of heaven. By another of the endless paradoxes that make religion useful, heaven enters our gates to become heaven-for-us. The Great Spirit descends through the east, where the sun rises. It comes from the west, where the sun beds down. We can feel it when we face north, where the quickening breeze stirs. It is lovely to the south, where summer sun retreats.

The sages prominent in Eastern religions have focused on human nature somewhat differently from the shamans, going inward rather than outward. Yogis want rest, not travel. Yogis exercise imageless awareness rather than imagination. So peculiar is human nature, though, that yogis have propped busy external cultures. Busy India, for instance, is unthinkable without its millennia of yogis.

However, yogis have made Indian activity reflect a cosmic maya and so be less serious than Western activity. They have led thousands of Indians to leave the marketplace and sit in the forest. Further, yogis were people who saw life as a stream, a great confluence of voiceovers and passing forms. From the ant to the king, one life-force streamed by, which the yogis heard sing a single "Om." It was the mantra of Brahman itself. To the wise, Brahman preexisted Shiva or Krishna. Thus, for Shankara, the great Trimurti (Brahma-Vishnu-Shiva) was but a symbol. Similarly, Buddha set nirvana beyond the gods, Nagarjuna put emptiness beyond all karma. By oneness, nirvana, and emptiness, Indian life became different from ancient or Western life.

Of course, Hinduism developed sages who were not pure yogis. Those behind the *Bhagavad Gita* were virtuosi (masters) who found *moksha* by several paths. Like the Buddha, they were "skillful in means" to save. For instance, they made Krishna an avatar of ultimacy and divine glory. As well, they made bhakti a common person's way. Shrewdly they saw that love could equal learning. Compassionately they left no one out. The *Gita*, then, became the most useful text of Indian religion. Following it, meditative types could sit in peace, intellectual types could pursue the moment of vision, emotional types could hear the unthinkable "You are dear to me," and active types could work in peace.

When Gandhi went looking to buttress *satyagraha*, his politics of truth-force, he settled on the fourth of the *Gita*'s yogas. Most useful to him was karma-yoga discipline—grasping ultimacy through selfless labor. He found it a high art, a trick hard to master. Can we engage in politics today as though spinning thread carelessly? Can an effective action not be concerned with the fruits of success? To Western ears, those are strange questions. On the other hand, is there any effective action that is attached, that is concerned with success? Don't we see again and again in the West that success mottles our work, that ego corrodes our politicians?

Thus, Gandhi's work dialectic sharpened his religion, honing it to a paradox. To become an instrument of truth, he saw, he had to lose self, ambition, concern. Bone weary with service, he had to count all his service as nothing. Yet, marvel of marvels, self-loss was energizing. It sent him on long marches to the sea, on long terms in prison. In his depths it evoked love for his enemies, help for those who persecuted him. Indeed, in his depths it did away with enemies and made his persecutors brethren.

If Gandhi had not freed a modern nation, we would count his *satyagraha* as so much hot air, but India used *satyagraha* to gain home rule (and then abused it to produce the Hindu-Muslim partition). Thus, we have to consider *satyagraha* quite real. In fact, we have to be humble enough to see in *satyagraha* one of Western religion's own truths about action: Work as though everything depended on God, and pray as though everything depended on yourself.

In the past few pages, we have taxed your patience, getting more than a little oracular in order to conjure how living religions actually speak. Such language perhaps shows a final utility that shamans, sages, and prophets have offered humankind—their capacity to shock sleepy humanity awake. The paramount religious figures have forced humanity to be more than animal by insisting that life is more than food and the body more than clothing. They above all have underscored the strange play of life and death that prompts deep reflection.

What is genuine living? What riches are valuable? Such questions can be cultural dynamite. For instance, if it is easier for a camel to pass through the eye of a needle

than for a rich person to enter the kingdom of God, what happens to Judaism's blessing for wealth, Hinduism's permission for *artha*, the Mormon Tabernacle, and St. Peter's in Rome? Similarly, if it were better for Chuang-tzu to drag his tail in obscurity, like a turtle in mud, what happens to ambition, even to service, let alone to Chinese bureaucracy?

Seers, founders, and saints all qualify our instinctive values. Instinctively we all tell the mirror, "Prosper, fill your barn, appease your loins." The saints answer, "You fool! This night God may require your soul." Because of saints, we have been prompted to think that money, sex, and fame are not all. Confucius kept China aware that it might be better to pay court to heaven than to the stove.

But is this shock really useful? Does it do anything more than upset the slothful majority and tempt the upsetters to pride? Our answers to that question say a great deal about our own values. If there is nothing but cradle to grave, religious persons are of all the most to be pitied. If there is no nirvana in samsara, Zen bipeds are of all the most wingless. The merit in teasing the mind over paradoxes, in disciplining the heart to search out reasons, stands or falls by whether the examined life is more than sound and fury. At bottom, there are just the two ways that Deuteronomy foresaw. One is death to humanity—to reflection, making a self, freedom, and love. It is the way that denies the examined life, that denies faith. The other way—reflection, freedom, love—makes real life.

The choice between the two ways, between death and life, is inalienable: No one can make it for you. Even not to choose is a choice—a choice to drift. There is a time to drift, as there is a time to come ashore. To drift too long, though, is to choose against the deeper spirit, against the deeper life. Religion has the (painful) utility of forcing us to hear that we are not what we eat. We are what we choose to be. In Augustine's terms, we can choose love of self unto contempt of divine mystery, or love of divine mystery unto contempt of self. In the *Dhamma-pada*'s terms, we can choose thoughts that form our selves to suffering or that form our selves to joy.

The contempt in the second half of Augustine's dichotomy is not self-hatred. It is not tearing the psyche to keep the ego important. Rather, it is letting go, opening up, saying yes to a world one did not make and does not finally control. At the end of the life cycle, Erik Erikson says, the "virtue" (power) we most need is wisdom. Wisdom, then, is the ability to love life in the face of death, to say yes in the face of nature's no. Before old age, wisdom often is the ability to say yes in the face of the senses' no. Accordingly, we are hardly wise if the senses have been our only tutors.

The religions say that the senses are splendid—when they serve the spirit, the mind, and the heart. Then, a tree is just a tree in a quite different way. In enlightenment, all trees are sacramentals. In the illuminative way, basic human acts (eating, intercourse, washing, anointing) are sacraments. They make life good enough to merit a profound love in the face of death. They make the golden mean, the Aryan middle way. The final utility of religion is that it can teach us how to die and how to live. For Plato, the love of wisdom was the art of dying. Plato was everything we require a religious sage to be. For Chuang-tzu, Taoism was the art of living. Chuang-tzu was everything we require a religious sage to be.

ON BEING AN AMERICAN CITIZEN OF THE RELIGIOUS WORLD

We have not paid special attention to America in this book, because in the full history of religion, America has only occupied a small fraction. In general handbooks such as the *Historical Atlas of the Religions of the World, Historia Religionum,* and *The Concise Encyclopedia of Living Faiths,* American religion does not receive 2 percent of the space. The first lesson that the world religions offer Americans, then, is that America is not as important as Americans tend to think. Our 400 years of religious experience are not much beside India's 5,000. If our 6 percent of the world's population and almost 40 percent of the consumption of the world's raw materials are disproportionate, we need all the help we can get to help us become less important.

We are not advocating the suppression of patriotism. Few existing cultures are very old. Europeans or Asians who sniff because their cultures go back more centuries than ours are hardly less ridiculous than we. All nations need a perspective on world history. All nations need to see things "under the aspect of eternity."

For most Americans, religion has been Christianity, and Christianity has often pivoted on Jesus and the founder of one's own sect. In some cases the dark ages between those two personages stretch 1,800 years. For such sects, Catholics are not considered Christians, and Orthodox are beyond the pale. True, Americans modified this intolerance by coexisting with their neighbors. Almost all Americans, though, need a deep breath of cosmopolitan air.

The root of provincialism is what Erik Erikson calls "pseudospeciation"—pretending that we are the only true human beings. In the past, that "we" has been Chinese, Japanese, and Eskimos. It has been Boston Brahmins and Oklahoma dirt farmers. It has been Catholics who would never darken a Protestant church door, Orthodox who would never visit a synagogue. Fortunately, we now know enough about the psychodynamics of pseudospeciation, largely through analyses of prejudice, to show that it has little to do with religion as such. In fact, we now know that genuine religion directly opposes pseudospeciation.

In most cases, pseudospeciation stems from a combination of fear and self-interest. We fear the universal humanity, the radical equality, that a pluralistic world implies. It would force us to shed our shells; it would snatch away our platform for boasting. Similarly, we fail to grasp notions such as the Christian Church because it is to our

Figure 32 The Underground Railroad, *Charles T. Webber,
courtesy of The Cincinnati Art Museum. Purchased from the
Webber estate by a popular subscription fund.*

advantage that "in Christ" there be male and female (Gal. 3 : 28). We fail to enact the notion of a union of all nations, because it is to our advantage to dictate prices to the world. Few of us are magnanimous willingly, textbook writers included.

If we Americans are to gain stature in religion's golden eye, we will have to become more realistic about time and space than we have tended to be. Throughout all time, most people have not been Americans, Christians, or whites, and any true God has blessed more lands than just ours. By today's standards, the colonial Puritans' "errand in the wilderness" was terribly naive. Those who launched it simply did not have our facts about human prehistory and human diversity. It was largely ignorance, then, that

led them to locate salvation in New England. The same is true of those who proposed that America be God's new Israel. Sober students of American history wonder to what extent such notions were used to justify ravaging the Indians. Historians of religion stumble over the obvious fact that God's old Israel was perfectly well.[12]

If we deflate our egos, we may see things in better perspective. From the vantage point of an astronaut or the sun god Re, Americans have never been *the* holy people. Long before the whites, reds revered every striking American locale. Shortly after the whites, blacks became America's suffering servants. Unbeknownst to our pioneers, peoples in Asia were living lives of grace under pressure.

The only holy people, in religious perspective, are of the single race, the single species. All divisions make but partial stories. There is a dictum in religious studies that he or she who knows just one religion knows no religion. By that dictum Americans urgently need to study world religions; if only to determine our own identity, we need to know what others have been, what alternatives there were.

In addition, the world religions can suggest what in American religious experience has been distinctive. This topic is immense, so we can only offer a few leads. First, the Reformation and Enlightenment had a marked effect on American religion. Together, they led to a peculiar blend of pietism and rationalism. Of course, pietism and rationalism have been present in other cultures. For instance, India embraced both bhakti and Vedanta; Islam embraced both Sufism and the law *(sharia)*. In America, the mixture tended to set the Bible against the brain. Evolution and the Scopes trial of 1925 brought this tension to the fore. In colonial times, Calvinists made syntheses that pleased at least themselves. During the drafting of the Constitution, it appears that reason ousted piety—unless we should call the founding fathers pietistic.

One way of looking at American pietism and rationalism is aesthetic. William Clebsch has recently elaborated that point of view.[13] In his opinion, thinkers such as Jonathan Edwards, Ralph Waldo Emerson, and William James tried to envision the world's beauty. Another way of approaching American religion is to emphasize American religious liberty. Sidney Mead has argued that the American experiment in religious pluralism has proven as momentous as the establishment of Christianity in imperial Rome.[14]

Both of these views owe much to the Enlightenment's advances on the Reformation. The Reformation set the principles of individual conscience and individual interpretation of scripture. The Enlightenment proposed that reason—nondogmatic thought common to all—should be judge when individual interpretations shattered civic peace. In this new land, where individual opportunity was rich, reason sat in the driver's seat.

In the matter of religious liberty through law, Americans made quantum leaps over their European forebears. There was much less than full political equality, as generations of blacks and women have underscored, but something novel was present that we have come to call pluralism. In religious terms, it was an attempt to live together as equals despite differences in creed. In secular terms, it was a search for a common sense to ensure economic and political cooperation. In theological terms, it conjured natural theology—speculation about God apart from scripture or dogma. For Roman Catholics, the implications of American pluralism only hit Europe in the "Decree on Religious Liberty" of Vatican II.

Despite its faults, America has done much that is commendable. In a world where the majority still seek basic human rights, including the right to religious liberty, America looks quite good. Even in the perspective of the world religions, our civic tolerance is remarkable.

At its most tepid, American religion has tolerated civic piety—mouthings on Memorial Day and the Fourth of July. However, it has also sponsored ecumenical debate, academic freedom, and political and religious dissent. The question now is whether pluralism is so inseparable from secularism that it condemns us to religious superficiality.[15]

Has our agreement to disagree about fundamentals relegated them to the private sphere? If religion is absent from the public places where we forge our national culture, our center may not hold. But if religion is only pursued by the pious, genuine traditionalists will not want it to hold. Eric Voegelin has said that a crucial mark of a culture is whether it enlists the best of its youth or alienates them. For both United States government and United States religion, that is now a hard saying.

We have become used to speeches telling us that our government has only to be as good as its citizens for America to prosper. In too many political assemblies, churches, and synagogues, that is a palliative. It brings no health or distinction to the speaker or the audience. To a religious guru, it shows that the speaker ignores the human condition—the beginner's mind, the nature of enlightenment. Unreflective, unmeditative, the speaker cannot be terse, poetic, evocative; he or she can only pour forth the old, stale, placating language. Ignorant of ignorance and sin, the speaker sees no tragedy. Lacking rigor, stupid in the reasons of the heart, the speaker thinks hope is found in good cheer.

Much the same is true of the audience, of ourselves. Not having gone down in spiritual death, we do not fly to the gods. Not set for spiritual combat, we do not resent that the seats are plush, the rhetoric easy. In part, that is because our culture tells us that only eggheads knit their brows and ponder. In part, it is because we are too lazy to live. It is a major accomplishment for us to endure ten minutes of silence.

From a religious perspective, the economics of American popular culture—the money we pay entertainers, athletes, and business executives—is obscene. Compared to what we pay the people who shape our nation's soul—the artists, scientists, nurses, teachers, and mothers—it is what Aeschylus called *nosos*—spiritual madness. Compared to how we treat the world's starving, it is beyond expression. Two thousand years ago, the *Book of Mencius* began by condemning profit. Wise persons would have taken that lesson and banked it. We, however, have built a culture on profit. It is what makes our Sammy and Sally run. When will we see that they are running in circles?

People who say things that others do not want to hear, no matter how true such things may be, will suffer for their indiscretion. Socrates stands as the paradigm of their fate, and Socrates shows that in the political realm, prophets and sages are one. He also shows that prophets and sages cannot live for audience applause. They must do what they have to do, say what they have to say,

because it is their truth, their good, their charge. Shamans, for instance, must sing—because it relieves their sadness, because it makes them whole. Plato's "Seventh Letter" says that the philosophical soul must live by a love of the Good, that it can only deny the Good by denying its self. Religious people, creative people, humanity's benefactors—they have all found something more precious than human praise. Better, they have all been found by something more precious.

That something is the sacred, the numinous, the holy, the really real. It is Wakan Tanka, the Tao, Buddha-nature, God. Commonly, it is the essence of any conviction significant in the ultimate order, in the world as it finally is. The world as it finally is is the one place where you get what you are. It is where someone may finally tell you, "If you do not believe in mystery, God, or the Tao, be honest about it." By doing so you will reap two benefits. First, you will not bring those realities into further disrepute. Second, you will take the first step in the pilgrimage toward wisdom—simple honesty.

A second step is no less simple or heroic. It is to love the truth that you see. That may be the truth that mystery is beautiful or the truth that the religions often cant. It may move you to sound the ram's horn or to void at the flag. The point is not so much the content as the act. The dynamic of human consciousness, on which any genuine wisdom takes its stand, is a movement from one's present light to wherever that light leads. "Lead kindly light," Cardinal Newman and others have prayed. Go to your light's source, Augustine and others have counseled. Your light shines in the darkness, and the darkness cannot overcome it—so long as you want to be human, so long as samsara is not your all.

Whatever is noble, whatever is good, whatever is honest—think on it, Paul said. Whatever is your current belief about American religion, face it and start to love it. If it is a solid truth, your personality will ripen, your social circle will take fire. If it is a rotten pseudotruth, you will hear a call to turn and change your heart. In the spiritual life, the only disaster is avoidance. Because they will not face their own beliefs, whether solid or rotten, many stay half-asleep.

Thus, human consciousness becomes intrinsically religious by pursuing the light to where it is love. Worthy religious traditions and patriotism have nothing to fear from this pursuit. The pursuer does have some things to fear, but they pale in comparison with what there is to gain. In Eastern terms, the pursuer learns about ignorance: how much is samsaric in his or her starting "truth." In Western terms, the pursuer learns about sin: how difficult it is to follow only the light. Why we do not know the good we should know, why we do not do the good we should do—they are among our deepest mysteries. Only when you ponder them can you call yourself mature, let alone wise. Still, understanding these mysteries is the major therapy that any self needs. Under-standing them is the heart of traditional political science.

However, the religions' dharma and prophecy illumine more than ignorance and sin. Ultimately they lead to enlightenment and grace. Enlightenment happens: It is an empirical fact. Light floods some people, bringing them inexpressible joy. Similarly, grace happens: There are marvelous saints. They love God with whole mind, heart, soul, and strength. They serve sisters and brothers more than themselves.

In a dark and troubled time (that is, in any historical time), saints and enlightened people save our beleaguered hope. Just one of them is stronger than all the rubbish, all the valid ground for cynicism. For a single really holy, really religious, really humane person says that what we want and need is possible. We want and need light and love. Light and love are possible. By definition, light and love are Buddha-nature and God, our center.

Study Questions

1. To what extent do the religions share a common attraction toward mystery?

2. Explain the following: "The final utility of religion is that it can teach us how to die and how to live."

3. What have been the principal strengths and weaknesses of American religion?

4. Write a brief definition of *religion* that takes into account the traditions' unity and the traditions' diversity.

Appendix A

One Hundred Key Dates in World Religious History

4.6 billion years ago	Formation of the earth
500,000 years ago	Homo erectus using fire
100,000 years ago	Homo sapiens: ritual burial
50,000 years ago	Homo sapiens in Australia
30,000 years ago	Prehistoric painting and sculpture; Mongoloid peoples cross Bering Strait
8,000–6,000 B.C.E.	Agriculture, domestication of animals, rise of towns
4500	Early Jomon period of hunting and gathering in Japan
4000	Casting of bronze
3500	Invention of wheel; Megalith cultures in Britain and Iberia
3100	Unification of Egypt; Invention of writing in Sumer
3000	Farming in central Africa
2750	Growth of civilization in Indus Valley
1600	Shang Bronze Culture in China
1570–1165	New Kingdom in Egypt
1500	Vedas, Rise of Iranian-speaking peoples
1200	Exodus of Hebrews from Egypt
1000	Colonization of Arctic
900	Nubian kingdom of Kush
800–400	Upanishads
750	Homer and Hesiod written down
750–550	Hebrew Prophets
ca. 628–551	Zoroaster
599–527	Mahavira, founder of Jainism
586	Fall of southern kingdom (Judah)
551–479	Confucius
536–476	Buddha
525	Persian conquest of Egypt
525–406	Aeschylus, Sophocles, Euripides
500–200	*Mahabhrata, Ramayana, Bhagavad Gita*
427–347	Plato
350	*Tao Te Ching*
331	Alexander conquers Palestine
273–236	Asoka
200	Rise of religious Taoism
80	Buddhist decline in India
50	Formation of Buddhist canon
5 C.E.	Building of Japanese National Shrine at Ise
30	Death of Jesus of Nazareth
50–95	New Testament writings
70	Romans destroy Jerusalem
80–110	Canonization of Hebrew Bible
220–552	Buddhist missions to China and Japan
304–589	Huns fragment China

325	First Ecumenical Council at Nicaea
400	Fall of Indian Gupta dynasty
451	Council of Chalcedon
500	Compilation of Babylonian Talmud
570–632	Muhammad
637	Islamic invasion of Persia
645	Taika reform—Japan takes Chinese model
650	Canonization of Qur'an
700	Golden Age of Chinese poetry
712–720	Shinto Chronicles
749	First Buddhist monastery in Tibet
750–1258	Abbasid caliphate
762	Foundation of Baghdad
787	Second Council of Nicaea
788–820	Shankara
800–900	Rise of Hindu orthodoxy
845	Persecution of Chinese Buddhists
966	Foundation of Cairo
1054	Mutual anathemas of Rome and Constantinople
1058–1111	Al-Ghazali
1130–1200	Chu Hsi, leading Neo-Confucian
ca. 1135	Maimonides
1175	First Muslim empire in India
1175–1253	Introduction of Pure Land, Zen, and Nichiren schools in Japan
1225–1274	Thomas Aquinas
1453	Ottoman Turks capture Constantinople
1469–1539	Nanak, founder of Sikhism
1473–1543	Nicolaus Copernicus
1492	Expulsion of Jews from Spain
1517	Luther's ninety-five theses
1526–1707	Islamic Mogul Dynasty in India
1549	Francis Xavier in Japan
1565	Roman Catholic colony at St. Augustine
1585	Matteo Ricci in China
1619	Beginning of black slavery in colonial America
1620	Mayflower Compact
1654	Jewish settlement at New Amsterdam
1734	First Great Awakening in New England
1801	Beginnings of revivalism in western United States
1809–1882	Charles Darwin
1818–1883	Karl Marx
1856–1939	Sigmund Freud
1868–1871	Meiji persecution of Buddhism
1869–1948	Mahatma Gandhi
1879–1955	Albert Einstein
1880–1913	Partition of Africa by Western powers
1893	World Parliament of Religions in Chicago
1893–1977	Mao Tse-tung
1894–1905	Japanese victorious in wars with China and Russia
1910	Beginning of Protestant ecumenical movement
1933–1945	Nazi persecution of Jews
1945	Japanese surrender; Disestablishment of Shinto
1947	Partition of Pakistan from India
1948	Creation of state of Israel
1954–1956	Sixth Buddhist Council, Rangoon
1962–1965	Second Vatican Council
1964	Civil Rights Act in United States

Appendix B

Membership Data on Major American Religious Groups (1979)

Adventists, Seventh Day	525,000
Baptists	26,000,000
Buddhists	60,000
Christian Church (Disiples of Christ)	1,260,000
Christian Churches and Churches of Christ	1,050,000
Church of the Nazarene	455,000
Churches of Christ	2,500,000
Eastern Churches (Orthodox)	4,050,000
Episcopal Church	2,820,000
Friends United Meeting (Quakers)	65,000
Jehovah's Witnesses	555,000
Jewish Congregations	5,775,000
Latter Day Saints (Mormons)	2,670,000
Lutherans	8,500,000
Mennonites	100,000
Methodists	13,500,000
Pentecostals	3,300,000
Presbyterians	3,600,000
Roman Catholics	50,000,000
Salvation Army	400,000
Unitarian Universalist Association	200,000
United Churches of Christ	1,800,000

Notes

Introduction

[1]This story is adapted from the Dutch Catholic bishops' work, *A New Catechism* (New York: Herder and Herder, 1967), p. 3.

[2]See Michael Polanyi, *Personal Knowledge* (New York: Harper Torchbooks, 1964); Stephen Toulmin, *Human Understanding* (Princeton, N.J.: Princeton University Press, 1977). For a discussion of Western religion and the distinctive rise of Western science, see Stanley L. Jaki, *The Road of Science and the Ways to God* (Chicago: University of Chicago Press, 1978).

[3]Philip Kapleau, *The Three Pillars of Zen* (Boston: Beacon Press, 1967), pp. 189–291.

[4]For example, Heinz Robert Schlette, *Toward a Theology of Religions* (New York: Herder and Herder, 1966).

[5]Another view of theology, geared to its easier practice in the university, is Shubert Ogden's "Theology and Religious Studies: Their Difference and the Difference It Makes," *JAAR*, 1978, 46(1):3–17.

[6]John Carmody, "Faith in Religious Studies," *Communio*, 1976, 3(1):39–49.

[7]Laurence G. Thompson, *Chinese Religion: An Introduction*, 2nd ed. (Encino, Calif.: Dickenson, 1975), pp. 3–15.

[8]Some of the usual methods of structural analysis are surveyed in Frederick J. Streng, *Understanding Religious Life*, 2nd ed. (Encino, Calif.: Dickenson, 1976). More directly influential on this work is Eric Voegelin, *Anamnesis* (Notre Dame, Ind.: University of Notre Dame Press, 1978).

[9]This cognitional theory is most fully elaborated in Bernard J. F. Lonergan, *Insight: A Study of Human Understanding* (New York: Philosophical Library, 1958).

Chapter One

[1]Shunryu Suzuki, *Zen Mind, Beginner's Mind* (New York: John Weatherhill, 1970), p. xxx.

[2]See John Bowker, *The Sense of God* (Oxford: Clarendon Press, 1973), pp. 57–58, 228.

[3]Sherwood Washburn, "The Evolution of Man," *Scientific American,* 1978, *239*(3):196–197.

[4]E. O. James, "Prehistoric Religion," in *Historia Religionum, I,* ed. C. J. Bleeker and G. Widengren (Leiden: E. J. Brill, 1969), p. 23.

[5]Mircea Eliade, "On Prehistoric Religions," *HR,* 1974, *14*(2):141.

[6]Eric Neumann, *The Origins and History of Consciousness* (Princeton, N.J.: Princeton University Press, 1971), pp. 5–101.

[7]Jacques Waardenburg, ed., *Classical Approaches to the Study of Religion* (The Hague: Mouton, 1973), pp. 3–78.

[8]Barre Toelken, "Seeing with a Native Eye: How Many Sheep Will It Hold?", in *Seeing with a Native Eye,* ed. Walter H. Capps (New York: Harper & Row, 1976), p. 9.

[9]E. G. Parrinder, "Religions of Illiterate Peoples," in *Historia Religionum, II,* ed. C. J. Bleeker and G. Widengren (Leiden: E. J. Brill, 1971), p. 550.

[10]James, "Prehistoric Religion," p. 23.

[11]Bowker, *Sense of God,* pp. 44–65.

[12]Merlin Stone, *When God Was a Woman* (New York: Dial Press, 1976), pp. 1–18. Behind this conception may well lie a more central role for women in biological evolution than they have hitherto been accorded. Recent studies suggest that women were the primary socializers of developing humanity, as well as the source of from 50 to 90 percent of its food. See Nancy Tanner and Adrienne Zihlman, "Women in Evolution, Part I: Innovation and Selection in Human Origins," *Signs,* 1976, *1*(3):585–608; Adrienne L. Zihlman, "Women and Evolution, Part II: Subsistence and Social Organization among Early Hominids," *Signs,* 1978, *4*(1):4–20.

[13]Adolf E. Jensen, *Myth and Cult among Primitive Peoples* (Chicago: University of Chicago Press, 1963), pp. 135–146.

[14]Mircea Eliade, *Cosmos and History* (New York: Harper & Row, 1959), pp. 8–16.

[15]Rudolf Otto, *The Idea of the Holy* (New York: Oxford University Press, 1958), pp. 12–40.

[16]G. Van der Leeuw, *Religion in Essence and Manifestation, I* (New York: Harper & Row, 1963), p. 23.

[17]Bruce Lincoln, "Treatment of Hair and Fingernails among the Indo-Europeans," *HR,* 1977, *16*(4):351–362.

[18]Manabu Waida, "Symbolisms of the Moon and the Waters of Immortality," *HR,* 1977, *16*(4):407–423.

[19]Mircea Eliade, *From Primitives to Zen* (New York: Harper & Row, 1967).

[20]Hartley Burr Alexander, *The World's Rim* (Lincoln: University of Nebraska Press, 1953), pp. 63–99.

[21]Joseph Campbell, *The Masks of God, I: Primitive Mythology* (New York: Viking, 1970), p. 151.

[22]Durango Mendoza, "Summer Water and Shirley," in *American Indian Authors,* ed. Natachee Scott Momaday (Boston: Houghton Mifflin, 1972), pp. 96–105.

[23]Clyde Kluckhohn, *Navaho Witchcraft* (Boston: Beacon Press, 1967), pp. 13–61.

[24]Ruth Underhill, *Red Man's Religion* (Chicago: University of Chicago Press, 1965), p. 51.

[25]Carlos Castaneda, *Tales of Power* (New York: Simon & Schuster, 1974), pp. 118–162.

[26]Annie Dillard, *Pilgrim at Tinker Creek* (New York: Harper's Magazine Press, 1974), pp. 163–164.

[27]Jensen, *Myth and Cult*, pp. 1–79. Also W. Richard Comstock, *The Study of Religion and Primitive Religions* (New York: Harper & Row, 1971), pp. 28–72; John J. Collins, *Primitive Religion* (Totowa, N.J.: Littlefield, Adams, 1978), pp. 55–158.

[28]Marcel Griaule, *Conversations with Ogotemmeli* (London: Oxford University Press, 1965), pp. xi–3.

[29]Bruce Lincoln, "The Indo-European Myth of Creation," *HR*, 1975, *15*(2):121–145.

[30]Victor Turner, "Sacrifice as Quintessential Process: Prophylaxis or Abandonment?", *HR*, 1977, *16*(3): pp. 189–215.

[31]Eliade, *Cosmos and History*, pp. 17–21.

[32]James B. Pritchard, ed., *Ancient Near Eastern Texts*, 3rd ed. (Princeton, N.J.: Princeton University Press, 1969), pp. 100–101.

[33]Joseph Epes Brown, ed., *The Sacred Pipe* (Baltimore: Penguin, 1971), pp. 116–126. Black Elk's exposure to Christianity makes it difficult to consider him a pure ancient spokesperson.

[34]Colin Turnbull, *The Forest People* (New York: Simon & Schuster, 1962), pp. 184–200.

[35]Mircea Eliade, *Myths, Dreams, and Mysteries* (New York: Harper & Row, 1960), pp. 174–175.

[36]Mircea Eliade, *Shamanism* (Princeton, N.J.: Princeton University Press, 1964), pp. 3–13.

[37]Odd Nordland, "Shamanism as an Experiencing of the 'Unreal,'" in *Studies in Shamanism*, ed. Carl-Martin Edsman (Stockholm: Almquist and Wiksell, 1967), pp. 166–185.

[38]Arthur Waley, *The Nine Songs* (London: Allen & Unwin, 1955).

[39]Ichiro Hori, *Folk Religion in Japan* (Chicago: University of Chicago Press, 1968), p. 181.

[40]I. M. Lewis, *Ecstatic Religion* (Middlesex, England: Penguin, 1971).

[41]John Neihardt, *Black Elk Speaks* (Lincoln: University of Nebraska Press, 1961), p. 20.

[42]Napoleon Chagnon, *Yanomamo: The Fierce People* (New York: Holt, Rinehart and Winston, 1968), p. 52.

[43]Carl-Martin Edmans, ed., *Studies in Shamanism* (Stockholm: Almquist and Wiksell, 1967).

[44]Robert E. Ornstein, *The Psychology of Consciousness* (San Francisco: Freeman, 1972), pp. 49–72.

[45]Robert Pirsig, *Zen and the Art of Motorcycle Maintenance* (New York: Morrow, 1974).

[46]Lewis Thomas, *The Lives of a Cell* (New York: Viking, 1974), pp. 69–74.

[47]John Courtney Murray, *The Problem of God* (New Haven: Yale University Press, 1964), sets the Western problem succinctly.

[48]Huub Oosterhuis, *Your Word Is Near* (New York: Newman Press, 1968), p. 151.

[49]See William Richardson, *Heidegger: Through Phenomenology to Thought* (The Hague: Martinus Nijhoff, 1967).

[50]Bernard Lonergan, *Method in Theology* (New York: Herder and Herder, 1972), pp. 101–103.

[51]Erik Erikson, *Toys and Reasons* (New York: Norton, 1977), pp. 67–118.

[52]Carol P. Christ, "Why Women Need the Goddess: Phenomenological, Psychological, and Political Reflections," in *Woman-*

spirit Rising, ed. Carol P. Christ and Judith Plaskow (New York: Harper & Row, 1979), pp. 273–287.

⁵³E. F. Schumacher, *Small Is Beautiful* (New York: Harper Torchbooks, 1973).

Chapter Two

¹Robert Coles, *Children of Crisis,* vol. 4, *Eskimos, Chicanos, Indians* (Boston: Little, Brown, 1977).

²Ibid., p. 522.

³See C. G. Jung, *Memories, Dreams, Reflections* (New York: Vintage, 1963), pp. 246–253.

⁴Weston La Barre, "Amerindian Religions," in *Historical Atlas of the Religions of the World,* ed. I. al Faruqi and D. Sopher (New York: Macmillan, 1974), pp. 51–57.

⁵J. R. Fox, "Religions of Illiterate People: North America," in *Historia Religionum, II,* ed. C. J. Bleeker and G. Widengren (Leiden: E. J. Brill, 1971), pp. 593–608.

⁶A. Clos, "Religions of Illiterate People: Asia," in *Historia Religionum, II,* ed. C. J. Bleeker and G. Widengren (Leiden: E. J. Brill, 1971), pp. 573–592.

⁷Mircea Eliade, *From Primitives to Zen* (New York: Harper & Row, 1967), p. 88.

⁸Paul Radin, *The Trickster: A Study in American Indian Mythology* (New York: Philosophical Library, 1956).

⁹Ruth M. Underhill, *Red Man's Religion* (Chicago: The University of Chicago Press, 1965), p. 104.

¹⁰Charles A. Eastman, *The Soul of the Indian* (Boston: Houghton Mifflin, 1911), pp. 6–8.

¹¹See La Barre, "Amerindian Religions," p. 52.

¹²Emory Sekaquaptewa, "Hopi Indian

Ceremonies," in *Seeing with a Native Eye,* ed. Walter H. Capps (New York: Harper & Row, 1976), p. 39.

¹³La Barre, "Amerindian Religions," p. 53.

¹⁴Dee Brown, *Bury My Heart at Wounded Knee* (New York: Holt, Rinehart and Winston), 1971.

¹⁵Carl F. Starkloff, *The People of the Center: American Indian Religion and Christianity* (New York: Seabury, 1974).

¹⁶Ake Hultzkrantz, "The Contribution of the Study of North American Indian Religions to the History of Religons," in *Seeing with a Native Eye,* ed. Walter H. Capps (New York: Harper & Row, 1976), pp. 86–106.

¹⁷Sam D. Gill, "Native American Religions," *The Council on the Study of Religion Bulletin,* 1978, 9(5):125–128.

¹⁸Ake Hultzkrantz, "North American Indian Religion in the History of Research: A General Survey," *HR,* 1966, 6(2):91–107; 1967, 6(3):183–207; 1967, 7(1):13–34; 1967, 7(2):112–148.

¹⁹Margaret Atwood, *Surfacing* (New York: Popular Library, 1976).

²⁰N. Scott Momaday, "Native American Attitudes to the Environment," in *Seeing with a Native Eye,* ed. Walter H. Capps (New York: Harper & Row, 1976), pp. 79–85.

²¹See Coles, *Children of Crisis,* vol. 4, pp. 216–217.

²²Kaj Birket-Smith, *The Eskimos* (London: Methuen, 1959), p. 161.

²³Franz Boas, *The Central Eskimo* (Lincoln: University of Nebraska Press, 1964), p. 175.

²⁴Ibid., pp. 178–179.

²⁵Birket-Smith, *The Eskimos.*

²⁶Knud Rasmussen, *Across Arctic*

America (New York: Putnam's, 1927), p. 385.

27Ibid., p. 386.

28Ibid., p. 81.

29Ibid., p. 86.

30Mircea Eliade, *Shamanism* (Princeton, N.J.: Princeton University Press, 1964), p. 58.

31Clos, "Religions of Illiterate People: Asia," p. 576.

32Birket-Smith, *Eskimos*, p. 166.

33John J. Collins, *Primitive Religion* (Totowa, N.J.: Littlefield, Adams, 1978), pp. 65–66.

34Peter Freuchen, *Book of the Eskimos* (Cleveland: World, 1961).

35Boas, *Central Eskimo*, p. 201.

36Rasmussen, *Across Arctic America*, p. 261.

37See Colin Turnbull, *The Forest People* (New York: Simon & Schuster, 1962), p. 252.

38John Mbiti, "Traditional Religions in Africa," in *Historical Atlas of the Religions of the World*, ed. I. al Faruqi and D. Sopher (New York: Macmillan, 1974), pp. 61–68.

39Ibid., p. 62.

40For moving literary presentations, see Hamidou Kane, *Ambiguous Adventure* (New York: Collier Books, 1969) on Islam and Chinua Achebe, *No Longer at Ease* (New York: Fawcett, 1969) on Christianity.

41Evan Zuesse, "Divination and Deity in African Religions," *HR*, 1975, 15(2):167, note 15.

42Henri Frankfort, *Kingship and the Gods* (Chicago: University of Chicago Press, 1978), pp. 33–34. (Originally published 1948.)

43Geoffrey Parrinder, *African Traditional Religion*, 3rd ed. (New York: Harper & Row, 1976), p. 17.

44Geoffrey Parrinder, "Religions of Illiterate People: Africa," in *Historia Religionum, II*, ed. C. J. Bleeker and G. Widengren (Leiden: E. J. Brill, 1971), p. 556.

45John Mbiti, *African Religions and Philosophy* (Garden City, N.Y.: Doubleday, 1969), p. 67.

46Parrinder, "Religions of Illiterate People: Africa," p. 561.

47W. Richard Comstock, *The Study of Religion and Primitive Religions* (New York: Harper & Row, 1971), p. 80.

48This paragraph is adapted from Denise Lardner Carmody, *Women and World Religions* (Nashville: Abingdon, 1979), p. 34. See Carol P. MacCormack, "Biological Events and Cultural Control," *Signs*, 1971, 3(1):93–100; also Mbiti, *African Religions and Philosophy*, pp. 165–171.

49Turnbull, *The Forest People*, p. 217.

50See Ian Barbour, ed., *Finite Resources and the Human Future* (Minneapolis: Augsburg, 1976), especially pp. 55–114.

51Parrinder, "Religions of Illiterate People: Africa," p. 564.

52Eliade, *From Primitives to Zen*, p. 269.

53Ibid., p. 268.

54Parrinder, "Religions of Illiterate People: Africa," p. 567.

55Zuesse, "Divination and Deity," pp. 158–182.

56Ibid., p. 167, note 15.

57See Parrinder, *African Traditional Religion*, p. 124.

58This is dramatically portrayed in the anthropological novel by Elenore Smith

Bowen, *Return to Laughter* (Garden City, N.Y.: Doubleday, 1964).

⁵⁹Geoffrey Barraclough, ed., *The Times Atlas of World History* (Maplewood, N.J.: Hammond, 1979), p. 236.

⁶⁰See Patrick White, *A Fringe of Leaves* (New York: Viking, 1977). Also, see White's earlier novel *Voss* (New York: Viking, 1957), especially pp. 237 ff.

⁶¹See Mircea Eliade, *Australian Religions* (Ithaca, N.Y.: Cornell University Press, 1973), p. 194.

⁶²T. G. H. Strehlow, "Religions of Illiterate People: Australia," in *Historia Religionum, II*, ed. C. J. Bleeker and G. Widengren (Leiden: E. J. Brill, 1971), pp. 609–628.

⁶³Emile Durkheim, *The Elementary Forms of the Religious Life* (New York: Free Press, 1965).

⁶⁴Eliade, *Australian Religions*, p. 68.

⁶⁵Eliade, *From Primitives to Zen*, p. 140–141.

⁶⁶Ibid., p. 162.

⁶⁷Rita M. Gross, "Menstruation and Childbirth as Ritual and Religious Experience in the Religion of the Australian Aborigines," *JAAR*, 1977, 45(4):1147–1181.

⁶⁸Eliade, *Australian Religions*, p. 88.

⁶⁹Ibid., p. 92.

⁷⁰Ibid., p. 122.

⁷¹Eliade, *From Primitives to Zen*, p. 424.

Chapter Three

¹Mircea Eliade, *A History of Religious Ideas*, vol. 1, *From the Stone Age to the Eleusinian Mysteries* (Chicago: University of Chicago Press, 1978).

²Ibid., p. 4.

³See Joseph Campbell, *The Masks of God: Primitive Mythology* (New York: Viking, 1970), pp. 173–176; Adolf E. Jensen, *Myth and Cult among Primitive Peoples* (Chicago: University of Chicago Press, 1963), pp. 107–112.

⁴Eliade, *History of Religious Ideas*, vol. 1, pp. 38–39.

⁵Ibid., p. 115.

⁶See Eric Voegelin, *Order and History, I: Israel and Revelation* (Baton Rouge: Louisiana State University Press, 1956), pp. 1–15.

⁷Helmut Ringgren, *Religions of the Ancient Near East* (Philadelphia: Westminster Press, 1973), pp. 1–123; W. H. P. Romer, "The Religion of Ancient Mesopotamia," in *Historia Religionum, I*, ed. C. J. Bleeker and G. Widengren (Leiden: E. J. Brill, 1969), pp. 115–194.

⁸R. Schilling, "The Roman Religion," in *Historia Religionum, I*, ed. C. J. Bleeker and G. Widengren (Leiden: E. J. Brill, 1969), pp. 442–494.

⁹Robert N. Bellah, *The Broken Covenant: American Civil Religion in Time of Trial* (New York: Seabury, 1975).

¹⁰H. R. Ellis Davidson, "Germanic Religion," in *Historia Religionum, I*, ed. C. J. Bleeker and G. Widengren (Leiden: E. J. Brill, 1969), pp. 611–628; Maartje Draak, "The Religion of the Celts," in *Historia Religionum, I*, ed. C. J. Bleeker and G. Widengren (Leiden: E. J. Brill, 1969), pp. 629–646; Fr. Vyncke, "The Religion of the Slavs," in *Historia Religionum, I*, ed. C. J. Bleeker and G. Widengren (Leiden: E. J. Brill, 1969), pp. 647–666.

¹¹Laurette Séjourné, "Ancient Mexican Religion," in *Historia Religionum, I*, ed. C. J. Bleeker and G. Widengren (Leiden: E. J. Brill, 1969), pp. 667–679; Antje Kelm, "The Religion of Ancient Peru," in *Historia Religionum, I*, ed. C. J. Bleeker and G. Widengren (Leiden: E. J. Brill, 1969), pp. 680–691.

[12]See John Fowles, *Daniel Martin* (Boston: Little, Brown, 1977), pp. 493–494.

[13]Henri Frankfort, *Kingship and the Gods* (Chicago: University of Chicago Press, 1978), pp. 15–214.

[14]See Voegelin, *Order and History, I,* pp. 88–95; John A. Wilson, *The Culture of Ancient Egypt* (Chicago: University of Chicago Press, 1956), pp. 58–60.

[15]Voegelin, *Order and History, I,* p. 99.

[16]C. J. Bleeker, "The Religion of Ancient Egypt," in *Historia Religionum, I,* ed. C. J. Bleeker and G. Widengren (Leiden: E. J. Brill, 1969), pp. 47–49.

[17]Voegelin, *Order and History, I,* p. 108.

[18]James B. Pritchard, ed., *Ancient Near Eastern Texts* (Princeton, N.J.: Princeton University Press, 1969), p. 370.

[19]Voegelin, *Order and History, I,* p. 86.

[20]Hans J. Klimkeit, "Spatial Orientation in Mythical Thinking as Exemplified in Ancient Egypt: Considerations toward a Geography of Religions," *HR,* 1975, 14(4):266–281.

[21]Frankfort, *Kingship and the Gods,* pp. 148–212.

[22]C. J. Bleeker, *Egyptian Festivals* (Leiden: E. J. Brill, 1967), pp. 91–123.

[23]C. J. Bleeker, *The Rainbow: A Collection of Studies in the Science of Religion* (Leiden: E. J. Brill, 1975), pp. 167–173.

[24]Pierre Montet, *Everyday Life in Egypt* (Westport, Conn.: Greenwood Press, 1974), p. 51.

[25]Vern L. Bullough, *The Subordinate Sex* (Baltimore: Penguin, 1974), pp. 32–33.

[26]Ibid., p. 39.

[27]John A. Wilson, *Culture of Ancient Egypt,* p. 78.

[28]James B. Pritchard, *Ancient Near Eastern Texts,* p. 34.

[29]Ibid., p. 35.

[30]Jacques Duchesne-Gullemin, *The Hymns of Zarathustra,* trans. M. Henning (Boston: Beacon Press, 1963), p. 1.

[31]R. Ghirshman, *Iran* (Baltimore: Penguin, 1954), p. 27.

[32]Arnold Toynbee, *Mankind and Mother Earth* (New York: Oxford University Press, 1976), pp. 91–116.

[33]Richard Frye, *The Heritage of Persia* (New York: World, 1963), pp. 19–20.

[34]R. C. Zaehner, *The Dawn and Twilight of Zoroastrianism* (New York: Putnam's, 1961), pp. 60–61.

[35]Duchesne-Gullemin, *Hymns of Zarathustra,* p. 135.

[36]Ibid., p. 137.

[37]Isma'il R. al Faruqi, "Zoroastrianism," in *Historical Atlas of the Religions of the World,* ed. I. al Faruqi and D. Sopher (New York: Macmillan, 1974), pp. 133–134.

[38]Eric Voegelin, *Order and History, IV: The Ecumenic Age* (Baton Rouge: Louisiana State University Press, 1974), p. 149.

[39]Ibid., p. 151.

[40]Ibid., p. 152.

[41]Zaehner, *Dawn and Twilight,* p. 99.

[42]Frye, *Heritage of Persia,* p. 190.

[43]Ghirshman, *Iran,* p. 269.

[44]On Manichaeanism, see J. P. Asmussen, "Manicheanism," in *Historia Religionum, I,* ed. C. J. Bleeker and G. Widengren (Leiden: E. J. Brill, 1969), pp. 580–610.

[45]Jacques Duchesne-Gullemin, "The Religion of Ancient Iran," in *Historia Religi-*

onum, I, ed. C. J. Bleeker and G. Widengren (Leiden: E. J. Brill, 1969), pp. 366–367.

⁴⁶Ibid., pp. 358–363.

⁴⁷Emily E. Culpepper, "Zoroastrian Menstruation Taboos," in *Women and Religion*, rev. ed., ed. J. Plaskow and J. A. Romero (Missoula, Mont.: Scholars Press, 1974), pp. 199–210.

⁴⁸Mary Boyce, "Zoroastrianism," in *Historia Religionum, II*, ed. C. J. Bleeker and G. Widengren (Leiden: E. J. Brill, 1971), pp. 228–229.

⁴⁹Eric Voegelin, *Anamnesis* (Notre Dame, Ind.: University of Notre Dame Press, 1978), p. 92.

⁵⁰John Fowles, *The Magus: A Revised Version* (New York: Dell, 1978), p. 69.

⁵¹Toynbee, *Mankind and Mother Earth*, pp. 77–78.

⁵²Phillipe Borgeaud, "The Open Entrance to the Closed Palace of the King: The Greek Labyrinth in Context," *HR*, 1974, *14*(1):1–27; Raymond Christinger, "The Hidden Significance of the 'Cretan' Labyrinth," *HR*, 1975, *15*(2):183–191.

⁵³Eliade, *History of Religious Ideas*, vol. 1, p. 136; K. Kerenyi, "Voraussentzungen in der Einweihung in Eleusis," in *Initiation*, ed. C. J. Bleeker (Leiden: E. J. Brill, 1965), pp. 59–64; M. Mehauden, "Le secret central de l'initiation aux mystères d' Eleusis," in *Initiation*, ed. C. J. Bleeker (Leiden: E. J. Brill, 1965), pp. 65–70.

⁵⁴B. C. Dietrich, *The Origins of Greek Religion* (New York: de Gruyter, 1974), pp. 191–289.

⁵⁵Eliade, *History of Religious Ideas*, vol. 1, pp. 247–250.

⁵⁶W. K. C. Guthrie, *The Greeks and Their Gods* (Boston: Beacon Press, 1955), pp. 73–87.

⁵⁷E. R. Dodds, *The Greeks and the Irra-tional* (Berkeley: University of California Press, 1966), pp. 76–82.

⁵⁸Ibid., pp. 270–282.

⁵⁹Eliade, *History of Religious Ideas*, vol. 1, p. 360.

⁶⁰Dodds, *Greeks and the Irrational*, pp. 6–8.

⁶¹H. J. Rose, *A Handbook of Greek Mythology* (New York: Dutton, 1959), pp. 91–94.

⁶²Edith Hamilton, *Mythology* (New York: New American Library, 1942), pp. 103–105.

⁶³Guthrie, *Greeks and Their Gods*, p. 318.

⁶⁴Ibid., pp. 217–253.

⁶⁵Ibid., pp. 254–306.

⁶⁶See A. W. H. Adkins, "Greek Religion," in *Historia Religionum, I*, ed. C. J. Bleeker and G. Widengren (Leiden: E. J. Brill, 1969), pp. 402–406, 411–422.

⁶⁷Gilbert Murray, *Five Stages of Greek Religion* (New York: Doubleday Anchor, 1955), p. v.

⁶⁸See Eric Voegelin, *Order and History, II: The World of the Polis* (Baton Rouge: Louisiana State University Press, 1957), pp. 203–331.

⁶⁹Ibid., pp. 332–373; Eric Voegelin, *Order and History, IV: The Ecumenic Age* (Baton Rouge: Louisiana State University Press, 1974), pp. 178–183.

⁷⁰John Carmody, "Plato's Religious Horizon," *Philosophy Today*, 1971, *15*(1):52–58.

⁷¹Voegelin, *Order and History, IV*, pp. 187–192; Werner Jaeger, *Aristotle* (New York: Oxford University Press, 1962), pp. 366–406.

⁷²Bernard Lonergan, *Verbum* (Notre

Dame, Ind.: University of Notre Dame Press, 1967).

[73]Jaeger, *Aristotle*, pp. 426–461.

[74]Murray, *Greek Religion*, pp. 119–165; Dodds, *Greeks and the Irrational*, pp. 236–269.

[75]M. J. Vermaseren, "Hellenistic Religions," in *Historia Religionum*, I, ed. C. J. Bleeker and G. Widengren (Leiden: E. J. Brill, 1969), p. 495.

[76]Sharon Kelly Heyob, *The Cult of Isis among Women in the Graeco-Roman World* (Leiden: E. J. Brill, 1975), pp. 111–127.

[77]See Vermaseren, "Hellenistic Religions," pp. 522–533.

[78]Ibid., pp. 523–528.

[79]See Mircea Eliade, *From Primitives to Zen* (New York: Harper & Row, 1967), p. 55.

[80]See Eliade, *History of Religious Ideas*, vol. 1, p. 256.

[81]See Bullough, *Subordinate Sex*, p. 59.

[82]Eliade, *From Primitives to Zen*, p. 540.

Chapter Four

[1]Troy Wilson Organ, *Hinduism* (Woodbury, N.Y.: Barron's, 1974), p. 40; see also Thomas Hopkins, *The Hindu Religious Tradition* (Encino, Calif.: Dickenson, 1971), pp. 3–10; A. L. Basham, *The Wonder That Was India* (New York: Grove Press, 1959), pp. 10–30.

[2]R. N. Dandekar, "Hinduism," in *Historia Religionum*, II, ed. C. J. Bleeker and G. Widengren (Leiden: E. J. Brill, 1971), p. 241; see also Wendy Doniger O'Flaherty, *Asceticism and Eroticism in the Mythology of Shiva* (New York: Oxford University Press, 1973), pp. 8–11.

[3]On the earliest history and religion of the Indian Aryans, see Mircea Eliade, *A History of Religious Ideas*, vol. 1, *From the Stone Age to the Eleusinian Mysteries* (Chicago: University of Chicago Press, 1978), pp. 186–199.

[4]Organ, *Hinduism*, p. 51.

[5]See Edward C. Dimock, Jr., et al., *The Literature of India: An Introduction* (Chicago: University of Chicago Press, 1978), pp. 1–2. Also Satsvarupta dasa Gosvami, *Readings in Vedic Literature* (New York: Bhaktivedanta Book Trust, 1977), pp. 3–4. For an overview of Vedic literature, see James A. Santucci, *An Outline of Vedic Literature* (Missoula, Mont.: Scholars Press), 1976.

[6]Most youths who received the classical training were male. However, there are some indications that in early Hinduism young women could be well educated. For a general view of women in Hinduism, see Denise Lardner Carmody, *Women and World Religions* (Nashville, Tenn.: Abingdon, 1979), pp. 39–65.

[7]On the polarity of the *asuras* and *devas* in Vedic religion, see F. B. J. Kuiper, "The Basic Concept of Vedic Religion," *HR*, 1975, *15*(2):p. 111.

[8]Stella Kramrisch, "The Indian Great Goddess," *HR*, 1975, *14*(4):235–265. As an introduction to the complexity of the Hindu order of the gods, see J. Bruce Long, "Daksa: Divine Embodiment of Creative Skill," *HR*, 1977, *17*(1):29–60.

[9]See Organ, *Hinduism*, p. 66.

[10]See Eliade, *History of Religious Ideas*, vol. 1, pp. 213–214; see also O'Flaherty, *Asceticism and Eroticism*, p. 83; J. Gonda, *Visnuism and Sivaism* (London: Athlone Press, 1970), pp.1–17.

[11]Hopkins, *Hindu Religious Tradition*, pp. 19–35.

[12]Mircea Eliade, *Histoire des croyances et des idées religieuses*, vol. 2, *De Gautama*

Bouddha au triomphe des Christianisme (Paris: Payot, 1978), p. 194.

[13]Robert Ernest Hume, *The Thirteen Principal Upanishads* (New York: Oxford University Press, 1971), pp. 5–13.

[14]Organ, *Hinduism*, p. 102.

[15]See R. C. Zaehner, *Hinduism* (New York: Oxford University Press, 1966), pp. 57–79; see also K. Sivaraman, "The Meaning of *Moksha* in Contemporary Hindu Thought and Life," in *Living Faiths and Ultimate Goals*, ed. S. J. Samartha (Maryknoll, N.Y.: Orbis, 1974), pp. 2–11.

[16]For a comparison of the Vedic and Upanishadic mystiques, see S. N. Dasgupta, *Hindu Mysticism* (New York: Frederick Ungar, 1959), pp. 3–57.

[17]Max Weber, *The Religion of India* (New York: Free Press, 1967), pp. 3–54.

[18]See Eliade, *Histoire des croyances*, vol. 2, pp. 151–153.

[19]Heinrich Zimmer, *Philosophies of India* (Princeton, N.J.: Princeton University Press, 1969),pp. 227–234.

[20]For a brief summary of Jainism, see Carlo Della Casa, "Jainism," in *Historia Religionum, II*, ed. C. J. Bleeker and G. Widengren (Leiden: E. J. Brill, 1971), pp. 346–371; see also A. L. Basham, "Jainism," in *The Concise Encyclopedia of Living Faiths*, ed. R. C. Zaehner (Boston: Beacon Press, 1967), pp. 261–266.

[21]See Dasgupta, *Hindu Mysticism*, pp. 113–168.

[22]Organ, *Hinduism*, p. 150; see also David R. Kinsley, *The Sword and the Flute* (Berkeley: University of California Press, 1975), pp. 1–78.

[23]See John Stratton Hawley, "Thief of Butter, Thief of Love," *HR*, 1979, *18*(3):203–220.

[24]See Kinsley, *Sword and the Flute*; see also Basham, *Wonder That Was India*, pp. 304–306.

[25]Franklin Edgerton, *The Bhagavad Gita* (New York: Harper Torchbooks, 1964), p. 105; see also R. C. Zaehner, *The Bhagavad-Gita* (New York: Oxford University Press, 1973), pp. 1–41; Ann Stanford, *The Bhagavad Gita* (New York: Seabury, 1970), pp. vii–xxvii; Juan Mascaró, *The Bhagavad Gita* (Baltimore: Penguin, 1962), pp. 9–36; Gerald James Larson, "The *Bhagavad Gita* as Cross-Cultural Process," *JAAR*, 1975, *43*(4):651–669.

[26]O'Flaherty, *Asceticism and Eroticism*, pp. 83–110. For specimens of later Dravidian devotional Shaivism, see R. K. Ramanujan, *Speaking of Siva* (Baltimore: Penguin, 1973).

[27]Dimock et al., *Literature of India*, p. 2.

[28]Organ, *Hinduism*, p. 182.

[29]See Cornelia Dimmitt and J. A. B. van Buitenen, eds., *Classical Hindu Mythology* (Philadelphia: Temple University Press, 1978), pp. 38–41.

[30]Zaehner, *Hinduism*, pp. 57–79.

[31]Selections in Sarvepalli Radhakrishnan and Charles A. Moore, eds., *A Sourcebook in Indian Philosophy* (Princeton, N.J.: Princeton University Press, 1957), pp. 184–189.

[32]On the "tripartite Indo-European ideology" (priests-warriors-farmers) that Georges Dumézil has found at the root of Aryan society, see Eliade, *History of Religious Ideas*, vol. 1, pp. 192–195.

[33]See Radhakrishnan and Moore, *Sourcebook in India Philosophy*, pp. 193–223.

[34]Sudhir Kakar, "The Human Life Cycle: The Traditional Hindu View and the Psychology of Erik H. Erikson," *Philosophy East and West*, 1968, *18*:127–136; see also Basham, *Wonder That Was India*, p. 158.

[35]Basham, *Wonder That Was India*, pp. 177–188.

[36]On the six orthodox schools, see Radhakrishnan and Moore, *Sourcebook in India Philosophy*, pp. 349–572; Zimmer, *Philosophies of India*, pp. 280–332 (Samkyha and Yoga), 605–614.

[37]Rudolf Otto, *Mysticism East and West* (New York: Macmillan, 1970).

[38]See Zaehner, *Hinduism*, pp. 36–56; see also R. C. Zaehner, *Hindu and Muslim Mysticism* (New York: Schocken, 1969), pp. 41–63.

[39]See Dimmitt and van Buitenen, *Classical Hindu Mythology*, pp. 59–146.

[40]Glenn E. Yocum, "Shrines, Shamanism, and Love Poetry," *JAAR*, 1973, *61*(1):3–17.

[41]See Zaehner, *Hindu and Muslim Mysticism*, pp. 64–85.

[42]On the Puranic Shiva, see Dimmitt and van Buitenen, *Classical Hindu Mythology*, pp. 59–146. On Shiva in the Tamil literature, see Glenn E. Yocum, "Manikkavacar's Image of Shiva," *HR*, 1976, *16*(1):20–41.

[43]Organ, *Hinduism*, p. 288.

[44]See Zimmer, *Philosophies of India*, pp. 560–602; see also Kees W. Bolle, *The Persistence of Religion* (Leiden: E. J. Brill, 1965); Mircea Eliade, *Yoga: Immortality and Freedom* (Princeton, N.J.: Princeton University Press, 1970), pp. 200–273.

[45]Ernest Wood, *Yoga* (Baltimore: Pelican, 1962), pp. 140–147; see also Eliade, *Yoga*, pp. 244–249.

[46]For a brief survey of Sikhism, see Kushwant Singh, "Sikhism," in *Historical Atlas of the Religions of the World*, ed. I. al Faruqi and D. Sopher (New York: Macmillan, 1974), pp. 105–108; see also John Noss, *Man's Religions* (New York: Macmillan, 1974), pp. 226–235.

[47]However, see Cyrus R. Pangborn, "The Ramakrishna Math and Mission," in *Hinduism: New Essays in the History of Religions*, ed. Bardwell L. Smith (Leiden: E. J. Brill, 1976), pp. 98–119.

[48]See Organ, *Hinduism*, pp. 319–325.

[49]Nervin J. Hein, "Caitanya's Ecstasies and the Theology of the Name," in *Hinduism: New Essays in the History of Religions*, ed. Bardwell L. Smith (Leiden: E. J. Brill, 1976), pp. 15–32; Joseph T. O'Connell, "Caitanya's Followers and the Bhagavad-Gita," in *Hinduism: New Essays in the History of Religions*, ed. Bardwell L. Smith (Leiden: E. J. Brill, 1976), pp. 33–52.

[50]See Edward C. Dimock, Jr., and Denise Levertov, trans., *In Praise of Krishna* (Garden City, N.Y.: Doubleday, 1967).

[51]Following are some representative works: Swami Prabhupada, *The Nectar of Devotion* (Los Angeles: Bhaktivedanta Book Trust, 1970); *Krishna: The Supreme Personality of Godhead*, 3 vols. (Los Angeles: Bhaktivedanta Book Trust, 1970). On the Hare Krishna movement, see J. Stillson Judah, *Hare Krishna and the Counterculture* (New York: Wiley, 1974).

[52]Radical feminist Mary Daly has recently exposed the full horror of suttee; see Mary Daly, *Gyn/Ecology* (Boston: Beacon Press, 1979), chap. 3.

[53]For brief selections from the leading Indian voices of the past century, see Ainslee T. Embree, *The Hindu Tradition* (New York: Vintage, 1972), pp. 278–348.

[54]See Walker G. Neevel, Jr., "The Transformations of Sri Ramakrishna," in *Hinduism: New Essays in the History of Religions*, ed. Bardwell L. Smith (Leiden: E. J. Brill, 1976), pp. 53–97.

[55]Joan Bondurant, *Conquest of Violence*, rev. ed. (Berkeley: University of California Press, 1965).

[56]Erik H. Erikson, *Gandhi's Truth* (New York: Norton, 1969).

[57]See Mohandas K. Gandhi, *An Autobiography: The Story of My Experiments with Truth* (Boston: Beacon Press, 1957).

[58]Eliade, *Yoga*, pp. 47–100.

[59]Dasgupta, *Hindu Mysticism*, pp. 3–30, 33–57, 141–168.

[60]Basham, *Wonder That Was India*, pp. 74–231.

[61]Kuiper, "Basic Concept of Vedic Religion"; see also Bruce Lincoln, "The Indo-European Myth of Creation," *HR*, 1975, *15*(2):121–145.

[62]Basham, *Wonder That Was India*, p. 153.

[63]Zaehner, *Hinduism*, p. 102

[64]Vern L. Bullough, *The Subordinate Sex* (Baltimore: Penguin, 1974), pp. 230–231.

[65]See Basham, *Wonder That Was India*, pp. 186–188.

[66]Noss, *Man's Religions*, p. 188. On the role model that the *Mahabharata* described for women in Draupadi, see Nancy Auer Falk, "Draupadi and the Dharma," in *Beyond Androcentrism*, ed. Rita M. Gross (Missoula, Mont.: Scholars Press, 1977), pp. 89–114. For a sensitive fictional treatment of the modern Indian woman, see Kamala Markandaya, *Nectar in a Sieve* (New York: Signet, 1954).

[67]Bullough, *Subordinate Sex*, p. 232.

[68]Reference in Organ, *Hinduism*, p. 387.

[69]Ibid., p. 29.

[70]For example, Gandhi, *Autobiography*, p. 8.

[71]See Basham, *Wonder That Was India*, pp. 324–325.

[72]A popular version is that by Swami Prabhavanada and Christopher Isherwood, *How to Know God* (New York: Mentor, 1969). The commentary is from the viewpoint of Vedanta, whereas Patanjali's own philosophy was Samkhya.

[73]See David Kinsley, "The Portrait of the Goddess in the Devi-mahatmya," *JAAR*, 1978, *46*(4):489–506.

[74]A good reminder that most Hindus have not directly known or followed the high literary tradition is found in Philip H. Ashby, *Modern Trends in Hinduism* (New York: Columbia University Press, 1974), pp. 7–24.

[75]See Rita M. Gross, "Hindu Female Deities as a Resource for the Contemporary Rediscovery of the Goddess," *JAAR*, 1978, *46*(3):269–291. On the methodological aspects, see Gross's "Androcentrism and Androgyny in the Methodology of History of Religions," in *Beyond Androcentrism*, ed. Rita M. Gross (Missoula, Mont.: Scholars Press, 1977), pp. 7–21. For a vivid study of Kali, see Kinsley, *Sword and the Flute*, pp. 81–159.

Chapter Five

[1]Phillip Kapleau, *The Three Pillars of Zen* (Boston: Beacon Press, 1967), pp. 10–11.

[2]Richard H. Robinson and Willard L. Johnson, *The Buddhist Religion* (Encino, Calif.: Dickenson, 1977), p. 13; see also Trevor Ling, *The Buddha* (London: Temple Smith, 1973), pp. 37–83; Mircea Eliade, *Histoire des croyances et des ideés religieuses*, vol. 2, *De Gautama Bouddha au triomphe des Christianisme* (Paris: Payot, 1978), p. 174.

[3]Edward Conze, *Buddhist Scriptures* (Baltimore: Penguin, 1959), p. 34; see also Eliade, *Histoire des croyances*.

[4]Conze, *Buddhist Scriptures*, pp. 48–49; see also Lowell W. Bloss, "The Taming of Mara," *HR*, 1978, *18*(2):156–176.

[5]Robinson and Johnson, *Buddhist Tradition*, p. 28.

[6]Ibid., p. 31; see also Edward J. Thomas, *The History of Buddhist Thought* (New York: Barnes & Noble, 1951), pp. 58–70; Henry Clarke Warren, *Buddhism in Translations* (New York: Atheneum, 1973), pp. 202–208.

[7]See William Theodore de Bary, ed., *The Buddhist Tradition* (New York: Vintage, 1972), pp. 15–20; see also Edward Conze, *Buddhism: Its Essence and Development* (New York: Harper Torchbooks, 1959), pp. 43–48; I. B. Horner, "Buddhism: The Theravada," in *The Concise Encyclopedia of Living Faiths*, ed. R. C. Zaehner (Boston: Beacon Press, 1967), pp. 283–293.

[8]See Winston L. King, *In the Hope of Nibbana: Theravada Buddhist Ethics* (LaSalle, Ill.: Open Court, 1964).

[9]Texts on wisdom, morality, and meditation are available in Stephen Beyer, *The Buddhist Experience* (Encino, Calif.: Dickenson, 1974); see also Conze, *Buddhist Scriptures.*

[10]Edward Conze, *Buddhist Meditation* (New York: Harper Torchbooks, 1969); see also Nyanaponika Thera, *The Heart of Buddhist Meditation* (London: Rider, 1969).

[11]John Bowker discusses this rather creatively; see John Bowker, *The Religious Imagination and the Sense of God* (Oxford: Clarendon Press, 1978), p. 244; see also Willis Stoesz, "The Buddha as Teacher," *JAAR*, 1978, *46*(2):139–158.

[12]See I. B. Horner, "The Teaching of the Elders," in *Buddhist Texts through the Ages*, ed. Edward Conze (New York: Harper Torchbooks, 1954), pp. 17–50. Also Warren, *Buddhism in Translations*, p. 392; Charles S. Prebish, ed., *Buddhism: A Modern Perspective* (University Park: Pennsylvania State University Press, 1975), pp. 16–26, 49–53; Conze, *Buddhism: Its Essence and Development*, pp. 53–69; Beyer, *Buddhist Experience*, pp. 65–73.

[13]On the laity, see Conze, *Buddhism: Its Essence and Development*, pp. 70–88.

[14]See Conze, *Buddhist Scriptures*, pp. 182–183.

[15]See Warren, *Buddhism in Translations*, pp. 351–353.

[16]See Robinson and Johnson, *Buddhist Religion*, pp. 34–38; on early Indian Buddhist folk religion, see Lowell W. Bloss, "The Buddha and the Naga," *HR*, 1973, *13*(1):36–53.

[17]See Prebish, *Buddhism: A Modern Perspective*, pp. 29–45; see also Edward Conze, *Buddhist Thought in India* (Ann Arbor, Mich.: Ann Arbor Paperbacks, 1967), p. 121; Janice J. Nattier and Charles S. Prebish, "Mahasamghika Origins: The Beginnings of Buddhist Sectarianism," *HR*, 1977, *16*(3):237–272.

[18]Robinson and Johnson, *Buddhist Religion*, p. 77; see also John S. Strong, "Gandhakuti: The Perfumed Chamber of the Buddha," *HR*, 1977, *16*(4):390–406.

[19]Robinson and Johnson, *Buddhist Religion*, p. 81.

[20]Mircea Eliade, *Yoga: Immortality and Freedom* (Princeton, N.J.: Princeton University Press, 1969), pp. 162–199; see also S. N. Dasgupta, *Hindu Mysticism* (New York: Frederick Ungar, 1959), pp. 85–109.

[21]Conze, *Buddhist Meditation*, pp. 100–103.

[22]For general overviews of Mahayana, see Edward Conze, "Buddhism: The Mahayana," in *The Concise Encyclopedia of Living Faiths*, ed. R. C. Zaehner (Boston: Beacon Press, 1967), pp. 296–320; *Buddhist Texts*, pp. 119–217.

[23]Edward Conze, *Buddhist Wisdom*

Books (New York: Harper Torchbooks, 1972), p. 77.

[24]See Joanna Rodgers Macy, "Perfection of Wisdom: Mother of All Buddhas," in *Beyond Androcentrism*, ed. Rita M. Gross (Missoula, Mont.: Scholars Press, 1977), pp. 315–333.

[25]Conze, *Buddhist Wisdom Books*, pp. 101–102.

[26]See Frederick J. Streng, *Emptiness* (Nashville: Abingdon, 1967), pp. 139–152.

[27]See Conze, *Buddhist Thought in India*, pp. 238–244; see also Prebish, *Buddhism: A Modern Perspective*, pp. 76–96; T. R. V. Murti, *The Central Philosophy of Buddhism* (London: Allen & Unwin, 1955).

[28]See Conze, *Buddhist Thought in India*, pp. 250–260; Prebish, *Buddhism: A Modern Perspective*, pp. 97–101; Thomas, *History of Buddhist Thought* pp. 230–248.

[29]Juan Mascaró, trans., *The Dhammapada* (Baltimore: Penguin, 1973), p. 1.

[30]D. T. Suzuki, trans., *The Lankavatara Sutra* (London: George Routledge, 1932).

[31]Conze, *Buddhist Thought in India*, pp. 270–274; Robinson and Johnson, *Buddhist Tradition*, pp. 116–127; Thomas, *History of Buddhist Thought*, pp. 245–248; David Snellgrove, "The Tantras," in Edward Conze, ed., *Buddhist Texts through the Ages* (New York: Harper Torchbooks, 1954), pp. 221–273; Conze, *Buddhism: Its Essence and Development*, pp. 174–199.

[32]Hellmut Hoffmann, *The Religions of Tibet* (London: Allen & Unwin, 1961); Herbert V. Guenther, *Treasures of the Tibetan Middle Way* (Berkeley: Shambhala, 1976).

[33]Beyer, *Buddhist Experience*, pp. 258–261; Eliade, *Yoga*, pp. 249–254.

[34]Robinson and Johnson, *Buddhist Religion*, p. 120.

[35]See Herbert Guenther, trans., *The Life and Teaching of Naropa* (New York: Oxford University Press, 1971), pp. 112–249.

[36]Guenther, *Naropa*, p. 43; see also W. Y. Evans-Wentz, ed., *Tibet's Great Yogi Milarepa* (New York: Oxford University Press, 1969), p. 93.

[37]See Beyer, *Buddhist Experience*, pp. 174–184, 225–229, 258–261.

[38]Stephan Beyer, "Buddhism in Tibet," in *Buddhism: A Modern Perspective*, ed. Charles Prebish (University Park: Pennsylvania State University Press, 1975), pp. 239–247.

[39]Hoffmann, *Religions of Tibet*.

[40]Evans-Wentz, *Milarepa*.

[41]On modern times, see David L. Snellgrover, "Tibetan Buddhism Today," in *Buddhism in the Modern World*, ed. Heinrich Dumoulin (New York: Macmillan, 1976), pp. 277–293.

[42]W. Y. Evans-Wentz, *The Tibetan Book of the Dead* (New York: Oxford University Press, 1960).

[43]There are major qualifications to this statement, of course. On Hinduism in Southeast Asia, see Robinson and Johnson, *Buddhist Tradition*, pp. 129–136; on Hinduism in Indonesia, see Clifford Geertz, *Islam Observed* (Chicago: University of Chicago Press, 1968), pp. 29–43.

[44]For overviews, see R. H. Robinson, "Buddhism: In China and Japan," in *The Concise Encyclopedia of Living Faiths*, ed. R. C. Zaehner (Boston: Beacon Press, 1967), pp. 321–344; C. Wei-hsun Fu, "Mahayana Buddhism (China)," in *Historical Atlas of the Religions of the World*, ed. I. al Faruqi and D. Sopher (New York: Macmillan, 1974), pp. 185–194. Space forbids consideration of the history of Buddhism in the many other Asian lands that it influenced. For treatments on this subject, see Prebish, *Buddhism: A Modern Perspective*. On contemporary issues, see Heinrich Dumoulin, ed.,

Buddhism in the Modern World (New York: Macmillan, 1976).

⁴⁵On Buddhist beginnings in China, see Arthur F. Wright, *Buddhism in Chinese History* (Stanford, Calif.: Stanford University Press, 1959), pp. 21–41. Also Kenneth K. S. Ch'en, "The Role of Buddhist Monasteries in T'ang Society," *HR*, 1976, *15*(3):209–230.

⁴⁶See Heinrich Dumoulin, *A History of Zen Buddhism* (Boston: Beacon Press, 1969), pp. 52–136.

⁴⁷Robinson and Johnson, *Buddhist Religion*, p. 161. For a full discussion of this sutra, see Philip B. Yampolsky, *The Platform Sutra of the Sixth Patriarch* (New York: Columbia University Press, 1967); see also Wing-Tsit Chan, *The Platform Sutra* (New York: St. John's University Press, 1963). Interesting background is Alex Wayman, "The Mirror as a Pan-Buddhist Metaphor-Simile," *HR*, 1974, *13*(4):251–269.

⁴⁸Dumoulin, *History of Zen Buddhism*, p. 88; Yampolsky, *Platform Sutra*, pp. 23–121.

⁴⁹Beatrice Lane Suzuki, *Mahayana Buddhism* (New York: Macmillan, 1969), pp. 63–65; T. O. Ling, *A Dictionary of Buddhism* (New York: Scribner's, 1972), pp. 15–16.

⁵⁰Holmes Welch, "Buddhism in China Today," in *Buddhism in the Modern World*, ed. Heinrich Dumoulin (New York: Macmillan, 1976), pp. 164–178; see also Donald E. MacInnes, *Religious Policy and Practice in Communist China* (New York: Macmillan, 1972).

⁵¹For an introduction to Hua-yen metaphysics, see Francis H. Cook, *Hua-yen Buddhism* (University Park: Pennsylvania State University Press, 1977).

⁵²Robinson and Johnson, *Buddhist Religion*, p. 175.

⁵³Francis H. Cook, "Heian, Kamakura, and Tokugawa Periods in Japan," in *Buddhism: A Modern Perspective*, ed. Charles S. Prebish (University Park: Pennsylvania State University Press, 1975), p. 223.

⁵⁴See Kapleau, *Three Pillars of Zen*, pp. 295–299.

⁵⁵See H. Byron Earhart, *Japanese Religion: Unity and Diversity* (Encino, Calif.: Dickenson, 1974), pp. 85–92; see also Robert N. Bellah, *Tokugawa Religion* (Boston: Beacon Press, 1970).

⁵⁶See Emma McClory Layman, *Buddhism in America* (Chicago: Nelson-Hill, 1976), pp. 52–80.

⁵⁷See, for example, D. T. Suzuki, *Zen and Japanese Culture* (New York: Pantheon, 1959).

⁵⁸Shunryu Suzuki, *Zen Mind, Beginner's Mind* (New York: John Weatherhill, 1970).

⁵⁹See Lama Govinda, *The Psychological Attitude of Early Buddhist Philosophy* (New York: Samuel Weiser, 1969), pp. 77–142.

⁶⁰For instance, Spiro found that the goal of Burmese Buddhists was not nirvana but a better rebirth; see Melford E. Spiro, *Buddhism and Society* (New York: Harper & Row, 1970).

⁶¹On the Buddhist shaping of Chinese folk religion, see Daniel L. Overmyer, "Folk-Buddhist Religion: Creation and Eschatology in Medieval China," *HR*, 1972, *12*(1):42–70.

⁶²Laurence G. Thompson, *The Chinese Way in Religion* (Encino, Calif.: Dickenson, 1973), pp. 77–129; see also Arthur Waley, trans., *Monkey* (New York: Grove Press, 1958); Daniel L. Overmyer, "Boatmen and Buddhas," *HR*, 1978, *17*(3–4):284–302. For Japan, see H. Byron Earhart, *Religion in the Japanese Experience* (Encino, Calif.: Dickenson, 1974), pp. 37–64; Ichiro Hori, *Folk Religion in Japan* (Chicago: University of Chicago Press, 1968), pp. 83–139.

[63]On the relation between Buddhism and the Japanese love of nature, see William LaFleur, "Sagyo and the Buddhist Value of Nature," *HR*, 1973–74, *13*(1,3):93–128, 227–248.

[64]Denise Lardner Carmody, *Women and World Religions* (Nashville: Abingdon, 1979), pp. 45–52; I. B. Horner, *Women Under Primitive Buddhism* (New York: Dutton, 1930).

[65]See Nancy Falk, "An Image of Woman in Old Buddhist Literature: The Daughters of Mara," in *Women and Religion*, rev. ed., ed. J. Plaskow and J. A. Romero (Missoula, Mont.: Scholars Press, 1974), pp. 105–112.

[66]Frank Reynolds, "The Two Wheels of Dhamma," in *The Two Wheels of Dhamma*, ed. Bardwell L. Smith (Chambersburg, Pa.: American Academy of Religion, 1972), pp. 6–30; Bardwell L. Smith, "The Ideal Social Order as Portrayed in the Chronicles of Ceylon," in *Two Wheels of Dhamma*, ed. Smith, pp. 31–57.

[67]King, *Hope of Nibbana*, pp. 176–210.

[68]Eric Voegelin, *Anamnesis: Zur Theorie der Geschichte und Politik* (Munich: R. Piper, 1966), pp. 179–222. This portion is not available in Gerhart Niemeyer's recent translation of *Anamnesis* (Notre Dame: University of Notre Dame Press, 1978). However, it first appeared under the title "The Mongol Orders of Submission to European Powers," in *Byzantion, Vol. XV* (1940/41), pp. 378–413.

[69]See Jane Bunnag, *Buddhist Monk, Buddhist Layman* (Cambridge: Cambridge University Press, 1973); see also Spiro, *Buddhism and Society*, pp. 396–421. On the more spiritual ties among members of the community, see Richard Gombrich, " 'Merit Transference' in Sinhalese Buddhism," *HR*, 1971, *11*(2):203–219.

[70]G. P. Malalasekera, "Theravada Buddhism," in *Historical Atlas of the Religions of the World*, ed. I. al Faruqi and D. Sopher (New York: Macmillan, 1974), p. 172.

[71]John B. Cobb, Jr., "Buddhist Emptiness and the Christian God," *JAAR*, 1977, *45*(1):11–25.

[72]Yoshito S. Hakeda, trans., *The Awakening of Faith* (New York: Columbia University Press, 1967).

[73]Kapleau, *Three Pillars of Zen*, p. 207.

[74]E. F. Schumacher, *Small Is Beautiful* (New York: Harper Colophon, 1973), pp. 50–58.

[75]D. T. Suzuki, *Zen Buddhism* (New York: Anchor Books, 1956), pp. 157–226. On the Taoist influence, see Chang Chung-yuan, *Creativity and Taoism* (New York: Harper Colophon, 1970).

[76]Conze, *Buddhist Thought in India*, pp. 122–134.

[77]The famous Zen ox-herding pictures display the progress toward this freedom. See Kapleau, *Three Pillars of Zen*, pp. 301–313.

[78]Chogyam Trungpa, "Foreword," in *Buddhism: A Modern Perspective*, ed. Charles S. Prebish (University Park: Pennsylvania State University Press, 1975), p. ix.

[79]John Bowker has recently discussed this matter in the illuminating context of information theory; see Bowker, *Religious Imagination*, pp. 244–307.

[80]This point is discussed further in John Carmody, "A Next Step for Roman Catholic Theology," *Theology Today*, 1976, *32*:371–381.

[81]On the broader question of hermeneutics, see Robert A. F. Thurman, "Buddhist Hermeneutics," *JAAR*, 1978, *46*(1):19–39; on the devotional implications of the Buddha's hermeneutical status, see Nancy Falk, "To Gaze on the Sacred Traces," *HR*, 1977, *16*(4):281–293.

[82]Alex Wayman, "Buddhism," in *Historia Religionum, II*, ed. C. J. Bleeker and G. Widengren (Leiden: E. J. Brill, 1971), pp. 393–395; see also Frank E. Reynolds, "The Several Bodies of the Buddha," *HR*, 1977, *16*(4):374–389; B. L. Suzuki, *Mahayana Buddhism*, pp. 52–63.

[83]For a discussion of Chinese Buddhism as religion, see C. K. Yang, *Religion in Chinese Society* (Berkeley: University of California Press, 1970). For a discussion of Zen as religion, see Kapleau, *Three Pillars of Zen*, passim.

[84]Suzuki, *Zen Mind, Beginner's Mind*, pp. 65–67.

[85]C. N. Tay, "Kuan-yin: The Cult of Half Asia," *HR*, 1976, *16*(2):147–177.

[86]Thomas, *History of Buddhist Thought*, pp. 119–132.

[87]On the history of mystery, see Eric Voegelin, *Order and History*, vol. 4, *The Ecumenic Age* (Baton Rouge: Louisiana State University Press, 1974), pp. 316–335.

Chapter Six

[1]See E. Zürcher, *The Buddhist Conquest of China* (Leiden: E. J. Brill, 1972); Kenneth K. S. Ch'en, *Buddhism in China* (Princeton, N.J.: Princeton University Press, 1964).

[2]Laurence G. Thompson, ed., *The Chinese Way in Religion* (Encino, Calif.: Dickenson, 1973), pp. 231–241; Donald E. MacInnes, *Religious Policy and Practice in Communist China* (New York: Macmillan, 1972).

[3]C. K. Yang, *Religion in Chinese Society* (Berkeley: University of California Press, 1970), pp. 294–340.

[4]Karl Jaspers, *The Origin and Goal of History* (New Haven, Conn.: Yale University Press, 1953), p. 2.

[5]Arthur Waley, trans., *Monkey* (New York: Grove Press, 1958).

[6]Laurence G. Thompson, *The Chinese Religion: An Introduction*, 2nd ed. (Encino, Calif.: Dickenson, 1975), pp. 3–15; Joseph Needham, *Science and Civilisation in China*, vol. 2 (Cambridge: University Press, 1969), pp. 216–345.

[7]David N. Keightley, "The Religious Commitment: Shang Theology and the Genesis of Chinese Political Culture," *HR*, 1978, *17*(3–4):213.

[8]Hans Steininger, "The Religions of China," in *Historia Religionum, II*, ed. C. J. Bleeker and G. Widengren (Leiden: E. J. Brill, 1971), pp. 479–482.

[9]*Chuang Tzu*, sec. 6; see Burton Watson, trans., *Chuang Tzu: Basic Writings* (New York: Columbia University Press, 1964), pp. 76, 81.

[10]Thompson, *Chinese Religion*, pp. 21–23; Needham, *Science and Civilisation*, pp. 354–363.

[11]Arthur Waley, *The Nine Songs: A Study of Shamanism in Ancient China* (London: Allen & Unwin, 1955).

[12]Eliade, however, stresses the Chinese shaman's magical flight. See Mircea Eliade, *Shamanism* (Princeton, N.J.: Princeton University Press, 1972), pp. 448–457.

[13]On the ritualistic side of early Chinese shamanism, see Jordan Paper, "The Meaning of the 'T'ao-T'ieh,'" *HR*, 1978, *18*(1):18–41.

[14]Anna Seidel, "Buying One's Way to Heaven," *HR*, 1978, *17*(3–4):419–431.

[15]Donald W. Treadgold, *The West in Russia and China*, vol. 2 (Cambridge: University Press, 1973), pp. 20–26.

[16]Quoted in Thompson, *Chinese Religion*, pp. 30–32.

[17]Mircea Eliade, *Histoire des croyances et des ideés religieuses*, vol. 2, *De Gautama Bouddha au triomphe des Christianisme* (Paris: Payot, 1978), pp. 11–12.

[18]Arthur Waley, trans., *The Analects of Confucius* (New York: Vintage, 1938), pp. 27–29.

[19]A. C. Graham, "Confucianism," in *The Concise Encyclopedia of Living Faiths*, ed. R. C. Zaehner (Boston: Beacon Press, 1967), p. 367.

[20]Thompson, *Chinese Way*, pp. 139–153.

[21]Wing-Tsit Chan, *A Source Book in Chinese Philosophy* (Princeton, N.J.: Princeton University Press, 1963), pp. 84–94.

[22]Ezra Pound, *Confucius* (New York: New Directions, 1969), p. 219.

[23]W. A. C. H. Dobson, trans., *Mencius* (Toronto: University of Toronto Press, 1963), p. 131.

[24]Lee H. Yearley, "Mencius on Human Nature," *JAAR*, 1975, *43*:185–198.

[25]See Eric Voegelin, *Order and History*, vol. 4 (Baton Rouge: Louisiana State University Press, 1974), pp. 272–299.

[26]On Hsun-tzu, see Chan, *Chinese Philosophy*, pp. 115–135; Sebastian de Grazia, *Masters of Chinese Political Thought* (New York: Viking, 1973), pp. 151–181. On Mo-tzu, see Chan, *Chinese Philosophy*, pp. 211–217; de Grazia, *Chinese Political Thought*, pp. 216–246.

[27]Arthur Waley, *Three Ways of Thought in Ancient China* (Garden City, N.Y.: Doubleday, 1956), p. 205.

[28]On this period, see Werner Eichhorn, *Chinese Civilization* (New York: Praeger, 1969), pp. 43–85; H. G. Creel, *The Birth of China* (New York: Reynal and Hitchcock, 1937), pp. 219–380.

[29]H. G. Creel, *What Is Taoism?* (Chicago: University of Chicago Press, 1970), pp. 37–47.

[30]Thomas Merton, *The Way of Chuang Tzu* (New York: New Directions, 1968).

[31]Arthur Waley, trans., *The Way and Its Power* (New York: Grove Press, 1958).

[32]Waley stresses the mystical; Wing-Tsit Chan's *The Way of Lao Tzu* (Indianapolis, Ind.: Bobbs-Merrill, 1963) stresses the pragmatic.

[33]Denise Lardner Carmody, "Taoist Reflections on Feminism," *Religion in Life*, 1977, *44*(2):234–244.

[34]Holmes Welch, *Taoism: The Parting of the Way* (Boston: Beacon Press, 1966), pp. 35–49.

[35]For a sketch of a utopia that is Taoist in spirit if not in origin, see Ernest Callenbach, *Ecotopia* (New York: Bantam, 1977).

[36]*Tao Te Ching*, chap. 5, in *The Way and Its Power* (New York: Grove Press, 1955), p. 147; Chan, *Lao Tzu*, (Indianapolis, Ind.: Bobbs-Merrill, 1963), p. 108, note 2, says: "Straw dogs were used for sacrifices in ancient China. After they had been used, they were thrown away and there was no more sentimental attachment to them."

[37]Current scholarly opinion, however, associates religious Taoism with preaxial religion. See *Encyclopedia Brittanica*, 15th ed., s.v. "Taoism," "Taoism, History of"; N. Sivin, "On the Word 'Taoist' as a Source of Perplexity," *HR*, 1978, *17*(3–4):303–330.

[38]Werner Eichhorn, "Taoism," in *The Concise Encyclopedia of Living Faiths*, ed. R. C. Zaehner (Boston: Beacon Press, 1967), pp. 389–391; Welch, *Taoism*, pp. 151–158.

[39]Welch, *Taoism*, pp. 130–135; K'uan Yu, *Taoist Yoga* (New York: Samuel Weiser, 1973).

[40]Kristofer Schipper, "The Taoist Body," *HR*, 1978, *17*(3–4):355–386.

[41]Edward H. Schafer, "The Jade Woman of Greatest Mystery," *HR*, 1978, *17*(3–4): 393–394.

[42]Chang Chung-yuan, *Creativity and Taoism* (New York: Harper Colophon,

1970), pp. 169–238; Albert C. Moore, *Iconography of Religions* (Philadelphia: Fortress, 1977), pp. 170–180; Raymond Dawson, *The Chinese Experience* (New York: Scribner's, 1978), pp. 199–284.

⁴³C. Wei-husn Fu, "Confucianism and Taoism," in *Historical Atlas of the Religions of the World*, ed. I. al Faruqi and D. Sopher (New York: Macmillan, 1974), p. 121.

⁴⁴Thompson, *Chinese Religion*, p. 123.

⁴⁵Yang, *Religion in Chinese Society*, pp. 265–272.

⁴⁶Graham, "Confucianism," p. 370.

⁴⁷See Chan, *Chinese Philosophy*, pp. 588–653.

⁴⁸This appears in Rodney L. Taylor, "The Centered Self: Religious Autobiography in the Neo-Confucian Tradition," *HR*, 1978, *17*(3–4):266–283.

⁴⁹Thaddeus Chieh Hang T'ui, "*Jen* Experience and *Jen* Philosophy," *JAAR*, 1974, *42*:53–65.

⁵⁰For an absorbing depiction of the tradition from 1661 to 1722, see Jonathan Spence, *Emperor of China: Self Portrait of K'ang-hsi* (New York: Knopf, 1974). As a link to the communist era, see Dawson, *Chinese Experience*, pp. 285–292.

⁵¹Steininger, "Religions of China," p. 468.

⁵²See Thompson, *Chinese Way in Religion*, pp. 231–241; MacInnes, *Religious Policy and Practice*. See also Yang, *Religion in Chinese Society*, pp. 341–404.

⁵³Stuart Shram, *Mao Tse-tung* (Baltimore: Penguin, 1967), p. 23.

⁵⁴Elisabeth Croll, ed., *The Women's Movement in China* (London: Anglo-Chinese Educational Institute, 1974).

⁵⁵Robert Jay Lifton, *Revolutionary Immortality: Mao Tse-tung and the Chinese Cultural Revolution* (New York: Vintage, 1968).

⁵⁶Mao Tse-tung, *Poems* (Peking: Foreign Language Press, 1976).

⁵⁷N. J. Giradot, "The Problem of Creation Mythology in the Study of Chinese Religion," *HR*, 1976, *15*(4):289–318; see also his "Myth and Meaning in the *Tao Te Ching*: Chapters 25 and 42," *HR*, 1977, *16*(4): 294–328.

⁵⁸Alvin P. Cohen, "Concerning the Rain Deities in Ancient China," *HR*, 1978, *17*(3–4):244–265.

⁵⁹See Helmut Wilhelm, *Change: Eight Lectures on the I-ching* (New York: Pantheon, 1960).

⁶⁰Richard Mather, "Buddhism Becomes Chinese," in *The Chinese Way in Religion*, ed. Laurence G. Thompson (Encino, Calif.: Dickenson, 1973), pp. 77–86.

⁶¹Heinrich Dumoulin, *A History of Zen Buddhism* (Boston: Beacon Press, 1969), pp. 52–136.

⁶²Philip Kapleau, *The Three Pillars of Zen* (Boston: Beacon Press, 1967), p. 205.

⁶³Steininger, "Religions of China," pp. 482–487; Creel, *Birth of China*, pp. 204–216.

⁶⁴See Arthur F. Wright, ed., *Confucianism and Chinese Civilization* (New York: Atheneum, 1964).

⁶⁵This is a major theme in Peter Weber-Schafer, *Oikumene und Imperium* (Munich: P. List, 1968).

⁶⁶Vern L. Bullough, *The Subordinate Sex* (Baltimore: Penguin, 1974), p. 249.

⁶⁷Mary Daly, *Gyn/Ecology* (Boston: Beacon Press, 1979), chap. 4. The reference to Dworkin is to her *Woman Hating* (New York: Dutton, 1974), p. 103.

⁶⁸Magery Wolf, "Chinese Women: Old

Skills in a New Context," in *Woman, Culture, and Society*, ed. M. Z. Rosaldo and L. Lamphere (Stanford, Calif.: Stanford University Press, 1974), pp. 157–172.

[69]Denise Lardner Carmody, *Women and World Religions* (Nashville: Abingdon, 1979), pp. 66–72.

[70]Ellen Marie Chen, "Tao as the Great Mother and the Influence of Motherly Love in the Shaping of Chinese Philosophy," *HR*, 1974, *14*(1):51–63.

[71]Yang, *Religion in Chinese Society*, p. 294.

[72]Max Weber, *The Religion of China* (New York: Free Press, 1968), pp. 173–225.

[73]Donald J. Munro, *The Concept of Man in Early China* (Stanford, Calif.: Stanford University Press, 1969).

[74]A. C. Graham, "Chuang Tzu's Essay on Seeing Things as Equal," *HR*, 1969, *9*:137.

[75]Chung-yuan, *Creativity and Taoism*, pp. 123–168.

[76]In her article "Is There a Doctrine of Physical Immortality in the Tao Te Ching?" (*HR*, 1973, *12*(3):231–249), Ellen Marie Chen argues that Lao-tzu did not propose immortality. She also argues against the Taoist character of *The Secret of the Golden Flower* because it is Confucian in emphasizing the yang principle (p. 246, note 22). For the psychodynamics of *The Golden Flower*, see C. G. Jung, "Commentary," in Richard Wilhelm, trans., *The Golden Flower* (New York: Harcourt, Brace & World, 1962), pp. 81–137.

[77]G. Van der Leeuw, *Religion in Essence and Manifestation*, vol. 1 (New York: Harper & Row, 1963), pp. 23–187.

[78]C. N. Tay, "Kuan-yin: The Cult of Half Asia," *HR*, 1976, *16*(2):147–177.

[79]On the original peasant mentality, see Marcel Granet, *The Religion of the Chinese People* (New York: Harper & Row, 1975), pp. 37–56.

[80]David C. Yu, "Chinese Folk Religion," *HR*, 1973, *12*:378–387. On the complexity of so small an item as a Taoist talismanic chart, see Michael Saso, "What Is the Ho-t'u?" *HR*, 1978, *17*(3–4):399–416.

Chapter Seven

[1]H. Byron Earhart, *Japanese Religion: Unity and Diversity*, 2nd ed. (Encino, Calif.: Dickenson, 1974).

[2]Johannes Maringer, "Clay Figurines of the Jomon Period," *HR*, 1974, *14*:128–139.

[3]Carmen Blacker, "The Religions of Japan," in *Historia Religionum, II*, ed. C. J. Bleeker and G. Widengren (Leiden: E. J. Brill, 1971), p. 518.

[4]Earhart, *Japanese Religion*, pp. 11–16.

[5]Ichiro Hori, *Folk Religion in Japan* (Chicago: University of Chicago Press, 1968), pp. 181–251. See also Carmen Blacker, *The Catalpa Bow* (London: Allen & Unwin, 1975).

[6]G. Bownas, "Shinto," in *The Concise Encyclopedia of Living Faiths*, ed. R. C. Zaehner (Boston: Beacon Press, 1967), p. 349.

[7]Ryusaku Tsunoda et al., *Sources of Japanese Tradition*, vol. 1 (New York: Columbia University Press, 1964), pp. 25–26.

[8]Bownas, "Shinto," p. 357.

[9]Ibid.

[10]Chinese culture began to penetrate Japan at least as early as 57 C.E. See Arnold Toynbee, ed., *Half the World* (New York: Holt, Rinehart and Winston, 1973), p. 184.

[11]Earhart, *Japanese Religion*, pp. x–xi.

[12]Francis H. Cook, "Japanese Innovations in Buddhism," in *Buddhism: A Modern Perspective*, ed. Charles S. Prebish (University Park: Pennsylvania State University Press, 1975), pp. 229–233.

[13]William LaFleur, "Saigyo and the Buddhist Value of Nature," *HR*, 1973–74, *13*:93–128, 227–248.

[14]Peter Beilenson, trans., *Japanese Haiku* (Mount Vernon: Peter Pauper Press, 1956), p. 11. Reprinted by permission.

[15]Ibid., p. 13. Reprinted by permission.

[16]Yasunari Kawabata, *Thousand Cranes* (New York: Berkley Medallion, 1968).

[17]Yasunari Kawabata, *The Master of Go* (Rutland, Vt.: Tuttle, 1973).

[18]Yasunari Kawabata, *The Sound of the Mountain* (Rutland, Vt.: Tuttle, 1971).

[19]Earhart, *Japanese Religion*, p. 73.

[20]See Tsunoda et al., *Sources of Japanese Tradition*, pp. 261–276.

[21]Shusaku Endo, *Silence* (Rutland, Vt.: Tuttle, 1969).

[22]Robert N. Bellah, *Tokugawa Religion* (Boston: Beacon Press, 1970), pp. 90–98.

[23]John B. Noss, *Man's Religions*, 5th ed. (New York: Macmillan, 1974), p. 324.

[24]Denise Lardner Carmody, *Women and World Religions* (Nashville: Abingdon, 1979), p. 84.

[25]Edwin O. Reischauer, *Japan Past and Present*, 3rd ed. rev. (Tokyo: Tuttle, 1964), pp. 108–141.

[26]H. Byron Earhart, *Religion in the Japanese Experience* (Encino, Calif.: Dickenson, 1974), pp. 201–210; see also Ryusaku Tsunoda et al., *Sources of Japanese Tradition*, vol. 2 (New York: Columbia University Press, 1964), pp. 131–210.

[27]Earhart, *Religion in the Japanese Experience*, p. 204.

[28]Joseph Kitagawa, "The Japanese *Kokutai* (National Community): History and Myth," *HR*, 1974, *13*:209–226.

[29]See Blacker, *Catalpa Bow*, pp. 130–132.

[30]Earhart, *Japanese Religion*, p. 112.

[31]Ibid., pp. 114–117.

[32]Y. T. Hosoi, "The Sacred Tree in Japanese Prehistory," *HR*, 1976, *16*:95–119.

[33]Manabu Waida, "Symbolisms of the Moon and the Waters of Immortality," *HR*, 1977, *16*:407–423.

[34]See Blacker, *Catalpa Bow*, and Hori, *Folk Religion in Japan*, for the shamanistic exceptions to this statement.

[35]See Lynn White, Jr., "The Historical Roots of Our Ecological Crisis," in *Ecology and Religion in History*, ed. David and Eileen Spring (New York: Harper Torchbooks, 1974), pp. 15–31. The other articles in this volume suggest the sort of qualifications one would expect in discussing Japanese ecology. See especially Yi-Fu Tuan, "Discrepancies between Environmental Attitude and Behaviour," pp. 91–113.

[36]On contemporary professional and business life in Japan, see Ichiro Kawasaki, *Japan Unmasked* (Rutland, Vt.: Tuttle, 1969); Nobutaka Ike, *Japan: The New Superstate* (Stanford, Calif.: Stanford Alumni Association, 1973).

[37]Earhart, *Religion in the Japanese Experience*, pp. 145–159.

[38]Kitagawa, "The Japanese *Kokutai*."

[39]Alan Miller, "Ritsuryo Japan: The State as Liturgical Community," *HR*, 1971, *11*:98–124.

[40]Manabu Waida, "Sacral Kingship in Early Japan," *HR*, 1976, *15*:319–342.

[41]Winston Davis, "Ittoen: The Myths and Rituals of Liminality," *HR*, 1975, *14*:282–321; 1975, *15*:1–33.

[42]Alfred North Whitehead, *Religion in the Making* (New York: Meridian, 1960), p. 16.

[43]Yukio Mishima has brought this lovely Zen temple into recent Japanese religious consciousness. See his *The Temple of the Golden Pavilion* (Rutland, Vt.: Tuttle, 1959).

[44]Patrick White, *The Vivisector* (New York: Viking, 1970).

[45]Chang Chung-yun, *Creativity and Taoism* (New York: Harper Colophon, 1970).

[46]G. Bownas, "Shinto."

[47]Carmen Blacker, "Religions of Japan."

[48]We would begin that business with Bernard Lonergan's *Insight* (New York: Philosophical Library, 1958), pp. 595–633.

[49]Bellah, *Tokugawa Religion*, pp. 107–132, 178–197.

[50]Mircea Eliade, *From Primitives to Zen* (New York: Harper & Row, 1967), pp. 452–454.

[51]Considering Shinran as a bodhisattva would force us to adjust this judgment. See Robert N. Bellah, "The Contemporary Meaning of Kamakura Buddhism," *JAAR*, 1974, *42*:7–9.

[52]See Shunryu Suzuki, *Zen Mind, Beginner's Mind* (New York: John Weatherhill, 1970), pp. 92–95, 102–104.

[53]Earhart, *Religion in the Japanese Experience*, p. 25.

Chapter Eight

[1]Michael Avi-Yonah et al., *Jerusalem* (Jerusalem: Keter, 1973); Robert L. Cohn, "Jerusalem: The Senses of a Center," *JAAR*, 1978, *46*(1), Supplement F; Giora Shamis and Diane Shalem, *The Jerusalem Guide* (Jerusalem: Abraham Marcus, 1973).

[2]Gerhard Kressel et al., *Zionism* (Jerusalem: Keter, 1973).

[3]Jacob A. Argus, "Judaism," in *Historical Atlas of the Religions of the World*, ed. I. al Faruqi and D. Sopher (New York: Macmillan, 1974), p. 156.

[4]R. J. Zwi Werblowsky, "Judaism," in *Historia Religionum, II*, ed. C. J. Bleeker and G. Widengren (Leiden: E. J. Brill, 1971), p. 1.

[5]Herbert May, ed., *Oxford Bible Atlas*, 2nd ed. (New York: Oxford University Press, 1974), p. 57; G. Widengren, "Israelite-Jewish Religion," in *Historia Religionum, I*, ed. C. J. Bleeker and G. Widengren (Leiden: E. J. Brill, 1969), p. 226.

[6]Isadore Epstein, *Judaism* (London: Penguin, 1959), pp. 12–14; Eric Voegelin, *Order and History*, vol. 1 (Baton Rouge: Louisiana State University Press, 1956), pp. 188–195.

[7]I. al Faruqi and D. Sopher, eds., *Historical Atlas of the Religions of the World* (New York: Macmillan, 1974), p. 286.

[8]John L. McKenzie, S. J., *Dictionary of the Bible* (Milwaukee, Wis.: Bruce, 1965), pp. 153–157.

[9]William Foxwell Albright, "The Biblical Period," in *The Jews: Their History*, ed. Louis Finkelstein (New York: Schocken, 1970), pp. 15–19.

[10]See Samuel Sandmel, *The Enjoyment of Scripture* (New York: Oxford University Press, 1972), pp. 164–175.

[11]For example, Roland Murphy, "Introduction to Wisdom Literature," *The Jerome Biblical Commentary*, vol. 1, ed. R. Brown, J. Fitzmyer, and R. Murphy (Englewood Cliffs, N.J.: Prentice-Hall, 1968), p. 487.

[12]John J. Collins, "The Jewish Apocalypse," in *Apocalypse: The Morphology of a Genre*, ed. John J. Collins (Missoula, Mont.: Scholars Press, 1979), pp. 21–59.

[13]Eric Voegelin, *Order and History*, vol. 4 (Baton Rouge: Louisiana State University Press, 1974), pp. 117–133, 153–165.

[14]Victor Tcherikover, *Hellenistic Civilization and the Jews* (New York: Atheneum, 1974), pp. 152–234.

[15]Joseph Fitzmyer, "A History of Israel," in *The Jerome Biblical Commentary*, vol. 2, ed. R. Brown, J. Fitzmyer, and R. Murphy (Englewood Cliffs, N.J.: Prentice-Hall, 1968), p. 692; Judah Goldin, "The Period of the Talmud," in *The Jews: Their History*, ed. Louis Finkelstein (New York: Schocken, 1970), pp. 121–129.

[16]*Encyclopedia Judaica*, s.v. "Talmud, Babylonian."

[17]See Jacob Neusner, "Form and Meaning in Mishnah," *JAAR*, 1977, 45(1):27–54; "History and Structure: The Case of the Mishnah," *JAAR*, 1977, 45(2):161–192.

[18]R. Travers Herford, *Pirke Aboth: The Ethics of the Talmud* (New York: Schocken, 1962).

[19]Renée Bloch, "Midrash," in *Approaches to Ancient Judaism*, ed. William Scott Green (Missoula, Mont.: Scholars Press, 1978), pp. 19–50; Nahum N. Glatzer, ed., *Hammer on the Rock* (New York: Schocken, 1962).

[20]Epstein, *Judaism*, pp. 121–194. On the Talmud's view of prophecy (which its law was somewhat trying to replace), see Nahum N. Glatzer, "A Study of the Talmudic-Midrashic Interpretation of Prophecy," in his *Essays in Jewish Thought* (University, Ala.: University of Alabama Press, 1978), pp. 16–35.

[21]See Jacob Neusner, *The Life of Torah* (Encino, Calif.: Dickenson, 1974), pp. 17–24.

[22]Epstein, *Judaism*, p. 140.

[23]See Robert Goldenberg, *The Sabbath Law of Rabbi Meir* (Missoula, Mont.: Scholars Press, 1978), pp. 159–264.

[24]For a contemporary view of the Sabbath, see Richard Siegel et al., *The Jewish Catalogue* (Philadelphia: Jewish Publication Society of America, n.d.), pp. 103–116.

[25]For an overview of the medieval period, see Jacob B. Argus, *The Meaning of Jewish History*, vol. 2 (New York: Abelard-Schuman, 1963), pp. 232–297.

[26]Epstein, *Judaism*, p. 180.

[27]On this whole question, see S. D. Goitein, *Jews and Arabs* (New York: Schocken, 1955).

[28]Epstein, *Judaism*, p. 191.

[29]See Julius Gutmann, *Philosophies of Judaism* (New York: Holt, Reinhart and Winston, 1964).

[30]Moses Maimonides, *The Guide for the Perplexed*, 2nd ed., trans. M. Friedlander (New York: Dover, 1956), p. 11.

[31]R. J. Zwi Werblowsky, "Judaism, or the Religion of Israel," in *The Concise Encyclopedia of Living Faiths*, ed. R. C. Zaehner (Boston: Beacon Press, 1967), pp. 45–48.

[32]Gershom G. Scholem, *Major Trends in Jewish Mysticism* (New York: Schocken, 1961).

[33]See J. Doresse, "Gnosticism," in *Historia Religionum, I*, ed. C. J. Bleeker and G. Widengren (Leiden: E. J. Brill, 1969), pp. 536–537.

[34]Werblowsky, "Judaism," p. 24.

[35]See Gershom G. Scholem, ed., *Zohar: The Book of Splendor* (New York: Schocken, 1963), pp. 12–21.

[36]Argus, *Jewish History*, pp. 300–485; Cecil Roth, *A History of the Jews* (New York: Schocken, 1961), pp. 235–424.

[37]Roth, *History of the Jews*, pp. 180–294.

[38]Leon Poliakov, *The History of Anti-Semitism* (New York: Schocken, 1974).

[39]See Elie Wiesel, *Souls on Fire* (New York: Vintage, 1973).

[40]Mark Zborowski and Elizabeth Herzog, *Life Is with People* (New York: Schocken, 1962).

[41]Martin Buber, *Hasidism and Modern Man* (New York: Harper Torchbooks, 1966).

[42]Abraham J. Heschel, *Man's Quest for God* (New York: Scribner's, 1954); *God in Search of Man* (New York: Farrar, Straus & Giroux, 1955).

[43]Argus, "Judaism," p. 152.

[44]Jacob Neusner, *The Way of Torah*, 2nd ed. (Encino, Calif.: Dickenson, 1974), pp. 68–71.

[45]Arthur Green, "The *Zaddiq* as *Axis Mundi* in Later Judaism," *JAAR*, 1977, *45*(3):327–347.

[46]Martin Buber, *Tales of the Hasidim*, 2 vols. (New York: Schocken, 1947–48).

[47]Elie Wiesel, *The Gates of the Forest* (New York: Avon, 1966), pp. 6–10.

[48]On this conflict in the United States, see Sydney Ahlstrom, *A Religious History of the American People* (New Haven, Conn.: Yale University Press, 1972), pp. 969–984; also Neusner, *Life of Torah*, pp. 156–203.

[49]Argus, "Judaism," p. 154.

[50]Eva Fleischner, "A Select Annotated Bibliography on the Holocaust," *Horizons*, 1977, *4*(1):61–83.

[51]See, for example, Rosemary Ruether, *Faith and Fratricide* (New York: Seabury, 1974).

[52]See McKenzie, *Dictionary of the Bible*.

[53]Werblowsky, "Judaism, or the Religion of Israel."

[54]Geoffrey Wigoder et al., *Jewish Values* (Jerusalem: Keter, 1974).

[55]Voegelin, *Order and History*, vol. 4, chaps. 1, 3, 7.

[56]Salo Wittmayer Baron, *A Social and Religious History of the Jews*, vol. 1, *Ancient Times*, 2nd ed. (New York: Columbia University Press, 1952), pp. 4–16.

[57]Sherry B. Ortner, "Is Female to Male as Nature Is to Culture?" in *Woman, Culture and Society*, ed. M. Z. Rosaldo and L. Lamphere (Stanford, Calif.: Stanford University Press, 1974), pp. 67–88.

[58]Phyllis Bird, "Images of Women in the Old Testament," in *Religion and Sexism*, ed. Rosemary Radford Ruether (New York: Simon & Schuster, 1974), pp. 41–88.

[59]Judith Hauptmann, "Images of Women in the Talmud," in *Religion and Sexism*, ed. Rosemary Radford Ruether (New York: Simon & Schuster, 1974), pp. 184–212. On Mishnaic menstrual taboos, see Jacob Neusner, *A History of the Mishnaic Law of Purities* (Leiden: E. J. Brill, 1977), pt. 22.

[60]I. Epstein, "The Jewish Woman in the Responsa: 900 C.E.–1500 C.E.," *Response*, Summer 1973, no. 16, pp. 23–31.

[61]For an overview of women in Judaism, see Denise Lardner Carmody, *Women and World Religions* (Nashville: Abingdon, 1979), pp. 92–112. For current issues, see Carol P. Christ and Judith Plaskow, eds., *Womanspirit Rising* (New York: Harper & Row, 1979); Elizabeth Koltun, ed., *The Jewish Woman: New Perspectives* (New York: Schocken, 1976).

[62]On this point, Robert L. Cohn reminded us of Hillel's saying, "Sever not thyself from the congregation" (*Pirke Avot*, 2:5).

[63]Richard L. Rubenstein, *After Auschwitz* (Indianapolis, Ind.: Bobbs-Merrill, 1966).

[64]Emil Fackenheim, *God's Presence in History* (New York: New York University Press, 1970).

[65]Hanna Arendt, *Eichmann in Jerusalem* (New York: Viking, 1965).

[66]See Elie Wiesel, *The Oath* (New York: Random House, 1973).

[67]See, for example, Joel Blocker, ed., *Israeli Stories* (New York: Schocken, 1965).

[68]Michael Polanyi and Harry Prosch, *Meaning* (Chicago: University of Chicago Press, 1975). That does not mean, however, that the Talmud did not meditate deeply on Jewish divinity. See A. Cohen, *Everyman's Talmud* (New York: Schocken, 1975), pp. 1–26. For a contemporary view, see Leo Baeck, *The Essence of Judaism* (New York: Schocken, 1961), pp. 83–150.

[69]See Lewis S. Ford, *The Lure of God* (Philadelphia: Fortress, 1978).

[70]Friedrich Heiler, *Prayer* (New York: Oxford University Press, 1932).

Chapter Nine

[1]For a brief study of Christianity that includes fine maps of its spread, see Gerald Sloyan, "Christianity," in *Historical Atlas of the Religions of the World*, ed. I. al Faruqi and D. Sopher (New York: Macmillan, 1974), pp. 201–236.

[2]One of the most thorough recent treatments of the critical and theological issues concerning Jesus is Edward Schillebeeckx, *Jesus* (New York: Seabury, 1979).

[3]See Raymond E. Brown, *The Birth of the Messiah* (New York: Doubleday, 1977).

[4]Geza Vermes, *Jesus the Jew* (London: Fontana, 1976), pp. 18–82.

[5]Joachim Jeremias, *New Testament Theology: The Proclamation of Jesus* (New York: Scribner's, 1971), pp. 29–36.

[6]Karl Rahner and Herbert Vorgrimler, *Theological Dictionary* (New York: Herder and Herder, 1965), pp. 236–241.

[7]A succinct discussion of New Testament ethics is J. L. Houden, *Ethics and the New Testament* (New York: Oxford University Press, 1977).

[8]Jeremias, *New Testament Theology*, pp. 250–257.

[9]See Eric Voegelin, "The Gospel and Culture," in *Jesus and Man's Hope*, vol. 2, ed. D. Miller and D. Hadidian (Pittsburgh: Pittsburgh Theological Seminary, 1971), pp. 59–101.

[10]Joseph A. Fitzmyer, "Pauline Theology," in *The Jerome Biblical Commentary*, vol. 2, ed. R. Brown, J. Fitzmyer, and R. Murphy (Englewood Cliffs, N.J.: Prentice-Hall, 1968), pp. 810–827.

[11]On the problems of writing the history of the realities of Christian faith, see Van A. Harvey, *The Historian and the Believer* (New York: Macmillan, 1966).

[12]Recent and readable is Stephen Neill, *Jesus through Many Eyes* (Philadelphia: Fortress, 1976). For a literary stress, see Leonard L. Thompson, *Introducing Biblical Literature* (Englewood Cliffs, N.J.: Prentice-Hall, 1978), pp. 213–307.

[13]Antonio Javierre, "Apostle," in *Sacramentum Mundi*, vol. 1, ed. Karl Rahner et al. (New York: Herder and Herder, 1968), p. 77.

[14]Raymond E. Brown et al., eds., *Peter in the New Testament* (Minneapolis, Minn.: Augsburg, 1973).

[15]See Maxwell Staniforth, trans., *Early Christian Writings* (Baltimore: Penguin, 1968).

[16]J. Doresse, "Gnosticism," in *Historia Religionum, I*, ed. C. J. Bleeker and G. Widengren (Leiden: E. J. Brill, 1969), pp. 536–537.

[17]Succinct information on personages such as these is available in F. L. Cross, ed., *The Oxford Dictionary of the Christian Church* (New York: Oxford University Press, 1966).

[18]See Jaroslav Pelikan, *The Christian Tradition, 1: The Emergence of the Catholic Tradition* (Chicago: University of Chicago Press, 1971).

[19]J. G. Davies, "Christianity: The Early Church," in *The Concise Encyclopedia of Living Faiths*, ed. R. C. Zaehner (Boston: Beacon Press, 1967), pp. 60–69.

[20]On patristic terminology, see G. L. Prestige, *God in Patristic Thought* (London: Society for the Promotion of Christian Knowledge, 1959).

[21]Bernard Lonergan, *The Way to Nicaea* (Philadelphia: Westminster, 1976).

[22]Eric Voegelin, *Science, Politics and Gnosticism* (Chicago: Gateway, 1968), pp. 22–28.

[23]William A. Clebsch, *Christianity in European History* (New York: Oxford University Press, 1979), pp. 29–84; Stephen Reynolds, *The Christian Religious Tradition* (Encino, Calif.: Dickenson, 1977), pp. 35–77.

[24]Thomas Merton, *The Wisdom of the Desert* (New York: New Directions, 1960).

[25]Nicholas Zernov, "Christianity: The Eastern Schism and the Eastern Orthodox Church," in *The Concise Encyclopedia of Living Faiths*, ed. R. C. Zaehner (Boston: Beacon Press, 1967), p. 86.

[26]Donald W. Treadgold, *The West in Russia and China*, vol. 1 (Cambridge: University Press, 1973), pp. 1–23.

[27]On classical Eastern theology, see Jaroslav Pelikan, *The Christian Tradition, 2: The Spirit of Eastern Christendom* (Chicago: University of Chicago Press, 1974); see also G. P. Fedotov, *The Russian Religious Mind* (Cambridge, Mass.: Harvard University Press, 1966).

[28]See Timothy Ware, *The Orthodox Church* (Baltimore: Penguin, 1964).

[29]Bernhard Schultze, "Eastern Churches," in *Sacramentum Mundi*, vol. 2, ed. Karl Rahner et al. (New York: Herder and Herder, 1968), pp. 120–133.

[30]C. W. Monnich, "Christianity," in *Historia Religionum, II*, ed. C. J. Bleeker and G. Widengren (Leiden: E. J. Brill, 1971), p. 65.

[31]Jaroslav Pelikan, *The Christian Tradition, 3: The Growth of Medieval Theology* (Chicago: University of Chicago Press, 1978), pp. 268–307.

[32]Anthony Kenney, ed., *Aquinas* (New York: Doubleday, 1969); see also H. Francis Davis, "St. Thomas and Medieval Theology," in *The Concise Encyclopedia of Living Faiths*, ed. R. C. Zaehner (Boston: Beacon Press, 1967), pp. 108–112.

[33]On the history of the notion of reform, see Gerhart B. Ladner, *The Idea of Reform* (Cambridge, Mass.: Harvard University Press, 1959).

[34]Erik H. Erikson, *Young Man Luther* (New York: Norton, 1962).

[35]*The New Columbia Encyclopedia*, s.v. "plague."

[36]See Pennethorne Hughes, *Witchcraft* (Baltimore: Penguin, 1965).

[37]John Kent, "Christianity: Protestantism," in *The Concise Encyclopedia of Living*

Faiths, ed. R. C. Zaehner (Boston: Beacon Press, 1967), pp. 117–149.

[38]Owen Chadwick, *The Reformation* (Baltimore: Penguin, 1964), p. 41.

[39]See Lewis Spitz, ed., *The Protestant Reformation* (Englewood Cliffs, N.J.: Prentice-Hall, 1966).

[40]C. W. Monnich, "Christianity," p. 72.

[41]See William A. Clebsch, *American Religious Thought* (Chicago: University of Chicago Press, 1973), pp. 11–56.

[42]James Brodrick, *The Origin of the Jesuits* (London: Longmans, 1940); *The Progress of the Jesuits* (London: Longmans, 1946).

[43]Sidney E. Mead, *The Lively Experiment* (New York: Harper & Row, 1976); *The Nation with the Soul of a Church* (New York: Harper & Row, 1975); see also Sidney E. Ahlstrom, *A Religious History of the American People* (New Haven, Conn.: Yale University Press, 1972), pp. 121–229.

[44]Harvey D. Egan, *The Spiritual Exercises and the Ignatian Mystical Horizon* (St. Louis: Institute of Jesuit Sources, 1976); Gaston Fessard, *La dialectique des exercices spirituels de saint ignace de loyola* (Paris: Aubier, 1956).

[45]Robert McAfee Brown, *The Spirit of Protestantism* (New York: Oxford University Press, 1965).

[46]Max Weber, *The Protestant Ethic and the Spirit of Capitalism* (New York: Scribner's, 1958).

[47]Heribert Raab, "Enlightenment," in *Sacramentum Mundi*, vol. 2, ed. Karl Rahner et al. (New York: Herder and Herder, 1968), p. 230; see also Crane Brinton, "Enlightenment," in *The Encyclopedia of Philosophy*, vol. 2, ed. Paul Edwards (New York: Macmillan, 1967), pp. 519–525.

[48]See the articles by Sidney E. Mead, Sydney E. Ahlstrom, Vincent Harding, and Robert Bellah in *Soundings*, 1978, 61(3):303–371.

[49]Eric Voegelin, *From Enlightenment to Revolution* (Durham, N.C.: Duke University Press, 1975).

[50]The breakthrough work was Gustavo Gutierrez, *A Theology of Liberation* (Maryknoll, N.Y.: Orbis, 1973). Especially provocative is Jose Miranda, *Marx and the Bible* (Maryknoll, N.Y.: Orbis, 1974). A fine survey that brings liberation thought to the United States is Robert McAfee Brown, *Theology in a New Key* (Philadelphia: Westminster, 1978).

[51]See Sergio Torres and John Eagleson, eds., *Theology in the Americas* (Maryknoll, N.Y.: Orbis, 1976).

[52]Martin E. Marty, *Righteous Empire* (New York: Dial Press, 1970).

[53]Robert Bellah, *The Broken Covenant* (New York: Seabury, 1975).

[54]See Voegelin, *Science, Politics and Gnosticism*; see also his *The New Science of Politics* (Chicago: University of Chicago Press, 1952).

[55]Carnegie Samuel Calian, *The Gospel According to the "Wall Street Journal"* (Atlanta: John Knox, 1975).

[56]See Sam D. Gill, "Native American Religions," *The Council on the Study of Religion Bulletin*, 1978, 9(5):125–128.

[57]Peter L. Berger, *A Rumor of Angels* (Garden City, N.Y.: Doubleday, 1969).

[58]Jorg Splett et al., "Nature," in *Sacramentum Mundi*, vol. 4, ed. Karl Rahner et al. (New York: Herder and Herder, 1969), pp. 171–181.

[59]Pieter Smulders et al., "Creation," in *Sacramentum Mundi*, vol. 2, ed. Karl Rahner et al. (New York: Herder and Herder, 1968), pp. 23–37.

[60]See Harold K. Schilling, *The New Consciousness in Science and Religion* (Philadelphia: United Church Press, 1973).

[61]Alfred North Whitehead, *Process and Reality* (New York: Harper Torchbooks, 1960).

[62]See Staniforth, *Early Christian Writings*, pp. 171–185.

[63]See Bernard Cooke, *Ministry to Word and Sacrament* (Philadelphia: Fortress, 1976).

[64]Edward Schillebeeckx, *Christ: The Sacrament of Encounter with God* (New York: Sheed & Ward, 1963).

[65]See Karl Rahner, *The Church and the Sacraments* (New York: Herder and Herder, 1963).

[66]Mary Daly, *Gyn/Ecology* (Boston: Beacon Press, 1979), chap. 6.

[67]Denise Lardner Carmody, *Women and World Religions* (Nashville: Abingdon, 1979), pp. 113–136; Carol P. Christ and Judith Plaskow, eds., *Womanspirit Rising* (New York: Harper & Row, 1979); Elizabeth Clark and Herbert Richardon, eds., *Women and Religion* (New York: Harper & Row, 1977); Rosemary Radford Ruether, ed., *Religion and Sexism* (New York: Simon & Schuster, 1974); Mary Daly, *The Church and the Second Sex* (New York: Harper Colophon, 1975).

[68]Steven Runciman, *The Orthodox Churches and the Secular State* (Auckland: Auckland University Press, 1971).

[69]Karl Rahner, *The Shape of the Church to Come* (New York: Seabury, 1974).

[70]See Vladimir Lossky, *The Mystical Theology of the Eastern Church* (Crestwood, N.Y.: St. Vladimir's Seminary Press, 1976); Alexander Schmemann, ed., *Ultimate Questions* (Crestwood, N.Y.: St. Vladimir's Seminary Press, 1977).

[71]John L. McKenzie, *The Power and the Wisdom* (Milwaukee, Wisc.: Bruce, 1965), pp. 252–255.

[72]See Bernard Lonergan, *Grace and Freedom* (New York: Herder and Herder, 1971).

[73]A handy collection of relevant texts on Barth is Karl Barth, *Church Dogmatics: A Selection* (New York: Harper Torchbooks, 1962), pp. 29–86. On Tillich, see his *Systematic Theology*, vol. 1 (Chicago: University of Chicago Press, 1967), pp. 71–159.

[74]Etienne Gilson, *The Elements of Christian Philosophy* (New York: Mentor-Omega, 1963), pp. 135–145.

[75]A profound interpretation is Karl Rahner's "Thomas Aquinas on the Incomprehensibility of God," *Journal of Religion*, 1978, *58*, supp.:107–125; see also Paul Ricoeur, " 'Response' to Karl Rahner's Lecture on the Incomprehensibility of God," *Journal of Religion*, 1978, *58*, supp.:126–131.

Chapter Ten

[1]There are good maps on the spread of Islam in Geoffrey Barraclough, ed., *The Times Atlas of World History* (Maplewood, N.J.: Hammond, 1979), pp. 104–105, 134–135, 138–139; see also I. al Faruqi and D. Sopher, eds., *Historical Atlas of the Religions of the World* (New York: Macmillan, 1974), pp. 237–281.

[2]Fernando Diaz-Plaja, *El espanol y los siete pecados capitales* (Madrid: Alianza Editorial, 1966), esp. pp. 17–122.

[3]On the Muslim quarter of Jerusalem, see Giora Shamis and Diane Shalem, *The Jerusalem Guide* (Jerusalem: Abraham Marcus, 1973), pp. 93–105. On Muslim history in Jerusalem, see Michael Avi-Yonah et al., *Jerusalem* (Jerusalem: Keter, 1973), pp. 48–142.

[4]Annemarie Schimmel, "Islam," in *Historia Religionum, II*, ed. C. J. Bleeker and G. Widengren (Leiden: E. J. Brill, 1971), p. 127.

[5]W. Montgomery Watt, *Muhammad: Prophet and Statesman* (New York: Oxford University Galaxy Books, 1974), pp. 45–55.

[6]We have used the translation by A. J. Arberry, *The Koran Interpreted* (New York: Macmillan, 1973).

[7]Watt, *Muhammad*, p. 7.

[8]On the pre-Islamic background, see Ignaz Goldziher, *Muslim Studies*, vol. 1 (Chicago: Aldine, 1967), pp. 11–44; Marshall G. S. Hodgson, *The Venture of Islam*, vol. 1 (Chicago: University of Chicago Press, 1974), pp. 103–145; M. M. Bravmann, *The Spiritual Background of Early Islam* (Leiden: E. J. Brill, 1972).

[9]Schimmel, "Islam," p. 129.

[10]Isma'il al Faruqi, "Islam," in *Historical Atlas of the Religions of the World*, ed. I. al Faruqi and D. Sopher (New York: Macmillan, 1974), p. 241.

[11]Charles J. Adams, "The Islamic Religious Tradition," in *Judaism, Christianity and Islam*, ed. J. O'Dea, T. O'Dea, and C. Adams (New York: Harper & Row, 1972), p. 166.

[12]H. A. R. Gibb, *Mohammedanism*, 2nd ed. (New York: Oxford University Press, 1962), p. 30.

[13]See Watt, *Muhammad*, pp. 229–231.

[14]H. A. R. Gibb, "Islam," in *The Concise Encyclopedia of Living Faiths*, ed. R. C. Zaehner (Boston: Beacon Press, 1967), p. 179.

[15]N. J. Dawood, trans., *The Koran* (Baltimore: Penguin, 1968), p. 10.

[16]Kenneth Cragg, *The House of Islam*, 2nd ed. (Encino, Calif.: Dickenson, 1975), pp. 30–34; Arberry, *Koran Interpreted*, p. 28.

[17]Arthur Jeffrey, ed., *Islam: Muhammad and His Religion* (New York: Bobbs-Merrill, 1975); Isma'il al Faruqi, "Islam," in *The Great Asian Religions*, ed. W. T. Chan et al. (New York: Macmillan, 1969), pp. 307–395.

[18]On the development of the *Hadith*, see Ignaz Goldziher, *Muslim Studies*, vol. 2 (Chicago: Aldine, 1975), pp. 17–251.

[19]Cragg, *House of Islam*, pp. 5–18.

[20]See Martin Lings, *A Sufi Saint of the Twentieth Century*, 2nd ed. (Berkeley: University of California Press, 1973), pp. 121–130; R. C. Zaehner, *Hindu and Muslim Mysticism* (New York: Schocken, 1969), pp. 86–109.

[21]W. Montgomery Watt, *The Faith and Practice of al-Ghazali* (London: Allen & Unwin, 1953), pp. 90–130.

[22]See Cheikh Hamidou Kane, *Ambiguous Adventure* (New York: Collier, 1969).

[23]Cragg, *House of Islam*, pp. 73–108; Frederick Mathewson Denny, "The Meaning of *Ummah* in the Qur'an," *HR*, 1975, 15:34–70.

[24]al Faruqi, "Islam," in *Historical Atlas*, p. 248.

[25]Bernard Lewis, *The Arabs in History*, rev. ed. (New York: Harper Torchbooks, 1966), p. 55; see also Edmund Bosworth, "Armies of the Prophet," in *Islam and the Arab World*, ed. Bernard Lewis (New York: Knopf, 1976), pp. 201–224; V. J. Parry, "Warfare," in *The Cambridge History of Islam*, vol. 2, ed. P. M. Holt et al. (Cambridge: University Press, 1970), pp. 824–850.

[26]Lewis, *Arabs in History*, p. 56.

[27]See Hodgson, *Venture of Islam*, pp. 187–217.

[28]See W. Montgomery Watt, *The Formative Period of Islamic Thought* (Edinburgh: University Press, 1973), pp. 253–278.

[29]Stephen F. Mason, *A History of the Sciences*, rev. ed. (New York: Collier, 1962), p. 95; see also A. I. Sabra, "The Scientific

Enterprise," in *Islam and the Arab World*, ed. Bernard Lewis (New York: Knopf, 1976), pp. 181–200; G. Anawati, "Science," in *The Cambridge History of Islam*, vol. 2, ed. P. M. Holt et al. (Cambridge: University Press, 1970), pp. 741–779.

[30]Albert C. Moore, *Iconography of the Religions: An Introduction* (Philadelphia: Fortress, 1977), pp. 213–226; see also Richard Ettinghausen, "The Man-Made Setting," in *Islam and the Arab World*, ed. Bernard Lewis (New York: Knopf, 1976), pp. 57–88; G. Fehervari, "Art and Architecture," in *The Cambridge History of Islam*, vol. 2, ed. P. M. Holt et al. (Cambridge: University Press, 1970), pp. 702–740.

[31]Schuyler V. R. Cammann, "Religious Symbolism in Persian Art," *HR*, 1976, 15:193–205.

[32]A. J. Arberry, *Aspects of Islamic Civilization* (Ann Arbor: University of Michigan Press, 1967); see also Charles Pellah, "Jewellers with Words," in *Islam and the Arab World*, ed. Bernard Lewis (New York: Knopf, 1976), pp. 141–160; Irfan Shahid et al., "Literature," in *The Cambridge History of Islam*, vol. 2, ed. P. M. Holt et al. (Cambridge: University Press, 1970), pp. 657–701.

[33]Oleg Grabor, "Cities and Citizens," in *Islam and the Arab World*, pp. 89–116.

[34]Arberry, *Aspects of Islamic Civilization*, p. 257.

[35]Ibid.

[36]Ibid., p. 111.

[37]See J. Schacht, "Laws and Justice," in *The Cambridge History of Islam*, vol. 2, ed. P. M. Holt et al. (Cambridge: University Press, 1970), pp. 539–568.

[38]Fazlur Rahman, *Islam* (Garden City, N.Y.: Doubleday, 1968), p. xxii.

[39]al Faruqi, "Islam," in *Historical Atlas*, p. 267.

[40]Martin Lings, *What Is Sufism?* (Berkeley: University of California Press, 1977), pp. 45–46; A. J. Arberry, *Sufism* (New York: Harper Torchbooks, 1970), p. 35.

[41]Watt, *Al-Ghazali*, p. 57.

[42]Ibid., p. 60.

[43]Idries Shah, *The Way of the Sufi* (New York: Dutton, 1970).

[44]Ibid., p. 162.

[45]Ibid., p. 169.

[46]Arberry, *Sufism*, p. 119.

[47]Richard M. Eaton, "Sufi Folk Literature and the Expansion of Indian Islam," *HR*, 1974, 14:117–127.

[48]Lings, *Sufi Saint*; see also Clifford Geertz, *Islam Observed* (Chicago: University of Chicago Press, 1971).

[49]See Roger Le Tourneau et al., "Africa and the Muslim West," in *The Cambridge History of Islam*, vol. 2, ed. P. M. Holt et al. (Cambridge: University Press, 1970), pp. 209–405; Benjamin Ray, *African Religions* (Englewood Cliffs, N.J.: Prentice-Hall, 1976), pp. 174–191.

[50]Lewis, *Arabs in History*, p. 144.

[51]See Norman Itzkowitz, "The Ottoman Empire," in *Islam and the Arab World*, ed. Bernard Lewis (New York: Knopf, 1976), pp. 273–300.

[52]Roger M. Savory, "Land of the Lion and the Sun," in *Islam and the Arab World*, ed. Bernard Lewis (New York: Knopf, 1976), pp. 245–272.

[53]S. A. A. Rizi, "Muslim India," in *Islam and the Arab World*, ed. Bernard Lewis (New York: Knopf, 1976), pp. 301–320; see also I. H. Qureshi et al., "The Indian Sub-Continent," in *The Cambridge History of Islam*, vol. 2, ed. P. M. Holt et al. (Cambridge: University Press, 1970), pp. 1–120.

⁵⁴Lewis, *Arabs in History*, pp. 158–159.

⁵⁵See Rahman, *Islam*, pp. 237–260.

⁵⁶Gibb, "Islam," p. 207.

⁵⁷See Wilfred Cantwell Smith, *The Meaning and End of Religion* (New York: Mentor, 1964), p. 79.

⁵⁸Anne Sinai and Allen Pollack, *The Syrian Arab Republic* (New York: American Academic Association for Peace in the Middle East, 1976); *The Hashemite Kingdom of Jordan and the West Bank* (New York: American Academic Association for Peace in the Middle East, 1977).

⁵⁹al Faruqi, "Islam," in *Great Asian Religions*, p. 308.

⁶⁰Ibid., p. 310.

⁶¹Ibid.

⁶²Schimmel, "Islam," p. 186.

⁶³al Faruqi, "Islam," in *Great Asian Religions*, p. 359.

⁶⁴Ibid., p. 366.

⁶⁵Ibid., p. 374.

⁶⁶Eric Voegelin, *Order and History, IV* (Baton Rouge: Louisiana State University Press, 1974), pp. 142–143.

⁶⁷Ibid., pp. 144–145.

⁶⁸See Schimmel, "Islam," pp. 160–166.

⁶⁹Ibid., p. 163.

⁷⁰For an overview, see Denise Lardner Carmody, *Women and World Religions* (Nashville: Abingdon, 1979), pp. 137–155. On current attitudes, see Elizabeth Warnock Fernea and Basima Qattan Bezirgan, *Middle Eastern Muslim Women Speak* (Austin: University of Texas Press, 1977).

⁷¹Joseph Graziani, "The Status of Women in the Contemporary Muslim Arab Family," *Middle East Review*, 1976–77, 9:48.

⁷²*Ms.*, March 1977, p. 112.

⁷³Kari Ka'us Iskander, *A Mirror for Princes* (London: Cresset, 1951), p. 125.

⁷⁴George Allgrove, *Love in the East* (London: Gibbs and Phillips, 1962), p. 128.

⁷⁵Mary Daly, *Gyn/Ecology* (Boston: Beacon Press, 1979), chap. 5.

⁷⁶Jane I. Smith and Yvonne Haddad, "Women in the Afterlife: The Islamic View as Seen from the Qur'an and Tradition," *JAAR*, 1975, 43:39–50.

⁷⁷See Goldziher, *Muslim Studies*, vol. 2, pp. 366–368.

⁷⁸On scholarship and saintliness, the Sufis somewhat sponsored women, though their overall view of women was ambivalent; see Annemarie Schimmel, *Mystical Dimensions of Islam* (Chapel Hill: University of North Carolina Press, 1975), pp. 426–435.

⁷⁹Watt, *Formative Period of Islamic Thought*.

⁸⁰See J. E. Esslemont, *Bahaa'u'llah and the New Era: An Introduction to the Baha'i Faith* (Wilmette, Ill.: Baha'i Books, 1970).

⁸¹al Faruqi, "Islam," in *Great Asian Religions*, p. 347.

⁸²Schimmel, "Islam," p. 179.

⁸³For a sensitive study of the meaning of *Islam*, more suitable for the end of our survey than the beginning, see Jane I. Smith, *An Historical and Semantic Study of the Term Islam as Seen in a Sequence of Quran Commentaries* (Missoula, Mont.: Scholars Press, 1975).

⁸⁴Schimmel, "Islam," p. 142.

⁸⁵On the Mutazila, see Watt, *Formative Period of Islamic Thought*, pp. 209–250.

[86] See S. Pines, "Philosophy," in *The Cambridge History of Islam*, vol. 2, ed. P. M. Holt et al. (Cambridge: University Press, 1970), pp. 780–823.

[87] Earle Waugh, "En Islam Iranien," *HR*, 1975, *14*:322–323.

[88] See Gustave Thaiss, "Religious Symbolism and Social Change: The Drama of Husain," in *Scholars, Saints, and Sufis*, ed. Nikki R. Kiddie (Berkeley: University of California Press, 1972), pp. 349–366.

[89] Fatima Mernissi, "Women, Saints, and Sanctuaries," *Signs*, 1977, *3*(1):101–112.

[90] Schimmel, "Islam," p. 168.

Conclusion

[1] C. G. Jung, *Memories, Dreams, Reflections* (New York: Vintage, 1963), p. 235.

[2] In our view, Mircea Eliade shows that persuasively; see his *Shamanism* (Princeton, N.J.: Princeton University Press/Bollingen, 1972); *Yoga* (Princeton, N.J.: Princeton University Press/Bollingen, 1970).

[3] See Wilfred Cantwell Smith, *The Meaning and End of Religion* (New York: Mentor, 1964); on the rise of the term *religio* with Cicero, see Eric Voegelin, *Order and History*, IV (Baton Rouge: Louisiana State University Press, 1974), pp. 43–48.

[4] See Joachim Wach, *The Comparative Study of Religions* (New York: Columbia University Press, 1961).

[5] Three recent works that illumine tradition are Huston Smith, *Forgotten Truth: The Primordial Tradition* (New York: Harper & Row, 1976); E. F. Schumacher, *A Guide for the Perplexed* (New York: Harper & Row, 1977); Peter Slater, *The Dynamics of Religion* (New York: Harper & Row, 1978). Our colleague Paul Wiebe's unpublished paper "Religious Tradition" has been a great stimulus on the question of tradition and modernity.

[6] This is a theme in John Bowker, *The Sense of God* (Oxford: Clarendon Press, 1973).

[7] See Voegelin, *Order and History*, pp. 330–335.

[8] Marcel Griaule, *Conversations with Ogotemmeli* (London: Oxford University Press, 1973).

[9] Huston Smith, "Frithjof Schuon's *The Transcendent Unity of Religion:* Pro," and Richard C. Bush, "Frithjof Schuon's *The Transcendent Unity of Religion:* Con," *JAAR*, 1976, *44*:715–719, 721–724.

[10] Voegelin, *Order and History*, pp. 300–335.

[11] See Karl Rahner and Herbert Vorgrimler, *Theological Dictionary* (New York: Herder and Herder, 1965). pp. 308–309.

[12] On religious interpretations of American destiny, see Conrad Cherry, ed., *God's New Israel* (Englewood Cliffs, N.J.: Prentice-Hall, 1971).

[13] William A. Clebsch, *American Religious Thought* (Chicago: University of Chicago Press, 1973).

[14] Sidney Mead, *The Lively Experiment* (New York: Harper & Row, 1976).

[15] On American pluralism, see *Soundings*, 1978, *61*(3), entire issue.

Annotated Bibliography

The following books ought to appeal to undergraduates, and we recommend them for further reading. Adventurous students may pursue other, often more specialized resources given in the chapter notes.

INTRODUCTION: ON THE STUDY OF WORLD RELIGIONS

Carmody, Denise Lardner. *Women and World Religions*. Nashville: Abingdon, 1979. A survey of female images and roles in the major religious traditions that describes what being religious as a female has meant in the past and means today.

Carmody, John. *The Progressive Pilgrim*. Notre Dame, Ind.: Fides/Claretian, 1980. An extended essay on the religious life, stressing its expression in education, prayer, play, marriage, and other primary zones.

Dunne, John S. *A Search for God in Time and Memory*. New York: Macmillan, 1969. A meditation on the autobiographical aspects of religion, stressing insights of Sören Kierkegaard, Bernard Lonergan, and C. G. Jung.

Eliade, Mircea. *The Sacred and the Profane*. New York: Harcourt, Brace & World, 1959. A concise statement of Eliade's view that human beings try to find meaning by making sacred the primary realities of their lives.

Novak, Michael. *Ascent of the Mountain, Flight of the Dove*. New York: Harper & Row, 1971. An exposition of religious studies as a personal exploration of the self, society, culture, and religious organizations.

CHAPTER ONE: THE ANCIENT RELIGIOUS MIND

Campbell, Joseph. *The Masks of God: Primitive Mythology.* New York: Viking, 1970. A readable interpretation of prehistoric culture from a Jungian point of view.

Carmody, Denise Lardner. *The Oldest God: Archaic Religion Yesterday and Today.* Nashville: Abingdon, forthcoming. A study of the ancient religious mentality from prehistoric times to the present.

Castaneda, Carlos. *Tales of Power.* New York: Simon & Schuster, 1974. Probably the most coherent of the controversial books by this anthropologist/novelist (all present an absorbing picture of what certain ancient experiences might have been like).

Lewis, I. M. *Ecstatic Religion.* Baltimore: Penguin, 1971. An anthropological study of spirit possession and shamanism that shows their function in modern peoples' social lives.

Maringer, Johannes. *The Gods of Prehistoric Man.* New York: Knopf, 1960. A dated but lucid reconstruction of religion from early Paleolithic to late prehistoric times.

CHAPTER TWO: RELIGIONS OF ORAL PEOPLES

Coles, Robert. *Children of Crisis.* Vol. 4: *Eskimos, Chicanos, Indians.* Boston: Little, Brown, 1977. Case studies of Eskimo, Chicano, and American Indian children that beautifully describe their current share of their rich traditions.

Eliade, Mircea. *Australian Religions.* Ithaca, N.Y.: Cornell University Press, 1973. A somewhat demanding application of Eliade's theories to the data available on Australian aborigines.

Rasmussen, Knud, *Across Arctic America.* New York: Putnam's, 1927. A first-hand account of Eskimo customs by an explorer sensitive to the richness of Eskimo religion.

Turnbull, Colin M. *The Forest People.* New York: Simon & Schuster, 1962. A study of the Pygmies of the Congo by an anthropologist who came to know and love them well enough to be adopted into their tribe.

Underhill, Ruth M. *Red Man's Religion.* Chicago: University of Chicago Press, 1965. A readable introduction, rich in details, to the principal beliefs and practices of American Indians north of Mexico.

CHAPTER THREE: RELIGIONS OF ANCIENT CIVILIZATIONS

Frankfort, Henri, et al. *Before Philosophy.* Baltimore: Penguin, 1949. A popular classic presentation of the mythical thought of Egypt and Mesopotamia.

Frye, Richard. *The Heritage of Persia.* New York: World, 1963. An informative if rather fact-laden history of ancient Iran.

Guthrie, W. K. C. *The Greeks and Their Gods.* Boston: Beacon Press, 1955. A thorough commentary on the religion of classical Greece.

Renault, Mary. *The Last of the Wine.* New York: Pocket Books, 1964. One of her several historical novels that absorbingly reconstruct the classical Greek world—in this case, that of Socrates and Plato.

Wilson, John A. *The Culture of Ancient Egypt.* Chicago: University of Chicago Press, 1956. A general history, not too difficult and good on the principal ideas.

CHAPTER FOUR: HINDUISM

Basham, A. L. *The Wonder That Was India.* New York: Grove Press, 1959. A readable and comprehensive study of Indian life before the coming of the Muslims.

Erikson, Erik H. *Gandhi's Truth.* New York: Norton, 1969. A psychoanalytic study of the modern founder and theory of militant nonviolence.

Hopkins, Thomas J. *The Hindu Religious Tradition.* Encino, Calif.: Dickenson, 1971. A brief and solid survey of the major religious developments.

Markandaya, Karmala. *Nectar in a Sieve.* New York: Signet, n.d. (originally 1954). A simple novel of Indian women caught in the crumbling of traditional culture.

Stanford, Anne, trans. *The Bhagavad Gita.* New York: Seabury, 1970. A fairly readable verse translation of India's most influential book.

CHAPTER FIVE: BUDDHISM

Conze, Edward. *Buddhism: Its Essence and Development.* New York: Harper Torchbooks, 1959. A compact treatment of the major sects of Buddhism.

King, Winston. *In the Hope of Nibbana: Theravada Buddhist Ethics.* LaSalle, Ill.: Open Court, 1964. A solid study of the framework and content of Theravada ethics, both individual and social.

Nyanaponika Thera. *The Heart of Buddhist Meditation.* London: Rider, 1969. A thorough study of the Buddha's way of mindfulness that reflects Theravada traditions.

Robinson, Richard H., and Johnson, Willard L. *The Buddhist Religion.* Encino, Calif.: Dickenson, 1977. A comprehensive survey of Buddhist religion throughout the world.

Suzuki, Shunryu. *Zen Mind, Beginner's Mind.* New York: Weatherhill, 1970. A lovely and penetrating vision of Zen by a contemporary master.

CHAPTER SIX: CHINESE RELIGION

Pound, Ezra. *Confucius.* New York: New Directions, 1951. An idiosyncratic but stimulating translation of major Confucian texts.

Thompson, Laurence G. *The Chinese Religion: An Introduction.* 2nd ed. Encino, Calif.: Dickenson, 1975. An overview of the major components of Chinese religious culture.

Thompson, Laurence G. *The Chinese Way in Religion.* Encino, Calif.: Dickenson, 1973. A good collection of original sources that represent the span of Chinese religion.

Waley, Arthur, trans. *The Way and Its Power.* New York: Grove Press, 1958. A readable version of China's most beguiling classic.

Wright, Arthur F. *Buddhism in Chinese History.* Stanford, Calif.: Stanford University Press, 1959. A straightforward survey of Buddhism's fortunes in the major historical periods.

CHAPTER SEVEN: JAPANESE RELIGION

Bellah, Robert N. *Tokugawa Religion.* Boston: Beacon Press, 1970. A somewhat demanding sociological analysis of Japanese religious culture on the verge of modernity.

Earhart, H. Byron. *Japanese Religion: Unity and Diversity.* 2nd ed. Encino, Calif.: Dickenson, 1974. An exposition of Japanese religious development from prehistoric times to the present.

Earhart, H. Byron. *Religion in the Japanese Experience*. Encino, Calif.: Dickenson, 1974. A good collection of texts that represent the many aspects of Japanese religion.

Hori, Ichiro. *Folk Religion in Japan*. Chicago: University of Chicago Press, 1968. A somewhat specialized study whose richness of detail, especially on shamanism, makes it of interest to the nonspecialist.

Kapleau, Phillip, ed. *The Three Pillars of Zen*. Boston: Beacon Press, 1967. A clear view of the practice of Zen in modern Japan.

CHAPTER EIGHT: JUDAISM

Cohen, A. *Everyman's Talmud*. New York: Schocken, 1975. A topical presentation of rabbinic Judaism's main teachings, rich in quotations and details.

Neusner, Jacob. *The Life of Torah*. Encino, Calif.: Dickenson, 1974. A selection of readings that illustrate basic aspects of Jewish faith, both traditional and modern.

Neusner, Jacob. *The Way of Torah*. 2nd ed. Encino, Calif.: Dickenson, 1974. A readable introduction to Judaism that delineates its classical structure, the Torah, and the modern situation.

Roth, Cecil. *History of the Jews*. New York: Schocken, 1961. A lucid presentation of Jewish experience from biblical times to World War II.

Zborowski, Mark, and Herzog, Elizabeth. *Life Is with People*. New York: Schocken, 1962. An absorbing portrait of *shtetl* life prior to World War II, based on interviews and personal reminiscences.

CHAPTER NINE: CHRISTIANITY

Brown, Robert McAfee. *The Spirit of Protestantism*. New York: Oxford University Press, 1965. A lucid analysis of the major emphases in Protestant theology and faith.

Carmody, John Tully, and Carmody, Denise Lardner. *Contemporary Catholic Theology: An Introduction*. New York: Harper & Row, 1980. A layperson's guide to the current state of Roman Catholic theology.

Clebsch, William A. *Christianity in European History*. New York: Oxford University Press, 1979. A somewhat demanding but stimulating view, set in terms of religious studies rather than church history.

Neill, Stephen. *Jesus through Many Eyes*. Philadelphia: Fortress, 1976. A good presentation of recent New Testament scholarship that shows the distinctive theologies of the different New Testament writers.

Schmemann, Alexander. *The Historical Road of Eastern Orthodoxy*. Crestwood, N.Y.: St. Vladimir's Seminary Press, 1977. A view of the development of Orthodoxy from New Testament times, originally written for Russian Christians.

CHAPTER TEN: ISLAM

Arberry, A. J. *Aspects of Islamic Civilization*. Ann Arbor: University of Michigan Press, 1971. Selections that illumine major themes of Muslim culture, including science, law, poetry, and mysticism.

Cragg, Kenneth. *The House of Islam*. 2nd ed. Encino, Calif.: Dickenson, 1975. An analysis of major topics in Islam, such as its view of God, the role of Muhammad, liturgy, and Sufism.

Geertz, Clifford. *Islam Observed.* Chicago: University of Chicago Press, 1968. A brief, somewhat difficult but rewarding analysis of religious development in Morocco and Indonesia by a leading cultural anthropologist.

Lings, Martin. *A Sufi Saint of the Twentieth Century.* 2nd ed. Berkeley: University of California Press, 1973. A somewhat cumbersome analysis of the impact and teaching of a leading North African sheik.

Rahman, Fazlur. *Islam.* Garden City, N.Y.: Doubleday, 1968. A solid, fact-filled history of Islam from Muhammad to the present.

CONCLUSION: SUMMARY REFLECTIONS

Ahlstrom, Sydney. *A Religious History of the American People.* New Haven, Conn.: Yale University Press, 1972. A massive, authoritative treatment of American religion from precolonial times to the end of the 1960s.

Carmody, John. *Theology for the 1980s.* Philadelphia: Westminster, 1980. Recent trends and prospects for Christian theology, set in an ecumenical horizon that includes the non-Christian religions.

Johnston, William. *The Inner Eye of Love.* New York: Harper & Row, 1978. Shows the contemplative foundations of religion, with special reference to Christianity and Buddhism.

Slater, Peter. *The Dynamics of Religion.* New York: Harper & Row, 1978. A rather conceptual but rich theory of how the religions configure and can best be analyzed.

Streng, Frederick. *Understanding Religious Life.* 2nd ed. Encino, Calif.: Dickenson, 1976. An analysis of methodology in religious studies, traditional ways of being religious, and the varieties of religious expression.

Glossary

aesthetic: concerning the beautiful or artistic

ahimsa: Hindu nonviolence or noninjury

Allah: Muslim God

anatman: Buddhist no-self

angakoq: Eskimo shaman

animism: ancient tendency to assume spirits in all things

anthropomorphism: personification; treating something nonhuman as though it were human

apostle: one sent forth; original Christian witness

archaic: old; premodern and prescientific

arhat: Buddhist term for saint; perfected one who has reached nirvana

asceticism: discipline; abstinence from self-indulgence

Askenazim: Jews of German origin

atman: Buddhist and Hindu term for self or substantial entity

baptism: Christian sacrament of initiation with water

bhakti: Hindu term for devotion

bodhisattva: Mahayana Buddhist term for saint or enlightened one

Brahman: Hindu term for ultimate reality

Brahmin: Hindu member of upper, priestly caste

Cabala: Jewish mystical tradition

cannibal: person who eats human flesh, usually for ritual reasons

caste: inheritable Hindu social class

cosmos: the universe conceived as an orderly system

dharma: the teaching of the Buddha; Buddhist doctrine and truth; Hindu social theory

dharmas: the ultimate constituents of phenomena

dhikr ("zicker"): Muslim term for recollection or remembrance (of God)

diaspora: Jewish term for dispersion or exile from Israel

divination: art of discerning future events

ecumenism: largely Christian term for movement towards worldwide or transdenominational unity

empiricism: philosophical outlook that stresses sense experience and limits speculation

Enlightenment: eighteenth-century European movement that stressed the untrammeled use of reason

enlightenment: Buddhist term for realization of the truth or attainment of the goal

eschatology: Christian doctrine regarding the final things, such as the end of the world, judgment, heaven, and hell

ethics: study or teaching concerned with morality or right and wrong

Eucharist: Christian sacramental meal of thanksgiving, based on Jesus' Last Supper

faith: belief; commitment or assent beyond factual surety or proof

fetish: object believed to have protective powers

Gemara: comments on and discussion of the Mishnah

Gnosticism: religious movement based on secret knowledge *(gnosis)* that contested with early Christianity

God: the Supreme Being; usually considered personal in the West

god: a being of more than human power

gospel: the Christian glad tidings or joyous message of salvation

grace: divine favor or free help

hadith: Muslim traditions about Muhammad

haggadah: Jewish stories or lore

hajj: Muslim pilgrimage to Mecca

halakah: Jewish legal tradition

Hejira: Muhammad's flight from Mecca to Medina in 622

henotheism: worshipping one god without denying others

Hinayana: older Buddhist sects that arose in India in the first four centuries after Buddha's death; "smaller vehicle"

holy: set apart and dedicated to the worship or service of the divine

imam: spiritual guide of Shiite Muslims

Incarnation: Christian doctrine that the divine Word was made flesh in Jesus of Nazareth

Islam: the faith, obedience, and practice of Muslims

jen **("run"):** Confucian virtue of humaneness

jihad: Muslim holy war

jinn: Arabic term for demon or spirit

jnana-marga: Hindu term for the way of knowledge

kami: Shinto gods or spirits

Karaism: movement among Middle Eastern Jews of the eighth to twelfth centuries who rejected oral Torah

karma: Hindu and Buddhist term for the physical law of cause and effect

kibbutz: collective, often agricultural settlement in Israel

kosher: fit, proper, suitable according to Jewish law

li: Confucian term for propriety and ritual protocol

maat: Egyptian notion of cosmic order

magi: ancient Persian and Zoroastrian priests

magic: attempts to control divinities for one's own use

Mahayana: branch of Buddhism that arose in the schism of the second century after the Buddha's death and that came to dominate East Asia; "greater vehicle"

meditation: Hindu and Buddhist interior exercises aimed at liberation

megalith: prehistoric monument constructed of huge stones

metaphysics: philosophical study of underlying causes

midrash: Jewish exegesis of scripture

mikvah: Jewish ritual bath

minyan: quorum of ten needed for Jewish worship

Mishnah: code of Jewish law formally promulgated around 200 C.E.

mitzvah: Jewish commandment; scriptural or rabbinical injunction

moksha: Hindu term for release, liberation, salvation

Muslim: submitter to Allah; follower of Islam and Muhammad

mystery: something that has not been explained or cannot be explained

mysticism: experience of direct communion with ultimate reality

myth: explanatory story, usually traditional

nature: physical reality in its totality; whatness or character

Neolithic: relating to the latest period of the Stone Age, beginning in southwestern Asia around 8000 B.C.E.

nirvana: Buddhist goal of liberation or fulfillment

ontology: the study of being or existence

oral peoples: those peoples whose cultures had or have no writing

orthodox: straight, correct, or approved in belief or worship

Pharisees: ancient Jews that defended oral Torah

prajna: Buddhist term for wisdom

Prajna-paramita: Mahayana literature concerned with the perfection of wisdom

prehistoric: prior to written history

priest: religious functionary who performs sacrifices, rites, interpretations, and so on

primitive: original or underived; undeveloped

prophet: spokesperson for God or a divinity

rabbi: Jewish title for teacher of oral Torah

Ramadan: Muslim lunar month for fasting

rasul: Muslim prophet or messenger

redemption: retrieval ("buying back"); deliverance from sin

religion: communion with, service of, or concern for ultimate reality

revelation: disclosure (of sacred truth)

ritual: prescribed, formalized religious action or ceremony

sacrament: sacred, empowering action, such as Christian baptism or Eucharist

sacrifice: an offering that "makes holy"; oblation of something of value (such as an animal) to God or sacred powers

Sadducees: ancient Jewish priests who stressed written Torah

salvation: saving from sin; making whole and healthy

samadhi: Indian term for highest state of meditation or yoga

samsara: Hindu and Buddhist term for the state of continual rebirths

sangha: Buddhist term for the community (especially of monks)

secularism: worldly view of life that tends to depreciate religion

Sephardim: Jews of Spanish origin

shaman: ancient specialist in techniques of ecstasy

Shema: Jewish proclamation of God's unity (based on Deut. 6 : 4–9)

Shia: sectarian Islam that opposes the Sunni orthodoxy

sin: offense against God; moral (culpable) error or misdeed

skandhas: Buddhist term for the "heaps" that temporarily comprise the "person"

sorcery: the use of power gained from evil spirits

Sufism: devotional, ascetic, or mystical Muslim tradition whose adherents are often members of a lodge or brotherhood

Sunni: majority sect of Islam

sunyata: Buddhist term for emptiness

sutra: Buddhist text or discourse, especially from the Buddha himself

synagogue: Jewish house of assembly, study, and prayer

Talmud: primary source of Jewish law and rabbinic learning; Mishnah plus Gemara

tantra: Hindu and Buddhist term for ritual manual; approach to liberation through ritualistic, symbolic, or magical means

Tao ("dow"): Chinese term for cosmic and moral "Way" or "Path"

theology: study or teaching about God or the gods

Theravada: older, conservative school of Pali Buddhism, in contrast to Mahayana; survivor of Hinayana branch

Torah: Jewish revelation or law

totem: animal, plant, or other object that serves as a clan emblem

tradition: teaching and practice that has been handed down

transcendence: going beyond the usual limits, often out to the divine

transmigration: the passing of the life force from one entity to another

Trimurti: Hindu divinity as Brahma-Vishnu-Shiva

Trinity: the Christian God as Father-Son-Spirit

Ummah: the community of Islam

Vinaya: the code of Buddhist monastic discipline

witch: one who performs sorcery or magic with evil intent; a wise woman in some feminist circles today

wu-wei: Taoist notion of active not-doing

yang: Chinese principle of nature that is positive, light, and male

yin: Chinese principle of nature that is negative, dark, and female

yoga: Hindu and Buddhist term for discipline, especially that which is interior and meditative

Yom Kippur: solemn Jewish holiday, Day of Atonement

zakat: Muslim almsgiving

Zen: Japanese school of Buddhism that stresses meditation

Zionism: Jewish movement to secure a state in Palestine

Zohar: prime text of Jewish Cabalists

Index of Names and Places

Index of Subjects